The Aesthetics of Mimesis

The Aesthetics of Mimesis

❉

ANCIENT TEXTS
AND MODERN PROBLEMS

Stephen Halliwell

PRINCETON UNIVERSITY PRESS

PRINCETON AND OXFORD

Library of Congress Cataloging-in-Publication Data
Halliwell, Stephen.
The aesthetics of mimesis : ancient texts & modern problems / Stephen Halliwell.
p. cm.
Includes bibliographical references and index.
ISBN: 978-0-691-09258-4 — ISBN 0-691-09258-3 (pbk. : alk. paper)
1. Aesthetics—History. 2. Mimesis in art. I. Title.
BH81 .H35 2002
111'.85—dc 21   2001056023

This book has been composed in Garamond Light

www.pup.princeton.edu

Printed in the United States of America

3   5   7   9   10   8   6   4   2

Contents

❋

Preface

THE CONCEPT OF MIMESIS lies at the core of the entire history of Western attempts to make sense of representational art and its values. This book sets itself a pair of aims: first, to undertake a searching reexamination of the ancient roots of that history, from the formative approaches of Plato and Aristotle to the innovative treatment of mimesis by the Neoplatonists of late antiquity; second (and not only in my final chapter), to engage with and elucidate the complex legacy bestowed on aesthetics from the Renaissance to the twentieth century by mimeticist ways of thinking.

My concern throughout is with philosophical theories and critical models of mimesis. It would be a very different task, of which Auerbach's book *Mimesis* remains the most famous exemplar, to investigate the specific kinds of artistic practice that various versions of mimesis might claim to explain or justify. Significantly for my purposes, Auerbach himself barely touched on the *theory* of mimesis. In particular, he had almost nothing to say about the role of mimesis in the philosophies of Plato and Aristotle, or about the recurrent influences, direct and indirect, positive and negative, that Platonic and Aristotelian paradigms of mimesis exercised on later thinkers. It is a relief, needless to say, not to be in competition with Auerbach.

In more recent times, as the extent of my (nonetheless selective) bibliography testifies, a mass of work has appeared on various facets of the whole phenomenon of mimeticism in aesthetics, as well as on other, partially related concepts of mimesis in psychology, anthropology, and beyond. My own book, however, offers the fullest reassessment yet attempted, I believe, of the ancient foundations of mimetic theories of art, and in the process it claims to correct and replace numerous misconceptions about not only the materials of those foundations but also the later edifices that have been erected (or superimposed) on them.

The book represents the culmination of many years' worth of thinking about Plato, Aristotle, and their importance for a revised history of aesthetics. The kind of history I have in mind, and to which this book is intended to make a contribution, is one that looks back beyond the crucial but in some ways philosophically narrow developments of the eighteenth century (when, in a nutshell, "aesthetics" was named and baptized with an identity so restricted as to imperil its connection with, and importance for, the rest of life), as well as beyond the diverse forms of antirepresentationalism thrown up by the twentieth century. It thereby endeavors to rediscover a structure of ideas at whose center lies a sense of the vital, mutually enriching bonds between representational art and human experience at large.

Mimesis is not only indispensable for any understanding of ancient views of representation in the verbal, visual, and musical arts; it is also essential, I maintain, for the entire history of aesthetics, including the invention of aesthetics so-called in the eighteenth century itself. This means that the book has a two-way perspective: it looks at antiquity from a viewpoint conscious of the later developments of mimetic theory; and it seeks to reinterpret certain features of those developments with a better informed awareness of the complexity of ancient ideas than is to be found in most of the existing literature on the subject. The ambition is too much, it goes without saying, for one person or one book. But I hope, in the terms of Blake's arresting proverb, I have driven my cart and plow sufficiently vigorously over the bones of the dead to stimulate and provoke those who may be able to modify or improve on parts of my argument. Because I deal with a very considerable and diverse amount of material, and advance a many-sided thesis, I have given in the last section of my introduction a relatively full summary of my ideas: I hope this will assist readers with a marked interest in particular chapters to orientate themselves in relation to my enterprise as a whole.

The groundwork of this project was laid by my books on Aristotle's *Poetics* in 1986–87, and my commentary on Plato *Republic* 10 in 1988 (see the bibliography for full details of all publications mentioned). I started to explore some of the wider implications of my views in an article on "The Importance of Plato and Aristotle for Aesthetics" (Halliwell 1991a), which was given as a paper to the Boston Area Colloquium in Ancient Philosophy and as a Mellon Fresh lecture in Aesthetics at Brown University in April 1989. For that and subsequent invitations to Brown, I am extremely grateful to Martha Nussbaum, who, in addition to the stimulus of her own outstanding writings, has often discussed my work with me and has lent crucial intellectual encouragement over the past decade and more. I am deeply indebted to her in many respects. Earlier statements of ideas that have found their way into this book, often in greatly transmuted form, were presented as lectures and seminars, over many years (and more than once in several of these locations), in Bergen, Cambridge, Chicago, Edinburgh, Harvard, Helsinki, Leeds, London, Los Angeles, Munich, Nottingham, Oslo, Oxford, Paris, Pittsburgh, Princeton, Providence (Brown University), Reno, Riverside, Rome, Tübingen, and Zurich. One of these invitations now arouses mixed emotions in me: Gianni Carchia was responsible for inviting me to Rome to give four Italian lectures in April 1998; I remember his kindness with affection, but his premature death in February 2000, when I was in the later stages of this project, caused me great sadness.

For the other invitations I have mentioned, for the dialectic that took place on those occasions, as well as for responses to my work in a variety of other contexts, I owe thanks to a very large number of friends and colleagues in different parts of the world. To list some of them may seem a mechanical act, but I hope they will all appreciate that my gratitude to them—for inviting me, arguing with me, or assisting me in other ways— is anything but perfunctory. They are: Deborah Achtenberg, Meg Alexiou, Øivind Andersen, Julia Annas, Elizabeth Asmis, David Blank, Luc Brisson, Thomas Buchheim, Myles Burnyeat, Terence Cave, Sir Kenneth Dover, Monique Dixsaut, Dorothea Frede, Simon Goldhill, Adrian Gratwick, Jon Haarberg, Malcolm Heath, Harry Hine, Ottfried Höffe, Johannes Hübner, John Hyman, Christopher Janaway, Daniel Javitch, Ian Kidd, David Konstan, Ismene Lada-Richards, Jonathan Lear, Bernd Magnus, Penny Murray, Gregory Nagy, Alexander Nehamas, Anthony Price, Christof Rapp, Amélie Rorty, Christopher Rowe, Dory Scaltsas, Heda Segvic, Juha Sihvola, Michael Silk, Mae Smethurst, Richard Sorabji, Robert Wallace, John Wilkins, Bernard Williams, Peter Woodward, and Bernhard Zimmermann.

I was given help in obtaining copies of relevant publications by Daniel Delattre (who generously showed me parts of his important new edition of Philodemus *De Musica* in advance of publication), Daniele Guastini, Fernando Bollino, Babette Pütz, and Richard Rutherford. Princeton's two readers, Cynthia Freeland and Paul Woodruff, gave me constructive criticisms and helpful suggestions that made it easier for me to improve parts of the book. I am also happy to acknowledge a Research Leave Award from the Arts and Humanities Research Board for the autumn semester of 1999, which greatly facilitated completion and revision of the project.

Finally, I must thank my family for continuing to endure living with me. My younger son, Edmund, has argued with me endlessly (about everything, including matters related to this book) and has shared more laughter with me (some of it mimetically incited) than anyone else; my older son, Luke, has provided expert technical advice and help with computers; and my wife, Ruth, has given love and support that exceed my entitlements to an embarrassing degree.

Acknowledgments

THE FOLLOWING CHAPTERS contain revised versions of previously published material, for which permission is acknowledged, as follows:

Chapter 2: M & P Verlag, Stuttgart, for parts of "Plato and the Psychology of Drama," from *Antike Dramentheorien und ihre Rezeption*, ed. B. Zimmermann = *Drama* 1 (1992): 55–73; and Transaction Publishers, New Brunswick, N.J., for parts of "Plato, Imagination and Romanticism," from *The Passionate Intellect: Essays on the Transformation of the Classical Tradition*, ed. L. Ayres (1995), 23–37.

Chapter 3: Oxford University Press, for "Plato's Repudiation of the Tragic," from *Tragedy and the Tragic*, ed. M. S. Silk (1996), 332–49.

Chapter 4: Edinburgh University Press, for "Plato and Painting," from *Word and Image in Ancient Greece*, ed. K. Rutter and B. Sparkes (2000), 99–116.

Chapter 5: the Editorial Board of the *Journal of the History of Philosophy*, for "Aristotelian Mimesis Reevaluated," from *Journal of the History of Philosophy* 28 (1990): 487–510.

Chapter 6: Princeton University Press, for "Pleasure, Understanding, and Emotion in Aristotle's *Poetics*," from *Essays on Aristotle's Poetics*, ed. A. O. Rorty (1992), 241–60.

Chapter 8: Leo S. Olschki, for "Music and the Limits of Mimesis," from *Colloquium Philosophicum* 4 (1999): 9–30.

Note to the Reader

ALL TRANSLATIONS in this book, from both ancient and modern languages, are my own unless otherwise indicated. Secondary literature is standardly cited in the notes by author's name and date (full details will be found in the bibliography). Abbreviations of ancient authors and titles mostly follow common conventions: for guidance refer to *The Oxford Classical Dictionary*, 3rd ed., ed. S. Hornblower & A. Spawforth (Oxford: Oxford University Press, 1996), or to LSJ. Some other works are abbreviated as follows:

DK   H. Diels and W. Kranz. *Die Fragmente der Vorsokratiker*. 6th ed. Dublin: Weidmann, 1951.

FGrH   *Die Fragmente der griechischen Historiker*. Ed. F. Jacoby. Berlin: Weidmann, and Leiden: E. J. Brill, 1923–58. References are given as author number plus fragment number (e.g., Duris 76 F1).

LSJ   *A Greek-English Lexikon*. Ed. H. G. Liddell and R. Scott. Rev. H. S. Jones. 9th ed. Oxford: Clarendon Press, 1940.

PCG   *Poetae Comici Graeci*. Ed. R. Kassel and C. Austin. Berlin: de Gruyter, 1984–.

PG   *Patrologiae Cursus Completus: Series Graeca*. Ed. J. P. Migne. Paris: Lutetiae, 1857–66.

PHerc.   Herculaneum papyri (numbered; no standard edition).

P. Oxy.   *The Oxyrhynchus Papyri*. Ed. B. P. Grenfell, A. S. Hunt, et al. London: Egypt Exploration Society, 1898–.

SVF   *Stoicorum Veterum Fragmenta*. Ed. H. von Arnim. Leipzig: Teubner, 1903–24. References are given as volume number plus fragment number (e.g., 2.130).

The Aesthetics of Mimesis

Introduction

❊

Mimesis and the History of Aesthetics

Mais la nature étant une, comment concevez-vous, mon ami,
qu'il y ait tant de manières diverses de l'imiter et qu'on les
approuve toutes? (Diderot)[1]

In October 1798, Goethe, with the cooperation of a few friends, founded a new journal of art criticism and bestowed on it the title of *Die Propyläen*. The choice of the Greek term "Propylaia" (or Propylaea), whose original meaning designated an architectural portal or gateway—most famously the entrance to the Athenian Acropolis—lent the project a culturally rich yet ambiguous resonance. While evidently signaling an approach to a classical past, the journal's title subtly evoked a view from outside and even from "below" (the view of the Acropolis on its western side was already becoming a familiar subject in late eighteenth-century art).[2] Such a nuance certainly suits the particular perspective of Goethe's own relationship to the classical heritage, as we can see from an item placed programmatically in the first issue of the periodical, a short dialogue "Über Wahrheit und Wahrscheinlichkeit der Kunstwerke" (On truth and verisimilitude in works of art—or, more effectively, On truth and the appearance of truth in works of art). It is my contention that this piece can be fruitfully read as a kind of condensed meditation on the whole tradition of mimeticism, and one whose interest is heightened by the circumstance that it was written not only in a period when neoclassical[3] models of art were coming under acute strain from new romantic paradigms of aesthetics, but also by someone whose own thinking amounts to a "negotiation" between competing ideas of art, both ancient and modern. Despite its brevity, Goethe's tersely thought-provoking dialogue can count as eloquent testimony to a line of thought that goes all the way back to the origins of classical Greek reflec-

---

[1] "But if there is only one nature, how do you suppose, my friend, that there are so many different ways of imitating it and that all of them are commended?" Diderot, *Salon de 1767* (Diderot 1957–79, 3:195).

[2] The Athenian Propylaia itself was still half-submerged at this date. On the founding of Goethe's journal, cf. now Boyle 2000, 609–11, who sees the title as a pointed retort to the Schlegels' *Athenäum*. Goethe's own introduction to *Propyläen* indicates several reasons for the journal's symbolic title (Goethe 1985–98, 6.2:9–10).

[3] Throughout this book I use "neoclassical" and "neoclassicism" in the broadest sense, to encompass the whole current of Greco-Roman influences on the culture of Europe from the Renaissance to the eighteenth century.

tions on (mimetic) art, at the same time as it foreshadows some distinctively modern preoccupations.[4]

The dialogue takes place in a German theater and is occasioned by an operatic stage set that itself depicts the interior of a theater, showing members of the imagined audience seated in boxes and apparently looking down on the actual stage below them. A real spectator in the theater is dissatisfied by the painting because it fails to meet his standards of visual realism, which he glosses as the striving of art to give an illusion of "the thing itself" (die Sache selbst), not merely an "imitation" (Nachahmung). A supporter of the scene painter persuades the spectator that there is a fine but critical difference between appearing to be true or real (wahr scheinen) and "possessing an impression or appearance of truth" (einen Schein des Wahren haben).[5] He uses the case of opera to obtain the spectator's agreement that it is possible to be completely convinced by and absorbed in a work of art—in fact, to be "deceived" (getäuscht) by it, as the spectator, after hesitation, agrees—without finding it strictly illusionistic or true-seeming.[6] Between them, though very much under the guidance of the artist's advocate, the two men proceed to agree that the capacity of an artwork to "deceive" and "enrapture" (entzücken) the mind depends not on making the subject of its "imitation" seem actual, but on the unity and harmony of the work with itself, on its "inner truth" (innere Wahrheit) and the laws of "its self-contained world" (eine kleine Welt für sich). "The truth or reality of art" (das Kunstwahre) and "the truth of Nature" (das Naturwahre) are different: art is "above nature," yet not "outside nature" (übernatürlich, aber nicht außernatürlich).[7] Only the uncultivated

---

[4] The text can be found in Goethe 1985–98, 4.2:89–95. See Boyle 2000, 549–50, on the context of the essay's composition in 1797.

[5] The complex concept of Schein (appearance, semblance, show, deception, etc.) is of great importance for eighteenth-century German aesthetics. Goethe's use of it here is probably influenced in part by Schiller: for a survey of the latter's usage of the term, see Wilkinson & Willoughby 1982, 327–29.

[6] The artist's advocate says that successful opera not only does not "wahr scheinen," but does not even "einen Schein des Wahren haben": this must, I think, be understood as a kind of hyperbole, for his larger case, as I stress in the text, depends on the maintenance of a canon of what can fully convince the mind.

[7] Übernatürlich does not here mean "supernatural" in a religious sense (the standard meaning in modern German); Goethe also uses it in the introduction to Propyläen (Goethe 1985–98, 6.2:13): the entry in Grimm 1854–1960, 11.2:435–6, does not cover this sense of aesthetic idealism. Compare Goethe's comment on Rubens's use of light in his Conversations with Eckermann for 18 April 1827 (Goethe 1985–98, 19:559–60): Rubens's artistry is above nature ("über der Natur"; lesser artists are "unter der Natur," ibid., 270: 20 Oct. 1828), though Goethe balances this (in a way that parallels the 1798 dialogue) with the principle that art should not arbitrarily dispense with the natural. Among eighteenth-century ideas that may have influenced Goethe in this area of his thought is Winckelmann's formulation of the status of the best Greek art, near the start of Gedanken über die Nachahmung der griechischen

expect sheer illusionism—like the famous birds reputedly tricked into pecking at Zeuxis's painted grapes. The genuine art lover responds to the inner perfection of "the artistic microcosm" (die kleine Kunstwelt), rather than looking only for "the truth of what is imitated" (die Wahrheit des Nachgeahmten).

The whole of this short but pregnant piece can be understood as a reinterpretation of mimesis *qua* "imitation of nature."[8] Goethe shrewdly uses a quasi-Socratic dialogue form to give himself scope to place contrasting considerations in delicately balanced, even somewhat teasing, juxtaposition. The main emergent line of argument—that art must rise above mere illusionism toward a kind of entrancing idealism—is eventually clear enough. But we need to register that the idea of *Nachahmung* remains a necessary, though not sufficient, condition for this position, a point in keeping with other evidence for Goethe's own aesthetic of art's relation to nature. The true lover of art is said to recognize *not only* the truth of "imitation"; and the motif of "deception," actually first mentioned by the spectator in connection with his naive requirement of artistic verisimilitude, is not discarded by his interlocutor but adapted and sustained in such a way as to underpin the suggestion that art needs the psychological power to draw its audience into its world, to offer something that is wholly convincing and absorbing in its own terms. While, therefore, Goethe apparently wishes to escape from what one might call a principle of phenomenal illusionism, an illusionism of "mere" appearances, he seems to want to replace it with a sort of spiritual illusionism, an illusionism of deep psychological engagement and entrancement. If this point borders on paradox (how can the effect of a painting not be a matter of appearances?), so does the idea (whose Neoplatonic inflection is not accidental) that art should be "above" but not "outside" or "beyond" nature. In the light of other evidence for Goethe's aesthetics, we might be inclined to treat this last proposition as meaning that the finest art must make contact with something more than the surfaces of nature, but must nonetheless do so by working *through* the representation of natural phenomena. In the intro-

---

Werke (1755), as even greater than nature, "noch mehr als Natur" (Winckelmann 1982, 3). For earlier precedents, cf. Bellori's introduction to his 1672 *Lives* of the artists, where idealistic art is said to be "above" yet nonetheless derived from nature (text in Panofsky 1968, esp. 156, 162, 172; cf. my chapter 12, section I), and Batteux 1989, 81–89 (= pt. I, chs. 1–2), where fine art is said to improve on nature yet to remain within its limits. As it happens, the Greek phrase "above nature" (*huper phusin*) occurs in Proclus's commentary on Plato's *Republic* (*In Remp.* 1.77.24 Kroll) in reference to the plane of divine or noetic reality that is conveyed by the best poetic myths (cf. Proclus *In Parm.* 956.32–33 Cousin; *In Tim.* 1.410.6–7 Diehl); cf. my chapter 11, section II.

  [8] On the complex history of ideas of "the imitation of nature," see my chapters 5, section I, and 12.

duction to *Propyläen* itself, the chief requirement for the artist is said to be the study and emulation of nature, and Goethe complains that most modern artists rarely even achieve "the beautiful exterior" (äußere schöne Seite) of things. But he takes the imitation of nature to involve striving to penetrate "into the depths of things" (in die Tiefe der Gegenstände), so as to produce an organic creation that can in some sense "rival" nature, appearing simultaneously part of the natural realm yet elevated above the common level of its outer show.[9]

What merits emphasis here is that Goethe, far from simply rejecting the "imitation of nature," has reinterpreted it so as to produce an aesthetic of idealism and creativity *from within* that older principle. He achieves this through four kinds of reorientation: by moving from nature as surface or phenomenon to nature as hidden system (an idea as old as Heraclitus: "Nature likes to hide herself," fr. 123 DK); by transforming truth or reality from a criterion of appearances to one of insight ("inner truth"); by spiritualizing the goals of artistic conviction and "deception," as observed earlier; and by making the artist a creator of a "world-in-itself," but a "world," an imagined reality, nonetheless. This last element obviously echoes earlier eighteenth-century ideas of the artistic "heterocosm" (Baumgarten's term) or fictional universe.[10] But like other aspects of the dialogue it also picks up strands from an older mimetic tradition. Just as Goethe reuses the notion of artistic "deception," a notion not only polemically attacked by Plato but stretching back to earlier Greek thinking about mimesis;[11] just as he grap-

---

[9] Goethe 1985–98, 6.2: 9–26, esp. 13–14. This stance can be analyzed as something close to a combination of two prominent strands in the history of the expression "the imitation of nature" (see the references in the preceding note): art as nature's "rival" (Goethe uses the verb *wetteifern*) implies an idea of teleological creativity, while at the same time Goethe retains a classicizing emphasis on the need for art to work through semblances of the natural world. This last point is foregrounded in an aphorism (no. 71) from the last section of *Wilhelm Meisters Wanderjahre*, bk. 2 (Goethe 1985–98, 17:524), which stresses the need for poetic representation "mit der Wirklichkeit wetteifern" (to rival reality) by vivid representation of "das Äußere" (the external). Cf. also Goethe's "Einfache Nachahmung der Natur, Manier, Styl" of 1789 (Goethe 1985–98, 3.2:186–91), where the finest art is said to go beyond "simple imitation" (close fidelity to appearances), and beyond an individual way of seeing (a "manner"), until a grasp of the inner nature of things is reached; but there too Goethe stresses the overlaps between his three categories. On Goethe and mimesis, cf. Berghahn 1997, 533–38.

[10] "Heterocosm" derives from Baumgarten 1735, 20, §§52–53 (the adjectival form "heterocosmica"); see Baumgarten 1954, 55. See Abrams 1953, 72–85, on the history of "heterocosmic" metaphors in poetic theory; cf. Ruthven 1979, 1–15. "Heterocosm" has not yet been recorded by the *Oxford English Dictionary*.

[11] See note 49 on the ancient origins of the motif; for a prominent instance earlier in the eighteenth century, see the preface to Lessing's *Laokoon*, where it is said that both painting and poetry deceive and enjoy deceiving: "beide täuschen, und beider Täuschung gefällt" (Lessing 1970–79, 6:9).

ples with questions both of verisimilitude and/or probability (Wahrschein-lichkeit) and of artistic unity that were salient in Aristotle's *Poetics* (a work he had been rereading just months before writing this dialogue);[12] just as his principle of penetrating beyond natural appearances to nature's inner truth has markedly Plotinean affinities (and Neoplatonism had been an early influence on Goethe's thinking);[13] so his idea of "die kleine Kunst-welt," the world *within* the work of art, has ancient antecedents too, the most notable of which is perhaps the concept of a literary microcosm de-veloped by Proclus.[14] In short, Goethe's dialogue is a fertile reworking of vital issues in a whole history of argument about the status of representa-tional "appearances" in art and their relationship to worlds both real and invented. That history is the history of mimesis.

Whatever the most immediate influences on this work of Goethe's may have been, the dialogue can usefully exemplify a claim I wish to make about the entire tradition of aesthetic mimeticism. Goethe's argument strives to strike a delicate balance between two fundamental views of art, and, by implication, two conceptions of mimesis. These are, in barest es-sentials, first, the idea of mimesis as committed to depicting and illuminat-ing a world that is (partly) accessible and knowable outside art, and by whose norms art can therefore, within limits, be tested and judged; sec-ond, the idea of mimesis as the creator of an independent artistic hetero-cosm, a world of its own, though one that, as in Goethe's case, may still purport to contain some kind of "truth" about, or grasp of, reality as a whole. These radically contrasting alternatives were present in the tradi-tion of thought about mimesis from a very early stage. The extent of their ramifications in the philosophy of art is perhaps the primary factor that has made mimesis so consequential a presence in the history of aesthetics. Mimesis, in all its variations, has quite simply proved to be the most long-lasting, widely held and intellectually accommodating of all theories of art

[12] See Halliwell 1992b, 419–20, for some discussion of the relevant correspondence with Schiller. Goethe had read the *Poetics* as early as 1767; he returned to it again in 1826, produc-ing his *Nachlese zu Aristoteles' Poetik* (publ. 1827; see Goethe 1985–98, 13.1:340–43).

[13] Grumach 1949, 2:815–21, documents Goethe's relationship to Plotinus. Note that Goethe subsequently incorporated several portions of Plotinus *Enn.* 5.8.1 (cf. chapter 11, section I) into the section of aphorisms, "Aus Makariens Archiv," at the end of *Wilhelm Meis-ters Wanderjahre* (Goethe 1985–98, 17:689–91): see von Einem 1972, 109–11 (cf. his 18–20); Gelzer 1979, 322–33.

[14] See Coulter 1976, 95–126; cf. Heath 1989, 129–31. It is doubtful whether the phrase *kosmos epeōn* (*vel sim.*), in Solon fr. 1.2 (West 1989–92), Parmenides fr. 8.52 DK, and Demo-critus fr. 21 DK (where Barnes 1987, 262, translates as "world of words"; similarly Guthrie 1962–81, 2:477, but contrast 2:50, and see Russell 1981, 72–3), should be understood as a poetic "world," a "linguistic universe" (Gentili 1988, 50), rather than an "order," "arrange-ment," or "adornment" of poetic language. On fictional "worlds" more generally see note 52.

in the West. To understand something of why that should have been so—
and to trace the major paths by which it has come about—still requires, at
the foundations, an encounter with ancient Greek texts and thinkers and,
above all, with Plato and Aristotle.

II

This book has two principal, overlapping aims. At its heart lies what I
believe is a more sensitive analysis than has previously been attempted of
the concepts and treatments of mimesis to be found in the writings of Plato
and Aristotle. But that core is supplemented and enriched, in ways I have
anticipated in my observations on Goethe's dialogue, by a broader view
of the whole history of mimesis as a concept (or rather a family of concepts)
of the representational arts, from classical Greece to the present—from
Plato, as one might aptly put it, to Derrida. This wider perspective is
opened up most obviously in part III of the book, but I have tried to foster
and maintain awareness of it, and to elaborate some of its details and connections, throughout the chapters on Plato and Aristotle as well. There are
two reasons for this method. In the first place, no modern approach to the
mimeticism of these two thinkers can escape the burden, the conceptual
weight, of the intervening history of mimesis, especially in its Latinized
form of *imitatio* and its various derivatives (as well as their equivalents in
other languages, such as German *Nachahmung* and *Nachbildung*): this
larger history—a history of both language and ideas—is built into the very
terms with which mimesis is now usually discussed.[15] The second reason
is that Plato and Aristotle themselves, whether directly or indirectly (and,
like all the greatest thinkers, their views have mostly been disseminated
at second hand), have remained immense shaping forces on the whole
evolution of this subject. In summary, this book tries to show that for "us,"
at this late stage in the history of Western thinking about art, the reading
of Plato and Aristotle, together with their ancient successors, and the interpretation of everything that has subsequently been made, both positively
and negatively, of mimesis, are mutually implicated tasks.

    As the very title of my book advertises, the viewpoint I adopt on mimesis
will throughout be situated within the framework of what I count as the

---

[15] Most scholars continue standardly to translate the Greek term *mimēsis* and its cognates
by "imitation," something I rarely do, and only with qualification, in this book; the perils of
equating mimesis with imitation are discussed later in this introduction. The most concerted
modern attempt to undermine the equation of mimesis with imitation is that of Koller 1954
(an outline in Koller 1980), but his book is severely marred by a forced theory of the history
of the term's origins and evolution in Greek: see my notes 30, 32, 39, 53.

study (and, once more, the history) of aesthetics.[16] Concepts of mimesis, art, and aesthetics are fully interlocked within the structure of my argument, and an underlying concern of the entire project is to demonstrate that the relationship between ancient and modern concepts of "art" is much more complex, even paradoxical, than orthodox accounts and received opinions might make us believe. One particularly influential account in this area is contained in a widely reprinted essay of Paul Kristeller, "The Modern System of the Fine Arts" (originally published in 1951–52), which maintains that the notion of "art" as we are now (supposedly) familiar with it (or still were, perhaps, half a century ago) was essentially an invention of the eighteenth century, and consequently that antiquity lacked any comparable notion.[17] This thesis, despite the abundant and impressive erudition that accompanies its presentation, seriously simplifies a far more intricate story in the development of ideas. My own contrasting view can be initially outlined in two complementary propositions. The first is that mimesis itself gave antiquity something much closer to a unified conception of "art" (more specifically, of the mimetic or representational arts as a class) than Kristeller was prepared to admit. By the fourth century B.C. it was already a widely shared judgment, as both Plato and Aristotle explicitly attest, that a certain range of artistic practices and their products—above all, poetry, painting, sculpture, dance, music, but also certain other activities too (including vocal mimicry and theatrical acting)—could be considered to share a representational-cum-expressive character that made it legitimate to regard them as a coherent group of mimetic arts.[18] While subject to some refinement and debate, mostly at the margins, this type of judgment remained part of the common currency throughout antiquity and was effectively revived by the neoclassicism of the Renaissance.

---

[16] A corollary of this is that I am concerned with other notions of mimesis only to the extent that they impinge on the question of representational art: for studies of mimesis with broader, though sometimes very loosely construed, terms of reference, see esp. Morrison 1982, Gebauer & Wulf 1992 (of which the English translation, 1995, is less than reliable), and Taussig 1993. Also outside my ambit is the relationship of mimesis to non-Western traditions of thought: see Liu 1975, 47–53, for a brief specimen of a comparative exercise.

[17] Kristeller 1980, 163–227: a valuably documented piece, but at its weakest on antiquity, where Kristeller simplifies much of the evidence and plays down the coherence of its mimeticist traditions.

[18] It is telling that at *Poet.* 8.1451a30 Aristotle refers to "the other mimetic arts" (*tais allais mimētikais*), implying a concept of a "family" of such arts; for later uses of the same plural, see Philo Jud. *Migr.* 167, Plotinus *Enn.* 5.9.11.2. By the time of Plotinus, in the third century A.D., it had become possible to refer to "the arts" (*hai technai*) as shorthand for "the mimetic arts": Plotinus *Enn.* 5.8.1.32–33, 5.8.2.1. For my gloss of mimetic as representational-cum-expressive, see note 31.

Moreover—and this is my second modification of Kristeller's thesis—the eighteenth century's establishment of a category of "fine art" or "the fine arts" (*les beaux arts*) was in the first instance, and especially in Batteux's pivotal work, *Les beaux arts réduits à un même principe* (1746), explicitly based on a mimeticist inheritance, that is, on a prevailing concept of art as, in the language of the time, "imitation." What misled Kristeller, and has misled others, is the paradox that having exploited the legacy of mimesis to build an integrated concept of art, the eighteenth century then took a sharp (though not complete) turn away from the general understanding of representational art as "imitation." To see beyond the surface of this paradox, what we need is not a radical separation of ancient and modern views of art but a more subtle and patient investigation of the ways in which elements in the tradition of mimeticist thought were transformed (but not simply abandoned) during the middle of the eighteenth century and in the subsequent era of romanticism.[19] Throughout this book, then, the concepts of art and mimesis will be interrelated and partly definitional of one another. Accordingly, I use the term "art" as equivalent to "mimetic arts," in a manner that makes it possible, I believe, both to do justice to the habits and patterns of ancient thinking and also to bring those patterns into significant relation with more recent positions and problems in aesthetics. At no point, I must stress, do my arguments entail the application to or imposition on ancient texts or contexts of an independently, let alone a timelessly, defined notion of "art." Nor, it is worth adding, do they force an outmoded model of art onto modern aesthetics, because, as I have already started to suggest, there is a significant degree of both historical and conceptual continuity (which is not, of course, the same as identity) between the traditional issues of mimeticism and modern debates about artistic representation.[20] The extent of that continuity, and of the large-scale framework for a history of aesthetics that it helps to put in place, is my constant preoccupation, whether overtly or implicitly, in this book.

Kristeller's thesis that the category of (fine) art(s) was an invention of the eighteenth century is the corollary of a much more widely touted proposition that aesthetics itself was a product of the Enlightenment. It is crucial to give some preliminary indication of how and why this book will distance itself from this proposition.[21] Now, it is undeniable that the term

[19] See chapter 12 for part of the historical foundations of such an alternative account.

[20] It is worth mentioning that ancient concepts of mimesis, while they focus preponderantly on poetry, pictorial art, and music, do not presuppose a closed set of activities or objects. One might say, in brief, that any sufficiently developed cultural activity will be eligible for mimetic status if it is susceptible to analysis in terms of the tripartite scheme of Aristotle *Poet.* chs. 1–3—that is, in terms of media, objects, and modes of representation.

[21] Halliwell 1991a is an earlier statement of my position on this issue.

"aesthetics," in the first instance in Latinized form, was coined by Alexander Baumgarten in his *Meditationes Philosophicae de Nonnullis ad Poema Pertinentibus* (Reflections on certain matters relating to poetry) of 1735 and later used by him as the title of a large but unfinished treatise. In addition to setting up a model of poetry as the domain of "heterocosmic" fictions, self-contained worlds produced by a human maker on analogy with the divine creator himself, Baumgarten used *aesthetica* to denote the "science of perception," the sphere of immediate and particular sensory cognition, as opposed to the general, abstract forms of conceptual or intellectual cognition.[22] In part from this terminological starting point, aesthetics gradually acquired a distinctness of demarcation and a new self-consciousness as a domain of critical and philosophical discourse, centering on a configuration of issues relating to fine art, beauty, and "taste." Far more important than the term aesthetics as such, however, or even than Baumgarten's own writings, is the eighteenth century's larger development of a new concept and model of an autonomous and "disinterested" realm of experience that came by many to be described as "aesthetic." Recent historians of ideas, especially Meyer Abrams, have traced the genesis of this new model in instructive detail, drawing particular attention to the way in which it came into being partly as a secularized derivative of much older (originally Platonic, later Christian) ideas of the disinterested contemplation of transcendent (i.e., divine) beauty and goodness.[23] Although Kant's *Critique of Judgment* (1790), which sharply distinguishes the judgments of "taste" from the operations of both pure (intellectual) and practical (ethical) reason, was a powerful landmark in the codification of this trend of thought, a doctrine of the autonomy and self-sufficiency of "the aesthetic" had grown steadily over the preceding decades. This doctrine poses a central issue for the construal of mimeticism's history that underlies my entire enterprise, and it will repay us to pause a moment to ponder some aspects of Kant's own version of it.

---

[22] Baumgarten 1735, 39 §116 (= Baumgarten 1954, 78) uses the Latinized form of the Greek adjective *aisthētikos*; he extended his use of the term in his unfinished *Aesthetica* of 1750–58: see Ritter 1971, 555–62, and Reiss 1994, 1997, for the evolution of the terminology in Baumgarten and his successors; on Baumgarten, cf. also Summers 1987, 195–97. For "heterocosmic fictions" see my note 10.

[23] See the fine essays in Abrams 1981 and Abrams 1989, 135–87; cf. Stolnitz 1961 on the contributions of Shaftesbury (but with the corrective of Mortensen 1994) and Addison; Woodmansee 1994, 11–33, takes a more radically historicizing tack. Earlier in the eighteenth century "disinterestedness" remained an essentially ethical concept entirely compatible with mimeticism; this is especially so with the Platonist Shaftesbury, whose concepts of mimesis and the "imitation of nature" couple representation (see, e.g., "represent mimetically" in his approving translation of Aristotle: Shaftesbury 1999, 88 n. 12) with the emulation of nature

Although the complex character of Kantian aesthetics as a whole is not my immediate concern, it needs to be appreciated that the idea of "pure" aesthetic judgment, as Kant himself designates it, is far from being the whole story of his third critique. Having set up, without any direct reference to art, an ostensibly clear-cut model of disinterested aesthetic pleasure and judgment in the early sections of part I, Kant later supplements it by allowing for "dependent" judgments of beauty that, unlike the pure variety, depend on concepts and may involve an emotional component. This qualification anticipates the specific treatment of the "fine arts" which he subsequently undertakes in sections 44–54. There Kant not only admits the involvement of concepts in the experience of those arts but treats them in a way that falls within the terms of the mimeticist tradition: that is, as fundamentally representational and embodying a relationship to natural appearances that Kant dubs the production of a "second nature" (eine andere Natur), a formulation that echoes the old motif of the artistic "imitation of nature."[24] What this shows is that even if we go no further into the ramifications of Kantian aesthetics (such as the treatment of the sublime or the complex role of imagination, Einbildungskraft, within it), we can see that Kant is committed to a recognition that the "pure," disinterested model from which he starts is inadequate to cope with art forms, whether verbal or visual, that have the evocation and exploration of human life at their basis.[25] The broader implication of this is revealing for my own project. The eighteenth century's invention of a new category of autonomous, disinterested aesthetic experience was incapable of making a complete break with earlier accounts of artistic experience. Try as various thinkers might do, both then and later, to disengage "the aesthetic" from its previously accepted intersections with ethics, emotion, and truth, this could only be done at the cost of making any resulting theory too narrow, too psychologically etiolated, to encompass and deal with the representational and expressive impulses that remained central to various forms of "fine

as a "plastic," creative force (ibid., 93, with the poet described as a "second maker," cf. my chapter 12, note 35).

[24] Kant's notion of dependent (abhängig) aesthetic judgments is introduced in Kritik der Urteilskraft §16 (Kant 1914, 299–301); for one analysis see Schaper 1979, 78–98. He speaks of fine art as representation (Vorstellung) especially in §§48–49 (ibid., 386–94), and of the making of a "second nature" in §49 (ibid., 389); on "imitation of nature," see my chapter 12. The imitation (Nachahmung) of which Kant speaks in §47 (ibid., 383–86), and to which he contrasts genius, is not representation but the emulation of previous art. Cf. Zaffagnini 1995 on the mimetic component of Kant's thinking in the third Critique, with my chapter 8 and its note 3 on Kant and music.

[25] For one critique (Schiller's) of Kant's aesthetics as inadequate to the "life interests" of representational art, see Wilkinson & Willoughby 1982, xxiii–vii; cf. the more general statement of the point in Abrams 1981, 101–2, with Eaton 2001 for a powerful critique of "separatist"-formalist conceptions of aesthetics.

art." In consequence, the conception of aesthetics of which the earlier sections of Kant's third critique remain paradigmatic did not and could not mark an end to older, more open-ended, and interpretatively richer ways of thinking and feeling about poetry, painting, or music. What it did do, however, was to expose, and set up in a sharper form than ever before, a possible polarity between standards and ideals of autonomy and heteronomy in the evaluation of representational artworks.

In the light of what has just been said, it ought to be apparent why I believe that any model of aesthetics that presupposes the foundational status of a quasi-Kantian model of pure, disinterested judgment of beauty places a serious impediment in the way of an adequate conception of the larger history of aesthetics. Yet it remains a widespread assumption that this history effectively started with, and should continue to take as its central reference point, the late eighteenth-century paradigm of "the aesthetic" as a self-sufficient category of experience, whether the objects and vehicles of such experience are taken to be those of art, nature, or both. But we need to be extremely clear about how much is at stake here. Such an equation of aesthetics with certain kinds of self-sufficient experience rests on no documentarily neutral historical facts, such as those relating to the creation of the term "aesthetics" itself. Rather, the strongest proponents of the idea of aesthetics as an Enlightenment invention (or, in their own terms, discovery) believe—in the wake of Kant—that aesthetics permits of an absolute conception of itself, and that it is accordingly possible to identify a historical moment at which this conception first came fully to light. One such proponent, Benedetto Croce, offers us a vision of the history of aesthetics that discerns only inchoate, confused movements toward a "true aesthetic" before the time of Vico (who, rather than Kant, is for Croce the discoverer of aesthetics proper). According to Croce, it is Vico's fundamental distinction between imagination, as the realm of poetic expression, and intellect, as the realm of truth, that opens up the perspective essential for a true aesthetic.[26] I single out Croce here only as a preeminent instance of a philosopher whose (in the older sense) historicist convictions about his subject lead him to esteem earlier figures to the degree to which they approximate to the criteria of pure aesthetics laid down by his own system.

Of all the branches of philosophy, it is only aesthetics, it seems, whose own practitioners are commonly tempted to equate the history of their

[26] Croce 1950, part 2, sets out the author's historical perspective on aesthetics: his treatment of Vico is at 242–58. Vico's distinction between imagination and intellect has something in common with Baumgarten's and Kant's distinctions between nonconceptual (aesthetic) and conceptual cognition, but Vico happily combined this distinction with a mimetic conception of poetry: see Vico 1968, 75–76 (§§216–19), with my chapter 6, note 5.

discipline with the discovery of its supposedly "pure" truths. No approach of this kind would make much sense for, say, the history of metaphysics, epistemology, ethics, or the philosophy of mind, in all of which it is necessary to acknowledge a history that embraces substantially, even radically, different ways of thinking, rather than making any one set of ideas or arguments definitional of the subject itself. To reject such an approach to the history of aesthetics, as I want to do, does not at all mean underestimating the significance of eighteenth-century developments; on the contrary, it means recognizing that the intellectual apparatus of a model of aesthetic autonomy and disinterestedness marks such an influential turning point that it requires a fuller historical perspective, a larger map of the subject's routes, to put it properly in its place without allowing it to occlude or distort the possibility of alternative ways of thinking. Indeed, any definition of philosophy that is more than self-servingly (not to say self-fulfillingly) teleological needs to frame its understanding of its own past not only in terms of questions and issues to which different answers have been given at different times but in terms of the possibility of asking different questions. In the case of aesthetics, therefore, we ought to find it wholly inadequate to suppose that we could treat a concept of a self-sufficient domain of "disinterested contemplation" as a profitable basis on which to tackle the many different styles in which philosophers and critics have tried to think about the experience of such things as poems, paintings, and pieces of music.[27]

The preceding remarks have started to broach some of the reasons for my fundamental contention that an understanding of the long and intricate legacy of mimeticism has a vital contribution to make to the task of making better and more inclusive sense of the history of aesthetics. At the risk of simplification, those reasons can be said to be exactly the inverse of those for which a proponent of a "pure" aesthetic would be likely to depreciate a mimetic conception of art. When, for example, the British Hegelian Bernard Bosanquet explicitly describes ancient notions of mimesis as aesthetically primitive because of their association with criteria of both truth and ethical value,[28] he is simply reformulating his conviction that aesthetic experience, and therefore the objects that make it possible, must be detached and isolated from engagement with the rest of experience. I suggest, however, that it is precisely a strength of the mimeticist tradition as a whole that, while permitting different interpretations of artistic representation, it has precluded any such clean detachment and has persistently kept open

---

[27] Tolstoy is among those to have stressed some radical differences between ancient and modern categories of aesthetics: see Tolstoy 1930, 91, 136–39. But Tolstoy had his own (religious) reasons for not looking to antiquity for a richer conception of the subject as a whole.

[28] Bosanquet 1892, 11 (though note the more qualified view of mimesis on 12).

the relationship between "life" and "art" for serious debate and scrutiny. This is not to say that ancient theories of mimesis (or their neoclassical and later descendants) were consistently inclined to ascribe either straightforward truth or unproblematic ethical value to mimetic works. On the contrary, the mimeticist tradition—which was, from the outset, a framework for argument and dialectic, not, as I hope to show, a doctrinaire continuum—was far too diverse and complex to allow of any such easy generalization, though Bosanquet, despite his own knowledge of Greek philosophy, is sadly typical of antimimeticist thinkers in his failure to appreciate that point. To trace and expose the complex diversity of mimeticism, from Plato to the present, is one of the guiding aims of my entire enterprise.

From the point of view occupied in this book, then, part of the importance of mimesis for the history of aesthetics lies not in any narrow or fixed conception of art, readily encapsulated in a slogan such as "the imitation of nature," but rather in the range and depth of the issues (cognitive, psychological, ethical, and cultural) that mimetic theories, through a long process of adaptation and transformation, have opened up for analysis and reflection. No greater obstacle now stands in the way of a sophisticated understanding of all the varieties of mimeticism, both ancient and modern, than the negative associations that tend to color the still regrettably standard translation of mimesis as "imitation," or its equivalent in any other modern language. There are problems here (and this consideration has not received anything like as much attention as it should have done) in which concepts, terminology, and translation are all interconnected, and often intertwined. Although it cannot be denied that the greater part of the history of mimeticism has been conducted in Latinized form (i.e., through the vocabulary of *imitatio, imitari,* and their derivatives and equivalents), it is now hazardous to use "imitation" and its relatives as the standard label for the family of concepts with which this book will deal.

Let me state this aspect of my case in a deliberately paradoxical form, because the paradox can help to focus attention on a crucial element in the conceptual and historical challenges posed by the subject. While it made some sense for, say, sixteenth-century Italian, seventeenth-century French, or eighteenth-century English writers to use *imitatione* (or *imitazione*), *l'imitation, imitation* to translate Plato's concept of mimesis in the *Republic* or Aristotle's in the *Poetics,* and at the same time to frame arguments applicable to contemporary issues of artistic representation in their own cultures, I believe that it no longer makes good sense for us to do either of these things. It is an extension of this point that we need to be extremely cautious before supposing that we can automatically grasp what neoclassical critics and theorists meant by "imitation" in their various languages. One cardinal consideration here, though largely ignored in litera-

ture on the history of aesthetics, is that throughout the neoclassicism of
the sixteenth to eighteenth century texts that employ the language of "imitation" often do so alongside, and interchangeably with, a cluster of other
terms, above all the language of "representation."[29] Such interchangeability, and the cross-fertilization of ideas that went with it, is no longer possible for us, I maintain, except within a self-consciously historicizing idiom,
for the simple but inescapable reason that the semantics of "imitation"
have been considerably narrowed and *impoverished* in modern usage
(and equally, so far as I can tell, in all modern languages).[30] Where once,
in a neoclassical intellectual setting, "imitation" could, in the hands of the
most subtle writers, possess a suppleness of meaning and resonance that
it "borrowed," so to speak, from the philosophical weight of tradition that
lay behind ancient mimeticism, the standard modern significance of imitation tends almost inevitably to imply, often with pejorative force, a limited
exercise in copying, superficial replication, or counterfeiting of an externally "given" model. Notions of this narrow type, even though they have
played some part in the history of mimesis (usually on the side of opponents rather than proponents of mimesis), cannot begin to do justice to
the difficulty of the issues about artistic representation and expression[31]
(their objects, modes, techniques, psychological effects, etc.) that have
been raised by arguments whose ancestry goes back to the writings of
Plato and Aristotle. So while it is hard to avoid using the terminology of
imitation in certain historical contexts, I maintain that it is preferable, because less question-begging, to keep the term "mimesis" itself as the general designator for the theories and models of art addressed in this book.

[29] I cite some salient examples in chapter 12, section I.

[30] Cf. Petersen 1992 on the force of this point in relation to German *Nachahmung* etc.
(though his larger reliance on Koller 1954 is unwise: cf. my notes 15, 32, 39, 53), with Velotti
1999, 146–47, and Jenny 1984 for statements from Italian and French perspectives. Some
awareness of semantic change in this area was already shown by Batteux in 1746 (Batteux
1989, 88–89: pt. 1, ch. 2), though he only glances at the point. Stern 1973, 68–72, distinguishes
between the sense in which "imitation" might be applied to representational art and the use
of the word in other contexts. Kaufmann 1969, 41–46, protests against equating mimesis with
"imitation," but his reasoning is not wholly reliable.

[31] I develop my twin theses that ancient ideas of mimesis often encompass a dimension
of what would now be counted, by many aestheticians, as expression, and that representation and expression are not mutually exclusive concepts in the interpretation of art, as they
have so often been taken to be (especially under the influence of Croce), in chapters 4, 5, 8,
10 (notes 23, 47), and 12. My own position, very roughly, is that expression is the sensory
representation of nonsensory properties (paradigmatically of affective, dispositional, and
evaluative states of mind); I also take artistic expression to encompass both properties of
represented states of affairs (e.g., of fictional characters) and of the perspective of a representational viewpoint (whether of an actual or "implicit" artist or viewer). It is unjustifiably narrow of Sheppard 1987, 15–17, to limit representation to direct objects of sense perception
(cf. chapter 4, section I).

III

Our evidence for pre-Platonic instances of mimesis terminology, as I have argued elsewhere, cannot be reduced to a chronologically neat semantic development. It does establish, however, that we need to allow for its usage in relation to at least five categories of phenomena:[32] first, visual resemblance (including figurative works of art); second, behavioral emulation/imitation;[33] third, impersonation, including dramatic enactment; fourth, vocal or musical production of significant or expressive structures of sound; fifth, metaphysical conformity, as in the Pythagorean belief, reported by Aristotle, that the material world is a mimesis of the immaterial domain of numbers.[34] The common thread running through these otherwise various uses is an idea of correspondence or equivalence—correspondence between mimetic works, activities, or performances and their putative real-world equivalents, whether the latter are taken to be externally given and independent or only hypothetically projectable from the mimetic works themselves. Although there is little surviving evidence for the theorizing of mimesis before Plato himself,[35] it is nonetheless worth

[32] See further details in Halliwell 1986, 109–16. My position remains more fluid than that of Else 1958 (whose translations tend to be doctrinaire; cf. note 42), Sörbom 1966 (whose useful survey is vitiated by some superficial consideration of individual texts), and Koller 1954, who has a wholly inadequate basis for his theory of the origin of mimesis in Dionysiac cult-drama, a theory often repeated uncritically by scholars in other fields (e.g., Riedel 1993, 91; Dahlhaus 1985, 17; Givens 1991a, 123–24; Tatarkiewicz 1970–74, 1:16–17; 1973, 226, the latter marred by several gross errors); to make "ritual" a basic part of the concept of mimesis, as Nagy 1989, 47–51; 1990, 42–45, continues to do, is unwarranted. For criticism of Koller, see esp. Moraux 1955. The brief comments of Flashar 1979, 79–83, rightly stress that "imitation" (*Nachahmung*) is an inappropriate translation for most fifth- and fourth-century applications of mimetic terminology to art. Kardaun 1993 is skimpy and erratic.

[33] The earliest instance of this usage is Theognis 370: "none of the unskilled will be able to emulate/match [*mimeisthai*] me." Though the reference in this context is unclear, the basic thrust of *mimeisthai* is not; Nagy 1989, 48 and Nagy 1990, 374, cannot be right to see here an idea of poetic-authorial "reenactment." The general sense of behavioral emulation also gave rise to the idea of artistic emulation of predecessors or rivals; see chapter 10, note 21.

[34] Aristotle *Met.* 1.6, 987b11–14; on metaphysical mimesis, see Halliwell 1986, 115–16. It is not easy to place here Hippocrates *De victu* 1.10–18 (of uncertain date: see chapter 11), which, in the context of a pseudo-Heracleitean mishmash (= Heraclitus C1 DK), posits micro- and macrocosmic mimesis between the human body and the cosmos, and mimetic relationships between human arts (*technai*) and human nature, as well as applying mimesis to visual art (cf. chapter 4, note 11). For various later examples of "metaphysical," nonsensory mimesis, see Michaelis 1942, 663–68 (esp. Philo); Cleanthes' description of humans as a "*mimēma* of (?)god," *Hymn to Zeus* 4 (= *SVF* 1.537, where the text has been much disputed: see Sier 1990, 96–98), with the same Stoic conception in Musonius Rufus fr. 17 (p. 90.4–5 Hense); and the other instances cited in chapter 9, notes 6, 30–33; chapter 10, note 28; and chapter 11.

[35] Xenophon *Mem.* 3.10, which scholars occasionally imagine as pre-Platonic, probably belongs to the 350s, though it can be regarded, with due caution, as retrospective evidence

underlining that the pre-Platonic material does not uniformly imply that
the object or model of a mimetic entity need be either particular or actual,
as opposed to a type, a general or universal substance, or an imaginary-
hypothetical state of affairs (what Aristotle was later to call "things that
could occur," *Poetics* 9.1451b5).[36] I make this point partly in order to signal
an issue whose implications will recur several times in this book, namely
the possibility that works or acts of artistic mimesis need not (always) be
thought of as corresponding to specific, empirical "originals."[37]

For this reason alone it is dangerous to rely on the translation "imitation"
even for most early Greek occurrences of mimesis and its cognates, and
far more fruitful to accept that from an early stage, when applied to poetry,
visual art, music, dance, and the like, mimesis amounts to a concept (or
family of concepts) of representation, which in this context can be broadly
construed as the use of an artistic medium (words, sounds, physical images) to signify and communicate certain hypothesized realities.[38] But because hypothesized realities are imagined possibilites of experience, the
Greek tradition, both before and after Plato, is greatly interested in the
effects of mimetic artworks on their viewers or hearers, and repeatedly
attempts to characterize the kinds of recognition, understanding, emotional response, and evaluation that such artworks can or should elicit in
their audiences. As will emerge in different parts of this book, the whole
history of mimeticism manifests a dual concern with the status of artistic
works or performances and with the experiences they invite or make available. The mimeticist tradition stands as a cumulative repudiation of anxieties over the so-called affective fallacy: if representational artworks are
communicative acts, as mimetic theories consistently hold, then it cannot
be fallacious to understand and evaluate them partly on the basis of the
emotional effects that they produce on their audiences.

---

for the intellectual-artistic ambience of Socrates himself: for this and some other fourth-century texts, see chapter 4, section I.

[36] In the case of Pythagoreanism, it looks as though mimetic entities are themselves particulars that stand in a relationship of mimesis to universals (numbers).

[37] For an example of confusion over this fundamental point, see Cantarella 1969, 193, who
equates mimesis with representation of "una realtà obiettiva," but then bizarrely takes the
latter to exclude the "things which might happen" of Aristotle *Poet.* 9.1451b5 (ibid., n. 21).

[38] It is no objection to regarding concepts of mimesis as concepts of representation to
point out, with Woodruff 1992, 90, and Heath 1996, xiii, that not all representation is mimetic:
mimesis is a family of kinds of representation; there are other kinds of representation too.
There is, besides, a closer fit between mimesis and English usage of "representation," though
not the verb "represent," than Heath acknowledges: one would not, I think, say that an
arbitrary cartographic symbol (Heath's example) is a "representation" of an airport. Heath
refers to problems with his own preferred translation of "imitation." As my own practice in
this book will demonstrate, I do not believe that there is a single English equivalent that
appropriately *translates* mimesis in all contexts (cf. Gomme 1954, 56–57; Kardaun 1993, 10–

The search for origins is always an alluring but often a fruitless enterprise. Although several scholars have been greatly exercised over the origins of the Greek concept of mimesis, the thinness of available evidence has doomed their undertakings to at best the speculative, at worst the futile. The etymology of Greek *mim-* terms is irrecoverable with any confidence and therefore of no help (if etymology ever is, where the history of concepts is concerned); and we know very little about the early history of the word group to which the noun *mimēsis*, itself not attested before the fifth century, belongs.[39] It is standardly supposed, though not securely demonstrable, that the oldest member of the mimesis word group was the noun *mimos*, which by the fourth century B.C. could certainly designate either the genre of "mime" (consisting of subliterary, low-life dramatic sketches, *not*—contrary to an occasional misapprehension—dumb mimes in the modern sense)[40] or the performer of such pieces, the specialized mime actor. But we have no occurrence of *mimos* earlier than a fragment from Aeschylus's tragedy *Edonians*, where, in an elaborate description of the orgiastic music accompanying the arrival of Dionysus in Thrace, it is used in reference to the booming sounds of the primitive musical instruments known as bull-roarers, called "bull-voiced . . . frightening *mimoi*."[41] Gerald Else convincingly rebutted Koller's belief that we have here a literal reference to actors in a Dionysiac cult drama, and argued for the meaning "imitations of the voices of bulls," which is a serious possibility, though "representation" would suit just as well as "imitation." But I suggest that we should also reckon with the bolder alternative that we have here a *metaphor*, whereby the sounds of the bull-roarers are characterized or personified as quasi-dramatic actors. On this reading, the relevant portion of the fragment might be translated along the lines of "terrifying, bull-voiced performers bellow from somewhere out of sight"—sounds heard offstage, so to speak (an idea that might be thought to have particular appeal for Aeschylus's dramaturgical imagination).[42] In this way we can

---

18, surveys the range of modern translations, though her own view of the *Grundbedeutung* of mimesis is badly flawed.

[39] On etymology, see the appropriate caution of Chantraine 1984–90, 2:704 and Koller 1954, 13–14; Manieri 1998, 19–20, is more confident. The earliest occurrences of the noun *mimēsis* itself are Democritus fr. 154 DK, at least in part with reference to music (see note 44), and Herodotus 3.37 (referring to visual likeness). Moraux 1955, 8–9, rightly asserts the impossibility of discovering an "original" sense of mimesis from the available evidence; contrast the talk of a *Grundbedeutung* etc. in Koller 1954, e.g., 13, 38, 79.

[40] As wrongly stated by, e.g., Brogan 1993, 1041.

[41] Aesch. fr. 57 Radt. Gentili 1988, 51, commits the fallacy of supposing that because the context here is ritual, the "very origins" of mimesis must also be so. Sörbom 1966, 53–57 doubts a reference to bull-roarers but on inadequate grounds; cf. Kaimio 1977, 172–73.

[42] Else 1958, 74–76, uses the passage to argue simultaneously (and not entirely without ambiguity) that *mimos* here means "imitation" or "mimicry" of sound, and also that in the

accept Else's insistence that the literal reference is to bull-roarers, while holding open the possibility of a connection between *mimoi* and dramatic performance or impersonation.

Whatever precisely we make of this passage, part of the force of the word *mimoi* is likely to come from an association with specifically musical performance, and that may be significant in itself. In the very earliest text where a member of the mimesis word group turns up in an artistic setting, the *Homeric Hymn to Apollo*, probably dating from around or shortly before 600 B.C., a chorus of Delian maidens is said to bewitch its audiences by the performance of hymns in honor of Apollo and other gods. The poet says of the maidens that they know how to represent (*mimeisthai*) the voices of all men and, literally, the sound of castanets (*krembaliastun*): "each person would say it was the sound of their own voice—so well put together is their lovely song."[43] At first sight these lines might be thought to suggest some sort of vocal mimicry; but mimicry of the most obvious kind (the kind, indeed, that Helen practices at *Odyssey* 4.279 by impersonating the wives of individual Greek heroes) is surely excluded by the musicochoral setting. Partly puzzling though the passage remains, it treats mimesis not as a mere clever trick or knack but as a type of artistic accomplishment—the mastery of different styles of (poetic) language, probably including different dialects, in a performance that is both musical and choreographic. Mimesis is here, therefore, some kind of representation, rather than simple simulation, of vocal and perhaps musical sounds. The idea that a hearer "would say it was the sound of his own voice" probably refers to regional or dialect styles, not to individual mannerism or idiosyncrasy (a ludicrous idea in this context); it is an extravagant way of identifying desired qualities of authenticity, vividness, and recognizability in the cho-

---

fifth century more generally it refers to the performance, not the actor, of mimes; but he simply overlooks the possibility of metaphor. We do not need to wonder, of course, about the appeal of "offstage" noises to Aeschylus's imagination (cf. Taplin 1977, 366–67, 371–74). I think it worth adding that Aeschylus's imagery could conceivably contain an allusion to "offstage" sounds in actual mime performances. Mimes may well have used the types of instruments (including pipes, cymbals, and strings) referred to in this fragment: for one example, admittedly of much later date, see *P. Oxy.* 413 col. 4 (text in Cunningham 1987, 42–47; cf. Page 1941, 336–49, for a partial text, with 338–39 for the possible use of tambourines, castanets, etc.). West 1992a, 122, collects other Greek references to bull-roarers.

[43] *Hom. Hymn Ap.* 162–64. One recent discussion, Colvin 1999, 46–47, prefers the reading *bambaliastun* (clattering sound) to *krembaliastun* in 162; but for a cogent defense of the latter as referring to "rhythmic form," see Barker 1984, 40 n. 4. Colvin, as others have done, posits choral singing in different dialects (Else 1958, 76–77, cites Aesch. *Cho.* 564 for the word *phōnē* (voice) in reference to dialect). Flashar 1979, 80, takes the point to be vocal representation of the sound of musical instruments, which could be *part* of what is meant (if we keep *krembaliastun*). Nagy 1989, 47 and Nagy 1990, 43–44, strains the passage by thinking in terms of the reenactment of myth; Puelma 1989, 69–71, sees a link with the chorus's telling of heroic myth (in line 159).

ral performance, a performance that is described as both bewitching and beautiful. On its first fleeting appearance in relation to an artform, mimesis already hints at complexities of representational style and effect that can hardly be captured by a jejune notion of imitation.

We can be confident, then, that by the time of Aeschylus words from the *mim-* root had already come to be associated with the musicopoetic arts in general (poetry, music, and dance, all embraced by the Greek term *mousikē*), a fact borne out by two passages of Pindar, in one of which the verb *mimeisthai* is used of choreographic representation of animals, whereas in the other it denotes the musical expression, through the plangent sounds of the aulos or reed pipe, of the sound of the dying Gorgon.[44] But beyond the complex of poetry, music, and dance that was so central to Greek culture, mimesis had by the first half of the fifth century become associated with visual art too. We know this from another fragment of Aeschylus, this one from his satyr play *Theōroi* (Spectators, or Ambassadors), in which a chorus of satyrs admires votive images of themselves for their remarkable degree of likeness, speaking of a particular "image" (*eidōlon*)—which is so like their form that it "only lacks a voice"—as "the mimetic work [*mimēma*] of Daedalus," a phrase in which the noun *mimēma* must refer to an object that is taken (however comically, in context) to be mimetic in the sense of rendering appearances in a lifelike or convincing manner.[45]

Although the passage poses several problems of interpretation, it is clear that the chorus is reacting to figurative images, painted with color (12),

---

[44] Pindar fr. 107a Maehler, where the dancer is instructed to match his or her steps to the movements of various animals; *Pythian* 12.21, on the music of the aulos: Belfiore 1992, 18–19, connects the latter to a Pindaric conception of poetry as making order and beauty out of the painful. In Pindar fr. 94b.15 Maehler, it is hard to tell whether *mimeisthai* means the chorus will emulate, or play-reenact the part of, the Sirens; but neither here nor in the other two Pindaric texts cited does "imitate" give more than a thin sense of what is conveyed. On all these passages of Pindar, cf. Else 1958, 77; Sörbom 1966, 59–63. A different fifth-century application of mimesis to music is to be found in Democritus fr. 154 DK, referring to the supposed origin of music in imitation of birdsong (cf. chapter 5, note 5).

[45] Aeschylus fr. 78a.1–12 Radt, with Diggle 1998, 11–15 for a reedited text; there is a text and translation by Lloyd-Jones in his appendix to Weir Smyth 1957, 550–56. The fullest recent treatment of this much discussed fragment is Stieber 1994, who links the passage to realism in late archaic sculpture, a claim disputed by Stansbury-O'Donnell 1999, 112–13, 211 n. 155; Keuls 1978, 20, sidesteps the implications of the passage for mimesis. For *mimēma*, see also Aeschylus fr. 364 Radt, where a Greek tunic is called a *mimēma* of a Liburnian cloak: whatever the exact point, this is another case of mimesis *qua* visual resemblance, though unlike fr. 78a.7 it does not imply intentional representation through image making. With the use of *eidōlon* (fr. 78a.6) in reference to visual works of art, cf. esp. Democritus fr. 195 DK, Alcidamas *Soph.* 27, with Halliwell 1988, 119, on Platonic usage. Stewart 1990, 1:73–85, discusses the general values of Greek visual art in relation to mimesis (which he too readily glosses [73] with "illusion").

whose supposedly startling resemblance to themselves is couched in terms of the artistry of the mythological sculptor Daedalus, popularly reputed to have made statues that could actually move.[46] Although many scholars have thought in terms of masks and/or architectural antefixes, the word *morphē* in line 6 better suits a full body-shape than a purely facial figuration.[47] In this fragment as in the *Homeric Hymn to Apollo* the motif of artistic vividness and credibility connects with a larger and older tradition of Greek thinking. One of the things the leader of Aeschylus's satyr chorus says about his image is that if his mother saw it she would "think it was actually *me*—that's how like me it is" (16–17). Mimesis can be praised, hyperbolically (and here, no doubt, absurdly: do satyrs have mothers?), for being confusable with the "real thing." This reminds us of the epic formula, found in both Homer and Hesiod, that describes various kinds of "falsehoods" or "lies" (*pseudē*)—including some sorts of poetry itself— as being "like the truth," that is, fictionally plausible and seductive. It is equally akin to expressions that characterize the products of figurative arts as "like living things."[48] In all of this, mimesis becomes associated with ideas that sometimes cluster around the motif of artistic "deception"—a motif fated to be picked up and given new force by Plato, and one that continues to resurface periodically, whether with positive or negative effect, in the later history of mimeticism, as we noticed with the dialogue of Goethe's cited at the start of this chapter.[49]

[46] See, e.g., Cratinus fr. 75 *PCG*; Aristophanes fr. 202 *PCG*; Plato *Euthyph.* 11c–d, 15b; *Meno* 97d, with Bluck 1964, 408–11; Morris 1992, 216–26.

[47] Cf. Aristotle *Pol.* 8.5, 1340a25, with chapter 6, note 23. Stieber 1994, 86 n. 4, moots the possibility of "full-length" images, but she does not comment on the use of *morphē*.

[48] "Lies like the truth": see esp. Homer *Od.* 19.203; Hesiod *Theog.* 27 (with chapter 1, note 31); anon. *Dissoi Logoi* 3.10 (poetry and painting), with Pratt 1993, 106–13; Finkelberg 1998, 156–60; and Walsh 1984, 26–33, for various interpretations. "Like living things" *vel sim.*: e.g., Hesiod *Theog.* 584; *Scutum* 189, 194, 244; Homer *Il.* 18.418; Pindar *Ol.* 7.52 (Rhodian sculpture); Empedocles fr. 23.5 DK ("forms like all things," in painting; cf. chapter 4, note 45); Xenophanes fr. 15.3 DK (painting); Xenophon *Mem.* 3.10.2 and 7 (painting: cf. chapter 4, note 17); Euripides fr. 372 Nauck; Plato *Phdr.* 275d; for similar topoi in later references to visual art, see Gelzer 1985, 102–9. Also pertinent here is the "as if present" motif (implying an imaginative "eyewitness" role for the viewer-audience of art), which appears as early as Homer *Od.* 8.491 (of the bard himself) and later becomes a commonplace for narrative-dramatic vividness: see, e.g., Plato *Ion* 535c1, Aristotle *Poet.* 17.1455a24 (with chapter 5, note 45), Josephus *Bell. Jud.* 7.146, Dionysius of Halicarnassus *Comp.* 20, Proclus *In Remp.* 1.164.5–6 Kroll; cf. chapter 12, note 70, for a modern instance. Burnyeat 1999, 263–66, stresses this last factor in Plato's treatment of mimesis.

[49] "Deception" is already implicit in the idea of "falsehoods" or "lies" (*pseudea*) at Homer *Od.* 19.203, Hesiod *Theog.* 27 (see note 48); cf. Solon fr. 29 West 1989–92 ("bards tell many falsehoods," *polla pseudontai aoidoi*, said to be a proverb at Aristotle *Met.* 1.2, 983a3–4.). The designation of *apatē* as an explicitly though paradoxically artistic value is found in Gorgias fr.

In both the fragment from Aeschylus's *Theōroi* and the *Homeric Hymn to Apollo*'s praise of the Delian chorus, the persuasive vividness of a mimetic work or performance is more than the achievement of a specious surface. It involves the creation of something that, through its sense of *life*, can affect the viewer or hearer emotionally too: in the case of the hymn, it is a matter of the power to "bewitch" or "enchant" (*thelgein*), a metaphor (if it is one) well embedded in the Homeric epics' descriptions of the emotional effect of musicopoetic arts and storytelling;[50] and in Aeschylus we find an emotional effect ascribed both to the orgiastic sounds of certain musical instruments and, however parodically, to the sight of the "Daedalic" images that so impress the satyr chorus of *Theōroi*.[51] These points pick up further strands in older Greek habits of thinking about the capacity of mimetic performances to make a psychologically powerful impact on their audiences. The traditions of mimeticism are firmly aligned with a recurrent Greek tendency to judge the impressiveness of artistic representations partly in terms of their success in drawing the hearer or viewer into a strong engagement with the possibilities of experience that they depict. Artistic mimesis is conceived of as the representation of a world in relation to which the audience imaginatively occupies the position of an absorbed or engrossed witness. That is one reason why concepts of mimesis, as we shall see throughout this book, inescapably raise

---

23 DK (cf. fr. 11.8–9): in tragic poetry "the deceiver is better than the nondeceiver, and the deceived wiser than the undeceived" (cf., respectively, "The truest poetry is the most feigning," Shakespeare *As You Like It* III.iii.16, and Coleridge's "willing suspension of disbelief"); see Verdenius 1981, Barnes 1982 for discussions, and cf. chapter 7, note 42. Anon. *Dissoi Logoi* 3.10 makes a similar point with reference to both tragedy and painting; cf. Pliny *NH* 35.65 (the famous competition between Zeuxis and Parrhasius), Philostratus min. *Imag.* proem 4, and Callistratus *Imag.* 7.2 for deception and painting, with chapter 4, note 10. But Gorgias was not as original as often assumed (on his links with earlier Greek poetry, cf. Buchheim 1989, XXI–XXV): Plutarch *Aud. Poet.* 15d couples Gorgias's remark with Simonides' quip that only the Thessalians were "too stupid to be deceived" by his poetry; related ideas appear in Pindar *Nem.* 7.20–24, where Homer's "falsehoods" (*pseudea*) and "artistry" (*sophia*) are said, with somewhat ambiguous force, to beguile (*kleptein*) the mind; cf. Pindar *Ol.* 1.28–29. The reference to deception at Empedocles fr. 23.9 DK, following the analogy with painting (cf. note 48), may allude to an existing motif of this kind. Note Plato's ironic references to mimetic deception at *Rep.* 10.598b–c, *Soph.* 234b; cf. my earlier comments on the motif of aesthetic deception in Goethe.

[50] See Walsh 1984, esp. 14–21, and, more speculatively, Entralgo 1970, 25–29, 60–64; cf. chapter 9, note 19.

[51] The emotional reaction indicated at Aeschylus fr. 78a.13–17 Radt, where a satyr's mother is envisaged as running away in alarm at the sight of the image, is particularly hard to interpret; it could be multiply comic: by playing on the idea that people have never seen such images before (if the play's scenario involves the mythological invention of figurative art); by alluding to the supposedly apotropaic force of certain images; or just by the (inadvertent) suggestion that even a satyr's mother might find the unexpected sight of his face disagreeable.

questions about the relationship between the world *inside* and the world *outside* the mimetic work.[52]

Our testimony for archaic and early classical usage of the mimesis word group is not substantial, and we should avoid claiming to be able to discern a tidy semantic development behind it; however, the passages I have reconsidered here are nonetheless sufficient to show that by the first half of the fifth century the terminology of mimesis could be applied to both the musicopoetic and the visual arts, so that by this stage there was already the basis for a grouping of all these arts together as mimetic—a conjunction attested also in Simonides' famous comparison of poetry and painting, and one that points to an emergent sense of the shared or overlapping representational-cum-expressive status of the arts in question.[53] This process in the aesthetics of archaic and classical Greece was to lead, by the fourth century, to the establishment of a unitary categorization of mimetic art, or the mimetic arts, as a general cultural datum. Plato and Aristotle both refer explicitly to the widely held status of this categorization in their own day, and both, in their different ways, take it as a starting point for their theoretical reflections on the arts in question.[54]

IV

It has already begun to transpire, as is borne out by my arguments elsewhere in this book, that the tensions I drew attention to in Goethe's essay "Über Wahrheit und Wahrscheinlichkeit der Kunstwerke"—tensions between art and nature, imitation and creativity, illusionism and idealism—have deep roots in the traditions of mimeticism as a whole. In fact, a principal contention of this book is that mimesis is an intrinsically double-faced

[52] Scodel 1999, 1–31, rightly reasserts the importance of credibility and verisimilitude in both ancient and modern traditions of literary fiction, against the skepticism of some recent schools of criticism. On the concept of the "world" of a fictional work, see Walton 1990, 57–67; cf. chapter 5, note 7.

[53] On Simonides' apophthegm, see chapter 4, note 3. The general applicability of mimesis to representational art is accepted by, e.g., Gentili 1988, 50–52, though I disagree with many of his individual claims; cf. De Angeli 1988. The thesis of Koller 1954, esp. 62–63 (followed with modifications by, e.g., Keuls 1978, esp. 9–22), that application of mimesis terminology to visual art was a late development, is untenable; cf. Halliwell 1986, 110–13, with chapter 4, note 12. Koller nowhere cites Aeschylus fr. 78a Radt; and it is conspicuous that he either overlooks or conveniently ignores Plato *Rep.* 2.373b (see chapter 1), whose reference to mimesis is also disregarded by Keuls 1978 (despite 126 n. 2). Webster 1939, 167–69 more plausibly considers mimesis a sixth-century concept (of literature and art) that gradually became standard in the fifth. Philipp 1968, 58–61, 67, in commenting on the relationship between the visual and musicopoetic arts, ignores the relevance of mimesis.

[54] See esp. Plato *Rep.* 2.373b, *Laws* 2.668b–c; Aristotle *Poet.* 1.1447a13–28; note also pseudo-Plato *Epinomis* 975d. Cf. chapter 1, note 19.

and ambiguous concept, which is a major reason for its long-lasting presence in the vocabulary of aesthetics and criticism. The history of mimesis is the record of a set of debates that form themselves around a polarity between two ways of thinking about representational art. The first of these places central emphasis on the "outward-looking" relationship between the artistic work or performance and reality ("nature," as it is often though problematically termed in the mimeticist tradition),[55] whereas the other gives priority to the internal organization and fictive properties of the mimetic object or act itself. Reduced to a schematic but nonetheless instructive dichotomy, these varieties of mimetic theory and attitude can be described as encapsulating a difference between a "world-reflecting" model (for which the "mirror" has been a common though far from straightforward metaphorical emblem),[56] and, on the other side, a "world-simulating" or "world-creating" conception of artistic representation.

On the first of these interpretations, mimesis incorporates a response to a reality (whether particular or general) that is believed to exist outside and independently of art. It engages with this reality, or at the very least with other experiences and perceptions of it, and has the capacity to promote and enlighten the understanding of it. On the second interpretation, mimesis is the production of a "heterocosm" (Baumgarten's term again), an imaginary world-in-itself, which may resemble or remind us of the real world in certain respects (and may thus in some cases be partly a matter of "worldlike" consistency or plausibility), but is not to be judged primarily or directly by comparison with it. These contrasting positions point respectively toward aesthetics of, on the one hand, realism (at the strongest, of "truth"), and, on the other, of fictional coherence or congruity: in the one case aesthetic values will converge on, or even be identified with, "life values" as a whole; in the other, they will move in the direction of a purely formal, sui generis satisfaction.

This schematized, somewhat stark structure of (potential) oppositions is certainly not intended to simplify the history of mimeticism. Over and above the obvious consideration that many thinkers have occupied midway or fluctuating positions between the alternatives indicated, or have tried to combine elements from both sides of the division, major variations are possible even within each half of the contrast. There are substantial differences between, say, a normative, Platonist conception of truth and the "scientific," sociological conception of truth underlying the literary naturalism of Zola; or, equally, among critics who reject an aesthetics of "truth" but nonetheless diverge appreciably in the extent to which (or the

---

[55] I note some fluctuations in mimeticist understandings of "nature" in chapter 12.

[56] See chapters 4 and 12, section II, for various interpretations of artistic mimesis as a mirror.

reasons why) they require artistic representation to be true-*seeming*, *vraisemblable*. But these and other modifications of the "world-reflecting"–"world-simulating" schema to be addressed in detail in later chapters only reinforce my claim that the history of mimeticism has been anything but the maintenance of a single, fixed reading of the relationship between art and world. It is a serious mistake to reduce mimeticist aesthetics to homogeneity, rather than seeing it as an entire "family," and an extended (as well as sometimes discordant) family at that, of aesthetic points of view. Textbook versions of the history of criticism tend to leave the impression, if only for reasons of classificatory tidiness, that "mimetic theories" are a relatively easily demarcated set of theories.[57] But conceptions of mimesis have proved capable of directing attention to the internal design and structure of artworks, to their emotionally expressive and communicative potential, and to the images of reality (actual, possible, ideal, or imaginary) that they are perceived to embody; and these axes of thought can vary considerably in emphasis and orientation according to where a particular theory situates itself within the field of force that exists around the polarity of world-reflecting and world-creating interpretations of artistic representation.

In part I of this book I set out to show that Plato's importance as the "founding father" of mimeticism is much more complex and much less easily condensed into a unified point of view than is normally supposed. Plato's relationship to mimesis has suffered from the common but poorly grounded conviction that he held an unchanging and consistently negative attitude to the subject. But from at least the *Cratylus* onward, and as late as the *Laws*, Plato introduces mimesis terminology in a remarkably large range of contexts, using it in connection with issues in epistemology, ethics, psychology, politics, and metaphysics, and applying it to both the musicopoetic and the visual arts, as well as to other human practices, including even aspects of philosophy itself. His purposes in doing so emerge, on the account given here, as far from straightforward or uniform.

Chapter 1 charts and elucidates some of the intricacies of Plato's various treatments of mimesis. Beneath an overarching concern with the bearing of mimesis on the general relationship ("primary representation") between the mind and a philosophically hypothesized mind-independent reality, Plato formulates a whole series of issues about the status of mimetic arts—principally poetry, but also music and visual art—as types of "secondary

---

[57] This is true even of such reasonable and helpful versions as those of Abrams 1953, 6–29; 1989, 3–30: while Abrams's distinction between mimetic and "expressive" (i.e., here, author-centered) theories is strong, the former cuts across his other two categories of theory, "pragmatic" (concerned with communicative effects on reader or audience) and "objective" (concerned with the internal world of the artwork).

representation," that is, representations of human experience (with the perceptions, attitudes, and values that belong to them) that are embedded in a highly mind-*dependent* reality and whose appeal is linked to the particular social and cultural settings in which their audiences come to them. Two main lines of approach run through the dialogues' handling of mimetic art: one fixes on the complex relationship of "likeness" between mimetic images and the features of the world they (purport to) represent, the other on the psychological implications and consequences of mimesis for its audiences. On the first of these matters, no single Platonic view of artistic mimesis establishes itself. The *Cratylus* seems to acknowledge the difference between mimetic works that do and those that do not stand in a readily discernible relationship to real-world particulars, and also explicates the "correctness" of mimetic art-objects as "qualitative" rather than "quantitative" (or "mathematical"). Books 2–3 of the *Republic* allow for an interplay between "truth" and "falsehood" (where both concepts move between descriptive and normative construals) in regard to mimetic works, and book 3 focuses (though not exclusively, as sometimes thought) on dramatic enactment as an especially intense mode of mimesis. Other passages of the *Republic* recognize the possibility of idealistic mimesis (where no real-world correlates exist to what is depicted), whereas book 10 provocatively employs (without, I argue, altogether endorsing) the implications of a "mirroring" conception of mimesis. The *Sophist* draws an important, though less than wholly lucid, distinction between literal (eicastic) and viewer-dependent (phantastic) kinds of mimesis. And the *Laws*, as well as citing the existence of culturally distinct traditions of mimetic art (the Egyptian and the Greek), draws together some of these multifarious threads by grappling with issues of mimetic "correctness" that are not reducible to a single criterion of aesthetic judgment. In investigating these and other ramifications of Plato's confrontations with mimesis, I repeatedly emphasize how the dialogues present exploratory, shifting, and inconclusive arguments on the subject, not at all the monolithic "doctrine" that has become, I believe, one of the supreme myths of modern histories of aesthetics.

In chapter 2 I pursue further Plato's interest in the psychology of mimesis, an interest framed by his overall sense of a necessary dialectic between pleasure and "benefit" in the experience of mimetic art. Central to this side of the question are the two great critiques of poetry in the *Republic*, the first of which concentrates (in book 3) on the psychology of imaginative self-assimilation, as practiced by the reciter or actor of poetry in the dramatic mode, and the second of which, in book 10, focuses on the powerful "sympathy" that can draw audiences of poetry into deep emotional absorption in the experiences of the characters depicted. In addition to reconsidering these two passages in detail, and to suggesting that an anxiety about psychological unity ("being one person instead of many") underlies them, I maintain that Plato's work as a whole allows us to construct a spectrum of positions, from detached critical judgment to complete "identification," on which different kinds of experience of mimetic art (including, by implication, the experience of his own dialogues) could in principle be placed. In the final reckoning, I argue, Plato's life-long and, we must surely believe, firsthand sense of the power of (the best) art to "penetrate to the interior of the soul," as the *Republic* puts it (401d), is a profoundly ambivalent aspect of his own philosophical (and creative) psychology, because it involves both a positive awareness but also a lurking fear of the power of imagination itself. For this reason I suggest here that Plato deserves to be ranked not as an outright opponent of art but rather as a "romantic puritan," a description that tries to capture his uniquely double-edged importance for the history of aesthetics. Plato's complicated attitude to the imagination (symbolized by the figure of the withdrawing lover at *Republic* 10.607e–608a), contains, I conclude, a challenge that is still highly germane to the cultural values that prevail in our own postromantic age.

Chapter 3 develops the thesis that the mimetic artform that interested and troubled Plato more than any other was tragedy. Plato should be counted, I claim, as the first thinker (and perhaps the *only* theoretical thinker in antiquity) to have articulated what can now appropriately be reckoned a concept of "the tragic," a concept of an essential worldview taken to lie at the heart of tragedy and/or the experience of tragedy (whether inside or outside art). On close inspection, I believe the underlying and unifying nub of concern in both the *Republic*'s two critiques of poetry is tragedy (in which Plato emphatically includes the Homeric epics). The reason for this is precisely that Plato understands tragedy to be the vehicle of a worldview, a worldview trapped in an incorrigibly human perspective that sees the fact of suffering and death as an ultimate, irremediable negation of the value of existence. This tragic "sense of life," with the grief-directed instinct from which it grows, is embodied at its most intense in the indignant, distraught heroes of Homeric and Attic tragedy; and by "surrendering" to pity for them, Plato's arguments suggest, the souls of spectators are themselves drawn into an implicit acceptance of a tragic mentality that can consequently seep into their psychological selves, corroding their capacity to take responsibility for their own lives or to seek the more-than-human truth that gives meaning to the world. Tragedy thus exhibits the power of mimetic art on two connected levels: it shows itself to be a potent communicative agent, the medium of a picture of reality that is, in some sense, a cultural rival to (Platonic) philosophy (as *Laws* 7.817b intimates); and it correspondingly demonstrates how the status of mimetic artworks is bound up inseparably with their psychological impact on their audiences. Tragedy is a prime witness to the Platonic case that the products of mimesis have a significant capacity to shape the ways in which people view and judge the world, and can therefore reveal things about the nature of the human mind itself.

At the heart of chapter 4 stands a denial that the notorious mirror of *Republic* 10.596d–e should be interpreted as a direct expression of Plato's attitude to painting in particular or mimetic art in general. That denial rests not only on a new reading of book 10's treatment of painting—a reading that tries to do justice to the rhetorically provocative strategy of the argument—but also on a reexamination of other references to visual art in the Platonic corpus. As early as the *Cratylus* we find Plato acknowledging some complexity to the kinds of relationship in which pictorial and figurative artworks can stand to visible reality. Socrates there makes the fruitful suggestion that this relationship is "qualitative" not "quantitative" or "mathematical"; he maintains, moreover, that the "correctness" of images cannot be legislated for by a set of necessary conditions. In later works Plato treats visual mimesis in ways that allow for a diversity of artistic possibilities, including the two species of representation ("eicastic" and "phantastic") distinguished in the *Sophist*, and the difference between Egyptian stylization and Greek visual naturalism referred to in the *Laws*.

Within the *Republic* there are several passages that contradict any simple thesis that Plato took figurative art to be necessarily or intrinsically mirror-like in its aspirations. What, then, is the status of the mirror in *Republic* 10? It is, I contend, part of an argument designed to suggest that an appeal to "the look of the real," to visual naturalism or verisimilitude, cannot provide a sufficient justification of pictorial art, and that something more than the reflection of the phenomenal world is needed to give value to visual, or any other kind of, mimesis. Although painting is not an object of interest entirely in its own right in *Republic* 10, where it serves as a partial analogy to poetry, the cumulative force of Plato's references to the art indicates that he regards it as subject, just as much as other varieties of mimesis, to ultimately ethical criteria of judgment. Several Platonic passages, not least the crucial remarks at *Republic* 3.401a, support the view that Plato recognized the full expressive capacities of visual art; such art is also covered by the intricate reflections found in *Laws* 2 on ethical form and beauty in mimetic works. Whatever else the mirror of *Republic* 10 may be (and I cite evidence from such thinkers as Leonardo and Samuel Johnson to illustrate the ambiguity of the mirror as a symbol of mimetic theories), it does not constitute the simple condemnation of mimesis that it has too often and too superficially been supposed to be.

Aristotle's views on mimesis, though substantially different from Plato's, are no less complex and have been subject to at least as much misunderstanding, however well intentioned. Part II of the book investigates these views in a series of stages that approximately parallel those of part I. Chapter 5 constructs a broad perspective on the relevant material in the following ways. First, it distinguishes Aristotle's specific conception of the mimetic arts (mimetic *qua* forms of intentional representation) from his quite separate and general principle of "the imitation of nature" by human productive craft (*technē*), the latter counting as "mimetic" not in terms of representation but by virtue of *analogy* or analogousness to natural processes of production. Second, I try to explicate the partially iconic sense of "likeness" that underlies Aristotle's concept of artistic mimesis and his associated construal of the "recognition," including *emotional* understanding, involved in appreciating mimetic works. Third, I argue that the *Poetics* permits us to see that Aristotle has a genuine if inchoate notion of mimetic "fiction," which helps him to divide mimesis from both "science" and history. Finally, I ascribe to Aristotle a "dual-aspect" model of mimesis that enables him to take account of both the artifactuality and the representational content of mimetic works, and thus to hold these two aspects in a creative tension that makes the *Poetics* neither formalist nor moralist in its essential outlook.

Chapter 6 attempts to make fuller sense of Aristotle's interpretation of the psychology of mimesis, in particular by maintaining that the elements of pleasure, understanding, and emotion are interrelated in the account he gives of the experience of poetry and other representational arts. Passages from elsewhere in the corpus, including the *Rhetoric*, *Parts of Animals*, and the difficult but important discussion of music in *Politics* 8, reinforce the evidence of the *Poetics* in making it possible to see that Aristotle regards the experience of mimetic art as resting on a strongly cognitive foundation. To understand a mimetic artwork is to recognize, understand, and, to a degree which varies according to the work and the recipient, "learn" (though not necessarily anything that can easily be paraphrased) from its representation of human action in a possible world. For reasons rooted in Aristotle's entire "anthropology," such cognitive activity is naturally pleasurable, but it is a pleasure that is enhanced and partly modified by awareness of the particular embodiment of the subject in the artistic media of representation. Moreover, because Aristotle takes recognition and understanding, where the stuff of human "actions and life" is involved, to entail appropriate affective and evaluative responses, his view of aesthetic experience does not posit the mere registering of "information," as some have wrongly supposed, but rather a rich perceptiveness that incorporates full scope for emotion, as the *Poetics*' discussion of tragedy amply bears out. This model of cognition must be adjusted further to accommodate the famous pronouncement in *Poetics* 9 that poetry "speaks more of universals" than history. In interpreting why Aristotle mentions universals in this context, I argue that his remark should not be pressed too hard: the universals of which he speaks are not fully formed truths that could be formulated as moral-cum-didactic propositions about the human condition; they are something more like the heightened intelligibility (in contrast to the contingencies of history) that the good poet can lend to his structures of action and character. Reference to universals is Aristotle's way of indicating the quasi-philosophical value he sees in poetry, but he nonetheless supposes that those universals must emerge from, and be discernible in, situations of vividly imagined particularity that constitute the primary fabric of mimetic art.

Chapter 7 offers a fuller analysis of Aristotle's approach to the experience of tragedy and, above all, his understanding of pity (whose centrality to the experience of tragedy was not a new insight but an idea he inherited from the Greek tradition). In order to supplement his relatively spare statements on the subject, the chapter places the pertinent Aristotelian material inside a more spacious perspective. This perspective starts from observations on Sophocles' *Philoctetes*, a tragedy in which the nature of pity forms a major theme (and a peculiar challenge for the audience), and incorporates a selection of other considerations, both ancient and modern, on the character and consequences of pity as experienced in the theater, including the views of the two greatest enemies of pity, Plato and Nietzsche. Within this larger perspective I make a case for seeing Aristotle's understanding of tragic pity as interwoven with his entire theory of the genre: it is embedded in his conception of tragedy as supremely "serious" (concerned with matters that bear on extreme possibilities of human action and suffering); it is hinged together with his account of "complex" plot structures (which expose the precariousness of human fortunes through patterns of tightly coiled paradox); and, in the substructures of the theory, it is subtly connected to his insistence on the need for poetic unity, because Aristotelian pity is no raw frisson of sentiment but part of a cumulative, integrated response to the mimetic representation of intelligible but intensely vulnerable human experiences. Pity is indispensable to Aristotle's vision of how tragedy can play its part in deepening our grasp of others', and consequently our own, humanity; it is also, therefore, the crux of his substantially anti-Platonic project of attempting to rationalize tragedy in a way that keeps it compatible with the positive aspirations of his own ethical and practical philosophy.

Chapter 8 brings us, in one sense, to the limits of mimetic theories of art. Most ancient thinkers appear to have counted even music as fundamentally mimetic, and similar convictions prevailed from the Renaissance until the middle of the eighteenth century. Yet opposition to such convictions has proved exceptionally vehement. My discussion of the issue is framed by examination of the views of a member of each of the opposing camps: on the one side Aristotle, whose model of music in *Politics* 8.5 is fundamentally mimetic; on the other the Epicurean Philodemus, whose assault on such ideas in his treatise *On Music* was utterly uncompromising. My analysis of Aristotle's position attempts to show that while he regards music's mimetic capacities (which I believe straddle modern distinctions between representation and expression) as rooted in a natural human affinity for melody and rhythm, his perspective on music nonetheless makes full allowance for the cultural elaboration of systems of musical composition, performance, and education. Aristotle's claim that music has a special capacity for the mimesis of "character" (*ēthos*) involves the supposition that elements of musical representation and expression can "kinetically" capture, and convey to a hearer's "sympathetic" feeling, something of the psychological dynamics (at root, of pleasure and pain) active in qualities of "character" and in emotions associated with them. The claim is complex, especially in Aristotle's compressed statement of it; but it certainly fits well with his larger theory that properties of mimetic works and the responses of their recipients are linked in a mutually explanatory manner. For Philodemus, however, all belief in the power of music to represent, express, and convey "character," and therefore to prove educationally useful, is an absurd self-deception. Epicurean physics requires music to be categorized as pure, "irrational" sound, necessarily incapable of making meaningful sense to the mind and able only to "tickle" the hearing. In tracing the implications of these contrasting positions, I argue that Aristotle builds a theory that attempts to keep touch with the phenomena of aesthetic experience in his culture, whereas Philodemus commits himself to explaining away these phenomena and thereby, I suggest, to losing a sense of the very things that make certain sounds into music for their hearers.

In part III I expand the book's horizons to take in a series of postclassical episodes (Hellenistic philosophy, Hellenistic and imperial literary criticism, Neoplatonism, and beyond) in mimetic theorizing in antiquity, most of which have not previously been investigated at any length. I also survey the contours of mimeticism's history from the Renaissance up to the present. Chapter 9 concentrates on the major schools of Hellenistic philosophy, Stoicism and Epicureanism, both of which broadly preserved the concept of mimetic art but with divergent interpretations of its cultural importance. Stoics, accepting poetry in particular as a kind of protophilosophy, regarded mimesis as a means of presenting instructive truths about life, and indeed about nature as a whole, in the form of vividly engaging images of the world, as we see especially from Strabo's treatment of Homer in the first book of his *Geography*. But to maintain his position, according to which Homer is a quasi-philosophical geographer and a general guide to existence, Strabo has to incorporate a recognition of elements of "myth" in Homeric poetry, and the resulting tensions illustrate a Stoic struggle (one consequence of which was some tendency to reinterpret mimesis in symbolic terms) with the ambiguous potential of mimetic image making. In sharp contrast, Epicureans started from their founder's trenchant dismissal of much if not all poetry as worthless, partly on account of its peddling of damagingly false views about the world. But some Epicureans, among them Philodemus, attempted to recognize the distinctively fictional status of mimetic art. I argue, however, that Philodemus's somewhat convoluted (and only fragmentarily preserved) views, built around a far from transparent conception of aesthetic pleasure, betray an unresolved tension between the status of truth and falsehood in, and therefore between different conceptions of the raison d'être of, mimetic art.

In chapter 10 I chart the wider currents of Hellenistic and imperial attitudes to mimesis (leaving largely on one side, as a substantially distinct subject, the sense in which the word was now commonly applied to the creative emulation of artistic or literary predecessors). During this long period the representational and expressive concept of mimesis was widened to include aspects of rhetorical and even historiographical writing. To trace this and other developments, the chapter concentrates on the work of Dionysius of Halicarnassus, Plutarch, and those medieval Homeric scholia that preserve vestiges of older Greek literary criticism (including a mixture of Platonic and Aristotelian elements). In all three cases we can detect a fluctuating construal of the relationship between mimetic works and the world (variously referred to as "truth," "reality," "life," and "nature"). Dionysius, for example, manipulates mimesis to fit the various ways in which he thinks rhetoric should reflect and conform to the supposedly constant traits of human behavior, but the result is sometimes a paradoxical superimposition of "art" and "nature," simulation and reality. Plutarch, as an eclectic, "soft" Platonist, grapples afresh with the problems raised in the *Republic*. He adopts the basic strategy of detaching mimesis from "truth," making *pseudos* not "falsehood" but "fiction"; but he cannot escape from a problematic (and itself Platonic) recognition that even invented stories raise vital questions about the *ethical* understanding of reality. Scrutiny of Plutarch's case extracts some important implications of the recurring contrast between "world-simulating" and "world-reflecting" models of mimesis.

Chapter 11 gives center stage to the far-reaching modifications of mimetic theory made by the Neoplatonists Plotinus and Proclus. Plotinus's hierarchical worldview is permeated by relationships that he calls "mimetic," meaning by this the reflection of higher by lower realities and the constant striving of the latter to assimilate themselves to the former. Within this scheme of things Plotinus manifests an ambiguous set of views on the

specifically mimetic arts. In a famous passage at *Enneads* 5.8.1, referring
to figurative art, he posits the capacity of artistic mimesis to reach beyond
natural phenomena to the underlying principles of nature, and he identifies the source of artistic beauty in the "form" that resides above all in the
mind of the artist. These and other indications of aesthetic "idealism" in
Plotinus are offset, however, by passages that seem to relegate much if
not most existing art to the level of mere, shallow simulacra of reality. This
ambivalence derives from a larger "dualism"—between soul and body,
between metaphysical and anthropocentric perspectives—in Plotinean
thought. Proclus too, two centuries later, is ambivalent about mimetic art.
In his fifth essay on Plato's *Republic* he counts all poetry as mimesis and
summarizes some of Plato's concerns with both "truth" and "goodness" in
mimetic works, though he has difficulty with the relationship between
descriptive and normative criteria in Plato's texts. In Proclus's sixth essay
mimesis becomes a classification for only the lowest of three kinds of
poetry, the highest ("inspired") and the second type ("didactic") being
supremely exemplified by Homer, whose profound affinities with Plato
himself furnish the real subject of the essay. Although Proclus sets up a
sharp distinction between mimetic and "symbolic" art, his argument is
complicated by a number of conceptual instabilities, among them his intermittent insistence that a salient feature of the kinship he celebrates between Homer and Plato is precisely the power of their mimetic artistry.
The relationship between the human images of mimesis and the transcendent truths of Proclus's theological philosophy remains deeply uncertain,
in part because of the influence of Plato's own shifting use of the concept
of mimesis. A further echo of Platonic thinking, filtered partly through
pagan Neoplatonism, is discussed in the penultimate part of this chapter,
where, as a coda to the entire story of mimeticism in antiquity (and before
noting the loss of mimetic models of art in the Western medieval tradition),
I briefly examine the philosophy of images found in the Byzantine iconophile John of Damascus.

My final chapter offers a wide-ranging though highly selective account
of some of the ways in which mimesis has remained a focus of attention
and argument, both positive and negative, in aesthetics from the Renaissance right up to the present. Much of this chapter is built around points
and gestures of resistance to received (and entrenched) opinions. Among
the main targets of my argument are the traditional notions that mimesis
was essentially a single identifiable model of art during the period of neoclassicism; that the slogan of art's "imitation of nature" is a univocal formulation of the shape of that supposed model; that the model in question
was decisively discarded by romanticism; and that the nineteenth and
twentieth centuries have distanced us irreversibly from mimetic thinking
about art. On the contrary, I argue, mimesis was always a locus of aesthetic

debate, particularly between supposedly "Platonist" and "Aristotelian" persuasions. Even when neoclassical critics seem to be using a standard, shared vocabulary (though in fact, as I indicate, the vocabulary itself was more variable than is usually realized), the interpretation of artistic "imitation," including the "imitation of nature," is subject to considerable fluctuations en route from fifteenth-century Italian humanism all the way to nineteenth-century French naturalism. Moreover, the relationship of romanticism to mimesis was tangled, because, as I illustrate from both German and English romantics, even the language of "imitation," with associated elements of the mimeticist tradition (including the mirror metaphor for art), was often adaptively reappropriated rather than simply rejected in this period. After the nineteenth-century polarization of attitudes to mimesis (with realism or naturalism and aestheticism at opposite ends of the spectrum), the twentieth century produced a bewildering range of aesthetic disputes and conflicting practices, many of which, I contend, continued to revolve around the world-reflecting–world-simulating contrast that has given impetus to so much of the history of mimetic thinking. That history, I believe, remains of compelling interest for anyone concerned with the status and value of representational art—past, present, or future.

These summaries have necessarily omitted not only a great deal of detail but also many of the subordinate claims and considerations I put forward in the following chapters. I hope, however, that in addition to proving useful for purposes of orientation, they also help to give a synoptic sense of the wealth, importance, and tenacious seriousness of the issues associated with the aesthetics of mimesis.

PART I

Chapter One

❊

Representation and Reality:
Plato and Mimesis

So we shall have to enlarge the city further . . . filling it with
numerous things which go beyond strict necessity, . . . for
example the practitioners of mimesis: the many who use
shapes and colors, the many who use musical forms, the
poets and their assistants (rhapsodes, actors, dancers,
theatrical impresarios), and the makers of multifarious
products, including women's cosmetics.
(Plato *Republic* 2.373b)

Everything we say must surely be mimesis and image making.
(Plato *Critias* 107b)

PLATO AND MIMESIS form a fateful conjunction in the history of aesthetics.
Not only was Plato the first Greek thinker to explore the idea of mimetic
art in a theoretically extensive and probing manner, engaging strategically
with themes and issues that, as we saw in my introduction, had been
voiced in various but unsystematic ways in earlier Greek poetry and
thought. He also took two momentous steps toward turning mimesis into
the backdrop for an entire philosophy of art. The first was to pose certain
fundamental challenges to the status and value of artistic mimesis—challenges that have remained unsettling and less than completely resolved to
this day. The second was to orientate questions of mimetic art around
larger philosophical concerns with the relationship between mind and reality: to bring what might be called the "secondary" representation of artistic mimesis (the images, poems, music that fill the city of luxury according
to Socrates' description in the *Republic*)[1] within the overarching framework of a philosophy of "primary" representation (as embodied in human
thought, perception, and language as a whole). In the broadest terms,
Plato's legacy to the history of mimeticism can be described as a combination of philosophical gravitas (mimesis cannot be divorced from the big-
gest, most serious problems that confront philosophy) with the disquieting, though inconclusive, suggestion that philosophy and art may be
somehow at odds with one another and even perhaps ultimately irrecon-

---

[1] With the implications of this image of cultural luxury, compare Plato *Soph.* 223e–24a,
which glances at the economic aspect of trade in *mousikē*, painting, etc.

cilable. It would be hard to overstate the consequences of this legacy, with
which ancient Neoplatonists, Renaissance idealists, romantics, and many
others have wrestled in their different ways. If we believe the arch anti-
Platonist of the late twentieth century, Jacques Derrida, Plato's treatment
of mimesis is central to the process by which "Platonism" has both dominated and blighted the history of Western thought.[2]

Derrida's view of the matter rightly seeks to register that we are faced
here with an aspect of Plato's writings that has had immense and far-reaching historical significance. But it also conspicuously illustrates a dangerous
temptation to which many writers on this subject have succumbed, namely
the assumption that it is feasible to identify a unitary, monolithic conception of mimesis at work in the dialogues. The study of Plato and mimesis
has suffered repeatedly from attempts to bring together into a neat, consistent synthesis the many different Platonic passages and contexts in which
mimesis is addressed. Whether Plato had a "doctrine" of anything at all, or
at any rate gave direct expression to doctrine in his written works, remains
debatable. That he had a doctrine of mimesis in particular is not a conclusion that can be confidently reached on the basis of a full and careful
reading of the dialogues.[3] Mimesis, I want to contend, is a classic case of
a concept that receives fluctuating and constantly revised treatment from
Plato. It is approached from various angles in different works and manifests the exploratory impulse that Aristotle shrewdly diagnosed as pivotal
to Plato's writing.[4] Nothing bears out this point more eloquently than the

[2] Derrida's view of "Platonic" mimesis is best seen in "La double séance," in Derrida 1972,
esp. 201–22; see my discussion in chapter 12, section III.

[3] The presence of the term "doctrine" is a telltale sign in the title of Verdenius 1949, a
standard modern work on the subject. Cassirer 1922–23 presupposes a seamless Platonic
attitude to mimesis, repeatedly speaking of Plato's thinking as a "system" and uncritically
glossing mimesis as "bloße Nachahmung" (e.g., 16, 19). The fullest examination of mimesis
in Plato is Zimbrich 1984, an elaborate attempt to relate the concept to Plato's own practice as
writer of dialogues; a philosophically adept discussion of many aspects of Platonic mimesis is
offered by Janaway 1995, 106–57. Asmis 1992e, 339, rightly refers to Plato "trying out various
approaches in different dialogues," though I do not always agree with her particular readings; McKeon 1957, 119–29, stresses the range of Platonic mimesis, as had Walter 1893, 441–
46; Laborderie 1978, 72–82, gives a developmental overview, at times too severe; Sörbom
1966, 99–175, provides a clear but sometimes conceptually unsophisticated survey. Philip
1961, 466, specifically denies that Plato held a "doctrine" of mimesis, but his own perception
of two main meanings of mimesis in the dialogues is too schematic; Melberg 1995, 10–50,
denies homogeneity in Platonic mimesis, but his intellectual presuppositions are very different from mine. Lodge 1953, 167–91, is an overspeculative jumble of claims. Otherwise interesting discussions are often marred by overreliance on "imitation," "copying," etc. (in various
languages): thus, e.g., Galli 1925, 287–313; Osborne 1987; and Brisson 1998, 66–74; by contrast, Woodruff 1998, 519, approves the retention of *mimēsis* untranslated. See also Büttner
2000, which reached me too late to be taken fully into account.

[4] Aristotle *Pol.* 2.6, 1265a10–12, referring to *to zētētikon*, the sense of inquiry and quest.

fact that at the end of the most notorious discussion of mimesis in Plato, *Republic* 10's critique of artistic mimesis as "twice removed" from the truth—a passage that has so often been turned into the cornerstone of accounts of Plato's supposedly unshakable, doctrinaire convictions about art—Socrates goes out of his way to draw attention to the provisional nature of the conclusions he has reached, and to the possibility of revising those conclusions in the light of further contributions from others (whether poets or lovers of poetry).[5] This is not only one of the most elaborate statements anywhere in Plato of the conditional standing of the arguments presented. It is also arguably the most pronounced invitation ever issued to Plato's readers to continue the debate themselves, in dialogue *with* as well as within the work. To that extent it is a crucial stimulus to my own arguments throughout this book.

To deny that Plato ever offers us a wholly fixed, let alone monolithic, doctrine of mimesis is not to deny that some recurrent, underlying anxieties are traceable beneath the surface of relevant passages in his text. The aim of this chapter, therefore, is to offer a fresh overview that does justice to the consistencies but also to the shifts and uncertainties that emerge from those discussions, while reserving closer examination of certain aspects of the subject for subsequent chapters. Analysis of the place of mimesis in Plato's oeuvre badly needs to escape from the deadening effect of received opinions. A good place to start is with the observation that mimesis was not always an explicit part of Plato's thinking about poetry. In three works, *Apology*, *Euthyphro*, and *Ion*, all of them now generally regarded as early,[6] Plato makes Socrates raise important concerns about poetry (and, in *Euthyphro*, other representational art too) without any mention of mimesis. In the *Apology* (22a–e) Socrates famously relates how he approached the poets (the tragedians among them) as a group of those regarded, by cultural consensus, as "expert" or "wise" (*sophoi*), but found that when he questioned them they were unable to explain "what they were saying" (*legein*), or "what they meant," in their works, so he could learn nothing from them. He drew two conclusions from this experience: first, that the poets created their poems not from wisdom or knowledge but by inspiration; second, that there was no basis for their belief (and the belief of others) that, as poets, they could lay claim to a more comprehensive authority.

It is worth noticing, however, that the *Apology* as a whole indicates an ambivalent attitude to poets. In the passage just paraphrased, Socrates

---

[5] Plato *Rep.* 10.607c–8b.

[6] I assume here, though without assigning it decisive importance for my case, a standard modern model of the relative chronology of Plato's writings; the best general statement of the model is in Brandwood 1990.

appears to allow that poets do say "many fine things" (*polla kai kala*, 22c3), and later on he invokes the Iliadic Achilles as an ethical exemplum (28b–d) and relishes the thought of conversing with poets like Homer and Hesiod in the (putative) afterlife (41a). Moreover, if poets are at least sometimes inspired, as Socrates suggests, presumably their inspired works may indeed embody valuable truths or insights, even if the hypothesis of inspiration prevents us from ascribing conscious understanding to the authors themselves. There are conundrums here that reappear in the *Ion*, Plato's fullest early discussion of poetry, where, in Socrates' purported exposure of the irrational status both of Ion's own performing-interpretative expertise in Homeric poetry and of poetry itself, we encounter much the same features as in the *Apology*: the contrast between knowledge and inspiration; the implicit questioning of a conception of the compendious wisdom or authority of the poets; but also a continuing acknowledgment that poets do say "many fine things."[7] The *Ion*'s celebrated middle section—where Socrates waxes lyrical about the poet as a "light, winged, sacred thing" (534b3–4) and elaborates his remarkable magnetism simile for the chain of inspirational effects that runs from Muse to poet, to performer, to audience—has made the work a central reference point in the history of ideas of artistic inspiration. But it is also the source of the work's elusive nature and has not unreasonably been found at least partly ironic by some readers (including Goethe).[8]

An integrated interpretation of *Ion* lies outside the scope of my present inquiry, but I want to offer a basic suggestion about how one might position the dialogue in relation to later, mimesis-centered treatments of poetry in Plato. A fundamental consideration is that the *Ion* brings to bear on poetic interpretation, and therefore implicitly on poetry itself, an extremely demanding model of what might count as skill (*technē*) and knowledge. In brief, Socrates treats poetry as constative, declarative discourse—discourse "about" (*peri*) the subjects it deals with;[9] he therefore ostensibly requires, in both the poet and his interpreter, knowledge of these subjects (such as warfare, medicine, and a host of other things) *in*

---

[7] *Ion* 534b8, the same phrase as at *Apol.* 22c3; *kalos* is also used of poetry at *Ion* 533e7;534a2, c2; cf. note 75. I take *Ion* to convey an implict questioning of the idea of authoritative poetic wisdom by its repeatedly ironic reduction of poetic discourse to fragments of material belonging to individual *technai* such as medicine, chariot-driving, and military strategy, even though the primary target of the irony is the rhapsode himself.

[8] A helpful recent treatment of this and related issues of interpretation can be found in Janaway 1995, 14–35. Flashar 1958 remains the fullest analysis, and one that finds much irony in the dialogue. Goethe's ironic reading of the work's account of inspiration is in Goethe 1985–98, 4.2:47–52 ("Plato, als Mitgenosse einer christlichen Offenbarung").

[9] Locutions involving *peri* (about) abound, forming a tricky thread in Socrates' apparent assumptions about poetry: e.g., 531a–b (nine times), 531c2–d4 (eight times).

their own right; and he thus develops a position that, if followed through, would yield only one criterion of poetic merit: systematically informative truth. A corollary of all this is that Socrates appears to rule out the possibility of any kind of fiction, or even of less-than-strictly-veridical poetic statements. When at one stage Ion edges toward a conception of the poet's art as involving the appropriate presentation of certain types of human character (540b3–5), the point gets lost in Socrates' renewed pressing of the model of *technē* as compendious knowledge of an independently identifiable discipline or expertise. But this detail only illustrates a larger problem about *Ion*: does the dialogue, as seems prima facie the case, press its extreme knowledge-inspiration dichotomy in order to exclude all other possibilities, or to produce reductive results (as in the ironic conclusion that Ion must be the best general in the Greek world) that might themselves stimulate a different line of approach? After all, Ion's abortive suggestion at 540b3–5, just mentioned, bears some similarity to Aristotle's explication of his notion of poetic "universals" at *Poetics* 9.1451b8–9. Did Plato mean Ion's idea to be more sustainable than Socrates seems to appreciate—a clue to a trajectory of thought that would escape the dialogue's apparently exclusive disjunction between inspiration and technical knowledge? Or did Plato overlook the potential of what he makes Ion say?[10]

My own view, briefly stated, is that *Ion* is the very reverse of a doctrinaire dialogue. It is a subtle Platonic exercise in the use of schematic dialectic to hint at much more than it ever states. It takes a particularly demanding criterion of poetic knowledge and uses it to find poetry (as well as poetry's interpreters) wanting, precisely because its subtext is an attack on culturally widespread but unexamined, or insufficiently substantiated, claims for the authority and wisdom of poets.[11] If poets are really to be counted as polymathic experts, then their works ought to be able to stand up to just the sort of hard-nosed scrutiny that Socrates applies in *Ion*. But it seems clear that they cannot, and surely should not. That is why the *Ion*, like the *Apology*, is ambivalent as well as undecided about poetry: it both exposes the demands that poetry cannot meet and leaves uncertain the basis of "the many fine things" that are still to be found in it, while simultaneously intimating, in its central section, that poetic power may be partly rooted in the capacity to arouse intense emotional responses in its audience. Whether or not Plato intended the idea of inspiration to be taken seriously, we need to recognize in any case that it cannot in itself solve

[10] For the adaptation of what Ion says at 540b3–4 in Hellenistic criticism, including its criticism by Philodemus, see Asmis 1992b, 410–12. Else 1986, 6–9, exemplifies a more negative reading of *Ion* than mine.

[11] Cf. the echo of themes from the *Ion* in the characterization of popular views of Homer's greatness at *Rep.* 10.598d–e; cf. too Xenophon *Symp.* 4.6–7, where Niceratus parrots the kind of views that are Plato's target in *Ion*.

all the problems posed by the *Apology* and *Ion*. At best, inspiration may give us a *causal* hypothesis about good poetry; it may purport to locate the source of some of what finds its way into such poetry. But that does not and cannot tell us what counts as, or how to appraise, good poetry, nor can it provide a more general understanding of the nature of poetry; inspiration is compatible with more than one criterion of poetic quality.[12] These questions were to remain of vital interest and importance to Plato, and it was to the concept of mimesis that he was to turn for assistance in tackling them.

In the earlier part of his career the widely held supposition of the poets' authoritative knowledge and wisdom formed the main root of Plato's partly skeptical attitude toward their credentials. The supposition, as Socrates puts it (*un*skeptically) at *Lysis* 214a, is that the poets are "our fathers and guides in wisdom"—wisdom being the *sophia* to which philosophers themselves, the "lovers of wisdom," had also come to lay claim.[13] We know that at least two of the pre-Socratic philosophers, Heraclitus and Xenophanes, had challenged such claims for poetry, thereby participating in what Plato was later to call the "ancient quarrel" between philosophy and poetry.[14] Apart from the *Apology*'s general account of the Socratic interrogation of the poets, the Platonic passage that most pointedly suggests that Socrates himself may have contributed to this debate is *Euthyphro* 6a–c, where Socrates links the charge against him of not believing in the city's gods with his doubts over the truth of the stories of divine conflict depicted by poets, painters, and other visual artists. The combination of poetry and painting recurs throughout Plato's work,[15] often in connection with mimesis, as we shall shortly see; and Socrates' objection to the depiction of

[12] Early Greek ideas of poetic inspiration (see esp. Murray 1981) were particularly associated with truth, but it is far from clear that Plato's references to inspiration always presuppose this. On the relationship between inspiration and mimesis in Plato, see Murray 1992 and 1996, 6–12, and Velardi 1989, 115–21, though I remain more agnostic than both these scholars. Woodruff 1982 presents a subtle account of Plato's position on poetic inspiration; most treatments, such as Tate 1929, 147–50, oversystematize the question.

[13] Plato never in fact stops being concerned about this idea of poets as "guides to life": for later critiques, see, e.g., *Rep.* 10.600a–e, 606e; *Laws* 9.858c–e, 12.964c; for contemporary references to such ideas, see Isocrates 2.3, 43.

[14] The main evidence for pre-Socratic critiques of poetry is in Heraclitus frs. 40, 42, 56–57, 104, 106 DK; Xenophanes frs. 1.21–4, 11–12, 14–16 DK. The "ancient quarrel" is at *Rep.* 10.607b5–6; cf. the idea of philosophy as "the greatest *mousikē*" (*Phaedo* 61a) and as "the truest tragedy" (*Laws* 7.817b, with chapter 3, section I). The arguments of Nightingale 1995, 60–67 (cf. Murray 1996, 231), that Plato invented this quarrel, are to be resisted: see Halliwell 1997b, 455–56, with Kannicht 1980 for a longer perspective on the quarrel.

[15] In addition to *Euthph.* 6b–c see esp. *Prot.* 311e; *Crat.* 423c–d; *Rep.* 2.373b, 377e, 6.493c–d, 10.597b ff.; *Tim.* 19b–e; *Soph.* 224a; *Polit.* 288c (cf. 299d), 306d; *Laws* 2.667c–9b, 10.889d; cf. *Epinomis* 975d. On the reference to figurative embroidery at *Euthph.* 6c, see chapter 4 note 18.

divine enmity and aggression has obvious, close affinities with the critique of poetry at *Republic* 2.377e–383c. So there are seeds here of themes that bulk much larger in later dialogues, and one can probably be confident that an authentic element of Socratic thinking informs such skepticism toward standard cultural estimations of poetry. But whether or not that is so, the philosophical challenge to the claims made (both by and on behalf of poets) for poetry's supposedly general but especially ethical authority is one that emerges in Plato's early works without reference to mimesis, but is then carried over to a whole series of works in which mimesis becomes the crux, the organizing focus, of the analysis.

It is probably no accident that the first dialogue in which mimesis starts to take on this role is *Cratylus*, a work many scholars have regarded as marking some sort of transition from "early" to "middle" Plato.[16] What was it that mimesis could bring to Plato's philosophical scrutiny of poetry that was lacking in the reflections on the subject he gives to Socrates in the *Apology*, *Ion*, and *Euthyphro* (and in further passages on poetry in *Protagoras* and *Gorgias*)?[17] Although I am committed to denying that we should expect a simple answer to this question, or, as already indicated, that mimesis ever occupied a fixed function in Plato's thinking, a preliminary observation may help to put in perspective the kind of role mimesis comes to play in the dialogues. In the broadest terms, mimesis allows Plato to construct a more elaborate framework of thought for the consideration not only of poetry but of the whole group of arts, both musicopoetic and visual, which, as we saw in my introduction, had come to be considered mimetic in the pre-Platonic tradition—exactly the group whose collective cultural status is foregrounded in Socrates' characterization of "the city of luxury." The complexity of this framework of thought, in comparison to, say, the overtly rather narrow terms of the *Ion*, resides in the way in which it makes room for the formulation of questions about the status of the "world" (the people and things) exhibited "inside" the mimetic work or performance, but also about the relationship of that world to reality as a whole, to the world outside the work. Mimesis, that is to say, permits issues of artistic representation to be framed both in their own terms and in terms of a larger scheme of truth and value. Reference to mimesis promotes the integration of concerns arising from the mimetic arts into an all-encompassing philosophical project; it even, as we shall see, comes to affect Plato's thinking about the basic conditions of such a project itself. All this

[16] See Guthrie 1962–81, 5:1–2; Baxter 1992, 2–3; Fine 1993, 292 n. 32; and Levin 2001, 4 n. 4, for a range of views and bibliography.

[17] It is unwarranted to see mimesis as implicitly adumbrated in the *Ion* itself, as do Vicaire 1960, 216–17, and Schaper 1968, 42; Flashar 1958, 87, thinks mimesis is deliberately "suppressed" in this dialogue. Note the cluster of visual arts, music, and poetry at *Ion* 532e–3c (with note 19).

may make it easier to discern why a concept of (artistic) mimesis first emerges in the *Cratylus*, which is likely to be the earliest dialogue in which Plato broaches overarching philosophical questions about the relationship between human understanding (language and thought) and reality (*ta onta*: everything that is the case, on Platonic premises, independently of human thought).

Mimesis makes brief but telling appearances in *Cratylus*. In the context of the dialogue's investigation into the relationship of language to "nature" (*phusis*) and "reality" (*ta onta*), Socrates develops an etymological model of the "correctness"—the accuracy and veridical reliability—of "naming." He pursues this model until he reaches the level of the basic elements, the "first" or primary names, which are not themselves reducible by further etymological analysis. The principle by which these primary names apprehend and communicate the nature of things (the posited functions of all naming) must therefore be different (422a–d). At this point Socrates introduces the concept of mimesis, applying it in turn to visual signification (including the kind of signing used by deaf mutes, he suggests)[18] and to spoken language itself. But he immediately distinguishes mimetic "naming" from the mimesis involved both in *mousikē*, the musicopoetic arts (including vocal mimicry), and in a visual art such as painting: the difference, he says, is that, whereas all these arts are concerned with the sensible properties—the sounds and appearances—of things in the world, language, in its strict "naming" function, is concerned with the "essence" (*ousia*) of things (423c–e). In addition to indicating an unproblematic acceptance of a broad grouping of mimetic arts, which by this date was probably culturally commonplace,[19] this passage sets out, in rudimentary form, a kind of "semantics" of representational art (parallel to the semantics of language that is Socrates' direct aim). Using "likeness," a defining property of all mimesis, these arts "show" (*dēloun*) and "signify" (*sēmainein*) a sensorily perceptible world;[20] but they do not address the "essence,"

---

[18] *Crat.* 422e–23a. The passage 422e3–4 contains the first known reference to the sign languages of deaf mutes: though these are not wholly mimetic, Plato was right to see a strongly mimetic dimension to them; cf. Sacks 1991, 122–23; Rée 1999, 119–20.

[19] The most straightforward indication of this is *Rep.* 2.373b; cf. my introduction, note 54, with Zimbrich 1984, 151–54. Many years later, at *Laws* 2.668b–c, Plato makes the Athenian say that the conception of all *mousikē* as mimetic is uncontroversial: the context as a whole shows not only that this term, as often, embraces all musicopoetic arts, but that the coupling of these with the visual arts, within a unitary category of mimetic art(s), is not in itself contentious. The point is corroborated by Aristotle, especially in the first chapter of the *Poetics* and at, e.g., *Rhet.* 1.11, 1371b4–10.

[20] Likeness: *Crat.* 423a5, 424d6–8; cf. 430c12, d6, and esp. 434a–b (where the natural, nonconventional status of (visual) likeness is stressed). *Sēmainein*: 422e4 (where its force should be applicable to the other kinds of mimesis discussed in the context). *Dēloun*: 422e3; 423a2, 5, b5, etc.

the true reality, of things, in the way that language-as-naming supposedly does. It seems that the suggestion here is that artistic mimesis, whether visual or musicopoetic, "pictures" things of the kind to be found in the actual world, but does not thereby tell us the (philosophical) truth about these things. Although Socrates' purpose at this point in *Cratylus* is to seek a way of holding together his account of language as a potential medium of philosophical truth (though he will eventually despair of this conviction),[21] it leads him to intimate a conception of mimetic art as both modeled on, and yet incapable of truly grasping, certain aspects of reality.

Two further passages in *Cratylus* help a little to give sharper edges to the dialogue's adumbration of a view of mimetic art(s). The first, at 430a–31d, picks up the earlier analogy between artistic and linguistic mimesis and appears to make the important admission that the relationship between a mimetic image or "likeness" and its object or model is not restricted to the copying of actual particulars in the world. Socrates refers specifically to paintings, and in addition to images such as portraits, whose definition depends on a relationship to specifiable individuals, he allows for images that represent imaginary members of classes such as "man" and "woman," or even, perhaps, depict the general properties of "man" and "woman" themselves.[22] This point matters in part because it serves to combat the common belief that Plato straightforwardly limits visual mimesis to the "mirroring" of visible reality, an interpretation I later dispute even for *Republic* 10. But there is a further strand to this passage. While Socrates compares the picture-object relationship to the name-object relationship, he distinguishes them by saying that in the latter case the "assignment" or "allocation" (*dianomē*) of name to object can be true or false, as well as correct or incorrect, whereas in that of a picture it can be only correct or incorrect.[23] Although it is difficult to press this distinction to a conclusive interpretation, it looks as though the difference Socrates asserts between acts of "naming" and the assignment of pictures to their objects depends on the idea that naming is always either explicitly or implicitly propositional in character, whereas pictures (or other mimetic images) are stan-

---

[21] This is a striking instance of how the reading of a Platonic dialogue must always be dynamic: the reader of *Cratylus* who takes Socrates' final hint ends up needing to start all over again. A new treatment of the *Cratylus*, construing its rejection of etymology as a critique of the literary tradition (from Homer to tragedy), is offered by Levin 2001, 13–98.

[22] *Crat.* 430a–31d: 430e5 refers to portraits, but the section as a whole allows for images of "tokens" and perhaps even of "types"; cf. esp. the implications of 430c, plus 431a3–4.

[23] *Crat.* 430c–d; see Baxter 1992, 32–37 for the problematic status of truth and falsity in this context. Notice that the metaphorical "images" and "paintings" in the soul at *Phlb.* 39b–40e are described as being either true or false: these are construed as mental representations of thoughts that have a propositional content (by virtue of being *doxai* or *logoi*, 39b–c, 40a6). That does not, of course, explain why in the *Cratylus* real pictures should be construed, as I suggest in the text, as nonpropositional.

dardly taken to stand in a relationship to reality that is other (and less) than propositional. Pictures, it might be thought, lack the kind of semantic articulation needed for propositional assertions.[24]

If that is right, and if the "picture-model" were applied to all arts of mimesis, it would mean that mimetic art does not purport to make determinate statements about the world and does not constitute a medium of truth (or falsehood) about that world, yet represents things that may be congruent with, and be recognizable on the basis of, experience in general. "Correctness," a concept we shall encounter again in Platonic treatments of mimesis, seems, on this reading, to be something different from truth: perhaps "truth-to" the general appearances of things, rather than truth about their underlying nature.[25] It is important to emphasize, however, that what we have here is a distinction that plays a part in the *Cratylus*'s provisional (and ultimately rejected) account of language, not one, as will emerge progressively, we can safely extrapolate to Plato's understanding of mimesis *tout court*. In particular, the dialogue's emphasis on the picture-model of artistic mimesis leaves the applicability of some of its arguments to the verbal art of poetry hard to discern: the status of poetic mimesis is a problem that the *Cratylus* leaves in the wings.[26]

The last passage of *Cratylus* calling for attention in this context is 432a–d, which enunciates a "qualitative" conception of visual images and rejects the need for mimesis to justify itself in terms of replicatory fidelity. Here the "correctness" (*orthotēs*) of an image is said to be qualitative in the sense that while any adjustment, any addition or subtraction, is critical where "mathematical" objects are concerned (i.e., objects whose essential properties are quantifiable or measurable), the overall quality of an image does not require such exactitude—indeed, if such exactitude *were* required, its fulfillment would yield a duplicate, not an image at all. "Do you see, then, my friend," says Socrates, "that we must look for a different standard of correctness for images . . . and not make the presence or absence of particular features a necessary condition for something to be an image? Surely

---

[24] For such a view see, e.g., Gombrich 1987, 246–47, and cf. Scruton 1974, 196–97. This is not to deny that pictures can sometimes be given a sufficiently "dense" contextualization to allow them to serve as propositions (e.g., with certain kinds of traffic signs).

[25] It may be relevant that the relationship of picture to object is framed in terms of "appropriateness" (*to proshēkon*) as well as likeness (430c12, 435c8). Cf. esp. *Rep.* 4.420c–d, where the analogy between the unity of the ideal city and the unity of a human figure in sculpture or painting perhaps suggests that "appropriateness" modifies the requirement of likeness by putting it in the context of a mimetic work's structure and coherence (cf. *Gorg.* 503d–e). But appropriateness may sometimes be synonymous with close likeness, as with eicastic mimesis at *Soph.* 235e1.

[26] Poetry is surely covered by the reference to *mousikē* at 423d, but it receives explicit attention only as a source of linguistic examples: on this separate aspect of the subject, see Vicaire 1960, 27–30.

you realize that images are far from having the same properties as the things whose images they are?" Although, once again, Socrates' argument bears principally on the semantics of language (and whether a change in the form of a name changes its status as a name), it seems to incorporate a recognition that the kinds of correspondence or correlation that qualify images in the mimetic arts as cases of "likeness" (*homoiotēs*) cannot be reduced to a "mathematically" strict set of requirements.[27] Whether this should count as a positive or negative recognition, however, is less easy to decide. It is certainly compatible with an appreciation that the nature of mimetic representation will vary according to (among other things) the materials and techniques of individual arts, as well as the cultural traditions that grow up around these arts; and other passages in Plato manifest an awareness of these factors.[28] But it might also be thought to point in the direction of a suspicion about the usefulness of images. Within the design of *Cratylus*, in fact, it helps to prepare the way for Socrates' ultimate loss of faith in the power of language to unlock the truth about the abiding reality that, he is convinced, must underlie the apparent flux of the world. No further consequences are explicitly drawn in the dialogue for the mimetic arts as such. But when taken together with the earlier passages already considered, Socrates' sense of the inescapable difference between images and their objects leaves the status and value of artistic mimesis in some uncertainty.

The *Cratylus* is not normally thought of, and has rarely been discussed, in connection with Plato's treatment of representational art.[29] But as the preceding comments should have established, it does deserve some reflection in this setting. Although the dialogue cites mimetic art only for the purposes of comparison and contrast with the hypothetically mimetic nature of language, it allows us to see that in picking up the traditional concept of mimesis, as applied to both the musicopoetic and visual arts, Plato was drawn into integrating his use of it into a larger and more complex configuration of ideas. This process can be described as the treatment of artistic mimesis as "secondary" representation, in subordination to the "primary" representation existing (as *Cratylus* itself pervasively accepts)

---

[27] The passage need not even imply that mimetic images aim at "the maximum amount of verisimilitude," as asserted by Baxter 1992, 168, who should be consulted further on the linguistic implications of this passage.

[28] See, for instance, chapter 4, section II, on the evidence of the *Laws* for a Platonic recognition of important differences between the representational traditions of Egyptian and Greek art.

[29] One exception is Vicaire 1960, 217–20, who also detects ambiguity in the dialogue's treatment of mimesis, though in somewhat different terms from mine. Koller 1954, 48–57, is skewed by his *parti pris* on the history of mimesis as a concept (see my introduction, notes 15, 30, 32, 39, 53).

in the fabric of human language and thought. In part the *Cratylus* gestures toward ways in which a distinction of this kind might be turned into a perception of how mimetic art calls for criteria other than the strictly truth- and knowledge-centered model ostensibly offered in *Ion*. This is particu- larly so with the suggestions, first, that artistic mimesis stands in a relation- ship to reality that is not one of (unqualified) truth or falsity (430c–d), and, second, that the relationship between mimetic images and their objects is not "mathematical" but "qualitative" and therefore variable (432a–d). These thought-provoking hints are ultimately submerged, however, be- neath a more negative sentiment. At the end of the dialogue Socrates ex- presses the conviction that the sort of truth that would satisfy his philo- sophical requirements could be gained only from "things in themselves," not from their "images" in language (439a–b): philosophical truth, in other words, would have to transcend representation altogether. But if this opens a problematic gap between even "primary" representation and the reality it aspires to make contact with, where does that leave the "second- ary" representation of artistic images? If primary mimesis is inadequate for philosophical truth, how much more so must be the secondary mimesis of painting or poetry? The *Cratylus*, we are now in a position to see, contains oblique intimations of thoughts that receive more trenchant formulation, with direct reference to mimetic art, in *Republic* 10: on my own preferred chronological hypothesis, this makes the former a shadowy prefiguring of the latter, though other ways of construing the relationship remain open.[30]

II

Regardless of chronological hypotheses, it is to the *Republic*, with its two distinct but related discussions of mimesis, that we must now turn. My initial treatment of these two passages will be necessarily selective, leaving specific aspects of them for closer scrutiny in later chapters. Part of the interest of the relevant sections of books 3 and 10 of the *Republic* is that they bring together questions of education, culture, politics, psychology, and even metaphysics. In consequence, they both require and reward ex- amination from a variety of standpoints. This has implications for the treat- ment of mimesis as such, which in both parts of the work is handled in a manner that simultaneously draws on earlier Greek thinking yet is innova- tive in important respects, bearing out my earlier claim that Plato's ap- proach to mimesis is neither static nor monolithic but subject to dynamic development. What I want to concentrate on here are the main conceptual lines of the two discussions of mimesis in the *Republic*, in an attempt to

---

[30] On the chronological issue, cf. note 16.

draw out certain points that have not always been well appreciated in the abundant literature on the subject.

The *Republic*'s first discussion of mimesis constitutes the later part of Socrates' blueprint for the contribution of "stories" (*muthoi*), which means above all poetry, to the education of the young Guardians. Poetry merits such prominent attention in the construction of the hypothetically ideal city (itself, we must always remember, a large-scale paradigm for the mind, "the city in the soul") on account of its educational and cultural prestige in the Greek world, not least in Athens. Widely deemed a repository of wisdom, as we have already seen, poetry was one of the most influential forms of discourse in the traditional life of the polis. The early scenes of the *Republic* itself dramatize a series of illustrations of the importance of poetry: the gravity Cephalus attaches to its myths and sentiments (330d–31a); Polemarchus's reliance on a definition of justice taken from Simonides (331d–e); Adeimantus's description of the culturally powerful hold of religious and ethical ideas embodied in poetry (363–65); and Socrates' own reference to the salience of poetic mimesis in the life of the city of luxury (373b). All this material signals some of the respects in which poetry impinges on people's lives and beliefs, and thereby prepares the ground for the examination of the place of *mousikē*, musicopoetic art, in the education of the future Guardians. The examination starts at 2.376c and proceeds from the premise that poetic stories or myths form a subclass of *logoi* (statements, arguments, narratives, forms of discourse)—the subclass essentially of "falsehood" or "fiction" (a possible ambiguity lurking beneath the noun *pseudos*, as well as the adjective *pseudēs*), but one that must nonetheless be judged, precisely because of its educational-cum-cultural influence, partly by (normative) standards of "truth," especially in the spheres of the ethical and the religious.[31] Storytelling, Socrates accepts, need not involve literal, factual truth, but its narratives are, even so, quasi-propositional in form and function: through their works the poets "say" or "mean" (*legein*) certain things (a motif we recall from the *Apology* and

---

[31] Here, as on some other points relating to the *Republic*, I condense arguments developed more fully in Halliwell 1997a. For the inclusion of poetry in the category of *logoi*, cf. *Gorg.* 502c; and with the truth-falsehood dichotomy of *Rep.* 2.376e11, note *Crat.* 408c (with chapter 3, section I). Belfiore 1985b argues for the importance of Hesiod's *Theogony* (cf. my introduction, note 48) to Plato's critique of "falsehood" in poetic theology. Weinstock 1927, 124, notes the ambiguity of *pseudos* in the *Republic*'s first critique of poetry; cf. Scolnicov 1988, 114–19, on the "global," nonliteral truth or falsehood of myths in this perspective. Murray 1996, 135–36, resisting the point, produces the awkward claim that Plato is concerned with "truthful and untruthful lies." Yanal 1999, 13–14, denies flatly that Plato recognized fictionality, but his argument rests on the erroneous premise that Plato thought mimesis always used a particular model. Cf. Carlisle 1999 for a survey of *pseud-* words, and their association with an emergent idea of fictionality, in Homer.

Ion), conveying ideas about and attitudes to the world that can in turn impress themselves on the minds of their audiences, especially the soft, malleable minds of the young, though not theirs alone.[32]

This complex combination of thoughts about the nature of *muthoi* explains how Socrates can start from the apparently neutral premise that *muthoi* belong in the class of false or fictive discourse (*pseudos*, 376e11), yet go on, notoriously, to maintain that extensive stretches of Homeric poetry constitute gross religious and ethical "defamation" (*katapseudes-thai*—the compound verb being necessarily pejorative) in their depiction of gods and heroes. As the crucial ambiguity attaching here to words of the *pseud-* root indicates, Plato does not have separate terms to denote what we now readily distinguish as "fiction" and "falsehood." But before we complain that he fails to articulate an appropriate concept of fiction, we must allow for the possibility that he would have seen reason to *resist* a clear-cut falsehood-fiction distinction. We might, indeed, count it an insight, not a limitation, that his argument assumes that the influence of works of art on their audiences' beliefs and feelings does not depend solely, or even principally, on the literal or factual status of their contents, but can operate also, and no less potently, through the normative or exemplary force of what they represent. This, then, is why he here gives Socrates a critique of poetic *muthoi* that treats them as the value-laden bearers of implicit *logoi* and appraises their content by standards of normative not "narrative" veracity. The result is a complex interplay, and a sort of cross-fertilization, between the criteria of truth(fulness), goodness, and (psychological) benefit to which Socrates makes appeal at different stages of the discussion.[33]

The crucial link between this first stretch of books 2–3's critique of poetry and the subsequent introduction of mimesis is provided by the prem-

[32] It is vital to see that the import of the discussion is not restricted to the young, but develops a general model of aesthetic experience and values: see esp. the various clues to this at 378d, 380c, 387b, with Halliwell 1991a, 329–30; Ferrari 1989, 113–4; Burnyeat 1999, 256, 262 (plus his repeated emphasis on "the total culture"). On the idea that poets "say" (*legein*) things, cf. *Apol.* 22b4, *Ion*, e.g., 530c5, with note 33.

[33] See Halliwell 1992c, 56–58, for the tension between fiction and falsehood, and the criteria of truth, goodness, and benefit, in this part of the work; cf. chapter 5 on Aristotle's contrasting position. Gill 1993 takes an interesting but somewhat different line on the problems of falsehood versus fiction in Plato. Both echoes of and developments beyond Plato's position can be traced in the characteristically paradoxical passages at Augustine *Solil.* 2.9.16, 2.10.18: cf. Barish 1981, 54–57; Eden 1986, 119–24. (The earliest verbally explicit distinction between fiction and falsehood may be at Isidore *Differ.* 20.) For a broader perspective on the Platonic treatment of poetry as always implicitly propositional (i.e., the medium of *logoi*, or of what the poet "says," *legein*), based on his practices of quotation, see Halliwell 2000a. Plato was never concerned with "the historical untruth of art," *contra* Carritt 1949, 54; Skillen 1992, 205, gets this right; cf. also Tate 1929, 145–46, on the complexities of "truth" in *Rep.* 2–3.

ise that (poetic) narratives induce and shape belief in their audiences,[34] a premise reinforced by the consideration that gods and heroes, the central characters in so many myths, have a paradigmatic standing in the value systems of the culture. At one point Socrates speaks of the need to censor out from poetry scenes of heroic grief and similar behavior, in order to prevent future Guardians from "acting like" (*homoia poiein*) such unworthy role models (2.377e–78a). The notion of "acting like" or emulating foreshadows the treatment of mimesis proper that begins at 392c, where Socrates suggests that the discussion of "*what* things should/may be said [sc. by poets]" now needs to be complemented by consideration of *lexis*, which he glosses as "*how* things should/may be said." Starting from the premise that all poetry is *diēgēsis*, (narrative, in a logical rather than strictly formal sense), he distinguishes two chief poetic modes or forms (which can, of course, be combined): "simple/pure narrative," in third-person form; and "narrative through mimesis," where mimesis—temporarily, it must be stressed—is limited to representation in direct speech (a sense not original with Plato).[35] Two questions are then posed in rapid succession: do we want mimetic poets in our city (394d), and do we want our future Guardians themselves to be "mimetic" (394e)? Socrates' answer to both is a qualified negative. The principle of social specialization, as set out in book 2 of the *Republic* (370, 374), is invoked to support the idea that just as the same person cannot *do* more than one thing well (cannot live more than one life, we might say),[36] so no one can engage in effective mimesis, or dramatic representation, of "many things" (394e). This is buttressed by the argument that, because mimesis involves "self-likening" or psychological assimilation, it follows that the young Guardians should be exposed to the mimetic mode of poetry largely for the presentation of virtuous characters. There will be no place, in the well-ordered city, for

[34] Poetry induces beliefs and "persuasion": e.g., *Rep.* 2.377b, 378d–e; 3.391d–e.

[35] I say "temporarily" because (a frequently overlooked point, wrongly downplayed by Cauer 1920, 163–64) a wider sense of mimesis, applicable to *all* poetry and other representational arts, occurs both *before* (2.373b, 388c) and *after* (3.401a) this passage, as well as, arguably, *within* it (note the implications of *mimeisthai* at 3.396b, 397a, 398a2); cf. also the application of mimesis terms to music (3.399a7, c3, d5, 400a7, with chapter 10, note 3), which goes beyond the strict sense defined at 393c (as does 2.382b9, though that is a separate issue). Aristophanes *Thesm.* 156, 850, testify to a strongly "enactive"-dramatic sense of mimesis already in the fifth century, a usage that can itself be regarded as an intensification of the general "behavioral" sense of mimesis terms; see the analysis of Stohn 1993, with Halliwell 1986, 113–14; cf. my introduction, note 33. Thus the claim (e.g., Most 1998, 381; Burnyeat 1999, 267–68, but cf. his 271 n. 27) that the impersonatory sense of mimesis was original in Plato *Rep.* 3 is mistaken. Adeimantus's initial uncertainty over Socrates' scheme at *Rep.* 3.392d should not be construed as implying that the sense of mimesis here is itself entirely strange.

[36] See chapter 2, section II, for the force of this idea in connection with (especially dramatic) poetry.

poetry involving constantly changing representation of different sorts of people and behavior: such poets will be politely but firmly denied admission (398a), because the imaginative variety of their art would imperil the fixity of social roles in the just polis.

The concept of mimesis as dramatic representation or impersonation introduces a distinction between authorial and character's utterances that played no part in the earlier discussion, where examples of both types, side by side, were subjected to the same kinds of evaluative criticism (e.g., 386c–87a). Mimesis is first explained by reference to the poet himself, who is pictured as a kind of imaginative stage performer (393c), but then almost abruptly applied to the (young) recipients of poetry: the transition occurs at 394d–e. But this transition is designed to convey the important idea (reminiscent of, but modifying, the *Ion*) that the mimetic mode is such as to carry over, with peculiar psychological efficacy, from poet(ry) to audience-*qua*-performer. To understand this idea we need to recognize that in addition to stage performances and public recitals Plato takes for granted normal Greek practices of reading aloud and reciting poetry, practices that effectively make the "reader" into a kind of performer.[37] These practices, inculcated through education, invite the reciter to step with imaginatively rich feeling into the roles of the poetic agents, much more so than with the habits of silent reading. Plato suggests, we might say, that "reading" dramatic poetry is always a kind of dramatic *acting*.

The concept of mimesis used in this section of the work, as applied to both the poet (393c) and the recipient or reciter (396a–b, 396d), entails "self-likening" or assimilation to the figures of poetry. In experiencing poetry in the dramatic mode, the mind orientates itself to, and positions itself "inside," the viewpoint of the speaker. This model of close psychological identification allows a deepening of the earlier concern with poetry's effects on the mind. We see this notably at 396d–e, where Socrates recommends that the decent man will not be prepared to recite mimetic poetry depicting immoral behavior, but will refuse "to mold and fit himself to the forms of rather evil characters." This echoes the original imagery, first at 377b, of the plasticity or malleability of the (young) soul, and of poetic stories as the carriers of *tupoi*—"molds," "stamps," or "images"—that can

---

[37] The term *rhētōr* at 396e10, which normally means "public speaker," is significant in this respect; cf. 7.536c7. Among the kinds of recital Plato may have in mind here are official recitations from epic and other poetry by boys at the Apaturia: Plato *Tim.* 21a–b; cf. Herington 1985, 192–200. On the psychology of Greek recitation reading, see Havelock 1963, 36–60, 145–64, though I do not share his larger thesis of a specifically oral "technology" and mentality; cf. Herington 1985, 3–40. My comments in Halliwell 1997a, 322–23, were not meant to exclude choral performances (*pace* Gastaldi 1998, 367 n. 40), though Plato's text puts no stress on them. Cf. chapter 2, note 20.

be impressed on the soul.[38] Where poetry uses the dramatic mode, the reciter is drawn intensely into, and thereby takes on, the mental and ethical cast of each speaker. So mimesis functions here as a process whereby the world of the poem *becomes* the world of the mind imaginatively (re)en-acting it. This point highlights a continuity, at the level of concern over the psychological influence of poetry, between the earlier scrutiny of poetic *muthoi* and the present analysis of poetic "form." It ought also to show us that Plato's questions can connect with problems that are still ours.

Plato makes Socrates relentlessly pursue the insight that, through and beyond their literal narrative content, stories can endorse a point of view, an expressive or affective stance, a way of thinking and feeling about the world. Ideas of this kind have now acquired considerable currency in modern cultural criticism, and they play an intermittent part in wider de-bates about creative freedom, censorship, and the influence of art. But part of our difficulty in coming to terms with the Platonic perspective on these matters is that we approach them from a culture that is itself uneasily divided between, on the one hand, traditions of political liberalism and a postromantic faith in the aesthetic imagination and, on the other, urgent anxieties about the power of mass-media entertainment.[39] If most of us— confident, for reasons we are unlikely to interrogate, that the reading of *Homer* could never harm us—find *Republic* 2–3 uncomfortably blunt and censorious in this area, this is partly because its own presuppositions are largely free of internal tension. Plato's arguments move from the acknowl-edged educational status and cultural influence of poetry within his own world to a statement of the need to control poetic content in the interests of ethical ideology, individual psychological development, and the social order as a whole. The anxiety this case standardly arouses in modern read-ers is as much a reflex of the unresolved tensions in our own cultural makeup as of intrinsic problems in Plato's arguments themselves.

What is at stake throughout this stretch of the work, then, is the artistic projection of ideas (embodied in images of divine and human behavior) capable of shaping the souls of those exposed to them: the education of the young is a paradigm of more general processes of psychological and cultural self-formation. The heightened degree of absorption induced by

---

[38] Gorgias fr. 11.13, 15 DK (*Helen*) applies such language to the psychological effects of both persuasion and sense experience; cf. Segal 1962, 106–8 and 142 n. 44, with my note 55. I am baffled how Porter 1996, 613, can say that for Gorgias "poems are not to be evaluated in relation to what they mean": Gorgias fr. 11.8–12 DK is all about the impact of (poetic) *logos* on the mind or belief of the hearer.

[39] Burnyeat 1999, an important contribution to the debate on Plato and poetry, offers a rich set of reflections on this side of the subject. Nehamas 1988, 220–30, relates some of Plato's ideas on mimesis, esp. in *Rep.* 10, to modern criticism of television.

the mimetic mode means a heightened danger. "Haven't you noticed," Socrates asks, "that mimetic acts [*mimēseis*], if allowed to continue from youth onward, establish themselves in the habits and nature of the person's body, voice, and mind?" (395d1–3). The question exploits the general semantic association of *mimēsis* with imitative or emulatory behavior; Socrates links the mimetic mode of poetry with the notion of character formation through habituation.[40] Where poetic mimesis encourages close identification with the figures depicted, the experience of poetry acts as a "rehearsal" for life itself. From these premises Socrates can reach only one answer to the question he posed at 394e. The future Guardians of the city should be exposed to mimetic poetry—and, to that extent, should themselves be "mimetic"—only where representation of the virtuous is concerned.[41] But why should *anyone* in a just society be exposed to anything other than this? That Plato's argument renders this a rhetorical question is confirmed by the eventual exclusion from the well-ordered city, and implicitly from the life of the well-ordered soul, of poetry that uses the mimetic mode indiscriminately (398a).

Distinctions between narrative modes and their points of view have now become the common fare of narratological and related kinds of criticism.[42] But Plato's argument is not focused on technicalities as such: at its heart is an anxiety over the heightened states of mind—the self-likening, absorption, and identification—(allegedly) entailed by participation in the dramatic mode. It is legitimate and instructive, I believe, to read this aspect of the dialogue as a radical attack on the workings of imagination itself, where imagination is to be understood as a dimension of the mind's capacity to explore the possibility of *difference* in its own life. This suggestion, together with my paradoxical proposal that we should think of Plato as a "romantic puritan," will be expounded in more detail in the next chapter. But it is worth stressing here two basic reasons for distinguishing the attitudes to mimetic-imaginative experience expressed in *Republic* 2–3 from

---

[40] See chapter 2, section I, for further discussion of this point. Danto 1986, 121–22, is badly mistaken in thinking that Plato's concern over dramatic mimesis rests on the idea that words spoken by actors are "real words" (and still more in generalizing this point to Plato's view of "mimetic representations as a class"): the argument of *Rep.* 3, as I have explained, is psychological not ontological.

[41] The virtues at 395c echo the earlier part of the critique: courage (cf. 386a ff.), self-discipline (389d ff.), piety (377e ff.), and "freedom" (387b5, 391c5).

[42] Hawthorn 1992, 58–61, summarizes some modern developments of Plato's distinctions, though like many others, including Genette 1988, 18, he strictly misstates Platonic usage (in which *diēgēsis* is the genus of which *mimēsis* is one species, equivalent to "pure *diēgēsis*"); for one "refurbishment" of Plato's typology, see Tarot 1970. Jenny 1984, 174–83, and Kirby 1991, esp. 118–19, discuss the relationship between Plato's (and Aristotle's: cf. chapter 5, note 46) categories of mimesis and the narratology of Genette. Lowe 2000 is a recent attempt to study Greek literature through narratological models.

REPRESENTATION AND REALITY

most later varieties of "puritanism" in aesthetics: first, because Plato's arguments are presented in a form—a Socratic dialogue of inexhaustible subtlety—that is itself deeply imaginative, and self-consciously so;[43] second, because they contain overt acknowledgments of the pleasures of poetry (e.g., 387b, 390a). Both these points direct us toward a broader observation of substantial significance, namely that all of Plato's dealings with poetry come from a position not of uncomprehending hostility toward, but profound appreciation of, as well as extensive indebtedness to, the traditions of poetry themselves.[44]

In view of this last remark, it is revealing that the *Republic*'s second treatment of mimesis, in book 10, is framed by quasi-confessional expressions of Socrates' (and, at some level, Plato's) closeness to the poetry he criticizes. At 595b Socrates admits to a love and respect, ingrained from childhood, that inhibits him from speaking adversely about Homer; in formulating "the greatest charge" against poetry at 605c–d he says that "even the best of us" are unable to resist the emotional power of Homeric and tragic poetry;[45] and at the end of the section, having again declared a personal susceptibility to the allure of poetry (607c), he goes on to speak in the language of a regretful, nostalgic lover, withdrawing from a *grande passion* yet only able to relinquish it with immense psychological effort (607e–8b). This recurrent tone invites us to see that book 10's critique of poetry and mimesis is really aimed at *lovers* of Homer who are willing to face a philosophical scrutiny of their love: it is written, and needs to be read, from a position of intimate knowledge of poetry, not severe detachment from it. An outright puritan might well be suspicious of Plato's own text.[46]

---

[43] This self-consciousness borders on the paradoxical at *Rep.* 2.376d9, where the discussion of *muthoi* is preceded by Socrates' description of the conversation itself (Plato's work) as a *muthos*; cf. 6.501e4.

[44] Various strands of Plato's own quasi-poetic artistry, and his reworking of poetic traditions, are explored by Rutherford 1995, Nightingale 1995 (both with further bibliography); see Gifford 2001 for Platonic adaptation of dramatic and tragic irony. On the relationship of Plato's criticisms of dramatic mimesis to his own dialogic practice, see chapter 1, section I.

[45] Barish 1981, 5, justifiably calls this passage a "haunting acknowledgement" of the power of theater. Robb 1994, 228, is typical of many in missing the tone of the passages cited in my text when speaking of "the depth of Plato's hostility to poetry" (cf. "contempt," 220) and his supposed aim of making it leave the city "ignominiously"; cf., likewise, Gould 1992, 17 ("at war"), 25 ("ferocious hostility"). Contrast, e.g., Laborderie 1978, 81; Burnyeat 1999, 287; and, in a different way, Nietzsche (see chapter 2).

[46] Particularly when one reaches Plato's own use of myth at the end of the *Republic*: Epicurus's friend Colotes of Lampsacus accused Plato of hypocrisy for attacking poetic myths in *Rep.* 2–3 but then writing a quasi-poetic myth and "falsehood" (*pseudos*) of his own, in particularly "tragic" style to make matters worse, in the myth of Er. Colotes' attack, which fits with Epicurus's own attitudes to poetic myths (cf. chapter 9, section II), is reported by Proclus *In Remp.* 2.105.23–106.14 Kroll; cf. chapter 3, note 38. Where Burnyeat 1999, 292–96, posits an

The second critique refers back to the first, but it widens the terms of inquiry by seeking a definition of "mimesis as a whole" (595c7; cf. 603a11). Instead of book 3's restriction to the dramatic mode, book 10 (re)expands the concept of mimesis to cover *all* representation in both poetry and the visual arts—not as disquieting a change of terminology and focus as many have found it, because even in books 2–3, as I noted earlier, the language of mimesis is used in both broader and narrower senses.[47] Many interpreters have been puzzled by the fact that the *Republic* returns at all to the subject of poetry and mimesis; this is one reason for speculative attempts to date book 10 considerably later than, and to see it as somehow partly "detached" from, the rest of the work.[48] But the design of the *Republic* is not determinable a priori, so to speak; it follows an exploratory course, blown by the wind of dialectical argument (3.394d), and turns back on itself at various points (e.g., the start of book 5). Book 10 refers several times to earlier passages of the dialogue. Above all, and unlike books 2–3, it partially, though problematically, presupposes both the form-centered metaphysics of books 5–7 and the concept of conflict between soul parts (4.439c–44lc). Its function is best understood as a complex coda to the main structure.[49] If we press further the question why the dialogue should return to poetry rather than any other topic, we must be satisfied with the thought that Plato perceives poetry as a potent cultural rival, an opponent in what Socrates famously calls the "ancient quarrel" (607b). It is in large part to test once again the established and widely accredited claim that poets are ethical experts—a claim we saw earlier as the root of his earliest engagements with the subject—that Plato constructs the arguments of 595–608, although we can hardly ignore the further consideration that these arguments are soon to be followed by the alternative and antitragic "poetry" of Plato's own philosophical myth.[50]

---

implicit audience of philosophers for the first part of *Rep.* 10, I would prefer to think in terms of (philosophical) lovers of poetry: perhaps we might agree on "philosophical lovers of poetry."

[47] See note 35. Belfiore 1984 puts the case for a tighter consistency between mimesis in books 3 and 10; cf. Nehamas 1982 (though his denial, 52–53, of a back reference to book 3 at 595a cannot be right) and Ferrari 1989, 120–41; Tate 1928, 16–19 (cf. Tate 1932, 161–63) has to manipulate Plato's text to find an underlying contrast between "good" and "bad" mimesis in both books. I continue to think that the model of narrower and broader senses, as suggested by the phrase "mimesis as a whole [*holōs*]" at *Rep.* 10.595c7, yields the best correlation between the two books.

[48] See Halliwell 1988, 194–95, for further references, with Babut 1983 for an excellent defense of the book's unity and its integral connections with the rest of the dialogue. Even if it were demonstrable, a later dating would not explain book 10's place in the work's structure.

[49] Burnyeat 1999, 289 n. 9, objects to such descriptions; but he understands "coda" to mean a distinct, nonintegral unit, where I understood a quasi-musical supplementation and drawing together of what has gone before.

[50] See chapter 3; but cf. note 46 here.

The second critique's *point de départ* is a notoriously metaphysical argument, which applies the concept of a "form" (*eidos, idea*: 596a–b) to classes of objects such as couches or tables, rather than, as in books 5–6 or the *Phaedo*, to properties like beauty or justice. This is not the place to attempt a resolution of a problem that has often exasperated specialists in Plato's so-called theory of forms.[51] But I stress three general interpretative factors in this connection. First, the exposition of the tripartite schema (forms, particulars, mimesis) is highly rhetorical in tone and emphasis, even (like later parts of the critique) satirical: this shows itself in the choice of bed or couch as an example, the irony of 596b–e (which introduces the notorious mirror analogy), and the language of 598b–c (with its talk of "children and stupid adults" as the gullible audience of visual art). It is imprudent to interpret the passage without taking account of Socrates' provocative tone in this regard and of its consequences for the direction of his arguments.[52] Second, Socrates' use of the tripartite schema need not depend on any one construal of "forms": provided that *some* concept of nonsensory truth and reality occupies the top tier of the schema, then the latter provides an arguably useful mechanism for posing questions about representational art. Finally, the top tier of the schema in any case ceases to carry much weight in the argument after 597e: apart from the linking reference at 598a, the metaphysics of forms is never directly mentioned again, despite a final glimpse of the tripartite schema at 599a.

The first part of book 10, with its application to mimesis of the language of "simulacra" (*eidōla*) and "apparitions" (*phantasmata*), is loosely reminiscent of the spirit of the Divided Line and the Cave, and to that extent it evokes one of the *Republic*'s governing thoughts, that truth and reality lie beyond the realm of the sensory. But it is nonetheless notable that this vocabulary, which belongs to a general Platonic idiom of ontological hierarchy (between "original" and "image"), cannot be used to match up book 10 precisely with the divisions of Line and Cave.[53] Nor is such a match easy

---

[51] Two recent, rather different approaches to the "forms" in *Rep.* 10 can be found in Fine 1993, 110–13, 116–19, and Burnyeat 1999, 245–49.

[52] I give a fuller statement of this point, with particular reference to the notorious mirror analogy of 596d–e, in chapter 4, section III.

[53] *Phantasma* at *Rep.* 10.598b3–5, 599a2 (cf. note 63), might prima facie be thought to match the level of physical images and reflections in the Divided Line (6.510a1); but it also corresponds to reflections in water etc. *outside* the Cave (7.516b5, 532c1). Likewise, the term *eidōlon* (10.598b8, 599a7, d3, 600e5, 601b9, 605c3) was used both for objects in the Cave (7.520c4; cf. 532b7, c2) *and* for reflections in the world outside it (516a7). Whatever overall interpretation of Line and Cave one adopts, mimesis in book 10 cannot be neatly correlated with their metaphysics, and that remains true even if the relationship between the two lower sections of the Line is conceptualized as mimesis at 6.510b4 (though the text is uncertain: see Adam 1963, 2:66). Burnyeat 1999, 240, includes the products of mimetic art among the shadows on the wall of the Cave. *Rep.* 10.596a6 is the nearest thing to a cross-reference to

to discern in other respects: for one thing, the physical images in the bottom section of the Line stand in a necessarily one-to-one relationship to particular objects, whereas neither *Republic* 10 nor any other Platonic text suggests anything of the kind for the mimetic products of painting or poetry; and although there is more scope to accommodate mimetic art within the allegory of the Cave, Plato gives his readers no prompting to recall the latter within book 10 itself. It is therefore not surprising that, while book 10 repeatedly refers back to earlier parts of the dialogue, Plato here provides no direct cross-reference to the metaphysics of the middle books. Taken as a whole, the second critique of poetry does not depend on an unequivocal set of metaphysical premises.

A further source of interpretative difficulty in book 10 is the analogy between poetry and painting that features in a series of stages from 596e to 605a. Because I examine this aspect of the passage more closely in chapter 4, together with other references to visual art in the dialogues, I limit myself here to the brief statement of some essential claims about this part of the work. In the first place, while the analogy with painting partly trades on the strong aspiration to visual naturalism in the contemporary art known to Plato, and while the notorious term *skiagraphia* (literally "shadow-painting") at 602d2 may (but need not) allude to a definite pictorial technique, the passage as a whole will not support the commonly adopted supposition that Plato is here primarily targeting one or more particular styles or schools of graphic art: painting simply plays too basic a role in the argument for that. However, that is not at all to concede another common view, that Plato has no real interest in painting in its own right but merely uses it as a convenient analogue to poetry. Painting, with other visual arts, is in fact mentioned and treated as a source of ideas and imagery throughout Plato's writings, and we have grounds for attributing to him a far from simple conception of its character or possibilities. Contrary to a standard but uncritical paraphrase, *Republic* 10 does not directly suggest that painting is *limited* to the "mirroring" of the sensory world (a view with which other passages in the dialogues are actually incompatible). Book 10's provocative slighting of the art of pictorial images is calculated to advance the formulation of a larger, integrated view of mimetic representation. At the center of that view, I believe, lies the important thought that the achievement of a convincing artistic semblance of reality is neither valuable in itself nor an indication of knowledge (of reality) on the part of the artist. A cogent justification of mimesis, Plato invites us to see, must appeal to something *more* than verisimilitude, of which visual

the metaphysics of the middle books, but not that near (cf. Halliwell 1988, 109, though I would now put the point even more cautiously) and in any case not directly evocative of either Line or Cave.

naturalism is one variety. When applied to poetry, this point leads to the conclusion that the apparently comprehensive familiarity with the phenomenal world, with the "surfaces" of life, exhibited in the works of Homer and others (598e) cannot in itself vouch for anything that deserves to be regarded as knowledge or wisdom. What is ultimately at stake here, as often elsewhere in Plato, is not the intrinsic nature of mimetic images but the use made of them and the basis of understanding on which that use rests.

One implication of this critique of mimesis is the need to distinguish the *ethical* credentials of poetry (or any representational art) from its *technical* accomplishment as representation. On my reading, the analogy from painting, with its repeated emphasis on mere appearances, is functionally more important and less tendentious than some interpreters have taken it to be. It underlines the argument's thrust that verisimilitude, the look of the real, should not be confused with veracity, a grasp of the real itself. Plato's argument suggests that a self-contained defense of artistic truth-to-life, appealing only to technical achievement and the creation of convincing impressions, is a defense not worth having. Ascription of value to artistic realism leaves open the question of what, if any, fuller or deeper truth about the world the mimetic artist might lay claim to: that is the import, satirically conveyed, of the reference to painting's deception of "children and foolish adults" at 598b–c. Sections 595–602 are a cumulative denial of the equation of representational convincingness with humanly significant knowledge or understanding. This denial does not remove, and may indeed make more urgent, the need to bring ethical criteria to bear on poetry. It is not inconsistent of Socrates to disparage the worth of poets' representational skills while continuing to be anxious about the insidiously expressive powers of what they produce. That is why, despite the doubts of some interpreters, the satirical, mocking tone of the first part of book 10 can coherently be followed by the somber scrutiny of (tragic) poetry's psychological hold over "even the best of us" (605c10). If there is an element of paradox here, it resides not in the structure of Plato's own thought processes but in the object of his attention—the mimetic capacity of major artworks to impress themselves on minds that know them to be, in some sense, pretenses.[54]

At 603 Socrates switches to the psychological angle which he had signaled at the start of the book (595a–b). Sections 603–6 offer both a renewal and an extension of the case made against (much) poetry in books 2–3.

---

[54] Annas 1981, 341–44, with Annas 1982, complains about the structure of the argument itself, but her case is vitiated by an impatience that prevents her from seeing an underlying (and coherent) challenge. I do not deny, however, that problems of detail remain in this section; cf. Halliwell 1997a, 328.

Continuity and development are present in the suggestion at 606b that sympathetic contact with the experiences of others "infects" a person's own psychological habits, an idea later taken up by such different thinkers as Augustine and Nietzsche.[55] This suggestion renews the impetus of the case made in books 2–3, where poetic *muthoi* were taken to be the carriers of *logoi* that "persuade" their hearers and shape their beliefs. It also, more specifically, echoes 3.395d, quoted earlier in this section, where mimesis was linked with character formation through habituation. But book 10 moves beyond that earlier context in two main ways. First, it no longer foregrounds, though it hardly forgets about, the special "assimilation" induced by the dramatic mode, but instead places an unqualified emphasis on the power of poetry to express attitudes and emotions that function, in relation to its audience, as the vehicles of religio-ethical values. Second, it refers back, at 603d, to book 4's psychology of the divided mind. It becomes clear, I maintain, that the target of the new argument is nothing less than a worldview, a worldview essentially identifiable as tragic, though in this respect too there is some continuity with books 2–3.[56] The divided mind is now seen to contain an element whose attachment to human life (in the form of a belief that life is supremely important, and death an irredeemable evil) makes it acutely prone to grief and pity.[57] It is precisely this psychic element that is fostered by tragedy (including Homeric poetry: 605c, 607a; cf. 595c, 598d). The Homeric-tragic tradition presents conspicuous images of heroes whose sufferings stand in profound contradiction to the proposition that "nothing in human affairs is worth much seriousness" (604c). When Socrates brings his "greatest charge" against poetry (605c–d)—that even the good find it hard to resist "surrender" to pity—it is Homer and tragedy he has in view, even though the sequel indicts comedy and other kinds of poetry too for their subversively emotional effects.

[55] I justify the translation of *apolauein* as "infect" at Halliwell 1988, 149 (cf. Hippocrates *Cap. Vuln.* 15.1 for a medical parallel); there is a direct echo here of 3.395d, with a further echo of Gorgias (cf. note 38), fr. 11.9 DK (*Helen*). This Platonic principle was taken up by Augustine, *Confessions* 3.2–4, in his discussion of the paradoxical pleasure of watching painful events in theatrical plays (Augustine *Civ. Dei* 8.13 has an explicit reference to Plato's banishment of the poets, on which see, e.g., Barish 1981, 52–54; Stock 1996, 35–37; O'Connell 1978, 126, here implausibly detects familiarity with Aristotle's concept of catharsis. A very different echo of the Platonic principle occurs in Nietzsche, *Menschliches Allzumenschliches* 1.212 (Nietzsche 1988, 2:173); cf. chapter 7, notes 66–67.

[56] Cf. the echo of 387–88 at 603e.

[57] Note, though, that nothing in book 10 specifically cites, or even requires, a tripartite soul: 604a ff. employs a bipartite model of reason (*logos*) versus emotion (*pathos*), and this holds good for the context as a whole; cf. 606d's blurring of book 4's distinction between *epithumia* and *thumos*. Book 4's discussion of psychic conflict turns out, after all, to be only a broad underpinning for book 10's argument; Belfiore 1983, 50–56, and Burnyeat 1999, 222–28, offer different views.

There is also a salient political dimension here; hence the references to mass festivals and theatrical audiences at 604e–5a.[58] Part of the potency of poetry is located by Plato in its performance on public occasions where it functions as ideological rhetoric for the polis as a whole, and his attitude to tragedy may well be influenced by a sense of the phenomenon of *mass* emotion that prevailed both in the theater and, as a well-known passage of *Ion* indicates (535b–e), at epic recitations too. This and other details of book 10 will have to be revisited when we look at Plato's treatment of tragedy more closely in chapter 3.

III

Even in the kind of condensed overview of parts of *Republic* 2–3 and 10 I have attempted here it is possible to see the subtlety and complexity with which the dialogue broaches educational, psychological, cultural, political, ethical, and metaphysical issues generated by the existence of mimetic art. To some extent these issues look back to the pre-Socratic misgivings of Heraclitus and Xenophanes about poetic myths; at the same time, they foreshadow in various respects the rejection of traditional poetic *paideia* by Epicurus, the moralism of Stoic attitudes to literature, and the efforts of Neoplatonism to reach a rapprochement between opposing sides in the "ancient quarrel."[59] For these and other reasons, the *Republic*'s two treatments of poetry are a defining point in the long history of attempts by ancient philosophy to subject representational art to its own interpretative control.

But at least three factors ought to prevent us from reifying these parts of the *Republic*, and especially book 10, into a rigid, uncompromising exposition of Plato's "essential" attitudes to poetry or art. The first is that the texts themselves, as I earlier emphasized, are exploratory and probing, rather than the statements of conclusive views: they pose more questions than they can answer, and even the most emphatic pronouncements made by Socrates in these contexts are best read (as 607c–e encourages us to see) as being at the service of ongoing, incomplete processes of reflection. The second reason is that further references to mimesis in the *Republic* convey nuances of judgment about the possibilities of artistic representation and thereby complicate the work's overall treatment of the subject. Particularly striking is a series of five passages in the central books that use the idea of philosophical "painting" analogically or metaphorically. I say more about these in chapter 4, but I mention them here to emphasize that while their implications for Plato's view of painting as such are debat-

---

[58] Cf. references to "the many" at 599a, 601a, 602b.
[59] See chapter 9 on Epicureanism and on the Stoics, and chapter 11 on Neoplatonism.

able, and have indeed been much debated, they do indicate a Platonic
awareness of the variable relationship between a painter's "model" (*paradeigma*) and reality, both visible and imagined, and they acknowledge
that a crucial part of the process of representation takes place in the mind
of the artist.[60] Different again, but equally important, is the portion of *Republic 3*—actually the tailpiece to the discussion of poetry's place in education—that states a general principle of "ethical form" applicable to mimetic and other products of human culture and, by doing so, enunciates
in embryo a theory of mimesis as expression, linking the form and beauty
of artworks to their ethical content (their "character," *ēthos*).[61] The cumulative weight of these passages means that anyone reading the entire *Republic* cannot, and certainly should not, interpret the mirror analogy of book
10 without recalling the diversity of ideas about mimesis that have
emerged at earlier stages of the dialogue. The effect of recalling those
earlier passages, I submit, is to reinforce the impression that book 10 itself
offers a particular challenge to one conception of mimesis, not an exhaus-
tive analysis of the subject.

The third and final reason for not "reifying" the treatment of mimesis in
Republic book 3 and, more especially, book 10 into a definitive Platonic
doctrine is that Plato indubitably did not stop thinking about the problems
of mimesis after writing the *Republic*. He returns to the topic on several
further occasions, and it is with some brief observations on the more important directions of thought found in these later dialogues that I now
want to deal.

It is an obvious move to turn first to the *Sophist*, which shares some
themes with *Republic* 10 and is likely to be chronologically close to that
book. What is particularly significant for my purposes is that while the
Sophist uses the concept of mimesis as part of its devastating critique of the
"sophist" as an intellectual and cultural impostor, it nonetheless includes
several indications of a less than monolithic view of mimetic art. Most
germane here is the dialogue's distinction between two kinds of mimesis
or image making, the "eicastic" and the "phantastic," marking the difference between images that are faithful to the (three-dimensional) proportions (*summetriai*) and surface features of what they depict and, on the
other hand, those whose representational properties are viewer-relative,
adjusted to take account of the perceptual point of view from which a

---

[60] For references and discussion see chapter 4, section II.

[61] *Rep.* 3.401a–d; see chapter 4, section II. Asmis 1992e, 346, speaks aptly, in a different
connection, of Plato's "subordination of linguistic to moral form" in poetry. The ethical
beauty of form in mimetic art is not fully covered by the remarks of Most 1992, 1344–45, in
his useful summary of ancient views of beauty.

human observer will contemplate them.[62] This passage of the *Sophist* places most painting, and indeed most mimesis, in the second category (236b9–c1), the category of distorted *phantastikē* or "semblance making," and it is actually difficult to see what kind of painting could count as "likeness-making," *eikastikē*—presumably, only paintings of two-dimensional objects. This could in principle be taken as a damning consideration against painting as a whole, on the assumption that only the eicastic variety of mimesis has any value at all.

Now, this interpretation would be equivalent to supposing that *Republic* 10's model of mimesis is implicitly that of *phantastikē*, and there are some prima facie grounds for this. Above all, in *Republic* 10 the language of appearances (*phainomena*), "apparitions" (*phantasmata*), and the like is prominent, and Plato here (unlike other parts of the *Republic*) avoids referring to the products of mimesis as "images" (*eikones*) or by any other term from the *eik-* root.[63] Moreover, there are several close motivic parallels between the *Sophist* and *Republic* 10, and it is broadly true that the latter's critique of artistic mimesis supplies some of the key ideas (the pretense of knowledge, deception of gullible audiences, and the production of speciously convincing artifacts) that structure the later dissection of the sophist's false pretenses.[64] But even so we cannot simply project back the *Sophist*'s eicastic-phantastic distinction onto *Republic* 10, because in the latter painting stands unequivocally as a paradigm for mimesis in general, whereas the eicastic-phantastic distinction is a division *within* the category of mimesis. What we can say, however, is that the critique of painting in *Republic* 10, with the critique of the simulation of appearances more generally, is offered not as a definitive judgment on all forms of mimesis

[62] Plato *Soph.* 235d–6c; cf. my comments with note 70. Notomi 1999, 147–55, is a helpful recent discussion. In view of the difficulty of interpreting the full scope of *eikastikē*, one should not say that instances of it correspond to their originals "in all particulars" (Eden 1986, 65; similarly Assunto 1965, 95), which would contradict the principle enunciated at *Crat.* 432c–d. Philip 1961, 459, goes too far in calling *eikastikē* "a class without members": Plato is likely to have included in it, for example, at least some Egyptian sculpture (cf. chapter 4, note 26). As regards *phantastikē*, one positive ancient recognition of the "approximative" nature of some large-scale sculpture can be glimpsed in Strabo's simile at *Geog.* 1.1.23.

[63] See Halliwell 1988, 118–9, with note 53 here, on the language of *phantasmata* and *eidōla*; for parallels between *Rep.* 10 and the *Sophist*, cf. Notomi 1999, 127–28. That *Rep.* 10 is concerned with *phantastikē* was the view of Proclus (see chapter 11, note 46), but for objections to this reading, see Palmer 1999, 122 n. 6.

[64] See note 63. Note also the motif of mimetic "play" (*paidia*) at *Soph.* 234a–b, 235a6, matching *Rep.* 10.602b8. *Laws* 2.667d–e suggests that mimetic art can count as "play" when it is a matter of pure pleasure, without possibility of ethical benefit or harm; cf. *Polit.* 288c. Other Platonic passages apply the term "play" more generally to representational art, in contrast to the "seriousness" of true philosophy: see esp. *Laws* 2.656b3, c3; 7.796b; 10.889d1, with chapter 2, note 25; cf. Sargeaunt 1922–23 on various aspects of the concept of "play" in the *Laws*.

but rather as the criticism of one conception of mimetic representation, a conception that makes ostensible verisimilitude (the look of the real) a supreme artistic value.

So despite the fact that the eicastic-phantastic distinction in the *Sophist* is deployed for pejorative effect against sophistry itself, it would be wrong to draw from it a decisively negative inference regarding mimetic art as such. Most important, it is not an implication of this passage that representational art is intrinsically defective whenever it fails, or is unable, to achieve exact correspondence between depictions and relevant (kinds of) objects in the world. I have already pointed out that some earlier Platonic texts, including parts of the *Cratylus*, specifically acknowledge that mimetic images need not always be understood in terms of close or literal correspondence, and I have also argued that *Republic* 10 can best be interpreted as a *critique* of the idea that verisimilitude at the level of appearances could provide mimetic art with self-sufficient value. It can now be added that there are other passages too that corroborate a Platonic acceptance of standards of depiction that are not reducible to the criterion of maximal, or even uniform, correspondence. One of these is the reference to variations in standards of acceptable pictorial "likeness" at *Critias* 107a–8a; another, perhaps the most remarkable, is the contrast between Greek and Egyptian styles of figurative representation in *Laws* book 2, in a passage that actually implies the existence of criteria by which heavily stylized forms of mimesis might be preferred to naturalistic genres of art.[65]

One thing that emerges clearly from the *Sophist* is the possibility of identifying different varieties and facets of mimesis, even if parts of the analysis (such as the applicability of the "eicastic" category beyond sculpture) are left in suspension. The dialogue's analysis of mimesis starts from the broad class of "the mimetic" (*to mimētikon*, 234b), which Theaetetus calls "a multifarious and extremely diverse category," and which turns out to include both painting and the sophist's pseudophilosophical sciolism. In the concluding section of the work (264b–68d), where the definition of the sophist is set out in its fullest form through a whole series of divisions of the genus *technē* (skill, art, and technique), mimesis is defined as "a sort of productive activity [*poiēsis*], but the production of simulacra [*eidōla*] not of things themselves" (265b1–2). This definition allows the concept to cover any activity that deals in, or brings into being, "products" that can be categorized as secondary, illusory, or false in relation to some primary, authentic, or true reference point. Not only does the reassertion of the eicastic-phantastic dichotomy mean that some of the products of mimesis

[65] *Laws* 2.656d–7b (cf. 7.799a), with my chapter 4, section II. The arts in question, both figurative and "musical," count in the *Laws* as fundamentally mimetic (see note 67), regardless of stylization.

have a prima facie legitimacy as "images" (*eikones*), but even the further subdivision of *phantastikē* turns out to leave room for arts such as painting and sculpture (alluded to at 267a3), or acting and vocal mimicry (267a, a definition reminiscent of *Republic* 3.393c), which are not implicated in the moral condemnation of the sophist's pernicious duplicity. All this shows that the work's final typology of mimesis progressively pushes mimetic art to one side, in order to identify a specific and specifically fraudulent species of mimesis that finally "traps" the sophist. And that is itself only one index of a larger point, that the *Sophist* does not offer a blanket condemnation of mimesis but something more like a philosophical "grid" on which many different kinds of human representation, including mimetic art, can be mapped.

We come back, then, to a cardinal observation made much earlier in the chapter, that mimesis was a concept that led Plato to place and appraise mimetic art within an intricate framework of issues about the relationship between human thought and (mind-independent) reality. Although the *Sophist* is not primarily concerned with mimetic art itself (there is, for example, no reference to poetry in this connection), it gives some valuable hints of a Platonic recognition of the need to avoid a monolithic treatment of mimesis and to make room for several variables in the operation of mimetic activities. This recognition of diversity and complexity is borne out by the most extensive of Plato's late reflections on artistic mimesis, which are to be found in the *Laws*, above all at 2.653–71. Both the style and the train of thought in this section, as elsewhere in the *Laws*, are frequently awkward and sometimes densely obscure. One has the impression that Plato is here renegotiating ground he had traversed in *Republic* 2–3 and, to a lesser extent, *Republic* 10. We see this, for example, in the dialogue's insistence on a factor of psychological "likening" or assimilation that belongs to the experience of mimetic art, as well as in its contrasting criteria of pleasure and benefit.[66] In *Laws* 2 the Athenian is concerned to expound, within a broader discussion of education, the rudiments of what deserves to be called an ethical aesthetics: a set of concepts and standards for the evaluation of mimetic art (here including poetry, music, dance, and visual art)[67] that center on the possible benefit or harm to the character, *ēthos*, of those who either perform or experience the performance of such art. But the Athenian's moral tenor does not make his arguments merely moralistic. At 667–71 he attempts to weave together three criteria of quality

---

[66] Psychological assimilation: *Laws* 2.656b, with chapter 2, notes 11, 15, 39. Pleasure in relation to benefit: esp. *Laws* 2.667b ff.; cf., e.g., *Rep.* 3.387b, 390a; 10.607d, with Halliwell 1991a, 329–39. On the larger educational context in *Laws*, see Morrow 1960, 297–318.

[67] See 655d5–7 (dance), 667e10 (image-making arts as a whole; cf. c9–d1), 668b2–10 (*mousikē*, here the musicopoetic arts as a whole), 668d7, e5 (general); 669d2, e4 (music); cf. the passing reference to musical mimesis at *Phileb.* 62c2.

in representational art: "correctness" (*orthotēs*) of relationship to the represented model or original, "benefit" (*ōphelia*) to the minds of the recipients
of the art, and pleasure (*hēdonē*) or "attractiveness" (*charis*). The function
of pleasure in the experience of representational art is a crucial, if difficult,
strand in the argument. Pleasure, which the Athenian thinks is too widely
and readily treated as a self-sufficient justification for the experience of
mimesis, is seen by him as possessing an intrinsically unstable status: it is
able to operate in conjunction with other elements of experience, for example by reinforcing certain ethical feelings, or, equally, to become a subversively independent psychological force; and it is anyway individually
variable, because it is in part a concomitant of the interplay between what
is represented in any artwork and the character or disposition of the particular viewer or hearer.[68] The need to anchor pleasure to a principle of ethical value keeps worrying the Athenian, and we are entitled to suppose
that Plato thought this need should worry his own readers.

But it is not only pleasure that has a somewhat ambiguous and shifting
role in the argument. The only one of the three criteria of artistic merit that
seems entirely unequivocal is "benefit," an idea that was prominent in the
critique of poetry in *Republic* 2–3 too. Benefit clearly counts as a general
test of the ethical acceptability of the experience of a mimetic work or
performance, but how is it to be integrated with appreciation of the representational status of mimesis? Here the crux is the concept of representational "correctness," a concept we met earlier in the *Cratylus*, where it
was distinguished, as a property of pictorial mimesis, from truth.[69] That
distinction poses an immediate difficulty for us, as "correctness" in the
Laws seems to be *equated*, or at any rate closely correlated, with truth
(667d–68a). This correlation is associated, furthermore, with language
reminiscent of the *Sophist*: first, the mimetic arts are called "eicastic"
(667c9–d1, 668a6), a term otherwise found (among Plato's works) *only* in
the *Sophist*'s discussions of mimesis; second, the desired correspondence
of these arts to their models or originals is called "proportionality," *to sum-
metron* (668a2), which reminds us of the *Sophist*'s definition of the eicastic
variety of mimesis as faithful to the *summetriai*, the (physical) proportions,
of the depicted object.[70]

---

[68] See esp. 655b–56a (with 657e, 658e) both for the individual variability of pleasure (cf.
7.802c–d) and for the idea that pleasure is accepted by many people as a self-sufficient criterion of artistic merit (cf. 3.700e, a symptom of "theatrocracy"), 658e–60a for the ideal of
pleasure *in* virtue, and 667b ff. for the capacity of pleasure to function as a dangerously
independent force. The earlier parts of the work have already established that learning to
feel pleasure and pain *correctly* is the goal of education (and virtue): see esp. 653b–c, and
cf. chapter 8, note 12.

[69] See section I.

[70] *Soph.* 235d. This "symmetry" is also termed "equality" (*isotēs*) at *Laws* 2.667d5, 668a1.

The double alignment between this passage of the *Laws* and the *Cratylus* and *Sophist* creates a conundrum. If we think of *Cratylus*, we may be reminded of that work's stress on the differences between mimetic works and their objects, as well as its related contrast between "mathematical" and "qualitative" relationships of correspondence. Yet the connections between the *Laws* and the *Sophist* suggest that the former is now treating all mimesis as (ideally) "eicastic," and therefore insisting on a rather close and literal criterion of representational match. The problem only deepens when we register that this passage of the *Laws* implies that the notion of mimesis *qua* "eicastic" representation is just as applicable to *music* as to any other art (668a–671a). This reminds us of the difficulty we noted apropos the *Sophist* itself in extrapolating from sculpture, the dialogue's own paradigm of three-dimensionally eicastic mimesis, to other kinds of artistic representation. But in the case of the *Laws*, the equation of mimesis in general with *eikastikē*, as well as the combination of correctness with criteria of benefit and pleasure, makes it hard to avoid the supposition that eicastic mimesis is here to be understood less strictly than in the earlier work, yet nonethelesss in a way that attaches importance to representational fidelity.

In trying to incorporate that point into a coherent view of this stretch of *Laws* 2, we find ourselves facing a further interpretative challenge. The greater the emphasis placed on the "eicastic" notion of mimesis, and accordingly on the need for a close "correctness" of representational match, the more the relationship between such correctness and the criterion of ethical "benefit" becomes problematic. To put the point most succinctly, it can be no more true of "correctness," *qua* representational fidelity, than it is of pleasure that it should count as a self-sufficient criterion. A mimetically "correct" (let us say, highly recognizable) depiction of something wrong or evil might, depending on its presentation, surely be the reverse of beneficial: that, after all, was central to the ethical critique of poetry in *Republic* books 2–3. That Plato is only too well aware of this difficulty is precisely, I suggest, why he makes the Athenian wrestle to *integrate* correctness with benefit, and indeed with pleasure, in his account of how mimetic art should be judged. We can see the effort of integration at a juncture such as 668a–b, where, immediately after describing all *mousikē* (here, as often, referring to musicopoetic art in general) as "eicastic and mimetic art" (*eikastikēn . . . kai mimētikēn*, 668a6–7), the Athenian says that such art should certainly not be judged by pleasure (sc. alone), but must be required to manifest "likeness to the representation of beauty."[71] Although this last phrase is

---

[71] *Laws* 2.668b1–2, *homoiotēs tōi tou kalou mimēmati*; for this peculiar phrasing, cf. 669e4, with England 1921, 1:321, 327–28. Verdenius 1949, 18 n. 1, translates "which gets its likeness from its being a representation of Beauty," but idealism, which Verdenius discerns generally

somewhat problematic, it is clear that likeness is here being joined to a consideration of "beauty" (*to kalon*) that is not, and cannot be, contained within the notion of representational accuracy itself. If such integration of value could be achieved, it would render mimetic art consistent with the examples of food and learning used at the beginning of this whole section (667b–c): healthy nourishment, the Athenian indicates, is both the "correctness" *and* the "benefit" of food (667c1), and likewise truth fulfils both criteria simultaneously in the case of learning or understanding, *mathēsis* (667c6). But such a fusion seems to elude the Athenian in the case of mimetic art, where his emphasis on "eicastic" accuracy draws attention to the way in which representational correctness, construed in terms of resemblance, remains potentially independent of "benefit."

Quite apart, then, from Plato's identification of the unstable nature of aesthetic pleasure (dependent as it is on an interplay between the variables of the spectator's mind and the properties of the mimetic object), the argument in this portion of *Laws* 2 throws into relief the uneasy relationship between a fundamentally "technical" criterion of artistic value (the artwork's success in embodying a faithful "appearance") and a fundamentally ethical criterion (the harm or benefit that experience of the artwork causes a spectator). Highlighting this point, 668e–69a stresses that a grasp of correctness is not a sufficient qualification for a judgment of what is (ethically) "beautiful" or "fine," *kalos*, in art.[72] The argument does not ultimately claim that this tension can be resolved by any kind of identification or merging of correctness and benefit (as in the examples of food and learning); instead, it insists on the desirability of combining and perhaps balancing them in critical judgment. "So, then, is it not true that as regards each image, in painting, music, and every other case, anyone who is to be an intelligent judge must be able to grasp three things: to recognize, first, what is [sc. represented], then how correctly [*orthōs*] it has been represented, and thirdly how well [*eu*] each image has been rendered?" (669a7–b2)[73] If we ask what the relationship is between these three criteria and the earlier division of pleasure, correctness, and benefit (667b), part of the answer is that pleasure, whose variable and unstable status has already been noticed, no longer has a direct role in the second of the two passages, whereas correctness explicitly belongs in both lists, and "how well . . . rendered" in the second list must be correlated with benefit in the first.

This still leaves the first criterion at 669a–b, knowledge of "what is represented," unaccounted for. To interpret it as the simple identification of the

in Plato's mimeticism, is not quite the point: this whole section of the *Laws* discusses mimesis without any reference to ideal forms (cf. Summers 1981, 556 n. 5).

[72] Cf. Saunders 1972, 10–11, for the correct interpretation of this passage.

[73] I follow England 1921, 1:325, who brackets the words *rhēmasi . . . rhuthmois* at b2–3. Webster 1952, 13, badly garbles the thrust of this whole passage (and much besides).

subject of a mimetic image would make the inclusion of the criterion in the list superflous, because it would amount to something logically presupposed by the ability to judge correctness. A clue to the fuller force of this point was supplied a little earlier, in fact, when the Athenian spoke of the need to understand the nature of each mimetic work in terms of recognizing "what it means/intends [*bouletai*] to be and of what it is actually an image": indeed, in this same context, he glossed correctness itself as "correctness of intention" (*orthotēta boulēseōs*).[74] Although, as with so much else in the argument, these are only passing hints, they do strongly suggest that the Athenian takes account of the fact that the representational character of a mimetic work can and must be partly interpreted from the point of view of its maker's intentions, in accordance with the embodiment of these intentions in the work itself. The significance of this implication is that it enriches the scope of the statement of three criteria at 669a–b. That statement can now be seen to constitute an elaborate model of aesthetic judgment that holds up a mimetic work to the (indefinite) test of reality (thereby evaluating the work's "correctness"), but does so in the light of a sense of the work's own representational goals ("what it means/intends to be," 668c6), and, moreover, judges the entirety of its representational character against fundamentally ethical standards ("how well . . rendered"). It is a model of judgment, in other words, that, despite its less than limpid formulation, has the potential to move in complex ways between the "inside" and "outside" of a mimetic work, bringing together technical and external, descriptive and normative, criteria of artistic success.

The Athenian's statement of the intelligent judge's three criteria at 669a–b is explicitly meant to explain what is needed for the estimation of mimetically rendered "beauty" or "fineness," *to kalon* (669a3–6), which has in fact been the guiding concern from the start of the discussion of artistic education (654b–d). When he later refers back to his triad of criteria, he revealingly calls the third of them ("how well . . . rendered") itself a matter of "beauty," *to kalon* (670e5). The upshot is a conception of mimetic art in which factors of representational choice and technique (the achievement of "correctness") are taken into the reckoning, but in subordination to considerations of ethically shaped form and significance.[75] The underlying position is essentially the same as in *Republic* 3, where Socrates, as the climax to an argument that repeatedly equated "beauty" with the ethical

---

[74] *Laws* 2.668c4–8; cf. England 1921, 1:322–23. For a modern model of "correctness," tied to a sophisticated notion of authorial intention, in the understanding of visual art, see Wollheim 1987, 47–51, 85–96.

[75] Ethical form and significance do not entail representation only of the good; mimesis of the bad is envisaged at, e.g., 2.655d–e (cf. the later reminiscences at 7.798d–e and 7.812–17), but acceptable depiction of vice requires an appropriately negative expression (see 814d ff. on dance, 816d–17a on comedy, with chapter 2 on the latter).

shaping of a work's narrative material,[76] contemplated requiring poets and other mimetic artists "to embody the image of the good character" in their works. In *Laws* 2 as in *Republic* 2–3, there is much that a modern liberal aesthetic is bound to find uncomfortable, but that should not lure us into the mistake, which my next chapter discusses more fully, of taking Platonic mimeticism for a simple variety of puritanism. In both of Plato's major discussions of mimesis within the educational framework of a hypothetical city, we can trace an intricate recognition of the various strands that go into the making, the experience, and the cultural status of representational art. In *Laws* 2 this recognition is conveyed by the Athenian's attempt— inconclusive but unmistakably earnest—to weave together the themes of correctness, benefit, and pleasure in his treatment of mimetic art, and by his final statement of the three criteria for good judgment of such art at 669a–b. In these respects, the passage can stand as an apt illustration of some of the complexities I have tried to diagnose in Plato's prolonged and profoundly ambivalent relationship with mimesis.

That relationship stems, I suggest in conclusion, from two main roots, which are partly, perhaps inevitably, entangled. One is Plato's critical attention to the workings and influences of cultural forces in his society, especially in the domain of the musicopoetic arts (with all their educational prestige) but also in relation to the images of figurative art forms. The other consists of his various and unending attempts to grapple with larger philosophical questions of representation and truth, questions embracing the whole relationship between human thought and reality. Mimesis increasingly insinuated itself into those attempts, eventually reaching the point, in his late works, where he could allow the idea to be voiced that "everything we say must surely be mimesis and image making."[77] The result is a history of complex fluctuations in the way mimesis is treated and regarded in the dialogues, fluctuations that scholars have often been too keen to smooth out and neutralize. But such complexity is connected to a characteristic tension between discrepant impulses in Plato's thinking. The first, a kind of "negative theology," which leads sometimes in the direction of mysticism, is that reality cannot adequately be spoken of, described, or modeled, only experienced in some pure, unmediated manner (by *logos*, *nous*, *dianoia*, or whatever).[78] The second is that all human thought *is* an attempt to speak about, describe, or model reality—to pro-

---

[76] *Rep.* 3.401b: note the equation of *eu* and *kalōs* at 400e2–3, with various earlier references to an ethically charged concept of beauty (2.377c1, d9, e7, 378e2; 3.389e4, 390a1, 400d2).

[77] *Critias* 107b (which need not be restricted to truth to *particulars*, *contra* Osborne 1996, 187–89), leading directly into an analogy with painting: note the same phrasing (*mimēsis* plus *apeikasia*) with reference to *mousikē*, including poetry, at *Laws* 2.668b10–c1.

[78] E.g., *Phdr.* 247c, *Crat.* 438–40, *Rep.* 6.510b, 7.533a (dialectic's journey beyond images).

duce "images" (whether visual, mental, or verbal) of the real.[79] On the first of these views, mimesis, of whatever sort, is a lost cause, doomed to failure, at best a faint shadow of the truth. On the second, mimesis—representation—is all that we have, or all that we are capable of. In some of Plato's later writing this second perspective is expanded by a sense that the world itself is a mimetic creation, wrought by a divine artist who, at one point in the *Timaeus* (55c6), is expressly visualized as a painter. That being so, philosophers are not only, as the *Republic* would have it, painters in a different medium, or, as the *Laws* suggests, writers of the truest tragedy. They are also interpreters of a cosmic work of art.[80]

[79] In addition to *Critias* 107b, quoted in the text, see, e.g., *Tim.* 29b–d (where images, *eikones*, are equated with "likelihood," *eikos*, as opposed to truth), *Laws* 10.897d–e (the use of an image as a substitute for the impossible task of gazing at the sun of reason); cf. also the various contrasts between truth or reality and earthly images or mimesis in the myth of *Phaedrus*, esp. 250a–51a. On further implications of images in Platonic philosophy, see, e.g., Gallop 1965, Patterson 1985.

[80] Philosophical "painters": chapter 4, section II; philosophy as tragic drama: *Laws* 8.817b, with chapter 3, section II. On the *Timaeus*'s idea of the cosmos itself as the mimetic work of the "demiurge," see chapter 4, notes 22, 51 (with Philostratus maj. *Imag.* proem. 1, and Philostratus *Vita Ap.* 2.22, for a notion of the natural world as a divinely wrought work of visual art; cf. chapter 10, note 56).

Chapter Two

❋

Romantic Puritanism: Plato and the Psychology of Mimesis

> Otherwise, my dear friend, we shall have to act like people
> who have been passionately in love with someone but who,
> when they think their passion is doing harm, force themselves
> to withdraw from the relationship. (Plato, *Republic* 10.607e)

ACCORDING TO Friedrich Nietzsche in the *Genealogy of Morals*, Plato stands as "the greatest enemy of art Europe has yet produced."[1] In framing this description Nietzsche was, in his own peculiarly incisive way, paying a formidable compliment to a writer he placed in the select company of those whose thought constitutes "a passionate history of their soul" (eine leidenschaftliche Seelen-Geschichte) and embodies the product of a life that "burns with the passion of thinking" (in der Leidenschaft des Denkens verbrennt).[2] The "greatness" of Plato's perceived enmity to art was, for Nietzsche, no crude extreme of antipathy but a measure of what he rightly recognized as the philosopher's deep sense of the dangerous power of art. Nietzsche, much of whose own aesthetics (with its defiantly celebratory invocation of illusion, intoxication, and "lies") can be read as an implicit, sometimes explicit, response to Plato, was compelled to feel a sardonic respect for the fact that Plato had acknowledged art as something *worth* his earnest antagonism. "What right at all does our age have," he bitterly exclaims in *Human, All-Too-Human*, "to give any answer to Plato's great question about the moral influence of art? Even supposing we have any art—where can we find the influence of art, *any kind* of influence?"[3] Plato's

---

[1] *Zur Genealogie der Moral* 3.25 (Nietzsche 1988, 5:402): "dieses grössten Kunstfeindes, den Europa bisher hervorgebracht hat"; cf. chapter 11, note 40. This passage was surely at the back of Croce's mind when he described Plato as "autore . . . della sola davvero grandiosa negazione dell'arte" (Croce 1950, 172).

[2] *Morgenröte* 5.481 (Nietzsche 1988, 3:285).

[3] "Aber welches Recht hat unsere Zeit überhaupt, auf die grosse Frage Plato's nach dem moralischen Einfluss der Kunst eine Antwort zu geben? Hätten wir selbst die Kunst, —wo haben wir den Einfluss, *irgend einen* Einfluss der Kunst?" (*Menschliches, Allzumenschliches* 1.212, Nietzsche 1988, 2:173–74). Nietzsche's quasi-Platonic insistence on art's embodiment of value-laden affirmations can be seen well at, e.g., *Götzen-Dämmerung*, "Streifzüge eines Unzeitgemässen" 24 (Nietzsche 1988, 6:127–28). Barish 1981, 404–13, provides one reading of some complex connections between Nietzsche's own and Plato's aesthetics; cf. chapter 1, note 55; chapter 7, notes 64, 66–67.

"great question" remained, for Nietzsche, both a challenge and a kind of reproach. It may well be that they should still be both of these things for us, too.

Plato's "great question," and indeed the greatness of his alleged enmity to art, often gives a markedly psychological slant to its moral anxieties. For Plato, the connection is intimate, because morality is conceptualized by him partly in terms of the internal order and health of the psyche. We saw in the previous chapter that both the *Republic*'s critiques of poetry rest substantially on psychological considerations. In books 2–3 and book 10, despite differences that receive fuller attention in this chapter, Plato's arguments are directed against the power of poetry to enter the mind, to take hold of its beliefs and emotions, and to mold the personalities of those exposed to it. In fact, at the conclusion of the first critique of poetry Plato signals that his concern is with a transformative psychological power that can be attributed, in some degree, to *all* mimetic art. This conviction first becomes plain in the discussion of music at 3.398b–400e, where the art's expressive-cum-representational nature is classified as mimetic and explained in terms explicitly indebted to the fifth-century Athenian theorist Damon.[4] It is then accentuated by the eloquent passage at 401a–d, which refers to the whole material fabric of a culture, including its visual and musical artifacts, and suggests that this fabric is pervaded by ethical "images" and mimetic expressions of character (*mimēmata*, 401a8) whose potent influence cannot be ignored by any serious inquiry into the educational and cultural formation of either individuals or social groups.[5] Furthermore, this last passage, where music in particular is said to "penetrate to the interior of the soul" (*kataduetai eis to entos tēs psuchēs*, 401d6–7), points to a crucial feature of Plato's dealings with the psychology of mimesis: the interweaving of unease over its dangers with a rich, half-admiring sense of its transformative power. Plato's ambivalent relationship to poetry is not altogether unlike Nietzsche's relationship to Plato himself.

Because the *Republic* outlines an authoritarian scheme for censoring whole tracts of the greatest Greek poetry, Plato has sometimes been regarded as severely dogmatic—in political terms, nothing less than totalitarian—in his attitude to representational art. To modern readers, heirs to the

[4] Music's mimetic character: 3.399a7, c3; 400a7; see Moutsopoulos 1959, 245–58. Damon: 400b1, c4; cf. 4.424c6, with my chapter 8, section II, and its note 24 on the Damonian tradition.

[5] This passage in fact extends mimesis to a wider range of activities and artifacts than any other in Plato: 401a mentions painting, figurative embroidery, architecture, and the making of every kind of artifact, as well as the human body itself and other organisms: while the passage's rhetorical sweep makes it hard to infer much from this, it certainly reinforces my claim (see chapter 1) that Plato does not have a fixed or static concept of mimesis. On the "expressive" scope of mimesis at 401a8, see chapter 4, section II.

romantic conviction that the imagination is a central and invaluable element of the mind, the Platonic critiques of poetry can seem irredeemably
negative and unsympathetic—indeed, essentially puritanical. To invoke a
paradigm of aesthetic puritanism in this context, one might think, for example, of the attempts made by the Plymouth Brethren parents (especially
the mother) of Edmund Gosse, as subsequently related in his *Father and
Son* of 1907, to expunge any fiction or imaginative storytelling from their
child's life in the interests of "the simplicity of truth" contained in the
Bible.[6] But, as I remarked in chapter 1, Plato's position is different from,
and more intricate than, the standards of such puritanism in three salient
ways: in the richly exploratory, imaginative character of the dialogues
themselves (with their own appeal to sympathetic imagination, to which
I shall return); in Plato's repeated acknowledgments, sometimes "confes-
sional" in form, of the alluring pleasures of poetry and other art; and in
the extensive literary indebtedness of Plato's forms of writing, including
his myths. It is not just that Plato is himself one of the supreme philosophical "stylists," and his work a lasting challenge to any neat distinction between philosophy and literature. It is also, and more important, that the
attitudes to poetry and other mimetic arts that he presents in his writings
stand, when everything is taken sensitively into account, in an ambivalent
relationship to the understanding of the psychology of artistic experience.
Plato's fear of the imagination[7] is that of a thinker and writer who does not
simply stigmatize certain kinds of art as dangerous or corrupting but who
claims to appreciate, to know *from the inside*, just how seductive the transformative experience of art can be. To express this thought most piquantly,
we might say that Plato himself must, at some level of sensibility, be the
reluctantly withdrawing lover of *Republic* 10.607e. For this reason, I propose that we can appropriately think of Plato, in full relish of the paradox,
as a romantic puritan.

To begin to grasp the force of this contention, we need to return to
some of the details of the discussions of mimesis in *Republic* books 3 and

---

[6] See Gosse 1970, esp. 20–22; cf. his parents' insistence on the literalness of the Bible itself
(49–50), and Gosse's diagnosis of his parents' lack of sympathetic imagination (50, 85, 204,
219), though one should add that the accuracy of parts of Gosse's account has been questioned by some scholars. As regards the partial affinities between such puritanism and Plato's
aesthetics, note Gosse's father's objection to the "falsehood" of Scott's novels (162), and
apropos my later argument regarding Plato's fear of imagination as a way of thinking differently and discovering other lives observe how fiction gave the young Gosse a sense of possible "escape" from the conditions of his own life (143–44).

[7] I have argued for the justification of speaking of "imagination" in this context, despite
Plato's lack of a single term corresponding to this concept, in Halliwell 1995a, esp. 26–29.
One recent account of imagination (as mental simulation) is that of Currie 1995, 141–63:
note, apropos the Platonic position I present in this chapter, Currie's comments (162–63) on
how imagination might spill over into real belief and desire.

10. We saw in the preceding chapter that the relevant stretch of book 3 adopts a restricted sense of mimesis for poetry, limiting it to the dramatic or impersonatory mode of first-person speech by the characters of poetry, though we should not forget, as scholars often have, that both before this (2.373b) and soon afterward (3.401a8) Plato permits himself to use mimesis terminology in a broader sense for both poetry and other representational arts. The narrower sense of mimesis in part of book 3 is designed, as we saw, to allow a sharp focus on the particularly heightened state of "self-likening" (*aphomoioun hautous*, 396a3), or psychological assimilation, which is ascribed first to the author (393c, 394d, 395a) and then to the reciter or actor (395a–b, 396b–e) of poetry in the dramatic mode, whether epic, drama proper, or other kinds. But Plato links this usage of mimetic vocabulary to the more general concept of mimesis as behavioral emulation and imitation through Socrates' suggestion that repeated indulgence in imaginative enactment of behavior (i.e., in mimetic role playing) shapes the disposition of the agent. "Haven't you noticed," Socrates asks, "that mimetic acts [*mimēseis*], if allowed to continue from youth onward, establish themselves in the habits and nature of the person's body, voice, and mind?" (395d1–3). The argument endows the self-assimilaton of poetic performance with a character-forming power comparable with that of behavioral patterning in life at large.[8]

The vital premise of this argument is a refusal to accept that when the mind engages in (fictional) role playing, in dramatic impersonation, this is a merely external or superficial event. Rather, Plato wants to insist, it is something which happens *to* and inside the mind of the role player. Moreover, some of the force of the case made by Socrates at this point in *Republic* 3 stems from a convergence between his psychological model of self-likening and the idea of poetry's normative or paradigmatic status on which the earlier parts of his critique of poetry had relied. If the characters of poetry, especially the heroic characters, carry a special prestige and weight in the ideals and value systems of the culture, then anyone who enacts their part in poetic performance may be liable to an especially poweful pull of psychological-cum-ethical attraction and assimilation. It is not difficult to see how this combination of factors might convert the externals of poetic performance into an act of internalization inside the performer's mind.[9]

---

[8] See, e.g., *Rep.* 4.444c10–d1, e4–5, for the principle (later adapted by Aristotle) that action is formative of dispositions.

[9] Burnyeat 1999, 271–74, detects a predominant concern with the *writing* rather than the reciting or acting of plays by Guardians in *Rep.* 3's treatment of mimesis, but I find his interpretation strained; the treatment of the Guardians as a uniform group counts against it (cf. Stohn 1993, 202). Sicking 1998, 94, erroneously applies the mimetic identification of *Rep.* 3

The dynamics of self-likening are not invoked by Plato solely for the negative purpose of restricting the scope for mimetic performance on the part of the young Guardians of the hypothetical city. Psychological and behavioral assimilation is a phenomenon he acknowledges in various contexts of his writings. It appears elsewhere in both positive and negative applications: for example, in the fascinating claim in *Republic* 8 that the pervasive freedom of a democratic culture leads to a kind of psychological (and specifically "mimetic") exchange of roles between fathers and sons; but also in the philosophical ideal of "likening oneself to god," which has a long legacy within ancient and later religious ethics, and in the *Republic*'s image of the true philosopher's "modeling" (*mimeisthai*) and self-likening (*aphomoiousthai*) of himself in accordance with the eternal realities on which he fixes his mind.[10] Plato's approach to the psychology of mimesis is grounded in the assumption that there is continuity, even equivalence, between our relations to people and things in the real world and to people and things presented in mimetic art. A direct acknowledgment of this principle occurs as late as the *Laws*, where the Athenian forcefully compares the effect on the soul of keeping and enjoying the company of bad characters with taking pleasure from the depiction of similar characters in poetry.[11] The soul's character is perpetually formed by the pleasure or pain, with the consequent attraction or repulsion, that it feels toward the environment of its experience, and Plato is reluctant to allow any fundamental separation in this respect between experience of empirical reality and experience of mimetic representation.

That last statement calls, however, for some qualification, because *Republic* 3 itself concentrates on the psychology of the performer, the actor or reciter, in such a way as to leave open the possibility that the position of an audience proper might be somewhat different. Part of the complexity of relationship between the *Republic*'s two critiques of poetry resides in the fact that whereas book 3 focuses directly on the mentality of the roleplaying performer, and links this point to its more specific concept of mimesis as direct enactment or impersonation, book 10 broaches the issue of audience psychology in broader terms and in connection with its wider perspective on mimesis "as a whole" (*holōs*, 595c7). Yet there are also several strands of continuity between the two arguments.

---

to "pure narrative." On some of the intricacies in book 3's classification of poetic types, see esp. Dyson 1988.

[10] Democratic fathers and sons: *Rep.* 8.562e, with 563b1 (where the verb *mimeisthai* is used of the fathers). "Likening oneself to god": e.g., *Rep.* 10.613b1, *Tht.* 176b1, with chapter 9, note 29. The philosopher's mimesis of eternal reality: *Rep.* 6.500b–c. Lear 1992 discusses some of the ramifications of "internalization" in the psychology and politics of the *Republic*.

[11] *Laws* 2.656b, in a context whose emphasis, as in *Rep.* 3, is on the performer's relationship to the poetic work, though not exclusively so; see my subsequent text and cf. note 39.

In book 10 Plato again couples the speeches of epic with the forms of theatrical drama (esp. 605c10–11), and his argument again assumes that poetry deals with (mythological) characters whose cultural reputation gives them an exemplary, paradigmatic force.[12] But now the psychological consequences seem more extensive than in book 3. Socrates here predicates of the audience in general a "sympathetic" response (*sumpaschein*, 605d4) that he describes as a sort of pleasurably emotional yielding or surrender (605d3). Such ideas probably had a more-than-philosophical currency: the tough-minded Athenian politician Cleon, for instance, as portrayed in Thucydides' Mytilenean debate of 427, warns the Assembly of the danger of the Athenians' "surrendering to pity," and in doing so he uses the same verb (*endidonai*) as Plato.[13] But the case analyzed by Socrates is of an explicitly "aesthetic" emotion, a grief or pity felt in response to an artistic spectacle that does not impinge directly on the spectator's own life. On the psychological model used by Socrates, a model related to but not identical with that of the middle books of the *Republic*, the soul surrenders to a pleasurably vicarious grief and, in order to overcome the resistance of reason, implicitly justifies the experience by telling itself that "these are *other people's* sufferings/emotions [*allotria pathē*]" (606b1), a motif that may consciously recall a passage in Gorgias's *Helen*.[14] When Socrates summarizes the consequences of this type of experience, we are strongly reminded again of book 3: the imaginative and emotional closeness to others that (tragic) poetry creates is said to "infect" our own lives after all, "since, when one has nurtured and strengthened one's capacity for pity on the lives of others, it is difficult to suppress it in one's own

[12] This is implicit in the linked references to "heroes" at 605d1 and a "good man" at 606b2. Wehrli 1957, 46, is badly wide of the mark in saying that the *Republic*'s two critiques of poetry have "nothing to do with one another"; he is misled partly by a serious confusion over the status of epic in book 3 (see 393b, 394c for evidence contradicting his own claims), and his suggestion that Plato expects the reader of book 10 to have *forgotten* the earlier passage is singularly unsophisticated.

[13] Thucydides 3.37.2. For the same verb, of yielding to desire, see *Rep.* 8.561b2, with the similar use of *paradidonai* at *Phdr.* 250e4.

[14] Gorgias fr. 11.9 DK: "the audience of poetry is overcome by fearful shudders, tearful pity and a longing for grief, and the soul is induced by the words to suffer an experience of its own *at the affairs of others* [*ep'allotriōn te pragmatōn*]"; on this whole context see Segal 1962, esp. 120–27, with Halliwell 1988, 148, for the possibility that Aristotle picked on this passage in a lost treatment of katharsis (most probably in *On Poets*: see Iamblichus *Myst.* 1.11 = Aristotle fr. 81 Rose, fr. 893 Gigon 1987, but classed as a fragment of the lost book of the *Poetics* in Kassel 1968, 52, fr. V; cf. now Sorabji 2000, 284–87). There are several possible echoes of this piece of Gorgias at *Rep.* 606a–b, as earlier at *Ion* 535d–e, and Gorgias in his turn looks back to the old epic motif of the "longing for grief" (e.g., Homer *Od.* 4.102, 183, with chapter 7, note 68). With the notion of emotional reactions to others' lives compare the idea of "the fortunes-of-others emotions," in a context of cognitive psychology, at Ortony, Clore, & Collins 1988, 92–108.

sufferings [*pathē*]" (606b7–8). The echo of book 3, especially of 395d1–3 (quoted earlier), is striking. In both cases the argument posits what amounts to a circle of reinforcement between responses to art and experience of life as a whole, a circle in which the former both draws on and in turn nourishes the latter.[15]

There will be more to be said, in the next chapter, about the specifically tragic dimension of *Republic* 10.605c–6b. Here I am interested in the overall psychological implications of the passage (whose main thrust, we need to remember, applies to comedy as well as tragedy, 606c). It seems a plausible prima facie inference that Plato is here expanding into a general audience psychology the kind of consideration which in book 3 Socrates linked to the mimetic mode in its narrower, enactive-impersonatory sense. What was there the perfomer's "self-likening" now seems to have become the emotional assimilation of the entire theater audience (or, equally, the audience of an epic recital, 605c10–11). Something similar is to be found in a passage of *Laws* 2 (655b–56b), mentioned earlier for the parallel it draws between responses to characters in life and in poetry, and where, notwithstanding a central concern with performers, the Athenian speaks of the emotional reactions of audiences in general.[16] Even so, there remains an important distinction to register between the psychological models that *Republic* books 3 and 10 apply to the experience of mimetic poetry. Book 10, I contend, stops short of the strong form of identification posited for poets and performers (reciters or actors) in book 3. Unlike the earlier model of self-likening, it makes room for at least a subconscious degree of mental dissociation between the hearer and the poetic character, positing "sympathy" or "fellow feeling" (*sumpaschein*, 605d4) where it is more appropriate to speak of "identification" in the case of book 3's argument,[17]

[15] Tragedy, for example, can only arouse powerful feelings of "sympathy" in its audience by tapping a "natural" propensity to grief (606a5) that has been already fostered by the formation of deeply valued attachments to other people. The stress on differences between art and life at *Rep.* 10.605d-e cuts across this point.

[16] See esp. *Laws* 2.655d–e; the context reworks material from *Rep.* 3 and 10 (note, e.g., the phrase *chairein te kai epainein* at *Laws* 655e2, with *Rep.* 605e6); cf. chapter 1, section III.

[17] "Sympathy" and "identification" are often, of course, used as practically synonymous in English; cf. section II. The distinction I draw (with which compare Heath 1987, 15) is sometimes blurred in discussions of Plato himself: Ferrari 1989, 98 (cf. 134), uses "identification" of both performers and audiences; Havelock 1963, 45, 160, uses "identification" and "sympathy" as synonymous, and elides differences between poet, performer and audience; I myself regrettably wavered in usage in Halliwell 1988, 147–49. The issue is more than terminological: see, e.g., Vernant 1991, 176, whose description of the audience of poetry having "the illusion of itself living out what is said" does not properly fit *Rep.* 10.606a–b; likewise with Robb 1994, 232 ("as though we were they"). Carroll 1998, 259, rightly links Platonic "identification" to the acting of roles but then (259–61) blurs the point by running Plato's position together with that of critics concerned about identification on the part of audiences. Helpful

and allowing for the soul's sense "that these are *other people's* sufferings/emotions [*pathē*]" it is watching (606b1). So, if there is an underlying affinity between the two analyses of what is entailed by the experience of mimetic poetry (in first a narrower and then a broader sense), and if the further consequences of such experiences are said to be essentially the same in both contexts, we should nevertheless try to preserve the contrasting nuances of the two passages. The importance of doing so is, in part, that it enables us to see why, contrary to common opinion, Plato does not have an undifferentiated conception of the psychology of mimetic experience.

We can, in fact, go further. In book 3 Plato refers to another dimension of the experience of poetry, one that involves neither identification nor sympathy. Socrates there says at one point that the future Guardians "must recognize/understand [*gignōskein*] both deranged and evil characters, whether male or female, but they must neither do nor even impersonate [*oude mimēteon*] any such thing" (396a4–6). This warning is presented as part of the argument for avoiding mimesis (in the narrower sense, i.e., dramatic impersonation) of certain sorts of characters but for nonetheless allowing the narrative representation of such characters in poetry, provided their ethical nature is unequivocally displayed. The principle is later reiterated in a more comprehensive form in a passage that states that education in *mousikē* should produce an ability to recognize virtues and vices in all their various forms and embodiments, including artistic "images" (*eikones*) of them (402b–c). Book 3 thus alludes, briefly but intriguingly, to the possibility that artistic representation might be productive of ethical understanding, though it insists on the separation of such understanding from the kind of full psychological immersion in a character that is involved, from the performer's point of view, in what is here classified as the mimetic mode. The idea that artistic representations might promote or enrich an ethical understanding of different sorts of human lives is revisited by Plato in the *Laws*, where the Athenian says of comedy: "without the comic it is impossible to understand [*manthanein*] the serious (and likewise with other pairs of opposites), if one is to become prudent; but, equally, one must not be able to *act* in both ways, if one is to have even a small amount of virtue; and that is why one must come to understand [*manthanein*] these things, in order to avoid ever doing or saying laughable things out of ignorance" (7.816d–e). Significantly, in view of the relevant passage of *Republic* 3, this quotation belongs to an argument for permitting the staging of comedy in the well-regulated city but for barring

---

in this connection is the detailed distinction between "empathy" and "sympathy" drawn by Feagin 1996, 83–142; cf. the comments of Tan 1996, 153–56, 189–90, on the concept of "identification" in relation to film.

citizens from performing in it and for leaving this task to slaves and aliens. Together, then, these two texts suggest that what Plato means by recognition and understanding (*gignōskein, gnōrizein, manthanein*) in these contexts must be construed essentially as a matter of rational ethical judgment, rather than understanding a character "from the inside." The latter is precisely what Plato fears about the mimetic mode in *Republic* 3, though the conclusion to that argument does notably leave this mode available—and, with it, the possibility of understanding *through* self-likening—in the case of paradigmatically good characters (397d4–5).

We can elucidate this last point, and probe further into some of the intricacies of Plato's approach to the experience of mimesis, by combining the various passages so far discussed into a hypothetical model (never systematized by Plato into a unified theory) of a series of psychological positions that can be occupied in the experience of poetry—a series of grades of imaginative absorption in the mimetic world that extends from the adoption of a quasi-participant point of view to the holding of an attitude of critical detachment. At one end of this range we can accordingly locate the intense assimilation, the self-likening identification, of *Republic* 3, which takes place when a performer's (or, we must remember, a poet's) mind plays out the role of a character, whether in first-person verbal recitation or in physical enactment. This experience, which partially recalls the *Ion*'s description of the performing rhapsode as "outside himself,"[18] involves something close to a wholly "participant" point of view and, on one understanding of the term, a strong degree of "empathy":[19] a point of view, in other words, from which the mind experiencing the poetic representation is so immersed in the mind of the character as to have no room for emotional or critical dissociation. But if my preceding interpretation is correct, this is not a class of experience which Plato ever ascribes to *audiences* of poetry in the strict sense, only to reciters and actors, though we should recall, as I mentioned earlier, that the argument of *Republic* 3 probably entertains the idea that the performer's self-likening role could be occupied even by an individual reader who actively "shapes himself to" (396d7–e1) the parts of individual characters.[20] For audiences as

---

[18] *Ion* 535b7 (linking with the poet's psychology posited by Socrates at 534b), which connects with older ideas of imagining oneself present "at the events themselves" (535c1, with my introduction, note 48); that the idea is undercut by what Ion goes on to say (535e) is a separate point.

[19] Note, however, that "empathy," as a translation of the German *Einfühlung*, has often been associated in modern thinking with a larger conception of mental "projection" onto aesthetic objects, including inanimate objects: see Carritt 1949, 187–91, and Gauss 1973 for summary guidance. "Participant" point of view: for some shrewd insights, see Harding 1968; also, with different nuances, Gill 1990, 16, and Gill 1996, 116–18.

[20] The terms of 396c5–e2 might be taken to cover both individual reading and more public forms of recitation or performance; cf. chapter 1, note 37. Gould 1992, 23, refers the mimetic

such, *Republic* 10, no doubt drawing on genuine scrutiny of the behavior of mass audiences in the Athenian theater, posits a psychically deep engagement with characters, and a "surrender" to the emotions they evoke, but one that takes the form of "sympathy" rather than "identification" and leaves some degree of (sub)conscious dissociation from the characters ("these are *other people*'s sufferings," 606b1). Audiences of tragedy, at any rate, are thus conceived of as engaged observers or "witnesses," but not quasiparticipants.[21]

At the opposite end of Plato's scale from complete self-assimilation, with its quasi-participant point of view, belongs a perspective of wholly rational judgment on the represented characters and events, a perfect philosophical fulfillment of the principle of ethical recognition and understanding that I have cited from *Republic* 3.402b–c and *Laws* 7.816d–e. In the case of evil characters, for whom it would be appropriate to feel outright disapproval and even, in some cases, "disgust,"[22] such recognition or understanding would have to be without any taint of emotional sympathy, let alone the assimilative role playing in recitation or performance whose dangers *Republic* 3 diagnoses. "Understanding," in this setting, would be a process of critically detached judgment: Plato does not regard a process of *gignōskein* or *manthanein*, in this respect, as entailing any kind of imaginative compromise with the object of understanding.[23] Such judgment

---

psychology of book 3 to "the audience" as a whole, but without argument, and I made the same false move in Halliwell 1988, 4, 149; contrast Dyson 1988, 44–45.

[21] The historical applicability of this model of theater (and recitation) audiences to classical Athens would be a large subject in its own right, and a conclusive answer to the question would be difficult to achieve. Lada 1993 undertakes a rich exploration of available evidence and argues for the essentially anti-Platonic conclusion that Greek/Athenian audiences were able to enjoy a fusion of emotion and judgment in "empathic understanding"; Lada 1996 restates her case with anti-Brechtian (but it could just as easily have been anti-Platonic) emphasis. Wallace 1997 offers a more sociological account of Athenian audiences, looking rather askance at Plato's "elitist sensibilities" and blaming the repressed behavior of modern theater-audiences on Platonic ideology.

[22] *Rep.* 10.605e6: *bdeluttesthai* is a term of remarkably strong detestation, associated in Greek comedy with a virtually physical feeling of revulsion (e.g., Aristophanes *Ach.* 586, *Wasps* 792); cf. *misein* (to hate) for the appropriate reaction to certain kinds of "comic" material at *Rep.* 10.606c4 (with *Laws* 2.656b2 for the equivalent in life).

[23] For the ostensibly very different view that all "understanding" of (historical) human behavior involves implicit identification with it, see the appendix to Primo Levi's great book, *Se questo è un uomo* (Levi 1989, 347): "'comprendere' . . . un comportamento umano significa . . . contenerlo, contenerne l'autore, mettersi al suo posto, identificarsi con lui" (to "understand" a piece of human behavior means to contain it, to contain its author, to put oneself in his position, to identify oneself with him). But it is interesting that Levi here speaks in terms close to those of *Rep.* 3's model of assimilation through mimesis. Isaiah Berlin, denying that "tout comprendre, c'est tout pardonner," takes the contrasting view that the imaginative understanding even of extremes of evil behavior can be valuable as a counterweight to intolerance and fanaticism (Jahanbegloo 1993, 37–38).

would not, however, necessarily be dispassionate, given the vehemence of disapproval marked as "disgust" at *Republic* 10.605e6; so that even at this end of the spectrum Plato envisages a psychological experience in which the force of reason is animated by a pressure of strong evaluative feeling. Besides, it is important to notice that Plato seems to believe that there is one context in which a correct response of ethical judgment is sometimes evoked in ordinary audiences by some existing poetry.

Because *Republic* 10.606 juxtaposes tragic and comic theater, and makes it clear that emotional "surrender" can take place in relation to both, it is easy to overlook a crucial asymmetry between Plato's attitude to the two genres. In essence, Plato's antitragic scheme of things, as my next chapter shows in detail, renders tragedy in anything like its traditional forms altogether redundant: it makes no sense to think of an acceptably modified version of the existing genre, as opposed, perhaps, to a philosophical replacement for it. But the same is not true of comedy. *Laws* 7.816d–e, already mentioned, specifies that comedy does have a valuable role to play in a culture: "without the comic it is impossible to understand the serious." There *is* an acceptable form of comedy, one in which the moral deficiencies of the agents are made unambiguous, so that an audience is invited to laugh *against* them, with clear recognition of their faults, and not in any sense *with* them. It is the latter, the comic equivalent of sympathizing with tragic suffering, that is condemned at *Republic* 10.606c. By contrast, the passage of *Laws* 7 just cited is in line with the definition of true comedy given by Socrates at *Republic* 5.452d–e, where "the laughable" (*geloion*) is equated, bluntly, with "the bad" (*kakon*).[24]

Even *Republic* 3, in fact, makes a cautious concession to comedy, entertaining the possibility of the mimetic mode in relation to defective characters provided it is used only "for the sake of play" (*paidias charin*, 396e2).[25] This passage shows that Plato can contemplate a more innocent kind of comic enjoyment, though the scope of this concession, phrased almost as an afterthought, is hard to assess. All that seems certain is that we have

---

[24] The bluntness needs qualifying, in turn, by the point made at *Phileb.* 49b–c, that the defects of comic characters must be kept within limits that separate them from the threatening and truly harmful: this anticipates the definition of the comic given at Aristotle *Poet.* 5.1449a32–37.

[25] The glossing of this as "satirical" (Ferrari 1989, 119; Nehamas 1988, 215) is, I think, inappropriate; that description would better fit the ethically directed laughter of *Laws* 7.816d–e. See Murray 1996, 178–79, with Halliwell 1988, 132, and my chapter 1, note 64, on other Platonic references to mimetic play; cf., more generally, Arnould 1990, 120–21. For comic "play" (*paizein*), and its exclusion of satire of individuals, see also *Laws* 11.935d–e, a passage that betrays the influence of comedy's special festive status in Athenian culture (so Halliwell 1991b, 67–68). Mader 1977 gives an overview of Plato's treatment of laughter and comedy, a subject made more complex, as with so much else, by Plato's own practice as a writer: see Brock 1990, and cf. Jouët-Pastré 1998 on the philosophical value of laughter.

here a marginal acknowledgment that role playing can sometimes be separated from the psychological internalization that is otherwise treated as an entailment of engagement in the mimetic mode. In the case of good characters, however, book 3 is more confident, though still not altogether without caution, in permitting the mimetic mode, and with it the full force of self-likening, on the part of the reciter or performer. But there is a complication to be registered here too, as later signaled in book 10. On the accounts given by Socrates in both book 3 and book 10, the perfectly good character would be a paragon of an antitragic view of the world, one whose unemotional response to the superficial misfortunes of life (even to such potentially "tragic" events as the loss of a loved one) would make him so unchanging and impassive as hardly to be a possible subject for poetic, let alone dramatic, representation at all (604e). The composed self-consistency of the rationally virtuous character would be almost a negation of the idea of dramatic, "human" interest. "Alles Stoische ist untheatralisch": all Stoicism is untheatrical, as Lessing laconically put a variant of this point in *Laokoon*; and others, including Hume and Rousseau, have made comparable observations.[26] Awareness of this point apparently puts Plato in the paradoxical position of reserving the mimetic mode in *Republic* 3 for the dramatization of characters who, as *Republic* 10.604e later concedes, might provide a dramatist with little *worth* dramatizing, at any rate for audiences other than the exclusively philosophical. Such audiences would find such subjects hard to "understand" (*katamathein*, 604e4), which indicates that just as the perfect philosopher (the member of a tiny class, *Republic* 10.605c7–8) would be immune to the emotional appeal of existing poetry, so the existing audiences of poetry would find it impossible to accommodate themselves to the emotional "austerity" (cf. *Rep.* 3.398a8) of such hypothetical representations of virtue.

Now, if one asks (as such reflections readily prompt one to) in what relationship Plato's own dialogues stand to such philosophical ideals, a cogent answer will need to take account of a whole set of factors.[27] On

[26] Lessing, *Laokoon* §1 (Lessing 1970–79, 6:16); Lessing's point was anticipated in particular by Dubos' *Réflexions critiques* (1719), pt. I, ch. 5 (Dubos 1748, 1:37: "a Stoic would certainly make a very wretched figure in a tragedy"), a work Lessing knew. Rousseau: see his *Lettre à d'Alembert* (Rousseau 1959–95, 5:3–125, at 17). Hume, in a note to "Of Tragedy" (1757), comments that "complete joy and satisfaction" do not allow for enough "action" to interest poets as much as distress and painful subjects (Hume 1993, 361). Two ancient texts which note poetry's preference for variety, however achieved, rather than an austere simplicity or purity are Plutarch *Aud. Poet.* 16a–b, 25d (note proximity to the contrast at 25c between Homeric poetry and Stoicism's black-and-white ethics), and pseudo-Plutarch *Hom.* 2.5, 218 (pp. 8, 116–17 Kindstrand). Cf. Skillen 1992, 203: stories "tend to delight through exciting, implicitly putting it across that the 'dramatic,' conflict-ridden, exciting life is the desirable life."

[27] Ferrari 1989, 141–48, provides an interesting discussion of this question; Tate 1932, 166–67, rightly stresses that Plato's own practice does not purport to implement ideal principles;

one side, the dialogues generally escape "austerity" by juxtaposing and mixing the philosophically admirable (especially in its Socratic form) with many varieties of human weakness, error, and emotion: they are therefore, taken in their totality, remote from the hypothetical depiction of virtuous rationality posited at *Republic* 10.604e. But that does not explain, indeed it tends to make all the less obvious, how Plato might have thought that his own work could meet the standards of *Republic* 3.398a–b, where the scope for dramatic representation (for the mimetic mode) is, as we have seen, severely constricted. Yet it is open to us to suppose that Plato never intended to meet precisely those standards, because he is not after all committed to following through all the consequences of an ideal model that he puts in the mouth of Socrates in one of his own works. That is no mere evasion, on Plato's behalf, of the question posed, for we must be on guard against the naive assumption that we can unequivocally extract an authentic Platonic "doctrine" from one part of his text.[28] We need to ponder more cautiously, then, how Plato might have thought his work related not only to the analysis of the mimetic mode given in *Republic* 3, but to the whole range of possibilities, from rational criticism to imaginative assimilation, which the arguments I have been considering allow us to discriminate on a Platonic spectrum of psychological responses to mimesis.

Although the ramifications of this reformulated question reach beyond the ambit of my own argument, there is an essential observation to be made here. Plato's own practice as a writer (that whole "passionate history of a soul" of which Nietzsche, his reluctant admirer, speaks) thrives on a teeming variety of ideas, characters, and subject matter; its purview takes in everything from sexual desire to the contemplation of eternity. Moreover, in its narrative, dialogic, and mythopoeic diversity (what Sidney called its "skin . . . and beauty"),[29] it self-consciously borrows, adapts, and transmutes elements taken from a whole host of literary and rhetorical sources, including Homeric, tragic, and comic poetry. So Plato's writing in itself bespeaks a necessarily elaborate, multilayered sense of the possibilities of responding to, and being shaped by, its own mimetic nature, and it

---

Kosman 1992 sees "mimetic displacement" (85) and "a valorization of mimesis" (87) as marking all of Plato's own writing. Note that *Rep.* 3.397c itself indicates that the preceding analysis of narrative types is applicable to other kinds of discourse than poetry.

[28] On the more general implications of this view for mimesis, cf. chapter 1, with note 3 there.

[29] Sir Philip Sidney, "Defence of Poesy" (Duncan-Jones 1989, 213). In antiquity, Plato's poetic qualities were recognized by, e.g., Longinus *Subl.* 13.3–4 (stressing his "Homeric" cast), Proclus *In Remp.* 1.196.9–13 Kroll (Platonic mimesis in emulation of Homeric poetry: see chapter 11, section II), and, with hostility, Colotes the Epicurean (chapter 3, note 38). Later views of Plato as poet occur in, e.g., Shaftesbury 1999, 114 n. 42, and Shelley *Defence of Poetry* (Jones 1916, 127). For Plato's own characterization of his work as a rival to tragedy, see chapter 3, section I; for some modern discussions, see chapter 1, note 44.

supplies us with our best reason to complicate further the implications of
the psychological spectrum I have constructed from various Platonic texts.
Plato the writer, in other words, intimates that we should not treat the
bands of this spectrum as a series of fixed or discrete phenomena, but
rather as a model of states of mind that stand, in reality, in a dynamic
relationship to one another. Plato's own practice arguably communicates
a more generous awareness of how engagement with a (dramatic) text
can become a function of "dialogue" *between* the interpreter and the text,
and thereby gives us the best reason of all for not taking the particular
remarks I have been examining as Plato's definitive word on the subject.

To derive a moral of this kind from Plato's own writing is not to override
the salient features of the concepts of critical detachment, emotional sympathy, or psychological assimilation that emerge in the passages with
which we have been concerned. Even within these passages themselves,
we have encountered numerous nuances of subtlety and complexity in
the positions I have designated as those of the detached critical judge,
the sympathetically engaged witness, and the quasi-participant mimetic
impersonator. These nuances reside not only in the distinctions drawn in
both the *Republic* and *Laws* between performers and audiences, between
different kinds of audiences, and between positive and negative kinds of
self-likening. They can also be detected in the shifting permutations that
consequently come into play in the relationships between performers, audiences, and dramatic characters, as well as in such details as the asymmetry between the status of tragic and comic emotions, or the underdevel-
oped suggestion that there is a mode of experience, namely "play"
(*paidia*), which might in principle be exempted from the stricter ethical
criteria that are otherwise applied to the mimetic arts. All these factors lend
to Plato's cumulative perspective on the experience of mimesis a richness
and depth that make it a still fruitful source of consideration for theories
of aesthetic experience. In order to foreground further some of the ways
in which this is so, I look selectively in the second part of this chapter at
three positions from more recent phases of aesthetics that make worthwhile points of comparison for the model I have ascribed to Plato, and I
proceed from there to expand on my reasons for wanting to locate a kind
of "romantic puritanism" at the heart of Plato's aesthetics.

II

In his *Theory of Moral Sentiments* (1759), a work that addresses much
more than responses to art but is nonetheless illuminating in this connection, Adam Smith explains "sympathy" (alias "altruism" or "fellow feeling")
in terms of imagination but gives an account of the sympathetic imagination that seems suspended between self-regarding and other-regarding

considerations. Smith tells us that we need imagination, when reacting to the experiences of others in social life as well as in fiction, to conceive "what we ourselves should feel in the like situation"; but he also claims that "by imagination . . . we enter as it were into his [i.e., another person's] body, and become in some measure the same person with him," thus "changing places in fancy with the sufferer."[30] As these latter quotations indicate, Smith's "sympathy" is hard to distinguish from identification, where the latter is defined, as I have already defined it in the first part of this chapter, in terms of a quasi-participant or intensely vicarious point of view. The synonymy of sympathy and identification reflects a more diffuse eighteenth-century use of these two terms as largely interchangeable, and that has in turn left its mark on general modern usage, with the exception of certain technical applications (especially in psychoanalysis).[31] In addition, however, Smith argues that sympathy in its strongest forms depends on understanding, reason, and judgment of a situation, on knowing the causes of another's suffering, so that it is not at all a purely instinctual reaction but manifests cognitive interpretation.

In effect, therefore, Smith presents a compound notion of imagination that, stimulating though it is for a wider inquiry into the basis of moral feelings, elides distinctions of the kind I have extracted from Plato's thinking and leaves us with the difficulty of how to separate different degrees of psychological closeness or emotional affinity in responses to the experiences of others (whether in life or in art). If it is a possible complaint against the Platonic model I have presented, though a complaint I have tried to some extent to defuse, that it draws excessively sharp lines of demarcation on the psychological spectrum, Adam Smith's account of related matters seems insufficiently alert to the shifting shades of evaluative and emotional feeling that can inform the perception of others' lives. In particular, Smith's position might make us wonder how becoming "in some measure the same person as another," which implies a psychological loss of self, can be reconciled with the stance of the attentive, judicious spectator from which, as Smith himself argues, ethical judgments need to be made.[32] It may be that

---

[30] Smith 1976, 9–13 (pt. I, sec. i, ch. 1). On the problematic importance of the fictional (esp. theatrical) model for Smith's thinking, see Marshall 1986, 167–92, with Bate 1961, 129–59, and Marshall 1988 for the broader eighteenth-century context of ideas. Nussbaum 1990, 338–47, penetratingly analyzes Smith's views more fully than I can do here, and in relation to her own ethical model of reading fiction.

[31] Wollheim 1973, 54–83, esp. 73–79, discusses Freudian "identification" in relation to other imaginative processes. Harding 1968, 308–9, criticizes the often loose and unhelpful use of the term "identification."

[32] The point applies in reverse if we remember that Smith suggests we can judge *ourselves* only by trying to adopt a spectator's point of view toward our lives (Smith 1976, 109–10: pt. III, ch. 1).

Smith's theory can be saved by regarding the element of identification not as a discrete state of mind but a tacit *hypothesis* which takes place whenever sympathy occurs. But even if that is so, the effect of his argument is to blur the distinction between two possible psychological relationships: that of the person who actively shares in, say, the grief of a sufferer, and that of the person who, in the same situation, feels pity *for* the sufferer.[33] This distinction, which corresponds to two processes of imagination, is the difference between the enactive, self-likening mimesis of Plato *Republic* 3.393c–398b and the sympathetic response of the audience of tragedy at 10.605c-6b. It is a distinction that matters greatly to both individual and cultural perceptions of artistic representation.

In contrast to the way in which Adam Smith, typically for his period, tends to condense the concept of sympathy, the modern literary theorist Hans Robert Jauss, occupying the historically relativizing perspective of a theory of "reception aesthetics," has constructed a scale of five major types of what he generically calls "identification."[34] Jauss's range runs from active "cultic participation" to the comparative detachment of "aesthetic reflection," although he also argues for the possibility of combining emotional engagement and aesthetic distance within a single response. Although Jauss does not link his psychological categories to those of Plato, and in fact makes more use of Aristotelian concepts, his scheme could be shown to cover a range analogous to Plato's and to embrace the fundamental distinctions I have already traced in the latter's dialogues. Thus, at one pole, Jauss's "associative identification," which involves the active assumption of a role, corresponds to Plato's conception of performative, self-likening mimesis.[35] Similarly, Jauss's "admiring identification" closely matches the concern with emulation of heroic role models that is conveyed by Plato in such passages as *Republic* 3.387d–88b. Where Jauss principally differs from Plato is in his willingness to multiply categories along the psychological spectrum of responses, and to take account of a very large number of artistic forms. These differences are chiefly an index of the cultural width of perspective adopted by Jauss, a perspective that generates a characteristically modern form of pluralism that was neither available (for historical reasons) nor congenial (for conceptual reasons) to Plato.

Given this contrast between Plato's position and a modern liberal-pluralist aesthetic, my last comparative example has been deliberately chosen with an instructive paradox in mind. Wayne Booth's *The Company We*

[33] Aristotle applies this distinction at, e.g., *Rhet.* 2.8, 1386a17–23; cf. chapter 7, section I.
[34] Jauss 1974.
[35] At the other pole, however, Jauss 1974's "ironic identification" (313–17), misleadingly labeled, involves an aestheticist withholding of engagement that is very different from anything in Plato (even from the latter's marginalized concept of "play"—see note 25—which can hardly be a case of "disinterested contemplation"); cf. note 42.

Keep develops a moral psychology of reading whose approach to the ethics of literature deserves to be counted, however paradoxically, as a liberal
variant on the Platonic paradigm I have been discussing in this chapter.
Booth is happy to invoke Plato explicitly at certain points, and he uses
language that has close affinities with some of Plato's terms, though he
often puts it to evaluatively different ends. Thus, Booth can write, reminis-
cently of *Republic* 10.605c–6b: "The essential first step [in reading fiction]
. . . can only be that primary act of *assent* that occurs when we *surrender*
to a story and follow it through to its conclusion."[36] Booth modifies his
"Platonism," however, in two principal respects. In the first place, he
works with a much more extensive and carefully refined range of terms
and criteria. Employing a characteristically modern "contextualism," which
Plato may have had his own reasons for resisting, he takes explicit account
of potential divergence between an authorially internalized control of a
text (the "sense of life" associated with the "implied author") and the properties of individual characters depicted in the work, a divergence that Plato
understood from the inside in his own writing but to which he seems
reluctant to attach weight where poetry is concerned.[37] Second, Booth argues for an ethics of reading that entails, as he puts it, "both surrender and
refusal" (136), an openness to sympathy tempered by critical control—a
combination that falls within the bounds of Platonic possibilities, but not
one in which any individual Platonic argument invests much confidence.

Yet Booth also sometimes moves toward a more uncompromisingly Platonic position, partly because he tends to assume that individual imaginative works project unitary sets of values. At one point, for instance, he
writes that, "insofar as the fiction has *worked* for us, we have lived with
its values for the duration: we have been *that kind of person* for at least
as long as we remained in the presence of the work."[38] Three things are
particularly remarkable here: one, that Booth applies something like *Republic* 3's self-assimilation, enactive paradigm ("we have *been* that sort
of person") to *all* reading of fiction, thereby going beyond Plato's own
psychological model; second, the unqualified phrase "its values," used
with reference to the totality of a literary work; finally, the overtones of
"lived with," which of course echoes the title of Booth's book and gives
a further Platonic dimension to the enterprise, because the comparison
between works of art and personal "company," as I earlier noticed, is

---

[36] Booth 1988, 32; only "assent" is italicized by Booth himself, who elsewhere uses "surrender" repeatedly. For explicit affiliation to the Platonic paradigm, see esp. Booth 41.

[37] On the nature of the Platonic anticontextualism that explains this reluctance, see Halliwell 2000a.

[38] Booth 1988, 41 (his emphasis).

found as a metaphorical motif in Plato too.[39] It is significant that here, and not only here, Booth skirts perilously close to an implicit notion of what amounts, in the terms of my earlier argument, to "identification," even though he also shows some caution about such a concept.[40] The ultimate reason for this, I think, is that despite the critical detail and evaluative finesse of many of his individual readings, Booth's psychology of reading rests on a theoretical foundation that is, however surprisingly, narrower than Plato's. Although, as already mentioned, Booth advocates a type of reading that can *combine* "surrender and refusal," it is also the case that he tends to see these two categories as fully defining the basic attitudinal options available to a reader, and supposes *all* reading to require at least a stage of surrender or succumbing.[41] Booth's general psychological schema can be faulted for not providing a sufficiently supple model of the stances which a reader might adopt or explore toward a fictional text, and in that respect the Platonic model, with its distinguishable categories of critical judgment, sympathy, identification, and even "play," actually acknowledges a wider range of possibilities, even if it does not ostensibly encourage reflection on ways of maximizing opportunities to exercise them in aesthetic contexts.

That anything like a self-conscious variant on Plato's psychology of art can be found in a liberal American literary critic is only one, but a very striking, illustration of the complex bearing that Plato's arguments in this area can have on the configurations of modern thought. Nietzsche's diagnosis of Plato's paradoxical importance for aesthetics, from which this chapter started, continues to be borne out in unexpected ways. In the remainder of the chapter I want to offer further thoughts on the relationship between Plato and some of the more prominent contours of modern aesthetics and, in doing so, to move closer to what I see as Plato's position vis-à-vis a central conviction of recent Western culture, namely romanticism's faith in the positive, wholesome power of imagination.

Now, it is easy enough to see, from one angle, how Plato's orientation in the passages examined earlier can be considered as a serious counterbalance and corrective to a modern notion that contrasts sharply with full-blooded romantic ideals of imaginative absorption in works of art—the notion of aesthetic "distance," a derivation from the idea of "disinterestedness" so important to Enlightenment and subsequent theories of aesthetics, as discussed in my introduction. I have already indicated that Plato

[39] See esp. *Rep.* 10.603b1 (where the imagery evokes a sexually dangerous woman: Halliwell 1988, 135), 605b1; *Laws* 2.656b (with note 11).
[40] See esp. Booth 1988, 138–42, where he appears to question the concept of identification as "misleading" and "excessive," but continues to use the term and to describe reading as "a kind of submersion in other minds."
[41] See esp. Booth 1988, 140.

himself sometimes legislates for a kind of distance, with the consequent possibility of conscious judgment, in the experience of artistic representation. But such distance has nothing in common with aesthetic "disinterestedness," because, unlike the latter, it rests on direct attention to the ethical content of works of art. Moreover, Plato suggests that marked aesthetic distance can be achieved only in carefully controlled circumstances, and only by suitably educated individuals. He does not at all treat it as the usual psychological state in which fictional works are apprehended; indeed, he seems to acknowledge, in more than one passage, that it is in the power of much of the greatest art to *command* an emotional absorption that is destructive of rational detachment. By contrast, theorists of aesthetic distance, such as Edward Bullough, have tended to exaggerate the feasibility, as well as the ideal nature, of states of aesthetic experience that are largely sui generis and isolated from the general, "nonaesthetic" workings of the mind.[42] There is probably no simple middle ground between these divergent points of view; they stand as irreconcilable accounts of ways in which certain works of art either are or could be experienced by some, suitably attuned people. But it remains plausible to affirm, with Nietzsche, that Plato's concern over the psychology of deep emotional engagement in artistic representations raises issues that cannot simply be dealt with by a prescriptive declaration that places such engagement outside the boundaries of the aesthetic.

Moreover, the cultural relevance of those issues seems hardly to have diminished with time, and it would be unwarranted to suppose that Platonic views of both audience and performer psychology are simply remote from modern ways of thinking. In fact, we can find analogues for the basic components of these views in many areas of more recent discourse about art, from popular argument about the dominant art forms of film and television to the language of more abstract theories of theater. Two brief examples will have to suffice. Alexander Nehamas has intriguingly contended that the essential pattern of Plato's ideas about drama in *Republic* 10 depends on a view of the "transparency" of mimesis (representation *qua*, as it were, an open window on the world) that is often retraced in certain kinds of intellectual criticism of television and other forms of mass entertainment.[43] Nehamas is right to stress that, in one sense, the Athenian the-

---

[42] Bullough 1957, 91–130 (first published 1912), is still a standard text on aesthetic distance (note his revealingly antimimeticist slant at 106–7); cf. Markowitz 1998 for some discussion. Ferrari 1989, 138, seems to me misleading in claiming that *Rep.* 10 involves an attack on aesthetic distance: the kind of dissociation indicated at 606b is embedded in an emotional experience radically different from what is normally understood by aesthetic distance. Cf. note 35.

[43] Nehamas 1988: but where he sees a metaphysical view of the nature of mimetic objects (219–20), I would prefer to say that Plato's critique targets the actual inclination of audiences

ater was a form of "popular entertainment" in Plato's own culture, although I think his argument needs qualifying by a recognition that the differences between that culture and modern democratic societies means that Athenian drama cuts across the sort of distinction between "highbrow" and "popular" that is now so familiar (and controversial). Plato's critique of the psychology of mimesis in *Republic* 10 cannot, at any rate, be so easily correlated as Nehamas proposes with "entertainment" as opposed to "art." On the contrary, it addresses issues of emotional absorption and engagement that are in principle equally applicable to the experience of any art form that dramatizes subjects of sufficiently compelling human interest. When the Socrates of *Republic* 10 says that the experience of tragedy affects "even the best of us," this is Plato's very revealing way of acknowledging that he is offering something more than an élitist repudiation of the psychology of the masses.

From a related but slightly different angle it is pertinent and useful to observe the significantly common ground between the thinking of Plato and the dramatic theories of Bertolt Brecht, despite the very different purposes behind their arguments. So far as I can see, Brecht himself was unaware of any affinity with Plato, but in fact his theory of "non-Aristotelian," epic theater coincides at several key points with ideas I have been investigating in this chapter: in its hostility to forms of theater that induce close, sympathetic absorption in the characters; in its rejection of styles of acting that depend on some kind of illusionism and require total psychological immersion and identification on the part of the actor; and in its advocacy of a type of drama that allows, indeed necessitates, the retention of a capacity for consciously ethical and social judgment by the spectator.[44] Brecht is just as disturbed by collective emotional empathy on the part of "bourgeois" theater audiences as Plato had been by the shared emotional engagement of democratic audiences in classical Athens. Both thinkers, despite the huge discrepancy between their ultimate motivations, are equally troubled by the power of certain kinds of successful ("popular") art to use emotion to express and promote mentalities that their own models of rationality categorize as both ethically and politically degenerate.

But we need to see beyond individual affinities of this kind in order to observe a much more extensive point about Plato's relationship to psy-

---

to *treat* mimetic representations as unmediated cases of what they represent. Carroll 1998 offers a full perspective on the aesthetics of popular art; cf. esp. 250–61 on the "Platonist" cast of some modern critiques of mass art, but see note 17.

[44] On Brecht's broader relationship to mimetic theories of art, see chapter 12, section III, with Halliwell 2002 on Brecht's anti-Aristotelian dramaturgy. Nussbaum 1993, 144–45 compares Brecht to the model of "critical spectatorship" (136–45) which she ascribes to some Stoics (and which could be regarded as a development of one part of the Platonic spectrum of psychological responses to poetry discussed in my text).

chological positions that have been occupied in the varied landscape of
modern aesthetics. It is hard for us, as postromantic readers of Plato, to
escape from the impression that his dealings with the psychology of mimetic art are perpetually shadowed by a sensibility of quasi-puritanical
anxiety. This is, I am convinced, only half the truth about Plato, but it is
an important half truth nonetheless. Although my earlier analysis tried to
uncover points of complexity on Plato's spectrum of psychological responses to mimetic works, it did not dispel the sense that he remains
predominantly inhospitable to the idea that imaginative engagement, as
aroused by poetic fiction at any rate, can itself be a medium or agency of
understanding. In *Republic* 10, indeed, understanding (*gignōskein*) and
mimesis (in the wider sense of artistic representation) are effectively set
up as mutually exclusive activities; that point is conveyed by the tripartite
scheme of user, maker, and mimetic artist at 601c–2b. But there is a further
reason why Plato wishes to deny to the imagination, as exercised in the
experience of dramatic fiction, a capacity to enlarge or enrich the discernment of its audiences, and it is one that is connected to a persistent Platonic preoccupation—a central theme of the entire *Republic*—with the
unity of the soul or the person.

In *Republic* book 4, after the matching tripartite schemes of citizen
classes and parts of the soul have been set out, we reach a crucial passage
where Socrates suggests that justice depends on the ordered, harmonious
integration of the elements that exist in every individual's mind. He invokes once more the twin principles of "one person, one function," and
"keeping to one's own business," which had earlier been presented as the
foundation of civic or social justice; and he now contends that these same
principles are the key to psychic and individual justice too. Justice in this
sense, he says, "is not a matter of external actions, but concerns inward
activity, indeed it concerns the person himself and his internal/intrinsic
affairs" (443c–d). Justice, along with the other three cardinal virtues, requires a condition of soul in which complete and structured unity is at-
tained—in which, to put the point in its most succinct and telling form,
the individual "becomes one person instead of many" (*hena genomenon
ek pollōn*, 443e1).

The integrity of the person, an ideal that is equally psychological and
ethical, stands as Plato's ultimate reason for mistrusting the arousal of the
imagination by poetry and drama. The importance of this idea is directly
signaled in *Republic* 3, at 394e, where the principle of "one person, one
function" is used to ground the conclusion that young Guardians should
not be given to free, wide-ranging indulgence in dramatic impersonation—should not, as we are entitled to rephrase the point, learn to be

imaginative.[45] The Guardians, like all citizens of a just state, and (for the same basic reason) like all just individuals, must have only one social or political function, and must therefore have harmoniously integrated characters that equip them for this function. Unless carefully controlled—which means, above all, restricted to selected models of virtue—the identification involved in performing or reciting dramatic poetry represents a threat to the soul's unity, because the operation of "self-likening," the enactment of experiences fictionally other than one's own, requires the mind to discover within itself, so Plato believes, the nature of what it is brought to imagine.[46] Drama invites and leads us to discover *other possible lives* and, in the process, to make them psychologically our own.

Although this passage of *Republic* 3 refers principally to the psychology of performance and recitation, we can again observe a degree of continuity between it and the account of the spectator's experience of dramatic poetry given in book 10. The spectator's experience involves something less than complete (empathetic) identification, yet the intense imaginative sympathy that it paradigmatically creates still constitutes, on Plato's premises, a compromise to the integrity of the individual, thereby threatening, in some degree, to turn "one person" into "many." This point emerges in book 10's own emphatic allegation that drama, both tragic and comic, can induce its audience to suspend psychological standards to which they profess allegiance outside the theater: part of the "yielding" or "surrender" contained in the experience, part of what it means to "follow" the emotional force of a dramatic portrayal, is precisely, according to Plato, to take on the underlying attitudes and values of the figures with and for whom one feels, and hence, to that extent, to imperil one's true self.

Republic 10 adds a further disquieting consideration to this argument. Plato finds the drama of both Homeric epic and Attic tragedy to have a particular interest in characters who are themselves far from psychically integrated, characters—like Homer's Achilles and Sophocles' Ajax—given to emotional turbulence and sharp shifts of mental mood, as opposed to the composed self-consistency of the rationally virtuous man (who is him-

---

[45] The passage immediately following this, 395a–b, seems to involve some ambiguity in the idea of "impersonating/acting many things" (*polla mimeisthai*), which could mean either acting many roles or acting in different genres (and which anticipates the motif of mimesis *qua* "making everything," *panta poiein*, in book 10: see chapter 4, section III). But this does not obscure the main line of argument.

[46] Note, by contrast, the conception of judges at *Rep.* 3.409a–b as people who have no personal or *internal* sense of evil, only external, slowly accumulated knowledge of its nature. On the connection between exercising the imagination through fiction and discovering "other lives," cf. note 6. Schubert 1995, 150–58, gives a skeptical reading of the educational psychology of *Rep.* 3; Ferrari 1989, 108–19, argues a position parallel with my own.

self, as we saw that Plato recognizes, less than ideally suitable for dramatic treatment). In this context Plato applies both to volatile characters and to the poetry that dramatizes them a term, *poikilos* (heterogeneous, constantly shifting), which helps to accentuate what is at stake for him in this entire issue.[47] If the *Republic*'s model of the mind or soul is one that makes unity the supreme condition of virtue and happiness, it is one that equally regards all forms of variety and versatility as subversive of virtue. Psychological heterogeneity is the antithesis of "self-control," *sōphrosunē* (cf. 3.404e): if the latter is the virtue that embodies integration and harmony, heterogeneity fosters the conditions in which each of us will continue to live not as one but as many people. Nothing, as Plato sees it, is more characteristic of the poetic imagination than fascination for, and an implicit invitation to, psychic volatility (and therefore instability). It is in the nature of the variety on which the imagination thrives that it can take us "outside ourselves," transposing us not only in terms of the physical and temporal settings of experience but also in terms of the emotional and ethical factors that partly constitute what that experience might mean for us.

The upshot of this line of reasoning is that the psychological core of Plato's critique of poetry and drama, with the moral and political authoritarianism it brings with it, is rooted ultimately in a fear of the imagination as such, a fear of what imagination can enact within each of us ("the city in the soul") as well as, by extension, within whole communities. The many selves into which the soul can be diffracted exist potentially within each person; Plato's philosophical psychology declares that the possibility of this disordered or constantly changing multiplicity is given by the very nature of the human mind. Plato's fear is that the imagination, in the peculiarly potent forms activated by compelling fiction, can easily serve to foster these different selves and the desires on which they live.[48] Except under specially limited conditions, he seems to believe, the imagination must be dangerously inimical to reason, precisely because its dynamics are those of self-transformation: for what can transform the self or the soul can subvert and destroy its chances of happiness.

But that way of putting the point allows one to see, I think, why it is justifiable to describe Plato not simply as a puritan but, however oxymo-

---

[47] See 604e1, with Halliwell 1988, 140. *Laws* 2.665c6 (contrast 7.812d–e) is a rare concession of the need for some *poikilia* in the experience of art. Heath 1987, 105–6, cites other Greek views of literary *poikilia*; cf. Heath 1989, 28–30, with my chapter 11, note 34.

[48] Because the dramatic imagination involves the supremacy of desire over reason (605b5, 606a–b), it is tempting to refer to the comparable account of dreams at *Rep.* 9.571c–d, where the result, at least for one kind of soul, is a grim orgy of sexual and violent crimes of precisely the type found in some tragic myths. But the experience of tragedy, even on Plato's most pessimistic reckoning, cannot mean surrender to desires of this kind, which are incompatible with the centrality of pity at 605c–6b; see Halliwell 1995b, 86–88, against Lear 1995, 68–72.

ronically, as a romantic puritan. I mean by this that Plato's mistrust of the imagination stems from perceptions of its potency which are paradoxically comparable to those that made it such a vital and insistent part of so much romantic ideology.[49] Romanticism and Platonism are both devoted, in part, to a quest for the spiritual harmony and integrity of the individual. But for the romantics that integrity requires the imagination as one of its primary agencies, because imagination carries with it a potential for self-creation, self-exploration, and self-renewal, which is taken to be indispensable for spiritual growth and fulfillment. The many selves that Plato sees lurking in every mind, and which he thinks need to be integrated into a single, stable self under the rule of reason, become, for romanticism, nothing less than an essential source of freedom and discovery. In one of his *Kritische Fragmente* of 1797, Friedrich Schlegel—using the kind of imagery that constantly recurs in this period—speaks of the need for the free spirit to be able to "tune" itself, like a musical instrument, to any "mode" of mind, while Shelley, employing something of a romantic cliché, compares the human mind to an Aeolian lyre and speaks of the "ever-changing melody" produced on it by the constant flow of external and internal impressions.[50] Plato too speaks of the mind in the language of music, but when he does so it is in order to define *sōphrosunē* as the harmonious unity of the parts of the soul, and this harmony is not a shifting range of possibilities (a chromaticism of mental music), but a single, fixed "tuning" of virtue.[51] Similarly, when Thomas de Quincey undertakes the typically romantic task of trying to define the quintessence of poetry, his argument centers on the awakening of powerful feelings that open up, illuminate, and recreate the mind itself, "the world within."[52] The imagination that was, for Plato, potentially subversive of identity had become, for romanticism, formative and even partly constitutive of the self.

There are no doubt many respects in which this conclusion calls for qualification and refinement. It is certainly the case that the comparison I have drawn between Plato and romanticism is, inevitably, only one chapter of a much larger and more complex story. To make my case I have had to leave entirely on one side the very different uses of the imagination that can be traced at work within Plato's own philosophical thinking and

[49] Cf. here the enlightening arguments of Wind 1983, 1–20.

[50] Schlegel, *Kritische Fragmente*, no. 55, in Schlegel 1964, 13; Shelley *Defence of Poetry* (Jones 1916, 121). For a later instance of this romantic model of mind, cf. Jules Laforgue's essay on "Impressionism" (1883): "each man is . . . a kind of keyboard on which the exterior world plays in a certain way. My own keyboard is perpetually changing" (quoted in Nochlin 1966, 18–19).

[51] *Rep.* 4.430c3–4, 431e–2a, 443d–e.

[52] "Letters to a Young Man Whose Education Has Been Neglected" (1823), in Foakes 1968, 139–42.

writing—uses that, in their metaphysical and visionary settings, subserve what we might call an alternative, and very different, Platonic "aesthetic." As a result, I have been unable to take any account of what is, in the light of my own thesis, the historically ironic fact that many important romantic conceptions of imagination were themselves substantially indebted to a tradition of aesthetic idealism that can be traced back to Plato's own mythology (and visionary metaphysics) of transcendent beauty and truth.[53] But the argument I have tried to develop does, I think, validly concentrate on some significant points of affinity between Platonic and romantic interests in the imagination. Above all, I have suggested, we can observe here a common if finally divergent concern with the implications for the individual mind of the deepest aesthetic experiences of engagement in the lives and feelings of fictional characters. And I have tried to identify a belief, shared by Plato and the romantics though very differently evaluated by them, in the self-transforming powers of the imagination: a belief that when art allows its audiences a special intensity of involvement in dramatized patterns of thought and emotion, it opens and exposes them to the possibility of absorbing those patterns into their own existence.

Many of us, it seems beyond dispute, are still heirs to a romantic faith in the artistic imagination. But if this is so, then Plato's view of the dangers of such imagination places us in an instructively difficult predicament. There are many piecemeal ways in which we can object to elements of the Platonic views I have been examining. We can question whether there is so straightforward a causal link as Plato seems to suggest between what we encounter in art and what we will come to do in our own lives. On this point we might even prefer the view of Rousseau, who, for all his interest in and approval for Plato's attitudes to dramatic poetry, believed (and anticipated Brecht in doing so) that emotions experienced in the theater could create a tendency to passivity and complacent inaction in real life.[54] Equally, we might wonder whether Plato is too reliant on an atomistic, "one-to-one" model of an audience's relationship to the characters of dramatic art and ignores the possible complexity and even conflict that can color responses to the totality of a dramatic structure.[55] But what is above all required, in order to combat Plato's mistrust of the imagination,

[53] I touch on some strands of romantic Platonism in chapter 12. Others are discussed by, e.g., Abrams 1953, 126–32; Newsome 1974; and in several of the essays in Baldwin & Hutton 1994.

[54] Cf. chapter 7, section I. Rousseau compiled a pamphlet, eventually published in 1764 as De l'imitation théâtrale, in which he drew heavily on Plato's discussions of drama in both Republic and Laws (Rousseau 1959–95, 5:1196–1211).

[55] Plato's emphasis reflects the typical interest of both epic and tragedy in sharply highlighted heroic figures, but it is nonetheless arguable that this emphasis insufficiently allows for relationships between characters and for the resulting complexities of dramatic viewpoint.

is something that we can already observe Aristotle attempting in various ways to supply—a radical modification to a psychology that separates imagination from reason, feeling from judgment. Yet it remains a pressing question whether such a modification can really emerge from the legacy of romanticism, whose own near absolute trust in the imagination, underpinned by a very un-Platonic confidence in the authoritative nature of the artist, often involves its own versions of the division between imagination and reason. When combined with belief in the autonomy of aesthetic experience—a belief that has collected so many adherents in the past two centuries—unlimited faith in the imagination may find itself laying claim to complete immunity from ethical scrutiny and interrogation. So long as that claim is able to sustain itself with unquestioned confidence, as it is in certain quarters, we will have some reason to agree with Nietzsche that "the greatest enemy of art" has not yet been conclusively confronted.

Chapter Three

❀

Mimesis and the Best Life:
Plato's Repudiation of the Tragic

There is something which, for lack of a better name, we will
call the tragic sense of life, which carries with it a whole
conception of life itself and of the universe, a whole
philosophy more or less formulated, more or less conscious.
(Unamuno 1921, 17)

IN UNCOVERING the psychological infrastructure of Plato's engagement with
mimesis I suggest in chapter 2 that his unease over the transformative
power of mimetic art—its capacity to shape the minds of its audiences by
absorbing them imaginatively in the possibility of "other lives"—culmi-
nates in an acute anxiety over one particular kind of art, tragedy. It is
above all to tragic poetry, a category that Plato, on grounds that will soon
emerge, does not limit to Attic drama but treats as embracing the work of
Homer ("first of the tragedians") too,[1] that "the greatest charge" of *Republic*
10.605c6 relates: the charge that tragic poetry has the potency to command
emotional "surrender" from "even the best of us." Tragedy preoccupied
Plato's attention, I shall argue, not purely because it was one of the most
culturally prestigious phenomena of the Greek world (and one of which
he acquired an intimate knowledge from his own youth), and not only
because it aroused particularly intense passions in its audiences. The Platonic obsession (hardly too strong a term) with tragedy was driven by an
even more fundamental consideration than those. Tragedy mattered to
Plato, I maintain, because he believed it was the medium of a whole view
of the world—a view that, if it were true, would negate his own philosophical enterprise at its roots.

Conceptions of tragedy that base themselves on a theory of "the tragic"
(*das Tragische* or *die Tragik*) are associated especially with a line of
thought that derives from German idealism and romanticism, a line that
connects, in this respect, Schelling, Hegel, Schopenhauer, and Nietzsche,
to name the most prominent figures in the tradition. Theories that posit
the tragic as an overarching existential-cum-metaphysical category are,

---

[1] Homer's status as one of the tragedians is a leitmotif in *Rep.* 10: see 595c1–2, 598d8,
605c11, 607a3; cf. 602b9–10, *Tht.* 152e. It is not clear whether quite the same view is present
in Isocrates *Ad Nic.* 48–49 (which belongs to the late 370s), but it recurs, modified, in Aristotle's *Poetics* (see chapter 7, note 2) and later; cf. Herington 1985, 213–15.

after all, only one species within the genus of concepts of tragedy and, more particularly, represent only one type of approach to the kind of drama to which the description of tragedy belongs. One commonly drawn corollary of the Germanic cast of interest in the tragic is the claim that while ancient Greece created the first and most concentrated tradition of dramatic tragedy, it lacked anything that can be classified as an explicit notion of the tragic.[2] But I contend in this chapter that there are important grounds for ascribing to Plato the first conscious delineation of something we can coherently identify as "the tragic"—the first, at any rate, outside tragic poetry itself, though that, of course, is a complex reservation, depending as it does on an answer to the very question of whether tragedy itself is necessarily a vessel of the tragic. But to make good my thesis about Plato I start from the basic thought that in order to qualify as a version of the tragic, and to be distinguishable from the many other views of tragedy that, whatever their emphasis (formal, material, psychological, ethical, etc.), do not belong in this category, a theory of tragedy must diagnose an essential, all-embracing, and therefore, in some sense, metaphysical significance at the core of whichever phenomena the theory counts as truly "tragic." I take it, accordingly, as an obligatory condition for any conception of the tragic that it should suppose dramatic tragedy (at least in a paradigmatic version), or any other tragic art form, to intimate some ultimate vision of or insight into reality, and one with profound spiritual and ethical consequences for human beings' sense of their place in the world, even if it should turn out that the nature of such insight, on some accounts, needs to be characterized as inherently mysterious. As that condition perhaps already implies, where the tragic is framed in metaphysical terms the dramatic genre of tragedy will become subsumable under, rather than representing the exclusive carrier of, the larger vision or worldview at issue. It is even conceivable that little if any existing dramatic tragedy will satisfy the strict conditions of a particular conception of "the tragic"—such, at any rate, is one of the more paradoxical outcomes of parts of the peculiar body of theorizing that has built up around the definition of tragedy as art form and/or mentality.[3]

The case I develop in this chapter attributes the first (theoretical) formulation of the tragic to a thinker whose special motivation was precisely to challenge and contest it at a deep level of philosophical principle. But as regards the purely historical question of Plato's priority in articulating an

[2] See, e.g., Lesky 1966, 213–19, and Most 2000 (without proper discussion of Plato). Schmitt 1997 offers, by contrast, a recent attempt to locate a sphere of "die Tragik" in Greek tragedy itself.

[3] One instance of this extreme position is Richards 1928, 247, who deems the greater part of Greek and Elizabethan tragedy to be "pseudo-tragedy."

understanding of the tragic, within his larger concern with mimetic art, we might reasonably begin by wondering whether it is accidental that we possess no view of a comparable kind elsewhere in fifth- or fourth-century sources. Classical Athenian culture must, after all, have fostered a rich and widespread discourse of attitudes to tragedy. This inference is pressed upon us not just by the sustained tradition of performance at civic festivals (a performance tradition probably more than a century old at the time of Plato's birth), but also by the substantial size and mixed character of Athenian audiences, the attested explicitness of their reactions (both positive and negative) to performances of tragedy,[4] the creation of a theatrical system that involved preselection of plays and official competition between staged works, and, last but not least, the survival of two documents, Aristophanes' *Frogs* and Aristotle's *Poetics*, which in their very different ways afford glimpses of available or imaginable critical assessments of tragedy. A series of classical sources, from Herodotus to Isocrates, and including Aristotle's *Poetics*, attests that the experience of tragedy was consistently associated with the strong, open display of emotion—especially pity—by mass audiences.[5] But the "emotionalism" of tragic audiences in Athens falls far short of evidence for a full-blown conception of "the tragic" of the sort whose conditions I have already stipulated. And if we look further for traces of such a conception in the evidence for Athenian responses to tragedy either before or indeed anywhere outside Plato, it remains surprisingly hard to find much of salience.

In the first place, only a loose and general impression of tragic qualities is conveyed by most classical uses of the adjective *tragikos* itself. When not picking out features of the genre in purely technical terms, with reference to poets, costumes, choruses, and such like, the word's predominant connotations are (as they were long to remain) of high-flown solemnity or overwhelmingly lugubrious subject matter. Plato aside, there are very few cases indeed in which we have reason to discern more extensive implications than this, and the same is true of metaphorical senses of the noun *tragōidia*, the verb *tragōidein* and other members of the word family.[6] Perhaps the most striking exception to this generalization is Aristotle's

---

[4] On the behavior of Athenian theater-audiences, see the sources and analysis in Csapo and Slater 1995, 286–305, with 103–38 on the festival context; cf. Wallace 1997, Goldhill 1997, and Sommerstein 1997, 63–71, for discussion of various aspects of the cultural sociology of Athenian audiences.

[5] See esp. Herodotus 6.21, Gorgias fr. 11.8–9 DK, *Helen* (with chapter 2, note 14), Andocides 4.23 (with chapter 7, note 17), Isocrates 4.168 (with chapter 7), Xenophon *Symp.* 3.11 (on the mass weeping of audiences), with Stanford 1983, 1–20, for introductory considerations, and chapter 7 for the Aristotelian perspective. Lada 1993 and Griffin 1998 offer different views of the emotional behavior of tragic audiences; cf. chapter 7, section II.

[6] Some classical additions to LSJ's examples of figurative or semifigurative uses of these terms are: Aristophanes *Peace* 136; Aristotle *Rhet.* 3.3, 1406b8; *Meteor.* 2.1, 353b1 (*tragikos*); Menander *Sik.* 262–63 (*tragōidia*); *Asp.* 329 (*tragōidein*).

famous remark at *Poetics* 13.1453a29–30 that Euripides "is found the most tragic of poets" (*tragikōtatos . . . phainetai*) in the theater.[7] It deserves emphasis, because the point is so often ignored, that Aristotle is not in this phrase pronouncing categorically on Euripides' qualities but on the impression which many of his plays—those ending in extreme, unmitigated misfortune—make on contemporary audiences. This is important in part because it means that Aristotle's phrasing can be taken to attest at least an instinctive inclination, within Athenian culture of the mid-fourth century, toward identifying the spectacle of unrelieved calamity, and therefore perhaps of an associated pessimism, as an archetypally tragic phenomenon. However, this is not at all the same as inferring that Athenian audiences always expected or wanted this kind of experience from the genre: Aristotle's further observation, just two sentences later in the *Poetics* (1453a33–35), that audiences prefer plots that end with an ethically balanced resolution (rewards for the virtuous, punishment for the evil) is quite sufficient to block this further inference. But if such an inference is not open to us, that is in itself tantamount to saying that Aristotle's reference to the impact of particularly bleak Euripidean dénouements is not compelling evidence for a sharply articulated conception of "the tragic," or even a prevailing consensus on the subject, within fourth-century (or earlier) Athenian responses to tragedy.

This conclusion from a document that contains some broad reflections of contemporary theatrical values is complemented and reinforced by the *Poetics'* own stance toward tragedy. All the major features of Aristotle's treatment of the genre bear out the proposition that his interpretation of tragedy is independent of, and in some ways actually inimical to, what we might now deem, in the wake of the modern Germanic slant of theorizing about tragedy, to count as a metaphysically developed notion of the tragic. These features include an analytical framework (the "six parts" schema) that stems from a general theory of poetic art and could consequently be applied equally to comedy, as well as a fundamental interest in issues of structure, unity, and "narrative" coherence that are likewise much larger than tragedy (or even, potentially, than poetry) in their scope. Of course, Aristotle erects on these foundations a specific account of tragedy that incorporates a combination of elevated action and characters, the arousal of pity and fear, and the motif of movement or transformation (*metabasis*) between life-defining poles of prosperity and adversity, especially in the "complex" form involving reversal (*peripeteia*) and recognition (*anagnōrisis*). The *Poetics* thus elaborates a concept of tragedy that, as I explain more fully in chapter 7, recognizes the centrality of acute suffering and

---

[7] Aristotle's other uses of *tragikos* etc. in the *Poetics* are, when not plainly technical, relatively unrevealing: 13.1452b37 appeals to the criteria of pity and fear (cf. chapter 7), 14.1453b39 to the requirement of *pathos*; 18.1456a21 is deeply obscure.

vulnerability, a vulnerability that exposes the limitations on human agency, intentionality, and (self-)knowledge. Moreover, this aspect of Aristotle's account of the genre is further refined by the fact that he posits human fallibility (*hamartia*) as the key component in the great changes or shifts of fortune that characterize tragic plots.

But it is legitimate to hold that this theory of tragedy yields something appreciably different from a pronounced sense of the tragic, not least because Aristotle's model of the mutability of human experience repeatedly accommodates the possibility of movement from adversity to prosperity, as well as the reverse. In this respect, the *Poetics* adopts a position that is true to long-established patterns within Attic tragedy, and that alone should prevent us from diagnosing a shortcoming or blind spot in Aristotle's own sensibility. In a further respect, namely the downplaying of religious explanations of human suffering, Aristotle does markedly diverge both from the tragic tradition and, for different reasons, from the Platonic views that I shall presently discuss. But that important point, while complex in its entailments for Aristotle's approach to tragedy,[8] need not deflect us from drawing the crucial conclusion that the evidence of the *Poetics* as a whole, at the level of both documentation and theory, leaves us free to believe without paradox that it was entirely feasible within classical Athenian culture to speak about the nature and experience of tragedy without speaking in terms of the tragic.

This observation receives some oblique and provisional confirmation from the earlier evidence of Aristophanes' *Frogs*. There are many separate strands in the fabric of this play's famous contest of tragedians—among them, Aeschylus's supposedly militaristic ethos, his penchant for dramatic silences, his choral refrains, and his archaic verbosity; or, on the other side, Euripides' alleged fondness for beggar-heroes, his "democratic" realism, his devotion to new gods, and his stereotypically predictable prologues. But the competition is unified by an overlapping interest in, broadly speaking, stylistic and ethicopolitical factors. This pairing of subjects and criteria is signaled by the rare agreement between Aeschylus and Euripides, at the outset of the agon (1008–10), that a poet should be judged for both "skillfulness" (*dexiotēs*) and "edification" (*nouthesia*), which between them constitute the artistic excellence (*sophia*) that is at stake in the contest (882 etc.).[9] But this much-quoted passage can be used to under-

---

[8] See Halliwell 1986, ch. 7, and Hall 1996, 296. The counterconsiderations adduced by Heath 1991, 395–97, legitimately stress that there are ways in which divine involvement in a tragic plot could be consistent with Aristotle's general theory, but they do not require a serious amendment to the claim that the *Poetics* neglects the religious dimension of the genre. Jones 1971, 61, finds a "vestigial religious sense" in the *Poetics*, but his intimation of it is elusive.

[9] See Dover 1993, 12–15, for a good analysis of these elements in the work; on the *Frogs* and tragedy, cf. Schwinge 1997.

score what is, for my purposes, a significantly negative claim. The leading themes of the debate, precisely because they revolve around a generalized conception of the fine, civically useful poet, bring with them no genre-specific standards of distinctively tragic qualities, let alone a more abstract consciousness of "the tragic" as a form of *Weltanschauung*. The competition naturally contains reference to features, such as prologues and choral lyrics, that have a definable place within the conventions of tragedy; and there are various allusions to the particular heroes and myths that provide the stuff of the tragedians' works. But what is conspicuously missing— conspicuously even when viewed from the perspective of the *Poetics*, and still more so from that of Plato—is any prominent attention to the emotional states, other than general pleasure, aroused by tragedy, or to the heroically heightened sense of suffering embodied in many tragic agents, or, finally, to the intense aura of religious meaning (and/or mystery) in which the lives of these agents are characteristically shrouded. The nearest the discussion ever comes to such topics is perhaps in Dionysus's reminiscence about scenes of communal grief in Aeschylus's *Persians* (1028–29), or Dionysus's and Aeschylus's sarcastic remarks, apropos Euripides' quotations from the start of his *Antigone*, about the illusory happiness of Oedipus (1182–95). But these are moments of no special salience in the overall shape or tone of the competition.

There can, of course, be no question of relying straightforwardly on *Frogs* as a full or faithful image of late fifth-century Athenian attitudes to tragedy. Comic selectiveness and distortion rule out the feasibility of detailed inferences about what were no doubt the complicated habits of thought and feeling that informed contemporary experience of tragic theater. In particular, it is impossible to suppose that audiences of this period were blind to the religious ideas or the heroic values by which tragedy's mythical materials were typically saturated, although that is not to imply that awareness of these ideas and values would in itself suffice to constitute a strong sense of the tragic. An alternative hypothesis, which would allow us to integrate the partial evidence of *Frogs* and of other fifth-century sources[10] without resorting to implausibly extreme conclusions about Athenian audiences of tragedy, is that certain major elements of tragedy, however fundamental to the type of experience that the genre offered, were nevertheless left largely unvoiced in the general terms in which individual plays were discussed and the categories by which they were judged. This view has a positive corollary—namely that it was an active part of Plato's project to bring to the surface of argument, and to open up for reflective evaluation, dimensions of tragedy that had not previously received sustained recognition in the culture's critical discourse.

---

[10] Dover 1993, 25–27, cites other fifth-century references to tragedy, none of which contains any overt indication of what could count as a conception of the tragic.

Indirect support for this thesis can be derived from the observation that while, as already noticed, the terms *tragōidia*, *tragikos*, and the like had accumulated a range of metaphorical usage by the first half of the fourth century, we encounter in Plato a much more thought-provoking set of figurative applications of these words than in any other author of the period.[11] Because these applications occur mostly outside contexts in which the significance of tragedy is directly addressed, and because they have never been given connected consideration, it will be worthwhile to examine them before turning to other, fuller Platonic materials. As the first of these passages reveals, however, the employment of tragedy as an expressive trope cannot be disentangled from its status as an object of philosophical criticism. Toward the end of the *Philebus*'s discussion of mixed emotional experiences of pleasure and pain, of which tragic theater, where the spectators "derive pleasure from weeping," is held up as an instance (48a), Socrates declares: "So our argument shows that pains and pleasures are mixed together in outpourings of grief [*thrēnois*] and in tragedies—not only in stage-plays, but in the entire tragedy and comedy of life [*tēi tou biou sumpasēi tragōidiai kai kōmōidiai*]."[12] Metaphors of the life-as-the-ater variety have become so familiar a topos, even a cliché, that it is easy to underestimate the force of Plato's point in this passage.[13] Whether the imagery is original to him, which we do not know, its implication is that tragedy (as well as comedy) can be perceived as the vehicle of a highly distinctive sense of life—so much so, indeed, that it becomes equally possible to regard tragedy as an interpretation of life, and to conceive of life itself as a quasi-aesthetic phenomenon possessing the kinds of properties that are exhibited in their most concentrated form in theatrical works.

Apart from a connection with grief and lamentation, the content of tragedy's sense of life is left unspecified at *Philebus* 50b. But we edge a little closer to it in the playful yet revealing etymologizing of *Cratylus* 408b–d. Here, the double nature of the god Pan is linked to that of speech or language (*logos*), which has the capacity to signify "everything" (*to pan*— a traditional false etymology of Pan's name), both truth and falsehood.

---

[11] In addition to the cases discussed in my text, see those cited by Tarrant 1955, 83.

[12] *Phileb.* 50b1–4: I am not able to pursue, in the present context, the full implications of the apparent suggestion that "tragedy and comedy of life" denotes a hybrid concept of tragicomedy (a concept that appears as the title of comic plays in Plato's own lifetime: see *PCG* II, p. 9). Socrates' famous remark about an ideally joint capacity for the composition of tragedy and comedy at *Symp.* 223d is only tangentially related to this point; cf. note 16.

[13] Later imagery of this kind is cited by (e.g.) Curtius 1953, 138–44; Kelly 1993, 23–26, 79–81; and Kokolakis 1960; for one striking instance, cf. chapter 11 note 21. Plato is taken to have "invented" the metaphor by, e.g., Vicaire 1960, 61; Amphis fr. 17.4 *PCG*, referring to the city as a "theater" (where people's misery is on display), is rather different (*pace*, e.g., Dobrov 2001, 84 with 188 n. 75, where Plato is overlooked).

Whereas truth is "smooth and divine," falsehood represents the lower, "human" side of Pan, with the "harsh and tragic" features (*trachu kai tragikon*, in Plato's pseudo-etymologizing alliteration) that go with human existence: "for it is here [i.e., in the human world] that very many stories and falsehoods belong, in connection with the tragic life" (408c7–8). The self-conscious wit of the passage depends principally on the etymologizing recuperation of the goat (*tragos*) element in tragedy, so that what is "harsh and tragic" in human life can be correlated with the "rough and goat-form" side (*trachus kai tragoeidēs*), the (literally and metaphorically) "lower" half, of Pan's nature. But the verbal punning, for all its factitious ingenuity, contains a kind of philosophical enigma. Not only do we have the reference to a conception of life, "the tragic life" (408c8), which could be construed either as life in general seen in a tragic light (as at *Philebus* 50b), or as a specific pattern of life (that of the inhabitants of a tragic world). We must also register the unmistakable insinuation that, on either construal, this conception is a matter of myth and falsehood or fiction: that it *is*, in some as yet undefined respect, a myth and a falsehood, tied up with a harshly material humanness, an incorrigibly human way of looking at things, that is sharply opposed to the "truth" of the divine and is symbolized by the nondivine half of Pan's double nature.[14] The key to the enigma, as we shall discover, can be located elsewhere in Plato, in those very passages that elucidate philosophical reasons for repudiating any adherence to what might be framed as "the tragic life."

If *Cratylus* 408 hints in playfully allusive terms at the outline of a possible critique of tragedy, and one that Plato was soon afterward to work out in more detail in the *Republic*, we find an express contrast between "tragic" and "philosophical" interpretations of life expressed at a much later date in an intriguing passage of *Laws* book 7. Here, the Athenian envisages an encounter between the well-governed city's lawgivers (the persona occupied by himself and his companions in their philosophical discussion) and a traveling troupe of tragic actors who request permission to perform in the city.[15] The lawgivers' imagined response to the request is notable for its metaphorical and symbolic extension of the concept of tragedy, in a manner continuous with, but much clearer in its implications than, the idea of the "tragic life" in either the *Philebus* or the *Cratylus* passages

---

[14] The conjunction of "myth" (*muthos*) with terms from the *pseud-* root is strongly reminiscent of *Rep.* 2.376e–7a and the discussion that follows it: on this, and the falsehood-fiction tension it entails, see chapter 1, section II, with my subsequent discussion. On the *Cratylus*'s dealings with tragedy more generally, see Baxter 1992, 144–47; the dialogue uses the verb *tragōidein* (414c5, 418d4) to denote ostentatious verbal artifice. Pan's upper, divine half is associated with "internal beauty" in a very different Platonic context, at *Phdr.* 279b.

[15] The passage alludes to official procedures of selection that were followed in the actual planning of dramatic performances at Athens: see Wilson 2000, 2–3, 63, 289.

already considered. "Honored visitors," they say, "we ourselves aspire to be poets/makers [*poiētai*] of the finest and best tragedy; our whole state/constitution [*politeia*] is constructed as a representation [*mimēsis*] of the finest and best life—which is what *we* count as the truest tragedy [*tragōidian tēn alēthestatēn*]. So you and we turn out to be poets using the same materials, and we are your rivals and competitors in producing the finest drama."[16]

It would be defensible to maintain that in its highly pregnant but eloquent way this late passage discloses more than almost any other in Plato about the nature of the philosopher's confrontation with tragedy, because it indicates how that confrontation is not simply an opposition but an active attempt to transform and overcome tragedy within a new kind of philosophical thinking and writing whose own dramatically mimetic character is explicitly acknowledged here. At first sight Plato's terms may look paradoxical—prima facie it would be bizarre to suppose that Attic tragedy offers overt, unconditional paradigms of "the finest and best life." But the point is deeper, and very powerful. It can be provisionally adumbrated (along lines that we shall later see corroborated and clarified by other Platonic texts) by saying that philosophy perceives tragedy as inescapably committed to the affirmation of certain essential values precisely in virtue of what it incites its audience to mourn and grieve over. To lament what is lost or destroyed in suffering is implicitly to cling to a certain sense of what is worth having and preserving in life. On this model of interpretation, if tragedy's values are followed through to their logical conclusion, the genre can be seen as the expression of nothing less than a "life"—a conception of what is supremely worth living for. And that is why, in this the boldest of self-referential figures in Plato's writing, tragedy—"the truest tragedy"—can become the ultimate trope for philosophy itself and for its efforts to create an alternative vision of what "the finest and best life" might be.

One further passage, from the *Phaedo*, deserves to be added to those in which Plato exploits the idea of tragedy in at least a semifigurative fashion. Although the *Phaedo* as a whole can be justifiably regarded as a kind of tacit response to, and transcendence of, tragic drama, it contains only one direct reference to tragedy. This is the moment where, as the time to drink the hemlock approaches, Socrates tells his companions with the gentlest of ironies that they will follow him on some future occasion, before adding: "but as for me, 'fate' [*heimarmenē*], as a tragic man would say, now

---

[16] *Laws* 7.817b1–8; Pitcher 1966, 726, misses the point of this passage by treating it as a neutral comment on the nature of tragedy. Patterson 1982 discusses the relevance of this (78–81) and other passages, including *Symp.* 223d (cf. my note 12), to a conception of Plato's own writing as "true" tragedy and comedy. On Plato's dialogues as a form of "antitragic theater," see Kuhn 1941–42, Nussbaum 1986, 122–35; cf. Gifford 2001 on Platonic adaptation of tragic irony in parts of his own work.

summons me" (115a5–6). Commentators have mostly treated *anēr tragikos*, the "tragic man," as meaning a character in tragedy. But it could equally, I think, mean a person possessing or adopting a tragic view of (his) life (whether inside or outside a tragedy proper), so that *tragikos* here would be parallel to the "tragic life" of *Cratylus* 408c8 and the "tragedy" of life at *Philebus* 50b3.[17] At any rate, Socrates' remark involves the transferability of a tragic attitude from the theater to one's own life: if *he* were to behave with the convictions of a "tragic man," he would interpret the circumstances of his death, and thus feel about them, in a very different way from the philosophical equanimity and acquiescence that he has displayed throughout the dialogue. The ramifications of the point embrace not just Socrates as an imagined individual, but the nature of Plato's depiction of him and the response that this depiction both invites from and encourages in a reader. Just as a tragic presentation, a mimetic enactment, of a hero's death could convey a whole "world" of value at the point of grievous dissolution, so the *Phaedo*'s own dramatization of Socrates' death enacts and communicates a transvaluation of any possible tragic construal of the event. But to achieve this, it must allow the "tragic" reading to be heard, and it does that by its dramatic unfolding of a scene in which everyone *except* Socrates exhibits impulses toward tragic grief—that is, toward the experience of Socrates' death as an evil done to the fabric of human value, because an irreversible loss of something supremely treasured.[18]

The passages so far adduced, from *Philebus*, *Cratylus*, *Laws*, and *Phaedo*, though individually brief as well as widely spaced in the oeuvre, mark telling points on the trajectory of Platonic thinking about tragedy. Their metaphorical and figural applications of the idea of tragedy suggest important connections between tragedy in "life" and in drama, and thereby bring to light what I take to be four overlapping elements of a potential conception of the tragic: first, tragedy's perceived function as the medium for an overarching sense of life ("the tragic life") and, by extrapolation, a worldview; second, tragedy's embodiment of this worldview in myths (and falsehoods or fictions) exhibiting an alleged dependence on a restrictedly embodied perspective (symbolized by the lower, harsher part of Pan's nature) that excludes the "smooth" truth of the divine; third, tragedy's implicit expression of ultimate values and commitments (paradoxically designated "the best life" in *Laws*), to which philosophy must pose its own alternatives (whether in the life and transfigured death of Socrates, or in the more abstract expression of truths that look beyond the corporeal

---

[17] At *Rep.* 10.595c1 the *tragikoi* are the tragedians themselves; my main point would not be affected if we were to take *tragikos* at *Phaedo* 115a5 to mean either a tragic poet or a tragic character—or even, for that matter, a tragic actor (cf. Hegelochus fr. 8.4 *PCG*).

[18] I have given one reading of this aspect of *Phaedo* in Halliwell 1984, 56–58.

realm to which tragic grief attaches itself); fourth, tragedy's obsession with death, not as a raw datum about the world but as something whose interpretation is central to an evaluative attitude to life itself. In the texts already considered these elements are present only as momentary hints and pointers, albeit in a fascinating range of tones (the "tragicomic" slant of *Philebus*, the playful etymologizing of *Cratylus*, the assured antitragic gestures of *Phaedo*, and the somber but wistful "farewell" to the tragedians in *Laws*). For a fuller articulation of these components in Plato's circumscription and repudiation of "the tragic," we need to turn once more to the two great treatments of poetry in books 2–3 and 10 of the *Republic*.

II

The discussion of poetic stories or myths (*muthoi*) in *Republic* books 2–3, from 376e to 392c, is guided by a concern with the ethics and psychology of fiction. This concern manifests itself in a setting that is ostensibly educational but whose underlying principles, as I stressed in the two preceding chapters, are applicable to all cultural and individual self-formation.[19] Socrates' critique of poetry here focuses predominantly on Homeric texts. Of more than thirty quotations in this stretch of the work more than three-quarters are Homeric and only four (all Aeschylean) are taken from tragedy.[20] But while these proportions may reflect something of note about the paramount status of the Homeric poems in Athenian/Greek education, they do not blunt the relevance of the passage's main lines of thought to what I maintain to be Plato's delineation of the tragic. This relevance, which will later be unequivocally foregrounded in book 10, can be most readily appreciated by reminding ourselves of four primary propositions, or quasi-propositional attitudes,[21] which the argument identifies and condemns in the images of "gods and heroes" (377e1–2, 392a5) that are projected by many poetic *muthoi* (the vehicle of "rough and tragic" falsehoods or fictions, we recall, at *Cratylus* 408c).

The first is that gods are responsible for evil (379a–c; cf. 391d6), a theme on which the argument about divine metamorphosis and deception at 380d–83c can here count as a variation. Plato's association of this idea with tragic poetry needs no explanation, although it is worth commenting that *contestation* of the gods' responsibility for evil is itself sometimes enunci-

---

[19] See esp. chapter 1, note 32.

[20] The tragic quotations are at 380a3–4, 381d8, 383b1–9, 391e7–9.

[21] Plato's argument does not draw a distinction between these two things; it focuses on *muthoi* (stories) as bearers of *logoi* (see esp. 376e11, 378a7, d3 [*logopoiein*], 380a8), and the latter could be glossed as propositionally formulable views (though their poetic expression may be nonetheless implicit and affective): cf. chapter 1, section II, with Halliwell 2000a, esp. 103–4.

ated within Homeric and tragic poetry.[22] The second definingly "tragic" proposition is that death is an evil to be feared (386a–87c), not only, however, in the plain sense of being a direct cause of self-regarding apprehension, but also in the deeper sense of being a negation of everything worth living for—a conception of death voiced, for example, in Achilles' famous rejection of Odysseus's consolations, and his bitter melancholy over the emptiness of Hades, in the *Odyssey*'s underworld scene, part of which is quoted here by Socrates.[23] The third attitude contributing to a tragic perspective, and one obviously interlocked with the second, is that the greatest heroes regard the death of those they cherish as an ultimate loss (387d–88d), so much so that the warrior Achilles can roll around inconsolably on the ground or pour ashes in his hair in black grief, or King Priam throw himself on a dung heap in despairing distress (388a–b). Finally, and most succinctly, Socrates suggests it is a quintessentially tragic conviction of the poets that justice and happiness are not correlated: many unjust people are prosperous, and many just people reduced to wretchedness (392b). The world, in other words, is not made for goodness.

All four of these ideas reinforce factors that I earlier highlighted in the four passages where Plato employs tragedy as a trope and emblem of a certain conception of life. Together they configure a mentality that finds the organization of the world—governed by divine powers capable of ruthless destructiveness, and limited by the inevitability of a death that negates everything worth having—to be fundamentally hostile to human needs and values and irreconcilable with a positive moral significance. The rejection of this mentality, the mentality of an Achilles or a Niobe, is a prerequisite for the assertion of a religio-ethical interpretation of reality (including the assertion of unqualified divine goodness) that would be acceptable within the terms of the philosophical project pursued in the *Republic*, as Socrates' proposals for educational and cultural censorship make emphatically clear. Notwithstanding its wider frame of reference, then, it is possible to discern that the critique of poetry in books 2–3 provides a preliminary analysis and rejection of a specifically tragic sense of life. In the overall economy of the *Republic*'s argument, this conclusion is confirmed by the return to poetry in the last book of the dialogue.

As in books 2–3, the approach to tragedy in book 10 is intertwined with a critique of Homer. But because a conception of the tragic like the one I have already sketched has an intrinsic tendency to run beyond the genre

---

[22] Most famously in Zeus's programmatic remarks at Homer *Od.* 1.32–43, a passage to which, interestingly, Plato never refers, unless *Alcib.* II 142d–e is genuine. Denials of divine evil are particularly associated with tragic characters in Euripides, esp. *El.* 583–84, *HF* 1341–46, *IT* 391, *Bellerophon* fr. 292.7 Nauck.

[23] See Homer *Od.* 11.488–503; 489–91 is quoted disapprovingly at 3.386c, though Socrates finds occasion to adapt the same lines for his own purposes at 7.516d.

of dramatic tragedy as such, the Homeric material in both these parts of the *Republic* accentuates and enhances the scope of what Plato understands by a tragic sense of life. The tenth book's famous description of Homer as "teacher and leader of the tragedians" (595c1–2), and "first of the tragedians" (607a3), establishes that the Homeric epics themselves matter to Plato in this context primarily as texts that justify a tragic reading. This implication of the conjunction of epic and dramatic tragedy is corroborated at 602b8–11, where Socrates refers to those "who put their hands to tragic poetry, whether in epic hexameters or in iambics" as "mimetic artists par excellence." This sentence, together with another reference to tragedians at 597e6, helps to suggest that tragedy, *qua* vehicle of the tragic, is not only in the argument's sights throughout the first portion of book 10 (up to 605c), where artistic mimesis is arraigned on a series of charges of manipulating appearances to specious effect, but is actually the prime target of this argument: tragic poets are the first to be mentioned when Socrates explains, at the start of the book (595b4), why he wants to reopen the discussion of poetry; and at three junctures where the conversation passes from painting back to poetry (597e, 598d, 602b) it is tragedy that is placed at the head of the list.

If that is so, we have an incentive to ponder afresh the guiding relationship between the book's earlier arguments: between, that is, the critique of mimesis as "twice removed from the truth," and, on the other hand, the "greatest charge" argument presented at 605c–606d, whose relevance to tragedy (once more, both Homeric and Attic: 605c11) is explicit and concentrated. Approached from this angle, tragedy will be the paradigm, however paradoxically, *both* of the alleged limitation of mimetic poetry to the "surfaces" of life, *and* of poetry's capacity to corrupt the mind by encouraging emotionally and therefore ethically dangerous absorption in its dramatic world. Some scholars have found this combination and sequence of emphases—first on the production of supposedly mirrorlike simulacra, then on the potential for severe psychological harm—to be incongruous. But I have already explained in chapter 1 why that need not be so. Socrates begins by confronting (believers in) the power of mimetic representations to capture the truth, or to convey knowledge, about the nature of the world, as opposed to merely simulating the appearances, the surface phenomena, of things. But he then goes on to treat some forms of mimesis, above all tragic poetry, as capable of insidiously expressing and transmitting a whole set of feelings about, a whole evaluative attitude toward, the "life" whose appearances it represents. The case as a whole constitutes a paradoxical but not contradictory charge of *dangerous illusionism*. To see "tragedy," both Homeric and Attic, as the unifying object of attention at the deepest level of this critique makes it easier to recognize how the two halves of the critique cohere. If poetry manipulates a world of illusions or simulations, then it will become most dangerous at just the point at which those illusions involve things that are taken, by the makers and audiences of mimetic art, with the greatest seriousness. The central thrust of the critique will then be this: that tragedy is the poetic form, indeed the representational art form, that most potently exploits the false pretenses, the pseudoworld, of mimesis, so as to draw its audience into surrendering to an emotional acceptance of a whole view, an incorrigibly human view, of reality.

Before examining how this critique is brought to a head in the "greatest charge" argument, it is worth looking at the character of the immediately preceding passage, 603c–5c, in order to reinforce the claim that tragedy can be read as the major target throughout the treatment of poetry in book 10. For here the dialogue effectively makes a transition from the idea of mimetic illusion, which has predominated since the start of the book, to the ethical-cum-psychological anxieties that lead to the "greatest charge" itself. It does so by a sequence of thought that might seem, at first sight, curiously elliptical. At 603c4–7 Socrates offers a general statement, prefiguring Aristotle's definition of tragedy in the *Poetics*, of the human scope of poetry (and, by implication, other representational arts):[24] "mimetic art [*mimētikē*] represents humans engaged, we can say, in actions that are either involuntary or voluntary, and as a result of their actions believing themselves to have done well or badly, and in all these situations feeling either distress or pleasure." But Socrates then turns at once, without any direct reference to poetic characters, to the psychic conflict between reason and emotion that can affect any "good person" struggling to come to terms with the loss of one of the things—such as a son—"to which he attaches supreme value" (*hōn peri pleistou poieitai*, 603e3–4).

Two observations are required to make sense of this apparent elision. The first is that tragic poetry is recognizably the *subtext* of the argument. The example of bereavement at 603e3–5—though applying in the first instance to ordinary psychology, not to poetic figures—glances back to the third book's critique of extreme displays of grief by Homeric-tragic heroes.[25] The emphasis on *pathos* (604b1), which is simultaneously the objective cause (the "injury") and the subjective experience (the "emotion" or "passion") of "suffering," demarcates a fundamental characteristic of the material of tragic poetry (its obsessive manifestation of what Dostoevsky, in connection with convulsive grief, calls "a compulsion to keep reopening the wound"), and a characteristic soon to be picked up in the "greatest

---

[24] See my notes in Halliwell 1988, 136; here as elsewhere in book 10 Plato may be recalling Gorgianic ideas (see the reference to good/bad fortune in fr. 11.9 DK); cf. chapter 1, notes 38, 54, and chapter 2, note 14.

[25] *Rep.* 10.603e4 refers back to 3.387d–88e.

charge" argument itself (606b1–8).[26] Moreover, the suggestion—supposedly part of what *nomos* (law/tradition) prescribes—that "nothing human merits great seriousness" (604b12–c1) alludes to the idea, cited ironically in several Platonic passages, that tragedy is above all the genre of portentous "seriousness" (*spoudē*).[27] The presence of tragedy as a subtext to the remarks on the general psychology of grief is in due course clinched by the reference to (Athenian) theater audiences at 604e, where we hear of the "crowds and multifarious masses gathered into theaters" who crave, and are only able to appreciate, the dramatic mimesis of psychically turbulent characters.

But a second observation further clarifies the allusions to tragic poetry in this passage. Plato's argument can shift, without warning, from poetic images to general human psychology, and then back again to poetry, because the ground is being prepared for the claim, already touched on at 604e and to be developed in the "greatest charge" section, that the psychology of tragic audiences is involved in a mutual interplay with that of tragic characters. In other words, tragedy appeals to powerful grief-directed instincts in the psyche; and the psychology of audiences can in turn be influenced by, through being *assimilated to*, that of tragic heroes.[28] What is more, we can connect this point with the conception of the tragic, delineated in the earlier parts of this chapter, as a sense of life that finds its most potent expression in tragic poetry but is not confined to the particular forms of literary art. Both the appeal and the influence of tragedy reflect propensities of the human soul that are *prior* to, and in some sense waiting for, the creation of tragic art forms. On the Platonic view, "the tragic" could and would have existed as a response to life even if tragic poetry had never come into being, because such a response is rooted in the intrinsic (if disordered) possibilities of the soul. Nonetheless, the focus of the argument at this point is not on the structure of the psyche as such but on poetry's control over it, and this theme comes to a climax with the "greatest charge" at 605c6–606d.

The greatest charge against poetry is just this, that it has the psychological power to "maim" or "impair" the souls even of the good,[29] and to make

---

[26] Gould 1990, esp. 22–69, discusses *pathos* from an interesting range of angles; but his treatment of the concept vis-à-vis popular religion, in particular, needs cautious handling. Dostoevsky's words, which are reminiscent of the imagery of Plato *Rep.* 10.604c–d, come from *The Karamazov Brothers*, bk. 2, ch. 3 (Dostoevsky 1994, 61).

[27] Compare *Gorgias* 502b, *Laws* 7.817a2, 8.838c4, and see the seriousness of tragedy's audience at *Rep.* 10.605d4; the point was taken up, positively, in Aristotle's use of *spoudaios* in the *Poetics* (see chapter 7, section II).

[28] This is also a recurrence of one of the dominant psychological and educational topics in the treatment of poetry in books 2–3: see chapter 2, esp. section I.

[29] *Lōbasthai* (maim) at 605c7 echoes 595b5: the greatest charge has been in view since the return to poetry at the beginning of the book. The potential harm affects the "best part" (i.e.,

the lives of those exposed to it "worse and more wretched" (*cheironōn kai athliōterōn*, 606d6–7), drawing them, as those last words ironically imply, toward the self-fulfilment of a tragic evaluation of life.[30] The charge potentially covers all kinds of poetry (606c2–d7), but its main statement applies specially to tragic epic and drama, whose capacity to open up the emotions and to free them from rational inhibition affects even "the best of us" (605c10–11). As this last phrase intimates, a key aspect of this passage is its acknowledgment that the force of tragedy is not something artificial or aberrant: its secret is that it taps a universal, *ever present* possibility within the psyche. Tragedy can elicit what is described at 605d3 as emotional "surrender" precisely because the impulse to yield to grief (for oneself) and pity (for others) is entirely "natural" (606a5) and calls for actively *repressive* measures to keep it in check (606a3). Because it is taken for granted that the impulse to lamentatory grief (*to thrēnōdes*, 606b1; cf. *Philebus* 50b) and to pity (*to eleinon*, 606b8) is at root one and the same, it is implicit in the greatest charge that the passions aroused by tragedy involve the same values, the same attachments to life, that are expressed in the personal sorrows of bereavement. The tragic heroes envisaged at 605d1–2—Plato has no need to mention such names as Achilles, Ajax, Eteocles, Heracles, Oedipus, Priam, and many others, especially given the third book's citation of some prominent specimens—are ones whose uncompromising acuteness of anguish, projected by all the means available to poetic artistry, destroys the canons of moderation and self-control that were ascribed to the "good man" at 603e–604e. They are ultimate embodiments of a sense of life that makes the outpouring of grief an imperative, and which releases a pressure toward rage (*to aganaktētikon*) at the world's (or the gods') coldness to human aspirations.[31] To sympathize with these figures, to share compassionately in their suffering (*sumpaschein*), is consequently to accept the valuation of life that they represent.

The dynamics of psychological-cum-ethical influence posited by this argument are not uncontestable, if only because the relationship between experience of art and of life remains a fraught area in which we (both ancients and moderns) cannot claim to understand ourselves well. Even in Plato's own time there were, for example, Athenian observers who claimed to notice a disparity between emotional responses to tragic theater

---

reason itself), as 606a–b indicates (see Mastrangelo & Harris 1998 on the intricate grammar and sense of this passage).

[30] Compare the adjective *athlios* (wretched) at 606d7, whose resonances are very much of a tragic ethos, with the same word at 3.392b2, cited earlier; cf. Murray 1996, 167–68.

[31] The element of rage, and the part of the soul that feels it or responds to it in others, is referred to at 604e1–2, 605a5; cf. 604b10. Such heroic rage was later to be regarded by Nietzsche as the "more manly brother of pity," (diesen *männlicheren* Bruder des Mitleidens); *Morgenröte* §78 (Nietzsche 1988, 3:77).

and sometimes ruthless reactions to sufferings in the real world, while Rousseau is among those subsequent thinkers who have sustained or generalized such observations in relation to aesthetic experience as a whole.[32] But it is important here to draw a distinction between improbable claims of an automatic or simple transference from art to life, and a more subtle recognition of the involvement of art in the shaping, modification, and reinforcement of attitudes that can inform patterns of behavior. There is no good reason to take the "greatest charge" argument as an example of the first rather than the second. Although Plato's case refers to the inevitability of "infection" between our imaginative responses to tragic characters and the place of emotion in our own lives, there is an explicit appreciation that such responses represent no ordinary frame of mind but a heightened receptiveness, commensurate with the idea of "surrender" (605d3), to the dramatic projection of feeling (606a7–b8). The point is not that aesthetic experience has easily calculable or immediate consequences for our mental lives, but that a strong yielding to emotions expressed in an artwork amounts to the enactment and acceptance of an underlying valuation. It is hard to see how such a judgment could be confidently discarded without at the same time depriving tragedy, or any other art, of its "seriousness" (a recurrent motif, as we have seen, in Platonic references to tragedy) by severing its links with the realities of emotion as a psychological determinant of action.[33] That still leaves quite open, of course, the possibility of dissenting from the Platonic argument at the level of the proposition that the emotions are intrinsically "irrational" and dangerous, and therefore badly in need of the control of the "higher" function of reason. But an objection on that front would do nothing to diminish, and might even tend to strengthen, the suggestion that emotional responses to tragedy are the carriers of implicit values and thus hold the potential to generate, or intensify, a tragic sense of life, a tragic *Weltgefühl*.

It is worth emphasizing that in one fundamental respect Plato's position is aligned with a perspective sometimes explicitly assumed by Greek tragedy itself. One obvious but far-reaching fact about tragic suffering is that it is almost always witnessed and responded to within the dramatic context of tragedy, most often by the chorus. This means that suffering is not just

[32] The Athenian texts that discern the gap between theatrical and normal experience are Andocides 4.23, Isocrates 4.168: see my discussion in chapter 7, section I. One recent occurrence of a comparable point is in Steiner 1989, 144, though he then proceeds to endorse the strength of the Platonic challenge. For Rousseau's view of theatrical experience as sentimental and escapist, see chapter 2, with note 54, and chapter 7, section I.

[33] An eloquent statement of a quasi-Platonic position in this area is Booth 1988: see my chapter 2, section II. See now also Burnyeat 1999, esp. 249–58, 319–24, on the forcefulness of Plato's conception of the gradual and partly unnoticed operation of cultural influences that shape the ethos of society.

shown in its raw state but already to some extent *interpreted* in the immediate environment of the events. And one distinctively tragic interpretation
of suffering—the interpretation which Plato has in mind both in *Republic*
10 and in other passages mentioned earlier in this chapter—is the translation of a particular *pathos*, a particular injury to the fabric of life, into a
symbol of the limits on the human condition in general.[34] Perhaps the
aptest example of this idea is the final stasimon of Sophocles' *Oedipus
Tyrannus*, where the chorus treats Oedipus as in every respect a "model,"
a *paradeigma* (1193), for its understanding of man:

> O generations of mortals,
> I count your lives as equal
> To nothingness itself.
> For who, tell me who,
> Has happiness that stretches further
> Than a brief illusion
> And, after the illusion, decline?
> Considering you as my model,
> Considering your daimon, yours alone,
> O wretched Oedipus,
> I count no mortal blessed.

(1186–96)

Oedipus's life is here interpreted as a "model," a kind of measure or touchstone, in terms equally of what he had previously appeared to accomplish,
and of what he has now irretrievably lost: the curve traced by his rise and
fall, and beneath which the agency of a god (*daimōn*, 1194) can be felt,
is held up as a pattern definitive of the human condition.[35] Regarded in this
doubly and ironically paradigmatic light, his case encourages the chorus to
extrapolate to all "generations of mortals," and to conclude that all happiness or flourishing, *eudaimonia*, is a cruel mirage. The mentality of the
chorus, as it universalizes the implications of Oedipus's catastrophe, perfectly bears out the diagnosis that *Republic* 2–3 provides of tragedy's tendency to deposit a corrosive pessimism about human possibilities. The
mind that surrendered to this pessimism in a permanent way might indeed
find itself living a "worse and more wretched" life (*Republic* 606d6–7),
because it would be condemned by its own beliefs to abandoning any
hope that its highest endeavors could be meaningfully satisfied by the

---

[34] I have offered a general interpretation of tragic religion in relation to the idea of human
limits in Halliwell 1990b.

[35] This example adds weight to the force of Plato's reference to rivalry between philosophy
and tragedy over the definition of "the finest and best life" at *Laws* 7.817b: see my previous
discussion.

world. Such permanent surrender is part of what Plato elsewhere evokes, in the passages discussed in the first part of this chapter, by the notion of a "tragic life." If such outright pessimism really is the heart of what tragedy offers, and if the experience of it can be consistently translated into sustained impulses of thought and feeling, then the Platonic critique will continue to raise penetrating questions about its artistic, its mimetic, enactment and about its psychological consequences, however short the critique may fall of refuting tragedy's metaphysical presuppositions. Yet both of those conditionals contain permanently disputable propositions, whose validity is surely relative to individual and cultural variables that are not explicitly encompassed by the terms of Plato's argument. Even in the *Oedipus Tyrannus*, tragic pessimism is not necessarily definitive of tragedy; the play's final stasimon is not its last word.

It is arguable, then, that the most basic objection to the Platonic critique of tragedy is that it ignores the *manifold* nature of what tragedy can and does offer. Yet this objection may itself be, in a sense, misdirected, insofar as it draws attention to precisely what makes the critique, so I have argued, into a conception of the tragic. If, as I originally suggested, theories of the tragic, as opposed to more general perspectives on tragedy, are characterized by their perception of an essential, defining vision, the content of this vision need not be discoverable in all de facto members of the genre of tragedy. Equally, anything that qualifies as a definition of the tragic will do so by virtue of supplying not so much a useful framework for the analysis of tragedy, but something akin to the "whole conception of life itself," the "whole philosophy more or less formulated," to which Unamuno refers at the beginning of this chapter.[36] This consideration is especially pertinent in the case of Plato and allows us to regard in a richer light the idea—an idea explicitly prompted, as we earlier saw, by *Laws* 7.817b—that his response to tragedy, his repudiation of the tragic, is a vital dimension of his own philosophy. The Platonic disavowal of the tragic reflects an awareness, paralleled in antiquity only by the later and partly Platonizing views of the Stoics, that the tragic itself is *a philosophy in embryo*.[37] And it is precisely the strength of this awareness that makes tragedy, from the Socratic imperturbability of the *Apology* or *Phaedo* to the overt terms of *Laws* 817b itself ("we ourselves aspire to be poets of the finest and best trag-

[36] It is curious that while Unamuno himself frequently cites Plato, he does so always as an illustration of the yearning for immortality and nowhere as the repudiator of a tragic sense of life: note, however, the passing acknowledgment of Platonic complexities where Unamuno refers to "the serene Plato," before adding "but was he serene?" (Unamuno 1921, 45).

[37] For some apposite Stoic reactions to tragedy, engaging with it as a vehicle of ethical and psychological attitudes, see Chrysippus's views *apud* Galen *De Plac. Hipp. et Plat.* 3.3.13–22, 4.2.24–27, 4.6.19–22 (De Lacy 1978–84); Epicteus *Diss.* 2.17.19–22; Marcus Aurelius *Med.* 11.6; with Gill 1996, 226–35; Nussbaum 1993, 136–45.

edy"), a permanently important "adversary" to be confronted and resisted by the voices and the truth seeking of Plato's own writing.

If we return, with that thought in mind, to *Republic* 10, we should be well placed to see how appropriate it is that the book not only conveys direct antipathy to a tragic conception of life but also completes the entire work with a myth that has specifically antitragic resonance at several stages.[38] The myth of Er is, more than anything else, an allegory of the soul's responsibility for its own life. The Thyestes-like tyrant who finds that it is his "destiny"[39] to eat his own children and commit other execrable deeds, proceeds to pour out his grief in precisely the uninhibited manner (with breast-beating and lamentations) characterized earlier in the book as tragic, and to blame "fortune and the gods and everything *but* himself" (619c2–6). By this externalization of his self-imposed destiny he shows himself unable to grasp or face up to the supreme denial of the tragic incorporated in the priest's earlier pronouncement to the souls: "the responsibility lies with the chooser; god is blameless" (617e4–5). The case of this "Thyestes" figure is therefore a stark emblem of the Platonic contrast between two ultimate hypotheses about the world: the first, that human lives are governed by external forces that are indifferent to, and capable of crushing, the quest for happiness; the second, that the source of true happiness is located nowhere other than in the individual soul's choice between good and evil. To embrace the first of these is to open the floodgates to (self-)pity, and to interpret the world as a stage made for the tragedy (or perhaps, if we recall the *Philebus*, the "tragicomedy") of life. To follow, on the other hand, a belief in the soul's capacity to forge its own moral fate, is to entertain a hope that nourishes the psychological, ethical, and metaphysical aspirations of Plato's own dialogues. Whatever else may need to be said about the nature of this dichotomy, I hope to have shown that the Platonic consciousness of it is as remarkable for its identification of one version of the tragic as for its pursuit of a philosophical rationalism by which tragedy might be transcended.

---

[38] Colotes the Epicurean (chapter 1, note 46) complained that at certain points in the myth of Er (especially the horrors of 10.615d–16a) Plato hypocritically exploits motifs borrowed from tragic myth itself; but Colotes seems not to have been interested in the antitragic bent of the myth as a whole. Cf. Babut 1983, 48–54, on the underlying connections between the myth of Er and the work's earlier criticisms of poetry.

[39] *Heimarmenē*, 619c1. Exactly the same term as used by Socrates in his deprecation of a tragic gesture at *Phaedo* 115a5–6; its use here is subtly ironic, because the soul in question has already "chosen" its own life to be. For other Platonic uses, see Halliwell 1988, 187–88.

Chapter Four

❖

More Than Meets the Eye:
Looking into Plato's Mirror

La peinture est l'art d'aller à l'âme par l'entremise des yeux.
(Diderot)[1]

IF POETRY is the art form that occupies most space in ancient discussions of mimesis, it is equally true that the figurative arts, above all painting, constitute an almost ever present paradigm and point of reference for interpretation of the concept. This state of affairs goes back beyond Aristotle's *Poetics*, in which painting is cited as a parallel to poetry on a total of eight occasions, and even beyond Plato's own frequent comparisons of the two arts, not least in the momentous conjunction of painting and poetry in *Republic* book 10.[2] The aesthetic association of poetry and painting is at least as old as the poet Simonides, who near the end of the sixth century B.C. famously described poetry as "speaking painting" or "painting with a voice" (*zōigraphia phtheggomenē / lalousa*), painting as "silent poetry."[3] In doing so he provided some impetus to a line of thought that, via a long and influential tradition conventionally summed up by Horace's phrase, "ut pictura poesis," descends all the way to Lessing's *Laokoon* of 1766 and, beyond it, to continuing modern debates about the affinities and contrasts between various species of art.[4] Lessing's treatise begins with an explicit protest against the exaggerated influence of Simonides' aphorism, though not, significantly, against the aphorism itself. In fact, Lessing displays his own adherence to a mimetic conception of art precisely by his approval of the idea that underlies Simonides' saying. Lessing interprets this idea as

---

[1] "Painting is the art of gaining admission to the soul by means of the eyes": Diderot, *Salon de 1765* (Diderot 1957–79, 2:174; spelling modernized).

[2] See chapter 5, note 15, for the *Poetics*' references to painting and chapter 1, note 15, for Platonic comparisons of poetic and visual art.

[3] The four occurrences of this remark in Plutarch, with slightly different wordings, are at *Aud. Poet.* 17f–18a, *Quomodo Adul.* 58b, *Glor. Ath.* 346f, *Qu. Conv.* 748a; cf. chapter 10, note 34. On the context of Simonides' apophthegm, see Morris 1992, 311, with my introduction. It is unlikely that Democritus fr. 142 DK, which calls the names of the gods "speaking statues" (*agalmata phōnēenta*), plays on the same idea; cf. Cole 1990, 68 n. 17.

[4] Lee 1967 remains important for the Renaissance development of the painting-poetry *paragone*; cf. Braider 1999 (reading "Plutarch" for "Pliny" on 168). Steiner 1982, 1–18, traces the development as far as its modern revival; other treatments include Praz 1970, esp. 3–27; Graham 1973; Marshall 1997.

the insight that both poetry (i.e., on his definition, all the arts which use "progressive" or sequential means of representation) and painting (i.e., all visual arts) put before us, in the words of his preface, "absent things as present, appearances as reality" (Beide [Künste] . . . stellen uns abwesende Dinge als gegenwärtig, den Schein als Wirklichkeit vor), a formulation that could plausibly serve to encapsulate the nucleus of the entire tradition of mimeticism explored in this book.[5]

Although Lessing's primary concern in *Laokoon* is, of course, to identify and explicate the defining differences between poetic and visual mimesis, it is noteworthy, but not often enough actually noticed, that in the process he regularly combines and interchanges the concept of "imitation" (*Nachahmung*) with that of "expression" (*Ausdruck*). More important still, he insists on the free play of imagination as an indispensable factor within the workings of artistic mimesis. Speaking of the choice of a single moment that (supposedly) defines the representational scope of painting or sculpture, he writes: "That alone is fruitful which permits the imagination free play. The more we see, the more we must be able to supplement it in thought; the more our thought supplements it, the more we must believe we can see."[6] Lessing's aesthetic in *Laokoon* exhibits, among much else, the modification of a fundamentally mimeticist position by a stress on imaginative expression and suggestiveness; and in this respect he marks a tendency of thought and sensibility that is a harbinger of, and was soon to culminate in, romantic revisionism toward the whole notion of mimesis.[7] Unlike some full-blown romantics, however, Lessing does not seek to *replace* mimesis with imagination but considers the activity of the latter to be a necessary completion, a kind of interpretative realization, of the significance of the former. In section 6 of *Laokoon* he states: "That which we find beautiful in a work of art is found beautiful not by our eye but by our imagination operating *through* the eye."[8] Lessing stops short, we might remark, of the romantic move of supplanting the external eye with the

---

[5] *Laokoon*, preface (Lessing 1970–79, 6:9). Lessing's mimeticism is also flagged by his Greek quotation on the title page (ibid., 7), then repeated in the preface (ibid., 10), from Plutarch *Glor. Ath.* 347a (which follows one of Plutarch's citations of Simonides' apophthegm; see note 3): poetry and painting "differ in the materials and modes of their mimesis" (*hulēi kai tropois mimēseōs diapherousi*). Gebauer & Wulf 1992, 262–88, give one account of Lessing's mimeticism; cf. Berghahn 1997, 532–38, on Lessing's approach to mimesis in relation to other German thinkers of the period.

[6] "Dasjenige aber nur allein ist fruchtbar, was der Einbildungskraft freies Spiel läßt. Je mehr wir sehen, desto mehr müssen wir hinzu denken können. Je mehr wir dazu denken, desto mehr müssen wir zu sehen glauben." *Laokoon* §3 (Lessing 1970–79, 6:25–26).

[7] See further discussion in chapter 12, section II.

[8] " . . . was wir in einem Kunstwerke schön finden, das findet nicht unser Auge, sondern unsere Einbildungskraft, durch das Auge, schön" (*Laokoon* §6; Lessing 1970–79, 6:52). For the possible influence of Philostratus on Lessing, see chapter 10, note 57.

exercise of an internal, spiritual eye (a motif of Platonic and Neoplatonic ancestry).[9] He does not wish to discard the idea of sensory representation as the creative foundation of aesthetic possibilities.

Lessing's insistence on the free play of imagination in aesthetic experience adds complex depth to his programmatic declaration that both poetry and painting present us with "appearances as reality." In reading *Laokoon* we gradually realize that for Lessing the success of an artistic representation does not entail the creation of an exactly illusionistic appearance; rather, it invites and enables the viewer's imagination to fill out and complete the projective work of the artist. This feature of Lessing's aesthetic is all the more instructive, I want to stress, for having been formulated from within a mimeticist position. Far from impeding him, his conception of mimetic representation allows him to construct a flexible model of the relationship between artwork and spectator, between the object and the experience of representation. But the *Laokoon*'s augmentation of the idea of artistic "appearances" by a sense of active interpretative interplay between artwork and viewer might prompt us to wonder whether any mimetic theory of art can generate a credible aesthetics if it relies on a conception of artistic "appearances" alone. From this point of view, the traditional metaphor of a painting or other work of art as a "mirror" of reality could be thought to be doubly unfortunate, because it obscures the interpretative character both of representation itself (on which Lessing places great emphasis) and of the response of a cooperatively engaged viewer. Can a mimetic theory of pictorial art, in particular, be profitable, we ought to ask, without admitting the need to regard a painting as something more than a purely visual field, something more than a construction of (mere) "appearances"? If not, where does this leave the mimetic "mirroring" of reality? I hope to show in the course of this chapter that these questions are highly pertinent to understanding the famous Platonic treatment of painting in *Republic* 10, and I later draw attention to some interesting parallels, elsewhere in the legacy of mimeticism, to the points I have briefly highlighted in Lessing's treatise.

We can be confident that questions regarding the status and character of visual mimesis were under discussion in classical Athens even before Plato's incisive entry into the argument. Although direct evidence for fifth-century arguments about images is scarce, we have enough clues to make it reasonable to believe that there was much more of a culture of inter-

---

[9] The "inner eye" of romanticism appears in, e.g., remarks of Caspar David Friedrich, cited in Holt 1966, 84–85, and in Schelling's "Über das Verhältnis der bildenden Künste zur Natur" (quoted in chapter 12, section II): the Platonic antecedents of this motif go back to "the eye of the soul" at Plato *Rep.* 7.533d2, 540a7, and *Soph.* 254a10; an important Neoplatonic version of the theme is at Plotinus *Enn.* 1.6.8–9 (cf. Basil *Ad adolesc.* 2.30 for a Christian instance, echoing Plato).

pretative debate about visual art than we can now reconstruct in detail. Consider the implications of Plato *Ion* 532e–33b, where Socrates alludes in passing to the critical exposition or exegesis (*epideiknunai* and *exēgeisthai* are the verbs) of the productions of major painters such as Polygnotus. The reference, though embedded in a context of heavy irony about Ion's own credentials as poetic exegete, marks the recognition of a parallelism within established cultural practice between "expert" discourse about pictures and about poetry; and while Plato can be notoriously insouciant about historical consistency, it is implausible to suppose there could have been anything incongruous about making Socrates take for granted the existence of expert discussion of pictorial art. Moreover, the verb *epideiknunai* (literally "to give a demonstration") used in this passage, matching Ion's own hermeneutic activitives with poetry (530d5, 541e–2a), belongs to a word group that has strong associations with sophistic display-rhetoric, "epideictic" rhetoric no less. Sophistic discussion of visual art was surely more extensive than the hints in our sources now reveal. We have evidence that Hippias of Elis discussed painting and sculpture, while the *Dissoi Logoi* applies to painting, as well as tragedy, the paradox of aesthetic "deception" articulated in connection with poetry by Gorgias, who himself refers to painting and sculpture in his *Helen*.[10] Other possible echoes of pre-Platonic debates about visual art include Alcidamas *Sophists* 27–28, of disputed date though placed by many scholars in the 390s or 380s, where mimesis terminology is applied to visual art without any sign of novelty, and the "Hippocratic" treatise *De victu* 1.21, arguably of fifth-century origin, which states that sculptors produce mimesis of the human body "except for the soul" (*plēn psuchēs*), a remark whose resonance chimes with a passage of Xenophon shortly to be discussed.[11] It is wholly unwarranted to suppose that the application of mimetic terminology to pictorial art was an innovation of the fourth century, whether by Plato or anyone else.[12]

[10] Hippias A2 DK; anon. *Dissoi Logoi* 3.10 (cf. the mention of the sculptor Polycleitus at 6.8); Gorgias on deception, fr. 23 DK, with my introduction, note 49; Gorgias on visual art, fr. 11.18 DK (with my later note 45); cf. Philipp 1968, esp. 42–61, for a survey of pre-Platonic references to the visual arts. With *epideiknunai* at *Ion* 533a2, compare *Rep.* 10.598c3, *Soph.* 234b9, though these other passages seem to refer only to "exhibiting," not to expounding, paintings.

[11] On the long debate over the date of Alcidamas's treatise consult, e.g., Richardson 1981, 6–8 (with 5, 10 n. 40); O'Sullivan 1992, 23–31, with 63–65, 95; and cf. my note 42. For different views of the date of pseudo-Hippocrates *De victu* 1, see, e.g., Kahn 1979, 4 with 304 n. 12 (favoring the late fifth century), and Kirk 1954, 26–29 (favoring late fourth), with my introduction, note 34, on the work's larger concept of mimesis; the words *plēn psuchēs* quoted have been doubted by some scholars.

[12] Application of mimesis terminology to visual art is at least as old as Aeschylus fr. 78a.7 Radt: see my introduction, section III. The thesis that Plato innovated in this respect (Keuls 1978, 9–32; Tatarkiewicz 1970–74, 1:122) is therefore false; cf. Halliwell 1986, 110–12. Like-

The earliest non-Platonic text to give us a fuller flavor of discussion of the relationship between appearances and meaning in visual mimesis is the well-known passage of Xenophon's *Memorabilia* in which Socrates speaks to the painter Parrhasius and the sculptor Cleiton and invites both of them to ponder the representational capability of their art forms.[13] Although this text may have been written as late as the 350s, its rich vocabulary of visual representation is likely to give us a glimpse of issues and debates already under way in the previous century, even if the relationship of these issues to Socrates himself and to the actual artists concerned must remain a matter for speculation. However fictional Xenophon's elaboration of these conversations may be, they suggest that he expected his readers to recognize not just the possibility of informed discussion of visual images, but, more significantly, the emergence of philosophical considerations about mimesis from technical questions about figurative art. To that extent at least, these anecdotes open a window, I submit, on the background to certain Platonic arguments.

Socrates' questions to the artists focus on how one gets, or whether one *can* get, from the design of a visual field ("shapes and colors") to the representation or expression of nonsensory, perhaps nonmaterial properties.[14] With Parrhasius, Socrates starts from the premise that painting is "imaging/modeling of the visible world" (*eikasia tōn horōmenōn*) and moves to overcome the painter's initial doubt whether visual mimesis can depict "character" (*ēthos*) by proposing that painting can show character

---

wise with the common suggestion (Tate 1932, 162; Koller 1954, 62–63; Vernant 1991, 165; and Gebauer & Wulf 1992, 47) that Xenophon *Mem.* 3.10 (discussed in my text) *innovates* by applying the language of mimesis to figurative art: this book of the *Memorabilia* almost certainly postdates (e.g.) Alcidamas *Soph.* 27–28 (see my note 11) and Plato's *Republic* (see 373b, with my introduction, note 53). *Mem.* 3.5 is generally regarded as written after the battle of Leuctra in 371, and parts of book 3 might be as late as the 350s, though cf. Sörbom 1966, 80–81 (n.b., incidentally, that Sörbom's book nowhere mentions Alcidamas *Soph.* 27–28).

[13] Xenophon *Mem.* 3.10.1–8; note the detailed vocabulary of visual representation, especially the verbs *apeikazein, proseikazein, apomimeisthai, ekmimeisthai,* and *aphomoioun*; Tatarkiewicz 1970–74, I:101 (cf. 121–22) preposterously maintains that the noun *mimēsis* "was still not available" in the context of this discussion. Cf. note 12 here, with my introduction, note 39. On the relationship of the discussion to the practice of artistic realism, see Stansbury-O'Donnell 1999, 111–14; a possible link with the actual art of Parrhasius is seriously entertained by Robertson 1975, 1:412–13. Pollitt 1974, 30–31, links the passage to early fourth-century artistic "subjectivism," though his discussion is unreliable in several details. The fullest analyses of Xenophon's text are in Sörbom 1966, 80–98, and Preißhofen 1974.

[14] For my claim that mimesis here and elsewhere straddles matters of representation and expression, see the introduction, note 31, and chapters 8 and 12, with my notes 38, 59 here. Wollheim 1987, 80–89, gives a rewarding philosophical account of the problem of pictorial expression.

"through" (*dia*) its physical expression, especially on the face.[15] Socrates is here raising a basic question about the relationship of "appearances" (*phainomena*) to human meaning. In part, it is worth adding, this question is about "life" as much as about "art": the question how we can "see" or perceive character at all. In this connection Socrates' intransitive use of the verb *diaphainein* (to show through) at 3.10.5, of the link between outer bodily signs (including the face) and "inner" *ēthos*, is extremely interesting.[16] Character "shows through"; it is a sort of emergent property. This metaphorical transparency is first applied to the phenomenology, the direct experience, of character in general, and then turned by Socrates into a justification for ascribing to figural art the capacity (which Parrhasius had originally doubted) to depict or express character in its visual medium.

A bridge from life to art is constructed once more by Socrates' question to the sculptor Cleiton, "how do you produce/realize [*energazesthai*] the appearance of life (*to zōtikon phainesthai*) in your figures?" which crisply epitomizes a concern running through both earlier and later Greek ideas of what one might call the quasi-vitalistic quality of mimesis.[17] In the phrasing of this question, the adjective *zōtikon* identifies the simulation of "life" that a viewer may experience "in" an image, the sense of what might be termed its vividly "worldlike" properties, while the verb *energazesthai*, literally "to work into," contrastingly marks the artifactuality, the concretely "manufactured" status, of the image. These two things are held together, so to speak, by the concept of appearances (*phainesthai*). The notion of artistic appearance, semblance, or even illusion has a long history in aesthetics; it is the realm, for instance, of what eighteenth-century German aestheticians liked to call *Schein*, as we have already seen in Lessing's programmatic statement, in the preface to *Laokoon*, that both painting and poetry, notwithstanding their differences, "put before us . . .

[15] The aesthetics of facial or bodily expression becomes part of a long-lasting tradition in the interpretation of visual art: an ancient locus classicus is the proem to Philostratus maj. *Imag.* (note that Philostratus calls the interpretation of pictures both *hermēneuein* and *epideixis*, ibid., 5); for other views and reflections of the issue, cf., e.g., Plutarch *Qu. Conv.* 681e, *Cimon* 2.3, *Alex. Fort.* 335b, Philostratus min. *Imag.* proem, Callistratus *Imag.* 3.2, 5.1. A notable Renaissance instance is Alberti *De pictura* 2.41–44 (Alberti 1973, 70–79); Alberti was familiar with Xenophon *Mem.* 3.10 (see *De pictura* 2.31, Alberti 1973, 54–55).

[16] Compare, though with obvious differences, Aristotle *De sensu* 440a7–8 (colors appearing "through" one another: *phainesthai di'allēlōn*), with my note 19. I discuss Aristotle's own approach to the question of whether and how character can be depicted in visual art in chapter 5, section I, and chapter 8, section II.

[17] See, e.g., my introduction note 48, for some earlier cases of this motif, with chapter 10, note 43, and chapter 11, note 54, for other uses of *zōtikos*. With Xenophon's use of *energazesthai*, compare *enapergazesthai* at Plato *Soph.* 236a6.

appearances as reality" (stellen uns . . . den Schein als Wirklichkeit vor). Even within the limitations of the short conversations related by Xenophon in the *Memorabilia*, we can discern a tension—a tension that turns out, on my reading, to be pivotal to the entire legacy of mimesis—between divergent views of representational art as, on the one side, fictive illusion, the product of "deceptive" artifice, and, on the other, a reflection of and engagement with reality (that sense of "life"). We need not attribute to Xenophon a deep insight into fundamental issues of aesthetics in order to take Socrates' alleged conversations with a painter and a sculptor as at any rate oblique evidence for the development of a philosophical analysis of images in the intellectual climate of late fifth- and early fourth-century Athens. It was within that climate that Plato's thinking about visual mimesis evolved. And it is on Plato that we must now concentrate our attention.

II

It is worthwhile, in approaching the place of painting in Plato's conception of mimesis, to register that both he and Aristotle mention visual arts on many occasions and in many kinds of context—psychological, political, scientific, even metaphysical. Neither of them, however, addresses the subject in a sustained way, although Plato, in *Republic* 10, comes closer to doing so than Aristotle. For the most part their references to painting consist of analogies, metaphors, and obiter dicta. But that does not make them negligible: the analogies and metaphors of philosophers can be revealing, indeed partly constitutive, of their patterns of thought. Both philosophers refer often to figurative art partly because of its prominence in the surrounding culture, especially in Athens, where painting, sculpture and other visual arts had a pervasiveness reflected in Plato's description of the "city of luxury," with its pathology of cultural "fever," in *Republic* 2.[18]

Aristotle, as one might expect, generally mentions painting in ways that concede its respectable existence as an artistic activity: Aristotle, we can say, has no quarrel with painting. In keeping with this, he shows signs of careful observation of some of the things that painters do, noticing, for example (in a passage rather neglected by historians of Greek art), a technique involving the overlay of less vivid upon more vivid color for the depiction of objects under water or in haze; or citing the kinds of colors that painters can and cannot produce by mixing.[19] Plato, on the other hand,

---

[18] *Rep.* 2.373b (quoted in chapter 1). For visual arts other than painting and sculpture, note especially Plato's references to figurative textiles (both on cult statues and in domestic use) at *Euthph.* 6c1; *Rep.* 2.373a7, 378c4, 3.401a2; and perhaps *Hipp. Maj.* 298a2.

[19] Visual effects of water or haze: *De sensu* 3.440a8–10 (where it is said that colors show "through" one another: cf. my note 16); see my chapter 6, section I, and cf. Gage 1993, 15,

is often apparently dismissive of pictorial technique. Even when he seems to acknowledge its importance, as he tends to do in passing allusions to "good" painters or painting (e.g., at *Republic* 10.598c2), or when he touches on quasi-technical details, as in a series of highly controversial mentions of *skiagraphia*, literally "shadow painting," he rarely displays an Aristotelian interest in such things on their own terms.[20] But that, perhaps paradoxically, is precisely why Plato's references to painting (and, like Plato himself, I sometimes use "painting" as a synecdoche for the figurative arts as a whole) tend to be philosophically more far-reaching than Aristotle's, above all in the sense that they come to attach themselves to central elements in his own thinking and writing. Although Aristotle is respectful of the practices of pictorial and other visual arts, his remarks on them are almost always peripheral to his own thought. If painting had not existed, it would perhaps not ultimately have mattered much to Aristotle's philosophical scheme of things, but it would have deprived Plato of a recurrent and telling, if profoundly ambiguous, source of reflections on human attempts to model and interpret reality.[21]

From at any rate *Cratylus* onward, as I explained in chapter 1, Plato returns repeatedly to the idea and language of mimetic images in order to pose questions about how the nature of those images, both pictorial and otherwise, and particularly their relationship to putative originals or models, might be construed. Such concerns occur in some of the most memorable and widely discussed contexts of the Platonic dialogues, such as the unforgettable Sun, Line, and Cave analogies in *Republic* 6–7, or the *Timaeus*'s discussion of the creation of the world, by the demiurge and his assistants, as an image, in matter and time, of a timeless model—a work

---

for a rare art-historical citation of this intriguing passage. Colors: *Meteor.* 3.2, 372a5–8. A philosophically somewhat more sustained Aristotelian analogy from visual art is *De mem.* 1.450b20–31: cf. my chapter 6, section I.

[20] Some Platonic references to technicalities of graphic, pictorial, or plastic art: mixing of colors (*Crat.* 424d–e, with the reference to "flesh tints," *andreikelon*; *Rep.* 6.501b uses the same details as metaphor; cf. *Polit.* 277c2, and Empedocles fr. 23.3–4 DK); contrast between a sketch or outline (*perigraphē, hupographē*) and a finished or detailed work (*Rep.* 6.501a–b, 8.548c–d, *Polit.* 277b–c); erasure and correction (*Rep.* 6.501b9); adjustment of proportions to allow for angle of viewing (*Soph.* 235e–36a); clay modeling technique in sculpture (*Polit.* 277a–b); modification of already applied color (*Laws* 6.769a–b, with Rouveret 1989, 42–49). On the vexed question of *skiagraphia* see note 46. I leave aside the extremely remote possibility, asserted in ancient biographical texts (Diogenes Laertius 3.5, Apuleius *Dogm. Plat.* 1.2), that Plato had himself been a painter at one stage: see Riginos 1976, 42–43.

[21] Morgan 1990 attempts to explain why painting came to matter to Plato against a cultural background of increasingly self-conscious "representational viewing"; see also Janaway 1995, esp. ch. 5, for a probing analysis of the dialogues' ideas on painting. Of older writers, Schweitzer 1953 takes most seriously the influence of visual art on Plato's thinking and experience, though he overstates some aspects of Plato's affinities with it.

of cosmic mimesis.[22] Despite their frequently polemical tone, Plato's references to images and pictures become associated with anxieties that are
integral to his own lines of philosophical inquiry, especially in the later
dialogues. While taking some account here of this important factor, my
own aim is not to reexamine the independent philosophical uses to which
Plato puts the concept of images, both literal (visual) and metaphorical,
in his work. Nor do I want simply to try to extract art-historical information
from Plato, a task fraught with dangers and one that many others have
undertaken.[23] I want instead to foreground some of the various ways in
which pictorial art is approached in the dialogues, and thereby to counter-
act the common belief that Plato possessed both a unitary and a severely
reductive view of the status of visual mimesis. Central to my account is the
claim that Plato's attitude to the visual arts is more exploratory and fluid
than is usually realized. Standard accounts of Plato's supposed "hostility"
to painting, including many attempts to trace evolving patterns in his references to the art and its practitioners, are greatly simplified; they depend
on overdogmatizing readings of individual arguments, and they often miss
subtleties within those arguments. Crucial, of course, is *Republic* 10, in
particular the infamous mirror analogy of 596d–e. But as a prelude to a
fresh discussion of that most notorious of texts, I want first to construct a
broader chart of some of Plato's more philosophically important references to visual art.

Perhaps the nearest Plato comes to providing a definition of pictorial
mimesis is in the *Cratylus*, which may, as I suggest in chapter 1, be the
earliest Platonic dialogue in which the subject of artistic mimesis arises.
In the course of attempting to work out a hypothetical semantics of language (later rejected, we need to remember), Socrates here sketches an
analogous "semantics" of visual signification (*sēmainein, Cratylus* 422e4)
based on the idea of resemblance or correspondence.[24] Pictorial mimesis,
on this admittedly rudimentary account, uses a visually organized field
("shape and color") to produce "likenesses" (*homoia, homoiotētes*) of
things. But the *Cratylus* importantly acknowledges that the relationship

[22] See esp. *Tim.* 38a, 39e, 41c, 42e, 44d, 48e, 50c, 51b, 69c, 88d, with Theiler 1957, Curtius
1953, 544–46, for the concept of the demiurge. On the wider issues of images in Platonic
philosophy, cf. chapter 1, note 79.

[23] Art-historically orientated surveys of references to painting in Plato can be found in
(among others) Sartorius 1896; Steven 1933; Webster 1952 (a wildly speculative article);
Schweitzer 1953, esp. 83–87; Schuhl 1952; Demand 1975; Keuls 1978; and Rouveret 1989,
24–59, though all contain overconfident, and mutually discrepant, views on Plato's relationship to the art-historical background.

[24] Plato *Crat.* 422e–23e. Cf. the more general definition of mimesis at *Soph.* 265b ("a kind
of making, but the making of simulacra [*eidōla*] not of things themselves"), with chapter 1,
section III.

between a graphic image or likeness and its object or model is not confined to the copying of actual particulars in the world. In addition to images such as portraits, which are by definition correlated with individuals, there are images that represent imaginary members of classes such as "man" and "woman," or even, perhaps, the classes themselves.[25] This passage is therefore incompatible with the common belief that Plato consistently limits visual mimesis to the "mirroring" of visible reality, an issue that will later prove central to the interpretation of *Republic* 10. And there are two sides to this point: one touches the "semantic" status of an image's representational content (its relationship to identifiable items in the world); the other concerns the optical conditions of visual mimesis (the nature of the "likeness" of its perceptual properties to the perceptual properties of objects in the world). My denial that we can discover a uniform "mirror theory" of mimetic art in Plato applies in both these respects, as will later become clear.

It is highly germane in this connection to recall the admiration expressed by the Athenian in the *Laws* for Egyptian art as a paradigm of cultural stability and conservatism.[26] Whatever else Plato believed about Egyptian art, he must have known—although the Athenian does not comment expressly on this—that its pictorial traditions did not depend on the pursuit of optical naturalism through techniques of foreshortening, modeling, and the like, as employed by Greek artists in Plato's own time. So the Athenian's praise of Egypt implies the possibility of approval for at least some kinds of nonnaturalistic and heavily stylized figural art. Now, another much-cited Platonic text explicitly contrasts different types and conventions of visual representation, namely the *Sophist*'s distinction between two kinds of mimesis or image making, the "eicastic" and the "phantastic." However, this distinction (whose primary function is to enable the unfavorable dissection of the sophist's own intellectual pretensions) is not the same as that between naturalistic and nonnaturalistic images, but marks

---

[25] *Crat.* 430a–31d: see chapter 1, note 22.

[26] Plato *Laws* 2.656–57, 7.799a–b (cf. chapter 1, and its note 65): the Egyptians laid down obligatory standards of beauty and correctness in figurative arts and in *mousikē* (all of which count as mimetic: see 655d, 667c–69e; cf. chapter 1, note 67) which have allegedly not changed for ten thousand years. Davis 1979 considers Plato's familiarity with Egyptian art; Brisson 2000, 151–67, examines the broader status of Egyptian culture in Plato's work. For a later but related contrast between Egyptian and Greek art, see Diodorus Siculus 1.98 with Pollitt 1974, 12–14, 28–29; cf. Panofsky 1970, 90–100, on the difference between Greek and Egyptian treatment of human bodily proportions. Contrast, however, *Polit.* 299d–e on the need for inquiry and exploration, *zētein*, rather than mere written rules, in all *technai* (both mimetic and otherwise); cf. the reference to technical progress in sculpture at *Hipp. Maj.* 282a. Morrow 1960, 355–58, stresses that the *Laws*' remarks on Egyptian art and on the fear of artistic innovation (cf. esp. 2.657b, 7.798e), like the more famous passage at *Rep.* 4.424b–e, do not altogether rule out variety and change.

the difference between an image that preserves (measurable) ontological fidelity to the proportions (*summetriai*) and surface features of whatever it depicts, and, on the other hand, an image that is deliberately adjusted to suit the perceptual point of view from which a human observer contemplates it.[27] Precisely because this passage of the *Sophist* places most painting, and indeed most mimesis, in the second category (*phantastikē*), it actually corroborates my thesis that Plato does not take the pursuit of literal correspondence between depictions and objects in the world to be a necessary condition for visual mimesis per se. Furthermore, juxtaposition with the *Laws'* references to Egyptian art shows that the consequences of this point are not intrinsically negative.

It is instructive here to recall too the passage from *Cratylus*, discussed in chapter 1, which adumbrates a "qualitative" conception of visual images and rejects the need for mimesis to justify itself in terms of replicatory fidelity.[28] "Correctness" (*orthotēs*), the criterion of acceptable representational rendering, is there explicitly construed as something different from measurable ("mathematical") correspondence to the depicted object. That might in turn make us wonder how strictly Plato would have wanted to press the definition of eicastic mimesis in the *Sophist*.[29] But leaving that unanswerable question aside, my immediate point is that if we put the *Cratylus*'s "qualitative" conception of pictorial correctness together with the basic implications of the eicastic-phantastic distinction in the *Sophist*, what emerges is a Platonic recognition that the kinds of relationship to the world that qualify images as types of "likeness" (*homoiotēs*) are not unitary but artistically and culturally variable. These two passages thus give some broader conceptual support to the contrast drawn between the pictorial (and other artistic) traditions of Greece and Egypt in the *Laws*.

It is my provisional contention, then—provisional, because still to be tested against *Republic* 10—that Plato's argumentative strategies toward painting do not depend on the supposition that visual mimesis is intrinsically or necessarily mirrorlike in its aspirations, and do not suggest that such aspirations furnish the sole, or even the most important, criterion of the value of artistic images. There is no such thing, I maintain, as a single,

---

[27] Plato *Soph.* 235d–36c: mimetic art (*mimētikē*) or image making (*eidōlopoïetikē*) is subdivided into (a) "likeness making" (*eikastikē*, cf. *Laws* 2.667d1, 668a6, with chapter 1), which matches the proportions and surface attributes of its *paradeigma*, and (b) "semblance making" (*phantastikē*), which adjusts its properties, and thereby "distorts" its original, in order to produce a certain appearance when viewed from a particular position. Most painting falls into the second category (236b9); cf. chapter 1, section III.

[28] Plato *Crat.* 432a–d; see chapter 1, section I.

[29] Cf. chapter 1, section III, for various difficulties in making sense of the concept of *eikastikē*.

fixed Platonic paradigm for the evaluation of the images of figurative art. In fact, Plato's multifarious references to painting betray a recurrent tension between at least two models and standards of visual representation: the first, as for example in the *Sophist*'s concept of "eicastic" image making, that of a maximized match or fidelity between a mimetic image and the visible properties of its (supposed) original or exemplar; the second, as for example at *Cratylus* 432a—d, that of the artistic selection, manipulation, and "reconfiguration" of appearances, with a concomitant awareness of the image's inescapable divergence from the properties of its "original." The reasons for this tension reach down far into the foundations of Platonic philosophy.[30]

It is clearly pertinent in this context that a number of Platonic texts, including *Cratylus* 430a–31d (with its indication that not all depictions are of individuals), recognize that the objects of visual representation need not exist independently in reality, a principle Aristotle was to apply more thoroughly to the interpretation of mimesis in what he says at *Poetics* 25.1460b8–11. Particularly remarkable is the fact that we encounter this point in as many as five passages in the central books of the *Republic*, four of which include the term *paradeigma*—"model," "exemplar," but also "ideal." At 5.472d Socrates compares the status of his hypothetical city to a good painter's rendering of an ideal (*paradeigma*) of human beauty that might never be found anywhere in the flesh, and he proposes that such a representation would not for that reason be artistically any less valuable.[31] At 6.484c Socrates says that, unlike true philosopher-rulers, political leaders who lack philosophical knowledge "have no vividly clear *paradeigma* in their mind" to which they can constantly "look" and refer, as painters do, in trying to match their work with their models.[32] Shortly after this, in the prelude to his parable of the deaf shipowner and the

---

[30] Cf. chapter 1, section III.

[31] In Halliwell 1993a, 196–97, on 472c4 and 7, I suggested that the language of idealism in Plato is sometimes influenced by the terminology of the visual arts; cf., somewhat differently, Carpenter 1959, 107–8. Flasch 1965, 270, goes too far in speaking of mimesis of "the Idea itself" at *Rep.* 472d, though this passage may have encouraged such a line of thought in others (see chapter 11, section I); and Panofsky 1968, 15, is mistaken in saying of this passage that such an artist would be excellent "*precisely because* he could not prove the empirical existence" (my emphasis) of the man depicted. It is unjustified to see here, with Schweitzer 1953, 55, an allusion to Zeuxis.

[32] This passage could, in isolation, be construed without idealistic implications for the painter's side of the comparison; but such a construal would, I think, be forced, and we have seen idealistic painting clearly acknowledged elsewhere in the *Republic*. It remains unclear, however, whether and in what sense the words *eis to alēthestaton* ([looking] at/toward the truest object) at 484c9 are applicable to painters as such. I posit a possible echo of this passage in Philostratus *Vita Ap.* 6.19: see chapter 9, with its note 36.

unruly sailors, Socrates cites painting's invention of such fictive entities as goat-stags, compounded from different elements of reality.[33] In a more extended comparison between philosophers and painters, at 6.500e–501c, Socrates restates his program for philosopher-rulers by asserting that the city will never flourish in happiness "unless its form is delineated by the painters who use the divine model [*paradeigma*]."[34] And this fascinating sequence of passages is concluded at 7.540a, in terms that echo all the earlier ones, with a description of the climax of philosophical training as the moment when the mind's eye can be opened to the light of the good itself, which the philosopher-rulers will then take as their perpetual ideal model (*paradeigma*).

In addition to intimating that the *Republic* itself is a kind of philosophical word-picture,[35] the cumulative force of these analogies seems to converge on the thought that philosophers are painters in another medium, in the sense that they endeavor to give vivid realization or embodiment to ideals conceived in and held before their minds. The metaphorical character of these passages should not, of course, be allowed to obscure critical differences. The philosopher's *paradeigma* is putatively immaterial and, in some sense, transcendent; the painter's, even if fictive or imaginary, has to be linked to possibilities of the visible.[36] These passages, with others already cited, nonetheless confirm a Platonic awareness that the status of a painter's *paradeigma*, and therefore the significance of what he paints, is variable. Although they imply an effort to match a depiction as closely as possible to a model or "original," they leave entirely open the source and status of the latter in particular cases. Moreover, by recognizing that

[33] Plato *Rep.* 6.487e–88a; the idea of an image constructed from many exemplars, which becomes such a topos in later art criticism (see Jex-Blake & Sellers 1896, lxi–ii), was already familiar at this date: the phrasing of 488a5 is akin to Xenophon *Mem.* 3.10.2; cf. my notes 12–13. Aristotle *Pol.* 3.11, 1281b12–15, is germane but has a different emphasis; cf. chapter 5, note 17.

[34] Aissen-Crewett 1989, 269, rightly sees in this passage at least an oblique implication for painting's own scope, but misleadingly describes it as implying something *more* than mimetic; Tate 1928, 21, speaks too bluntly of "genuine painting." For different interpretations of the *Republic*'s philosophers as visual artists, see Zimbrich 1984, 293–300; Büttner 2000, 162–67.

[35] Cf. *Tim.* 19b–c, where the *Republic* itself is referred back to as a painting.

[36] *Polit.* 285e–86a suggests that immaterial (*asōmata*) entities cannot be visually represented, because they allow no perceptual "likeness" (*homoiotēs*) or image (*eidōlon*) to be produced, but can be grasped only by logos: see Rowe 1995, 211–12. The concept of representation here is implicitly mimetic, and excludes the possibility of symbolism (cf. Dio Chrysostom 12.59, where symbols are used to represent that which cannot be depicted by [sc. mimetic] images; cf. chapter 9, note 30). Thus *eidōlon* here lacks pejorative connotations and is equivalent to a mimetic image; cf., e.g., *Soph.* 241e3, with Halliwell 1988, 119, for Platonic usage, as well as my introduction, note 45.

the process from model to representation takes place, in part, inside the artist's mind, these texts broach possibilities that were to have momentous consequences for various types of Neoplatonist idealism in aesthetics—from antiquity, through the Renaissance, to romanticism. Some of those consequences are investigated in the last two chapters of this book.

The contention that Platonic texts do not reduce either the aim or the value of visual mimesis to that of mirrorlike reflection of the phenomenal world can be both reinforced and deepened by bringing into the reckoning some Platonic references to "beauty" (*kallos, to kalon*) in painting and other figural arts. Without attempting to harmonize the diverse contexts of these references into anything like a seamless doctrine, I suggest that we can detect behind many of them an earnest Platonic commitment to what might be called the ethics of form. This is perhaps most concisely, though not unproblematically, summed up by *Laws* 2.668e–69b, where the judge of the beauty of any mimetic image (*eikōn*) is required to know three things: first, the identity of the object shown; second, how "correctly" (*orthōs*) it is represented (though we have already seen that the criteria of such correctness need not be simple); third, how "well" (*eu*) it has been depicted. As I argued in chapter 1, it is reasonable here to recognize overlapping and connected criteria—the "what?" the "how?" and the "what for?"—of the beauty of representation, and this nexus of considerations entitles us to speak in terms of a concept of ethical form.[37] On this account, the beauty of a mimetic work (visual or otherwise, 669a8) depends not on straightforward, one-to-one correspondence to a (putative) model but on a complex relationship in which a certain kind of purposiveness ("what it [sc. an image] wants/intends/means," *ti pote bouletai*, 668c6) must be taken into account, and in which mimetic imaging turns from a technical into an ethical activity. This section of *Laws* 2 does not yield a wholly perspicuous theory of the connections between the representational form and the ethical significance of mimetic art, but it does unquestionably try to formulate an interplay between them, and thereby offers something much less unambiguous, in the case of the visual arts, than a concept of mimetic mirroring.

Something comparable can be seen at *Republic* 3.401a–d, a very important passage that stands as the culmination of the analysis of the use of poetry and music in education. As a tailpiece to that analysis Socrates generalizes the principle of ethical form to all mimesis—in fact, to the entire fabric of a culture—and in the process reextends the concept of mimesis, as I stressed in chapter 1, beyond the category of dramatic imper-

---

[37] See my fuller discussion in chapter 1, section III.

sonation previously defined at 392d–394c.[38] At 401 he states that painting is "full" of formal manifestations of "character" (*ethos*), and he speaks of mimesis in a way that should be construed, in part at least, as a concept of expression (matching the earlier, Damonian idea of music as "mimesis of life"),[39] saying that beautiful form (*euschēmosunē*) involves *mimēmata* of good character: beauty of form is a matter not just of appearances but of appearances that embody and convey ethical value. This last passage contains one of the most wide-ranging statements about mimetic art to be found anywhere in Plato, and it rests on the proposition that in the visual arts (and elsewhere) form is not neutrally depictional but communicative of feeling and value. Although the view Socrates puts forward here is not exactly the same as the one attributed to him in the passage of Xenophon's *Memorabilia* discussed earlier in this chapter, there is an intriguing kinship between them: it would be a bold, though not unsustainable, hypothesis that an authentically Socratic view lies behind them. In both cases we can see at work an idea of the enrichment of representation by an implicitly evaluative dimension: in Xenophon's anecdote it is a case of character (*ethos*) showing "through" the figures depicted; in *Republic* 3 it is a matter of the form of the mimetic artwork as a whole (including that of individual figures) serving as a medium for affective and ethical attitudes. In both contexts, but much more forcefully in the *Republic*, mimesis is taken to be inescapably engaged in making moral sense of the human world—not just *registering* appearances, but actively construing, interpreting, and judging them. That gives us a vital sense of why beauty in the figurative arts is regularly taken in Plato to entail something other, or more, than optically definable or apprehensible accuracy.[40] Mimetic beauty, for Plato, is an expressive form of ethical value.

[38] See chapter 1, note 35, where I point out what is often overlooked, that the narrower definition of mimesis at 3.392d ff. is both preceded (2.373b, 388c) and followed (399a–400a of music, plus 398a2, 401a) by a broader use of the term, and one whose applicability to music makes reference to some notion of expression inescapable. The fact that mimesis in this context actually covers nonfigurative art, including architecture (401a3, b6), only strengthens the case for seeing a concept of expression at work here. Mimesis at 401a is treated as a concept of "expression" by Bosanquet 1925, 105; Burnyeat 1999, 218, says, apropos 400d–e, "style . . . expresses . . . character" (though he continues to translate mimesis terms by "imitation"); Sörbom 1966, 127–28, concedes the point grudgingly, with an inadequate appreciation of what is at stake. Cf. note 14.

[39] *Rep.* 3.400a7; on the Damonian tradition underlying this passage, see chapter 8. Scruton 1997, 119, finds Plato "insensitive" to the distinction between representation and expression (which Scruton strangely thinks does not predate Croce); I would prefer to say that Plato has a stronger sense than Scruton permits of some of the overlaps and connections between phenomena that might be covered by these two concepts (cf. my introduction, note 31).

[40] Note here also the force of *Rep.* 3.402b–c, which refers to the need for future Guardians to be able to recognize the virtues both in themselves and in "images" (*eikones*, 402c6). Cf.

III

It is time to confront the longest and most notorious Platonic treatment of painting—the first part of *Republic* book 10. It is time, in other words, to face the specter of Plato's mirror, the mirror to which the painter's mimetic activity (and therefore that of the poet too) is, it seems to many, directly compared at 596d–e, a passage Ernst Gombrich suggested had "haunted the philosophy of art ever since."[41] *Republic* 10's use of the mirror motif, which we know was not original to Plato,[42] is part of a larger argument that relegates the products of both painting and poetry to a level "twice removed from the truth," making them in some sense inferior even to the artifacts produced by carpenters and others, let alone to the realm of truth and reality constituted by forms or ideas. One thing that needs saying immediately is that, although painting here serves an analogical function, and is certainly of secondary interest in relation to poetry, this does not give us justification for dismissing Socrates' remarks about painting as somehow lightweight, though that is precisely how they have often been treated. On the contrary, the question posed by Socrates at the very start of this section is: "What is the nature of mimesis *as a whole?*" or "of mimesis in general?" (*holōs*, 595c7; cf. 603a11). Poetry, for various reasons, is Plato's main concern; but the conjunction of two mimetic arts is nonetheless sig-

---

the later Stoic view that virtues and vices manifest themselves, and are therefore perceivable, in outward forms (Plutarch *Sto. Rep.* 1042e–f = *SVF* 3.85, *Comm. Not.* 1073b).

[41] Gombrich 1977, 83. Sartorius 1896, 133, interestingly speculates that 598d alludes to the actual use of mirrors by contemporary artists; I am not aware of any Greek evidence for this practice (which is, of course, well documented for the Renaissance: see section IV): Pliny *NH* 35.147 may refer to a mirror *in* a picture (see Croisille 1985, 257 n. 14).

[42] The most important earlier uses are Pindar *Nem.* 7.14 (the mirror of poetic glory) and Alcidamas *apud* Aristotle *Rhet.* 3.3, 1406b12–13 (the *Odyssey* as a "beautiful mirror of human life," *kalon anthrōpinou biou katoptron*, a metaphor deprecated by Aristotle). Note that neither of these passages treats the mirror as a pure or passive reflector; both imply some sort of artistic enhancement of life. On the Pindar, cf. Frontisi-Ducroux & Vernant 1997, 117–18. In Alcidamas's metaphor Richardson 1981, 7, finds a point about "ethical value" as well as "realism," O'Sullivan 1992, 74, an impressive "scale of vision in literary judgement." The contextless citation hardly supports either view. Indeed, "realism" may be precisely *not* the point: "a *beautiful* mirror" rather suggests idealization, something Alcidamas certainly ascribes to visual art at *Soph.* 28, where "real bodies" (*alēthina sōmata*) are contrasted with "beautiful statues" (*andriantes kaloi*), and the latter (ibid., 27) are nonetheless classed as mimesis (cf. note 11). As to whether Plato could have had Alcidamas in mind in *Rep.* 10, see the contrasting views of Richardson 1981, 6–8, and O'Sullivan 1992, 63–66, 95; Solmsen 1968, 2:139, certainly goes too far in taking Alcidamas's mirror metaphor as the chief spur to Plato's treatment of mimesis in that book.

For more general discussion of mirrors in ancient metaphors, see Mette 1988, 350–56, and Curtius 1953, 336 and n. 56; Grabes 1982 richly documents the longer legacy of mirror imagery. For later mirror motifs in aesthetics, see section IV, with notes 62–68. Frontisi-Ducroux & Vernant 1997 offer a cultural psychology of Greek mirrors.

nificant as a means of broaching larger themes about all mimetic representation. This will prove a key factor for the direction of my own argument.

Much that has been written about this section of book 10 has underestimated, and sometimes altogether missed, the rhetorical and even satirical dimensions of the passage.[43] What we come up against here is a testing instance of the need to read many, maybe most, Platonic arguments as more than formal structures of reasoning, and to take account of the tonal and attitudinal factors with which particular speakers, above all of course Socrates, put forward particular claims. It is a quality of Plato's writing in general—a quality plausibly to be thought of as inspired by his experience of Socrates' own personality[44]—that it calls for a constant alertness in its readers to the presence of "subtexts." In the present case the tone is set at the start by Socrates' paradoxical suggestion that "making everything" (a motif already found in connection with painting in Empedocles) is, where a mirror is involved, "not difficult" (596d8), a slur that cannot be applied literally to the visual arts themselves, because their status as *technē*, an accomplished skill, is conceded throughout the dialogues.[45] This semisatirical touch is sustained later both by the sarcastic gibe that trompe l'oeil effects can fool only "children and stupid adults" (598c2), and by the choice of cobblers and carpenters as objects of figural art (598b-c).

The significance of this last detail has been generally obscured by the mistaken assumption that Plato's argument here is about the kind of Greek painting we still have substantial access to, namely vase painting. But the idea of trompe l'oeil, with the requirement of distance viewing at 598c3,[46] establishes a reference to the major but largely lost forms of wall and panel painting in whose predominantly mythological and historical subjects (subjects, we need to remember, largely shared with poetry) the depiction

---

[43] Robb 1994, 230, detects humor and satire in the first part of book 10, but his interpretation of its thrust is rather different from mine.

[44] The idea expressed by Alcibiades at *Symp.* 221e–22a, that Socratic arguments have a sometimes enigmatic "outside" and a many-layered "inside," is especially germane here as an oblique clue to one of Plato's own aspirations.

[45] Pictorial *technē*: e.g., *Ion* 532e–33b; *Gorg.* 448b, 450c10; *Rep.* 7.529e; *Soph.* 234b7; *Polit.* 288c; *Laws* 2.668e7–69a1. Empedocles' reference to painting's production of "forms like all things" (*eidea pasin aligkia*) is in fr. 23.5 DK; Inwood 1992, 36–37, rightly surmises that this fragment may have influenced Plato (as it may also have done Gorgias fr. 11.18 DK: see Buchheim 1985, and Buchheim 1989, 172–73). Too 1998, 62 (cf. 61) blunders in taking the "sophist" who "makes everything" at *Rep.* 10.598c–d to be the divine demiurge, rather than the mimetic artist.

[46] The reference to distance viewing, paralleled at *Soph.* 234b, is elsewhere linked to *skiagraphia*: e.g., *Rep.* 7.523b, *Tht.* 208e, *Parm.* 165c, with Rouveret 1989, 24–26, 50–59, for the best analysis of the vexed issue of *skiagraphia*, a term that I do not believe Plato used with rigorous consistency. Distance viewing makes little sense for vase painting.

of low-grade artisans cannot have been at all typical.[47] Too many readings of *Republic* 10 have completely ignored the rhetorically provocative character of the argument about painting, and have consequently failed to consider the possibility of taking the mirror as part of a challenge to refine the conception of (pictorial) mimesis that is at stake here. To treat a Platonic argument as a challenge of this sort is hardly arbitrary: it is precisely what Socrates himself indicates later in book 10, in relation to the critique of poetry, when he invites the art's defenders or advocates to produce a new justification of it that takes account of the problems raised by the preceding discussion (607d–e).[48] It is certainly reasonable to suppose that it mattered much more to Plato whether such a challenge could be taken up in the case of poetry than in that of painting. But to ignore the equivalent possibility in the case of painting, and to take the earlier part of book 10 as an unequivocal condemnation of visual mimesis, is to run the risk of missing part of Plato's point.[49]

But how exactly can a recognition of rhetorical and satirical tone affect our interpretation of the arguments that Plato here gives to Socrates? My suggestion is that the rhetoric makes a specific difference if we see it as serving a provocative function—that is, as a way of issuing an intellectual challenge to those who hold certain unquestioned assumptions about mimesis. Even as regards the immediate implications of the mirror comparison itself, the force of the passage is more subtle and teasing than common paraphrase would make one believe. Socrates refers to the use of a mirror not as an exact analogue to what mimetic artists do, but as a provocative

---

[47] The point is blurred by, e.g., Burnyeat 1999, 300–301, who supplies an illustration from a vase painting of a carpenter. It is not clear, in fact, that Plato *ever* has vases in mind when he refers to painting; the only painters he mentions by name are Polygnotus (*Ion* 532e–33a, *Gorg.* 448b12), his brother Aristophon (*Gorg.* 448b11), Zeuxis (*Gorg.* 453c), and Zeuxippus (= Zeuxis?, *Prot.* 318c–d), who all worked in large-scale forms of mythological art (cf. Philostr. maj. *Imag.* proem 1 for the sharing of heroic myth by the visual arts and poetry). I offer the speculative suggestion that the proverbial story about Apelles and a cobbler at Pliny *NH* 35.85, including the artist's proverbial saying, "cobbler, stick to your last," may go back to someone who was reacting to Plato's provocative choice of example at *Rep.* 598b9. (A similar nuance may be present at Strabo 1.2.5: see chapter 9, note 21.) If Jex-Blake & Sellers 1896, lix, are right to link the anecdote to Duris of Samos, it is attractive to suppose we are dealing here with a Peripatetic response to *Rep.* 10, picking up on Aristotle's own assertion of the distinctness of mimetic art from the standards of other *technai* (*Poet.* 25.1460b13–21); on Duris and mimesis, see chapter 9. The cobbler is a standard example of the artisan in Plato *Rep.*, e.g., 1.332a, 2.374b–c.

[48] Cf. chapter 1, section III.

[49] I am here partly modifying the emphases of my own previous approach in Halliwell 1988, which I now consider too rigid in some of its formulations. Wehrli 1957, 44–45, is right to deny that *Rep.* 10 is Plato's "last word" on painting or that it offers a dogmatically conceived theory of art.

illustration of how "easy" it is (cf. 599a1), in a certain sense, to "make everything" (*panta poiein*, 596c–e; cf. 598b); at the same time, the passage introduces a cardinal (but also, note, a far from esoteric) ontological distinction between appearance and reality. It is crucial, therefore, to notice two things that the mirror simile (and its sequel) does *not* say or entail: first, that all painting actually purports to be a "mirroring" of the world, in the sense of striving for optimum optical fidelity to the appearances of things; second, that painters always or even normally aim to represent actual models in the world (a supposition that we have seen would clash with other passages of the *Republic*).[50] These two negative observations add weight to the claim I have already advanced that the introduction of the mirror analogy is presented as part of a deliberately provocative stance on Socrates' part. The assimilation of painting's capacity of "making everything" to something as easy and commonplace as holding up a mirror does not constitute a direct condemnation of painting as necessarily or limitingly mirrorlike, but issues a challenge to consider whether, and with what consequences, it is appropriate to think of painting as a reflector of appearances. The mirror is not a definitive conclusion but a dialectical gambit.

It is sometimes thought that book 10's arguments about painting depend so heavily on the metaphysics of forms, introduced at the start (596a–b, actually before painting has been mentioned), that those arguments must stand or fall *with* that metaphysics. But I want to insist, in the first place, that Socrates' use of painting as an analogy does not hang on any particular view of the so-called theory of forms. At 596e–97e Socrates puts forward a tripartite and hierarchical scheme of (i) perfect being, reality, and truth (the realm of "god" and "nature"), (ii) material particulars (including the products of artisan crafts such as carpentry), (iii) "semblances" or "simulacra," *phainomena, eidōla, phantasmata* (the realm of mimetic artists, *mimētai*). The status of the top tier of this scheme has often embarrassed Platonic specialists, both because it appears to posit metaphysical forms of general classes such as "couch," and because it appears to give even a carpenter mental or conceptual access to such forms (596b7).[51] Now, it is

---

[50] Janaway 1995, 119–20, states this second point forcefully, apropos 598a1–3; others, including Gombrich 1977, 83; Annas 1981, 336; D. Scott 1999, 34 ("imitation of a particular"); and Yanal 1999, 14, have got it wrong. On the status of the mirror analogy, cf. also Babut 1985a, 85 (though Babut 1985b, 135, is less satisfactory). For a later occurrence of the "make everything" motif, see chapter 11, note 16.

[51] It is one of several paradoxes about this passage that the carpenter's mental access to an idea or form (of what he makes) is reminiscent of the language used in the analogies between philosophers and painters at 5.472c–d, 6.501b (see section II); cf. also the general distinction between a craftsman's (*dēmiourgos*) use of an unchanging or changing "model" (*paradeigma*) at *Tim.* 28a–b, though that passage prepares us for the divine "demiurge." For

important to see that, whatever the thrust of Platonic metaphysics may be in other passages, Socrates' tripartite schema in book 10 can function as a stimulus to further scrutiny of the status of mimetic art (both visual and poetic) provided we can give *some* sense to the notion of a domain of truth and reality that goes beyond that of material or sensible particulars. If we call this domain the domain of philosophical truth, then one aspect of Socrates' analysis will be the double suggestion that such truth cannot be captured by an account of the material world alone, and that representational art, because embedded in experience of the world as empirical phenomenon, inevitably distances us from the search for philosophical truth. But the carpenter's grasp of a "form" or "idea" of his artifact, whether *qua* mental blueprint or a set of constitutive principles, shows that Plato cannot want the top tier of his schema to signify something exclusively philosophical, let alone transcendent of human experience. The carpenter's knowledge must be the summation of technical competence, not abstract intellectual insight.

It calls for some emphasis, in any case, that the second and third levels of Socrates' tripartition frame a problem that is, or can be made, independent of the top level itself. The suggestion that painting deals in "simulacra"—in insubstantial appearances that are ontologically secondary and inferior to the particulars of the material world—does not depend for its force on a "theory of forms" (in whatever version or interpretation), or even on a conception of strictly philosophical truth. It is often overlooked that most of what is said about painting in *Republic* 10 addresses the relationship between painting and the visible or material world, not that between mimesis and some "higher" domain of truth or reality. Even the second phase of the argument (598a–d) does not really depend on forms for its main point, namely that painting produces appearances that are, when judged in relation to relevant kinds of real objects in the world, mere simulacra (*phantasmata, eidōla*). We can get a purchase on this point by noticing the parallelism of language between 597a and 598b (which belong, respectively, to what I have called the first and second phases of the argument). In both cases an ontological contrast is drawn between that which is more and that which is less real or true; but whereas in the first passage the contrast is between forms (however construed) and the material world, in the second it is between the material world and the images of mimesis.

two recent, rather different approaches to the "forms" in *Rep.* 10, see Fine 1993, 110–13, 116–19, and Burnyeat 1999, 245–49, but neither of them resolves the issue of the craftsman's relation to the form at 596b7 (ignored by Fine 1993, 196), a problematic passage for many scholars: cf., e.g., Reeve 1988, 223, who simply "rewrites" the passage (his earlier treatment, 86, is also unsatisfactory: the expert user of an artifact is not a philosopher-king but the relevant specialist, e.g., the musician at 601d10). Steckerl 1942 relates the passage to subse-

When we reach the third and fourth phases of the inquiry into mimesis (601c–2b, 602c–3b), which arrive at the conclusions, first, that mimetic artists are themselves ignorant (regarding the things that their works purport to represent) and, second, that their works appeal to lower, irrational parts of the mind, there is no explicit role for "forms" at all. Moreover, the commonly made claim that book 10 treats mimetic works as "imitations of imitations" or "copies of copies" is seriously misleading.[52] No such formulation appears in Plato's text, nor can it capture the impetus of the arguments here. Book 10's conception of mimesis implies human intentionality: mimetic works are produced by painters, poets, and others who aim in some sense to model or fabricate images of (possible or imagined) reality. But this kind of mimetic intentionality cannot be a property of other objects (whether natural or humanly designed) in the material world. To suppose that it could is to conflate book 10 gratuitously with the *Timaeus*, where the material world as a whole is regarded as the "mimetic" creation of the demiurge, though even there it is never exactly asserted that each material particular (least of all, those produced by human artifice, like the carpenter's couch or bed in *Republic* 10) is an "imitation" or "copy."[53]

What all this comes to, I suggest, is that the treatment of painting in the context of book 10 operates as a critique of its relationship, *qua* paradigm of mimesis, not only or even principally to a putative realm of philosophical truth but to the world of human experience in general. More specifically, it becomes a critique of the *look* of the real—a critique, that is, of the status of visual verisimilitude or naturalism (or, in its extreme form, illusionism)—as a justification of pictorial mimesis. Seen from this viewpoint, what I earlier called the rhetorically provocative force of the mirror analogy can now be brought into sharper focus. By claiming that "making everything," in the sense of simulating the appearance of every kind of

---

quent developments in Platonism but without doing justice to its own contextual force.

[52] Such descriptions (anticipated, with reference to tragedy, as early as anon. *De philos. Plat.* 25.22–23: Westerink 1962, 47) have become a cliché of the literature; see, e.g., Tate 1928, 20 (and 1932, 164–65); Assunto 1965, 96; Babut 1985a, 82; Coulter 1976, 33; Hathaway 1962, 7; Murray 1996, 6; Schweitzer 1963, 1:53; Redfield 1994, 49; D. Scott 1999, 34; Sheppard 1994, 13; Watson 1988b, 212–3; White 1979, 248; Weinberg 1966, 701 (compounding matters with the false assertion that Plato thought poetry *imitated* the "Ideas" by imitating natural objects which were themselves imitations). *Rep.* 10.598b3, however construed, does not warrant the "copy of copy" claim, despite the supposition of such a luminary as Diderot in his *Salon de 1767* (Diderot 1957–79, 3:57). There is no good reason, in any case (and as *Crat.* 389a–b helps to show), for saying that the artisan "copies" or "imitates" the form to which he looks (e.g., Annas 1981, 336, and Hwang 1981, 35, the latter a seriously defective analysis), still less, *contra* Kosman 1992, 88, that he "imitates God in his making of a bed" (or that the poet "imitates" the artisan as such).

[53] The nearest to such a claim is at 50c, whose interpretation is uncertain; cf. Taylor 1928, 324. For the dialogue's other references to mimesis, see my note 22.

material entity, gives painting an aspiration that can already be easily accomplished with a mirror, Socrates issues a challenge to those who value
visual art, just as he later does to the lovers of poetry, to find a justification
for pictorial representation that will endow it with something other than
the cognitively redundant value of merely counterfeiting the "look" of the
real. The mirror analogy stands for the threat, not the final assertion, of a
reductive conception of visual mimesis. Stated in an inclusive form, the
message of Socrates' mirror analogy amounts to a denial that what I earlier
called the worldlike properties of artistic representation are worth having
for their own sake.[54] If the only (or main) justification for pictorial mimesis
is visual verisimilitude, then paintings are in danger of being as cognitively
superfluous as mirror images, in the case of which we almost always have
independent access to what they show. We cannot, in most circumstances
(at any rate, most circumstances envisageable by Plato), learn anything
from a mirror that we could not learn better in some other way.[55] Who
would choose to use a mirror where direct vision of an object was available? Contemplating what we can see in a mirror is for the most part a
trivial pastime.[56] Why should it be different with paintings?

If it is legitimate to interpret the treatment of painting in *Republic* 10 as
conducting a critical inspection of the idea that naturalism, the look of the
real, is a self-sufficient justification for mimesis, then the argument ought
to make provision for two alternative possibilities: one, that visual art (and,
by implication, other mimetic arts too) may just as usefully, if not more
usefully, turn to nonnaturalistic styles of representation as to the pursuit
of, at the extreme, illusionism (trompe l'oeil); the other, that naturalism, or
verisimilitude more generally, may have instrumental though not intrinsic
value. In the case of the first of these alternatives, we do not need to

[54] At the same time Plato's argument implicitly spurns the idea that artistic *skill* (cf. note
45) in achieving convincing visual likenesses is its own justification: an idea found, for example, in Adam Smith's "Of the Nature of that Imitation which takes place in what are called
The Imitative Arts," I §§5–18 (in Smith 1980, 176–209), where great stress is placed on the
difference of kind or medium between an artwork and its "model."

[55] But this might not be so with other *metaphorical* mirrors: one has limited access to
thought (except one's own) other than through language; but language is described as a
mirror of thought at Plato *Tht.* 206d.

[56] It perhaps needs spelling out that while Plato's argument leaves largely on one side the
commonest use of a mirror, namely, for self-inspection (something alluded to at 596e2, as at
Tim. 46b2; cf. *Alcib.* 132d–33b for an interesting reference to "the eye seeing the eye," and
Phdr. 255d5–6 for a remarkable erotic simile, seeing oneself in the "mirror" of the beloved),
this is not a problematic neglect: in terms of the analogy its implications would be limited to
self-portraits (and, what is more, to the artist's, not the viewer's, relation to a self-portrait).
However significant self-portraits have become in the subsequent history of painting, they
cannot count as paradigmatic of the nature of the art (or, more pertinently, of a viewer's
relationship to a painting), and the mirror motif serves to characterize the general relationship between (visual) mimesis and the (visible) world.

speculate about Platonic attitudes to types of artistic stylization, or even types of conceptual art, which were unknown at the time. Instead we can remind ourselves that at any rate later in his life, when writing the *Laws* (2.656–57), Plato allowed the Athenian to express strong admiration for the (supposedly) unchanging canons of one non-Greek artistic tradition, the Egyptian. Such admiration, from a Greek perspective, implies the recognition of stylization as a valuable artistic option, as well as the repudiation of naturalistic truth-to-appearances as an invariable desideratum of pictorial mimesis. This consideration connects with a more general Platonic tendency, which I count as his anti-aestheticism, to reject the idea of autonomous artistic criteria of value and, with it, the acceptability of appraising artistic styles or techniques from within a purely artistic perspective rather than from a wider angle of ethicocultural judgment.[57] As such, it leads on directly to the second possible response that might be prompted by the critique of painting in *Republic* 10, namely that it remains thinkable that artistic naturalism, the "look" of the real, is indeed potentially valuable to mimetic art, but in ways that contribute instrumentally to the overall psychological and social impact of the art forms in question.

Now it is true that because of the priorities of his text (in which poetry is the major target) Plato shows no immediate interest in pursuing this point vis-à-vis painting as such. But that need and should not prevent us from identifying the kind of direction in which we would have to move in order to satisfy the challenge implied by his discussion of painting. We can do that precisely because of the discussion's analogical function in relation to poetry, the focus of the larger argument. In the case of poetry, Plato's critique revolves around intertwined ethical and psychological considerations; the eventual invitation to the lovers of poetry to justify the object of their love calls for a defense that will show "the benefit, and not just the pleasure, that poetry brings to human societies and to individual lives" (607d). Equally, if pictorial naturalism can be valuable, on Plato's terms its value can only be instrumental, subject to judgment by "external" ethical, not artistically intrinsic or technical, criteria. This entitles us to say that an account of painting that satisfied the challenge of the Platonic argument in *Republic* 10 would have to be, at bottom, an ethical account, an account that took painting to involve something substantially more than the mirroring, the successful replication, of appearances.

That such an account could have been contemplated by Plato is shown, I submit, by several of the other references to painting in his work, both inside and outside the *Republic*, that I documented earlier in this chapter. I have drawn attention to the fact that in some of those passages it is accepted that there is more to painting than "meets the eye," and that a

---

[57] On Plato's anti-aestheticism, see esp. chapters 1 and 2, with Halliwell 1991a.

philosophically adequate approach to pictorial mimesis needs to accommodate such factors as ethical expression, idealization, and beauty. This emerges particularly strongly in a crucial passage of book 3, at 401a–d, where I earlier interpreted mimesis as in part a concept of expression.[58] That passage, which happens to come at the conclusion to the *Republic*'s first critique of poetry, places painting at the head of a list of arts said to be capable of embodying and communicating ethical qualities in mimetic form, not just reflecting appearances but filling them with meaning and value: painting is "full" of good and bad forms of "character" (*ēthos*), forms that are simultaneously a matter of visual representation and ethical expression and qualify as cases of mimesis in both these respects (401a8). It would no doubt be exorbitant to maintain that Plato took painting to have the same intensity of psychological-cum-ethical power as he ascribes to poetry. But given the general prominence of visual art in Greek religion and society, not least in classical Athens, we should not after all be surprised to find—as the total evidence of his references to it reveals—that Plato discerned in figurative mimesis the potential (and the obligation) to achieve much more than the simulation of appearances. Whatever else the mirror of *Republic* 596d–e bespeaks, it must be something other than a trope for the whole truth about painting.

The justification for looking to book 10's painting-poetry analogy for clues to a richer reading of the mirror simile is not, however, simply external. The reversibility of the analogy is actually entailed by its own logic, although this feature of the argument has been scarcely noticed by interpreters of the book, who have been understandably preoccupied with the text's own momentum toward its major target, poetry. But if, as 597e suggests (and in keeping with the aim of investigating "mimesis as a whole," 595c7), whatever is essentially true of the painter as a *mimētēs* (a representational artist) must be equally true of the poet as *mimētēs*, then it ought to be feasible to read other parts too of the analogy in reverse. The point of doing this, as I have maintained, would be to move beyond, and to engage dialectically with, the "rhetorical" downgrading of painting in the first part of book 10, and to make out the contours of a view of painting more in line with other Platonic passages examined earlier in this chapter.

Now, where poetry is concerned, Plato's arguments strongly urge the case for treating mimesis as something more than the simulation of appearances, or the production of simulacra capable of deceiving only "children and stupid adults." For the critique of poetry does not simply put the equivalent of the reductive trompe l'oeil model; if it did, it would need to maintain that only children and the stupid can be deceived by poems into taking dramatic fiction for reality. Rather, it contends, in ways I analyzed in

[58] See section II.

chapter 2, that poems are highly charged and expressively loaded bearers of meaning, whose projection and communication of human significance and ethical values are so great that they can affect "even the best of us" (605c10). Contrast this with the implications of the standard view that the first part of book 10 really does urge us to regard painting as mere mirroring of appearances. On the mirroring model, treated as a "straight" analogy, painting would actually be denied any expressive value, because expression, which I am here treating as one dimension of the concept of mimesis, requires recognizable traces of human intentionality and cannot be ascribed to the "raw" optical phenomena of mirror images[59]—hence, as we shall shortly see, the careful qualifications adopted by some later proponents of a "mirror theory" of artistic representation. But it is hardly open to us to suppose that this is evidence for outright Platonic insensitivity to the possible expressiveness or representational richness of pictorial art, because my previous arguments have established that Plato's works as a whole, including several earlier parts of the *Republic*, take account of much more than the strictly optical properties of works of visual mimesis, allowing for the painter's selection and interpretation of what he depicts and therefore for the importance of ethical character, idealization, invention and beauty in such art forms.

Moreover, I have also insisted on the provocatively "rhetorical" and even "satirical" tone of the first part of *Republic* 10, including Socrates' introduction of the mirror motif itself. If we now bring together this consideration of tone with the reversibility of book 10's painting-poetry analogy at the level of mimetic principle, and also with the collective evidence of Plato's references to painting, we are left with a powerful set of reasons for refusing to read the mirror simile at 596d–e as a conclusive depreciation of visual art. Instead, as I have already proposed, the consequence of looking into Plato's mirror, and of comparing its reflection with the arguments that follow it, should be to see the *insufficiency* of any conception of painting that emphasizes sheer appearances—including naturalistic verisimilitude, the "look of the real"—at the expense of representational and expressive significance. *Republic* 10 itself does not attempt to supply the developed and complex account of pictorial representation which book 3, 401, as well as other Platonic texts cited earlier, would ideally require. But on the interpretation I have put forward here it does add its own peculiar weight to the need for such an account.

---

[59] This is not to deny that mirrors might be *used* for quasi-expressive effect, by deliberate human design, e.g., in the arrangement of a room. Comparably, the presence of human intentionality allows (some) photographs, in contrast to ordinary mirror images, to be treated as expressive objects. Cf. my introduction, note 31.

IV

If the central thesis of my previous section is upheld, then the history of Western attitudes to visual art has been "haunted," in Gombrich's term, not so much by Plato's mirror itself as by a ghostly misapprehension about what it reflects. But if so, this state of affairs accentuates what might be thought a larger paradox to emerge from the reading I have offered of *Republic* 10's treatment of painting. On my interpretation, Plato's arguments offer a mimetic conception of art at whose core lies a critique of precisely those ideas—truth-to-appearances, verisimilitude, realism, illusionism—that have often been considered to define the mimeticist tradition in aesthetics. After all, the mirror motif itself, whether as "mirror of life" or "mirror of nature," has been repeated by numerous later thinkers in that tradition.[60] But it is only on the most simplified versions of the tradition that the mirror motif can be understood as committing a theory of representational art to the pure, self-sufficient reflection of appearances. I pointed out in the first section of this chapter that Lessing's view of visual art, though belonging to that tradition, certainly does not adopt such a model of representation, because it insists both on the selective, interpretative character of the artwork and on the active, interpretative response of the collaborative viewer. But even those mimeticist thinkers who have directly espoused a "mirror theory" of art have, in the most interesting cases, done so in a manner that shows them alert to the need to avoid treating naturalistic or realistic truth-to-appearances to be a supreme value in its own right. I would like now to glance at some striking illustrations of this claim.

My first example, which relates directly to literature but has wider implications, is taken from a *Rambler* essay of Samuel Johnson, a thinker whose aesthetic convictions are in part a kind of Platonism without the metaphysics. In the course of expounding the view that authors of realistic narratives ought to select their material on the basis partly of moral considerations, Johnson presents a combination of ideas that resembles the position I have attributed to Plato. Johnson grounds his case on a general statement of mimeticism, in characteristically neoclassical idiom ("it is justly considered as the greatest excellency of art to imitate nature"). He proceeds immediately, however, to demonstrate that his mimeticism is not a principle of pure or unqualified realism. Johnson sees very clearly that a literary or artistic aspiration to a perfect "surface" of verisimilitude, if taken as an absolute or unconditional aim, would necessarily prove self-confounding,

[60] In addition to the instances discussed here, see chapter 10, note 7, for antiquity, and chapter 12, notes 42, 50, 53–54 for later periods.

because the most complete achievement of this aim could only amount, *ex hypothesi*, to the duplication or reproduction of the appearance of such things as are in principle already available to our experience of the world. "If the world be promiscuously described," he writes, "I cannot see of what use it can be to read the account, or why it may not be as safe to turn the eye immediately upon mankind, as upon a mirror which shows all that presents itself without discrimination."[61] It is important to spell out the corollary of this point, which constitutes a less rhetorically slanted version of Socrates' notion that to "make" (the appearance of) "everything" can be easily accomplished with a mirror. Johnson recognizes that as soon as one attributes to a realistic art form, whether literary or pictorial, an aim that in some degree either diverges from or supplements the aspiration to perfect verisimilitude, there is an implicit recognition of artistic values that cannot be explained in exclusively technical terms (i.e., where "technique" is understood to imply an aspiration to illusionism). The mirror that "shows all . . . without discrimination" therefore designates something decisively inferior to a more famous Johnsonian mirror, that "faithful mirror of manners and of life" that Shakespeare "holds up to his readers" and whose status as an emblem of ethical art is signaled both by its concern with the general, not the particular, and by its direct attention to morality ("manners").[62]

But even if, as Johnson's case helps to confirm, the message of Plato's mirror can be incorporated into a fully mimeticist position, is it not also true, an objection might run, that the idea of a mirror as a metaphor of artistic excellence has often attracted both artists themselves and the theorists of mimesis? It is well known that as sagacious a thinker as Leonardo da Vinci actually recommends the use of a mirror by painters and, in addition, suggests more than once in his notebooks that the painter's mind should resemble a mirror in its openness to the appearances of things all around it.[63] But the practical or technical use of a mirror on the part of a painter need not imply agreement with an aesthetic of mimesis as direct copying of reality. It is interesting, in this connection, that when one of Leonardo's predecessors, Alberti, in the second book of his treatise *De pictura* (finished in 1435, and extant in both Latin and Italian versions), likewise says

[61] *Rambler* 4, 31 March 1750, in Johnson 1977, 155–59, at 157. Cf. Hegel's objection to the "superfluity" of art considered as *mere* "imitation of nature," Hegel 1975, 42 (but with chapter 12, note 46); see Halliwell 1993b, 6–8, for application (and qualification) of this point.

[62] Johnson, preface to Shakespeare (1765), in Johnson 1977, 299–336; the "manners and life" (301) reflected in Shakespeare's mirror are a matter of the "general nature" referred to just a little earlier by Johnson (ibid.) and surely echo the famous mirror simile at *Hamlet* 3.2.16–20. Cf. chapter 12, section I.

[63] See Richter 1970, 1:320–21 (nos. 529–30: the use of a mirror to test a painting's qualities), 1:306 (no. 493: the painter's mind like a mirror; cf. 1:310, no. 506).

that a mirror is a good judge of a painting, he seems to suppose that the mirror in some way heightens both the merits and the weaknesses of a pictorial composition. Alberti regards the mirror as an instrument by which the artist can refine and adjust his habits of viewing nature: indeed, he recommends using a mirror to *correct* the appearances of things taken from nature.[64] Like Leonardo, Alberti recognizes that a mirror presents and "frames" its images in a manner that is itself quasi-pictorial, lending them a form subtly different from the natural appearances of things. It is, after all, an optical fact—though one either unknown to, or ignored by, Plato— that even a completely flat mirror does not precisely reproduce appearances as experienced directly by the eye.[65] We can infer this much, at any rate, about Alberti's mirror, that it functions within a process that leads from natural appearances to *beautiful* appearances. And we know that Alberti does not consider the latter to be coextensive with the former, because he is prepared to reproduce a negative ancient judgment on excessive realism achieved at the expense of beauty, as well as arguing more generally for the importance of naturalistic technique (in the rendering of planes, volume, and light) not for its own sake but in the service of both beauty and a morally edifying, quasi-poetic use of *(h)istoria*.[66]

In the case of Leonardo, the question can be resolved more decisively, I think. In another passage in the notebooks he writes that the painter who relies exclusively on the eye, without the use of reason, is no better than a mirror, "which *reproduces without knowledge*."[67] By insisting on a distinction between raw perception—corresponding to the mirror as passive reflector—and a deeper kind of cognitive experience in which appearances are not just registered but interpreted and comprehended, Leonardo

[64] *De pictura* 2.46 (in Alberti 1973, 82–85, with parallel Italian and Latin texts).

[65] Plato never shows any doubt that a mirror produces an exact reflection, but Plutarch *Pyth. Orac.* 404c–d is an interesting ancient acknowledgment that even mirrors—plane as well as concave or convex—make a difference to the likenesses they reflect (cf. Sextus Empiricus *Pyrr. Hyp.* 1.48–49 for an argument from mirrors to the material relativity of perception).

[66] Alberti's negative judgment on the excessive realism of Demetrius of Alopece is at *De pictura* 3.55 (Alberti 1973, 96–97, and cf. Quintilian 12.10.9 for Alberti's source); 3.55–56 (Alberti 1973, 96–97) indicates more generally the subordination of naturalistic technique, as set out especially in book 1 of the treatise, to beauty (*pulchritudo, vaghezza, bellezza*). For the importance of quasi-poetic *(h)istoria*, see esp. 2.40–42 (Alberti 1973, 68–75), 3.54 (Alberti 1973, 94–95).

[67] Richter 1970, 1:119 (no. 20): "il pittore che ritrae per pratica e gviditio d'ochio sanza ragione è come lo spechio che in sé imita tutte le a sé cotraposte cose sanza cognitione d'esse" (Richter's punctuation slightly changed). This negative use of a mirror simile is overlooked by Gilbert & Kuhn 1953, 163–64, who also give a spurious quotation from Alberti; both points are then regrettably duplicated from them by Abrams 1953, 32. See Alpers 1989, 46–48 (which I found after forming my own argument), for a subtle discussion of the tension between "simple" and "selective" mirroring in Leonardo.

ostensibly comes close to the position I earlier traced out in the arguments of *Republic* book 10. The resemblance to Plato's argument is, however, only partial, insofar as Leonardo's conception of painting as a branch of "natural philosophy" requires him, more generally, to attribute importance to what can be learned by means of the eye (which he holds to be "the window of the soul") and then transferred by the painter into the intelligible and universal forms of his art. In a larger perspective it is sufficiently obvious that the view of painting held by Leonardo practically inverts the priorities indicated in the *Republic*, since his beliefs endow the phenomenal world, the world of appearances, with a significance that contradicts the values conveyed by Plato's argument. In Leonardo's writings the phenomenal world is an integral part of divine creation, whereas in the tenth book of the *Republic* Socrates ascribes to (a) "god" (597b6–7, whatever the rhetorical force of the term in this context) the creation not of the material world but of the "forms" or "ideas" that in some sense lie behind or beyond it.

This more general contrast, however, is secondary to my main contention, which is that even for Leonardo, whose naturalistic aesthetic and whose mimeticist presuppositions are beyond doubt, the notion of painting as a mirror is not after all unconditional.[68] Leonardo's observation that a mirror produces images without knowledge is, from the point of view of aesthetics, tantamount to affirming that however seductive may be the goal of artistic realism—the goal of fidelity to the appearances of nature—pictorial images must be something more than the images of a surrogate mirror. They need to be informed by, and correspondingly able to offer the mind of the viewer, ways of seeing that do not simply "register" appearances but interpret and make sense of them. Only in this way, Leonardo intimates, can observed phenomena be turned into the material of that "natural philosophy" which he believes to be the essence of painting; only thus can sight be turned into insight. Just as it is necessary for the soul to observe actively and attentively through the window of the eye, in order to grasp the truths discoverable and discernible in nature, so the painter's work ought to show us something that requires rational contemplation for its complete appreciation. We may doubt whether a Renaissance aesthetic of this kind would have convinced Plato of the capacity of painting to incorporate and communicate knowledge, just as, equally, we may suspect that the Platonic critique of the visual arts rests ultimately on too radical a renunciation of sensory perception. But if I am right, this is nonetheless an aesthetic that in its own way confronts the urgent issues raised by the simile of the mirror, and by its context of argument, in the last book of the *Republic*.

[68] On Leonardo's mimetic conception of painting, cf. chapter 12, notes 7, 15.

Plato's mirror has not been, and certainly does not deserve to be considered as, quite so oppressive a specter as Gombrich's statement might suggest, at any rate if we judge it in the light of the views of exponents of mimeticism as eminent and subtle as Leonardo and Samuel Johnson. For thinkers of such acumen, the symbol of the artistic mirror was always to some degree ambiguous, always an encouragement to ponder more deeply on the relationship of painting or literature to reality, rather than a naive formula for the aspiration to artistic verisimilitude. If this is true, it confirms that the traditions of mimeticism have always been capable of a self-critical attitude toward their own central doctrines. But that in turn prompts my final thought, that the Platonic analysis of painting, as I have interpreted it in this chapter, poses a permanently stimulating challenge, not only to philosophers but to all lovers of painting, to produce an aesthetic of the visual arts that can address questions of meaning and value without reducing them to the unprofitable terms of simulation or illusion.

PART II

Chapter Five

✻

Inside and Outside the Work of Art: Aristotelian Mimesis Reevaluated

Après tant de recherches inutiles, et n'osant entrer seul dans
une matière qui, vue de près, paraissait si obscure, je m'avisai
d'ouvrir Aristote. (Batteux)[1]

THE UNDERSTANDING of Aristotelian mimesis has suffered almost as much at
the hands of its ostensible friends as at those of its avowed opponents.
While the philosopher's concept of mimesis has played a vital role in the
long story of Western attitudes to artistic representation, that role has often
been mediated through the reworking and misinterpretation of his ideas,
especially those found in the *Poetics*. The critical balance of the treatise
has been prejudicially weighted down, at different times, either on the
side of a doctrinal didacticism or, equally distortingly, on that of a formalist
creed of pure artistic autonomy. Similarly, its compressed and intricate
arguments have too often been reduced to the neoclassical slogan of "the
imitation of nature," a phrase that, contrary to an alarmingly common misapprehension, is nowhere to be found in the *Poetics* or in any other Aristotelian discussion of poetry.[2] Partly in reaction against its earlier canonization, the *Poetics* has more recently been made to bear the brunt of modern
objections to naturalistic conceptions in both the theory and practice of
art; it has received, in certain quarters, the treatment appropriate for a
fallen idol. Against the background of a history of such shifting fortunes,
I propose in this chapter to undertake a fresh evaluation of some aspects
of the concept of mimesis in Aristotle's own writings but, at the same time,
to address some of the ways in which his views have become entangled
with a larger, more amorphous mass of ancient and neoclassical variants
of mimeticism. My primary aim will be to vindicate the critical integrity
and finesse of what, notwithstanding Plato, has proved the most influential
and most adaptable of all conceptions of mimetic art.

---

[1] "After so much fruitless inquiry, and not daring to undertake on my own a subject that
looked, on close inspection, so obscure, I decided to open Aristotle . . .": Batteux 1989, 74
(= préface).

[2] Egregious instances of this error are Boal 1979, 1 ("this statement [that art imitates nature]
. . . can be found in any modern version of the *Poetics*"), Clements 1963, 146 (the *Poetics*'
"famous prescription [*sic*] about art imitating nature"). Cf. note 6 and chapter 12 note 55.

Two basic but indispensable requirements for a better appreciation of Aristotle's perspective on mimesis, each of which will be clarified by subsequent parts of my argument, deserve immediate foregrounding. The first is to grasp the inadequacy of the still prevalent translation of mimesis as "imitation," a translation inherited from a period of neoclassicism in which its force had different connotations from those now available. As I stressed in my introduction, the semantic field of "imitation" in modern English (and of its equivalents in other languages) has become too narrow and predominantly pejorative—typically implying a limited aim of copying, superficial replication, or counterfeiting—to do justice to the sophisticated thinking of Aristotle, even if the extent of Latinization in the traditions of mimeticism means that we sometimes cannot avoid speaking of "imitation" in specific historical contexts. The second requirement is to recognize that we are not dealing here with a wholly unified concept, still less with a term that possesses a "single, literal meaning,"[3] but rather with a rich locus of aesthetic issues relating to the status, significance, and effects of several types of artistic representation. Given the range and subtlety of approaches (psychological, ethical, political, metaphysical) that Plato had taken to mimesis, as already explored in part I of this book, we might well expect to find some complexity in Aristotle's thinking on this subject. This chapter will argue that such expectations are indeed borne out by the evidence. At the center of my case will be the claim that the importance of Aristotle's understanding of mimesis rests on its "dual-aspect" function as a way of holding together the "worldlike" properties of artistic representation—its depiction, as he puts it (*Poetics* 9.1451a37), of things which *could* be the case—with its production of objects that possess a distinctive, though not wholly autonomous, rationale of their own.

Aristotle introduces the mimesis word group in a variety of contexts, but my virtually exclusive interest is in its attachment to a set of artistic activities—above all, poetry, painting, sculpture, music, and dance. This is, in fact, the predominant sense of the mimesis family in Aristotle, as illustrated by *Poetics* 1.1447a13–28, which mentions various kinds of music, visual art, vocal mimesis (the actor's impersonation), dance, as well as poetry, and by *Rhetoric* 1.11, 1371b4–10, which cites figurative art and poetry together as specimens of mimesis. The wider application of mimesis terms to nonartistic forms of human or animal behavior, or sometimes to inanimate objects, sheds little light on what mimesis means for artistic practices and products, with one major exception—the connection made by Aristotle between children's make-believe and artistic mimesis in *Poet-*

---

[3] McKeon 1957, 130.

ics chapter 4, a text that receives closer attention in my next chapter.[4] Aristotle speaks of mimesis both as a property of works and performances of art and as the product of artistic intentionality; the subject of the verb *mimeisthai* can be an individual work, a genre, an artist (the primary "maker"), or a performer (the executant) of an artwork. To call a performance or work "mimetic" is, for Aristotle, to situate it in a context of cultural practices that grow out of certain human instincts (cf. *Poetics* 4.1448b4–21) and develop into institutions that involve communication between artists or "makers" (such as poets or painters), performers (such as actors or musicians), and audiences (whether individuals or groups such as theater audiences). This means that the "intentionality" of mimetic works is not located simply in the specific designs of the particular artist but also in the shared conventions, traditions, and possibilities of a culture. The mimetic status of certain art objects is a matter of their having a significant content that can and, if their mimetic status is to be effectively realized, must be recognized and understood by their audiences.

This last point makes it easier to see why it is so important here to insist on a distinction that has often been either blurred or even overlooked in the legacy of Aristotelian ideas. The mimetic arts are certainly counted by Aristotle as belonging to the class of *technē* (craft, artistry) as a whole, and, more particularly, as forming a subdivision of *poiēsis* (making) or productive craft. As with all other varieties of human craft, artistry, or technical activity, Aristotle regards poetry, visual art, music, and dance as possessing, at any rate in their culturally developed manifestations, highly structured procedures for the achievement of their purposes. In that sense they presumably fall, with all *technē*, under the general Aristotelian principle that human craft or artistry, in its imposition of form on matter and in its ordered pursuit of ends, "follows the pattern of nature" (*mimeitai tēn phusin*, and similar Greek locutions), or, in the usual though now quite unhelpful translation, "imitates nature."[5] But it is imperative to distinguish

---

[4] See *Poet.* 4.1448b4–9, where I take him to be thinking mainly of children's play acting (cf. *Pol.* 7.17, 1336a33–34), with chapter 6, section I. Elsewhere, Aristotle recognizes several varieties of nonartistic mimesis: e.g., causal dependence (*Meteor.* 1.9, 346b36: cyclic processes in atmospheric moisture vis-à-vis the sun's movements), visual similarity (*Hist. Anim.* 2.8, 502b9: an ape's foot and a human heel), analogy (*Hist. Anim.* 9.7, 612b18: animal and human life, cf. note 5; *Metaph.* 1.6, 988a7; *Pol.* 2.2, 1261b3), and behavioral imitation or mimicry (*Hist. Anim.* 8.12, 597b23–26 [animal]; *Nic. Eth.* 3.7, 1115b32).

[5] Aristotle's formal and teleological principle of craft's analogousness to natural principles, on which see Solmsen 1968, 1:344–54, occurs at *Phys.* 2.2, 194a21–22, 2.8, 199a15–17; *Meteor.* 4.3, 381b6; *Protrep.* frs. 13–14, 23 Düring; cf. pseudo-Aristotle *De mundo* 5.396b12, which should not (despite its inclusion in Heraclitus fr. 10 DK) be treated as Heraclitean, *contra*, e.g., Koller 1954, 58; Grassi 1962, 48–49; Warry 1962, 103 (wayward, as often); Kugiumutzakis 1998, 82–83 (without indication of the source): see, rightly, Theiler 1925, 55–56; Jaeger

this fact from the more specifically mimetic character of the group of arts classified as such by Aristotle in the first chapter of the *Poetics* and elsewhere. It was not Aristotle but parts of the ancient tradition of mimeticism as a whole, and subsequently its neoclassical inheritors, that conflated the larger formal-cum-teleological principle with the more specialized idea of a particular group of mimetic arts.[6] As already mentioned, a crucial element in Aristotle's conception of the latter category of arts is that they produce objects whose representational significance calls for recognition and understanding. But the same is not true of the "mimetic" character of the many other activities that Aristotle believes exemplify his principle that human artistry follows patterns analogous to those of nature. A painting or a poem is mimetic *qua* the bearer of an identifiable representational content, but that is not true of, for example, the doctor's healing of a patient or the builder's making of a house.

Unlike medicine or house building, then, mimetic works or performances of art render and communicate intelligible images of what it is reasonable, though not unproblematic, to term a "possible world,"[7] given Aristotle's famous remark in *Poetics* 9, when contrasting poetry with history, that the former is concerned with "things which *could* be the case and which are possible in terms of probability or necessity" (1451a37–38). The status of the world depicted in a mimetic artwork is not, however, for Aristotle, something constant, as is made clear above all by his statement in *Poetics* 25 that mimetic art (and he cites visual art here alongside poetry)

1948, 75 n. 1; Else 1958, 82. This is to be distinguished from the idea of Democritus fr. 154 DK that humans learned certain crafts (including music) by imitation or emulation of animals, an idea Aristotle may be consciously correcting at *Hist. Anim.* 9.7, 612b18–22, where he observes the many *mimēmata* (here analogies, resemblances, but *not* "imitations") that exist between animal and human life; cf. Cole 1990, 53 n. 18, with 43, 57. The Democritean point recurs in Chamaeleon fr. 24 Wehrli 1969 (*apud* Athenaeus 389F), and at, e.g., Vitruvius *Arch.* 2.1.2; cf. Diodorus Siculus 2.52.7–8. Russell 1981, 101 with n. 4, seems wrongly to run together the Aristotelian principle with the Democritean. Different again is pseudo-Hippocrates *De victu* 1.10–17: see my introduction, note 34. Posidonius fr. 284.85–99 Edelstein-Kidd (= Seneca *Epist.* 90.22–23) turns the Aristotelian principle into a matter of conscious emulation of natural processes.

[6] Cf. Butcher 1911, 116–18; but Butcher himself, 154–58, later has problems with the distinction because of his idealistic interpretation of mimesis in art (cf. note 64). Instances of the common conflation of what are two separate ideas in Aristotle occur in e.g. Schaper 1968, 61; McKeon 1957, 131; Tatarkiewicz 1970–74, 1:141–42; Bate 1961, 10; Laborderie 1978, 74; Prendergast 1986, 41–42, 216; and Gernez 1997, XVI n. 17. Sörbom 1966, 179–80, has a firm statement of the distinction; cf. my chapter 10, and chapter 12, sections I–II.

[7] Palmer 1992, 27–34, gives a critique of the application to fiction of the notion of "possible worlds" as used in metaphysics from Leibniz onward; cf. Pavel 1975 for a technical treatment. To speak of "possible worlds" as the object of Aristotelian mimesis requires only a marginal qualification for Aristotle's partial allowance of "the impossible" (*Poet.* 24.1460a26–27, 25.1461b9–13). Cf. my Introduction, note 52.

can make any of three things the object of its mimesis: "the sorts of things that were or are the case, the sorts of things people say and think to be the case, or the sorts of things that should be the case."[8] Thus the relationship between the world within the work and the world of the artist or audience is variable and potentially complex; and its variations span a spectrum that runs from the true to the fictional, from the close reflection of known reality to the representation of the purely imaginary. But if anything is to meet the Aristotelian conditions for mimetic art, it must be possible, on the basis of what is recognized and understood in the work or performance, to predicate certain properties of the agents and objects in a hypothetical yet coherent world. In technical terms, all mimetic art is "internally" or necessarily relational (vis-à-vis a supposed state of affairs in the world); but the actual relation to reality is in each case "external" or contingently determined. While Aristotle in this way accommodates a more flexible, liberal set of artistic options than Plato often seems happy to contemplate, there is no doubt that he nonetheless maintains a position that makes it always appropriate to discuss the contents of a mimetic work in terms of configurations of essentially believable human experience, and, in that sense, a "possible world."

Aristotle, like Plato, is generally content to use what had become the traditional Greek language of "likeness(es)" in talking about mimetic art.[9] At *Politics* 8.5, 1340a, he claims that melodies and rhythms contain "likenesses" (*homoiōmata*, 18) of qualities of character (*ēthē*), and soon afterward that they are mimetic (that they contain *mimēmata*, 39) of these qualities. The two terms are here clearly synonymous, and this is confirmed by the use of "likenesses" (*ta homoia*, 23), in the same passage, as a compendious description of mimetic artifacts.[10] The primary concern with

---

[8] *Poet.* 24.1460b10–11. Since Aristotle says the poet or painter must depict one of these three things "at any one time" (*aei*), he allows for combinations of or shifts between the three within individual works. Marshall 1981 (a piece disfigured by badly misprinted Greek) rightly stresses that Aristotelian mimesis does not depend on a relationship to an existing object or to a "single level of 'fact.'" It is as wrong to find a straightforwardly realistic concept of mimesis in Aristotle (e.g., Freeland 1992, 111–12: "plot directly mirrors reality") as it is to ascribe some kind of aesthetic idealism to him (see note 64).

[9] For traditional designations of artistic representation as "like the truth" *vel sim.*, see my introduction, note 48; Aristotle uses "like the truth" as a gloss for *endoxa*, reputable or probable general opinions, at *Rhet.* 1.1, 1355a14–18; cf. Plato's use of the same idea for a plausible approximation, but with a religiously and ethically prescriptive twist, at *Rep.* 2.382d2–3 (with 377e1–3). On "likeness" and mimesis in Plato, see chapter 1, sections I and III. The suggestion of Barnes 1995, 274, that Plato and Aristotle may have "inferred" that poetry involved "likenesses" from their observation that pictures did so, is historically as well as conceptually untenable.

[10] Note, however, that Aristotle sometimes uses the adjective *homoios* (like) to pick out particular features of mimetic works: this is most obviously true in the *Poetics*, at, e.g., 2.1448a6 and 12, 15.1454b10 (all referring to poetic characters), where his exact meaning is

music in this passage (shortly to be examined in more detail) also reinforces the fact that for Aristotle, as for other Greeks, the language of "like-
ness(es)" could be applied to much more than the visual media of painting
and sculpture. The force of the terminology of "like(ness)" in Aristotle's
vocabulary has a logical basis: likeness is a matter of similar qualities or
attributes,[11] and as such can subsist in diverse modalities of experience.
Because all the mimetic arts employ perceptible media (of sound, rhythm,
color, etc.), Aristotle probably takes it that artistic "likenesses" always have
a sensory dimension, most easily exemplified by figural art, for which Aristotle, like Plato, assumes a "resemblance theory" of visual depiction.[12] But
it is important to notice that Aristotle does not restrict likeness to a sensory
or perceptual match. If he did, he could not regard musical sounds and
rhythms as standing in a mimetic relationship to qualities of ethical "character" (which are themselves patently not audible phenomena), as we
have already seen that he does.[13] Indeed, a model of one-to-one sensory
matching between a mimetic representation and its object(s) would not
account for the general conception of poetry as a form of mimesis. It is
clear that Aristotle considers poetry mimetic partly in virtue of its use of
linguistic *meaning* (the medium of *logos*; e.g., *Poetics* 1.1447a22) to construct representations of possible realities.[14] So while some forms of mimesis, including (dramatic) poetry, may depend in part on the employment
of directly sensory "likeness," sensory correspondence cannot capture
anything like the whole of what Aristotle understands by mimesis.

   As I noted earlier, Aristotle sees mimetic art as embedded within a cultural matrix that connects the makers, performers, and audiences of mimetic works. Mimetic likenesses entail an intentionality that is ultimately
natural in origin but becomes embodied in culturally evolved and institutionalized forms. This is one reason why not all likenesses are mimetic:
not all likeness has the intentional grounding that is a necessary condition
of artistic mimesis. Aristotle touches on this last point at *Metaphysics* 1.9,

---

open to dispute but it is nonetheless clear that he intends something narrower than he does
when referring to mimesis in general in terms of likeness at *Pol.* 1340a23.

   [11] See, e.g., *Cat.* 8.11a15–18.

   [12] On resemblance theories, cf. chapter 8, note 22.

   [13] See chapter 8, section II, for a fuller statement of this point.

   [14] It is therefore tempting to classify poetic mimesis, in Aristotelian terms, as a kind of
"signification" (*sēmainein*), but Aristotle himself never appears to make this connection explicitly: the only passage, so far as I am aware, where he links likeness and signification is
Topics 6.2, 140a8–10, referring to metaphor (cf. note 55). Aristotle does not consider language
per se as mimetic: *Rhet.* 3.1, 1404a20–21, should probably be construed as making not this
larger claim but the narrower claim that *poets use* language for mimetic purposes (the whole
context requires a point specifically about poetry); Janko 1987, 136 compounds confusion
by linking this passage to his misleading statement that in metaphor one name "represents"
another (cf. his 220).

991a23–26, in the course of criticizing (as "empty talk and poetic meta-phor") a quasi-Platonic account of metaphysical forms as "paradigms" in which sensible particulars "participate." Aristotle rejects the existence of metaphysical forms that material things can be said to resemble (to be "like"), and he observes that anything can be like anything else without being deliberately rendered like it or "made in its image" (*eikazomenon*). Although Aristotle's concerns are here logical and ontological, what he says about likeness and causal relationships has implications for his use of the concept of likeness elsewhere, and corroborates that intentionality, embodied in culturally developed practices, underwrites the significance that mimetic works carry for both their makers and their audiences.

The verb *eikazein* used in this passage of the *Metaphysics* is associated especially with painting and sculpture, the prime producers of "images" (*eikones*), and the connection between mimesis and images has further pertinence to my argument. At *Topics* 6.2, 140a14–15, in a context referring to both metaphorical and literal images, Aristotle states that an image (*eikōn*) is that which is produced by means of mimesis, that is, by inten-tional likeness making. Pictorial and sculpted images provide not only instances of visual mimesis but a basic Aristotelian reference point for the conceptualization of artistic mimesis as a whole. We can see this, for in-stance, at *Poetics* 25.1460b8–9, where Aristotle readily illustrates a point of generic relevance to mimesis by mentioning painting and other forms of "image making." Further passages of the *Poetics* confirm the paradigmatic status of the visual arts as examples of mimesis: the treatise contains in total eight references to these arts, and in every case a positive comparison is involved.[15] Mimetically rendered "likeness" is, then, typified by the case of visual depiction, though Aristotle is just as clear in the case of pictorial and plastic as in that of poetic art that mimesis need not involve a relation-ship to identifiable particulars and, in that respect, need not have a strictly referential function.[16]

It is perhaps tempting, therefore, to suppose that Aristotle might also have been prepared to extend to painting and sculpture the famous (though problematic) point he makes in *Poetics* 9 about poetry's tendency to "speak" (*legein*) of universals, though we do not find an acknowledg-

[15] The eight passages are: 1.1447a18–20; 2.1448a5–6; 4.1448b10–19; 6.1450a26–29, 1450a39–50b3; 15.1454b9–11; 25.1460b8–9, 1461b12–13; cf. also the reference to scene painting at 4.1449a18. I cite some other Aristotelian references to visual art in chapter 4, notes 16, 19.

[16] It is precisely the variable range of the "objects" of both visual and poetic art that prompts Aristotle's broadest comparison between them, at *Poet.* 25.1460b8–11. Note also that in his references to figural art Aristotle uses the noun *eikōn* (image) in two senses, roughly equivalent to the contrast between portraiture (involving a relation to an actual par-ticular) and depiction more generally: see chapter 6, with n. 20 there.

ment of this anywhere in the writings.[17] In any case, I suggest that the appeal of the visual model to Aristotle, in his thinking about mimesis, is that it provides arguably the most transparent illustration of his principle, enunciated most clearly at *Poetics* 4.1448b10–19, that experience of mimesis calls for and requires a process of recognition and understanding. This is not to say that the understanding of a painting or sculpture need have meant, for Aristotle, something intrinsically simpler than the understanding of a poem, only that there is a level on which, precisely because of the factor of (partial) perceptual match (a factor, I have stressed, not present in all forms of mimesis) between the "shapes and colors" of pictorial representations and the appearances of the (sorts of) objects they depict, it may be easier to specify the basic process of recognition, and therefore the salient features of the mimetic object itself, than in the case of, say, an epic or tragic poem.

But if visual art supplies an essential reference point for the concept of mimesis in Aristotle, it happens to be his comments on music in *Politics* 8.5, already mentioned, that give us some of our most valuable, if problematic, pointers to his interpretation of the concept. I discuss this text more fully from the point of view of music itself in chapter 8, but here I want to try to derive from it some more diffuse illumination of Aristotle's mimeticism. At *Politics* 1340a12–39 Aristotle follows his proposition that the tonal and rhythmical elements of music contain likenesses (*homoiōmata*) and mimetic presentations (*mimēmata*) of "character" (*ēthos, ēthē*), or perhaps "ethical feelings," with the explanatory claim that likenesses of character are strictly possible only in audible percepts, not in other sensory media— a statement that should certainly not be paraphrased as asserting that music is the "most mimetic," *tout court*, of the arts.[18] In visual media, he says, one can have signs or indices (*sēmeia*) of character, but not (or only to a slight degree—Aristotle equivocates) mimetic presentations of *ēthos*.[19]

---

[17] There are certainly Aristotelian passages that refer to idealization in visual art: see esp. *Pol.* 1.5, 1254b34–36, 3.10, 1281b10–15; *Poet.* 15.1454b9–11; cf. *Magn. Mor.* 1.19, 1190a30–32. But idealization should not be equated with the universals of *Poet.* 9.1451b4–9: see chapter 6, section II. The fact that universals can be perceived in particulars (*Post. Anal.* 2.19, 100a3–b5) ought, on Aristotle's premises, to increase the scope for universals in visual art; note too the possible ramifications of *Pol.* 8.3, 1338b1–2 (ability to draw, *graphikē*, makes one closely attentive, *theōrētikos*, to bodily beauty). See my fuller discussion of universals in chapter 6.

[18] This inaccuracy is widespread: e.g., Butcher 1911, 129; Sikes 1931, 95; Gilbert 1936, 565; Shorey 1930–35, 1:224; Ross 1949, 278; Kaufmann 1969, 42; Rudowski 1971, 81. Ong 1958, 173, calls the idea "a commonplace" and supplies it with a wholly specious explanation. Cf. chapter 8, section II.

[19] For the contrast of "likenesses" and "signs," cf. *De interp.* 1.16a3–8, where the former applies to the relationship between mental experiences and things in the world, while signs

A painter may depict bodily indications or correlatives of "character" but this, Aristotle maintains, does not fully meet the criteria of mimesis. So it emerges from *Politics* 8.5 that mimetic works may contain signs but are not mimetic in virtue of such signs. Not everything in a mimetic work need itself be mimetic, a point perhaps also implied by the remark at *Poetics* 1.1447a16 that various forms of poetry and music are, "taken as a whole" (*to sunholon*), mimetic.

The distinction between mimesis and *sēmeia* provides a clue to the nature of the former. In Aristotle, a sign is related to that of which it is (taken to be) a sign by providing a reason for an inference, either probable or necessary, about that to which it points. Externally perceptible states of the body may be signs of emotional and ethical qualities, as the passage from *Politics* 8.5 observes and as Aristotle discusses in more detail elsewhere.[20] Because the relationship between a sign and that of which it is an index may, in some cases, be natural, the difference between *sēmeia* and *mimēmata* cannot simply be that between the conventional and the natural. Mimesis must involve something more, or other, than a basis even for necessary inferences about what naturally obtains. Now, Aristotle asserts that there are likenesses of *ēthos*, here apparently designating the emotions and feelings that accompany (and are partly constitutive of) ethical character, "in" the tones and rhythms of music (*en tois rhuthmois kai tois melesin*). Musical mimesis is conceived of as an intrinsic capacity of musically organized sound to present and convey (affective) aspects of character; the patterns of music have properties "like" the emotional states that can, for that reason, be the objects of their mimesis. As evidence for this view Aristotle cites music's power to put its audiences into states of mind or feeling that contain, or are characterized by, these same emotions, so that musical mimesis seems to be a case that covers what might now be distinguished, by some philosophers, as representation and expression.[21] The experience of music appears, for Aristotle, to be a matter of experiencing emotions that are not just indicated or evoked (as they might be, on his view, in a painting) but are in some sense *enacted* by the qualities of the artwork. That these qualities are "in" the (musically organized) sounds themselves is inferred from music's capacity to convey emotional-cum-ethical feelings to the audience. Such feelings are, in part at least, a matter of movement, *kinēsis* (cf. 1340b8–10), perceived not as spatial

---

or indices constitute the relationship between spoken language and mental experience (as well as between writing and speech).

[20] See *Prior An.* 2.27, 70b7–32.

[21] For a fuller analysis of how Aristotle construes musical mimesis in this passage, see chapter 8, with note 5 there on the question of representation and expression.

change but as the experience of affective sequences or impulses, which elsewhere too Aristotle sometimes describes as "movements" of the soul.[22]

It seems legitimate to infer, then, that in this passage of *Politics* 8 Aristotle is committing himself to an interpretation of mimetic likeness as "iconic," an iconic "sign" (in Peirce's much-borrowed terminology) being one that "denotes merely by virtue of characters of its own" and involves similarity or analogy to the signified.[23] If the term is modern, the fundamental idea is not; Aristotle surely knew the explicit occurrence in Plato's *Cratylus* of the principle, exemplified by the use of color in painting, that mimetic likenesses share by nature (not convention) some of their properties with the things they signify.[24] Although there is no doubt that Aristotle regards musical mimesis as rooted in nature, I have already pointed out that reference to nature will not in itself account for the sharp distinction drawn in *Politics* 8 between mimesis and (indexical) "signs." It is in any case vital to keep in mind that the musical properties he discusses there are just that, properties of highly organized and culturally sophisticated systems of tone and rhythm, not properties of raw sound.[25] More important for the description of Aristotle's concept of mimesis in this passage as a case of "iconicity" is the fact, on which I have laid emphasis, that he considers music's capacity to embody "likenesses of character" as a matter of *intrinsic* qualities of tone and rhythm, qualities that are "in" the sounds. It is, I suggest, the intrinsic rather than the natural that is central to Aristotle's case; and the notion of the "intrinsic" can here perhaps best be explicated by the observation that if music is experienced as "containing" qualites of *ēthos* or ethical feeling, there is nothing outside the musical work (say, the composer's mind) on which this property is dependent or to which it needs to be referred for further justification.

But if Aristotle's treatment of music in *Politics* 8 qualifies as an iconic theory of mimesis, we need to supplement, enrich, and also modify this proposition by taking account of the philosopher's view that the nature of (musical) mimesis registers itself in its directness of effect upon listeners: "our souls are changed" (*metaballomen . . . tēn psuchēn*) as we listen to such music, as Aristotle puts it (1340a22–23). Now, it is no necessary part

---

[22] See, e.g., *Prior An.* 2.27, 70b11; *De mem.* 1.450b1; *Rhet.* 1.11, 1369b33; *Pol.* 8.7, 1342a8 (with chapter 8, note 24 on the last passage). If we take account of *De anima* 1.4, 408b1–33, such movements are semiphysiological. Note the "movements" of character at *Nic. Eth.* 4.14, 1128a10–12, and cf. ps.-Aristotle *Probl.* 19.29, 920a3–7 (which also uses the term *energeia* for this aspect of music: cf. chapter 6, note 37).

[23] See Peirce 1931–58, 2:156–60 (§§274–82), 5:50–52 (§§73–76); note Peirce's own association of icons with "likeness," e.g. 2:147 (§255), 2:159–60 (§§281–82). On Aristotle and iconicity, cf. Rey 1986, plus my chapter 8, note 17.

[24] See esp. *Crat.* 433d–34b, with chapter 1, section I.

[25] On the importance of this point, see further in chapter 8, section II.

of a Peircean conception of iconicity that iconic signs (as Peirce would call them) should register in this way. Yet this factor is clearly integral to Aristotle's position in this context, a position that seems to suppose that the hearer of music simultaneously recognizes the emotion "in" the music and is carried through its pattern of feeling in a response of "sympathetic" psychological engagement. The description of "sympathetic" is Aristotle's own (the hearers of musical mimesis, he says, become *sumpatheis*, at 1340a13), albeit in a passage where the text is controversial,[26] and it here fits together with the idea of emotions that are "in" the music but conveyed or transmitted to its audience, which thereby "feels *with*" the music (the literal meaning of the verb *sumpaschein*). Aristotle's musical aesthetic in *Politics* 8 does not *identify* musical mimesis with its emotive effect; in other words, it is not a sheer "arousal" theory of musical expression. But it is, as I maintain more fully in chapter 8, a theory of musical expression nonetheless, if "expression" is understood as embracing, and making a causal connection between, the perceived affective content of the musical work and the corresponding pattern of the listener's experience.

What this means, in sum, is that the *Politics'* discussion of music sets up a model of mimesis that is enactive in the double sense of positing both a representational tracing of emotion "in" the work (or performance) and, at the same time, the communication of that emotion to the audience (emotion being, for Aristotle as for Plato, in part a dynamic pattern of pleasures and pains). This model, which treats mimesis as not only a matter of the representational properties of an object, but also a form and vehicle of experience, matches the idea of "sympathy" used, for example, in Plato's critique of tragic and other poetry in *Republic* 10.[27] This is why it is so important to combine a judgment of the *Politics'* conception of mimesis as "iconic" with an awareness that it is also a concept of expression: Aristotle does not locate mimesis "in" tones and rhythms in order to set up an "objectivist" interpretation of musical representation but precisely in order to correlate the musical work or performance with the experiences of the mind that "sympathetically" receives it. Mimesis, on this reading, is constituted partly *by* the experiences that it opens up for, and induces in, its audience. To that extent the remarks on music in *Politics* 8 are a counterpart to the attitude to tragic emotion in the *Poetics*, where Aristotle indicates that the effect of pity and fear to be worked on the audience should be "embodied" in, built into, the dramatic construction itself:[28] pity and fear in the spectator (or hearer) are the emotional upshot of the recognition and understanding of the "pitiful and fearful" *in* the

---

[26] See chapter 8, with note 21.

[27] See my discussion in chapter 2.

[28] *Poet.* 14.1453b10–14 ("embody" here translates *empoiein*); cf. 19.1456b2–7.

imagined world of the drama. And in this respect—in their intertwining of representational content with the possibilities of experience made available to those who experience it—both the *Poetics* and the *Politics* are aligned with a much broader current in ancient mimeticist thinking.[29]

It needs now to be stressed that what has just been said about Aristotle's conception of musical mimesis has complex implications for his view of mimesis in general. Although Aristotle distinguishes music from painting, and mimesis from "signs" (*sēmeia*), in relation to the mimesis of *character*—though even here his position may have been less rigid than *Politics* 8.5 suggests[30]—he directly compares the mimetic standing of the two arts in other respects. The experience of emotion (forms of pleasure and pain) in response to mimetic works is, he says, close to being equivalently disposed toward "the truth" or "the real thing" (*pros tēn alētheian*, 1340a23–25). He then illustrates the point by suggesting that the pleasure taken in a human form depicted in a work of visual art entails that the equivalent physical form in a real body would give a closely similar pleasure.[31] One clear implication of this observation is that painting and sculpture are, at least in part, and as the *Cratylus* had suggested, iconic: their depiction of form involves a relationship of mimetic "likeness" (a directness of correspondence to the equivalent realities) of the same kind, on Aristotle's understanding, as arises in the case of music and *ēthos*. A painting of a man (whether or not of a real individual) represents him mimetically just insofar as it uses "colors and shapes" (cf. *Poetics* 1.1447a18–19) to put before our eyes something we can perceive, with regard both to spatial properties

---

[29] See my introduction, and cf. chapters 2, 10, and 11. The *Politics*' treatment of music need not imply that the emotions "in" the work are simply reenacted by the audience, as opposed to being "sympathetically" felt; the latter is compatible with varying degrees of critical awareness of the music's artistic structure. (Cf. once more the analogy with the sympathetic experience of mimesis in Plato *Rep.* 10, where the audience does not feel exactly the same emotions as the depicted characters: see chapter 2.) If "straight" emotional reenactment were meant, then the model of mimesis in *Pol.* 8 would entail the equivalent of the "identification" that I discussed in connection with *Rep.* 3's analysis of enactive mimesis: see chapter 2, section I.

[30] In fact, even within this very chapter, at *Pol.* 1340a37, Aristotle refers to the great painter Polygnotus as *ēthikos*, "full of character." There are also references to *ēthos* as an object of visual mimesis at *Poet.* 2.1448a5–6, 6.1450a26–29, 25.1461b12–13 (?). The likeliest explanation of this ostensible discrepancy is that in the *Politics* Aristotle makes a strict point about the inability of a visual medium to show character with any immediacy, while elsewhere he adopts a looser view that allows for character to be visually conveyed or expressed by the total "narrative" force of certain depicted actions; cf. chapter 8, section II. If this is right, Aristotle can be seen to have a complex response to a question—whether visual mimesis can depict strictly nonvisual properties—that we know to have been discussed as an artistic issue before him: see Xenophon *Mem.* 3.10, with chapter 4. On a higher level of philosophical abstraction, cf. Plato *Polit.* 285e, with chapter 4, note 36.

[31] *Pol.* 1340a25–28: for further discussion of this point, see chapter 6.

and to human significance, in ways that formally (though incompletely) match up with our perceptions of actual people. This is partly analogous to the manner in which, on Aristotle's model, music can offer its hearers affective patterns (of pleasure and pain) pertaining to *ēthos* in a form that activates their recognition, as well as eliciting their "sympathetic" experience, of related emotional feelings. If that is right, however, it follows that sameness of sense modality cannot be a requirement of the kind of "iconicity" I am ascribing to Aristotle.[32] The match between a mimetic art form and the features of the possible worlds that it represents involves, so *Politics* 8.5 suggests, a dimension of close correspondence but not necessarily at the level of the art form's physical media. In painting or sculpture, colors and shapes are used to represent the colors and shapes of imaginable objects; but in the case of music it is tones and rhythms that represent or express the emotions, feelings, or qualities of *ēthos* that are "movements of the soul."[33]

In painting as in music, then, Aristotle supposes that mimesis provides a formal equivalent of an imaginable reality, but also that it opens up the possibility of equivalence of *experience*, on the part of the audience, in relation to such reality: the "isomorphism" of artistic form is accompanied by a tight correlation of psychological, including emotional, response. Aristotle's theory places as much stress on the second as on the first of these things, and this, I suggest, is because of the more general connection he makes, as explained at *Poetics* 4.1448b4–19, between mimesis and the human need to understand the world.[34] Aristotle was, of course, aware that the aspects and elements of reality capable of being represented and/or expressed mimetically depend on the individual resources of particular arts. If music, on Aristotle's view, is much more powerful than painting (or other visual art) in its "kinetic" capacity to embody and express emotion, he knew that the reverse is true where the depiction of the material world, including human bodies and "frozen" moments of human action, is concerned. To judge by *Poetics* 1.1447a26–28, Aristotle apparently considered the art of dance to overlap with the representational fields of both visual art and music, because he says that it uses a combination of rhythm and visual forms (*schēmata*)—rhythms translated into visual form and movement—to provide mimesis of "character, emotions, and actions."[35]

---

[32] See further in chapter 8, section II.

[33] Note that Aristotle does not appear to regard musical mimesis as involving metaphorical properties, a view taken by some modern philosophers (e.g., Scruton 1997, 19–96).

[34] See chapter 6 for my interpretation of the ways in which pleasure, understanding, and emotion come together within Aristotle's theory of responses to representational art.

[35] There is an anomaly in Aristotle's classification of dance: because of its use of rhythm he seems to count it as a branch of the poetic art (unsurprisingly, if we think of its traditional association with poetry and music in the general Greek category of *mousikē*: cf. my introduc-

Of the handful of other references to dance in his work, however, there
is nothing to substantiate how much value he attributed to it. It is clear,
though, that the art to which Aristotle ascribed the richest, most wide-
ranging, and most culturally important mimetic capacities was poetry. Because the *Poetics* ensures that we have a fuller impression of his appreciation of poetry than with any other art form, it is to poetry that we must
now turn, both to test some of the claims already made about Aristotle's
conception of mimesis and to seek ways of enlarging our grasp of that
conception.

II

The evidence so far scrutinized, especially that of *Politics* 8.5, has disclosed
some intricacy within the structure of Aristotle's idea of mimesis. The *Poetics* adds further layers of complexity to this structure. I want to proceed by
setting out for reappraisal three passages of the *Poetics* in which Aristotle
advocates a firm separation between poetic mimesis and certain practices
that he believes to be sometimes confused with it.

   (a) 1.1447b13–20 affirms that mimesis is a necessary condition of poetry, but that its essential status has been obscured by the habit of classify-
ing poets according to metrical forms. (We can notice in passing that metrical form is not regarded as a sufficient basis for generic categories, though
it is subsequently accepted as one factor in the conception of genres such
as tragedy and epic: see 4.1449a21–28, 24.1459b31–60a1.) By this verse-
centered criterion Homer and Empedocles would belong together, as authors of works in hexameters; but for Aristotle they have "nothing in common *except* their meter," and Empedocles should be counted not as a poet
but as a natural scientist (*phusiologos*).

   (b) Chapter 9 offers a related distinction (which reiterates the inessential status of metrical criteria, 1451a38–51b4), this time between the poet
and the historian. Aristotle does not formulate this directly by reference to
mimesis, but rather in terms of a particulars-universals dichotomy. But he
concludes by saying: "So it is clear that the poet should be a maker of plot
structures rather than of verses, insofar as he is a poet in virtue of mimesis
and the object of his mimesis is actions" (1451b27–29, where both "poet"
and "maker" translate the one Greek term *poiētēs*). This seems to confirm
that the poet is distinguished from the historian too by the mimetic status of

tion and chapter 1), yet the reference to *schēmata* acknowledges its hybrid poeticovisual
character. For a later conception of dance within a mimeticist context, see chapter 11, note
16.

his work,[36] while perhaps also suggesting a possible connection between mimetic status and universals.

(c) 24.1460a5–11 praises Homer for speaking very little "in his own voice [or person]," unlike other epic poets; for it is not when or by speaking in this way, according to Aristotle, that the poet is a mimetic artist (*mi-mētēs*).

These three passages demarcate poetic mimesis from philosophy or science (a), history (b), and speaking in one's (the poet's) own person (c). What, between them, do they seem to tell us? The first maintains that mimesis is not concerned with conveying bodies of technical knowledge (such as natural science or medicine, 1.1447b16), though elements from such domains may of course enter "accidentally," as Aristotle would say (cf. *kata sumbebēkos*, 1460b16, 30–31), into a poem. This point is elaborated in chapter 25 of the *Poetics*, where poetry is broadly exempted from the need to meet the stringent criteria of truth that obtain within specific spheres of knowledge (1460b13–32). From the second passage, (b), we learn that there are other aspects of reality with which mimesis deals only insofar as they furnish suitable material for its own constructions. So historical events, *qua* history, fall outside its ambit, though they may provide material that poetry can nonetheless exploit—shorn, as it were, of their historicity. This contrast with history can be read, in part, as an application or extension of the previous demarcation of mimesis: history as such is excluded from poetry on at least one of the same grounds as underlie the exclusion of natural science—because of its distinct status as a discipline of inquiry. But there are two other strands to the contrast with history: one, a distinction between the actual and the (partially) invented that points toward a notion of fictionality, to which I shortly return; the other a matter of the contingency of much that is historically actual (as stressed separately at 8.1451a16–19, 23.1449a21–24), a contingency that makes it unsuitable for the unified plots on which Aristotle's theory insists.[37] The final contribution to the delimitation of poetic mimesis, in passage (c), relates, I want to argue, to the differentiation of its use of language from assertoric propositions about the world. Poetry, for Aristotle, does not consist of propositions with a determinable truth value (though such propositions may belong, again "accidentally," to poetry—for instance, when a poem contains a correct historical statement or a proposition considered true within a technical field such as medicine). But at 24.1460a5–11 he

[36] On the post-Aristotelian development of a concept of historiographical mimesis, see chapter 10, section I.

[37] For the connection between this point and "universals," see further in chapter 6, section II.

states the positive corollary of this exclusion by suggesting that the proper or ideal mode of poetry is personative or dramatic.

This triad of passages fills out our picture of what Aristotle understands by mimesis, even if the distinctions they delineate look at first sight predominantly negative in thrust. One way of turning this thrust in a positive direction is to say that Aristotle is feeling his way in these passages toward a notion of the fictional or fictive, at least in the basic sense of the "feigned" and invented,[38] and is marking off its boundaries both from particular areas of knowledge and inquiry (history, natural science, philosophy), within which specific methods and procedures would be appropriate, and from the truth-claiming character of the discourse belonging to such domains. Modern philosophical analysis of the concept of fiction has been broadly divided between, on one side, a concern with the (ontological) status of the inhabitants and contents of fictional worlds and, on the other, interest in the semantic-referential status of statements or utterances in fictional discourse.[39] Aristotle never confronts these issues directly, but his distinctions between mimesis, on the one hand, and "science," history, and declarative statements, on the other, generate a strong presumption that he is staking out a case, with both negative and positive components, for treating artistic mimesis as equivalent to fiction, if by "fiction" we here understand the modeling of a world whose status is that of an imaginary, constructed parallel to the real, spatiotemporal realm of the artist's and audience's experience: imaginary, in that it rests on a shared agreement between the maker and recipients of the mimetic work to suspend the norms of literal truth; but "parallel," in that its interpretation depends on standards of explanatory and causal coherence that are essentially derived from and grounded in real experience (hence the *Poetics*' repeated concern with "probability or necessity" in poetic plot structures). That prompts

---

[38] One example of the typical early neoclassical association of mimesis and fiction is Sir Philip Sidney's glossing of poetry as "imitation or fiction" (Duncan-Jones 1989, 216), an equation colored by the use of "fingere," "fictio," etc., in Latin for invention in both visual and verbal arts.

[39] Wolterstorff 1980, 231–34, gives an account of fiction, partly in terms of the "mood-stance" of its practitioners, that has affinities with my reading of Aristotle; Lamarque & Olsen 1994, esp. 29–52, 268–88, canvass various modern concepts of fiction. Most 1998, 382, confusingly ascribes to Aristotle the view that "the world portrayed by poetry is not a fictional world, but a recognizable version of our own real one" (a curious antithesis that would make many modern novels nonfictional), and that the possibilities mimetically presented are "real, not fictional" (but a "real" *possibility* is not incompatible with fiction). Aristotle himself consistently contrasts the mimetic with the "real" *qua* actual: see chapter 6, note 8. Petersen 1992, 27–32, finds a notion of fiction adumbrated in the *Poetics*; Yanal 1999, 15–16, offers a faulty case for his claim that Aristotle lacked a sense of fictionality. Rösler 1980 (see 308–19 on Aristotle) is the fullest account of the "emergence" of a Greek idea of fictionality, though the connection he makes with the change from an oral to a literate culture is not wholly cogent.

the further consideration, which I pursue in the next chapter, that the "universals" of *Poetics* 9 can be seen as an element in Aristotle's attempt both to demarcate poetic mimesis from factual-cum-scientific discourse and yet also to keep it connected to the ways in which human minds try to make sense of their world.[40]

If it is right that the conception of fiction adumbrated in the *Poetics* incorporates an acknowledgment that mimesis entails an exemption from the norms of truth applicable to both historical and scientific discourse, it is conspicuous in this connection that Aristotle generally eschews the noun *pseudos* (falsehood), together with its cognates, in characterizing the status of poetic mimesis.[41] A telling contrast can be made here with Plato, *Republic* books 2–3. There Plato moves some way toward giving *pseudos* and its congeners the standing of "fiction" when he declares all stories and myths to be essentially "false," *pseudeis* (376e–377a), though before proceeding to undermine the possibility of endowing this conception with much positive value by framing emphatic charges of ethical and religious "falsehood" against Homer and other poets. I suggest in chapter 1 that the position adopted in this section of the *Republic* can best be understood as involving some fluctuation between factual or historical and normative conceptions of truth, and therefore between divergent conceptions of falsehood.[42] I now suggest that it may have been precisely because of the ambiguities associated in Plato with the idea of poetic *pseudos* that Aristotle avoids the term in this connection, and instead allows something like a notion of fiction to emerge implicitly from an accumulation of observations that draw attention to the distinguishing characteristics, both positively and negatively defined, of poetic mimesis.

One such observation, already noticed in passage (c), is chapter 24's distinction between mimesis and the poet's speaking in his own voice or person. An immediate difficulty here is the apparent discrepancy between this remark, with its insistence that even the epic poet should properly be a "dramatist,"[43] and the earlier categorization of modes of mimesis in chapter 3 (1448a19–28), where the mode that presents agents in action (a model I shall call, interchangeably, the enactive, impersonatory, or dramatic

---

[40] See chapter 6, section II.

[41] The only ostensible exception is *Poet.* 24.1460a18–26, where he commends Homer for teaching other poets how to "tell lies" (*pseudē legein*, 19) in the way that poets should. But while the similar phrase at Hesiod *Theog.* 27 (cf. my introduction, note 48) might have been at the back of his mind, Aristotle does not seem to want the term *pseudē* (falsehoods or lies) to carry in itself an idea of "fiction" here, as we see from the repeated use of the noun *pseudos* in the same passage for logically fallacious inferences.

[42] See chapter 1, section II.

[43] Cf. the praise of Homer's "dramatic" (*dramatikos*) qualities at 4.1448b35–38, with 23.1459a18–19.

mode) is given no preference over third-person narrative, and where indeed Homeric technique is classified as a mixture of narrative and direct speech.[44] In chapter 24 Aristotle is clearly pressing a more stringent requirement for epic mimesis than elsewhere and doing so in order to emphasize Homer's superiority over other epic poets. Why, even so, should the "dramatic" be considered not only preferable to the narrative mode but also in some sense more mimetic? The point appears to be that direct speech, the enactive or impersonatory mode, more directly exhibits the imagined actions and events of the poem: the dramatic mode by definition employs speech to represent speech. On the other hand, Aristotle does not generally characterize poetry as the mimesis of speech but the mimesis of *action* (esp. 6.1450a16–17). Why, then, should the narrative mode of poetry be any less mimetic than the enactive?

At this juncture we should recall that an Aristotelian definition of human "action" has a strongly intentional cast: an action of the kind poetry is concerned with cannot be encompassed by a purely physical description, but must make reference to the reasons, desires, and choices of the agent. Now, poetic narrative must certainly be able to describe such action, though Aristotle may suppose that it is intrinsically less capable of "vividness" (*enargeia*) a quality he associates with bringing things "before the [mind's] eyes," or what might be called imaginative eyewitnessing.[45] More fundamentally, we have already seen in *Politics* 8.5 that Aristotle strongly inclines to an enactive conception of mimesis, and such a conception in *Poetics* 24 leads him to accentuate the need for poetry to exhibit rather than describe the world of human action.[46] This normatively expressed

[44] Rabel 1997, 8–21, revives the view that in ch. 24 Aristotle is not simply separating the dramatic mode from all first-person utterances by the poet, but making a distinction between passages such as proems, where the poet speaks specifically *in propria persona* (as it might seem), and passages of strict narrative, i.e., the recounting of events; cf. also Leigh 1997, 35 n. 52, and, more loosely, Gallop 1999, 83–84. This interesting interpretation still seems to me vulnerable to the criticism I made in Halliwell 1986, 126 n. 31. It might be worth adding that the basic distinction between the dramatic and narrative modes, yielding a tripartite scheme when the "mixed" mode is added to it (Plato *Rep.* 3.394b–c, with my chapter 2), remained standard in antiquity (see, e.g., Longinus *Subl.* 9.13, with chapter 10, note 41; chapter 11, note 30; and Haslam 1972, 20–21, for further references), so that modern narratological interest in differences of voice, technique, and point of view *within* third-person narrative has hardly any antecedents in ancient theory or criticism.

[45] See esp. *Poet.* 17.1455a22–26, *Rhet.* 2.8, 1386a28–b8, with Halliwell 2002; on the "as if present" motif in the first of these passages, see my introduction, note 48, with chapter 10, note 23, for the association of mimesis and *enargeia*.

[46] It is tempting to compare this point with the modern distinction, familiar in novel criticism since the time of Henry James, between "showing" and "telling," but recent narratology has exposed complications in the use of this contrast: see Genette 1972, 184–89 (= 1980, 162–69), and 1988, 44–46, with chapter 1, note 42, on the Platonic antecedent. Fusillo 1986

preference for the enactive mode of dramatic speech will consequently give us, for Aristotle's view of poetry, something like the factor of iconicity that we earlier saw in his remarks on musical and visual mimesis in the *Politics*. But here just as in that other context, Aristotle's conception of poetic mimesis makes the latter "iconic" only in a complex sense. The iconicity of the enactive or impersonatory mode need not involve a *perceptual* match between representational media and its objects; such a match will obtain only in full physical performance, which is not part of the definition of the dramatic mode as such and which Aristotle, notoriously, does not even make a requirement for drama proper.[47] The enactive mode is iconic, then, in the broadly Peircean construal I have brought to bear on Aristotle's position, not because it uses physical action to represent physical action (which it strictly speaking does not), or even because it uses speech to represent speech (which is true, but only a partial account of Aristotle's own conception of poetic mimesis), but because it uses represented speech to give a powerfully immediate and cognitively rich sense of imagined human "action(s) and life" (*Poetics* 6.1450a16–17). Finally, as I emphasized in my interpretation of the Aristotelian treatment of music in *Politics* 8, the power of this immediacy is both reflected in, and partly constituted by, the directness of recognition and response that it makes possible on the part of viewer or hearer.

What matters most, however, is not the strict question of whether Aristotle's view of poetic mimesis, or rather his view in chapter 24 (and not in chapter 3), can aptly be called "iconic"; that will doubtless hinge on just how tightly one construes the notion and the conditions of iconicity. More important is the clue to his larger interpretation of mimesis provided by the statement about epic at 24.1460a5–11. Here it is worth noticing what Lessing made of this passage in a letter to Nicolai of 26 May 1769, written against the background both of reactions to his own *Laokoon*, published three years earlier, and of a broader eighteenth-century interest in the distinction between natural and arbitrary signs. This distinction had already been treated by Lessing in his exploration of the representational capacities of poetry and painting within the mimeticist aesthetic of *Laokoon*, where we encounter the principle that "the signs [used in art] must have a close fit to that which is signified" (die Zeichen ein bequemes Verhältnis zu dem Bezeichneten haben müssen).[48] In the letter to Nicolai he returns

---

and Belfiore 2000b offer different perspectives on the relationship between Aristotelian *muthos* and narratological criticism.

[47] See, however, G. Scott 1999 for the argument that Aristotle does make performance an essential condition of tragedy. I have attempted a further reconsideration of Aristotle's much maligned attitude to theatrical performance of drama in Halliwell 2002.

[48] *Laokoon* §16 (Lessing 1970–79, 6:102–3).

to the question, producing a complex and slightly cryptic typology of both arbitrary and natural signs in painting and poetry. But whereas in *Laokoon* narrative had been accepted as a "natural" mode of poetic signification (and "imitation"), because of its (supposedly) sequential correlation with the actions it successively recounts, Lessing now turns to the Aristotelian precedent in the *Poetics* to support a new insistence that natural signification in poetry requires the dramatic mode. He cites both Aristotle's preference for dramatic over epic poetry and his characterization of the virtues of epic at its best as likewise dramatic. "The reason [Aristotle] gives for this," says Lessing, "is admittedly not mine; but it can be reduced to mine, and it is only by reducing it to mine that it can be safeguarded against false application."[49] In fact, on my view, Aristotle's reasons did anticipate the considerations that motivate Lessing here, insofar as both thinkers were concerned with the capacity of art forms, and more particularly their specific media and modes, to evoke aspects of imagined reality with a strong, quasi-enactive immediacy. In that sense, both were interested in what they saw as the ideally "iconic" character of mimesis. But as I explained earlier in discussing *Politics* 8.5, Aristotle does not straightforwardly tie his iconic model of mimesis to a concept of nature, and there is nothing in the *Poetics* to suggest that he would have regarded the dramatic mode of poetry as in any way more "natural" than narrative. To that extent, Lessing was wrong, I think, in claiming that Aristotle's view could be "reduced" to his own.

But the implications of Aristotle's normative remarks on mimesis at 24.1460a5–11 extend beyond an interest, partially shared with Lessing, in the directness or iconicity of representational modes. In asserting that the poet should say as little as possible in his own person, for that is not what makes him a mimetic artist (or, therefore, a poet), Aristotle indicates that he has reasons for wanting to exclude the poet's "own voice" from poetry.[50] As I have already suggested, this point needs to be bracketed with the distinction between mimesis and science in *Poetics* chapter 1, as well as with the distinction between poetry and history in chapter 9.[51] In the final analysis, chapter 24's preference for the dramatic over the narrative mode is a reflex of Aristotle's larger aim of demarcating off poetic mimesis, and thereby disengaging it, from kinds of discourse, including both "sci-

---

[49] Letter to Nicolai, 26 May 1769: text in Rudowski 1971, 93–96, whose monograph attempts a full contextualization; English translation in Nisbet 1985, 133–34. On the larger cultural context, see Wellbery 1984, 191–227.

[50] This may be a factor in the *Poetics*' general neglect of lyric poetry (outside drama), on which see Halliwell 1986, 276–85; cf. Johnson 1982, 80–83, for a rather different explanation (which the author himself obligingly calls "sheer fiction").

[51] In Greek, the formulation *ou gar esti kata tauta mimētēs* (24.1460a7–8), "it is not in virtue of this [i.e., speaking in his own person] that he is a mimetic artist," verbally echoes parts of those earlier chapters (see 1.1447b14–15, 9.1451b28–29).

ence" and history, to which it could easily be, and sometimes had been, assimilated in Greek culture. Within Aristotle's conceptual framework, the enactive mode recommends itself not only for its dramatic qualities as such but also because it supposedly erases the poet's own voice from the interior, from the world, of the poem, thus making it easier to say, against Plato and with Sir Philip Sidney, "the poet . . nothing affirms, and therefore never lieth."[52] While there remains, on my reading, an ineliminable discrepancy between chapters 3 and 24 of the *Poetics*, it is important to recognize that the tension manifested here does not disturb the argument of the *Poetics* as a whole, partly because it does not arise at all in the analysis of tragic drama, and partly because, when it does arise in connection with epic, it is smoothed over, in effect marginalized, by Aristotle's unequivocal and consistently signaled admiration for Homer the epic "dramatist."[53]

III

One of the most striking consequences of the Aristotelian perspective on mimesis is the distance it places between itself and the element of "transparency" that, as Alexander Nehamas has argued, Plato sometimes attributes to mimesis.[54] Although, as I maintained in earlier chapters, there is more than one attitude toward mimesis to be found in Plato's writings, prominent among them is anxiety over the danger of mimesis as a producer of morally and psychologically deceptive simulacra or pseudorealities. A partial, though also, as I argued in chapter 4, a problematic symbol of this anxiety is the mirror of *Republic* 10. But the idea of the mirrorlike status of (some) mimesis was probably not invented by Plato himself. We know that the sophist Alcidamas, probably earlier in the fourth century than the composition of the *Republic*, had called the *Odyssey* a "beautiful mirror of life," and we know this because Aristotle quotes the phrase as an example of frigidity of metaphor—which means, given Aristotle's read-

[52] Sidney, "Defence of Poesy" (Duncan-Jones 1989, 235). Note, however, that the use of the dramatic mode does not in itself protect poetry from Platonic criticism: for Plato's special concerns over this mode, see chapter 2, with Halliwell 2000a on the anticontextualist Platonic tendency to hear the poet's voice, to hear the poet speaking (*legein*), often *regardless* of poetic mode.

[53] Because, moreover, the criterion of "mode" is not the only means for distinguishing poetic mimesis from other kinds of discourse, Aristotle's remark about epic poets other than Homer can easily be read as a rhetorically emphatic statement of the latter's superiority over the former, rather than as a strict exclusion of other epic, or of narrative per se, from the class of mimesis.

[54] Nehamas 1988, 219; cf. chapter 2, note 43. By contrast, Woodruff 1992, who should be consulted for a number of views different from my own, argues that Aristotle's treatment of mimesis was largely independent of Plato's.

ing of metaphor as itself dependent on "likeness," that he saw no reason to take seriously the thought it expressed.[55]

The idea of mimetic mirroring dissatisfied Aristotle, and this fits with his general avoidance of a conception of mimesis as a counterfeiting of the real. At first sight, it might seem that the notion of iconicity I have employed in this chapter is Aristotle's own way of emphasizing the closeness of mimetic contact with reality. Yet the *Poetics* enables us to say with confidence that Aristotle's view of mimesis, even where it requires a kind of iconicity, involves combined and balanced consideration of the media as well as the "objects" of mimesis. In the place of the "transparency" that Plato had sometimes identified with mimesis (or, as I would prefer to say, had criticized as a putative justification of mimesis), I want to argue that Aristotle developed a theoretical approach that acknowledges two complementary aspects of mimetic representation: its status as created artifact, as the product of an artistic shaping of artistic materials, as well as its capacity to signify and "enact" the patterns of supposed realities. Plato was not simply blind to the first of these dimensions of mimesis, but he heavily subordinated it to his sense of the dangerous power of mimesis to draw the mind into, and mold it in the image of, its simulated visions of the world. But for Aristotle it is an aesthetic axiom that mimesis constitutes the materially embodied and internally organized identity of certain art forms at the same time as it designates the "outward-facing," representational significance of their contents. He accepts the need for ways of talking about works of art—methods, vocabularies, and standards of criticism—that keep the artifact and its meanings, the "materials" and the "object" of mimesis, *conjointly* in focus.[56] The resulting position can aptly be described as a dual-aspect mimeticism.

The contrast between Plato and Aristotle is not, therefore, a simple antithesis between conceptions of sheer artistic heteronomy and autonomy. Aristotle does not react to the absolutist tendencies of Platonic aesthetics by defining a realm of pure artistic self-sufficiency. That is precisely because he retains, and indeed builds his case on, a reinterpreted mimeticism. Among the major features of the *Poetics* that display this dual-aspect mimeticism is the explication of formal unity as a property inseparable from the substance, scale, and internal relations of a poem (form inheres in the poet's organization of his materials) and yet also an aspect of the

[55] *Rhet.* 3.3, 1406b4–14; cf. chapter 4, note 42. For metaphor and likeness cf. *Poet.* 22.1459a8, *Top.* 6.2, 140a8–10.

[56] Symptomatic of this feature of Aristotle's thinking is the use of the verb *suntheōrein*, "to contemplate [artistry] at the same time [as mimetic content]," at *Part. Anim.* 1.5, 645a12–13: see chapter 6, note 14. For a modern analogue, compare the twofold perception (of medium and of representation) associated with the idea of "seeing-in" in Wollheim 1980, 212–14.

imagined human action of the work.[57] Another, to be analyzed in detail in the next chapter, is the manner in which the notion of aesthetic pleasure (pleasure in mimetic art) both embraces and qualifies an understanding of possible responses, including emotional responses, to equivalent realities outside the work of art, so that the common Platonic premise of uniform correlation between responses to life and responses to art is modified yet not simply discarded by Aristotle. But I would like, in conclusion, to trace some other respects in which the argument of the *Poetics* constructs a dual perspective on poetic artworks by figuring them both as material constructions and as representations of imagined human actions.

In his analysis of the six "parts" of tragedy that forms the basis for his entire examination of the genre, Aristotle states his key tenets that a play's plot structure (*muthos*) is "the mimesis of the action," while characterization is "that in virtue of which we say that the agents have certain qualities" (6.1450a3–6).[58] These statements rest on the same principle as *Politics* 8's reflections on the mimetically expressive attributes of music, namely that there are components of an artwork that embody and convey an imagined ordering of possible realities. In a work of music one can talk of tones, rhythms, melodies, and much else besides, but one can also talk, according to Aristotle, of the emotional-cum-ethical qualities, the qualities of *ēthos*, that can be recognized "in" them and which constitute their significance in the developed forms of the musical art. Comparably, in a tragedy one has a plot structure, which is the intelligible design produced by the playwright (it is what he above all *makes*: 9.1451b27–28); and just as one can frame technical descriptions of a musical structure, so one can produce categorizations of a particular plot (that it is "simple," "complex," "double," to use some of Aristotle's own terminology), or about its specific properties (its scale, proportions, unity, dénouement, and so forth). But one can also speak of the actions and agents represented by the play, and for this one relies, according to the other half of the mimeticist premise, on the same range of concepts as are used in life outside the work of art—concepts, for example, of purpose and choice, success and failure, prosperity and suffering, good and evil, guilt and innocence. Nor, on this model, do we just speak descriptively of the work in these terms; we *experience* it through an understanding that depends on them, and we respond to it with evaluative judgments, hence with emotions, that presuppose and are informed by that understanding.[59]

---

[57] See Halliwell 1998 for a fuller exposition of this point.

[58] Silk 1994 restates the case for treating Aristotle's six parts in (partly) "processive-compositional" terms; I continue to regard them as conceptually analytical.

[59] See chapters 6 and 7 for further discussion of this psychological model of aesthetic experience.

This suggests, as Paul Ricoeur has argued, that the *Poetics*' interpretation of mimesis requires and draws on the preexisting intelligibility of action and life in the world at large: mimetic art may extend and reshape understanding, but it starts from and depends on already given possibilities and forms of meaning in its audiences' familiarity with the human world.[60] Yet that does not imply that mimetic significance duplicates or merely mimics the nature of the social world. Aristotle's terms and standards of analysis throughout the *Poetics* are irreducible either to a reading of the poetic work as a surrogate of the audience's world (a reading that had generated moralism such as Plato's), or to aesthetic absolutisms of the contrary kind (aestheticism, formalism, the semiotics of the autonomous text) that assert a self-sufficiency for the artwork's internal properties—hence what I have called Aristotle's dual-aspect mimeticism. This duality of perspective is a point of basic orientation that can be found even in some of the more schematic and unpromising passages of the treatise, for instance in chapter 15's four canons of characterization—goodness, appropriateness, likeness (i.e., here, essential humanity), and consistency. Each of these requirements presupposes a poetic contact with recognizable realities of human status, motivation, and disposition, and hence the legitimacy of critical propositions about dramatic character(ization) that invoke categories applicable to the understanding of persons in the world. Indeed, the very concepts of action and character as used in the *Poetics* assume such critical legitimacy at a foundational level. But the requirements of chapter 15 also collectively refer to the internal relationships and coherence of the artwork, so that to employ such standards in making critical judgments is not to appeal directly to matters of truth or morality, in quasi-Platonic manner, but to assess features of a constructed poetic fabric and its organization. This is even true of the stipulation of "goodness," which is not required for moralistic reasons but because Aristotle believes this to be a precondition of the kind of tragic plot patterns (conducive, above all, to the arousal of pity and fear) that are qualitatively constitutive of the genre.

It is worth developing a little further this contrast between moralistic criteria for works of art and criteria that, though requiring reference to life values for part of their application, rest on a sense of the distinctive identity and rationale of poetic genres. In chapter 4 Aristotle sketches a view of the development of poetry from its hypothetically primitive types to the highly evolved forms of tragic and comic drama in his own time. The

[60] See Ricoeur 1981, 18–20; Ricoeur 1983, 55–84 (1984, 52–87); cf. chapter 12, note 3. Note, however, that Ricoeur's "Aristotelian" view of narrativity goes far beyond Aristotle himself: in particular, by "poeticizing" social and cultural discourse in general, Ricoeur largely blurs Aristotle's distinction (*Poet.* 9) between poetry and *history*. For some discussion, see Clark 1990, 169–79.

historical basis for this reconstruction, which I believe to have been less robust than many have supposed, is not at issue here.[61] What is of interest to me is the way in which Aristotle confines to an early and long-super-seded stage in the process of cultural evolution the existence of artistic types (praise and blame poetry) that Plato had seen as paradigmatic of poetry's social and psychological functioning *in the present*. The original impulses to celebrate or denigrate in poetry and song have been, in the *Poetics*' account, absorbed and transformed into poetic genres, tragedy and comedy, in which they are no longer immediately recognizable as such. For although Aristotle suggests that comedy is a mimesis of base and inferior characters (the same types of figure who formed the targets of primitive blame poetry, it seems), he does not maintain that the dramatic genre is overtly moralizing in its treatment of them. And the equivalent point is evident in the case of tragedy, which Aristotle does not regard as celebrating or praising great men in any straightforward sense, in contrast to the Platonic inclination to see the genre as directly affirming certain values by projecting them onto the lives of supposedly admirable figures.[62]

The historical overview supplied in *Poetics* 4, then, implicitly rebuts a major premise of Plato's approach to the cultural function of poetry. It does so by reasoning in terms of the internal dynamics of Greek poetic traditions, whose character overrides and replaces the "primitive" im-pulses of praise and blame that are discerned behind the serious and comic branches of poetry.[63] Aristotle perceives a process of cultural evolution constituted by active experiment and concern with representational modes, story patterns, metrical forms, stylistic registers, and other matters of intrinsically poetic resources. In this way the relation between epic and tragedy, for example, which for Plato had been a matter of a shared (and defective) moral vision, assumes a place in an account whose terms are indefeasibly artistic. It is not that the element of "moral vision" has simply disappeared, for the treatise as a whole keeps ethical considerations cen-tral to the interpretation of poetry's treament of human action. But *Poetics* 4 indicates how the ethical has been incorporated, on Aristotle's terms of reference, into the complex historical development of poetry as a set of cultural practices and institutions.

This particular contrast with Plato can, if I am right, be traced back to the radical difference between a dominant belief in the "transparency" of

---

[61] See Cantor 1991 for an interesting analysis of *Poet.* 4 that finds Aristotle to hold a sophis-ticated model of generic development, midway between those of formalism and historicism. My own earlier discussion of the chapter is at Halliwell 1986, 92–96, 255–56.

[62] See chapter 3 for this reading of Plato's approach to tragedy.

[63] A salient feature of the medieval Arabic treatment of the *Poetics* is the attempt to reim-pose the praise-blame dichotomy onto the whole interpretation of the work: see chapter 11, section IV.

mimesis and Aristotle's dual-aspect conception of artistic representation. But to see this point more clearly still, one needs to reckon with Plato's apparent conviction that art, by purporting to show how things are in reality, implicitly endorses and reinforces the ethical burden of what it exhibits. Against this we must set Aristotle's determination, discussed in section II of this chapter, to exclude the assertoric and referential from poetry and to replace it with the fictional and the dramatic. Because mimetic images possess a humanly intelligible significance, they must, for Aristotle, remain open in certain respects to ethical understanding and judgment. But the application of this principle is made conditional on a sense that the images of poetry are constituted in artistic materials and forms that carry with them requirements and standards of value partly of their own. Aristotle argues this last position most directly in chapter 25 of the *Poetics*, where, as I earlier noted, he explicitly connects his rejection of a quasi-Platonic moralism to his understanding of the wide inventive and imaginative scope open to mimetic art. The guiding thought here is that because a poem or painting is an artifact of a particular kind, and one whose nature is fictively depictional, not declarative, it should be assessed by criteria that acknowledge and work with its internal aims and nature, including the range of choices that face mimetic artists: there is, for example, no support in this context for the claim, both neoclassical and modern (Butcher being its most prominent spokesman), that Aristotle holds an emphatically idealistic notion of mimesis.[64] We can see here, as clearly as anywhere, that in contrast to Plato's constriction of artistic freedom in the name of the supreme values of truth and goodness, the Aristotelian conception of mimesis is inherently liberal, though not for that reason automatically or necessarily preferable.[65]

[64] Butcher 1911, ch. 2, confuses the Aristotelian recognition and advocacy of idealization in particular types of mimesis—tragedy, epic, certain kinds of painting—with a conception of mimesis *tout court*; he has been followed by, e.g., Draper 1921. On Butcher's "romanticization" of the *Poetics*, cf. Kerrane 1968, 45–112, Halliwell 1987, 24–25, with my chapter 12, note 29, for neoclassical antecedents of the idealizing reading of Aristotle. The distance between Aristotle and modern idealist aesthetics is discussed by Galli 1925, esp. 346–51, 385–90.

[65] Cf. Halliwell 1991a for some further reflections on the choice between Platonic and Aristotelian paradigms in aesthetics.

Chapter Six

❀

The Rewards of Mimesis: Pleasure, Understanding, and Emotion in Aristotle's Aesthetics

> The appropriate business of poetry . . ., her privilege and her
> *duty*, is to treat of things not as they *are*, but as they *appear*,
> not as they exist in themselves, but as they *seem* to exist to the
> *senses*, and to the *passions*. (Wordsworth "Essay")[1]

> The province of art is all life, all feeling, all observation,
> all vision. (Henry James, "The Art of Fiction")

IT EMERGED in the preceding chapter that for Aristotle, just as much as for
Plato, a mature philosophical theory of artistic mimesis involves integral
consideration of the kinds of experience that mimetic artworks offer to
and invite from their audiences. The purpose of the present chapter is to
explore further this psychological dimension of Aristotle's mimeticism,
and more particularly to argue that his concept of mimesis, in the *Poetics*
and elsewhere, entails the interlocking functioning of three elements—
pleasure, understanding, and emotion—that have too often been separately discussed by students of this area of his thinking. The product of this
configuration of elements, I shall try to show, is a subtle and distinctively
Aristotelian perspective on the importance of representational arts to the
human mind and to the cultures that contain those arts. The route to be
followed here will take us to the heart of Aristotle's response to the challenge issued at the end of the critique of poetry in Plato *Republic* book 10
(607d), where Socrates appeals to the lovers and defenders of poetry to
demonstrate "the benefit, and not just the pleasure, which poetry brings
to human societies and to individual lives."

I start by examining the passage in *Poetics* 4, often wrongly regarded as
marginal or digressive, where Aristotle identifies two features of human
nature that he takes to explain the existence of poetry:

---

[1] Wordsworth, "Essay, Supplementary to the Preface" (1815), in Owen & Smyser 1974,
3:63.

Poetry in general can be seen to owe its existence to two chief causes, both of them natural. First, mimetic activity is instinctive to humans from childhood onward, and they differ from other animals by being so mimetic and by developing their earliest understanding through mimesis. [Second],[2] everybody takes pleasure in mimetic objects. A practical indication of this is that we take pleasure in contemplating the most precisely rendered images even of things whose actual sight we find painful, such as the forms of the basest animals and of corpses. The explanation for this is that understanding gives great pleasure not just to philosophers but similarly to everyone else, though their capacity for it may be limited. Hence people enjoy looking at images, because as they contemplate them they understand and reason what each element is (e.g., that this person is so-and-so).[3] Since, if one lacks prior familiarity with the subject, the artifact will not give pleasure *qua* mimetic representation but because of its craftsmanship, color, or some other such reason. (1448b4–19)

The pattern of thought here—statement, illustrative attestation, explanation, further confirmation—is highly characteristic: one close and particularly germane parallel is the opening of the *Metaphysics* (1.1, 980a21–7), where Aristotle makes his famous remark that all humans have a natural desire for knowledge. Also typical of the philosopher's mentality and method of reasoning is his conjunction of poetry with children's mimetic behavior, as well as his "ethological" contrast between humans and other animals (a comparative point, it should be stressed, since Aristotle does believe in animal mimesis).[4] By mentioning children's mimesis Aristotle means to cite not simple copying but make-believe or playacting, as the reference to young children's games at *Politics* 7.17, 1336a33–34, helps to confirm.[5] Reinforced by the comparison with other animals, this gives the

---

[2] Not all interpreters agree that this, as opposed to the instinct for melody and rhythm (1448b20–21), is the second "cause" meant by Aristotle: see Halliwell 1986, 71 and n. 35 there.

[3] "So-and-so" (*ekeinos*) is a placeholder for a particular, not a type. Moreover, Aristotle's phrase *houtos ekeinos* must refer to a person, *not* an object; it is wrong, though very common, to translate as "this is that" *vel sim.* (e.g., Golden & Hardison 1968, 7 [also turning the particular into the general, "this . . . is that kind of object"], Belfiore 1992, 46, 48; Lear 1988, 307; Sifakis 1986, 218; Nagy 1990, 44; Ferrari 1999, 186; as well as Lessing 1970–79, 6:154, *Laokoon* §24, and Croce 1950, 185), for which *tout(o) ekeino* (cf. *Rhet.* 1.11, 1371b9) would be needed: a case has sometimes been made for emending the former to the latter (see Gudeman 1934, 34, 119; Gallop 1990, 161–62, 167–68), but unnecessarily and unpersuasively in my view; cf. my note 34.

[4] See the references to bird mimicry at *Hist. Anim.* 8.12, 597b23–26; 9.1, 609b16; 9.49, 631b9.

[5] Note the preceding reference to stories, 1336a30, echoing Plato *Rep.* 2.377b–c (cf. Kraut 1997, 160); Gallop 1999, 79, overlooking *Pol.* 1336a33–34, ties *Poet.* 4.1448b7–8 to children's pictorial mimesis, which is certainly covered by Aristotle's point. Croce 1950, 184, thinking too narrowly (like Castelvetro 1978–79, 1:94–95; Warry 1962, 102) of following set examples,

context a force both anthropological and psychological. Mimesis, in its artistic but also in some of its nonartistic forms, involves modeling particular media (in the case of children, their movements and words, along with their feelings of pleasure and pain) so as to produce an object or a form of behavior that is intentionally significant of a piece of supposed or possible reality. Nothing said here erases the major differences between children's play and, say, a tragedy by Sophocles or a mural painting by Polygnotus. Yet Aristotle sees a common element between them, which he identifies as a natural human propensity toward imaginative enactment of hypothetical realities, with a concomitant pleasure in learning and understanding (the key verb *manthanein* embraces both things) from mimetic activity. The same link between learning or understanding (*manthanein*) and artistic mimesis recurs at *Rhetoric* 1.11, 1371a31–b12, as well as in the *Politics'* discussion of musical experience.[6] But before we can make progress with the implications of this important Aristotelian thesis, some other issues in this section of *Poetics* 4 need clarification.

If we can take pleasure in even detailed renderings of normally painful or unattractive subjects, it would seem that the contemplative attention— the act of *theōrein* (*Poetics* 4.1448b11, 16)—we direct to mimetic works can in some way convert, override, or at least supplement our common responses to equivalent features of reality.[7] Aristotle's point has an obvious

---

rather than imaginative make-believe in general, accuses Aristotle of confusion in linking art with childhood mimesis; but Vico, Croce's hero (ibid., 242; cf. my introduction, section II), makes exactly the same connection (Vico 1968, 75, 167, §§215–16, 498), as have a series of other thinkers: see, e.g., Burke, *Philosophical Enquiry*, pt. I §xvi (Burke 1958, 49); Schlegel 1962–74, 5:30; Dostoevsky, *The Karamazov Brothers*, bk. 10, ch. 4 (Dostoevsky 1994, 674–75); Walter Benjamin, "Über das mimetische Vermögen" (Benjamin 1972–89, 2.1:210; cf. 204–5); cf. chapter 12, note 64. The point, to which Plato *Laws* 1.643b–c is germane, remains a serious one: see Walton 1990, esp. 21–28, 209–12, for a modern philosophical adaptation, though one that barely acknowledges Aristotle (and cf. my note 7); also Harris 1998 on psychological continuities between children's and adults' responses to fiction. Modern research has established that children's imitative instincts begin very early: Meltzoff 1999 provides a summary, Nadel and Butterworth an interesting collection of essays; cf. Harris 1998, 336–39, for playing and appreciation of fiction. Freud's denial of a mimetic drive behind play, in the context of his own explanation of it in terms of emotional "abreaction," is in "Jenseits des Lustprinzips" §II (Freud 1989, 3:227; Eng. trans. in Freud 1953–66, 18:17), though he does in fact acknowledge the mimesis of play in "Der Dichter und das Phantasieren" (Freud 1989, 10:173; Eng. trans. in Freud 1953–66, 9:146); cf. my note 7.

[6] See *Pol.* 8.5, 1340a14–25, with chapter 8, notes 12, 14.

[7] It does not follow, of course, that painful emotions altogether lose this quality when experienced in aesthetic contexts; that they do remain painful is argued by Belfiore 1985a, esp. 349–50, 355–58; cf. Lear 1988, 302; Feagin 1983, 97–98 (who regards tragic pleasure as a metaresponse to a primary response of sympathy with tragic suffering). Schier 1983, 82, thinks the experience of tragedy is "not necessarily at all pleasurable" (cf. 79–81), but, not surprisingly, he equivocates on the point, and on 87 he is close to *Poetics* 4; Harding 1968, 306, challengingly contends that the pleasure of tragedy is a "pseudo-problem." Note that all

pertinence to tragedy, which affords pleasure through the dramatization of grievous human failures and sufferings. But we are for the moment concerned, as is chapter 4, with the wider application of the point. Aristotle clearly supposes that the pleasure in question depends on the perception of something *known* to be artistically mimetic: no one confuses a painting of a corpse with a real corpse.[8] So what faces us here is a view that has had many subsequent analogues, perhaps especially in the eighteenth century, when the problem raised by this passage was a recurrent topic of aesthetic discussion. Samuel Johnson, in his preface to Shakespeare, provides the concisest statement of the tenet: "The delight of tragedy proceeds from our consciousness of fiction." David Hume, in his short essay "Of Tragedy" (1757), takes over and endorses a similar point from the French critic Fontenelle, although Hume thinks this only one of a number of pleasures that convert what would otherwise be painful into pleasurable feelings. Kant too cited the capacity of art to produce beautiful descriptions even of the ugly, and his explanation of it seems to have been a variation on the function of fictional representation.[9] Several writers in this period made an exception to the principle for disgust and the disgusting. The *Poetics* too contains such an exception, but its concept of *to miaron* (the disgusting) covers only certain kinds of moral revulsion in the experience of tragedy and will therefore receive consideration in a separate context.[10]

The role of artistry in the transformation of painful into pleasurable experience is emphasized by Aristotle's reference to the detail or precision

---

the evidence suggests that Aristotle (and the ancient tradition as a whole) regards the emotions felt toward mimetic works as genuine emotions: Walton 1990, 249, despite the "mimetic" basis of his own theory of make-believe, therefore has no good reason for ascribing to Aristotle anything like his own conception of "quasi" emotions (on which cf. the criticisms of Carroll 1990, 68–79; Yanal 1999, 49–66). A Freudian version of the artistic conversion of pain to pleasure can be found in "Der Dichter und das Phantasieren" (Freud 1989, 10:172; Eng. trans. in Freud 1953–66, 9:144); cf. note 5 here.

[8] Aristotle never worries, in quasi-Platonic fashion, that a mimetic "likeness" might be mistaken for the real thing; cf. the force of such passages as *De anima* 2.1, 412b20–22; *Part. Anim.* 1.1, 640b35–41a3; *Meteor.* 4.12, 390a10–13, as well as the contrast between mimesis and "the real" (*alēthina*) at *Pol.* 3.11, 1281b12; 8.5, 1340a19, 24.

[9] Johnson, preface to Shakespeare (1765), in Johnson 1977, 312 (with my note 32); Hume, "Of Tragedy" (1757), in Hume 1993, 126–33 (at 127–28); Kant, *The Critique of Judgment* (1790), §48 (Kant 1914, 387). On Hume's psychology of weaker reinforcing stronger feelings (anticipated by Longinus *De subl.* 15.11: Hume knew this work), see Schier 1983, 74–82, 90–91. Also pertinent is the extended discussion of ugliness and disgust in art in Lessing's *Laokoon* §§24–25 (Lessing 1970–79, 6:152–65); for one modern treatment of disgust, see Pole 1983, 219–31, with Miller 1997 for a fuller perspective. Carroll 1990 argues that certain forms of disgust are central to the aesthetic of modern horror fiction.

[10] See chapter 7, note 50. Ferrari 1999, 185–86, confuses the relationship between *Poetics* 4 and 13: the former refers only to perceptually disagreeable appearances, while ch. 13's concept of "disgust" (*miaron*) is profoundly ethical; Ferrari's use of "disgust" for *both* passages (there is no common term in Aristotle's text) obscures this point.

of images at 1448b11.[11] In a related passage, *Parts of Animals* 1.5, 645a7–15, he talks of the conscious pleasure we can derive from contemplating the technical skill (*technē*), "whether pictorial or sculptural,"[12] that produces such images. But it would be wrong to infer that the pleasure envisaged in these passages is pleasure only in technical artistry (in, say, the delicacy of brushstrokes or exactness of chiseled patterns). That is actually precluded by the contrast drawn at *Poetics* 1448b17–19 between pleasure based on understanding of what is represented (and appreciation, therefore, of the work as *mimēma*) and enjoyment that is limited to features of craftsmanship or "finish" (*apergasia*, a term relating directly to artistic technique),[13] color, and texture, or other such material properties. To interpret Aristotle's position here correctly, we consequently need to distinguish between two ways in which aesthetic pleasure—pleasure taken in representational artworks—may arise in relation to artistic technique, the first, as *Poetics* 1448b11 implies ("we take pleasure in contemplating the most precisely rendered images"), being *mediated* through the artist's skilled accomplishment, the second being *restricted* to sensuous properties of the artifact.

Poetics chapter 4 presents this distinction both positively and negatively: positively, by grounding the pleasure taken in a mimetic work on a cognitive experience of the work's significance; negatively, by suggesting, as we have seen, that pleasure in workmanship, color, texture, and the like may become independent of the cognition of what is mimetically represented. In the *Parts of Animals* passage cited, it is worth noticing the use of the rare compound verb, *suntheōrein* (645a12–13), whose two other occurrences in Aristotle confirm the force of the prefix here: namely "contemplate or observe *at the same time*."[14] This verbal nuance indicates the desirability, implicit too in *Poetics* 4, of an aesthetic experience of mimetic art in which appreciation of both medium and "object," of the material

[11] The same verb, *akriboun* (to render precisely) is applied to literary art at 1450a36; cf. *Nic. Eth.* 6.7, 1141a9, with reference to visual art. On art-critical use of this terminology see Pollitt 1974, 117–26; Plato *Critias* 107c–d (cf. my chapter 1) is also germane.

[12] This phrase, and the similar reference to visual art at *Rhet.* 1.11, 1371b4–9, is one reason why Aristotle cannot be thinking of biological diagrams in the *Poetics* passage, a view taken by, e.g., Janko 1987, 74, and Gallop 1990, 161–67 (who ignores the references to art in *Part. Anim.* and *Rhet.*). A further, decisive consideration is that the logic of *Poet.* 1448b8–15 requires reference to the experience of *nonphilosophers* throughout. Contrasting approaches to the *Part. Anim.* passage are taken by Lear 1988, 308–9, and Sifakis 1986, 214–15; Heath 1996, xii, is right to say that it implies "a sophisticated observer."

[13] Many Platonic passages illustrate the technical sense of this word group: e.g., *Prot.* 312d; *Rep.* 6.504d7, 8.548d1; *Soph.* 234b7, 235e2, 236c3; *Laws* 2.656e.

[14] The other occurrences of the verb are *Prior An.* 2.21, 67a37, and *Eth. Eud.* 7.12, 1245b4–5 (referring to more than one person, but confirming the strong force of the prefix); LSJ s.v. translates correctly. Sifakis 1986, 215, treats the verb somewhat differently.

artifact and the imagined world that it represents, *coalesce* in a complex state of awareness.[15] This point, which will receive strong emphasis as my argument unfolds, corroborates the case for Aristotle's "dual-aspect" theory of mimesis that I developed in the last section of my previous chapter, and its ramifications for poetry will emerge further in the course of the present chapter. But because the visual arts too are in Aristotle's mind in the passages so far considered, it is worth registering what he implies about these arts at *De sensu* 3.440a8–9, where he refers to a painterly technique of color overlay used to render effects of haze or of objects seen under water: his description of such a case suggests that in responding to such paintings the viewer's eye might appreciate how the colors were productive and constitutive of the mimetic representation, so that pleasure in technique would accordingly mediate and merge with pleasure in the mimesis itself.[16]

It has sometimes been thought that to make full sense of Aristotle's attitude to representational art we need more than a distinction, such as the one just outlined, between material or technical properties of the artistic medium and recognizable properties of the the world depicted in the artwork.[17] A text that has been invoked in this connection is *De memoria* 1.450b20–31, where Aristotle, tackling the question whether memory experiences are of something present in the mind or of something absent, likens a recollection to a sort of internal painting and differentiates between a painted representation perceived as a figured or pictured form, *zōion*, and the same thing perceived as an *eikōn*, a term that can denote any pictorial "image" but must here mean a "portrait," that is, an image of an actual particular, as the example of a painting of "Coriscus" (a token individual) at 450b31 indicates. Aristotle is trying to illuminate the difference between a mental image "in itself" and a mental image that is the bearer of a true memory and that therefore corresponds to particulars experienced in the past.[18] His argument suggests that to contemplate a paint-

[15] Compare the views of Adam Smith, "Of the Nature of That Imitation . . .," pt. 1 (Smith 1980, 176–86), on the relationship between awareness of the object and the medium of mimetic art. Smith's position, unlike the one I ascribe to Aristotle here, tends to hold the two things rather firmly apart. *Poet.* 4.1448b17–18 is misunderstood by Lausberg 1990, 556, to imply that an "art critic" would concentrate more on color and line than on subject matter.

[16] Cf. chapter 4, notes 16, 19.

[17] See Halliwell 1992a, 243–45, for criticism of one such view, that of Belfiore 1985a, 351–55; Belfiore 1992, 48–66, modifies her position somewhat, but not, I think, in the crucial respects which I previously criticized. Sifakis 1986, 217–18, produces a wholly unwarranted distinction between *mimēma* and *eikōn* in *Poet.* 4; his quadripartite interpretative scheme contains multiple confusions, and depends (cf. 212–13) on rejecting the manuscript evidence at *Rhet.* 1.11, 1371b6 (for which the edition of Kassel 1976 is ignored).

[18] Sorabji 1972, 84, seems to me misleading when he says it is "only when we regard a picture as a copy [sic] that our attention is directed to the object depicted": Aristotle does not

ing as a *zōion* (literally "living thing," and a standard Greek term for any figural painting in its depictional status) is to recognize it as a determinate, intelligible form—that of a man, lion, house, or whatever—but not, unlike the special case of a portrait, to identify it as depicting something actual.[19] The difference between the two cases posited in *De memoria* lies not in the form of the depiction but in its referential status, that is, the relationship that the viewer understands it to have to reality.[20]

There are, then, both similarities and differences between this passage and the section of *Poetics* 4 already examined. In *De memoria* Aristotle's concern with memory means that he is interested in distinguishing between paintings regarded as figurative forms "in themselves" and, on the other hand, as figurative forms (such as portraits) that correspond to actual instances of things in the world. In *Poetics* 4 he draws the larger distinction between regarding a mimetic or figural form *as* a representation (which requires recognition and understanding of what it depicts) and regarding it nonrepresentationally, that is, only as a technical artifact. This means that in the latter passage Aristotle's reference to mimetic images must include, but is not restricted to, portraits or other depictions of actual particulars. Potential confusion in the interpretation of both passages stems from the term *eikōn* itself, which, as I have already mentioned, can refer to pictorial images in general or, more specifically, to portrait-type images.[21] *Poetics* 1448b11–12 ("images [*eikones*] . . . such as the forms of the basest animals and of corpses") shows that here the term cannot be used in its narrower sense; and although the later example ("this person is so-and-so") readily suggests the case of a portrait, it cannot be limited to portraits: the sentence as a whole, with the phrase "understand and reason what *each element* is" (16–17), must have wider applicability, including mythological figures. I shall return to this point. *Eikōn* in this passage has conse-

---

argue that we direct our attention any less "to the object depicted," if that means the object *in the picture*, when contemplating a pictured form, a *zōion*, than when recognizing such a form as a portrait (or equivalent).

[19] *zōion*: cf. e.g., *Gen. Anim.* 2.4, 740a15; *Pol.* 3.13, 1284b9; *De somn.* 2.460b12, referring to hallucinations, is interesting in this connection. The word cannot mean an abstract or purely geometrical configuration, *contra* Belfiore 1985a, 352.

[20] This is the distinction between what Budd 1995, 66–67 terms "relational" and "non-relational" paintings; in different usage, however, all mimetic images might count, on Aristotelian premises, as "relational" (cf. chapter 5, section I). On the *De memoria* passage, see now Everson 1997, 193–203.

[21] For *eikōn* as a portrait or copy of a particular, see (in addition to *De mem.* 1.450b21–451a15) *Pol.* 5.12, 1315b19; *Rhet.* 1.5, 1361a36, 2.23, 1397b29; and cf. *Poet.* 15.1454b9. For the sense "image" *tout court*, see *Poet.* 4.1448b11–15, 6.1450b3; *Top.* 6.2, 140a14–15; *Phys.* 2.3, 195b8; *Meteor.* 4.12, 390a13; *Part. Anim.* 1.5, 645a11; *Pol.* 1.5, 1254b36; and cf. *Poet.* 25.1460b9. Aristotle fr. 118.3 (Gigon 1987), = Alexander of Aphrodisias *In met.* 82.11, shows the term fluctuating between these two senses.

quently to apply to any mimetic image, whereas in *De memoria* it refers only to images of identifiable particulars, such as portraits. For Aristotle, any "image" is a case of visual mimesis and, therefore, as we saw in the preceding chapter, of representational "likeness," but only in certain instances is it possible and necessary to recognize the likeness of an image as a depiction of something that actually exists, or has existed, in the real world.[22]

To return, then, to the exposition of Aristotle's conception of the psychology of mimetic art, we are left with *Poetics* 4's basic dichotomy intact between (a) the cognitively grounded pleasure derived from recognizing the representational significance of a mimetic object, and (b) other pleasures that, though linked to experience of a mimetic work, are potentially independent of its representational character. But we are now in a position to expand an earlier observation. *Poetics* 4.1448b10–12 explains that the cognitively grounded pleasure taken in mimesis means that even the representation of painful or ugly objects can be aesthetically satisfying. *Rhetoric* 1.11, 1371a31–b12, repeats and confirms this: the pleasure in such cases depends on grasping the mediated fact of representation and is not a direct response to *what* is represented. At *Politics* 8.5, 1340a23–28, however, Aristotle states that it is sometimes the case that we take pleasure in the features of the represented reality as such: his example is the beautiful physique of a person depicted in a pictorial or sculptural image. The corollary of this, as indicated in this same passage and exemplified in complex form by the theory of tragedy in the *Poetics*, is that our response to a representation of the painful should involve emotions of the painful kind we would expect to feel toward comparable events in life. How, then, are we to combine what look as though they may be two distinct and possibly incompatible ideas: the first, that the full cognitive experience of a mimetic work encompasses, and is *modified by*, the fact that the object is not real but a product of artistic construction; the second, that responses to mimetic works are in general closely aligned with those toward equivalent realities in the world?

I suggest that far from contradicting the principles of *Poetics* 4 and *Rhetoric* 1.11, the passage from *Politics* 8.5, with its example of what might be called perceptual transference or transitivity, actually presupposes those principles. On Aristotle's account, we could not appreciate the form of a beautiful person in a picture except by grasping and understanding (*manthanein*) the mimetic representation or "likeness," that is, by recognizing how the work's form exhibits an example or specimen of human beauty, a recognition behind which, moreover, there will lie cultural concepts and

[22] For images and mimesis, see *Top.* 6.2, 140a14–15; for "likeness" and mimesis, *Pol.* 8.5, 1340a18–39, with my chapter 5, section I; cf. the next note.

standards of such beauty.[23] But Aristotle here treats the link or parallelism between reactions to an artwork and to equivalent realities as "necessary" (*Politics* 1340a26) *only* on the assumption that there are no further factors involved: "if one enjoys looking at an image of someone *for no other reason than* the bodily shape [depicted] . . ." (1340a25–26). His formulation implies that once contemplation of the image is enriched by a more subtle awareness of the relationship between representational medium and "object," between the artifact and what it represents, so the act of understanding, and its concomitant pleasure, will acquire a richer character. Aristotle is certainly committed to maintaining a vital connection between experience of art and of life, but not, as *Poetics* 4 indicates, to a theory of invariable equivalence. In the *Politics*, therefore, he leaves room for a more complex interaction, of the kind referred to in the *Poetics* and *Rhetoric*, between real-life responses and responses to mimetic representations, an interaction in which continuities between the two realms of experience are modified by the aesthetic conditions in which an artistic work or performance is contemplated.[24]

Between them, accordingly, these three texts yield the bipartite view that responses to mimetic works must always (if they are responses to mimesis as such) rest on the cognitive recognition of representational significance, and must therefore be *informed* by experience of comparable realities in the world at large; but also that such responses constitute a *compound* reaction to, and make possible an interplay between, representational content and its artistic rendering. The compound quality of aesthetic experience, so conceived, contains the important implication that it is wrong to regard the two components as properly independent: the separation at *Poetics* 1448b7–19 is presented precisely as a case of defective, incomplete aesthetic experience ("if one lacks prior familiarity with

[23] The physical *morphē* (shape) in Aristotle's hypothetical image at *Pol.* 8.5, 1340a26, cannot mean an abstract or schematic figure (cf. notes 18–19 on *zōion*): the noun denotes the sensuous form of a human body seen as handsome, strong, or beautiful in some other way; note the *morphē* depicted in a portrait at *Poet.* 15.1454b10, with the *morphai* of animals and corpses at *Poet.* 4.1448b12; cf. Aeschylus fr. 78a.6 Radt, with my introduction, note 47. Hence Belfiore 1985a, 353–54, cannot be right to treat *Pol.* 1340a23–28 as a case of viewing something "in its own right . . . and not *qua* likeness" (or "not as an image," Belfiore 1992, 65), or Jenny 1984, 184, to say that mimesis has no part in such an experience: Aristotle is there making a point *explicitly* about responses to "likenesses" (*en homoiois*, 23). *Rhet.* 1.5, 1361b7–14., illustrates some of the ways in which the perception of human beauty would involve concepts and standards.

[24] Aristotle's position is therefore not straightforwardly incompatible with the views of Budd 1995, 74–82, who stresses the differences between viewing a picture and viewing the equivalent scene in reality; cf. my notes 29–30. Givens 1991a, 130–32, while rightly seeing that Aristotelian mimesis involves elements of transformation, badly misconstrues *Poet.* 4 as part of an "antimimetic" aesthetic.

the subject, the artifact will not give pleasure *qua* mimetic representation").[25] When we feel pity and fear at a tragedy, and enjoy the experience because it is focused on an artistic representation and consequently makes possible a process of "understanding," it is not that we first feel painful emotions but then have them tempered by the pleasurable recognition that the events are only mimetic; still less that the latter recognition is followed by the painful emotions. Rather, we only experience the emotions, which may indeed still be in some way or degree painful, because we recognize in the represented actions and sufferings the kind of human possibilities that call for them. But, equally, grasping the mimetic significance just *is* in part, for Aristotle, apprehending the "pitiful" and the "fearful" in the events of the play.[26]

Although, therefore, Aristotle does not spell out the point unequivocally in the *Poetics*, we can see, by integrating the evidence of the passages so far marshaled, that he must take emotion and recognition, and, where appropriate, pleasure and pain, to be somehow *fused* in aesthetic experience. That is entirely consistent with the impression created by his reference to the pleasure people can take in contemplating detailed images of disagreeable animals or of corpses. More importantly, it fits perfectly with the most specific reference to the appropriate pleasure of tragedy later in the treatise: "the pleasure from pity and fear through mimesis" (*tēn apo eleou kai phobou dia mimēseōs . . . hēdonēn*, 14.1453b12). Aristotle's exploitation of a resource of Greek word order, enclosing both the qualifying phrases between article and noun (literally "the-from-pity-and-fear-through-mimesis-pleasure"), accentuates the unity of the experience thus designated.[27]

We have, then, in passages of the *Poetics*, *Rhetoric*, and *Politics*, the highly compressed kernel of a concept of aesthetic pleasure that, in stark contrast to the influential Kantian notion of such pleasure as subjective and noncognitive, can be described, if somewhat drily, as both objectivist and cognitivist, because it seeks to explain aesthetic experience in terms of the features of aesthetic objects (mimetic or representational works) and of the processes of recognition and understanding that such objects require and afford. What I now want to undertake is an attempt to fill out,

[25] Donini 1997, 11, rightly observes that the two kinds of pleasure at *Poet.* 1448b15–19 are not to be thought of as irreconcilable.

[26] Belfiore 1985a, 360, gives the impression of discrete stages in aesthetic experience: "We weep while viewing Oedipus. . . . We also view the tragedy *qua* artifact. . . . Finally, *because* we shudder and weep . . . we realize that it is an imitation" (emphasis in original). This seems to me both psychologically and exegetically false, and I have similar qualms about Lear 1988, 302: "it is just that *in addition to* the pity and fear . . . one is also capable of experiencing a certain pleasure" (emphasis added). "In addition to" hardly corresponds to "pleasure *from* pity and fear" at *Poet.* 14.1453b12.

[27] Denniston 1960, 52–53, gives other examples of this resource of Greek word order.

beyond the spare illustration given in *Poetics* 4, some of the implications of this important and inadequately appreciated view. There is no doubt that Aristotle's typical economy of statement bears some responsibility for creating the impression that in this passage he has only an elementary process of cognition in mind. But this does not really justify those critics who have stressed the simplicity of the illustration and lost sight of the larger purpose—namely, an explanation of the origins and causes (the term *aitiai* embraces both senses) of poetry and, indeed, as the *Rhetoric* passage shows, of mimetic art in general. Thus D. W. Lucas, a normally shrewd interpreter, struggles to fathom what Aristotle might have in his sights: "when we have learnt what already familiar thing a picture represents," he writes, "we have not learnt much"; and after considering further possibilities, he concludes that there is nowhere any hint that Aristotle has a conception of the power of literature to extend our comprehension of life.[28] Similarly, Malcolm Budd complains that "the information that a picture depicts such-and-such" is "too trivial" to explain pleasure in depiction. But Budd's complaint rests on two interpretative mistakes: the first (which he shares with Lucas) is to *reduce* Aristotle's point to one of "information," and thereby to miss the rich potential of the philosopher's verb *manthanein*, indeed his whole phrase *manthanein kai sullogizesthai* (to "understand and reason," 1448b16), about which I shall have more to say shortly; the second is the errant supposition that Aristotle ignores the importance of the "manner of depiction," even though the reference to pictorial art in this context actually takes immediate account of the medium and manner of depiction as a factor in aesthetic responses ("we take pleasure in contemplating *the most precisely rendered* images," 1448b11), while the *Poetics* as a whole bears out this point repeatedly in its treatment of tragedy as a poetic art form.[29] That Budd fails to do justice to Aristotle's position is brought out somewhat ironically by the fact that Budd himself regards a kind of "understanding" as lying at the center of the experience of representational art, while seeming not to realize that the concept conveyed by Aristotle's verb *manthanein* (and, elsewhere, the noun *mathēsis*) might have a comparably serious status.[30]

[28] Lucas 1968, 72–73; cf. Lear 1988, 308–9. Even Twining 1812, 1:280–88, is unusually reductive in his treatment of this passage, and in citing the *Rhetoric*'s treatment of metaphor he misses its indication of a spectrum of possible forms of understanding (see my note 38). By contrast, Donini 1997, xxxv, rightly speaks of "un apprendimento e una comprensione" in connection with *Poet*. 4.1448b13.

[29] On the art-critical verb *akriboun* at 1448b11, cf. note 11. See Budd 1995, 48–49, for his criticisms of Aristotle, which are based on too narrow an interpretation of the *Poetics* and are hard to square with some of Budd's own claims (see next note, with note 24).

[30] See, e.g., Budd 1995, 69, stating that pictures have an "artistic meaning" which "the spectator needs to *recognize* if he is to *understand* the picture" (emphasis added). Moreover, Budd 63, "Perhaps nobody knows what the subject of Piero della Francesca's *Flagellation* is; if so, nobody understands it or can properly evaluate its success as a realization of that

Once we acknowledge that Aristotle's reference to painting in *Poetics* 4 is a characteristically "shorthand" analogy, it becomes interpretatively literal-minded and narrow to restrict Aristotle's point in this passage, and in the even briefer passage of *Rhetoric* 1.11, to the mere identification of the subject of a picture, poem, or other mimetic work—as if being able to put some sort of label on the work's content were all that could be meant. Martha Nussbaum has rightly observed that this section of *Poetics* 4 should be taken to cover a whole range of possibilities, from simple to much more complex responses to works of art.[31] In order to elucidate something of the nature of these possibilities, I want now to bring together a number of Aristotelian texts that provide a nexus of thoughts within which to situate the hints I have so far been considering. I hope thereby to demonstrate how some of the major tenets of the *Poetics* can be read afresh in the light of the model of aesthetic experience that emerges from my argument.

Mimetic works such as poems and paintings can be said, in Aristotle's (and indeed in general Greek) vocabulary, to embody "likenesses." As we saw in the last chapter, Aristotle is prepared at *Politics* 8.5, 1340a23, to apply the term *homoia* ("likenesses," "like things") generically to the products of artistic mimesis. The cognitive pleasure afforded by the contemplation of mimetic works is accordingly a pleasure in the recognition and understanding of likenesses. But a likeness need not be of an individual or specifiable model. Most mimetic works are not, and are not assumed by Aristotle to be, renderings of actual, independently existing particulars; only certain types, especially visual portraits, fall into this category. Yet all mimetic works are likenesses, and they are so by virtue of having been made to represent imaginable realities in the perceptual and semantic properties of their particular media (colors and shapes, words, rhythms, choreographic patterns, etc.). It is accordingly possible to discern in them features of the kind possessed by, or predicable of, things in the world.

---

subject," is remarkably close to Aristotle's own formulation at *Poet.* 4.1448b17–18. On the nature of Aristotelian *mathēsis* (understanding), see my subsequent discussion with note 38.

[31] Nussbaum 1986, 388; in addition to my own earlier treatment of this point, Halliwell 1986, 70, see Cope 1877, I:218–19; Sifakis 1986, 216–17; Frede 1992, 214 and n. 43; and Kannicht 1980, 34, for sensitivity to the pregnant compression of Aristotle's formulation. Gallop 1990, 161 n. 24, takes the point too, but his own interesting interpretation differs considerably from mine (cf. note 12), and I cannot accept his case for a pleasure in tragedy that is primarily enjoyed *after* the play is over (an emphasis wholly absent from the *Poetics*). Ferrari 1999, 185, refers to my reading of *Poet.* 4 as "massively spiced," but he is wrong to call the larger interpretation to which it belongs "didactic" (184, 188), and his own treatment of ch. 4 ("all that Aristotle is in fact doing in this passage is to analyse the lowest common denominator of the pleasure we take in fictions," 185) is hopelessly reductive, as is Most 2000, 23 (with a bizarre misquotation of the Greek): these scholars completely ignore, for one thing, the philosophical weight of *manthanein kai sullogizesthai*. Petersen 1992, 22, mistakenly detects textual corruption in the first part of *Poet.* 4.

When we observe ordinary cases of likeness, we observe common properties or qualities. When we engage appreciatively with mimetic works, we recognize and understand the ways in which possible features of reality, possible forms of human experience, are intentionally signified and embodied in them. In the words of Samuel Johnson, "imitations produce pain or pleasure not because they are mistaken for realities, but because they bring realities to mind."[32]

Perceiving or grasping likeness is interpreted by Aristotle as an important mode of discernment for both philosophers and others. He discusses its relevance to a range of types of philosophical argument, including inductive reasoning "to" universals (*Topics* 1.13, 108b7–12; cf. *Rhetoric* 3.11, 1412a11–12), sees it as the essence of (producing) metaphor (*Topics* 6.2, 140a8–10; *Rhetoric* 3.10, 1410b10–19, 3.11, 1412a9–12; *Poetics* 22.1459a5–8), and notes its involvement in a variety of other contexts, such as the interpretation of dreams (*De divinatione somniorum* 2.464b5–12) and the construction of rhetorical analogies (*Rhetoric* 2.20, 1394a2–9). When Aristotle mentions the observation of likeness in these settings, it is evident that he does not have in mind a superficial or passive matter of merely registering the existence of similarities: in philosophy, metaphor, the interpretation of dreams, and in mimetic art too, it is something that not everyone can do, or not equally well. The discernment of likenesses means at its best an active and interpretative process of cognition—a perspicacious discovery of significances in the world or in representations of the world. This point has implications for both the makers and the audiences of mimetic art.[33]

There is a further, special factor that Aristotle seems to regard metaphors and mimetic works as having in common. A metaphor, as *Rhetoric* 3.10, 1410b19, puts it, asserts that "this *is* that" (*touto ekeino*). The same phrase occurs elsewhere, in an already cited passage of the *Rhetoric* (1.11, 1371b9), and we have met a variant of it (*houtos ekeinos*, "this person is so-and-so," literally "this person is that person") used at *Poetics* 4.1448b17 to explain the basis of the pleasurable process of recognition entailed in understanding a mimetic representation.[34] The common element appears

---

[32] Johnson, preface to Shakespeare (1765), in Johnson 1977, 312; cf. my note 9, with Smith 1983, 122, for a close analogue to Johnson's position. See chapter 5, for a fuller account of the Aristotelian position summarized in the present paragraph.

[33] *Nic. Eth.* 10.9, 1181a19–23, refers to the difference between expert and "amateur" understanding in fields such as painting and music; the point is in part technical, but it nonetheless suggests the general possibility of levels of understanding in the experience of mimetic arts. On the interpretative *effort* implied by Aristotle's view of mimesis, see Tracy 1946; cf. Gallop 1999, 80.

[34] On *Poet.* 4.1448b17, cf. note 3. Aristotle's *houtos ekeinos* may have a colloquial ring (cf. *hod' ekeinos*, "there he is!" or "this is him!," at Aristophanes *Knights* 1331), but *pace* Sifakis

to be this: in both cases it is not that a comparison is drawn or a similarity recorded, but rather that something is seen or comprehended *as* something else. In the case of metaphor, Aristotle is analyzing what might be regarded as an aspect of its creativity—the quality that makes him say of it, at *Poetics* 22.1459a6–7, that "this alone [sc. among linguistic techniques] cannot be learned from another and is a sign of natural talent [*euphuïa*]." At any rate, he expressly denies at *Rhetoric* 1410b19 that a *simile* "says this *is* that." If Pericles really said that the death of Athens's young warriors was like the removal of the spring from the year (which is how Aristotle twice records the saying, though calling it a metaphor in one context),[35] then his audience would be offered a simile or analogy. But if, speaking of the war dead, he said "the spring has been removed from our year," then his words would, on Aristotle's model, have an intensified force: the dead, we could say, become, or are felt as, the disappeared spring. Aristotle does not, in fact, consistently attach such importance to the difference between metaphor and simile;[36] but the foregoing passage nonetheless hints at something material to the status of mimesis, because the latter *embodies* or *enacts* its "likeness(es)" in its own organized form and, to that extent, is closer in character to metaphor than to simile. Here it is striking that Aristotle attaches particular weight to metaphors that place things "before the mind's eye" (*pro ommatōn*) and which therefore involve *energeia*, a sense of "activity" or "actuality." Not only are these qualities that he elsewhere associates with mimetic works; in the *Rhetoric* itself he tellingly asserts that such vivid "actuality" *is* a type of mimesis.[37] Finally, it is highly pertinent that Aristotle describes the experience of metaphor (and, to a lesser extent, that of simile) in terms of the same process of "understanding" or "learning" (*manthanein, mathēsis*) in which he elsewhere grounds the experience of mimesis, while making it clear that such understanding is *not* a matter of merely registering what was already known.

These parallelisms between mimesis and metaphor help to clarify Aristotle's view that in the case of mimetic art we see (or hear, depending on the art) a significance figured in the mimetic object: "this is that," "this

---

1986, 218, the specific colloquial idiom *tout' ekeino*, meaning something like "just as I thought/said" (see, e.g., Aristophanes *Ach.* 41, *Peace* 289, *Birds* 354; Plato *Charm.* 166b7), is irrelevant, as it must also be at *Rhet.* 3.10, 1410b19, with reference to metaphor's "identity statements."

[35] *Rhet.* 1.7, 1365a31–33; 3.10, 1411a1–4; see Cope 1877, I:145–46 for the historical evidence.

[36] *Rhet.* 3.4, 1406b20–26, 1407a10–14, assimilate the two figures; see McCall 1969, 24–53, for full discussion.

[37] Metaphors that place things "before the eyes": *Rhet.* 3.10, 1410b33, 1411a27–28, 35, 1411b4–22, 25 (on the same motif in the *Poetics*, see 17.1455a22–30, and cf. *Rhet.* 2.8, 1386a28–b8, with Halliwell 2002). For the term *energeia*, see *Rhet.* 3.10, 1410b36; 3.11, 1411b25–12a9; *energeia* as mimesis, 1412a9; cf. chapter 5, note 22.

person is so-and-so," and similar phrases are Aristotle's deliberately short-hand, rudimentary way of illustrating such cognitive experience, though without thereby implying, as I have already insisted, that the experience itself is limited to the rudimentary. As with metaphor, we do not so much consciously observe or make a connection; rather, we see one thing (the artistically shaped materials of the work or performance) *as* another (the representational field, the represented world). If this is right, a crucial en-tailment here is that Aristotle's conception of mimesis allows from its very foundations for the necessity and centrality of the mimetic medium: repre-sentational works do not offer us deceptive pseudorealities, as Plato had sometimes mooted, but the fictive signification of possible reality in artistic media that allow such reality to be recognized and responded to coher-ently. Moreover, because mimetic works need not, and usually will not, represent independently attested particulars or individuals, aesthetic un-derstanding cannot be limited to matching a "copy" with a known original, nor can it be reduced to the merely factual and immediate registering *that* a certain kind of thing has been represented.

If we now glance back at the *Rhetoric*'s treatment of metaphor, we can derive illumination from a combination of affinities with and differences from the experience of mimetic artworks. Aristotle is there concerned with what can be "learned" or "understood" from individual figures of speech (especially with witty "bons mots") in oratorical contexts, and it is there-fore unsurprising that he foregrounds the need for metaphors that lend themselves to "quick," though not instantaneous, appreciation. But at the same time he reveals that he takes "understanding," *mathēsis*, to encom-pass a whole spectrum of possibilities, from the very superficial (where the mind hardly moves beyond what it already knows or what is "obvious to anyone") to the most complex (which involve psychological effort and "searching," *zētein*).[38] If we bring this idea of a spectrum of possibilties to bear on Aristotle's view of mimetic art, the justifiable inference is that he would expect a good tragedy or painting to provide understanding of a much more complex, cumulative, and less rapid sort, and to involve much more of a process of "searching," than he thinks good rhetorical metaphors require. While understanding a particular rhetorical metaphor needs, in its setting, to be reasonably "quick," understanding a dramatic speech, a whole scene, a character, or an entire play will inevitably be a "slower" but more concentrated process.

But we do not need to rely on these hints from the *Rhetoric*, helpful though they are, to make a strong case for the potential complexity of

---

[38] *Rhet.* 3.10, 1410b10–26, indicates the parameters of the spectrum; see 21 for "quick" learning, and note esp. 10–15, 21–26, for the clear implication that *manthanein* cannot be limited to registering that which is already known; cf. Halliwell 1986, 73 n. 38. For *manthan-*

Aristotle's cognitive model of the experience of mimetic art. In *Poetics* 4 itself, notwithstanding what I have called the "shorthand" force of the pictorial example (where the mind recognizes that "this person is so-and-so"), there are sufficiently clear signals of the ramifications of what Aristotle has in mind. In addition to the telling fact that he is prepared, however loosely, to assimilate the general experience of artistic representation to a philosophical concept of "understanding," *manthanein*, we have to reckon with the suggestive force of the phrase "understand and reason what each element is."[39] In the case of a tragedy, the phrase "each element" can encompass every strand in the dramatic totality of actions, characters, events, emotions, arguments, and so forth, with all their various facets and interrelationships; and to "reason" or "infer," *sullogizesthai*,[40] will accordingly imply an intricate, unfolding process of attentive comprehension, including the kind of considerations later mentioned in chapter 25, where judgment of what is said or done in a poem calls for carefully contextualized regard to the identity of the agent, the recipient, the situation, the means and the end of the deeds or words in question (1461a4–9). To "understand" in this way is to discover an accumulating structure of significance in the work; and while each component may be a "likeness" in the sense of something we require an existing grasp of reality to comprehend, this does not entail that the drama as a whole is similar to anything we have previously experienced. Nor is there any reason to avoid the supposition that, mutatis mutandis, Aristotle would acknowledge the possibility of an

---

ein implying the use of existing knowledge, see, e.g., *Nic. Eth.* 6.11, 1143a12–13. *zētein* (search or investigate): *Rhet.* 3.10, 1410b19, 23.

[39] *manthanein kai sullogizesthai ti hekaston*, 1448b16–17; further discussion in Halliwell 2001. Cf. *Top.* 6.2, 140a22, where a reference to obscurity of details in "the old painters" forms an analogy to possible obscurities in a philosophical definition. The phrase *ti hekaston*, "what each (element) is," is elsewhere used by Aristotle in connection with processes of *philosophical* reasoning: see *Top.* 1.18, 108b1; *De anima* 2.4, 415a16; *Metaph.* 13.3, 1077b23–24; *Nic. Eth.* 7.14, 1154b33; *Pol.* 1.3, 1253b8. The link between *manthanein* and philosophy appears also in the *Rhetoric*'s treatment of metaphor, at 3.11, 1412a11–12.

[40] To find a suggestion of cognitive weight and seriousness in *sullogizesthai*, it is unnecessary (as well as dubious) to take it here in its strictly logical sense (of formal deduction), as do, e.g., House 1956, 118; Goldschmidt 1982, 402; Redfield 1994, 54; and Sifakis 1986, 215–20, the latter producing, as he admits (220), a peculiarly jejune form of inference. For comparably looser use of *sullogizesthai*, see, e.g., *Nic. Eth.* 1.11, 1101a34; *Metaph.* 8.1, 1042a3; cf. the *sullogismos* associated with rhetorical antithesis at *Rhet.* 3.9, 1410a21, and the use of both noun and verb in connection with enthymemes at *Rhet.* 3.17, 1418b3–6; for something a little closer to a formal syllogism (*within* a play), see *Poet.* 16.1455a4–8, and cf. Nussbaum 1978, 183–84. The medieval Arabic tradition represents the extreme case of the view that Aristotle took poetry to have a quasi-logical status: see chapter 11, esp. note 90. A sensitive modern attempt to argue something analogous has been made by Packer 1984, esp. 144; but I prefer a less strict yet richer model of aesthetic understanding, along the lines of Savile 1982, ch. 5; cf. Sherman 1989, 168. It is worth adding, however, that the syllogism proper is, in Aristotle's terms, a highly formalized point on a continuum of human reasoning.

equivalently extended process of understanding in the case of visual art too, despite the ostensible simplicity of his comment at *Poetics* 4.1448b17.[41]

So it is entirely legitimate, indeed essential, to discern a depth of theoretical perspective behind the compressed statements in this part of chapter 4. Furthermore, it is surely no coincidence that a closely similar conjunction of points—a comparison to philosophy, as well as the application of philosophically marked terminology to the experience of mimesis—occurs in a celebrated passage of chapter 9 of the *Poetics*. We have good warrant, therefore, for mobilizing what is said about poetry's quasi-philosophical status and about "universals" in chapter 9 to fill out and substantiate the implications of the section of chapter 4 we have so far been examining.

II

In approaching Aristotle's famous remark that "poetry is more philosophical and more serious than history, because poetry speaks more of universals, while history speaks (more) of particulars" (1451b5–7), we must start by accepting that, contrary to a common paraphrase, Aristotle does not say unqualifiedly that poetry *is* a mimesis of universals. In the treatise as a whole he repeatedly takes it to be a mimesis of actions and their agents, of "action(s) and life."[42] The characters of poetry are, at least prima facie, fictive particulars; they have names, perform individual actions,[43] and are contextualized in specific situations. Indeed, one poetic virtue acknowledged unequivocally by Aristotle is vividness of just the kind that belongs to actualities: the poet who aims for such vividness needs to think in terms of what it would be like in the presence of "the events themselves" (17.1455a22–25). Yet the remark just quoted from chapter 9 suggests that universals are somehow conveyed by poetry, at least more so than in history. This passage has become a locus classicus—often cited approvingly even by those who feel no general attraction to the *Poetics*—because it looks as though Aristotle is here expressing something of profound interest about poetry; and it seems right to try to do justice to that impression. Equally, however, it would be judicious to take account, as has often not been done, of the comparative and tentative phrasing of the passage.

Three aberrant interpretations, to which I shall add others in due course, can be rapidly cleared out of the way: the universals in question are not

---

[41] Cf. the kind of sophisticated viewing of visual art envisaged at *Part. Anim.* 1.5, 645a7–15, with my previous comments and note 12.

[42] *Poet.* 6.1450a16–17: the wording here, that tragedy is a mimesis "not of people but of action(s) and life," represents a normative principle for the priorities of (tragic) drama, elevating action over (static) characterization; it does not, of course, mean that people are not part of the object of representation (cf. Palmer 1992, 9–11); cf. chapter 7, section II.

[43] Actions are a matter of particulars: *Nic. Eth.* 2.7, 1107a31; 3.1, 1110b6–7.

quasi-Platonic ideas that transcend the realities of our experienced world; nor are they moralistically or didactically formulable principles; nor, finally, are they generalized abstractions.[44] Universals can play a part in human thought in more than one way, or on more than one level. They *can*, in the philosopher's hands, be abstractions, as the subject of definition, for example; and some universals can be arrived at or grasped only by fully philosophical knowledge: they are extremely remote from sense perception, as *Metaphysics* 1.2, 982a24–25, puts it. But, equally, other universals are to some degree present, according to *Posterior Analytics* 2.19, 100a3–b5, even in ordinary sense perception.[45] They emerge in and through the perception of particulars; they inhere, so to speak, as categories of discrimination and understanding, in perceptual cognition that is built up out of memory and experience.[46]

The poet—Aristotle's dramatic poet, that is—does not deal in abstracted universals, as the philosopher does. But nor can the remark in *Poetics* 9 be simply limited to the minimal sense in which universals are present in sense perception, because this would give no grounds for the distinction between poetry and history: "poetry speaks more of universals, while history speaks (more) of particulars" (1451b6–7). Universals should enter into poetry, it seems to follow, on a level somewhere between abstraction and common sense-experience. Chapter 17 perhaps gives us a clue to what is involved. There Aristotle starts by stressing that the composing poet's search for consistency and vividness will be served by strong imagination (mentally supposing oneself present "at the events themselves," a traditional formula).[47] But he then proceeds to suggest that one stage in composition—an earlier stage than the one that requires such imagination to flesh out the details of the play—should involve setting out the skeleton of the plot "in general terms," or as an overall structure, and only then filling it out with episodes. "In general terms" is here the same word, the adverb *katholou*, that Aristotle uses in his term for universals (*ta katholou*). Some commentators have denied that this connection is significant, but I contend that it must be. Confirmation of its pertinence comes from the fact

---

[44] For Renaissance versions of the first two of these misinterpretations, see Hathaway 1962, 129–43. Gulley 1979, 170, leans strangely toward abstraction in saying "it is part of [the poet's] job to make generalizations," a claim badly at odds with, e.g., *Poet.* 24.1460a7–8: even if Aristotle's position implies (which is not clear) that generalizations could in principle be *extracted* from poetry, he nowhere commits the naive mistake of supposing that such generalizations would themselves contain the value of poetry.

[45] But note the different emphasis of the formulation earlier in the *Post. Anal.*, at 1.31, 87b29–33: universals as such cannot be the object of perception.

[46] For the emergence of universals through memory and experience, see esp. *Post. Anal.* 2.19, 100a3–b5; *Metaph.* 1.1, 981a6–7. In deliberation, universals can be recognized as instantiated *in* particulars: *De anima* 3.11, 434a17–19.

[47] Cf. my introduction, note 48.

that the passage in chapter 17 closely echoes part of chapter 9 itself: both, crucially, refer to a process of plot construction followed by addition of the characters' names (1451b12–14, 1455b12–13); and both relate the force of *katholou* to probability or plausibility (*eikos*), which represents the more-than-particular basis of dramatic conviction.[48]

The universals of chapters 9 and 17 are built into the plot structure of a dramatic poem, into the causal network of actions and events that it comprises. As such, they also necessarily concern the agents, and chapter 9 makes this explicit: "'universal' means the sorts of things that it fits a certain sort of person to say or do according to probability or necessity."[49] So universals are not inherent in the raw stuff—the particular agents and actions—of a tragedy or comedy, not, at any rate, in a way, or to an extent, that differentiates these particulars from those of real life or of history. Poetic universals are embodied and discernible only in and through the organized mimetic structure of "action(s) and life" that the poet makes: this causally and intelligibly unified design of the artwork differentiates poetry, as Aristotle insists in chapters 8 and 23 as well as in chapter 9, from (many) ordinary events and hence from (much) history.[50] This means that universals are related to causes, reasons, motives, and intelligible patterns of human life in the structure of a dramatic poem as a whole.[51] Encouraged by the similar remarks in chapters 4 and 9, we can conclude that whatever Aristotle implies by the pleasure of learning or understanding in the case of mimesis (chapter 4), it ought, in the case of dramatic poetry, to have something to do with universals.

But it is in any attempt to extrapolate from these spare hints that the dangers of the aberrant readings I mentioned earlier, as well as of other misleading interpretations, loom up. One danger here is that of reducing Aristotle's doctrine to some sort of faith in the dramatic "type" and the typical.[52] This sort of interpretation threatens to take one in the direction

[48] Cf. Armstrong 1998, 453–54, for another angle on the connection between chs. 9 and 17.

[49] *sumbainein* at *Poet.* 9.1451b8 (contrast the use of the verb at 8.1451a25) must indicate an idea of appropriate fit or connection; cf., e.g., Heath 1996, 16 ("is consonant with"); Gernez 1997, 35 ("convenir"). Translations such as "turn out" (Golden & Hardison 1968, 17; Ferrari 1999, 183), French "arriver" (Magnien 1990, 98) or Italian "accadere" (Rostagni 1945, 52) blur Aristotle's point.

[50] See *Poet.* 8.1451a16–19 (part of the train of thought that leads up to ch. 9's remarks on universals), 23.1459a21–24 (poetic unity contrasted with historical contingency).

[51] An interesting argument regarding character and universals, though independent of Aristotle, is put by Lamarque 1983.

[52] The standard use of "type" or "typical" to refer to merely characteristic specimens needs to be distinguished from more philosophical usage. Armstrong 1998, who provides an incisive review of the issue, argues that the universals of *Poet.* 9 are "action-types" and indeed plots (453–54); on this, see further in Halliwell 2001.

of too much abstraction, too little concern with dramatic vividness and conviction. But it also pulls the idea of poetic universals toward the humanly "normal" and predictable, which is certainly compatible with some kinds of dramatic poetry (Aristotle's reference to comedy at 9.1451b12–15 shows that this part of his theory covers a wide spectrum), but cannot integrate the *Poetics*' repeated recognition that tragedy and epic deal with characters and actions that are, in certain respects, *out* of the ordinary: characters that are somehow "better than us" (chapters 2, 13, 15), and scenarios that call for a sense of "wonder" or "awe" (*to thaumaston*), best aroused by events that occur "contrary to expectation yet on account of one another" (9.1452a4) and that thus lend themselves to the powerful intricacies of the "complex" plot. But if reducing poetry's universals to the typical, normal, or merely characteristic cannot do justice to the thrust of *Poetics* 9, an equal pitfall is that of supposing them to yield readily formulable moral truths or didactic lessons.[53] Had Aristotle believed this, he would not have failed to say so unequivocally, especially against the background of Plato's ethical mistrust of poetry. We should register, moreover, that chapter 17's example of a plot set out "in general terms" gives no support to this hypothesis: there is no trace here of any moralizing thrust to the conception of the plot's sequence of action, only an attention (sketchily annotated) to its overall shape and coherence.

Similarly, there is no ground at all for *idealizing* Aristotle's universals, for treating them as ideal exemplars or models of possible realities. Butcher, by doing so with quasi-Hegelian solemnity, allows us to see what is so wrong with this reading: any interpretation that can turn the universal into "nature's ideal intention," "a correction of [nature's] failures," and "the manifestation of a higher truth," seems to have lost sight of the fact that these universals are posited by Aristotle in the fabric of *tragedies* (where things go so badly wrong) and *comedies* (where exhibitions of the "ugly" or "shameful" take center stage).[54] A variant on the idealizing reading is to equate the universals of *Poetics* 9 with possibilities that are "universal" in the sense of common to all human experience across time and space, transhistorically and transculturally capturing an "immutable human con-

---

[53] It is misleading of Ricoeur 1981, 26, 27, 30, and Ricoeur 1983, 109, 241 (1984, 70, 170), to talk repeatedly (and as though quoting Aristotle) of poetry as "teaching" ('enseigner') universals.

[54] See Butcher 1911, 158, 154, 160. Idealized universals appear also in, e.g., Dupont Roc & Lallot 1980, 222, who speak of the universal as an "exemple" and "modèle universel," citing *Poet.* 25.1461b13 for the term *paradeigma*, which refers there, however, not to mimetic art in general but to the idealizing style of particular artists and works (and therefore to only the third of the three possible objects of mimesis at 25.1460a9–11). More cautiously, Frye 1957, 84, speaks of Aristotelian universals lying "between the example and the precept," but also as "exemplary."

dition."[55] Aristotle never thinks or speaks in such terms, and it is unjustified to assume that he would have wanted to do so. Indeed, we can see from his *Rhetoric* that he recognized clearly the degree to which canons of "probability" and plausibility, which are central to this definition of universals in *Poetics* 9 (1451b9), are dependent on—and must therefore vary according to—the social, political, cultural, and personal background of individual audiences. The implication of this point is that Aristotle's conception of the kinds of explanatory or causal connection between characters and words or deeds that will give a poetic structure something of the "universal" in significance (1451b8–9) does not commit him to the supposition that such connections have an absolute or timeless basis in human nature.[56]

Let us, then, try to move toward a more modest but sustainable account of what Aristotle might mean by the "universals" of poetry. These universals are, in the first place, not a constant or consistent factor in all poetry; the cautious phrasing at 1451b6–7 ("poetry speaks *more* of universals") intimates that the universal import of poetry will fluctuate according to the quality of poetic design and execution. A bad poem might, by Aristotle's criteria, convey nothing "universal" at all; a great one might provide a depth of insight that could qualify as seriously "philosophical." Moreover, insofar as universals are present in a work, they will be present as implicit, "embodied" properties of a poem, not explicit, let alone propositional, elements. This means, among other things, that they are not a matter of the content of reflective or moralizing sentiments expressed by characters *in* the work; such reflections (which would be covered by Aristotle's notion of "thought," *dianoia*, *Poetics* 19.1456a33–56b8) could in principle draw out or reinforce the universals conveyed by the poetic design as a whole, but Aristotle nowhere shows much concern with this consideration, any more than he does for the moralizing component in many choral

---

[55] See, e.g., Hall 1997, 94, who attacks readings of Greek tragedy based on this idea of universality without doubting that this was what was "postulated by Aristotle"; similarly Wiles 1997, 6. Lear 1988, 312–14, criticizes the equation of "universal" with "the essence of the human condition," though his conclusion, that "the universality Aristotle has in mind . . . is not as such aiming at the depth of the human condition, it is aiming at the universality of the human condition" (314), is confusing.

[56] Even if a poet could succeed in making the explanatory or causal connections in his work consistently "necessary" and not just probable or plausible, it would not follow that he would be incorporating "timeless" universals, because the varieties of character and action involved might themselves not be timelessly possible. In any case, the very fact that Aristotle in ch. 9 and elsewhere relies on the joint formula, "probability and/or necessity," indicates, I think, how little the truly "necessary" enters into human affairs (cf. *Rhet.* 1.2, 1357a22–32): for different approaches to "necessity" in the *Poetics*, see Halliwell 1986, 99–106; Belfiore 1992, 111–19; and Frede 1992. Gallop 1991 tests the Aristotelian requirement of probability against modern works of fiction.

odes of Greek tragedy. Because the universals posited by *Poetics* 9 must be essentially implicit, it may be useful, furthermore, to think of them as, in modern terminology, "emergent" aesthetic properties: features not ready-made, present on the surface of the work, but dependent on an active, interpretative understanding (chapter 4's process of *manthanein*) on the part of spectator or reader.[57] The idea that universals do not simply lie on the surface of the work, but require engaged interpretation, can be supported by a somewhat neglected passage from *Poetics* 19 (1456b2–8) that stresses the way in which dramatic meanings and effects—including both emotional effects and the plausibility that holds a plot structure together—should be inherent "in the events" and should not require explicit statement, *didaskalia*, literally "teaching." This last observation should count decisively against all attempts, including that of Schopenhauer, to take the universals of *Poetics* 9 as a matter of "instruction" in general truths of human nature.[58]

It begins to appear that part of the enterprise of the *Poetics* is the effort to locate a domain for poetry that lies somewhere (though not at an exact midpoint) between neighboring but contrasting territories, territories whose character, if too closely approximated, would be deleterious to the enactive quality of mimesis that Aristotle identifies above all with drama. The paradigms of these other territories are philosophy and history, with their associated planes of the "pure" universal and the contingent particular. Poetry stands closer to philosophy than to history, according to chapter 9, yet at the same time its quasi-philosophical status is embedded in dramatic fictions composed of vividly imagined particulars that bring with them, as we have seen Aristotle insisting at 17.1455a22–26, the need for a sense of concrete immediacy and credibility. Moreover, Aristotle wants to steer poetry away from didactic statement, indeed from "statement"—the authorial voice—*tout court*, which he seems to regard as strictly incompatible with mimesis;[59] and he makes clear near the outset that he regards

----

[57] Yanal 1982, who rightly links his reading with *Poetics* 4's model of cognitive experience, treats universals as emergent properties. Gallop 1999, 82–83, stresses that poetic universals will be implicitly suggested, not directly asserted, but he still considers them to be "general truths" (cf. Pappas 2001, 20–22, with an implausible illustration). One might here compare, if obliquely, the subtle way in which particular judgments and general principles interact in Aristotelian moral reasoning: for two accounts, see Cooper 1975, esp. 1–88, and Broadie 1991, 242–60, with Burnyeat 1980 on the relation to Aristotle's view of the development of ethical character; cf. Halliwell 2001.

[58] Schopenhauer, *Die Welt als Wille und Vorstellung*, vol. 2, ch. 38, cites *Poet.* 9 in support of the idea that poetry offers knowledge of, and instruction ("Belehrung") in, human nature (Schopenhauer 1989, 2:510). In the same chapter Schopenhauer interestingly aligns history with the particularity of the novel (a genre he appears not to count as art proper in his own terms); he overlooks Aristotle's own requirement of poetic particularity in *Poet.* 17.

[59] *Poet.* 24.1460a5–11: see chapter 5, section II, for my discussion of this vexed passage.

philosophy in verse as philosophy, not poetry. The delicacy of Aristotle's attempt to place poetry in dual relation to history and philosophy should be considered as a productive tension in the arguments of the treatise, and it can help to put the role of chapter 9's universals in perspective. The implication of Aristotle's theory in its entirety is that poetry needs the convincingness of vivid particulars precisely in order to open up for its audiences the quasi-philosophical scope of comprehension and discernment that it is capable of providing. The extent to which universals can be discovered in a work will depend on an interplay between the depth and richness of the poem's imagined world (the complexity of the work's explanatory-cum-causal pattern of human action and experience) and the degree of engaged understanding that is brought to it by the mind of the spectator or reader.

It should by now be apparent, I hope, that the readings of chapters 4 and 9 of the *Poetics* I have proposed can be mutually illuminating. The cognition of mimetic works entails, in essence, the perception and understanding of their representational content and structure, of the possible or supposed realities they display (chapter 4). But what they represent is not, except in occasional cases, actual particulars; and chapter 9 suggests that, for poetry at least, even the use of such particulars—historical data—must be transformed by the poet into the material of unified (and, in the process, fictionalized) plot structures. This does not mean that the narrative content of poetry ceases to be particular. On the contrary, the characters and actions of an epic or dramatic poem remain fictive particulars, but they are particulars that work together, through the requisite degree of causal and explanatory unity expounded in chapters 7–8, to make exceptionally intelligible patterns of human experience, and therefore exceptionally rewarding material for aesthetic contemplation. Consequently, to "understand and reason what each element is" (4.1448b16–17), for a given mimetic work, cannot be—or cannot be only—a matter of identifying particulars, but must, on Aristotle's account, involve comprehension of how those particulars make cogent sense within a larger grasp of reality. Such comprehension, as chapter 9 intimates, brings into play implicit reference to "universals," the general conceptual structures that emerge within our experience, and give underlying order to our understanding, of the world. The process of reasoning (*sullogizesthai*) that is contained in Aristotle's model of responses to mimetic representations thus bears out the principle that "it is impossible to reason at all without universals" (*Topics* 8.14, 164a10–11).

The role of universals in poetry, and therefore in the adequate cognition of poetry, should not be pressed too hard. We should probably not, for example, assimilate it too closely to a conscious process of philosophical

argument such as the use of likenesses in dialectical induction.[60] Perhaps
the most prudent conclusion is to see the cognition of poetry as suspended
between ordinary processes of intelligent sense experience and the fully
articulated structures of philosophical thought. Poetic fictions offer (or
should do: the idea is normative) more than the simulation of ordinary
particulars in the world, because they are constructed in unified patterns
of probability or necessity. In this respect, there is more of the universal
visible in them, and they are accordingly more intelligible. Appreciative
engagement with such works will correspondingly draw on a stronger
awareness of universals than is always the case in perception of ordinary
events: given chapter 8's argument about the difference between a unified
poetic "action" and the often fragmented contingencies of life, poetic structures of action will seem *to make better or richer sense* than much actual
experience does. At the same time, poetry falls short of, or cannot—as Aristotle would see it—aspire to, the articulation, system, and surety of good
philosophical arguments. One probable implication of this is that Aristotle
need not consider poets themselves to be figures of quasi-philosophical
sagacity or insight, although his theory does commit him to supposing that
they possess a level of human perceptiveness and acumen that can be
adapted to the design of effective plot structures. If he might well have
gone further than this in the case of Homer, for whom his admiration is
profound, or perhaps that of Sophocles, it nonetheless remains salient that
he nowhere shows much inclination to claim back for poets themselves the
cachet of wisdom that Greek culture had traditionally allowed them and
that some Platonic texts had strenuously contested. It is in poetic structures,
not in their authors, that Aristotle locates the cognitive value of poetry.

In the case of a complex work such as a tragedy, our sense of the universals implicit in the work's structure will operate in respect of all three of
the "objects" of mimetic significance given in chapter 6—actions, character, and "thought" (1450a11). This means that to follow, appreciate, and
respond to tragedies, we must utilize (and understand how the work itself
uses) a wider sense of what it is for people to be agencies in the world,
what it is, more especially, for them to be ethically motivated agencies,
and what it is for them to express their thoughts in speech. We require,
that is, a fund and a grasp of already existing experience of life that is
itself quasi-universal, which has at least the seeds of universals within it—
always bearing in mind my earlier caveat that these universals are unifying
structures of thought, not suppositions of a timeless human condition. But
does Aristotle imply that poetry can do more than merely confirm or codify
such experience? The formulation in chapter 4 need not preclude the notion that what emerges from our encounters with, say, tragedy is some-

---

[60] See, e.g., *Top.* 1.18, 108b7–12, *Rhet.* 1.2, 1356b13–14, 1357b28–29.

thing that builds on but also, in part at least, enlarges our already acquired understanding. That is why I have laid repeated emphasis on Aristotle's use of the verb *manthanein*, to be translated as "understand" and/or "learn." But we have to be prepared to do some appropriate extrapolation from Aristotle's spare phrasing. What has often seemed to interpreters to be a rather narrow stress in this context on the need for a preexistent familiarity with the subject of a mimetic work ("if one lacks prior familiarity with the subject, the artifact will not give pleasure *qua* mimetic representation," 1448b17–18)[61] is tailored to the rudimentary case of visual identification—say, of the figure in a portrait—that Aristotle gives as a token instance of recognizing a pictorial representation. But if the argument purports, as it does (4.1448b4–5), to explain the roots of poetry as a major cultural practice, the point cannot be restricted to such cases; it needs to be capable of an amplification that will cover the full scope of the most ambitious types of mimesis.

In the case of tragedy, Aristotle's whole theory suggests that an audience needs to have sufficient experience of life to understand various kinds of action, intention, and character; to be able to distinguish degrees of innocence, responsibility, and guilt; to know, in an effectively mature way, what merits pity and fear; to have a grasp of human successes and failures, of the relationship between status and character, and so forth. All of these things, and much else besides, would contribute, in other words, to a complex form of the process that in chapter 4's general terms is described as a matter of understanding and inferring the significance of each element in a mimetic work. But tragedy does not just confirm its audiences in preexisting comprehension of the world. It provides them with imaginative opportunities to test, refine, extend, and perhaps even question the ideas and values on which such comprehension rests. Admittedly, Aristotle does not set himself to pursue all the ways in which tragedy might accomplish this. But there are nonetheless some suggestions in the *Poetics* of an awareness of this dimension of tragic experience, not least in the importance assigned by the treatise to effects of wonder and surprise (especially in the complex plot). I shall argue in the next chapter that even Aristotle's conception of pity may contain an idea of how the experience of tragedy can actively shape and potentially change an audience's perception of its relationships to others.[62]

Mention of the emotional charge central to the Aristotelian model of tragedy brings me to the final step in my present argument. For if we have

---

[61] A link with the acquisition of universals through experience (e.g., *Post. Anal.* 2.19, 100a3–8) may be implicit here, but Aristotle's terseness makes it hard to draw out the point. Cf. Sifakis 1986, 218–19, with the qualification in my note 40.

[62] See chapter 7, section II.

in *Poetics* 4 and *Rhetoric* 1.11 the core of a general conception of the cognitive pleasure taken in mimetic artworks, we also have in the *Poetics* as a whole a distinctive conception of the pleasure arising from the experience of tragedy. It should by now be clear why, on my interpretation, tragic pleasure—"the pleasure from pity and fear through mimesis" (14.1453b12)—must be a genre-specific application of the general account of aesthetic pleasure given in chapter 4. If that is so, we can observe how the somewhat schematic and simplified form of the general statement takes on a richer color and greater depth when set in the interpretation of a tradition of mimesis as highly elaborated as that of Greek tragic poetry. What was stressed in chapter 4 was the interrelation of cognition and pleasure; what comes into the foreground in the detailed case study of tragedy is the integration of pleasure, cognition, *and emotion*. The fact that our passage in chapter 4 says nothing of emotion in connection with cognition is due merely to the concision of Aristotle's argument at that point, although it is imperative to notice how the connection is taken for granted in the ensuing account of poetic evolution, where the "serious" and "comic" traditions of poetry are defined in terms of ethical categories that bring with them, for Aristotle, appropriately emotional evaluations. But the argument anyhow leaves full scope for emotion to be combined with cognition, and that is exactly what we find provided for in the specifics of the theory of tragedy, where Aristotle refers the tragic emotions, in keeping with his psychological outlook as a whole, to the types of belief that give them their focus and content (13.1452b34–53a7).

I offer a more extensive exploration of Aristotle's approach to tragic pity in the next chapter, but what needs underlining here is the compatibility of the work's stress on emotion with the cognitivist model of aesthetic pleasure set out in *Poetics* 4. The complete experience of a tragedy will necessitate the understanding of the work's significant structure of "action(s) and life" (6.1450a16–17), the ethical characterization of the agents, the rationale of their expressed thoughts, and so forth. But this cannot be a coldly cerebral process of ratiocination; it is the necessarily evaluative engagement of the mind with imagined human actions and experiences of a deeply serious and, for Aristotle, a justifiably emotion-inducing kind. It is for this reason that Aristotle speaks interchangeably of, on the one hand, the "pitiful" and "fearful" as properties of a tragic plot structure itself and its component events (e.g., 9.1452a2–3), but also, on the other, of pity and fear as the appropriate response of the spectator (or reader) who attends to and is absorbed in this structure of events (e.g., 11.1452a38–39). These emotional qualities, equally expressible in terms of the work itself or of a fitting reaction to it, provide the central criteria for the prescriptive treatment of the genre's values and ideals. There is, in this conception of tragic experience, no divorce between understanding and emotion, thought and feeling, because to feel in the right way toward the right things just *is*, on an Aristotelian psychology, one integral part of understanding their human sense and meaning.[63] So to suggest, as one scholar has, that the cognitive pleasure of tragedy "is a step that occurs en route to the production of the proper pleasure of tragedy," where this pleasure is said to arise *from* pity and fear through mimesis, is to separate elements that we should expect to find fused, given Aristotle's view (to be explored more fully in the next chapter) that the emotions themselves are cognitively grounded.[64]

The experience of tragedy reflects a duality that we earlier encountered in Aristotle's broader conception of aesthetic experience. On the one hand, it matches the principle stated in *Politics* 8.5 that there is a close congruity between responses to mimetic "likenesses" and responses to events in the world. We can observe this principle in operation, for example, in *Poetics* 13–14, where the ideal aims of tragedy are categorized in terms—simultaneously ethical and aesthetic—of the kinds of agents, actions, and sufferings that will elicit the requisite emotions. On the other hand, pity and fear are painful emotions, yet the experience of tragic drama is strongly pleasurable. Here, then, we have the supreme exemplification of the fact, noted briefly but pointedly in *Poetics* 4, that the nature of mimetic art can transform and integrate painful emotions into aesthetic pleasure. And this transformation, as we earlier saw, is traced back by Aristotle to the root cause of experiencing an intelligibly designed artifact, an artistic representation. So the duality in question, which I analyzed more fully in connection with *Poetics* 4, both acknowledges the "artificial" status of mimetic fictions and yet keeps intact their capacity to explore possibilities of reality.

We are now well placed to see the force of my central contention that pleasure, understanding, and emotion are interlocking concepts in the scheme of the *Poetics*. Pleasure in mimesis rests on a cognitive foundation (chapter 4), and that tenet inevitably points us toward the remarks on poetry and universals in chapter 9. The "proper pleasure" of tragedy

[63] For a modern analogue to this position, see Schier 1983, 89–90 (interestingly, an effectively Aristotelian conclusion to what starts [86], but has difficulty maintaining itself, as a Kantian argument).

[64] The quotation is from Lear 1988, 311; on 310 Lear calls pity and fear themselves only a "step along the route towards the proper effect." Although I cannot engage fully with Lear's case on catharsis (which he associates with the noncognitive, nonemotional "proper effect" of tragedy), I note that despite his avowedly anticognitivist stance this case ultimately rests on the "consolation" that tragedy occurs in a world presented as rational (325, and cf. 318 on disgust and the irrational). Such perception of a rational worldorder would appear to make catharsis entail, after all, a significantly cognitive dimension. Cf. note 70. The involvement of tragic pleasure *with* tragic emotion is rightly stressed by Neill 2001, 364–65.

(chapter 14) conforms to this basic model, for it is a pleasure for which Aristotle specifies the mimetic medium (*"through* mimesis . . .," 1453b12). But the pleasure of tragedy also revolves crucially around powerful emotions, and these complete the (virtuous) theoretical circle by drawing us back round to the cognitivist view that Aristotle takes of the emotions. These connections should have emerged prominently enough from the analysis I have offered, but they can be most suitably and conveniently reiterated, in conclusion, by way of contrast with an old and still strongly held view about the *Poetics,* namely that it offers a purely "hedonistic" conception of the experience of tragedy, that is, a conception of this experience as involving a pure form of pleasure.

The error of what I am calling the hedonistic reading of the *Poetics* can be pinpointed in the treatment of Aristotle's references to the end, *telos* (used five times), or the function, *ergon* (three times), of tragedy.[65] Proponents of the hedonistic reading typically claim or assume that all these passages corroborate the unequivocal proposition that tragedy's end or function is to give pleasure.[66] But this is misleading. To be sure, the *telos* and *ergon* of tragedy must incorporate or serve pleasure, but it is as significant as it has often been obscured that Aristotle nowhere says without qualification that pleasure is the end or function of tragedy. In fact, he only once says unreservedly what the *telos* is, and that is in chapter 6: the plot structure is the end of tragedy (1450a22–23; cf. 1450a18). In two other passages pleasure is mentioned as one aspect of the end and function, but not in such a way as to identify it exclusively with them (1462a18–b1, 1462b12–15). In four other passages there is no explicit mention of pleasure, and every reason to regard Aristotle as thinking of something more than pleasure—either of plot structure again (1450a31), or specifically of emotive effect (1460b24–26), or of some combination of these and other elements (1452b29–30).

The point I want to press is that the end or function of tragedy is not presented by Aristotle as a matter of some single, discrete factor. It involves, rather, the complete, harmonious fulfillment of the "nature" of the genre, and that is something that embraces all the major principles set out in the *Poetics*—principles of structure and unity, of agency and character, of the arousal of the genre's defining emotions. The peculiar pleasure that tragedy affords will thus be of a compound kind ("the pleasure from pity

[65] *Telos:* 6.1450a18, 22–23; 25.1460b24–26; 26.1462a18–b1, 1462b12–15. *Ergon:* 6.1450a31; 13.1452b29–30; 26.1462b12–13.
[66] One such instance is Heath 1987, 9–10. Heath 1996, xxxv–xliii, rightly recognizes multiple pleasures in the *Poetics,* but he ultimately declines to explain the "proper pleasure of tragedy" beyond linking it to Aristotle's acceptance of the traditional "paradox" of enjoying poetry on painful themes.

and fear through mimesis"), and one that, as I have argued, exemplifies those general principles of mimetic pleasure which are indicated in *Poetics* 4 and *Rhetoric* 1.11. We should, therefore, avoid ascribing to Aristotle the bare, unqualified view that the aim of tragedy is to give pleasure. It is essential to the whole cast of Aristotelian thought and evaluation that such a proposition requires suitable qualification in order to situate the idea of tragic pleasure within a fuller appraisal of the genre: only so will it become clear what differentiates tragic pleasure from other pleasures ("it is not every pleasure, but the appropriate pleasure, that one should seek from tragedy," 1453b10–11).

If, accordingly, we ask what, on Aristotle's reckoning, poetry (or any other culturally advanced form of mimesis) is *for*, the answer will be (like the ideal tragedy) complex, not simple.[67] We can be confident that Aristotle would wish to stress, with due explanation, that poetry is "for its own sake," not in any absolute way but in the sense that its aims are not directly instrumental to some externally specifiable goal.[68] Equally, an Aristotelian answer to the question will have to refer centrally to pleasure, because pleasure, as opposed to a biologically necessary or practical purpose, is indispensable to the existence of all mimetic art. This pleasure might be analyzed further into a range of pleasures, many of which I have not been able or concerned to deal with in this chapter.[69] But Aristotle speaks firmly of the pleasure peculiar and proper to individual genres, and this is the pleasure that, exemplifying and refining the general conception sketched in *Poetics* 4, lies at the heart of his theory of poetry. Such pleasure, I have been contending, is considered by Aristotle to arise from the exercise of our capacities for both understanding and emotion in the engagement with the fictive possibilities that art dramatizes. The proper pleasure of an activity, on the mature view of *Nicomachean Ethics* book 10, is the consummation of the nature of the activity. If we wish to grasp a particular pleasure, we must accordingly grasp the activity to which it belongs and which it completes. On the arguments I have put forward in this chapter, this means that the best answer we can construct on Aristot-

---

[67] When, in a context of politico-educational thought, Aristotle poses such a question explicitly for music at *Pol.* 8.5, 1339a11–42b34, his answer encompasses factors of play and relaxation, emotion and ethical character, as well as *diagōgē*, a form of cultivated and pleasurable "leisure" (cf. Kraut 1997, 144, 188–89). Babut 1985a, 89 n. 74, wrongly supposes that to refer to pleasure is to say all that needs to be said about Aristotle's conception of poetry's value.

[68] Cf. Aristotle *Protr.* fr. 77.63 (Gigon 1987), = fr. 44 Düring, where an intrinsic justification for attending dramatic performances ("purely for the sake of watching/contemplating") forms a comparison for the idea that the study of philosophy requires no external reward.

[69] See Halliwell 1986, 62–81, for a more compendious account.

le's behalf to the question, What is poetry for? must accommodate and
integrate all three elements of my title—pleasure, understanding, and
emotion—within a composite notion of aesthetic experience. Whether,
or in what respect, such an answer would also have something to say
about catharsis, is a topic on which I here elect, very deliberately, to remain (almost) silent.[70]

[70] Halliwell 1992d gives a summary of my own (increasingly skeptical) position on catharsis; cf. Halliwell 1986, 184–201, for a more protracted struggle. The huge disproportion between the slender evidence available to us and the mountain of (often depressingly self-
confident) secondary literature on catharsis makes a temporary moratorium on discussion of
the subject a consummation devoutly to be wished. Among the more helpful of recent treatments, however, are Zierl 1994, 72–85; Ford 1995; Kraut 1997, 208–12; and Donini 1998
(the latter denying that Aristotle takes catharsis to be the essential function of tragedy). The
interpretation of Gallop 1999, 86–90 (catharsis is "spiritual peace" induced by the spectacle
of "exemplary magnanimity or dignity in face of undeserved suffering") is ruled out by Aristotle's flat dismissal of plots based on the sufferings of morally distinguished characters (*Poet.*
13.1452b34–36, 1453a7–8). Sorabji 2000, 288–300, looks for echoes of Aristotelian catharsis
in later ancient sources. Cf. my note 64, and chapter 7, note 36.

Chapter Seven

✸

Tragic Pity: Aristotle and Beyond

LEAR: But we made the world, out of our smallness and
weakness . . . and we have only one thing to keep us sane: pity,
and the man without pity is mad. (Edward Bond, *Lear* III.3)

Mitleiden aber ist der tiefste Abgrund: so tief der Mensch in das
Leben sieht, so tief sieht er auch in das Leiden. (Nietzsche)[1]

FOR ARISTOTLE as for Plato, the deepest, most significant and most philosophically interesting of all mimetic artforms was tragic poetry.[2] That tragedy should attract such attention from both philosophers was a reflection
not only of the genre's cultural prestige in classical Athens, but also, and
more fundamentally, of the scope of its ethical and psychological engagement with extremes of human experience and suffering. Plato, as I argued
in chapter 3, counted tragedy as a kind of embryonic (though profoundly
mistaken) philosophy: the vehicle of a set of attitudes and values capable
of being translated into a worldview that, if taken seriously, would negate
his own search for a transcendent understanding of reality. There is no
indication that Aristotle ever felt impelled to judge tragedy in this manner
as a *rival* or a threat to philosophy, and every reason to believe, as the
preceding chapter maintained, that he esteemed tragedy as the finest form
of poetry's quasi-philosophical concern with "universals." But if that is so,
there are further questions worth asking about the specifically emotional
dimension that Aristotle attributed to the experience of tragic drama. At the
center of tragedy, for Aristotle, lies the mimesis, the dramatic enactment, of
"the pitiful" (*to eleeinon*) and "the fearful" (*to phoberon*), and at the heart
of the experience of tragedy, therefore, lie pity and fear themselves.
Thanks to the enshrinement of this thesis in the famous definition at the
start of *Poetics* 6, tragic pity, in particular, has acquired an entrenched,
indeed canonical status as a marker for theories of the genre. Yet our direct
evidence for Aristotle's own interpretation of the psychology of tragedy's

---

[1] "Pity is the deepest abyss: the deeper man looks into life, the deeper too he looks into
suffering": Nietzsche, *Also sprach Zarathustra* 3, "Vom Gesicht und Rätsel" 1, Nietzsche 1988,
4:199.

[2] By discussing epic and tragedy separately in the *Poetics*, and ranking them comparatively
(in ch. 26), Aristotle dilutes Plato's great idea that Homer was "leader of the tragedians" (see
chapter 3, note 1). But Aristotle nonetheless regards Homer as a quasi-tragic poet (even, I
maintain, in the *Odyssey*): see esp. *Poet.* 4.1448b34–49a2, with Halliwell 1986, 254–56, 262–
64.

audience remains rather slender. That is a prime reason for my decision
to adopt a fresh perspective on the subject in this chapter by constructing
a larger framework of ideas and issues within which to work out a reading
of the Aristotelian model of tragic pity (and to a lesser extent, for reasons
that will emerge in due course, of tragic fear). In this spirit, I begin by
invoking a remarkable and revealing case of an individual tragedy whose
very action comes to revolve around the operation of pity.

In Sophocles' *Philoctetes*, the young Neoptolemus, son of Achilles, is
initially and reluctantly persuaded by Odysseus to employ stealthy deception for the capture of Philoctetes and his bow. Neoptolemus's reluctance,
which Odysseus overcomes by appealing to a heroic desire for glory (112–
20), has nothing to do with his attitude toward Philoctetes himself. At this
early stage Neoptolemus shows no signs of regarding the abandoned hero
at all differently from the way in which Odysseus regards him. Both men
accept the legitimacy, even the imperative, of striving to take control of
Philoctetes, together with his bow, in the best interests of the Greek army
at Troy. They disagree only, in the first place, about the methods to be
used. One consequence of this shared view is that there is no hint in the
first scene of *Philoctetes*, even as Neoptolemus shows resistance to Odysseus's strategy for deception, that the wounded, outcast hero might be an
appropriate object of pity.[3] Odysseus, we soon sense, holds a perception
of Philoctetes that assimilates him to the state of a dangerous wild animal[4]—a prey too powerful and potentially ferocious to be captured by
head-on confrontation and therefore needing to be outwitted by cunning.
Neoptolemus too seems to understand this conception (cf. 116), and he
accepts the appropriateness of treating Philoctetes as an object of quasi-
military planning and, if necessary, aggression. His own initial preference,
after all, was for the use of force (90, 104–6).

But something changes; and it starts to change once Neoptolemus is left
alone with his sailors (the chorus) to carry out the instructions given him
by Odysseus. In its entrance song, the chorus expresses sentiments that
had been suppressed in the opening exchanges between Odysseus and
Neoptolemus. It begins to feel and to voice the possibility of pity (169–
75). In the first instance this seems a very basic, instinctive reaction to the
thought that *any* human should have to endure such isolation, depriva-
tion, and pain (hence its generalized exclamations about the human race

---

[3] Odysseus's abrupt deflection from the subject of Philoctetes' pain at 11 might, however,
be subtly read (or acted) as a deliberate suppression of the thought of the rejected hero's
suffering, and thus of the option of pity.

[4] This is an overtone of the adjective *agrios* (wild) from the very start (9 etc.), and perhaps
also of *phorbē* (43, cf. 162, 708–11, 1108), standardly used of animal food. Later in the play
the theme of Odysseus as hunter (609; cf. 839, 1005–7) is explicit.

at 177–79).[5] This is, however, no abstract, detached thought, but a direct response to the present situation: it is the sailors' immediate experience of conditions on the deserted island, as well as the bleak sight of Philoctetes' cave, that prompts the impulse to pity. It is not simply when, unlike Odysseus, they remember the humanity of Philoctetes, but precisely when they try to *imagine* the nature of his life, that their pity comes into play. And once the basic impulse to pity is given, it can be developed into a more concentrated judgment. The chorus goes on to pity Philoctetes more especially for suffering not as an ordinary human being but as a Greek hero of noble status (180–81), and therefore, by implication, as a figure especially undeserving of such a fate.[6]

Neoptolemus is exposed to the possibility of pity, then, almost as soon as his companions join him. But that possibility quickly expands, growing in vividness and detail, when he is confronted by Philoctetes himself. Pity, in fact, is virtually the first thing for which Philoctetes appeals (227), and his appeal echoes the chorus's thoughts in the parodos by starting from the basic expectation of sympathy for someone whose plight is so desolate, but then becoming intensified by the sense of shared Greekness and the prospect of *philia*, of emotionally charged kinship and friendship, which that evokes (234–44). The dramatic psychology of Neoptolemus's reactions to both the implicit and the explicit appeals to pity that stem from Philoctetes runs right through the core of the play.[7] I would like to make just three brief but important points about this psychology. First, it is an extraordinary feature of *Philoctetes* that it invites its audience to recognize the increasing aptness of pity (and thereby the increasing dilemma facing Neoptolemus) without having access, until much later, to Neoptolemus's own reactions. This means that individual spectators or readers are forced to imagine the internal drama in Neoptolemus's mind on the basis of their own reactions to Philoctetes, and then, subsequently, to test their reactions against those to which Neoptolemus eventually confesses at 895 onward (and esp. 965–66). The play challenges its audience, in other words, to correlate its own feelings with those which it can only, for some time, project hypothetically (and far from confidently, given Neoptolemus's established mythological persona)[8] onto one of the characters. In

---

[5] Cf. the similar but fuller thoughts at Sophocles *OT* 1186–96, discussed, in connection with Plato, in chapter 3, section II.

[6] The judgment is eventually made explicit at 685, *anaxiōs* (undeservingly); cf. Aristotle's linkage of tragic pity to one who is *anaxios* at *Poet.* 13.1453a4–5, with, e.g., Isocrates 16.48.

[7] There are further cues for pity at 501, 507, 756 (cf. 308–9, a reference to previous visitors to the island); see Whitlock Blundell 1989, 193–95, with Winnington-Ingram 1980, 283–88, on the concealed development of Neoptolemus's reactions to Philoctetes.

[8] Since Neoptolemus's involvement in this story was a crucial innovation of Sophocles, his firmly established association with ruthless violence at Troy (see Schefold 1992, 281–87;

that process, I suggest, the spectators of *Philoctetes* are compelled, if only subconsciously, to face urgent questions about the nature of pity itself.

Second, the pity that gradually and, as we later discover, irresistibly overcomes Neoptolemus's will-to-deceive is inseparable from how Neoptolemus comes to perceive Philoctetes as a person. It is inseparable, that is to say, not just from Neoptolemus's observation of the terrible pain tormenting Philoctetes (harrowing though that experience is for the observer), but also from the recognition of the complex relationship that starts to unfold between them—a relationship that draws on the former comradeship between Philoctetes and Achilles (with all that this means for Neoptolemus's sense of himself as the son of Achilles), as well as on the profound, almost desperate *need* for new bonds of friendship (*philia*) that Philoctetes manifests from his first cry of greeting onward.[9] The chorus of sailors had spontaneously felt an impulse of pity toward Philoctetes' plight simply as a case of human suffering. But Neoptolemus, as well as the chorus itself (676–729), comes to feel pity of a much more concretely focused kind, for *this* particular person suffering in *this* particular way. Pity may grow from deep roots of compassion, but its developed forms depend on sensitivity to individual, personal circumstances.

My third and final point corroborates, from a rather different angle, the fact that pity in the *Philoctetes* is not just presented as a raw or generalized instinct but as an emotion conditional on specific perceptions and judgments. At a much later stage of the play than I have so far mentioned, after Neoptolemus has yielded to pity and has ceased to treat Philoctetes as an object of deception (ceased to treat him as means to an end, and started to treat him as an end in himself), Philoctetes' intransigence over returning with the Greeks to Troy starts to reverse the direction of Neoptolemus's feelings, to tilt the scales of his sympathy away from him. Once again the chorus is implicated in this emotional movement. The chorus first expresses a withdrawal or qualification of pity at 1095–1100, speaking of Philoctetes as now responsible for his own misfortune and as the cause of the impasse that has arisen. Its reproachful attitude is, so to speak, that of "Heracleiteans" who accuse Philoctetes of turning into his own fate and misfortune, allowing his character to become his *daimōn*.[10] Neoptolemus subsequently spells out the point at 1316–23, distinguishing between unavoidable (god-sent) and voluntary suffering, and asserting that sympathy

---

Gantz 1993, 649–59; and chapter 8, note 18, for the mythological traditions) would hardly have induced an audience to anticipate that he would eventually "crack" with pity in this play.

[9] *Philia* is marked out as an intense and vital theme from Philoctetes' first appearance (224, 228–29, 234, 237, 242, etc.); see Whitlock Blundell 1989, 184–225, and, with emphasis on guest friendship (*xenia*), Belfiore 2000a, 63–80. Konstan 1999a takes a different line.

[10] See Heraclitus fr. 119 DK, *ēthos anthrōpōi daimōn*: "human character is destiny".

and pity should be withheld in cases of self-chosen affliction. Pity can be withdrawn, Neoptolemus implies, just as it can be granted, because the pitier always makes a judgment, however tacitly, about the situation and merits of the person concerned.

My first reason for beginning a chapter whose principal concern is Aristotle's conception of tragic pity with some remarks on Sophocles' *Philoctetes* is to invoke an exceptionally thought-provoking instance of a tragic situation in which pity itself functions as a catalyst between the play's central characters. The case of *Philoctetes* is one that, so I have suggested, challenges its audience to discern the pressure toward tragic pity in a way that creates a paradoxical relationship between its own feelings and those of Neoptolemus; in doing so it calls simultaneously for both strong emotional absorption and a highly reflective attitude on the part of spectators.[11] In watching *Philoctetes* we face an implicit choice between thinking and feeling like Odysseus or like Neoptolemus. But to understand what it means to feel like Neoptolemus—and this is the heart of the paradox—we have to become aware of pity in ourselves *before* we discover (for we could not know it in advance) that Neoptolemus himself is in the grip of it. To feel pity for Philoctetes only retrospectively, once Neoptolemus himself has admitted to it, would amount to something very different, something far from consonant with the viewpoint that comes to prevail inside the drama. Sophocles challenges his audience, in effect, to interpret the place of pity within the play through the medium of its own openness to such emotion. If these contentions are justifiable, *Philoctetes* makes an apposite point of comparison for various facets of Aristotle's own conception of tragic pity to be considered in the course of this chapter.

Sophocles' play, then, usefully supplies part of the larger perspective (the element of "beyond Aristotle" in my title) within which I think it is most fruitful to place the philosopher's own views on pity, views that afford a particularly rich set of connections with ideas that precede and follow them in the history of interpretations of tragedy. The larger perspective I want to delineate in this case is both Greek (involving reference to Plato and other intellectual predecessors, as well as to the types of poetry with which the *Poetics* is concerned) but also more-than-Greek. By bringing Aristotle's views into conjunction with other philosophical and critical attitudes to pity, we have a better chance of making sense of his own historical position, while at the same time engaging in a kind of ongoing historical dialogue with him.

As a further contribution to this fuller perspective, I want at this point to introduce a large but potentially instructive question about the psychol-

[11] See Nussbaum 1999, 257–59, 267–69, for some related considerations, though she does not highlight the special challenge posed to the audience by Neoptolemus's concealed reactions to Philoctetes.

ogy of pity. Is there a sense in which pity can and should be regarded as a particularly "theatrical" emotion? Might it be that pity lends itself especially aptly to theatrical experiences, not only in strict relation to dramatic performances but also in the broader, but also etymological, sense of experiences in which we occupy an observer's or spectator's, rather than a participant's, role—the role of an onlooker or witness rather than an agent? Some such thought seems to have occurred to Goethe, one of whose maxims tells us: "The man of action is always free of conscience; the only person with a conscience is the observer" (Der Handelnde ist immer gewissenlos, es hat niemand Gewissen als der Betrachtende).[12] It seems obvious, of course, that pity can be a motivating factor in all sorts of situations of action, not just in observation of others, and, conversely, that a failure to act or intervene in certain contexts can be a telling criterion for the absence of pity. After all, the example of Neoptolemus's behavior in Sophocles' *Philoctetes* is precisely a case in point: it is pity, as he eventually admits (965–66), that causes the crisis in his attitude to, and treatment of, Philoctetes.[13] Yet it is worth adding that we might think that the force of pity in *Philoctetes* overcomes Neoptolemus partly because he finds himself in a kind of agonized suspension between the roles of agent (in the first instance, as servant of Odysseus's plan and the army's needs) *and* observer (as witness of the harrowing suffering, both physical and mental, of his father's former friend). Pity works its way, as it were, into the space between these two psychological stances vis-à-vis the wounded, abandoned hero.

The general question, then, retains some relevance. Does pity lend itself particularly well to theatrical experience, in both the narrower and the wider senses of the term? If Lessing was right (in echoing a Platonic thought) to say that all Stoicism is untheatrical,[14] is pity, by contrast, crucial to the engrossing theatrical interest of pain and suffering? On the Greek front, several considerations give some substance to this possibility. In the first place, not just Aristotle but a much larger Greek tradition, attested in, among others, well-known passages of Gorgias's *Helen* and Plato's *Ion* to which I shall return, appears to have taken it as a basic datum that pity lies at the center of the experience of tragic poetry. Furthermore, there is the salient though in some ways puzzling importance of pity to the Homeric picture of the gods in the (tragic) *Iliad*.[15] Those gods are, of course,

---

[12] Goethe 1985–98, 17:758 (no. 241).

[13] There are other factors, especially shame (906–9), in Neoptolemus's great dilemma, and my remarks on this dilemma are necessarily partial: but this does not affect the central, acknowledged function of pity.

[14] See chapter 2, with its note 26.

[15] Divine pity in Homer is puzzling insofar as we might wonder how divine beings can feel pity at all for humans. Psychological accounts of pity, both ancient and modern, explain

agents as well as onlookers, and the pity they feel does sometimes motivate action, as when their collective pity for Hector's corpse leads them to
intervene against Achilles' maltreatment of it (24.23ff.; cf. 24.19). But the
Iliadic gods seem to feel pity above all when they look down as observers
of the human scene—when, in terms that the poem itself recognizes, they
view the human world as a spectacle of which they themselves form the
theater audience.[16]

Finally, as regards the Greek tradition, two statements found in classical
Athenian writers seem to support a case for what, in the sense already
adumbrated, could be called the theatricality of pity. Both in the speech
Against Alcibiades ascribed to Andocides (a work whose authenticity remains controversial but which is probably classical in date) and in Isocrates' *Panegyricus* (of around 380) we find passages that rebuke Athenian
civic audiences for being more susceptible to pity in the theater than in
actual political life[17]—thereby contradicting, we may note in passing,
Plato's premise in *Republic* 10 that exposure to emotion in the theater
conduces to an increased, not a diminished, susceptibility to the equivalent emotions in one's own life.[18] Andocides, complaining about Alcibiades' alleged fathering of a son on an enslaved woman from Melos, suggests that when they see such things on the tragic stage—and it is
presumably Trojan War plays he has particularly in mind—the Athenians
find them horrifying (*deina*, a term Aristotle uses in at least one passage
of the *Poetics* to indicate the arousal of tragic fear),[19] but are unmoved

---

the emotion in terms of a capacity for fellow feeling, more specifically (an Aristotelian point,
this, made in the *Rhetoric*, but echoed by later thinkers too: see note 55) a capacity to sympathize (*sumpaschein*) with the kinds of suffering to which we are vulnerable ourselves. Can
divine pity be explained in these terms? Perhaps, given the strongly anthropomorphic conception of the Homeric gods. But the question needs more explication than it has so far
received. By the same token, the ascription of a capacity for pity to the Christian god raises
an equivalent but perhaps more acute problem. See, on this and much besides, Konstan
2001 (published too late for me to take account of it).

[16] See Griffin 1980, 179–204, though he does not address the problem formulated in my
previous note.

[17] Andocides 4.23 (the latest discussion of the speech is Gribble 1997, who locates it in
the late fourth century), Isocrates 4.168 (cf. note 19). Lada 1996, 95–97, cites the latter but
seems to me to sidestep its claim; for different readings of the Andocides passage, see Griffin
1998, 61; Wilson 1996, 320–21.

[18] By contrast, Plato's point about yielding in the theater to emotions we might try to
resist in our own lives (*Rep.* 10.605d–e) is consistent with the observations of Andocides and
Isocrates. For ambiguities in Athenian attitudes to pity, as revealed by rhetorical texts, see
Stevens 1944.

[19] See Aristotle *Poet.* 14.1453b14, and cf. the implications of 13.1453a22, 14.1453b30,
19.1456b3. In Andocides as in the *Poetics*, *deinos* marks something other than normal, self-
regarding fear: see my subsequent comments, with Plato *Ion* 535c7, where *deinos* connects
with the effect of imaginative "amazement," *ekplēxis* (cf. *Ion* 535b2), which in turn is part of

by their occurrence in life. In similar terms, Isocrates claims that theater audiences weep tears of pity when watching tragedy's dramatization of the sufferings caused by war (including the confusions of friendship and enmity, a detail pertinent to *Philoctetes*), yet the same people can even feel *Schadenfreude* ("they enjoy the miseries of others") when witnessing such sufferings in real life. Like Andocides, Isocrates detects a kind of *sentimentality*—an emotional experience that carries no real commitments with it and is manipulated by the poetic designs of the tragedians— in the phenomenon of tragic pity. We should not, however, disregard the manner in which both writers exploit this point with a rhetorical hyperbole that may make it less than wholly transparent evidence for the cultural psychology of actual Athenian theater audiences.

"It is not good to stay too long in the theatre," as Francis Bacon was to put it. In the long, intricate history of "antitheatrical" attitudes in Western culture anxieties over pity and related emotions have surfaced many times.[20] A position interestingly akin to the one that underlies the passages just cited from Isocrates and Andocides can be found in Rousseau's critique of the theater, especially in his *Lettre à d'Alembert* of 1758. Rousseau there refers to pity experienced in the theater as "a transient and vain emotion, a sterile pity that has never produced the slightest act of humanity" (une émotion passagère et vaine . . .; une pitié stérile, qui . . . n'a jamais produit le moindre acte d'humanité). Emotion felt in the theater, according to Rousseau, leaves spectators feeling self-satisfied with their own virtuous sentiments; but far from providing a spur to benevolence or virtue outside the theater, this self-satisfaction is actually conducive only to a sluggish complacency in the face of all those real social evils that call insistently for practical remedy.[21] Whatever else one might make of such convictions (which form a partial antecedent of Brecht's critique of "Aristotelian" theater and the political apathy it supposedly encourages), they seem to reinforce the supposition that pity, alongside related kinds of sympathetic or

---

the "pity and fear" complex; on *ekplēxis* (see *Poet.* 14.1454a4, 16.1455a17; Sicking 1998, 105, bafflingly claims that the term is "definitely not Aristotelian") cf. Heath 1987, 15–16; Belfiore 1992, 216–22; and, in connection with *anagnōrisis*, Cave 1988, 43–45. Isoc. 4.168 uses *deinos* of the events in life for which the Athenians fail to feel *pity*: he thus clearly links pity and fear, and alludes, I think, to a standard conception of tragedy that linked them too; note the conjunction of pity and *deinos* at, e.g., Sophocles *Phil.* 501–2. See also notes 33, 35.

[20] The Bacon quotation is from *The Advancement of Learning* (1605), bk. 2 (in Vickers 1996, 188). The antitheatrical theme is searchingly documented and analyzed by Barish 1981.

[21] Rousseau 1959–95, 5: 3–125 (quotation on 23); cf. chapter 2, section II. Rousseau's views of the theater are discussed in Banerjee 1977, Barish 1981, 256–94, with further references; the particular focus on pity should be compared with the famous passage at Augustine *Conf.* 3.2 (see chapter 1, note 55). Differences between pity felt toward fiction and in life are remarked on also by William Wordsworth in his postscript of 1835 (in Owen & Smyser 1974, 3:247, 266–7).

compassionate feeling, is particularly suitable for the concentrated but artificial spectatorship of theater. But if this is right, the essential inference to
be drawn, I suggest, concerns the psychology of pity itself, not the nature
of theater, at any rate in the strictly institutional sense. The point I want to
emphasize is that pity seems to make itself available in a rather intense
form in contexts where no immediate question of acting upon the emotion
arises. If so, pity arguably differs in this respect from many other emotions,
such as anger, envy, hatred (and also, I would say, fear, in its normal,
wholly self-regarding reference),[22] whose occurrence, though still modifi-
able for the vicarious experience of theater, is paradigmatically much more
closely linked to particular kinds of action than is the case with pity. It
may be too that Plato's anxieties about the indulgence of pity in a theatrical
context (where the soul enjoys the experience partly by telling itself "these
are other people's sufferings it is watching") rests on a recognition of pity's
peculiar tendency to flow freely in settings, especially involving mass audiences, where it belongs exclusively to the viewpoint of an observer, not
an agent.[23]

There is one final refinement I would like to add to this thesis before
finally turning to Aristotle's own treatment of tragic pity in the *Poetics*. It
was a subtle insight of Aristotle—not in the *Poetics* but in his fuller account
of emotions in the *Rhetoric*—that pity maintains a rather delicate balance
between psychological involvement and distance. Later thinkers who
have interested themselves in the subject of pity have sometimes overlooked what is at stake here. Take Rousseau again, but this time in his
broad view of pity as the most basic human impulse apart from self-love,
and therefore as the source of all social virtues. When Rousseau expounds
this view in part I of his *Discours sur l'origine et les fondements de l'inégalité parmi les hommes*, he writes at one point, with a formulation that
encompasses other sentient beings than humans: "compassion [*la commiseration*, here synonymous with *la pitié*] will be all the more powerful,
the more closely the animal observing identifies itself with the animal that
suffers."[24] But there is an important objection to this unqualified proposition, and it is, as I have indicated, an Aristotelian objection. In implying
that pity can be intensified indefinitely while still remaining pity, Rousseau's argument (and this is clear, I think, from the context as a whole)

---

[22] But see my later discussion, with note 32, for qualification of this point in relation to
tragic "pity and fear."

[23] For *allotria pathē*, "other people's sufferings," see *Rep.* 10.606b1, with chapter 2, section
I, and note 14 there for the Gorgianic precedent. On mass audiences (in Athens), see chapter
2, section I and chapter 3, note 5.

[24] "La commiseration sera d'autant plus énergique que l'animal spectateur identifiera plus
intimement avec l'animal souffrant," Rousseau 1959–95, 3:111–236, at 155. Although Rousseau is speaking principally of humans, his phrasing alludes to a conviction that other animals too can feel pity to some extent.

elides a distinction between sympathy and identification.[25] This elision or
blurring, as I argued in chapter 2, occurs in other eighteenth-century writings too, including Adam Smith's account of sympathy in his *Theory of
Moral Sentiments*,[26] but what it blurs is a distinction that, in their different
ways, both Plato and Aristotle insist on. Aristotle makes the point apropos
pity in the *Rhetoric* by observing that pity is not felt toward those who are
so close and important to us that their sufferings *become* ours too.[27] In
such cases pity gives way to full immersion in grief (or, say, anger, depending on circumstances). At the other extreme, of course, no one would
contest the fact that too much distance, too much detachment (or too
little imagination), is also incompatible with pity: think again—aptly—of
Odysseus in Sophocles' *Philoctetes*.

Pity, in sum, seems to involve a degree of sympathy or fellow feeling
(*sumpaschein* and its cognates are Aristotle's, and other Greeks', regular
terms in this connection), but a sympathy that does not erase the sense of
difference between oneself and the object of pity. Pity, and perhaps above
all tragic pity, draws its audience close to the sufferings of others, but
allows and requires it to perceive those sufferings in ways that are necessarily distinct from the sufferer's own standpoint. Suffering, we might say,
entails a very strong kind of subjectivity, as exemplified in, though not
confined to, the nature of physical pain. When we feel pity, we do not
share the sufferer's subjectivity: however much we may draw emotionally
near to it, or move vicariously with its psychological expression, we remain, *qua* feelers of pity, outside the immediate, "first-person" reality of
the pain, whether physical or mental.[28] And that degree of psychological
space, so to speak, allows pity to take on a particularly free but also intense
form in theatrical settings, where, however engaged or absorbed an audience may become, it can never lose at least a subliminal awareness of its
spectatorial role.

II

In moving from this general, deliberately open-ended framework of ideas
to Aristotle's terse arguments in the *Poetics*, we face a prima facie difficulty.
Aristotle's repeated references to pity and fear as the twin defining ele-

---

[25] Dent 1992, 52–53, carefully qualifies Rousseau's stress on compassionate "identification"; but he does not, I think, fully meet the point made in my text.

[26] See chapter 2, section II.

[27] Aristotle *Rhet.* 2.8, 1386a18–23; cf. Macleod 1983, 3–4, 8.

[28] For one interpretation of this point, see Nietzsche, *Morgenröte* 2.133 (Nietzsche 1988,
3:125), where Nietzsche develops the extreme view that there is always an element of *unconscious* self-regard in pity. Cf. also *Die fröhliche Wissenschaft* 4.338 (Nietzsche 1988, 3:565–
68).

ments of the experience of tragedy have become a prominent landmark in the history of accounts of the genre. But an immediate impediment to seeing the relationship between the landmark and the rest of the terrain is placed in our way by the fact that the *Poetics* itself provides no definition of these emotions, still less of their peculiarly tragic combination—nothing, at any rate, beyond chapter 13's minimal statement that pity is felt for characters who do not deserve the misfortune they suffer, and fear for those who are "like" ourselves (1453a5–6).[29] I call the combination of pity and fear "peculiarly tragic" because most cases of real-life pity are not accompanied directly by fear, and vice versa. It is with this normal psychological perspective in mind that in book 2 of the *Rhetoric*, where we do find definitions and substantial analyses of the two emotions, Aristotle observes at one point that fear can actually drive out pity.[30] That goes to show, first, that those who think fear in the *Poetics* is principally a self-regarding (as opposed to a vicarious) emotion have a serious exegetical problem, because Aristotle appears not to believe that pity and overtly self-regarding fear belong together; and, second, that not everything said about the emotions in the *Rhetoric*, illuminating though I take its relevant chapters to be, is necessarily or straightforwardly transferable to the interpretation of tragic pity and fear.[31] Having discussed elsewhere the relationship between the *Poetics*' and the *Rhetoric*'s treatments of these emotions, I want here to concentrate on how they fit into the *Poetics*' overall theory of tragedy, despite the work's own relative lack of direct explication. Moreover, although I shall continue to make reference to the combination of emotions, my interest here is predominantly in pity, and I leave the debate about tragic fear very largely on one side, though not before reaffirming my view that fear is secondary to pity, and "parasitic" on it, in Aristotle's scheme.[32]

---

[29] Although the idea of "likeness" is stipulated specifically for fear at 1453a5–6, it effectively applies just as much to pity, as a comparison with *Rhet.* 2.5, 1383a10, 1386a24 shows. This reinforces the convergence and synthesis of the two emotions in the powerfully "sympathetic" experience of tragedy; cf. note 32.

[30] Aristotle *Rhet.* 2.8, 1386a21–23; cf. 1385b33–34. One striking instance of grief (not pity) combined with self-regarding fear occurs in the description of the emotional turmoil of the Athenians toward the dead and wounded at Thuc. 7.75.3–4.

[31] Two differently nuanced accounts of the relationship between the *Poetics* and *Rhetoric* 2's definitions of pity and fear are Nussbaum 1992 and Nehamas 1992; my own view of the matter is set out in Halliwell 1986, 172–84.

[32] I take the tragic fear of the *Poetics* to be essentially other-regarding, felt not directly for oneself but vicariously "for" (*peri*, *Poet.* 13.1453a5–6) the tragic agents; it is therefore not so much a distinct impulse as an index, in the experience of mimetic art, of the intensity of the impulse to pity. It is, however, an entailment of Aristotelian psychology, as indicated in the *Rhetoric* (2.8, 1386a26–28; cf. 1385b14–15), that pity contains an implicitly self-regarding fear (which may, of course, be more or less prominent, more or less conscious, in particular

A historical consideration should be foregrounded at once. Aristotle's omission of an explicit justification for positing pity and fear (or, perhaps preferably, pity-and-fear) as the core emotions in the experience of tragedy has an obvious enough explanation. Passages of Gorgias's *Helen* and Plato's *Ion* strongly suggest that this view of the psychology of tragic audiences was already well established long before the *Poetics* was composed. Not only do these passages involve a close coupling of the two emotions within descriptions of the experience of serious poetry (epic in the case of *Ion*, unspecified in that of Gorgias), but both also imply, unmistakably I think, that the nature of such emotional responses was recognized as such in the culture at large.[33] When Gorgias states that mass audiences of poetry feel "a fearful shuddering and a pity that brings floods of tears," or when Socrates and Ion are able to agree that the hearers of epic recitals find their hair standing on end, become highly excited, and weep profusely, both authors purport to be giving readily recognizable images, not idiosyncratic interpretations, of commonly observed cultural behavior. A case can even be made for seeing such descriptions as belonging to a tradition that goes all the way back to the Homeric epics, where experiences of both pity and fear seem to play a part in the accounts of individual responses to poetic storytelling.[34] And because we have ample confirmatory evidence in classical sources of the expectation that Athenian spectators of tragedy, in particular, would indulge in open weeping,[35] it is plausi-

---

instances). So there is a sort of convergence of the two emotions under the special conditions of the aesthetic-imaginative experience of tragedy. I give a fuller statement of my views in Halliwell 1986, 168–201. Cf. note 29.

[33] Gorgias fr. 11.8–9 DK (cf. chapter 2, note 14), Plato *Ion* 535b–e. Recall, too, that the passages from Andocides and Isocrates cited earlier—the Isocrates certainly and the Andocides conceivably earlier than the *Poetics*—both use the adjective *deinos* (suggestive of "fear" as a response), and the Isocrates speaks directly of pity: see note 19. The treatment of Aristotle in Konstan 1999b needs somewhat modifying in the light of this evidence for a cultural consensus, though it is anyway doubtful whether Aristotle should be taken as *limiting* tragic emotions to pity and fear. Nietzsche's criticism of Aristotle, in *Die fröhliche Wissenschaft* 2.80 (Nietzsche 1988, 3:436), for ascribing the desire for pity and fear to tragic audiences, is particularly perverse (cf. section III).

[34] The Homeric evidence is discussed by Shankman 1983; cf. Halliwell 1986, 170 n. 3, for some other indications of pre-Aristotelian couplings of pity and fear, noting esp. Sophocles *Phil.* 500–503 in view of my earlier discussion of this play.

[35] The passages of Gorgias and Plato already cited (note 33) both specify profuse audience weeping, which is also understood as the accepted response to successful tragic performances at, e.g., Xenophon *Symp.* 3.11; Plato *Phileb.* 48a6, *Rep.* 10.606a; Isocrates 4.168 (cf. notes 17, 19); cf. also Herodotus 6.21.2 (notwithstanding the special circumstances), with Wallace 1997 on the general demonstrativeness of Athenian theater audiences. Stanford 1983, 23–26 notes the "visceral intensity" often associated with pity in Greek sources. Schadewaldt 1955 (followed by, e.g., Flashar 1972, Fuhrmann 1982, 161–64) appeals to this intensity to make a case for sharply separating Greek from later (Christianity-influenced) ideas of pity, but he stresses the "primitive," physical aspect of *eleos* and *phobos* at the expense of the

ble that something very like the formula of "pity and fear" had general
currency within the theatrical culture of fifth- and fourth-century Athens,
and was therefore taken as an uncontentious psychological datum by Aristotle in the *Poetics*.

Just as in other areas of his philosophy, however, we can expect Aristotle to have added something, from his own processes of reflection and
analysis, to ideas that he took over from existing currents of thought. As
it is, the juxtaposition of pity and fear in chapter 6's definition with the
notoriously controversial concept of catharsis (which, by contrast, we
have no good reason to suppose was part of the common currency of
existing thought about tragedy) confirms that the *Poetics* contains an approach to the experience of the genre that goes beyond the merely familiar
or given.[36] So while pity and fear are first mentioned by Aristotle in chapter
6's definition, it is worth asking whether there is anything in the preceding
chapters of the *Poetics* that prepares the way for them. I submit that there
is. After his general classification of mimetic arts in chapters 1–3, Aristotle
offers a schematic "history" of Greek poetry, in chapters 4–5, which accentuates a great bifurcation between serious or elevated (*spoudaios*) and
comic or low poetic traditions. In treating the *Iliad* and *Odyssey* as precur-
sors of tragic drama, and Homer as the true discoverer of tragedy, Aristotle
partially follows Plato (and perhaps others too) in discerning a domain of
serious subject matter and preoccupations that bridges different generic
forms.[37] For Aristotle, the understanding of this domain rests on the concept of seriousness or elevation (*ta spoudaia*; cf. 1448b34), a concept that
has given rise to a good deal of polarized debate but which I take to be a
matter *both* of ethical gravity *and* of "tone" in the action and characters
depicted—ethical gravity itself being the (main) cause of tragedy's serious
or elevated tone. We get a clue to one of the implications of "seriousness"
in Aristotle's remark on the contrasting paradigm of "the comic/laughable"
(*to geloion*, also supposedly discovered by Homer's genius, 1448b36–7)
in chapter 5. When he says that the truly comic deals with matters of ugliness and shame (the adjective *aischros* is used twice, and the noun *aischos*
once) that nonetheless "avoid pain and destruction," we are entitled to
infer that pain and destruction are dimensions of human experience that

---

ethicocognitive value attached to the emotions by Aristotle. See Dilcher 1996, Kerkhecker
1991, for criticism of Schadewaldt, with Zierl 1994, 18–58, for a detailed review of interpretations of the two emotions.

[36] On catharsis, see chapter 6, note 70. I do not mean to deny that *katharsis* terms had
been used as psychological and intellectual metaphors before Aristotle (see Halliwell 1986,
185–88 for Platonic and other usage); but we do not know that they had been specifically
applied to the experience of tragic emotion.

[37] On this point, cf. note 2 and my later discussion. See chapter 5, with its note 61, on the
status of the poetic "history" in *Poet.* 4.

properly belong on the other, "serious" side of poetry's great division. And pain and destruction evidently orientate us in the direction of pity and fear.[38]

"Seriousness"—as Aristotle's overarching concept of the domain of epic and tragic poetry, as well as of what he supposes, more specifically (in chapters 2–3, 5, and 6), to be the defining property of the action and characters of tragedy—contains and communicates, I want to claim, a recognition that the search for virtue and happiness (*eudaimonia*) inescapably brings human beings up against the risk of suffering and misfortune ("pain and destruction," in Aristotle's shorthand). The contemplation of this aspect of the (human) world, when dramatized in tragic plots that have the vividness of particularity but also the larger resonance of "universal" structures of action and experience, activates tragic pity. The closest Aristotle comes in the *Poetics* to spelling out this broad but powerful implication of his concept of "seriousness" is in a somewhat vexed passage of chapter 6 where he addresses the relationship between action and character—the only passage in the entire work, in fact, where the term *eudaimonia* or any of its cognates occurs. What that passage says, with some glosses of my own inserted, is as follows: "The most important of these things [i.e., the six components of tragedy] is the structure of events, because tragedy is mimesis not of people as such but of action(s) and life; and happiness and unhappiness consist in action, and the goal [the goal of life, I take it, but therefore *also* of the mimesis of serious life] is a certain kind of action, not a qualitative state: it is in virtue of character that people have certain qualities, but through their actions that they are happy or the reverse."[39] Although the authenticity of this passage has sometimes been suspected, I see no cogent grounds to doubt that what we have here is Aristotle's clearest indication in the entire treatise that tragedy is a poetic exploration of affairs which bear, at a potentially profound level, on the possibility of "happiness," *eudaimonia*.

That passage in chapter 6 comes a little after the definition of tragedy, in which the concept of seriousness—a "serious action"—is placed alongside the arousal of pity and fear. It is itself followed shortly afterward by a passage that helps to give sharper focus to Aristotle's position; this is the statement at 1450a33–35 that "tragedy's most potent means of emotional

<hr/>

[38] Held 1984 rightly uses the concept of "the comic" to help elucidate that of "the serious"; but his account of both concepts as "teleological" is unhelpful. On the very different tenor of Plato's references to tragic "seriousness," see chapter 3, with its note 27. On the Homeric-tragic dimension of Aristotelian "seriousness," cf. Else 1957, 73–78.

[39] *Poet.* 6.1450a15–20. On the logic of the passage, see Horn 1975; Nussbaum 1986, 378–88, with 500–501 n. 2, rightly uses it to elucidate Aristotle's perspective on the ethics of tragedy; cf. Smithson 1983, esp. 7, and, for an interesting but harsher assessment of Aristotle as critical moralist, Freeland 1992.

effect"—that is, the things most calculated to arouse pity and fear—are the plot components of reversal (*peripeteia*) and recognition (*anagnōrisis*).[40] One marginal observation worth making on this statement is that it precedes by a long way the definition of the terms *peripeteia* and *anagnōrisis* in chapter 11; so we need to notice here, as often elsewhere, how Aristotle regularly presupposes more than he makes immediately explicit. But more important for my main concern is that Aristotle attaches maximum emotional power, and therefore supreme tragic efficacy, to plot components which by their very nature, and in a piquantly concentrated form, expose the precariousness of the control that human beings try to exercise over their lives.[41] *Peripeteia* marks a direct contradiction of intentions and expectations, an ironic rupture of the normal consequentiality of action. *Anagnōrisis* by definition occasions an increase in knowledge or understanding, but this knowledge is often irredeemably negative (where it brings to light what has already been committed in ignorance), and, even where it occurs in time to prevent such action (as in the averted catastrophes of plays like *Iphigeneia in Tauris*, discussed in *Poetics* chapter 14), it nonetheless draws attention sharply to the insecurity and unpredictable consequences of supposedly informed human agency.

But if reversal and recognition expose grave limitations on tragic agents' command over the results of their own agency, and therefore over their own lives, they equally, and for the very same reason, represent moments of illumination for the spectators of tragedy. Here it is crucial to remember that the *Poetics* commits Aristotle, as we would anyway have expected on the basis of his philosophical psychology as a whole, to an interpretation of emotion as cognitively grounded.[42] Pity and fear, whether felt in response to actual events in life or to the depiction of events in mimetic art (and this correlation, as we have seen in previous chapters, is part of what makes mimesis what it is for Aristotle), require an active perception and understanding of human realities, not just a raw or instinctual response to

[40] The idea is later found in a generalized form, linking surprise and emotion in poetic stories, at Plutarch *Aud. Poet.* 25d.

[41] The notion of pity (and related emotions) taking a sudden, keen hold of the mind is sometimes found in tragedy itself: one powerful instance is Soph. *Ant.* 801–5, where the elders experience a kind of involuntary surge of pity at the sight of Antigone being led away to her death.

[42] On the cognitive dimension or grounding of emotions within Aristotelian psychology, see Sherman 1989, esp. 44–50, 165–71; cf. chaper 6. Note that Gorgias too appears to have shared the idea that tragic emotions rest on a cognitive basis. His riddling remark that "the deceiver is better than the nondeceiver, and the deceived wiser than the undeceived" (fr. 23 DK; cf. my introduction, note 49), looks like an attempt to intimate that in responding emotionally to tragic suffering we are not just exercising pre- or unreflective instincts but are guided to a deeper understanding of certain human possibilities: cf. Taplin 1978, 167–71 (whose own position is more Aristotelian than he seems to realize).

suffering (a view of pity espoused, for example, by Rousseau, at least in part).[43] That observation connects Aristotle's view of the tragic emotions with the dramatization of pity in Sophocles' *Philoctetes*, which I earlier examined: in both, emotion is embedded in a fully contextualized awareness of the predicament of others. In one way it is enough here to remind ourselves that even the supremely paradoxical twists of the "complex" (*peplegmenos*) plot must, on Aristotle's principles, be integral to a unified structure of action that makes sense as a whole. The experience of pity and fear at the revelation of human vulnerability may reach a special level of intensity at certain critical turning points in a plot, as the remark quoted earlier about reversal and recognition in chapter 6 (1450a33–35) suggests. But such moments of heightened experience do not, on the Aristotelian model, constitute self-contained frissons of feeling; they are, rather, the peaks of a cumulatively unfolding response to the intelligible significance of the plot in its entirety. In short, and however surprisingly, the implications of pity and fear are inseparable from the requirements of unity that Aristotle prescribes for tragic plays.

A passage that helps to bring out this connection between unity of plot and the arousal of the tragic emotions is the section of *Poetics* 9 where Aristotle advances directly from criticizing "episodic" plots, which fail to satisfy the canons of probability or necessity, to a remark about the nature of pity and fear themselves. What he says is: "Given that mimesis [in tragedy] is not only of a complete action but also of fearful and pitiable matters, the latter arise above all when events occur contrary to expectation yet on account of one another" (1452a1–4). He then expands this point by suggesting that even the creation of a sense of awe or wonder (*to thaumaston*) is best achieved not by inexplicable interventions of chance, but by at least the appearance, and preferably the substance, of causally coherent significance.[44] More than one issue might be pursued in relation to this Aristotelian position: is it, for example, entirely hospitable to the partly obscure workings of religious causation as we encounter it in many surviving Greek tragedies? But all I want to emphasize for the purposes of my present argument is that Aristotle is clearly concerned to connect even the

---

[43] In both the preface and part I of his *Discours sur . . . l'inégalité* (see my note 24), Rousseau refers to pity as a psychological impulse prior to reason or reflection, "antérieur à la raison," "antérieur à toute réfléxion" (Rousseau 1959–95, 5:126, 155). Elsewhere, especially in *Émile*, he seems to accept that pity can involve perceptions and judgments that go beyond the brute facts of suffering. But his notion of natural pity apparently makes it essentially instinctual. On natural versus "social" pity in Rousseau, cf. Ansell-Pearson 1991, 65–68.

[44] The force of *kai* (even) at *Poet.* 9.1452a6 ("even among chance events the greatest wonder is aroused by those that *seem* to have occurred by design") shows that Aristotle does not regard such events as making ideal plots (because they lack a true causal nexus): the thrust of Aristotle's point in this passage is obscured by Ferrari 1999, 191–92.

most paradoxical hinges of tragic action (above all, the startling movements marked by reversal and recognition), and therefore the emotions
evoked by them, to the underlying principle of intelligibility (through
unity) in the construction of plot.

It is important to add that Aristotle is not denying in chapter 9 that
random or chance events could cause us to feel pity and fear for those
affected by them. Indeed, his argument precisely allows for that possibility by claiming that these emotions are aroused "above all" (or "most,"
"best": *malista*) by events that combine a quality of paradox ("contrary
to expectation") with the maintenance of causal continuity ("on account
of one another"). Causal continuity and coherence at the level of plot,
Aristotle believes, provide the conditions for cognitive clarity, and *therefore* emotional power, at the level of audience response. Or, to put it
another way, the more *meaningful* the sequences of actions and events
that generate tragic suffering, the stronger will be the affective responses
of a suitably sensitive audience. The better we (think we) understand
what happens, the fuller and more appropriate will be our emotional
engagement in it.

This link between unity of action and the strength of an audience's pity
and fear is forged partly out of Aristotle's conviction—which he holds so
fundamental as to require no explicit justification—that all tragedies, at
any rate all those classifiable as either "simple" or "complex," dramatize
major transformations, great changes of fortune, in the patterns of human
lives.[45] For the emotional potential of such transformations to be effectively
realized, we need not just the full impingement of the immediate changes
themselves, not just the brute impact of physical or mental afflictions, but
a sufficient context in the lives of those affected—a context of "action(s)
and life," in chapter 6's terms. This context provides the framework within
which the crucial junctures of action, and the corresponding emotional
peaks in the audience's response to them, will carry an intensity that gath-
ers up the significance of the plot structure as a whole. What is at stake in
tragedy, on this Aristotelian model, is not just the depth of suffering involved but the intelligibility of life itself at precisely those moments when
the control exercised (or aspired to) by human agency is exposed to extreme jeopardy. It is not difficult, against this background, to see why
Sophocles' *Oedipus Tyrannus* should have appealed greatly to Aristotle:
it is a classic case of the tragedy of a *whole life*—a whole life, to be sure,
not in the sense of the entirety of its contents (something Aristotle specifi-

---

[45] Aristotle's basic term for such a transformation or transition is *metabasis* (see esp.
10.1452a16); for the accentuated twists of transformation constituted by reversals and recognitions, he prefers *metabolē* (1452a23, 31): but he is not terminologically altogether scrupu-
lous in this respect; cf. Halliwell 1986, 206 n. 7.

cally thinks militates against unity of plot structure, 8.1451a16–22), but rather as a pitifully and fearfully meaningful shape of a life considered as a totality.[46]

The *Oedipus Tyrannus* also provides an instructive illustration of the difference between probability (*eikos*) and chance (*tuchē*) in the scheme of the *Poetics*.[47] In chapter 11 Aristotle takes his example of *peripeteia* (and consequent *anagnōrisis*) from this play, with the following observation (which slightly telescopes the facts of the drama but not in a way that matters for my present argument): "the person who comes to bring Oedipus joy, and intends to rid him of his fear about his mother, creates the opposite effect by revealing Oedipus's true identity."[48] In one sense we might be tempted to object that it is surely coincidence that the messenger who comes from Corinth happens to be the same person who years earlier received the infant Oedipus from the Theban herdsman charged with exposing him on Mount Cithaeron. But Aristotle would hold, I think, and would be right to hold, that Sophocles' play requires us to see that this is no coincidence at all: the two men are one and the same precisely because the slave's earlier rescue of the infant Oedipus gives him a special motivation for wanting to be the person who now brings Oedipus the news that Corinth intends to offer him its kingship.[49] That in turn sets up a situation in which events can take such an unexpected yet ultimately intelligible turn, when the messenger realizes that Oedipus's ignorance of his true identity, combined with his fear of what Apollo's oracle has foretold, now stands in the way of his return to Corinth. So the scene brings closer the terrible convergence of various threads in the fabric of the larger "action," the determining events, of Oedipus's life, and thus the disclosure of the appallingly pitiful truth that was latent in and intrinsic to the situation from the outset. Sophocles' play offers a consummate exemplification of Aristotle's principles by its creation of a plot in which each element, every stage of the action, is consistent with the probability of human reasons, desires, and intentions (Oedipus's relentless desire for the truth about himself, Jocasta's readiness to dismiss the oracle, the messenger's naive trust that it

---

[46] It is important to grasp *both* that nothing in Aristotle's theory of a unified action requires tragedy to deal with the pattern of a life as a whole, *and* that it allows for plays that do deal with such subjects to have a particularly powerful design (which explains why in ch. 13 he tacitly assumes that the best tragedies will center on transformations in the lives of individuals, 1453a7–12).

[47] Frede 1992 is the most helpful elucidation of this whole aspect of the treatise.

[48] *Poet.* 11.1452a25–26.

[49] Contrast the kind of occurrence Aristotle cites in other places to illustrate chance, where a person luckily encounters a debtor for whom he was not looking at the time and while pursuing a quite different purpose: e.g., *Physics* 2.4, 196a3–5. In the *Oedipus Tyrannus* it was *always* the messenger's intention to give Oedipus good news, and it is precisely his misguided pursuit of that intention that leads to the next step in the tragic disclosure.

can only bring Oedipus pleasure to hear the details of his origins), but whose overall sequence produces a result that nobody foresaw or wanted. Thus reversals and recognitions that are integral to the plot structure, as Aristotle reiterates later in chapter 11 (1452a36–b3), will most effectively arouse pity and fear. And because reversals and recognitions are necessarily unexpected events (for the agents), and yet the most emotionally charged parts of plays (for both agents and spectators), it would appear, a fortiori, that pity and fear will in general best be served by tragic material that does not sacrifice causal coherence or cloud the cognitive clarity that conduces to emotional intensity on the part of the audience.

Within this configuration of ideas we need to place what has sometimes seemed to readers of the *Poetics* to be Aristotle's strange exclusion, when discussing the ideal pattern of tragedy in chapter 13, of the misfortunes of "decent" (*epieikeis*) or "good" characters (1452b34–36)—misfortunes that, he suggests, would make us feel "disgust," not pity and fear.[50] This can be reasonably explained, I believe, only if it is taken to refer to characters covered by Aristotle's phrase a few lines further on, "preeminent in virtue and justice" (1453a8).[51] In other words, Aristotle must be excluding plots that dramatize the misfortunes of those who, by definition, can carry no ethical culpability for, and be involved in no degree of *hamartia* regarding, the adversity that befalls them. But if that is right, it gives us a pointer to the larger implications of Aristotle's theory. Such plots, we can infer, would exhibit the phenomenon of utterly unintelligible and therefore meaningless suffering, since they would represent a radical fissure between the teleology of human goodness and the nature of reality: precisely the kind of worldview that, as I maintained in chapter 3, Plato discerned and feared in tragedy. But everything in the *Poetics* contributes to the supposition that tragedy should help to make sense of the world, and to make

[50] Aristotle's concept of "disgust" (*to miaron*)—one variant on a recurrent anxiety in aesthetics (cf. chapter 6, notes 9–10)—would presumably be applicable to the same sorts of tragic situations in which the agents themselves would express what Plato at *Rep.* 10.604b, e, 605a, calls "rage" or "indignation" (*aganaktein*): cf. chapter 3, with its note 31. But Plato accepts the possibility of *both* pity (on the audience's part) *and* indignation (on the characters') within the same sphere of tragic experience, whereas for Aristotle *to miaron* would represent a degree of existential "nausea" that his theory of tragedy is not designed to embrace: for this factor in Aristotle's attitude to tragedy, see Halliwell 1984, 60–67; Lear 1995, 76–84, offers a different angle on Aristotle's "rationalization" of tragedy (see my reservations in Halliwell 1995b).

[51] I give a fuller version of this argument in Halliwell 1986, 219–20, with n. 24 there; see 215–25 for my account of *hamartia*, a term I regard as covering all the ways in which characters can be partially implicated in responsibility for their own misfortunes, and as therefore being crucial for the *ethical intelligibility* of suffering. Stinton 1975 remains the most important modern discussion of *hamartia*; cf. also Sherman 1992; Nussbaum 1986, 382–83; Schütrumpf 1989.

sense of it precisely at those extremes or limits of experience where we
are forced to contemplate, and thus to pity and fear, the precariousness of
informed human agency (the very conception of agency on which Aristotle's whole understanding of ethics is built). To put the point the other way
round, Aristotle's theory of tragedy—or, more strictly, his view of the ideal
pattern for tragic drama—cannot readily accommodate any case in which
the disparity between ethical agency and suffered misfortune is so drastic,
so morally repugnant, that nothing could be learned from it but the ultimate inhospitability of the world to human virtue.[52] His conception of tragedy entails that the genre will reveal some of the most extreme ways in
which lives and fortunes can go wrong, but not that it will confront us
with the stark idea that the world is radically blind to or heedless of human
aspirations to happiness. If that is right, then we can draw an extremely
important conclusion within the context of my present argument. For Aristotle, both the possibility of and the need for pity—pity, what is more, in
its full tragic intensity—*depend* on the general intelligibilty of life and the
larger "rationality" of existence.

To pursue further these claims, both positive and negative, would involve an appraisal of much more than the *Poetics*, for we have here
reached the juncture at which what is under scrutiny is, by implication,
Aristotle's entire (ethical) philosophy. But there is one further observation
to be made on this aspect of the *Poetics*. Whether or not we think Aristotle's
worldview, and consequently his conception of tragedy, is vulnerable in
this regard (perhaps because insufficiently pessimistic), I nonetheless contend that it is difficult to identify a single Greek tragedy built around a
character who would count, in Aristotle's terms, as "preeminent in virtue
and justice," or who, by the same token, would be incapable of going
wrong in one of the ways covered by Aristotle's requirement of *hamartia*.
Most of our surviving plays focus, rather, on figures who are certainly
exceptional in terms of (often, though not exclusively, heroic) status, as
Aristotle himself suggests (*Poetics* 13.1453a10), but who cannot be regarded as paragons of "virtue and justice" and whose characters and circumstances allow for "a great *hamartia*" (1453a16): such, to name some
obvious instances, are Aeschylus's Xerxes, Eteocles, and Agamemnon;
Sophocles' Ajax, Creon, Oedipus, and Heracles; and Euripides' Hippoly-
tus, Hecuba, and Pentheus. An arguably prima facie exception such as the
heroine in Euripides' *Alcestis* constitutes no real exception at all, because

---

[52] The case of Priam, cited at *Nic. Eth.* 1.10, 1100a8; 1.11, 1101a8, does not contradict this
proposition: it is invoked as a case of the extreme misfortunes not of the perfectly good man,
but of the person who has enjoyed most of a lifetime of prosperity before a final catastrophe;
cf. Nussbaum 1986, 327–30. Murnaghan 1995 diagnoses several ways (not all of which I
would agree about) in which the *Poetics* aims to "distance" audiences from the full horror of
tragedy.

even if we leave aside the larger question of whether such a woman can satisfy Aristotelian criteria for preeminence in virtue, we need to reckon with the fact that Alcestis chooses her own death; and because that choice is an *expression* of virtue, its consequences cannot constitute extreme misfortune for *her*. As 13.1453a7–10 indicates, what is at stake here for Aristotle is a pair of distinct but conjoint conditions for pity and fear: the involvement of characters who, because not "preeminent" in virtue (and therefore, loosely speaking, "like us"), are capable of eliciting our pity and fear, rather than "disgust," if they fall into extreme adversity; and, second, the involvement of these characters, by virtue of some sort of error (*hamartia*), in a chain of causation and responsibility which leads precisely to their adversity. Between them these two conditions create a substantial disparity between the ethical "worth" and the sufferings of the characters. The possibility of the extreme misfortunes of exceptionally virtuous agents is certainly not one that often appealed to the Greek tragedians; and to that extent Aristotle seems justified in having excluded it from his conception of the ideal tragedy.

In trying to explore the rationale that underpins Aristotle's brief statements on tragic pity, I have inevitably picked out several central strands from the arguments of the *Poetics* without being able to tie up each of the loose ends left by my analysis. By way of summing up this part of my argument, however, I want to reiterate that for Aristotle pity is both a cognitively grounded and an ethically charged emotion: it occurs (or should occur), that is to say, when someone (implicitly) judges certain things to be the case, and judges them to be so in an ethically evaluative light. For this reason, Aristotle builds pity into an account of tragedy that places great emphasis not on abstract or "pure" form, as has sometimes been mistakenly supposed, but on humanly significant form—the form of plot structures that convey extreme and disturbing, yet fundamentally intelligible, pictures of certain possibilities of experience.[53] Moreover, if we draw on the relevant passages from *Rhetoric* 2, we can clarify this account with the recognition that Aristotle's interpretation of pity forges a deep connection between our conception of ourselves and our conception of others. We pity in the sufferings of others what we could imagine ourselves, or those very close to us, suffering (*Rhetoric* 2.8, 1385b14–15), and we pity in the lives of others what we fear for ourselves (1386a26–28). This core insight, which Aristotle may have derived in part from tragedy itself,[54] has been reformulated and endorsed in various ways by many other thinkers, not least in the eighteenth century, when it became the basis of an entire

---

[53] I have attempted an overview of Aristotle's conception of artistic form in Halliwell 1998.

[54] See, e.g., Sophocles *Phil.* 500–503; *OC* 560–68, 1333–37; Euripides *Med.* 344–45; *Suppl.* 55–58, fr. 130 Nauck.

ethic of compassionate "sympathy," but also earlier, by Hobbes, and later, by Schopenhauer.[55] And to make that point is to see, I think, that Aristotle's cognitivist model of emotion is entirely compatible with a sense of how pity stems from a deep human instinct but in a way that remains open to the shaping influence of ethical beliefs and attitudes prevailing in particular cultural conditions.

It is a source of frustration to an interpreter of the *Poetics* (certainly to this one) that Aristotle, who gives us after all the fullest evidence we possess for possible Athenian reactions to tragic drama, does not do more to elaborate the implications of his view of pity. But at the risk of putting words in his mouth, I want to take one final, somewhat speculative step toward the elucidation of his position.[56] One source of illumination in this whole area is the contrast between Aristotle, on the one side, and the two greatest philosophical critics of pity, Plato and Nietzsche. I have discussed at length Plato's attitude to tragedy, and what might be called his negative metaphysics of pity, in chapter 3, and I shall shortly offer some thoughts on Nietzsche and pity as an epilogue to this chapter. But we can say with confidence about both these thinkers that their hostility to pity grows from an insistent recognition that pity is an intrinsically potent *solvent of psychological self-sufficiency*. The positive correlate of this, from the point of view I ascribe to Aristotle, is that pity brings with it a capacity to create an expanded awareness of humane and ethical affinities, and to override the sharp-edged criteria of likeness and difference that standardly operate in most forms of social life. As we recall, it is precisely the power of tragic pity to induce "surrender" to sympathy for the sufferings of others that stands at the center of the Platonic critique in *Republic* 10.[57] But what is pictured there as a regrettable yielding to the irrational pleasure of imaginative compassion can be revalued, on Aristotelian premises, as an openness to emotions that engage and activate a full ethical sensitivity. Plato and Aristotle might have agreed, in other words, that pity involves a responsiveness to others that carries the potential to contribute to the reshaping of one's own sense of moral identity. They might even have been able to agree that pity is central to what makes us *human*, and to our

---

[55] Hobbes, *Leviathan*, bk. 1, ch. 6 (pity "ariseth from the imagination that the like calamity may befall himself," Hobbes 1991, 43), represents the direct influence of Aristotle's *Rhetoric*, which Hobbes had paraphrased in 1637: see Harwood 1986, 80 for Hobbes's version of Aristotle's definition. Schopenhauer, *Die Welt als Wille und Vorstellung*, vol. 1 §67 (Schopenhauer 1988, 1:485–87), argues that weeping is self-compassion ("Mitleid mit sich selbst"), even when ostensibly focused on others' afflictions.

[56] I am here restating a point made in Halliwell 1995b, 93–95.

[57] *Rep.* 605c–6b: the ironic force of the idea that the mind watching or hearing tragic poetry tells itself "these are other people's sufferings" (606b1) lies precisely in the mind's ignorance of what the experience is doing to *itself*. Cf. chapter 3, section II.

recognition of the humanity of others. But where they radically disagree is over the desirability of cultivating, or alternatively striving to transcend, this "humanity."

The idea of pity as a force that can change those who feel it by opening them to the sufferings of others lay close to the heart of the Greek tragic tradition.[58] One representative aspect of this Greek tradition—a tradition in which, as both philosophers perceived it, Homer was the essential pre-cursor of Attic tragedy—serves to make this point concisely. It is crucial to Greek experience of tragic poetry (though it has been downplayed in much recent writing about the genre) that it encompasses an exposure to the sufferings of characters who do not simply match the predominantly male-citizen status of an audience such as that of classical Athens. Most tellingly, tragedy invites imaginative sympathy even for female and non-Greek characters. In some of their most extraordinary efforts of imagina-tion, the tragedians, like Homer, deliberately dramatize the potency of pity as a molder of perceptions of human value in situations that involve characters of these other, "inferior" types. This thread runs, to name only some obvious instances, through the encounter between Achilles and Priam in *Iliad* 24, the mythologization of Xerxes' and his people's tragedy in Aeschylus's *Persians*, and the treatment of Hecuba and her companions in Euripides' *Trojan Women* or, similarly, of Andromache in *Andromache*. In these and many other cases, the Greek tragic tradition discerns in com-passion the power to expand and *transform* the apprehension of others as "like ourselves." From this perspective, pity need not simply answer to a preconceived sense of identity and affinity; it can impinge upon an audience's self-image, by eliciting feelings, and their concomitant judg-ments, that cut across the practical norms of political and social life in the Greek polis.

But even if what I have just said, with necessary brevity, is true of the tragic tradition as a whole, is it true of Aristotle's own theory of tragedy? I do not want to claim that we can give an unproblematic answer to that question, but it would be equally wrong to underestimate the weight of the *Poetics*' central and repeated stress on pity-and-fear as the defining experience of tragedy. It is highly pertinent here that Aristotle's category of tragic characters who are "like ourselves" is never closely specified.[59] When he elaborates this factor in pity in the *Rhetoric* (2.8, 1386a24–25), it is significant that he mentions several criteria of "likeness" (age, character,

[58] The locus classicus for this is Sophocles *Ajax* 121–26, where Odysseus (here an "Aristo-telian spectator," Konstan 1999b, 5) feels pity for his enemy Ajax when he recognizes in the latter's ruin the downfall of another human being, in whom he therefore recognizes "himself" (cf. Schopenhauer, *Die Welt als Wille und Vorstellung*, vol. 1 §67 [Schopenhauer 1988, 1:486], on recognizing all humanity, and therefore oneself, in another's suffering).

[59] On the pertinence of the criterion of "likeness" to pity as well as fear, see note 29.

disposition, reputation, family/race). If we bear in mind that his perspective in the *Rhetoric* is necessarily geared to the practical aims of political and forensic oratory,[60] we can see that the criteria of "likeness" that he might have been prepared to apply to tragic characters could have been extremely broad. This is especially so given that the *Poetics'* notion of characters "like us" appears to mark a condition whose status is psychologically descriptive, not normative, and therefore relative to the kinds of responsiveness that a playwright is able to tap in his audience. Moreover, such responsiveness presupposes an audience not of atomistic individuals but of those who, to borrow another revealing detail from the *Rhetoric*, "have parents, children or wives" (2.8, 1385b28)—a detail that exemplifies the dependence of pity on the capacity to imagine not only what one might suffer oneself, but on what those who matter most to us might suffer. In these respects, then, the framework of the *Poetics'* theory of tragedy allows for, even if it does not spell out or pursue, the possibility that the experience of pity-and-fear will have a "sympathetic" scope that goes beyond the exclusive and predefined ethical self-image of a Greek, male audience of tragedy. We may, needless to say, agree tentatively to ascribe a sense of this possibility to Aristotle while reserving the right to doubt (in deference to Rousseau, let us say) whether the possibility was commonly realized in classical Athens.

III

To put in place the final element of a wider perspective on Aristotle's attitude to tragic pity in the *Poetics*, I turn in conclusion to the greatest modern enemy of pity, Friedrich Nietzsche. To devote just a few paragraphs to the subject of Nietzsche and pity is certainly to risk extreme superficiality. Notoriously, Nietzsche mentions pity in numerous and diverse contexts; his reflections on it—not all of which can be easily harmonized—reach into all the corners of his thinking. But while Nietzsche's thoughts on pity have attracted extensive discussion, little or none of it seems to have been addressed to what I see as a centrally paradoxical aspect of them.[61] It is to this paradox that I want to draw attention here. In

---

[60] In a particular rhetorical context the question of *whether* "likeness" should be recognized with a particular group might well be itself at issue: Thuc. 3.40.3, where Cleon tries to block the Athenians' pity for the Mytileneans, is a case in point.

[61] Staten 1990, 102–5, and ch. 8, esp. 153–55, offers one analysis of Nietzsche's views of pity, but without any direct reference to tragedy (although Staten does see Nietzsche's rejection of pity as linked to his renunciation of the Schopenhauerian basis of *The Birth of Tragedy*; for a different angle on this last point cf. Nussbaum 1991). Nussbaum 1994 is an important exploration of the Stoic cast of Nietzsche's thinking about pity, complemented by Cartwright 1984 on the influence of Kant. Apropos tragedy, it is worthwhile comparing

broad terms, Nietzsche sees pity as especially associated with an ethic of altruism, philanthropy, and benevolence, and this, for him, is a life-depressing ethic of weakness for which Christianity, the "religion of pity," is chiefly responsible.[62] Ancient Greek culture, by contrast, provides Nietzsche with the supreme paradigm of a very different ethic, an ethic that encourages the pursuit of excellence and self-realization by strong, noble souls that remain immune to the corrosiveness of sympathy. Yet Nietzsche was only too well aware that pity was regarded by the Greeks as central to the experience of tragedy; and because he was prepared to see tragedy as the expression of an entire cultural era ("das tragische Zeitalter der Griechen," the tragic age of the Greeks, as he called what we would now classify as the archaic and early classical periods),[63] it seems inescapable that there should be a tension attaching to pity within the framework of his thought as a whole.

Of several ways in which this paradox might be tackled, I want to highlight just one, namely what I take to be Nietzsche's attempted resolution of it in a section of *Daybreak*. Here Nietzsche writes: "Men of a fundamentally warlike disposition, as for example the Greeks in the time of Aeschylus, are *hard to move*; and when pity does for once overcome their hardness it grips them like an ecstasy and like a 'demonic force'—. . . a religious shudder. Afterward they feel uncertain about this condition, but while they are in its grip they enjoy the rapture of being outside themselves. . . . It is to souls which are sensitive to pity in this way that tragedy addresses itself, to hard and warlike souls . . . for whom it is useful to grow *soft* from time to time. But what is the point of tragedy to those who stand as open to the 'sympathetic affections' as sails to the winds!"[64] Nietzsche goes on,

---

Nietzsche's views with those of Hegel, who distinguishes between ordinary pity, which he considers incompatible with nobility and greatness of mind, and the deeper sympathy called for by tragedy: see Hegel 1975, 2:1197–98. Silk & Stern 1981, 270–71, register the uncertain status of pity in *The Birth of Tragedy*.

[62] Among the most pertinent of Nietzsche's critiques of pity are *Morgenröte* 2.132–39 (Nietzsche 1988, 3:123–31), *Der Antichrist* 7 (Nietzsche 1988, 6:172–74), *Die fröhliche Wissenschaft* 4.338 (Nietzsche 1988, 3:565–68).

[63] His essay *Die Philosophie im tragischen Zeitalter der Griechen*, unpublished in his lifetime, can be found in Nietzsche 1988, 1:801–72 (there is a translation in Cowan 1962). It does not, however, discuss tragedy as such.

[64] *Morgenröte* 3.172 (Nietzsche 1988, 3:152–53); cf. the last sentence of *Götzen-Dämmerung*, "Streifzüge eines Unzeitgemässen" 24 (Nietzsche 1988, 6:128), where the experience of tragedy is said to be for "the warlike" element in the soul and for "the heroic man." The autobiographical resonance of this section of *Daybreak* is hard to miss, as too is the implicit response to Plato *Rep.* 10.605c–d, a text that greatly interested Nietzsche: cf. *Menschliches, Allzumenschliches* 1.212 (Nietzsche 1988, 2:173–74), with my notes 66–67. Note that Nietzsche's notion of pity as a religious "shudder" (cf. the verb "schaudern" in *Die Geburt der Tragödie* 22, Nietzsche 1988, 1:141) must owe something to Gorgias's famous characterization of the emotional power of poetry in his *Helen* (fr. 11.9 DK), cited earlier, although

in this same section, to mention Plato and fourth-century philosophical complaints about the harmfulness of tragedy. He is here undoubtedly picking up the *Republic*'s critique of tragic pity, and his response to it, as we have just seen, involves a historical hypothesis—or, more aptly, a historical myth[65]—according to which the true value of pity is accessible only to those who are normally *without*, or fiercely resistant to, pity.

But why should those warlike Greeks, those hard "Aeschylean" souls, have found pity "useful" at all? Why, indeed, should such Greeks, who appear on the evidence of *Human, All-Too-Human* I.96 to have formed the appropriate audience of tragedy, have been *sensitive* to pity at all, given Nietzsche's comments in *The Birth of Tragedy* 22 about the nonaesthetic status of any response to tragedy that involves such emotion.[66] It is surely implausible that in his reference to Aeschylean men Nietzsche is thinking here of a kind of outlet for otherwise unwanted emotions, which happens to be the conception he holds, inadvisedly in my view, of Aristotelian catharsis.[67] However surprisingly, he does appear, after all, to recognize some real value in the experience of pity, an experience in which he discerns both a sense of something "wonderful" (das Wunderbare) and "the bitterest wormwood of suffering" (das bitterste Wermuth des

---

there the term *phrikē* is associated with fear rather than pity; cf. Aristotle *Poet.* 14.1453b5, Sophocles *OT* 1306. Gould 1990, esp. chs. 9 and 17, refurbishes the idea of an emotional "shudder" as part of his psychological-cum-religious account of Greek tragedy and myth, although he does not bring Nietzsche into the reckoning in this respect.

[65] This is one of several places where we can see traces of Aristophanes' *Frogs* (with its image of Aeschylus as the poet of warlike men, esp. 1013–42), a play that influenced Nietzsche's thinking about tragedy rather deleteriously.

[66] *Menschliches, Allzumenschliches* 1.96 (Nietzsche 1988, 2:92–93), *Die Geburt der Tragödie* 22 (Nietzsche 1988, 1:140–44). Note also that Nietzsche's endorsement of the Platonic principle (from *Rep.* 10.605c–6b; cf. my note 64) that the exercise of psychological drives *increases* susceptibility to them (*Menschliches, Allzumenschliches* 1.212, Nietzsche 1988, 2:173), makes it harder still to understand why "warlike" Greeks should have needed to succumb to pity in the theater at all.

[67] Nietzsche rejects Aristotelian catharsis, understood as a principle of emotional "purgation" (Purgativ) or "discharge" (Entladung), at, e.g., *Die Geburt der Tragödie* 22 (Nietzsche 1988, 1:142), *Menschliches, Allzumenschliches* 1.212 (Nietzsche 1988, 2:173; cf. my note 66), *Götzen-Dämmerung*, "Was ich den Alten verdanke" 5 (Nietzsche 1988, 6:160), and in a note from 1888 (Nietzsche 1988, 13:409–11). Cf., however, *Der Antichrist* 7 (Nietzsche 1988, 6:174), where Nietzsche seems half-accepting of the idea (for which cf. *Morgenröte* 2.134, Nietzsche 1988, 3:127–28, with reference to "the Greeks" rather than Aristotle) that it was good to allow occasional alleviation of such a sick and dangerous emotion as pity: the partial similarity of this passage to that quoted in my text from *Morgenröte* 3.172 suggests that there may, after all, have been some subliminal connection between the latter and Nietzsche's understanding of catharsis. *Die Geburt der Tragödie* 21 (Nietzsche 1988, 1:134) itself speaks positively of the "purifying and discharging power of tragedy" (der . . . reinigenden und entladenden Gewalt der Tragödie).

Leidens).[68] This reading is confirmed, I think, by a passage in *Human, All-Too-Human*, where Nietzsche suggests that benevolence and pity have always been perceived, despite other changes in ethical outlook, as "good for something" (gut wozu) or "useful" (nützlich).[69] This usefulness is linked by Nietzsche, both here and elsewhere, to the fundamental needs of a *community*, and relatedly, as we see especially in *The Birth of Tragedy* 21, to a clear attention to the *individuality of others*.[70]

For all his vehement espousal of the ethic of life-affirming strength and self-realization, Nietzsche surely understood that a world peopled only by souls taking such individualism to its extreme could not be a shared or social world at all, could not ground a *culture* (whether Greek or otherwise), and so could hardly belong to the realm of the human at all. Moreover, because Nietzsche accepted the idea, which we have seen in both Plato and Aristotle, that pity is not straightforwardly an emotion of self-forgetting but contains a latent conception of one's own vulnerability,[71] the "usefulness" of pity to his hard Greek souls must be, in however necessarily small a degree, a reminder to them of their lack of self-sufficiency. I do not know whether Nietzsche would have regarded the Odysseus of Sophocles' *Philoctetes* as conforming to his type of the hard, warlike Greek soul—very possibly not, given Odysseus's timidity at certain points in the play. But if he had, then his recognition of the "usefulness" of pity should have allowed him to see that the remarkable experience of Neoptolemus in that same play, from which this chapter began, is symbolic of a deep psychic need, even on the part of the warlike, to respond to the sufferings of kindred spirits and thereby to acknowledge the mutual needs entailed in being fully, or even "all too," human. This would still, of course, leave Nietzsche a long way from Aristotle, as well as from Sophocles. But not quite as far as is usually supposed.

---

[68] This is a Nietzschean acknowledgment of the Greek topos of the mixture of pleasure and pain within certain kinds of emotion: cf. the Homeric motifs of desire for and pleasure in lamentation (e.g., *Il.* 23.10, 14, 98, 108; *Od.* 4.102, 183; 11.212), or the pleasure of anger (*Il.*18.108–9); Gorgias fr. 11.9 DK ("grief-loving longing," *pothos philopenthēs*); Plato *Philebus* 47d–48a, 50b (including reference to tragedy: cf. chapter 3, section I); Aristotle *Rhet.* 1.11, 1370b25–30 (citing Homer on grief); 2.2, 1380b1–9 (citing Homer on anger).

[69] *Menschliches, Allzumenschliches* 1.96 (Nietzsche 1988, 2:92–93).

[70] For pity's link with community, see, e.g., *Menschliches, Allzumenschliches* 1.45 (Nietzsche 1988, 2:67–68). On the other hand, *Morgenröte* 1.18 (Nietzsche 1988, 3:30–32) seems to envisage early communities of strong souls who managed to live without pity. *Die Geburt der Tragödie* 21 (Nietzsche 1988, 1:137) suggests that the Apolline element in tragedy attaches our pity to the individuals depicted in the myths.

[71] See esp. *Morgenröte* 2.133 (Nietzsche 1988, 3:125–27): but Nietzsche here carries the point further and in the process transforms it; cf. my note 28.

Chapter Eight

✵

Music and the Limits of Mimesis: Aristotle Versus Philodemus

Just as my fingers on these keys
Make music, so the selfsame sounds
On my spirit make a music, too.
Music is feeling, then, not sound.
(Wallace Stevens, "Peter Quince at the Clavier")

THE NATURE OF MUSIC is perhaps the most intractable, as well as one of the most fascinating, of all problems in aesthetics. It has been debated voluminously and often polemically since antiquity, and far from becoming worn out the subject has in recent years seen a spate of publications from contemporary philosophers, especially in the English-speaking world.[1] However intellectualized the questions that cluster around the topic may have become, their roots are unmistakably "anthropological." Every known human culture not only possesses music but develops ways of using it that consistently manifest both an association with special categories of events and activities (from marriage to death, love to war, religion to sport), and a correlative tendency toward the arousal of affectively heightened states of experience. Yet it is probably an equally valid generalization that in all cultures music remains at least partly mysterious, eluding a fully convincing explanation of why such a degree of importance should be attached to it. While music lacks the overt semantics or syntax of language, the representational organization of figurative art, and the functional definiteness of architecture (tempting though critics often find it to compare music to all three of these things), it elicits responses which for many performers and listeners in many societies are the most emotionally charged that art of any kind produces in them. The nontransparency of music's power has sometimes been interpreted as an argument for its purity and its intrinsic self-sufficiency as a vehicle of aesthetic experience.

[1] Important recent contributions include Budd 1985; Budd 1995, ch. 4; Davies 1994; Kivy 1993 (and earlier books); Krausz 1993; Levinson 1990; and Scruton 1997. Bowman 1998 provides an extensive historical survey of philosophical theories of music. Tanner 1985 offers some usefully incisive thoughts on the difficulties of talking (and thinking) about music. Raffman 1993 tackles the question of musical "ineffability" (more specifically, the ineffability of musical perception) from the angle of cognitive science, although her brisk skepticism toward musical expression of emotion (56–60) strikes me as psychologically and culturally superficial.

When Walter Pater pronounced, famously, that "all art constantly aspires towards the condition of music,"[2] he was expressing a quintessential, if extreme, attitude of nineteenth-century aestheticism—an attitude, moreover, that embodies a specific reaction against the long-dominant tenets of mimetic conceptions of art.

One factor in Pater's model of music as a paradigm of artistic autonomy is something even mimeticist thinkers cannot easily deny, namely the peculiarly intangible and elusive character of musical meaning. On the other hand, it was the positive ability of music to merge form and content in a perfect synthesis or "interpenetration" which led Pater to single it out as paradigmatic for his aesthetic argument. In doing so he was acknowledging, in part, music's tendency to stimulate especially concentrated kinds of experience. We have the basis here, then, of what might well be thought a deep paradox, and one that seems to hold cross-culturally. Commonly experienced as the most intense and irresistible of art forms, music is yet the least susceptible to interpretation by rational understanding, except at a wholly technical level. Irreplaceably significant though it often is in the lives of both individuals and social groups, it remains enigmatic in what sense, if any, that significance can be construed as a direct or internal property of music itself. Regrettably, much of the history of aesthetics shows that the result of this profound difficulty has too often been a polarization of positions, pushing irreconcilably far apart those theorists who wish to maintain the meaningfulness of music, and those who, by contrast, regard it as nothing more than, in a phrase from Kant's *Critique of Judgment*, "die Kunst des schönen Spiels der Empfindungen," the art of the beautiful play of sensations.[3] I shall be concerned, later in this chapter, with a remarkable ancient demonstration of the philosophical consequences of such polarization.

Strange though it now seems to many, the concept of mimesis has played a fundamental and tenacious part in shaping the history of Western philosophies of music. Until the major shift of attitudes constituted by the romantic movement, mimesis had long been central to attempts to resolve the enigma of music. That music is, in some sense, a mimetic art, alongside poetry, painting, sculpture, and dance, was the prevailing, though not unquestioned, orthodoxy of the ancient tradition from at least the time of

---

[2] Walter Pater, "The School of Giorgione," in Pater 1901, 135 (orig. publ. in *Fortnightly Review*, Oct. 1877). The statement is sometimes misattributed to Mallarmé (e.g., by Brogan 1993, 1038).

[3] *Kritik der Urteilskraft* (1790), §51 (Kant 1914, 400). Although *Empfindungen* sometimes means "emotions," Kant's use of it here is limited to sense impressions, albeit ones appreciated partly in terms of form. Kant's views on music are complicated, however, by what he goes on to say in §§53–54: see e.g., Kivy 1993, 250–64; Bowman 1998, 84–91. On Kant, mimesis, and aesthetics more generally, cf. my introduction, section II.

Plato onward. This tradition was strongly revived by neoclassicist theorists from the sixteenth to eighteenth century, when a combination of ancient philosophical and rhetorical ideas lay at the foundation of the dominant view that music was above all the language of emotional expression and arousal.[4] This historical observation ought in itself to make us careful about how we describe the change in attitudes that occurred in the eighteenth and early nineteenth centuries, when mimesis (or, as I would prefer to stress, the vocabulary and mentality of mimeticism) became the target of much opposition in aesthetics. If we say, as is commonly done, that the later eighteenth century rejected a mimetic model of music for an expressivist model, we at once face the perplexity that neoclassicist conceptions of musical mimesis had all along made use of the idea of "expression," together and interchangeably with "imitation" and "representation." Two prominent examples of this phenomenon, from earlier and later stages of the entire neoclassical era of musical theory, are Vincenzo Galilei's much-cited *Dialogo della musica antica e della moderna* of 1581 and Johann Mattheson's *Der vollkommene Capellmeister* of 1739, the latter a highly influential treatise in the tradition of the so-called *Affektenlehre* or doctrine of music as the arousal of the passions. Both these works find it possible to juxtapose and mix the vocabulary of imitation, expression, and representation without any need for explanatory comment.[5] Let me spell out the implications of this in terms that will immediately foreground my own historical thesis. Despite the language of "imitation" widely employed in

[4] Berger 2000, 120–33, describes the revival of a mimetic model of music from the mid-sixteenth century onward; he does not discuss the concept of mimesis per se, but I note that he uses "imitate" and "represent" equivalently.

[5] See the extracts from Galilei quoted in the discussion by Carapetyan 1948, 53–58. For *Der vollkommene Capellmeister*, see Mattheson 1739, esp. 145 (2.5.75–78; translation in Harriss 1981, 318); Mattheson repeatedly uses "ausdrücken" (his form is "ausdrucken") and "vorstellen" interchangeably; on p. 331 (3.15.4, translated in Harriss 1981, 637) he gives the representation of all "natural objects and emotional feelings" as one of three senses of *Nachahmung* (the others being musical emulation and melodic voice imitation); Kivy 1993, 229–49, interprets Mattheson's language from a somewhat different angle. Other salient instances of the mixing of imitation and expression can be found in Batteux's treatment of music in *Les beaux arts* of 1746, esp. pt. 3 §3 chs. 1–4 (Batteux 1989, 231–46), and in the famous account of music in Diderot's *Le neveu de Rameau* (in Diderot 1983, 104–14). The influence of rhetorical thinking on neoclassical musical theory meant that there was always an inclination to link the representation or depiction of emotion with both its feeling or expression by the composer (on the "si me vis flere . . ." principle of Horace *Ars Poetica* 102) and its arousal in the listener; cf. note 50. But for some of the complexities that developed in this sphere, both terminologically and conceptually, in the eighteenth century, see Lessem 1974, Iknayan 1983, 8–12, with Lippman 1992, 83–136, for fuller (though sometimes superficial) documentation. An earlier exception to the rule of overlap between the vocabulary of "imitation" and "expression" in musical theory is the *Della poetica* (1586) of Patrizzi ("the arch-dissenter of Renaissance criticism," Babbitt 1910, 16): see Palisca 1985, 402–5; Hathaway 1962, 9–22. Cf. chaper 12, section I.

this period, the neoclassicist aesthetics of music, like its ancient antecedents in the writings of Plato, Aristotle, and others, rested on a concept of
mimesis within which it is both difficult and anyway, I submit, misguided
to distinguish sharply between ideas of representation and expression.[6]
And if this is right, whatever else we may say about the undoubted shift
of emphasis in the language and standards of musical aesthetics in the
second half of the eighteenth century, it cannot be regarded without qualification as one in which the role of mimesis was straightforwardly replaced
by expression in prevailing conceptions of music.

I return briefly in the final part of this chapter to the question of what
was involved in the rejection of explicit mimeticism in later eighteenth-
century treatments of music.[7] But my prior concern here is with an older
part of the story: more precisely, with a contrasting pair of ancient versions
of musical aesthetics—those of Aristotle and Philodemus—which themselves involve radically divergent evaluations of the relevance of mimesis
to music (and vice versa). Part of what I hope to show is that attention to
the very different positions occupied by these two thinkers can help us
reflect on a central element in what has recurrently been at stake in the
aesthetics of music. That claim is not, however, meant to disguise my belief
that the aesthetics of music, like all other forms of aesthetics, is historically
embedded in and contingent upon particular cultural contexts. In interpreting Aristotle's and Philodemus's views on musical mimesis, we are primarily engaged in reconstructing the relationship between their ideas and their
own world. At the same time, partly because those ideas belong to a tradition that has been immensely influential on later ways of thinking, and
partly because ideas enjoy a life which can in some measure transcend
their origins, it is worth our while to revisit older aesthetic arguments in
the hope that they may shed some illumination on problems that at a
certain level are still (or, rather, have become) ours.

II

In the last book of his *Politics* (book 8, chapters 4–7), Aristotle addresses
the subject of music within the broader context of a discussion of certain
aspects of education. The principal questions he poses here are what psychological and cultural functions music can fulfill, and what kinds of music

---

[6] Cf. Carapetyan 1948, a piece whose naive opening belies some useful historical observations. The nature of the mimeticist tradition in musical aesthetics, both ancient and neoclassical, is somewhat distorted in the brief remarks of Kivy 1997, 2–9.

[7] Morrow 1997 gives a detailed account of the displacement of a mimetic paradigm of
music. Barry 1987 discusses ways in which rejection of musical mimesis had wider consequences for aesthetics, especially in encouraging a model of aesthetic indeterminacy and a
sense of the need for the recipient of an artwork to supply an active, imaginative response;
cf. Lessem 1974, 327–30.

are appropriate for the formation of the citizens of the model polis. It is clear that in framing such questions Aristotle was following the lead of Plato, who in both the *Republic* (book 3) and the *Laws* (especially books 2 and 7) pursued lines of argument that had been broached by the pioneering Athenian musical theorist Damon in the mid-fifth century. The succession of Damon, Plato, Aristotle laid the foundations of an approach to music that was to remain important throughout antiquity, at least as late as the third century A.D. (if that is where Aristides Quintilianus belongs). Whatever exact ideas were held by the now shadowy figure of Damon himself, there is no serious doubt that he started a system of theorizing that depended on the attribution of "character" (*ēthos*) to musical works and to the tunings, scales, and melodic patterns (all of which can be covered by the Greek term *harmoniai*) which they employed.[8]

"Character," in this context, embraces a range of qualities or properties (courage, self-discipline, anger, mildness, enthusiasm, and others) of the types standardly ascribed to individual persons, so that what appears to be involved here is a claim of correspondence, equivalence, or correlation between some of the properties of musical works or styles and some of the properties of people—a formulation that encapsulates the kernel of the predominant ancient (and neoclassical) inclusion of music within the category of mimetic art. In this respect, *ēthos* theory is one instance of a much more widely documented phenomenon, namely the tendency of human beings to hear traces of psychological "life" in musical works or performances, and to (re)enact that life in the patterns of feeling that constitute responses to music. There is less distance than one might have expected, therefore, between Aristotle's approach to music and a modern psychological theory of musical experience which speaks in terms of the hearer's imagining a "virtual person" within a piece of music.[9] In Plato and Aristotle, in fact, and probably for most later *ēthos* theorists too, a pressing ethical-cum-political issue forms itself around the implications of the "character" of different kinds of music for the characters of those who listen to them, as though the experience of music were cognate to

---

[8] Anderson 1966 provides a book-length, though uneven, treatment of the *ēthos*-tradition of musical theory; see also Lord 1982, 203–19, and West 1992a, 246–53 (an exemplary outline). Ritoók 2001 is the most recent treatment of Damon; cf. Moutsopoulos 1959, 73–77, 183–97, 245–58. On the background to Aristotle's interest in *ēthos* theory, and the latter's relationship in the classical period to the other two main forms of Greek musical theory (Pythagorean number speculation, and technical "harmonic science"), see Wallace 1995.

[9] The idea of a "virtual person" as the imaginary subject of a piece of music has recently been advanced in experimental psychology by Watt & Ash 1998; compare the idea of a musical "persona," as the subject of emotions expressed in music, in Levinson 1990, 320–22, 338–39, 349, 374; Levinson 1996, 107, 122 n. 80. Cf. Scruton 1997, 76 ("the background in music is heard as a kind of life"). Such ideas must be distinguished from the view that in listening to music we are encountering the personality of the composer (see, e.g., Storr 1992, 112–21).

exposing oneself to the influence, or "keeping the company," of another human being.[10] On this model, responding to music means entering and becoming part of a world of musical feeling whose ethically charged pleasures and pains pass through, and have the capacity to shape, the hearer in the act of listening. Such considerations supply the guiding motivation of Aristotle's discussion of music in *Politics* 8, and they lead him to make some more general remarks on the nature and value of music—in short, to offer the rudiments of an aesthetics of music.

There are many intriguing as well as problematic details in this stretch of the *Politics*, to some of which I devoted preliminary attention, from the point of view of Aristotle's overall understanding of mimesis, in chapter 5. Here the focus of my inquiry will be the conception of music itself, though even so I will have to leave a number of issues on one side. The latter include the important fact that for Aristotle the mimetic-cum-expressive scope of music is actually wider than the category of musical *ēthos*, because his later acceptance of a classification that distinguishes melodies of character from those of action and passion (8.7,1341b32–42b34) implies that *ēthos* is not the only possible object of musical mimesis. However, it is Aristotle's reflections on *ēthos* that give us our best insight into the sense in which he believes music to be a mimetic art form. The framework of Aristotle's exposition of his views on music is a tripartite scheme of the uses of the art and its products: first, for education (*paideia*), second for entertainment or relaxation (*paidia*), and third for *diagōgē* (a difficult term, covering the cultured exercise of leisure in ways sufficiently serious to contribute to happiness).[11] In connection with the first of these three categories, education, which he understands quasi-Platonically as a training in virtue, Aristotle introduces his linked ideas on musical *ēthos* and musical mimesis. Although he touches on technical matters relating to the methods of musical education (above all, the extent to which it is desirable that young citizen males should learn to play instruments), Aristotle subordinates these to the central ethicopolitical question of how far, and in what way, music has the power to contribute to an education in "feeling pleasure and pain" (*lupeisthai kai chairein*) correctly.[12] His answer to this

---

[10] Plato uses the image of "keeping company" for the experience of a work of art at, e.g., *Rep.* 10.603b1: see my note on this passage in Halliwell 1988, 135; cf. *Rep.* 6.500c5–7 for the underlying principle, with my chapter 2 on behavioral-psychological assimilation in Plato. For a modern development of such thinking, but with only passing reference to music, cf. Booth 1988 (with my chapter 2, section II).

[11] Kraut 1997 gives a careful treatment of philosophical issues in this part of the *Politics*, though he devotes little space to Aristotle's conception of musical mimesis and character. Depew 1991, 362–80, deals with the larger political context.

[12] This idea, whose Platonic credentials are conspicuous at Plato *Laws* 2.653b–c, is most explicit at *Pol.* 8.5, 1340a14–25 (cf. *Nic. Eth.* 2.3, 1104b4–5a16): observe here the stress on learning, *manthanein* (16), to feel the right emotions, which involves "judging well" (*krinein*

question, in keeping with the "Damonian" tradition, is that music does
indeed possess "character," which can in turn arouse and shape ethically
significant feelings in the listener, and that music is accordingly an educationally potent force. What I want now to examine carefully is the concept
of musical mimesis that we find at work in Aristotle's presentation of the
position he adopts on these matters.

The most direct reference to musical mimesis occurs at 1340a18–42, a
passage worth quoting extensively.

> Rhythms and melodies contain likenesses [homoiōmata] that are especially
> close to the real nature of anger and mildness, as well as courage and self-
> discipline, and their opposites, and all other ethical traits [ēthika]. This is clear
> in practice, because our state of mind is changed [metaballomen . . . tēn
> psuchēn) as we listen to such music. Habituation to feeling pain and pleasure
> in response to likenesses [homoia] is close to being disposed in the same way
> toward reality [alētheia] itself. For instance, if someone enjoys contemplating
> an artistic image [eikōn] of someone for no other reason than because of the
> form depicted, he will necessarily find pleasurable the actual contemplation
> of the person whose image it is. It happens that in other sense modalities
> (tōn aisthētōn en men tois allois] there is no natural likeness to qualities of
> character—for instance, in objects of touch and taste. Objects of sight do pos-
> sess such likeness to a slight extent, because there are visible forms that have
> such qualities, but only to a small degree, and not everyone can perceive
> such things. Besides, these things—the forms and colors involved in states of
> character—are not really likenesses but only signs [sēmeia] of character; they
> are features of the body in emotional states [pathē]. Nonetheless, insofar as
> there is a difference even regarding the contemplation of these [i.e., visual]
> arts, the young should not contemplate the works of Pauson but those of
> Polygnotus and of any other painter or sculptor whose work is rich in charac-
> ter. By contrast, melodies themselves contain mimetic equivalents [mimēm-
> ata] of character, and this is readily clear from the fact that the scales [harmon-
> iai] possess natural qualities that make each of them have a different effect
> on listeners.[13]

Despite its typically compressed and parenthetic style, this argument is
rich in aesthetic implications. Two fundamentals are clear enough. The
first is that Aristotle draws a distinction between mimetic likenesses (repre-

orthōs, 17); cf. 8.6, 1340b38–39. In other words, the emotions involved in musical experiences are cognitively based (cf. chapter 6, and chapter 7, note 42).

[13] There are a number of problems of text and translation raised by this passage which
cannot receive full discussion here. The contention of Schütrumpf 1970, 18–20, that the passage refers only to dispositions of character and not to related emotions or affects is unduly
constricting: the psychological "change" referred to at 1340a22–23 is a kind of emotion (cf.
the definition of pathos at Rhet. 2.1, 1378a20–21).

sentational-cum-expressive equivalents or correlates, as I maintain), on
the one hand, and "signs" or "indices" (*sēmeia*), on the other: where qualities of "character" (*ēthos*) and ethical traits or feelings (*ēthika*) are concerned, he ascribes mimetic properties to music but not, or only to a slight
degree, to figurative art. The second is that Aristotle bases this distinction
on the kinds of experience made available by certain types of art. The
properties he is prepared to ascribe to music are identified in it by parallelism to the kinds of psychological states that music causes or evokes in its
listeners: music possesses certain "ethical" qualities because it makes "*us*,"
as we hear it, recognize and (learn to) feel equivalent qualities "sympathetically."[14] The connection between these two points is evidently, for Aristotle, a matter of nature. It is the "nature" of music that Aristotle is investigating (1340a1); musical likenesses are very close to the real "nature" of
the ethical qualities they correspond to (1340a19); the "nature" of different
scales, tunings, and melodic types (*harmoniai*) creates distinguishable effects on their listeners (1340a41); and human beings, as Aristotle adds at
the end of the chapter, have a natural instinct for tones and rhythms.[15]

We should hesitate, however, before supposing that Aristotle's naturalism here is naively or absolutely a priori. Rather, it serves to give explanatory underpinning and cohesion to an argument that moves from actual
(culturally attested) forms of experience to the properties of the objects
that occasion and ground those experiences. Provided we accept, as I
think we must, that Aristotle is not inventing, imagining, or distorting the
"data" of musical experience to which he refers, then we should be able
to see that his aesthetic naturalism is coherent in its own terms. Far from
invoking nature in order to avoid reckoning with the processes of culture,
Aristotle is engaged in embedding his understanding of the former within
his observation of the latter. There is, to put the point from a different
angle, nothing purportedly "timeless" about the perspective of Aristotle's
argument in this passage. That is because he works from within a shared
cultural phenomenology of music, in keeping with a philosophical
method that requires him to take account of the perceptions mediated by
common experience.[16] Still less is he claiming that the materials of music
exist quite independently of human culture. The properties of music he

[14] If music fits the general model of mimetic experience at *Poet.* 4.1448b4–19, as I expounded it in chapter 6, then listening to it will be, to varying degrees (depending on the
music itself as well as on individual hearers), a matter of *manthanein* (cf. note 12), *qua* both
learning and understanding: emotional responses to music will draw on existing psychological experience, but will actively add to and shape that experience.

[15] *Pol.*8.5, 1340b17–18, cf. 1340a4–6, *Poet.* 4.1448b20–21, and Plato *Laws* 2.653d–4a.

[16] Note especially the references to the empiricism of earlier musical theorists at 1340b5–
7, to general "agreement" about the melodies of Olympus at 1340a11, and to the experience
of "everyone" at 1340a13 (but with my note 45).

discerns are just that, properties of culturally elaborated rhythmic and tonal systems, not of "raw" sound; but with music as with language, there is no incompatibility between a hypothesis of natural underlying causes and the fact of cultural variation in specific forms. Furthermore, what Aristotle takes to be the natural grounding of musical expression does not entail a supposition that the art's mimetic "likenesses" are automatically self-evident to any and every hearer, as opposed to requiring relevant experience and sensitivity for their proper perception and appreciation. The importance of this last consideration will be all the more evident when we come later to what I shall contend is the reductive attitude of Philodemus to the nature of musical sound.

But even if nature operates here principally as the causal or explanatory connection between musical performances or works and musical experiences as evidenced in Aristotle's own culture, and not as an a priori and absolute point of reference, we might still wonder about the fine details of his case. We need, in particular, to scrutinize his distinction between mimetic "likenesses" and nonmimetic "signs" or indices. This distinction construes mimesis, it appears, as a matter of intrinsic rather than extrinsic significance, and also as a relation of close equivalence or resemblance to, rather than a more oblique and looser association with, its objects. Together these features seem to give us something like Peirce's notion of "iconic" signs, though it is worth remarking in passing that Peirce's terminology has ancient antecedents.[17] But there are difficulties in explicating Aristotle's position further.

Correlates of ethical qualities, he says, are contained by (exist "in") rhythms and melodies (1340a19, 38; cf. 28), in a sense allegedly not predicable of the materials of visual art. Yet he nonetheless acknowledges that paintings and sculptures can in some way, or to some degree, convey features of character. They can give us, he suggests, indications (which fall short of being mimetic likenesses) of ethical qualities. He means by this, I think, that while a painting by, for example, the great Polygnotus may allow us to interpret the scene it displays as evidence for the characters of those involved (say, for the bloodlust of Neoptolemus on the morning after the sack of Troy),[18] this requires a larger framework of suppositions for its justification—among other things, a narrative framework, that

---

[17] An iconic sign is one that "denotes merely by virtue of characters of its own" (Peirce 1931–58, 2:143, §247, cf. 5:50, §73) or "represent(s) its object mainly by its similarity" (2:157, §276); cf. chapter 5, note 23. Peirce's use of "sign" for the genus of which icons are a species is of course quite distinct from Aristotle's own use of "sign," *sēmeion*, in the passage under discussion. The notion of an "iconic" sign is partly anticipated in Proclus's *In Timaeum*: see Coulter 1976, 39–72 (but with reservations expressed in chapter 11, note 55).

[18] Some Athenians would have seen Polygnotus's painting of the scene in the Lesche at Delphi: Pausanias 10.25–26 (see 26.4 for Neoptolemus, and cf. chapter 7, note 8).

is (in the terms of the *Poetics*), an implicit structure of "action." The perception of character is such cases will be a process of discursive inference, a "reading" of the implied relationship between action and character, rather than a recognition of an intrinsic property of the ordered "shapes and colors" of the material artwork. The qualities of music, by contrast, are taken by Aristotle to have a direct communicative effect on the mind and emotions of the (appropriately receptive) hearer, who does not infer that the music embodies certain ethical traits but seems to experience the appropriate feelings as a necessary part of attending to the music: the listener's mind is "changed" in the very act of listening, and this change is constitutive of what it means, in the fullest sense, to hear the music. It is worth emphasizing, though, that Aristotle's distinction between mimetic likenesses and nonmimetic indices ("signs") does not seem to be a difference between the natural and the conventional; nothing in his analysis excludes the possibility that at any rate some of the class of indexical "signs" may be natural.[19]

At this juncture a point of historical clarification is called for that might be thought to undermine Aristotle's position. Most Greek music was written to accompany a verbal text, and it could therefore be argued that the supposedly intrinsic musical properties that Aristotle identifies were in fact themselves the result of traditional association with the semantic and narrative elements provided by poetry. Even Plato, as is often noticed, had voiced doubt about the capacity of purely instrumental music to carry expressive significance without the support of a text,[20] and we shall see that this doubt was taken much further by the Epicurean philosopher Philodemus in his critique of musical *ēthos* theory. The importance of the "marriage" of music and poetry in Greek culture cannot be overstated, and it is plausible to suppose that it was historically influential in forming the patterns of experience that gave rise to *ēthos* theory. Nevertheless, I want to suggest that this observation does not simply dispose of Aristotle's claims in the passage in question. Even if we were to formulate this observation in its strongest form as an objection to Aristotle's position—that is, as the thesis that the alleged qualities of musical rhythms and melodies

---

[19] Mimesis, as we have seen, has an explicitly natural basis: cf. the "natural affinity" for rhythm and harmony, *Pol.* 8.5, 1340b18, with *Poet.* 4.1448b20–21. But it does not follow that indexical "signs" could not also be natural; cf. the bodily features that can serve as signs of character at *Prior An.* 2.27, 70b6 ff.

[20] Plato *Laws* 2.669e: the Athenian does not say that "pure" music lacks expressive or mimetic significance, only that its significance becomes hard to understand. Longinus *Subl.* 39.1–3 acknowledges the intense emotional power of music, but describes it as devoid of strict significance (the sounds of a kithara are *ouden haplōs sēmainontes*, lacking in meaning; its effects are "illegitimate surrogates" [*mimēmata notha*] of persuasion) and implies, somewhat contradictorily, that it touches "the hearing alone," not the soul itself.

were purely the result of historical association—it would still be open to Aristotle to respond that this historical association was not entirely contingent but was itself amenable to explanation in terms of the "natural" potential of music's resources. An Aristotelian defense could continue to ground this appeal to nature, as in fact the passage we are considering does, in the strength and cultural ubiquity of the psychological experiences afforded by particular species of music. Aristotle's argument as a whole makes it clear, in my view, that he cannot have been persuaded that the association with poetry was a wholly contingent matter and therefore capable of explaining *away* the apparent properties of musical mimesis. His emphasis throughout is on music as such, not on music as an adjunct to poetry—so much so that when at 1340a13–14 the text runs, "when listening to mimetic performances [*mimēseis*] everyone feels a sympathetic response, and [or even] apart from the rhythms and melodies themselves," we are virtually obliged to accept the thrust of Susemihl's emendation of the Greek, which gives us instead: "everyone feels a sympathetic response through the rhythms and melodies themselves, even apart from <the words>."[21] Without this textual alteration, it remains opaque why Aristotle, when trying to show that music can change its hearers psychologically, would here wish to cite the power of words to elicit emotional sympathy *independently* of rhythms and melodies.

Let us return, then, to my contention that Aristotle's concept of mimetic likenesses, as opposed to nonmimetic "signs," involves properties that he takes to be both intrinsic to musical structures and instances of affective resemblance or equivalence. The notion of resemblance has been discussed by aestheticians mostly in connection with visual art, where, in the wake of Goodman's well-known critique, it remains a tenable if contestable basis for a concept of representation.[22] But whatever Aristotle under-

---

[21] See the apparatus in Immisch 1929, 282. The emendation is supported by pseudo-Aristotle *Probl.* 19.27, 919b26–27 (cf. 918b16–18). See Anderson 1966, 125–26, 186–88; Reeve 1998, 235, construes similarly, without commenting on the text; Kraut 1997, 194, misses the difficulty; Newman 1887–1902, 1:362, 3:537, unconvincingly finds a reference to "imitative sounds" not involving melody or rhythm, while Koller 1954, 70, 101–2, speciously discerns a distinction between performers and audience; Gigon 1973, 256, translating too loosely, finds a reference to music "without dance and song"; Galli 1925, 367 n. 1, sees but does not resolve the problem; Simpson 1998, 269–70, offers a muddled conspectus. Note that Aristotle explicitly recognizes the existence of purely instrumental music at 1339b21; it is wrong to think, with, e.g., Kristeller 1980, 169, 172, that Aristotle (and others) did not conceive of music at all as a separate art. On the "sympathetic" aspect of musical experience, cf. note 34.

[22] One of the most sophisticated treatments of this whole subject is Schier 1986, who links the notion of resemblance to the kinds of cognition (the "recognitional abilities") that depiction relies on—a line of argument anticipated, however sketchily, in Aristotle's general approach to mimesis: cf. chapter 5 for Aristotle's emphasis on "recognition" in the experience of mimesis. For (qualified) vindications of "resemblance theories" of pictorial art, see also

stands by "likeness" in connection with music, it is vital to notice that he cannot mean by it the purely aural counterpart to visual resemblance. The reason for this is that whereas the types of subject depicted in visual art do paradigmatically exhibit "colors and shapes," the various qualities embraced by the category of *ēthos* and treated by Aristotle as the objects of musical mimesis—qualities such as anger, self-discipline, enthusiasm— are not themselves constituted in sound. Music cannot contain, therefore, the match of sense modality that exists in the cases of painting and sculpture; and, as I pointed out in chapter 5, if a notion of (Peircean) "iconicity" is applicable to Aristotle's view of musical mimesis, it cannot be in virtue of such a match.

Yet Aristotle himself draws an analogy with visual art in this passage of the *Politics* (1340a25–28), evidently intimating that (notwithstanding the difference between them in relation to *ēthos*) he sees a conceptual parallelism between figural and musical mimesis. The parallelism appears to be a matter of both quasi-semantic and affective correlation, such that elements of the mimetic work create powerful psychological equivalences to the experience of (certain) features of the relevant phenomena in the real world, phenomena that are themselves closely associated with, and in some cases partly constituted by, affective properties. Although the significance of a mimetic work is necessarily communicated through its media, there need not be a complete correspondence between these media themselves and the objects they serve to represent; hence a continuity of sense modality between media and objects is a property of only some mimetic arts. Where poetry is concerned, the *Poetics* shows that Aristotle leans toward, without consistently adopting, an "enactive" conception of mimesis that posits an ideally close match between poetry's dramatic mode and the nature of human action, though here too the basis of equivalence cannot be complete continuity of sense modality.[23] In the case of music, Aristotle's account leaves us to infer that mimesis entails something like a kinetic or dynamic correspondence between the use of rhythms, tunings, and melodies, on the one hand, and the psychological states and feelings belonging to qualities of "character," on the other: the music "moves" emotionally, and we "move" with it.[24] And as we have seen,

---

Pole 1983, 135–47; Neander 1987; Sartwell 1991; and, most recently, Hopkins 1998, esp. 71– 93 (stressing the idea of experienced resemblance), Lopes 1996, 15–36.

[23] See Halliwell 1986, ch. 4. Kivy 1984, 17–18, takes "representation" but not "imitation" to be independent of resemblance within a particular sense modality; but this distinction cannot be projected back onto the historical use of mimeticist vocabulary.

[24] On this type of psychological "movement," see chapter 5, note 22; cf. Woodruff 1992, 91–92. A Damonian connection seems plausible here: there is a reference to movement of the soul in Damon fr. 6 DK (= Athenaeus 628c). Cf. Philodemus *Mus.* col. *82*.39–43 (Delattre 2001; cf. my note 32), = 3.37.13–17 Kemke, for Theophrastus's insistence on the "kinetic"

this correspondence or equivalence is supposed, in the final reckoning, to be a datum of common testimony within Aristotle's own culture.[25]

It is worth adding a rider at this stage. If the mimetic capacity of music in relation to *ēthos* manifests itself partly in the strength of emotional experience it affords, and if the visual arts, as *Politics* 8.5 claims, are limited to conveying *ēthos* by means of "signs" (*sēmeia*), we might expect Aristotle to suppose that painting and sculpture's nature will be negatively evidenced by an inability to arouse (strong) emotion. This is in fact confirmed by a passage from *De anima* (3.3, 427b21–24), where it is remarked that paintings of, say, "frightening" scenes leave those who look at them emotionally unaffected. Aristotle is there judging by the standards of powerful emotions in life, and he may be simplifying somewhat in the interests of highlighting his point about the difference between believing that there really is a frightening *x* in front of me and imagining myself confronted by a frightening *x*. So he need not mean that (fictional) paintings never arouse any trace of emotion in response to what they depict.[26] But the passage is certainly consonant with the contrast between music and visual art in *Politics* 8. The latter suggests that only an art that has an affective immediacy of correspondence to its objects can elicit a "sympathetic" response (cf. the adjective *sumpatheis*, 1340a13) of the kind that traces and follows the force of those objects—in this case, the pleasurable or painful feelings associated with particular traits of "character"—in the minds of its audience. The *Poetics*, we know well, regards poetry as capable of sustaining this kind of relationship vis-à-vis the fabric of human "action(s) and life" (1450a16–17) as a whole. For Aristotle, poetry is ideally an imaginative enactment of possible structures of action (and suffering), and the emo-

---

properties of music, with, e.g., cols. *38*.1–6 (= 1.22.1–6 Kemke), *43*.7–8 (= 1.27.7–8 Kemke), 117.42–45 (= 4.3.42–45 Kemke) for the same idea in Diogenes of Babylon; note a connection with mimesis in both cols. *38* and *82*. Philodemus criticizes this position in cols. 121–23 (= 4.7–9 Kemke). Budd 1985, 37–51, rigorously examines the senses in which music itself might be said to "move," and their relation to the expression of emotion.

[25] One should perhaps add that throughout his treatment of music in *Politics* 8 Aristotle presupposes an engaged attention to music, worthy of the description of *theōria/-ein*, contemplation, on the part of the listener: see esp. 1340a26–27, 37, 1341a23, and cf. *Poet.* 4.1448b11.

[26] "Fictional" is a necessary qualification: Aristotle would presumably accept that a painting linked to one's own life would have a different potential (cf. the incidental reference to a case of this sort at *Poet.* 16.1455a1–2, with Virgil *Aen.* 1.450–97 for a famous later instance). In any case, *De anima* 427b23–24 need only exclude strong, "real-life" emotions from the experience of painting: one does not feel, e.g., immediate fear *for oneself* when looking at a painting of a dangerous animal. Cf. Belfiore 1985a, 357–58, for the suggestion that contemplating a painting could still produce involuntary physiological concomitants of emotion. Aristotle allows that pictures may arouse feelings of pleasure at beauty, *Pol.* 8.5, 1340a25–26, and he probably implies at *Pol.* 7.17, 1336b12–16 (cf. ibid., 5–6, for the principle of influence) that figurative artworks can stimulate sexual feelings.

tions tragedy can arouse in its audiences are emotions that closely match what are taken to be complex properties of the human experience exhibited in a play.[27] Analogously, Aristotle takes (some) music to trace patterns of "character," which no doubt may become attached, where music accompanies text, to an explicit narrative framework, but which in purely instrumental music will nonetheless constitute processes of emotion and feeling that focus on a kind of *implicit* narrative, a meaningful structure of mimetic expression, carried by the rhythms, tunings, and melodies employed. Aristotle does not offer a psychological analysis of this putative capacity of music, but his whole section on the place of music in education rests on his acceptance of its existence and importance.

Notice, moreover, that we cannot make further headway with Aristotle's argument by attempting to separate representation and expression, for it seems to make equally good sense to say that he ascribes to music the capacity to represent and/or to express certain ethical qualities or feelings. Even if we wish (contestably) to say that representation is a matter of properties belonging to a work of art itself, while expression involves an essential effect on one who experiences the work, we still have to recognize that Aristotle himself binds representation and expression indissolubly together in his account of musical mimesis, because we have seen that the core of his case is an inference *to* the properties of music *from* the nature of its effects upon its hearers.

This is itself a far-reaching conclusion about Aristotelian mimesis, and one that has implications for the influence of the concept on Renaissance and post-Renaissance construals of the "imitation of nature," a principle whose history is much more complex and even ambiguous than is often realized.[28] The account of musical mimesis in *Politics* 8 requires us, I have suggested, to think of artistic representation and expression as very closely related and even overlapping. In this connection, it is interesting to place Aristotle's view of musical mimesis in relation to later concepts of musical expression, of which there have been three dominant varieties: first, expression, sometimes termed "transitive" expression, as the "arousal" of emotion in the listener (an idea that prevailed in the *Affektenlehre* of the sixteenth to eighteenth century); second, ("intransitive") expression as an "objectively" depictional or illustrative property (an idea that continues to appeal to some philosophers of music, including Peter Kivy); third, expression as *self*-expression on the part of the composer (an

[27] Pity and fear, that is, match the play's element of the "fearful and pitiful": for this point, cf. chapter 6. Hepburn 1984, 75–87, offers some sensitive remarks, with partial reference to music, on the relationship between emotional qualities of artworks and emotions experienced in response to them.

[28] See chapter 12.

idea still popularly prevalent, though philosophically somewhat out of favor).[29] Of the last of these there is no trace in Aristotle, I think, and very little trace at all in most ancient conceptions of mimesis, which are not for the most part preoccupied with the personal point of view, let alone the inner life, of the artist, but much more with the status of artistic works or performances and the kinds of experience they generate in their audiences.[30] But both the other two varieties of expression are, I believe, present in Aristotle's conception of mimesis. Indeed this conception can be read as not just a combination but a virtual *fusion* of the two. What this proposition amounts to is that for Aristotle the significance of a mimetic work or performance cannot be properly accounted for without reference to the response of a hypothetical or ideal hearer or spectator. Equally, though, the nature of this response is to be explained and justified by reference to intrinsic properties (the "nature") of the work itself. If "objective" and "emotive" theories of musical significance have often been regarded as opposed, for Aristotle they are integrated, and function as mutually explanatory, within a single theory.

This interpretative "loop" makes it, moreover, difficult if not impossible to apply to Aristotle's argument in *Politics* 8.5 the distinction between description and evaluation that has exercised some modern aestheticians. From one point of view, Aristotle's position looks obviously normative to us, because it implicitly assumes certain standards of judgment. At the same time, it builds its case, in *Politics* 8 as in the *Poetics*, on what are taken to be substantially shared experiences of mimetic art; and it holds these experiences, as we earlier saw, to be grounded in certain possibilities (capacities of the human mind, as well as a special affinity between the mind and the materials of music) made available by nature. We can certainly make allowance for some schematic tidiness in Aristotle's argument: part of his aim is to encompass, with music as with tragedy, certain areas of culturally prevalent and convergent experience, and this no doubt leads him to marginalize the extent to which disagreements about art actu-

[29] Levinson 1996, 90–125, offers a detailed survey and critique of modern philosophical positions on musical expression; Kivy's (somewhat fluctuating) interpretation of the issue is perhaps best seen in Kivy 1980. Matravers 1998, esp. 145–87, offers the most sophisticated defense yet attempted of an "arousal" theory; Sharpe 2000, 3–83, is skeptical about arousal and makes a balanced case for a "cognitivist" position. Dahlhaus 1985, 23, speaks loftily of the idea of a composer's musical *self*-expression as a "misleading and trivial [*sic*] belief propagated in popular aesthetics": odd, then, that such a "trivial" notion has been propagated by many composers themselves (cf. note 9). Twining 1812, 66–93, recognizes the need to talk of "expression" when speaking of ancient views, especially Aristotle's, of music as mimetic.

[30] One very specific kind of ancient interest in the operations of the artist's mind concerns the mental "form" that precedes the making of an artwork; on this, see chapter 11, note 6. Otherwise the major exception to the claim made in my text is, of course, the protoromantic Longinus *On the Sublime*, on whose qualified mimeticism, see chapter 10, section III.

ally did arise within his culture.[31] But it remains clear, I think, that such disagreements would not disturb the foundations of Aristotle's aesthetic model. According to this model, mimesis involves a communicative process in which the significance of an artwork is realized only through the response of one who traces and is moved by the pattern of experience embodied within it. Mimesis fulfills itself in the mind's active encounter with, its cognitive and emotional grasp of, a possible reality configured in an artistic form.

III

The most concentrated ancient attack on the kind of aesthetics represented by *Politics* 8 occurs in the treatise *On Music* (*Peri mousikēs*) of Philodemus of Gadara, a prolific Epicurean philosopher of the first century B.C.[32] Largely, no doubt, because of its extremely fragmentary condition (the result of having been partially recovered, as with some of Philodemus's other treatises, from the charred remains of Herculaneum papyri), this work has received very little attention from historians of aesthetics. But we can reconstruct enough of its critique of *ēthos* theory to make particularly instructive a juxtaposition of its ideas on music with those of Aristotle.[33] It does not matter for my purposes whether Philodemus had read *Politics* 8 as we now have it; as it happens, Aristotle's name does not appear in the remains of the treatise. Philodemus was undoubtedly concerned to criticize a whole range of earlier thinkers, from Pythagoras and Damon onward. His most prominent target in the work as it survives is the Stoic Diogenes of Babylon/Seleucia (c. 230–140), whose own treatise on music had incorporated views of the art taken over from the earlier philosophical tradition. But whatever Philodemus's main sources were, or the exact intel-

---

[31] The *Poetics* does make some reference to such disagreements (esp. 13.1453a30–31), but they are peripheral to its project. In *Pol.* 8, notice Aristotle's stress on the idea of musical "judgment" (*krinein* etc.): 1340a17–18, b25, 36, 39. Such judgment, which is probably meant to embrace a combination of technical and ethical factors (cf. Kraut 1997, 199–200), is implicitly normative.

[32] All references to *On Music* (*Mus.*) follow the column numbers in the new edition of Delattre 2001, which importantly assigns *all* the surviving fragments to book 4; for some readers' convenience I add references to the old book and fragment numbers in Kemke 1884. Note that Delattre italicizes column numbers 1 to 113, whose order is still hypothetical; furthermore, some of these numbers have changed since the provisional statement of his editorial method in Delattre 1989 (whose numbers I cited in Halliwell 1999).

[33] Philodemus's treatise is discussed, not always reliably (the translations are often loose), in Anderson 1966, 153–76; see also Koller 1954, 152–57; I have not seen Plebe 1957. More recently the work's specifically Epicurean presuppositions have been analyzed by Rispoli 1991; cf. Delattre 1997 on Philodemus's Epicurean appeal to the self-evidence of the senses in his rebuttal of Diogenes of Babylon.

lectual affiliations between them, it is clear that ideas very like Aristotle's in *Politics* 8 were in Philodemus's sights. We can be confident that if Philodemus had not read the *Politics* itself, he had at any rate made use of later Peripatetic texts that closely echoed its arguments.[34]

I want so far as possible to try to step delicately around the formidable difficulties that beset the detailed papyrological reconstruction and interpretation—an ongoing task—of *On Music*. I rely here on what I think we can securely identify as the central elements in the work's critique of *ēthos* theory, which by Philodemus's time had evidently become an orthodoxy broadly subscribed to by Academics, Peripatetics, Stoics, and Pythagoreans. This critique is probably to be viewed as part of a larger Epicurean alienation—prompted by Epicurus himself—from the established traditions of *paideia* (education), in which music and poetry bulked so large, even though the nature of that alienation was not as clear-cut as has sometimes been thought.[35] What is beyond doubt is that in *On Music* Philodemus repeatedly and disparagingly rebuts belief in the paideutic value of music. He does so because he rejects the principle that music can affect and change the psyche for good or bad and, in particular, that it can do so by expressing and transmitting qualities of "character" (*ēthos*) or the emotions associated with them. Not surprisingly, therefore, he repudiates the whole idea that music is a mimetic art, one that can incorporate "likenesses."[36]

As that very brief summary intimates, every important element in the musical aesthetics I earlier examined in Aristotle's *Politics* is emphatically contradicted by Philodemus. In the place of this aesthetics, and the coalition of mimesis and *ēthos* theory that is its hallmark, Philodemus's treatise sets up a conception of music as consisting of pure, nonsignificant sound

---

[34] For a denial of the idea of musically aroused *sumpatheia*, which is basic to the view taken of music in *Pol.* 8.5 (cf. my earlier comments, with note 21, and chapter 5, section I), see Philodemus *Mus.* col. 147.1–11 (= 4.33.1–11 Kemke); cf. col. 27.18 (= 1.15.18 Kemke). Possible Peripatetic intermediaries between Aristotle and Diogenes/Philodemus include Theophrastus (col. 81.1 = 3.35.1 Kemke, col. 82.39 = 3.37.13 Kemke), Heraclides Ponticus (col. 137.30 = 4.23.30 Kemke), Dicaearchus (col. 49.21 = 1.32.21 Kemke), Aristoxenus (col. 109.15 = 3.76.15 Kemke, col. 143.16 = 4.29.16 Kemke; for his *ēthos* theory, cf. Strabo *Geog.* 1.2.3 = fr. 123 Wehrli 1967) and Chamaeleon (col. 47.5 = 1.30.5 Kemke, col. 131.32 = 4.17.32 Kemke). Nussbaum 1993, 115–21, places the evidence of Philodemus *Mus.* on Diogenes of Babylon's views within the larger context of Stoic attitudes to poetry and music, though I have reservations about her thesis that Diogenes held an essentially noncognitivist view of music. Cf. now Sorabji 2000, 81–92.

[35] Several of the essays in Obbink 1995a offer reassessments of this question.

[36] Philodemus's rejection of musical mimesis can be seen esp. at col. 82.33–34 (= 3.37.7–8 Kemke), col. 91.1–12 (= 3.55.1–11 Kemke), col. 94.27–41 (= 3.62.6–20 Kemke), col. 117.23–42 (= 4.3.23–42 Kemke), col. 136.27–32 (= 4.22.27–32 Kemke); cf. col. 38.19 (= 1.22.19 Kemke).

whose only capacity is to provide the ears with sensory pleasure (a "tick-ling of the senses"), and, in standard Epicurean terms, an "unnecessary" or inessential pleasure at that.[37] What is more, where Aristotle had played down the importance of music's common combination with poetry, Philo-demus dwells on this connection as the source of those *apparent* expres-sive powers of music, which have given rise, in his judgment, to mistaken philosophical interpretations of the art. In several surviving passages Phi-lodemus asserts that, where music does appear to carry significance, it does so only in virtue of its conjunction with a verbal text. Yet in such cases, he insists, the significance belongs strictly and exclusively to the ideas and thought content of the text.[38] In addition, Philodemus will not even allow that music can enhance or intensify the significance of a text it accompanies. He goes so far as to suggest at one point that music can actually be a distraction from the verbal sense of a poem.[39] Although this view is perfectly plausible for some individual cases, it nonetheless looks as though Philodemus treats the music-poetry association as being so arbi-trary and contingent that his theory may have no way of explaining the historical extent and strength of that association.

Philodemus's conception of music, as it starts to emerge from both the negative and the positive propositions already outlined, benefits from being understood in relation to his Epicurean philosophy as a whole. At the same time, it represents a position that could be formulated indepen-dently of Epicureanism and can indeed be paralleled in more recent aes-thetics. Seen from an Epicurean angle, Philodemus is proposing a "scien-tific" account of music as constituted by mere sound. In one important fragment he asserts that "in the case of the hearing there is no difference at all [sc. between different hearers], but everyone's hearing receives the

[37] "Tickling of the senses" (the Greek verb is *gargalizein*): col. 78.30–31 (= 3.27.5–7 Kemke), apparently a favourite Epicurean motif (see Epicurus frs. 412–14 Usener). Philode-mus repeatedly marks the nonsignificant status of musical sound by calling it "irrational," *alogos*, and by applying the same adjective to the sensory experience of music; cf. Philode-mus *Poems* 5.xxiii.21–xxiv.11, xxvi.29–xxvii.2 Mangoni. Observe, for what it is worth, that Lucretius's account of the origin of music at *De rerum nat.* 5.1379–91 (with its echo of De-mocritus fr. 154 DK at 1379–81; cf. chapter 5, note 5) refers both to aural pleasure (1381) *and* an effect on the mind (1390).

[38] See col. 119.13–37 (= 4.5.13–37 Kemke), col. 120.2–26 (= 4.6.2–26 Kemke), col. 128.4–29 (= 4.14.4–29 Kemke), cols. 131–34 (= 4.17–20 Kemke), col. 140 (= 4.26 Kemke), col. 142 (= 4.28 Kemke). It should be added that Philodemus is not actually sanguine about the ethical value even of poetic texts: see esp. col. 140.4–6 (= 4.26.4–6 Kemke).

[39] Col. 140.9–14 (= 4.26.9–14 Kemke), cf. col. 142.22–35 (= 4.28.22–35 Kemke). At the same time, Philodemus rejects the idea that poetic form, with or without music, can itself enhance the force of what can be expressed in prose; he states, in typically polemical fash-ion, that "it is hard to find anything more ridiculous" than the view of the Stoic Cleanthes that meter, rhythm, and melody can improve the moral efficacy of religious thoughts (col. 142.1–22 = 4.28.1–22 Kemke = *SVF* 1.486; cf. chapter 9, with note 14 there).

same impression from the same melodies and takes very similar pleasure from them" (col. 116.9–15 = 4.2.9–15 Kemke). If people do experience the same music in different ways, it must be because of their beliefs, not their sensory perception as such (17–19). The various qualities that people ascribe to music do not belong to it in reality; they are mere projections of cultural preconceptions, not apprehensions of music's own nature (19–36). It is the tenets of Epicurean physics that prompt Philodemus to make a radical distinction between the natural reality of sound and the cultural constructions (amounting, for him, to factitious interpretations) that are put on that sound by many theorists and philosophers of music.

We know from Epicurus's own writings that his philosophy readily lends itself to a separation of, and potential tension between, uninterpreted sense data (whose reality is purely atomic) and the beliefs, true or false, that the mind develops in response to, and through interpretation of, those data.[40] There are certainly general problems with the psychological and epistemological implications of this Epicurean model of mind. My only concern at present, however, is with the application of the model to the aesthetics of music. Here the crucial point, I think, is that Epicurean science (or scientism) leads Philodemus into an aesthetic reductionism that runs the risk of being self-confounding. The essence of a powerful objection to Philodemus's argument, at any rate as that argument is visible in the fragments, is as follows. To listen to, and therefore to recognize, something *as music* is already to have at least a latent or implicit concept of its status as something more than sound *tout court*.[41] Conversely, to construe music as mere sound is no longer to apprehend or categorize it as music at all. The distinction between purely sensory pleasure, on the one hand, and mental pleasure channeled *through* the senses, on the other, here becomes acutely important. In the case of poetry, as we know from his treatise on the subject, Philodemus opposed a euphonist, sound-centered stance on poetic pleasure and value by insisting precisely that poetry works on the mind, the *dianoia* and *logos*, not merely the senses. Yet in the case of music Philodemus drives a wedge between the mental and the sensory, thus conforming to an Epicurean view, known to have

---

[40] See esp. Epicurus *Epist. Herod.* 50–51. Annas 1992, 157–73, and Asmis 1999 provide overviews of Epicurean philosophy of mind.

[41] This claim is not invalidated by the responses of infants and young children to music (a subject often noted in antiquity; Philodemus refers to Diogenes of Babylon's views on this subject at *Mus.* col. 27.6–14 = 1.15.6–14 Kemke). Such responses, though interesting, cannot be the key to adult experiences of music within a musical culture, a point taken by Aristotle at *Pol.* 8.6, 1341a13–17 (cf. 8.5, 1340a2–6), where the "common" (*koinos*) or "basic" aspect or pleasure of music (available even to some animals) is something like the purely sensory factor isolated by Philodemus's theory.

been criticized in antiquity, that the pleasures of sights and sounds belong purely to the senses not the mind.[42]

But does Philodemus actually construe music as mere sound? Twice in the fragments of *On Music* he refers to melodies as having nothing more than the status of (vocal or instrumental) sound (*phōnē*).[43] The noun *phōnē* normally denotes an entire class of audible phenomena, those produced by human (or, in principle, animal) voices, and elsewhere it standardly embraces speech sounds. But Philodemus's use of it in these passages is obviously meant to exclude the latter, because in the one case he is drawing a contrast with *logos* (meaningful discourse) and in the other with "thoughts" (*dianoēmata*) and "words" (*onomata*). In both cases, therefore, he is anxious to emphasize that the musical qualities of the melodic voice, though the product of controlled tonal articulation, are entirely empty of significance. Far from carrying a positive acknowledgment of the distinctive status of musically shaped sound, these two passages underline the entirely negative thrust of Philodemus's case. It is true that his formulation does not expressly reduce musical sound to merely physical sound. It is also true that his argument leaves him able to recognize the status of musical sound in very general cultural terms, by distinguishing its humanly controlled production from sounds that arise in other ways. But I want to contend that Philodemus's overall treatment of music, so far as we can reconstruct it, nonetheless amounts to an empty reduction of musical sound to pure (physical) sound.

To see why this should be so, it is worth reminding ourselves of Philodemus's claim, mentioned earlier, that "in the case of the hearing there is no difference at all [sc. between different hearers], but everyone's hearing receives the same impression from the same melodies and takes similar pleasure from them" (col. 116.9–15 = 4.2.9–15 Kemke). Now part of Philodemus's purpose in the passage from which this comes is to strip away from music the putative qualities (of *ēthos*, emotion, etc.) ascribed to it by various theorists and philosophers, and to leave it with nothing other than the status of aurally pleasing sound. This position constitutes a heavily normative conception of the "nature" of music (cf. col. 116.35–36 = 4.2.35–36 Kemke). But unlike the normative element that I earlier identified in

---

[42] Criticism of this Epicurean position is attributed to the Cyrenaic school at Plutarch *Quaest. Conv.* 674a–b. On Philodemus and euphonist conceptions of poetic value, see chapter 9, note 4, and cf. note 52 here.

[43] Col. 127.19–20 (= 4.13.19–20 Kemke), col. 128.16–17 (= 4.14.16–17 Kemke). *Phōnē* probably also means "sound," with reference to the tonal properties of both vocal and instrumental music, at, e.g., *Mus.* col. 137.16 (= 4.23.16 Kemke), col. 142.29 (= 4.28.29 Kemke), and *Poems* 4 col. viii.4, 10, 12 (see chapter 9, note 57); for earlier examples, see Plato *Crat.* 423d4–e3, *Phileb.* 17c1, with Diogenes Laertius 7.55–57 for Stoic conceptions of *phōnē* that include sounds other than human speech.

Aristotle's arguments in *Politics* 8.5, Philodemus's conception defiantly contradicts extensive areas of musical experience in his own culture. Philodemus is effectively engaged in explaining these experiences *away*, and by doing so he is indeed reducing music to the status of mere sound. For the only propositions that his Epicurean perspective allows him to admit about such sounds are, first, strictly physical observations on their source, duration, and the like,[44] and, second, statements about the extent to which these sounds are found pleasing by the ear. If it is true at all that "everyone's hearing receives the same impression from the same melodies," it can be true only as a proposition of physics (and, even then, only in stricter acoustic conditions than Philodemus appears to appreciate).[45] But that is exactly Philodemus's point, if I am interpreting him correctly: the only true understanding of music is one that comes via (Epicurean) science.

Philodemus has, accordingly, severed the standards of musical excellence from the conditions of a musical culture—the conditions without which, I submit, it is not even possible to define or identify music in the first place. He aspires to judge music from outside, where Aristotle saw the need to come to terms with it from within, so to speak. For Aristotle, in the *Politics*, musical judgment is something that can be the subject of education, cultivation, and experience. This means that, notwithstanding what he takes to be the natural roots of music, its practice and appreciation are the subject of mature cultural development, and in keeping with this Aristotle intimates some esteem for informed, professional expertise.[46] Philodemus, by contrast, is committed to reducing the success or failure of particular pieces of music, or of the tonal or rhythmic systems on which they depend, to a brute fact about the amount of aural pleasure they give to the ear; and he shows a general contempt for attitudes to music that are

[44] Notice, however, that unlike some other philosophers, especially Pythagoreans, Epicureans seem to have had no real interest in the physics of musical sound.

[45] It is important to register that when Aristotle appeals to a shared susceptibility to music (e.g., *Pol.* 8.5, 1340a13, "everyone"), he is not strictly claiming that any given piece of music will provide the same pleasure to all hearers: indeed, his discussion as a whole makes it clear that the individual listener's age, education, and character will all be capable of influencing his or her response to particular types of music. Diogenes of Babylon's observation of variations in emotional responses to music is indicated at Philodemus *Mus.* col. *38.*4–6 (= 1.22.4–6 Kemke), with col. *29.*7–14 for his Stoic view of the training of perception and judgment by painting and music; cf. also his distinction between natural (*autophuēs*) and "scientific" (*epistēmonikē*) perception (*Mus.* col. *36.*3–8 = 1.21.3–8 Kemke, col. 115.28–38 = 4.1B.28–38 Kemke), which goes back to Speusippus (see Sextus Empiricus *Adv. Math.* 7.145–46) and recognizes the idea of a trained musical sensibility; cf. Rispoli 1983. For a later recognition of variation in the effects of musical mimesis, see Aristides Quintilianus *Mus.* 2.4.

[46] Flashar 1999, 927, stresses that the pursuit of musical "research" flourished in Aristotle's own school. The dependence of some kinds of musical pleasure on (partial) training in the elements of musical culture is particularly clear at *Pol.* 8.6, 1341a13–17 (cf. note 42).

incompatible with his basic scientific premises. For Philodemus, it will be neither the musician nor the musical theorist, but the Epicurean philosopher, who is best equipped to pronounce on these matters. After all, it was Epicurus himself who had said that only the wise man—that is, the believer in his own doctrines—could discourse correctly about music and poetry.[47]

I return, in conclusion, to Philodemus's view that the apparently expressive properties of music are entirely the contingent result of association with semantic texts (of poetry). In this respect Philodemus was arguably the first person to make a mistake that has blighted the aesthetics of music on many occasions: that is, the supposition that the common conjunction of music and words justifies us in *discounting* the experiences offered by works involving this combination of media as evidence for music's own capacities. Such a view deserves to be stood on its head. Far from subtracting from the power of music as such, the ubiquitously manifested liaison between music and language actually gives us grounds to take all the more seriously the idea that music has authentic expressive powers of its own. The profound suitability of music as an accompaniment to certain uses of words (a suitability that seems to be a cultural universal) is a reason for believing that music can in some way answer to, or make indispensable contact with, at least part of the field of human meanings verbalized by language.[48] Nothing like the same degree or intensity of bond with language holds good for either tastes (cuisine) or odors (perfumes), to which Philodemus more than once cheaply compares music—nor, one might add, is it true of colors (which Philodemus himself does not mention), despite a long and tangled history of attempts to forge a connection between the experience of these and of music.[49] In short, the rhetoric of the comparison with tastes and odors betrays a failure on Philodemus's part to see why a model of music as mere auditory stimulus cannot begin to do justice to the emotional value attached to it in the Greek (or any other) tradition. As Rousseau was to put it: "comme donc la peinture n'est pas l'art de combiner des couleurs d'une manière agréable à la vue, la musique n'est pas non plus l'art de combiner des sons d'une manière agréable à l'oreille. S'il n'y avait que cela, l'une et l'autre seraient au nombre des

[47] Diogenes Laertius 10.120.

[48] Steiner 1997, 63–77, argues for an essentially conflictual relationship between music and language; but his case depends on a somewhat specious metaphysics (and some dubious inferences from myth).

[49] See, e.g., *Mus.* col. 133.23–24 (= 4.19.23–24 Kemke), col. 147.8–11 (= 4.33.8–11 Kemke) for Philodemus's comparisons with tastes and odors: Aristotle would have countered these analogies with the point made at *Pol.* 8.5, 1340a28 ff. As regards colors, see, e.g., the remarks of Rée 1999, 25–33, on ventures (some of them downright cranky) into "color-music," i.e., a "music" *of* color.

sciences naturelles et non pas des beaux arts." (Just as painting is not the
art of combining colors in a visually pleasing manner, no more is music
the art of combining sounds in a manner pleasing to the ear. If there were
no more to them than that, both would belong to the class of natural sciences, not of fine arts.)[50]

IV

If the tendency of all formalism in aesthetics is toward the idea that artistic
forms lack any significance outside their own construction or arrange-
ment, then Philodemus is not only the first formalist we can identify by
name in the history of musical aesthetics but also arguably one of the
most reductive.[51] Philodemus's outlook, which I have had to treat in a very
compressed and selective way, rests in part on a sweeping rejection of the
idea of musical mimesis. This rejection covered the weaker thesis (apparently held by Diogenes of Babylon) that music involves affective and ethical correlates ("likenesses") at an "epiphenomenal" level, as well as the
stronger claim—akin to the position exemplified in Aristotle's *Politics*—
that music involves intrinsic representation and/or expression of "character" and emotion.[52] It is important to understand that formalism of the se-

---

[50] *Essai sur l'origine des langues*, ch. 13, in Rousseau 1959–95, 5:414 (spelling modernized). Cf. Rousseau's remark, near the start of ch. 15 (ibid., 5:417), that "les sons, dans la
mélodie, n'agissent pas seulement sur nous comme sons, mais comme signes de nos affections, de nos sentiments; c'est ainsi qu'ils excitent en nous les mouvements qu'ils expri-
ment, et dont nous y reconnaissons l'image" (melodic sounds do not work their effects on
us *only* as sounds, but as signs of our affections, our feelings; it is thus that they arouse in us
the movements that they express and whose image we recognize in them), a sentiment that
combines musical representation or expression with "arousal" in a way that matches my
earlier account of Aristotle's position in *Pol.* 8.5. The scope of Rousseau's musical mimeticism
is discussed by Corbelli 1994.
[51] We know, however, that Philodemus had Greek predecessors in this respect (including
the anonymous author of the Hibeh Papyrus 1.13: see West 1992b, 16–23), and his views
were later echoed in the skeptic Sextus Empiricus *Adv. Math.* bk. 6: see, most recently, Blank
1998, xli–iv.
[52] See col. 117.23–35 (= 4.3.23–35 Kemke) for the distinction between "epiphenomenal"
(here something like "supervenient"?) and (intrinsically or strictly) mimetic qualities, where
the contrast must belong to a position adopted by Diogenes and contested by Philodemus.
Because other parts of Philodemus's treatise indicate that Diogenes *did* generally espouse a
mimeticist theory of musical representation or expression (see esp. *Mus.* col. 136.27–32 =
4.22.27–32 Kemke, and cf. col. 94.27–36 = 3.62.6–15 Kemke, col. 91.1–10 = 3.55.1–10
Kemke), the present passage should refer to a partial modification of Diogenes' stance, not
an outright rejection of a model of musical mimesis (*contra* Neubecker 1986, 129, and West
1992a, 250); the translation of this passage in Delattre 2001 puzzles me. The (transitive) verb
epiphainein in this context, which may or may not have been used by Diogenes himself,
seems to denote "cause/allow to appear" (so that *epiphainomena* are properties supervenient on more fundamental properties): cf. *Mus.* col. 33.11–12 (= 1.18.11–12 Kemke), *Poems*

verity found in Philodemus (and one might notice that Philodemus anticipates Hanslick in his polemical, dismissive tone, as well as in the
"scientific" bent of his reasoning) differs fundamentally from the various
denials of musical mimesis that were subsequently formulated in the
course of the aesthetic debates of the eighteenth century. Those philosophers and critics in this period who became increasingly dissatisfied with
the idea of musical mimesis or, in the by then trite formula, the "imitation
of nature," nonetheless preserved a vital link between music and emotion
(or "the passions"), however difficult they may have found it to specify,
let alone explain, the nature of this link. And romanticism, far from abandoning an older, indeed ancient, interest in the symbiosis of music and
poetry, revivified it in a freshly potent form.

But the language of musical aesthetics undoubtedly changed irrevoca-
bly in the later eighteenth and early nineteenth centuries, and one element
in this process of change was the obsolescence of the vocabulary of musical mimesis. A new language was inevitable, one can see with hindsight,
given the far-reaching transformation of sensibilities in this period, a transformation reflected in, and encouraged by, developments in the character
of music itself. The terminology of mimesis fell largely into disuse as regards music (though less so as regards both poetry and the visual arts) for
two principal reasons. The first is that it was too closely bound up with
vocal music—and accordingly with the traditional theory of music as inti-
mately related to the natural expressiveness of the human voice[53]—to be
able to survive in an era in which instrumental, and especially orchestral,
music had acquired such importance for both composers and audiences.
The other reason is that the concept of mimesis gave too little scope for
the attribution of self-expression to composers themselves, an idea that
became hugely important for romantic aesthetics of musical creativity. But

---

5.xxiii.28, xxiv.31 Mangoni (the last two referring to poetic euphony), with Asmis 1992a, 143
n. 15. Note that Philodemus does strictly allow at *Poems* 4 col. viii.9–13 (Janko 1991, 15) for
one, narrow kind of musical mimesis, namely the mimesis *of* sounds *by* sounds ("Tonma-
lerei"); but this passing concession in itself shows that he construes the concept of artistic
mimesis as encompassing in general much more than simple "imitation": see chapter 9, notes
57, 59.

[53] The possible complexities of this view, often overlooked by modern scholars (see, e.g.,
Abrams 1953, 91), can be glimpsed in Dubos' *Réflexions critiques* of 1719, bk. 1, ch. 45
(Dubos 1748, 361–62), where the expressiveness of the human voice seems to waver between being the *object* and the *source* of musical expression (the "passions" being the true
object of expression in the latter case); cf. Diderot's famous passage on music in *Le neveu
de Rameau* (see note 5 above), surely influenced by Dubos (and perhaps also by Plato: see
O'Gorman 1971, 118–35). One late ancient trace of the idea of music (in this case, musical
instruments) as linked to the expressiveness of the voice can be found in John Philoponus
In Aristot. De Anim. Comm. 15.375–76. Budd 1985, 131–50, rejects vocal expressiveness as
a model for musical expressiveness in general.

CHAPTER EIGHT

that is not at all the same as saying that expression *tout court* took the place of mimesis within the structure of musical criticism and aesthetics, because, as I earlier insisted, the traditions of mimeticism had always involved reference to some notion of expression—explicitly, in the views of music prevailing between the sixteenth and eighteenth centuries, and implicitly in the ancient traditions of *ēthos* theory, as I have tried to show in my discussion of Aristotle's *Politics* 8.5.

For most of Greco-Roman antiquity, and for some three hundred years after the Renaissance, mimesis served, under a variety of interpretations, as the focal point of attempts to make sense of musical meaning. If the framework of mimeticist thinking eventually failed to cope with the demands of romanticism in music, partly because of a shift from interest in the expression of well-defined "affections" to that of more fluid and indeterminate realms of feeling, that need not prevent us from seeing that older traditions of thought had been a response to a real need for something more satisfying than a wholly formalist account of music. In that important sense, romanticism reorientated and partly refashioned the language of musical aesthetics, but it did not discard the fundamental preoccupation with musical meaning that had motivated mimetic concepts of the art. Mimeticists and romantics were equally antiformalist in their convictions.[54]

If we are prepared to understand the idea of expression in a suitably flexible way—*au fond*, as something like a sense of the psychological "life" that is perceived or felt as moving within, and communicated by, music—then we might well conclude that the issue of expression is and always has been at the heart of the recalcitrant problems of musical aesthetics, and as such forms a bridge between mimeticist and postmimeticist models of music. For the issue of musical expression can be translated into the question—both anthropological and philosophical—of how and why music, in all its varieties, can mean so much to human beings, can seem to connect with some of their deepest capacities for feeling, and yet can remain so hard to elucidate in rational terms. This way of putting the point brings with it, I believe, the realization that formalism is not, in the

---

[54] Some threads of connection between the mimeticist tradition and romantic expressivism in music emerge from the discussion of Dahlhaus 1985, 16–29, though his own attempt to draw a neat distinction between "imitation" and "expression" (esp. 23) is historically incorrect (cf. note 5). Berger 2000, 133–52, offers a stimulating account of the postromantic conflict between "mimetic" and "abstract" models of music; Wallace 1986 shows that romantic attitudes to music were in practice more complex than standard versions sometimes suggest. Goehr 1992, 120–75, taking a rather different tack from mine, explores the relationship between music's eighteenth-century "emancipation from the word" and the break with traditional conceptions of music as mimetic, though her comments on mimesis as such are sometimes too conventional.

final analysis, a serious option in the aesthetics of music, however formidable the difficulties that confront those who try to see beyond it. If that is right, and all the more so if, as I have suggested, the concept of expression cannot be completely separated from that of representation, then there is an important respect in which the problems of mimesis in music (but not there alone) remain *our* problems. In narrowly terminological terms, and even in those of cultural psychology, the theory of musical mimesis may have reached its limits—the limits of its usefulness—in the mid-eighteenth century. But its abiding legacy is in part a challenge to grasp some underlying continuities, as well as major shifts of mentality, in the history of aesthetics. In that sense it is still worth our while to try to hold onto the delicate thread that connects us to the musical aesthetics (and the musical ethics) of Aristotle's *Politics*, despite the attempts of Philodemus, and of others like him, to snap it once and for all.

PART III

Chapter Nine

※

Truth or Delusion? The Mimeticist Legacy in Hellenistic Philosophy

The excellence of the poet is nothing other than the artistic
mimesis of life in language. (Strabo *Geography* 1.2.5)

Hoist the sails of your little boat, my happy friend, and flee from
all educated culture [*paideia*]. (Epicurus)[1]

IN THE DOMAIN OF aesthetics, moving on from the writings of Plato and Aristotle to the rather patchily preserved evidence for Hellenistic attitudes to
mimetic art is somewhat like descending from a mountain range into a
large but indefinitely sprawling plain. It is appropriate to begin this journey, however, by observing that extensive areas of the plain are irrigated
by waters that run down from the peaks above. One aspect of the impact
of both Plato and Aristotle—an aspect given little attention by historians
of philosophy but an immensely important one in the long run of the
history of ideas—is reflected in the fact that by the Hellenistic period the
vocabulary of mimeticism had become part of the lingua franca of Greek
criticism and philosophical aesthetics. In this as in other areas, the influence of Plato and Aristotle was diffused in various ways, both direct and
indirect. In Plato's case it is clear that the *Republic*, like other dialogues,
remained widely accessible and known.[2] But in Aristotle's case we have
to allow for three factors whose effects are no longer quantifiable: first, the
availability of his now lost dialogue *On Poets*, which may have included a
more "popular" statement of some of the ideas contained in the *Poetics*;
second, the existence of his large work on *Homeric Problems*, also now
lost, which probably made extensive application to the Homeric poems
of the principles set out in chapter 25 of the *Poetics*; and, third, the work
of a succession of Peripatetic thinkers, from Theophrastus onward, who
took over but also developed some of the basic tenets that the founder of

---

[1] Epicurus fr. 163 Usener (cf. note 38).

[2] For some possible Hellenistic and imperial echoes of passages of Plato's *Republic* dealing with mimesis see, e.g., notes 7 (Zeno), 12 (Posidonius), 21 (Strabo and his sources),
and 50 (Philodemus) here, with chapter 10, notes 30–31 (Plutarch), 49–50 (Homeric scholia,
deriving from Hellenistic criticism). Weinstock 1927 traces the repercussions, *pro* and *contra*,
of Plato's critique of Homer. For a case where we know that Plato's remarks on mimesis in
the *Laws* were taken up, see Philodemus *Mus.* col. 51 Delattre 2001 (cf. chapter 8, note 20), =
1.1 Kemke, where Diogenes of Babylon, reported by Philodemus, quotes parts of *Laws* 2.669.

their school had enunciated. Between them, these three factors compensate for the apparent circumstance that the *Poetics* itself was little known in the Hellenistic period or, indeed, during antiquity as a whole.[3] But they also introduce a substantial element of uncertainty into the evolution of Aristotelian mimeticism after Aristotle's own lifetime.

Although the views of Hellenistic and later thinkers on mimetic art tended, as we shall see, to generate arguments often polarized between positions that might now be characterized as formalist, on the one side, and moralistic, on the other, our evidence allows us to see that there was, with some important exceptions, a general acceptance of mimesis as a fundamental and unifying concept of aesthetics.[4] But the sources relevant to any attempt to chart some of the salient points and lines of development in postclassical mimeticism are themselves anything but unified. They are scattered, often fragmentary, and in many cases preserved only by indirect transmission, as for example with the traces of Hellenistic literary criticism embedded in the medieval scholia on the Homeric epics. For this reason, I propose to give separate attention, in this and the following chapter, to two very broadly conceived blocks of material: first, the schools of Hellenistic philosophy, principally (in this context) Stoicism and Epicureanism; and, second, the work of both Hellenistic and imperial scholars and literary critics.

[3] *On Poets*: for the fragments, see Gigon 1987, 263–67; Laurenti 1987, 1:211–300; cf. Janko 1987, 56–65 (a more conjectural reconstruction), and Janko 1991, esp. 35–59, but with my note 56, on the dialogue's possible use by Philodemus in *On Poems*; McMahon 1929 thinks the standard definitions of tragedy and comedy throughout antiquity and up to the early modern period go back to *On Poets*. *Homeric Problems*: see Gigon 1987, 526–39, for the fragments, with Erbse 1960, 59–69, for its possible use by Porphyry in the third century A.D. On the critical interests of the early Peripatetics in general, see Podlecki 1969, though there is little actual trace of mimeticism in the fragments; for contrasting treatments of Theophrastus, see Grube 1952, Dosi 1960, Koster 1970, 85–92, and cf. chapter 10, note 3. The neglect of the *Poetics* itself in antiquity is noted in Halliwell 1986, 287–88; cf. Kyriakou 1997 (too narrowly in certain respects) on the lack of influence on Hellenistic philosophy. Guthrie 1962–81, 6:59–65, gives a useful conspectus of evidence and views on the Hellenistic fate of Aristotle's writings in general; Lord 1986 offers a critical reappraisal. On possible elements of "Aristotelianism" in Hellenistic aesthetics, see notes 22, 43, 48, 54, and chapter 10, notes 3, 14–15, 35, 40, 44, 46, 55, 57, 60; cf. Rostagni 1955, 188–237 (a now somewhat dated overview).

[4] One of the most important exceptions, Philodemus's rejection of musical mimesis, has already been examined in chapter 8. Janko 1998, 104, claims that mimesis was abandoned by those advocates of a euphonist poetics whom Philodemus (*Poems* 5.xxi.16–17, xxvii.7–8 Mangoni; *PHerc*. 1676 col. 6.1–11), apparently following Crates of Mallos, refers to disparagingly as "the critics" (*hoi kritikoi*): but we do not know this; their view of euphony as an (exclusive?) criterion of poetic *value* need not entail rejection of the basic idea that poetry makes use of mimesis. (There is a devastating rebuttal of unqualified formalism of the kind represented by an extreme euphonist stance in Richards 1929, 231–33.) On the *kritikoi* themselves consult, most recently, Porter 1995b and Porter 1996, though I am not yet convinced

This arrangement is more a matter of convenience than of strict demarcation, and it is certainly not designed to preclude the observation of a larger network of connections between texts of various kinds. The distinction between philosophy and scholarship or criticism is not one which can always be superimposed unproblematically onto ancient patterns of thought and writing. Some compromises are necessary: thus, a figure like Crates of Mallos, whose philosophical connections are debatable and who called himself a "critic" (*kritikos*), appears in the present chapter, whereas Plutarch, whose philosophical background and standpoint are much clearer (if markedly eclectic), is discussed in the next. But much of the interest of mimetic models of art in antiquity lies, in any case, in a culturally powerful current of assumptions and habits of mind that cuts across precise intellectual "professions" or affiliations. The picture I want to construct over the next two chapters, therefore, does not aspire to the status of either a conceptually tidy or a chronologically progressive synthesis of the evidence. It aims to uncover and expose to analysis some of the major features on the large and now partly overlaid landscape of Hellenistic and imperial mimeticism.

In the case of the Stoics, to whom I turn first, the school's sustained commitment to a highly integrated, even monolithic, system of doctrine means that the loss of vast quantities of Hellenistic Stoic writings does not altogether impede us from piecing together a coherent account that can incorporate both the attested views of individual philosophers and the overall tendency of Stoic teaching. In the first place, some Stoics were prepared to assert a naturalistic view of language, and thus of etymology, of the kind which had been expounded (though ultimately discarded) in Plato's *Cratylus*, and this involved the claim that the first or earliest language, coming into existence "by nature," involved mimesis of reality.[5] Although this conception of the origins of language as natural representation was sometimes qualified by doubts about the philosophical value of etymology as such, Stoics subscribed to a view of language that could lend itself to a general understanding of mimesis as some sort of correct picture of reality. We get a glimpse of this point in the claim attributed to Chrysippus that Stoic wisdom, as the supreme art ("the art of arts," *technē tech-*

---

we can extract a fully coherent account of their position(s) from Philodemus's mangled, polemical remarks.

[5] Chrysippus *SVF* 2.146 (from Origen *Contra Celsum* 1.24); cf. Dawson 1992, 29–35, on Stoic theories of "mimetic" etymology. On mimesis in Plato *Cratylus*, see chapter 1, section I and chapter 4, section II; cf. chapter 5, note 14, on Aristotle *Rhet.* 3.1, 1404a20–22. Stoic doubts about the value of etymology appear at Diogenes Laertius 7.83 (*SVF* 2.130): the Stoic wise man or dialectician would have nothing to say about "correctness of names." On the larger Stoic view of language, see Long 1971, Barnes & Schenkeveld 1999.

nōn), is "a *mimēma* [a representation, model, or microcosm?] and close image [*apeikonisma*] of nature."[6] This passage involves a self-conscious comparison between Stoic wisdom and the mimetic arts. The direction of thought is confirmed by the fact that the sentence just quoted belongs to the same context as an analogy with the work of the sculptor Phidias, who is here said to have stamped his artistry on all the different materials he employed, just as Stoicism itself, drawing on its "mimetic" alignment with nature, stamps its form on all the materials of life. The analogy counts on a recognition that visual mimesis sometimes aims to produce images that successfully capture something of the truth about their subjects, and it more generally indicates acknowledgment of the cultural prestige of the mimetic arts, though without implying that they themselves have the capacity to embody or convey Stoic "wisdom" directly. Despite some evidence that Zeno of Citium, the founder of Stoicism, expressed reservations about the traditional education (*paideia*) to which appreciation of mimetic art belonged,[7] Zeno himself chose to write extensively on poetry, and serious respect for poetry, music, and the visual arts certainly became a feature of Stoic orientation toward the traditions of Greek culture, in stark contrast to the often deeply negative judgments of Epicureanism.

Although Stoics, as we have just seen, could apply the terminology of mimesis to the (original) condition of language as a whole and to the wisdom of their own school in particular, they were nevertheless able to accept a more specific sense of mimesis that characterized the status of poetry (called "the artistic mimesis of life in language" by the Stoic geographer Strabo), music (treated at length as at least a partially mimetic art in Diogenes of Babylon's treatise *On Music*), and the visual arts (the source of Chrysippus's metaphor for Stoicism itself as a kind of mimesis).[8] Unsurprisingly, poetry received the most explicit and frequent attention from

---

[6] *SVF* 3.301 (= Philo *De ebr.* 88); for a Stoic conception of the virtuous life as itself an "art," *technē*, cf., e.g., Strabo *Geog.* 1.1.1, Marcus Aurelius *Med.* 4.2, 11.5. Possibly germane here is Cleanthes *Hymn to Zeus* 4, where humans are called a *mimēma* of (?)god (see my introduction, note 34), and Epictetus *Diss.* 2.5.27 (note 32).

[7] Diogenes Laertius 7.32, reporting the hostile account of Cassius the Skeptic, attests a negative treatment of *paideia* in Zeno's *Republic*, one of several features of this work that appear to involve (modified) Platonic elements: see Schofield 1999, 756–60, and cf. my note 38 on Epicurus's attitude to *paideia*. Zeno's own writings on poetry are attested at, e.g., Dio Chrysostom 53.4–5 (cf. notes 24, 43).

[8] Poetry: Strabo *Geog.* 1.2.5. Music: the fragments of Diogenes' treatise are in *SVF* 3, pp. 221–35; see chapter 8 for my discussion of Philodemus's use of this work, with note 52 there for the evidence that Diogenes partly qualified his adherence to a mimetic model of music, and cf. Strabo 9.3.10 for another reference to music as mimetic (but with note 28 here). On visual art, note that Zeno's negative attitude to statues (and temples) reported in *SVF* 1.264 is purely religious (see Armstrong 1966 for the influence of such Stoic ideas, with chapter 11, note 63). Zagdoun 2000, 147–70, takes a different tack on Stoic views of mimesis.

Stoic thinkers, including Zeno, Chrysippus, and other major figures in the succession of the school's leadership, many of whom quoted poetic texts abundantly in their own writings and strongly tended toward the Platonizing principle that poetry should be judged, in large measure, by the truth and ethical value of its "thought" or (quasi-)propositional content, as well as by poetry's impact on the emotions.[9]

In this connection a much-cited fragment of Posidonius, the prodigiously polymathic Stoic scientist, is particularly arresting. Posidonius, we are told, defined *poiēma* (a piece of verse) as "metrical or rhythmical speech whose elaboration goes beyond the form of prose," and *poiēsis* (poetry or a poetic work) as "verse that carries significance [*sēmantikon poiēma*] in virtue of containing mimesis of divine and human matters [*mimēsin . . . theiōn kai anthrōpeiōn*]."[10] The purpose of this definition appears to be to explain poetic mimesis in terms of "signification," a point not unique to Stoicism but one especially telling given the Stoic view that all language (*logos*) is a vehicle of meaning.[11] Posidonius, while taking over the by now traditional concept of poetry as mimetic, nonetheless seems to understand mimesis in such a way as to align poetry with the function of language in general (whether or not he follows the doctrine of language as itself mimetic in origin), rather than treating it as the marker of an independently "artistic" category. One implication of this is that Posidonius offers a definition of poetry that does not require anything like a distinct concept of fiction. On the contrary, his definition of poetry as "verse that carries significance," that is, as a poem *qua* vehicle of signification, looks designed to maintain the function of poetry as one means of asserting the truth. For a Stoic, "signification" implies the capacity of language to capture true states of affairs, to describe reality. Poetry, Posidonius's definition tells us, does not deny itself this capacity, even though a "piece of verse" (*poiēma*), as opposed to "poetry" or a poetic work (*poiēsis*), can be understood in terms of formal considerations of meter and style. Poetry's meaning, it appears, is not of a fundamentally different

[9] De Lacy 1948 gives a good overview of Stoic attitudes to, and uses of, poetry; Nussbaum 1993 undertakes a more nuanced study of competing Stoic views of the effects of poetry on the emotions. It goes without saying that I am not myself here attempting anything like a complete reappraisal of Stoic (or Epicurean) poetics.

[10] Diogenes Laertius 7.60 = Posidonius fr. 44 Edelstein-Kidd. Gigante 1961 is the fullest discussion, but he places too much stress on putative connections between the fragment and Longinus *On the Sublime*; Porter 1995a, 108–11, gives a summary of various views. There is insufficient reason to take Posidonius's definition of *poiēsis* as applying particularly to epic poetry, as does, most recently, Schenkeveld 1999, 224. A good discussion of the Hellenistic distinction between *poiēma* and *poiēsis* can be found in Brink 1963, 58–69; cf. Asmis 1992d.

[11] See, e.g., Diogenes Laertius 7.56–57. For non-Stoic occurrences of the idea that mimesis is a kind of signification, see, earlier, Plato *Crat.* 422e–23b (with chapter 1, section I), and, later, Plotinus *Enn.* 5.5.5, Ammonius *In Ar. De Interp.* 31.17.

kind from that of language in general. Indeed, its meaning has far-reaching scope, because the second element of Posidonius's definition—"in virtue of containing mimesis of divine and human matters"—employs a formulation elsewhere associated with a Stoic definition of philosophy itself.[12] The subject matter of poetry is no different from that of philosophy, and embraces the cosmos as a whole: Posidonius would, it appears, have agreed with at any rate the spirit of Batteux's much later pronouncement that "tout l'univers appartient aux beaux arts."[13]

Posidonius's definition of poetry reaches us without much of its immediate context of argument, but it was certainly in line with orthodox Stoic attitudes to poetry. It is redolent, for example, of the early Stoic Cleanthes' view, derided by Philodemus in his treatise on music, that poetry could use its formal resources of meter and heightened linguistic expression, as well as the support of music, to give particularly forceful expression to philosophical ideas (regarding "matters divine and human"—the same phrase as Posidonius's) and to contribute to "the truth of contemplation of the divine."[14] But for a fuller sense of the kind of readings of poetic texts to which Posidonius's position would readily have lent itself, we need to turn to the discursive work of the geographer Strabo, writing at Rome in the first century B.C. and the early first A.D., who knew Posidonius and his work and from whom I have already quoted the definition of poetry— more precisely, of poetic excellence—as "the artistic mimesis of life in language."[15] This definition is incorporated within Strabo's larger view, which undoubtedly had something in common with Posidonius's attempt to explore all branches of human knowledge from a Stoic perspective, that philosophy encompasses the understanding of all reality, divine and human, celestial and terrestrial. Strabo's own primary topic of geography

---

[12] A similar designation, "divine and human affairs," occurs in Cleanthes *SVF* 1.486 (Philodemus *Mus.* col. 142.7–8 Delattre 2001 = 4.28.7–8 Kemke) with reference to the domains of both philosophy and poetry; see my next paragraph. It reappears at Strabo *Geog.* 1.1.1, here again designating the subject of philosophy and evidently intended as a familiar formulation. It is likely that Posidonius fr. 44 also echoes the similar language used by Homer's admirers to describe the scope of the poet's knowledge at Plato *Rep.* 10.598e1–2 (rather than 607a4 ff., *pace* Kidd 1988, 1:199), which may itself look back to Hom. *Od.* 1.338; cf. also Plato *Ion* 531c. Posidonius may additionally have been influenced, at any rate indirectly, by the Theophrastean definition of epic ("a medium [*periochē*] of divine, heroic and human affairs"), *apud* Diomedes *Ars gramm.* 3.1 (Keil 1857–80, 8:484). Note, finally, that Posidonius's distinction between *poiēma*, *qua* poetic form, and *poiēsis*, *qua* significance, essentially separates out the two elements in Gorgias's definition of poetry as "language [*logos*] with meter" (fr. 11.9 DK; cf. chapter 1, note 38).

[13] Batteux, *Les beaux arts* (1746), pt. 3 §3 ch. 5 (Batteux 1989, 249).

[14] Cleanthes *SVF* 1.486 (cf. Seneca *Epist.* 108.10 = *SVF* 1.487); see my note 12, plus chapter 8, note 39, with Gigante 1961, 45; Asmis 1992b, 400–401.

[15] *tēn mimētikēn tou biou dia logōn*, Strabo *Geog.* 1.2.5. For the earlier history of the motif of "mimesis of life" in art, see chapter 10, note 3.

is specifically designated, in his very first sentence, as integral to philosophy, and Homer is announced, near the outset, as both the founder and master of geography (as of much else besides).[16] Strabo explicitly couples Homer's supposedly all-embracing knowledge with his supreme excellence as a poet (1.1.2), so that what starts to emerge from the early chapters of the *Geography* is a configuration of ideas that simultaneously makes Stoicism a polymathic system of thought, poetry an instrument of philosophical knowledge, and Homer a polymathic proto-Stoic. Within this framework Strabo's reference to poetic mimesis must be positioned. By the time Strabo reaches that later definition of poetry (1.2.5), he has already extracted from the Homeric epics, by various techniques of inference,[17] an overall "geography," a picture of the earth and its peoples; and one of his references to Posidonius establishes that, despite disagreement on points of detail, Strabo has here been following principles of poetic interpretation—above all, the premise that poetry aims to give, and is capable of giving, a true and instructive account of reality—which his Stoic predecessor had also adopted.[18] Thus the occurrence of mimesis in both Posidonius's and Strabo's definitions of poetry is hardly coincidental: it fits in with a more widespread Stoic inclination to regard poetry as capable of representing important truths about the world.

Strabo's definition of supreme poetic excellence as "the artistic mimesis of life in language" occurs, in fact, as one step in a sequence of argument that has first set out Homer's credentials as a philosopher-geographer (1.1.1–10), and has then proceeded to a robust rebuttal of the thesis, espoused by the early Hellenistic scientist Eratosthenes, that all poetry aims at "enchantment" (*psuchagōgia*) rather than "instruction" (*didaskalia*).[19]

---

[16] See Schenkeveld 1976 for a general analysis of Strabo's interpretation of Homer as a kind of "historical exegesis"; French 1994, 12–34, discusses the implications of Strabo's conception of geography as philosophy.

[17] Strabo feels confident about inferring Homer's "knowledge" of geography from a whole host of cited passages, but his inferences vary between those based on direct statements or descriptions and those which involve the assumption that Homer sometimes communicates his knowledge by indirect hints (n.b. especially the verb *ainittesthai* at 1.1.3, 1.1.10, which is sometimes associated with allegory but is here a matter only of obliqueness).

[18] Strabo 1.1.7 (= Posidonius fr. 216 Edelstein-Kidd), referring to Posidonius's detection of allusions to flow tides in certain Homeric phrases. Posidonius's estimation of Homer's value as a geographer need not have been as high as Strabo's (cf. Kidd 1988, 2:766–77), but that does not affect my claim that the two Stoics shared assumptions about poetic mimesis.

[19] Eratosthenes' position is first contradicted at the end of the discussion of Homeric geography (1.1.10), then picked up again at 1.2.3–5. Eratosthenes' concept of poetic *psuchagōgia* may have been entirely traditional, because the idea (which echoes an old theme of poetic bewitchment: see my introduction, note 50) had been used by various earlier authors, esp. in connection with emotional effect: see pseudo-Plato *Minos* 321a (with Plato *Phdr.* 261a, 271c); Isocrates 2.49 (with a contrast between *psuchagōgia* and instruction, n.b.), 9.10; Aristotle *Poet.* 6.1450a33; Timocles fr. 6.6 *PCG*, with Halliwell 1986, 64 n. 24. So it is certainly

By this declaration of literary didacticism or moralism Strabo aligns himself strictly with earlier Stoics, as well as other individual thinkers, who had asserted the status of poetry as "first" (i.e., preliminary or rudimentary) philosophy.[20] The concept of poetry as mimesis of life, introduced at 1.2.5, is then given a particular twist that allows it to fill out this Stoic aesthetic. After offering his definition of poetic excellence, Strabo asks rhetorically—and in implicit answer to the arguments of Plato *Republic* 10, especially 598–600—how the poet could achieve such excellence if he lacked experience and understanding of life; and this enables him—given the (to a Stoic) inescapably ethical dimension of knowledge and understanding—to reach the typically Stoic proposition that "one cannot be a good poet without first being a good man": poetic excellence, he insists, "is tied to human excellence."[21] The concept of mimesis thus completes the interlocking framework of ideas on which Strabo's use of Homer's poetry rests and is itself necessarily associated with the veridical and ethical value bestowed on poetry within this framework as a whole. Poetry can only fulfill its didactic-cum-philosophical function if it is grounded in knowledge, and that commits Strabo to a view of mimesis as the truth-bearing and morally informed representation of reality. Although Strabo's own subject requires him to foreground the geographical knowledge supposedly to be found in Homer, he appreciates nonetheless that the main material of poetic representation is the fabric of human life—"character(s), emotions, and actions," as he puts it, in a phrase reminiscent of Aristotle.[22]

But there is a further layer to Strabo's treatment of poetry, and one that brings us closer to a tension within Stoic attitudes to the mimetic arts. When, in the section of his argument beginning at 1.2.7, he returns to the

---

gratuitous of Porter 1996, 613, to suggest of Eratosthenes (as of Gorgias: see chapter 1, note 38) that he detached poetic value altogether from *meaning* (as opposed to truth). The polemical tone of Strabo's references to Eratosthenes' view of poetry is not necessarily a safe guide to the latter's intentions, a factor ignored by, e.g., Meijering 1987, 6–7.

[20] See, once more, 1.1.10 and 1.2.3: the reference to "our own [sc. thinkers]" (*hēmeteroi*) at 1.2.3 shows that Strabo is invoking Stoic sources, though we cannot identify them precisely.

[21] *hē de poiētou sunezeuktai tēi tou anthrōpou* (1.2.5, where I prefer to take *tou anthrōpou* as generic rather than individual: cf., e.g., Plato *Rep.* 3.395b4, 10.602c4). Stoics were inordinately fond of formulations of the kind "only the (Stoic) sage can be a good *x*," "one cannot be a good *x* without first being a (Stoic) sage"; Strabo had already cited the Stoic sentiment that "only the sage is a poet" at 1.2.3. For the implicit response (likely to derive from earlier Hellenistic criticism) to Platonic arguments in *Geog.* 1.2.5, note (i) the argument from depiction of *x* to knowledge of *x*, (ii) the rejection of the idea of poetry as magic or wizardry, *goēteuein*, and (iii) the distinction between poetry and the work of handcraftsmen, *tektones* (cf. chapter 4, note 47), all of which seem to cluster around a repudiation of Plato *Rep.* 10.598b–e (with verbally close reaffirmation of the position noted at 598e3–5).

[22] Strabo 1.2.3, citing exactly the same triad as Aristotle *Poet.* 1.1447a28—an example of a Peripatetic vein in the vocabulary of Hellenistic mimeticism, but hardly to be taken as an instance of the influence of the *Poetics* as such (cf. note 3).

subject of Homeric geography and to conflicting estimates of its reliability, Strabo now admits that it is excessive to expect complete, literal accuracy in the poet's picture of the world. There is in Homer, he concedes, an element of *muthos*, of fictional discourse. *Muthos* he describes at one point as a use of language that "does not speak of things as they actually are, but of alternative states of affairs";[23] and he goes on to describe the capacity of myths both to satisfy the human desire to learn and to impinge on the psychological makeup of humans by arousing either positive or negative emotions in response to their narrative content. Strabo is struggling to maintain a stable position here. On the one hand he takes the view that *muthos* is suitable for those (especially women, children, and the uneducated) whose reason is not sufficiently developed to be susceptible to philosophy: philosophy is for the few, poetry for the many (1.2.8). On the other hand, he has already committed himself to the claim that some poetry, especially Homer's, is at least protophilosophical, and he will soon undertake an elaborate extension of his earlier contention that Homeric geography is essentially truthful. Strabo had, in fact, acknowledged at an earlier stage of his argument that Homer's poetry contained "an admixture of fiction [*muthōdē*] among the things he says in a historical and instructive manner [*historikōs kai didaskalikōs*]" (1.1.10), but this very formulation betrays his anxiety not to yield too much space to a conception of poetic *muthos* that might break altogether free of the constraining values of truth and goodness. This priority he reasserts at 1.2.9, where he goes back to the controversy over Homer's knowledge of geography and related matters. Strabo settles for a position that sees the core of the poetry as true, and the element of *muthos* as a kind of outer layer of embellishment. What this means is that while he purports to have a confident sense of the distinction between Homeric fact and fiction, he feels a strong pressure, arising from his Stoic tenets, to protect the poetry from any suggestion, such as Eratosthenes', that it is fundamentally or pervasively concerned with something other than truth.[24]

All of this helps to draw out the force of Strabo's definition of poetry as "the mimesis of life" at 1.2.5. Strabo's Stoic mimeticism has been formed

---

[23] *ou ta kathestēkota phrazōn, all' hetera para tauta* (1.2.8). Just before this, at 1.2.7, Strabo refers to the idea of allegorical myth, but surprisingly never develops this further: for a reassessment of Stoic use of allegorizing interpretation, see Long 1992, and cf. my notes 30–31.

[24] Strabo's distinction between truth or history and fiction or myth probably owes something to a Stoic tradition that goes back to the founder Zeno himself, whose writings on Homer drew a distinction (aimed at blocking charges of self-contradiction: note 43) between elements of truth and opinion (*doxa*) in the poems (Dio Chrysostom 53.5 = *SVF* 1. 274; cf. my note 7); see Long 1992, 59–62. For a wider view of Stoic methods of textual interpretation, see Pollmann 1999, 261–70 (though her understanding of "fictionality" differs from mine).

under the pressure of concerns (in origin Platonic) about the danger and the uselessness of "falsehood." If poetry (or any other mimetic art)[25] is to have genuine cultural value, it must work in the service of (Stoic) truth, which means that its mimetic status must be construed, normatively at any rate, in terms of faithful correspondence to reality. Given Strabo's geographical interests, it is appropriate that perhaps the most striking use of mimetic terminology elsewhere in his work occurs in a passage that refers to the possibility of "representing [*mimoumenon*] the truth" about the earth by constructing a spherical model of it.[26] Strabo patently does not believe that a globe can reproduce or duplicate all the data of terrestrial geography, only that it can produce a visually scaled equivalent, a coordinated set of correspondences, to certain surface features of the earth. This qualifies as one way of signifying "the truth," and it is an application of the vocabulary of mimesis that turns up in other writers too.[27] But when we move back from the visible properties of a particular object to the whole mass of human life, we have already seen that Strabo's desire to keep a strongly veridical sense for mimesis leads him into a struggle with what he himself admits to be the mixture of truth and fiction to be found even in the poetry of Homer.

Strabo's geographical preoccupations mean that in the final analysis he cannot give us more than a one-sided sense of how the Stoics grappled with the issues of artistic mimesis. The evidence of his discussions of poetry in the first book of the *Geography* suggests that to some extent his mimeticism was hemmed in by his twofold fixation with factual accuracy and poetic instruction, for he is nowhere able to elucidate how such a model of mimesis—the model, as it were, of the geographical globe—could be adapted to the multifarious human subject matter (the "characters, emotions and actions") of poetry. Only one other brief example of

---

[25] Strabo 1.2.8 (a reference to painting and sculpture, in connection with the same myths as are found in poetry) indicates Strabo's adherence to the conventional parallelism between poetry and the visual arts: note his unique use of the verb *huposēmainein* (to signifiy by implication, at the level of "subtext"?), which, even if not necessarily connected to Stoic ideas of signification (see my earlier remarks on Posidonius fr. 44), shows his belief in the capacity of images to convey quasi-narrative, possibly even quasi-propositional, meaning. *Huposēmainein* is sometimes found elsewhere with reference to allegory: see esp. Heraclitus *Alleg. Hom.* 24.6, 25.6, 34.4, 49.4; cf. my notes 23, 30–31.

[26] Strabo 2.5.10; cf. the globe of Billarus at 12.3.11, with Clarke 1999, 212, 236. It is possible that the use of *mimeisthai* at 2.5.10 owes something to Crates of Mallos, whose globe is mentioned here (= Crates fr. 6 Mette 1936); cf. further, with note 31, on Crates' description of Agamemnon's and Achilles' shields in Homer as a "*mimēma* of the cosmos." The term *mimēma* is used of astronomical models as early as Plato *Tim.* 40d2.

[27] See Lucian *Nigr.* 2, where the philosopher's reed globe is called "apparently made to represent the cosmos" (*pros to tou pantos mimēma*).

mimetic terminology in Strabo gives a hint of different possibilities, but it is nonetheless intriguing.[28]

In the course of a digression in book 10 on the ritual dancers known as Kouretes, Strabo remarks that the "mystic secrecy" of certain religious rituals produces a more elevated sense of the divine by virtue of, in some sense, representing or matching (*mimoumenē*) the way in which the nature of the divine escapes our sense experience (10.3.9). Strabo offers a general account of religious celebration that stresses how different components (festivity, frenzied dancing, music, etc.) function as means of bringing the mind of worshipers into a relationship with the divine, and his observation of the element of mystic or initiatory concealment in certain rituals is cognate with this argument. Although it is impossible to extrapolate from this passage to Strabo's assumptions about the mimetic arts as such, his use of the verb *mimeisthai* to denote a relationship of likeness, match, or correspondence between religious secrecy and the nature of the divine does help to show that his concept of mimesis need not be limited to literal or factual conformity. Moreover, Strabo's train of thought in this context is undoubtedly influenced by older traditions of philosophico-religious thinking, because he goes on, just two sentences later, to employ the same verb *mimeisthai* to refer to the idea that humans are capable of in some way "becoming like" the gods, an inherited usage that can be regarded as a special adaptation of the common sense of mimesis as behavioral emulation, but one that at the same time treats mimesis as a link between material (visible) and spiritual (invisible) orders of reality.[29] In the case of the relationship between ritual secrecy and the nature of the divine, it is clearer still that mimesis ties together visible and invisible, material and spiritual, and that it denotes here some sort of symbolic, even "mystic," equivalence. The background of this statement of Strabo may lie partly in allegorical interpretation of mystery religion, but it is reasonable also to see a connection with an older Pythagorean conception of "metaphysical" mimesis.[30] In this connection, it may be no coincidence that Strabo cites

[28] I leave aside 9.3.10, a reference to musical mimesis (cf. note 8), which is at any rate consistent with a literalist notion of mimesis, since it refers to the instrumental depiction of the sounds of a dying dragon!

[29] The tradition of "becoming like (a) god" is attested at, e.g., Plato *Theaet.* 176b; *Rep.* 10.613b; *Phdr.* 252d, 253a–b; *Laws* 4.716b–d; Epicurus *Ep. Men.* 124; Philo (e.g.) *Spec. Leg.* 2.225, 4.73; Epictetus *Diss.* 2.14.12–13; Plotinus *Enn.* 1.2.1–3; for the later Christian adaptation of this motif, see Ladner 1959, 777–79; Merki 1952; Wyrwa 1983, 173–89, with the *theom-* *im-* compounds referenced in Lampe 1961, 629.

[30] For the link with allegory, see Burkert 1987, 79 (though he mistranslates Strabo's sentence, which refers not to "Nature" [*sic*] but to "the nature of the divine"). Burkert also adopts the dubious, if widely shared, assumption that Strabo is here following Posidonius (the reference to Posidonius at 10.3.5 looks back to the preceding topic and has no bearing on the

Pythagorean doctrines (of philosophy as "music," and of the cosmos as itself a musical structure, *harmonia*) in this very same passage of his work. The notion of either allegorical or symbolic mimesis has often been identified in a fragment of another thinker usually believed to have had Stoic allegiances. Crates of Mallos, the second-century B.C. scholar associated with the library at Pergamum and famous for a visit to Rome that made an impression on the city's intellectual life, is reported to have called the shield of Agamemnon in *Iliad* 11 a "*mimēma* of the cosmos," and he is standardly supposed to have said the same about the more conspicuous shield of Achilles in *Iliad* 18.[31] There is more than one possible sense which this claim of Crates' might have underwritten. Because Crates is known to have argued that Homer was aware that both the earth and the cosmos were spherical, he may have regarded the shields as cosmologically symbolic partly in virtue of their circularity, thus treating the circle as a two-dimensional representation of sphericity and the mimetic relationship as one of partial geometrical correspondence:[32] he seems indeed to have re-

---

Kouretes digression as such). Kardaun 1993, 31, rightly objects to the translation of *mimeisthai* as "imitate" at Strabo 10.3.9, suggesting "symbolize" or "express" instead. Elsewhere, mimesis and symbolism are sometimes contrasted, most emphatically at Proclus *In Remp.* 1.198.15–16 Kroll (see Lamberton 1986, 190, 214–15, 287–88, with my chapter 11, section II); cf. also Dio Chrysostom 12.59 (with chapter 4, note 36), where "symbol," *sumbolon*, is opposed to implicitly mimetic images, although the use of *mimeisthai* at 12.74, 78, modifies the contrast. For the phrase *mimeisthai tēn phusin* [of *x*], see, e.g., Plato *Crat.* 423a2–3, Dio Chrysostom 12.54, 74 (the last two in connection with the difficulty of depicting the divine, as just cited; cf. Dio Chrysostom 4.85, 12.44). On the older Pythagorean-cum-Platonic tradition of metaphysical mimesis, see my introduction, note 34. Koller 1954, 45, gratuitously finds a reference to a form of "Mysterienspiel" at Strabo 10.3.9.

[31] Crates fr. 23 Mette 1936 (derived from Σ T Hom. *Il.* 11.40 and other sources), with Mette 1936, 30–51, for discussion. Crates' view is regarded as a case of allegory by, e.g., De Lacy 1948, 257, 261–62; Buffière 1956, 164 (with 155–65 for allegorical interpretations of the shield of Achilles); Russell 1981, 44; and Kennedy 1989, 209. The qualified nature of Crates' Stoic affiliations is well assessed by Asmis 1992a, 139–40, though her estimation of Crates' critical theory seems to me greatly inflated; cf. Pfeiffer 1968, 238–46 (with the reservations of Porter 1992, 71–73) for an overview of Crates' scholarship. For Crates' practice of allegorical criticism, see further frs. 6, 20, 22, 30, 34 Mette 1936; the claim of Struck 1995, 227, that allegorist critics wished to displace mimesis altogether, is not applicable to Crates at any rate. On the earlier development of Greek allegorical criticism, see Richardson 1975, Ford 1999.

[32] This point is exemplified by the possible echo of Crates in Asclepiades of Myrlea, *apud* Athenaeus 11.489d (= Crates fr. 26a Mette 1936), who suggested that round tables were designed "as a *mimēma* of the cosmos"; at a later date Alexander of Aphrodisias *Probl.* 3.12.6 refers to the egg as a "*mimēma* of the cosmos" in virtue of both its shape and its mixture of the four elements (cf. the Orphic doctrine at Plutarch *Quaest. Conv.* 636e)! Cf. the use of mimesis for the partly symbolic relationship between a map and the geographical features it represents at Ptolemy *Geog.* 1.1–4 Müller (with a comparison to visual art at 1.2). The human city is a *mimēma* of the cosmic "city" in Stoic thinking at Epictetus *Diss.* 2.5.27 (cf. my note 6).

inforced this point by equating the "ten bronze circles" of *Iliad* 11.33 with various astronomical circles. Allegoresis or allegorical interpretation of Homer was an old critical tradition by Crates' time, even though we have relatively few well-attested classical or Hellenistic instances of its practice. It is possible, then, that in calling the shield of Achilles (or of Agamemnon) a *mimēma* of the cosmos Crates was using the term to cover an allegorical or symbolic significance that combined elements of both visual and nonvisual correspondence. Whether this would have constituted a new meaning for the language of mimesis is questionable, and it is preferable here, as in the related case of Strabo's reference to mystery religion already considered, to see a partial continuation of Pythagorean-cum-Platonic traditions of metaphysical mimesis.[33]

The thinness of our evidence makes it difficult to detect an entirely consistent Stoic attitude to artistic mimesis. I suggested earlier that the combination of Posidonius fragment 44 with Strabo's definition of poetic excellence as "artistic mimesis of life in language" in the context of his defense of Homer as a protophilosopher can give us a sense of how mimesis could be made to conform to a central Stoic tendency toward the evaluation of (good) poetry as an "instructive" form of discourse capable of conveying a reliable picture of reality. On this Stoic view, mimesis is a form of signification that can serve as a means of expressing cardinal truths about the world. But any medium of truth, whether linguistic or otherwise, must also be capable of falsehood. The Stoics inherited some of Plato's anxieties over the implications of this principle for the mimetic arts, as we saw in Strabo's uneasiness over the relative amounts of truth and fiction, history and myth, to be posited or found in the Homeric epics. One response to such anxiety was the application of a notion of at any rate partly symbolic or allegorical mimesis, whereby deeper meanings, linking the human with the cosmic, could be discovered behind the prima facie phenomena of artistic representation. But Stoic reliance on allegoresis has probably been exaggerated, and it is anyhow easy to see why some members of the school may have retained reservations, again along Platonic lines, about

---

[33] Porter 1992, 94–95, argues for Crates' extension of the meaning of mimesis, but he does not consider the older usage of mimetic terminology for metaphysical relationships between visible and invisible, material and immaterial, human and cosmic; cf. my introduction, note 34. A little later than Strabo, cf. Josephus *Antiq.* 3.123, where the Jewish Tabernacle is called a mimesis of the nature of the universe (*mimēsin tēs tōn holōn phuseōs*) in virtue of the symbolic equivalence between its internal division and the sections of the universe (the inaccessible sanctuary corresponding to heaven, the rest to earth and sky). Cf. the mimetic relationships between microcosm (human head or body) and macrocosm at Plato *Tim.* 44d, [Hippocrates] *De victu.* 1.10 (with my introduction, note 34), and, much later, at Rufus Eph. *De part. corp.* 1.

any art that depended on the simulation of life and thus on the creation of appearances that might be illusory or deceptive.

One instance of such suspicion surfaces in Marcus Aurelius's reference to Greek Middle and New Comedy as involving a decline of the genre (from the morally useful outspokeness he ascribes to Old Comedy!) into an obsession with mimetic artifice or virtuosity.[34] By putting together the ideas of mimesis and of technical ingenuity (*philotechnia*), Marcus's criticism imputes to fourth-century comedy a kind of clever but amoral preoccupation with the simulation of life—an absorption in the production of beguilingly lifelike surfaces. His judgment has to be understood against the background of, and as a pointedly disapproving reaction against, what by this date was the conventional wisdom that New Comedy, especially in the plays of Menander, was an effective "mirror" and faithful expression of life.[35] Marcus's Stoic values prompt him to scrutinize poetic works in search of a directly ethical and instructive purpose, and this leads him to be suspicious of a dramatic genre that, in its prominent cultivation of (ostensibly) realistic representation, supposedly lost sight of just such a purpose. His position is therefore not out of line with Strabo's definition of poetic excellence as the "artistic mimesis of life in language," because I explained earlier how Strabo ties that definition to a Stoic conception of human and philosophical excellence in general and interprets the mimesis of life as entailing a morally informed and essentially correct picture of the world.

In the final reckoning, Stoicism could only come to terms with mimesis, it would seem, either by construing it in morally strict and factually literalist terms, or by saving its would-be philosophical credentials through elaborate meta-interpretations of the knowledge and thought it embodied beneath the surface. What we find no sign of, however, is any Stoic attempt to redefine the problems of a quasi-Platonic moralism by opening itself to more liberally nuanced critical strategies and distinguishing, as Aristotle had done, between different "objects" of, different purposes for, or different pleasures derivable from, mimetic art.[36] Even in the absence of fuller

[34] "The virtuosity that stems from mimesis" (*tēn ek mimēseōs philotechnian*), Marcus Aurelius *Med.* 11.6. Cf. Nesselrath 1990, 57, though he does not quite catch the force of Marcus's remark when talking of comedy "losing contact with the real world." Rutherford 1989, 26–28, presents a broader picture of Marcus's reading habits.

[35] See chapter 10, notes 2, 3.

[36] Nor, it is worth adding, did the Stoics turn to their concept of *phantasia* (sense impression or mental presentation) as an alternative to mimesis. When we find *phantasia* apparently pitted against mimesis at Philostratus *Vita Ap.* 6.19, the position is not purely Stoic (*contra*, e.g., Imbert 1980, 183–84; Kennedy 1989, 211) but essentially Platonizing, with a Stoicizing admixture: Plato *Rep.* 6.484c9 may be echoed here; cf. also *Rep.* 5.472d, with chapter 4, section II, chapter 10, notes 55–58; on Stoic *phantasia* as such, see Watson 1988a, 44–58.

evidence for the school's aesthetics, we are on safe ground in concluding that the Stoic worldview was too monolithic, and too uncompromising in its ethical requirements, to tolerate the immersion of mimetic art forms in the full multiplicity of that life whose whole truth Stoicism itself professed to know.

II

Epicurean sensibilities toward poetry, though radically different in thrust from those of the Stoics, were no less marked by ambivalence. The problems may well reach back in origin to the founder Epicurus himself, who seems to have bequeathed a double-edged legacy to his followers in this area. Treading partly in Plato's footsteps in the *Republic*, Epicurus was unequivocal in rejecting traditional poetic myths and stories that he took to be the vehicles of importantly false and damaging beliefs about the world. This was especially so where religious beliefs were concerned, because it was integral to his own philosophy to rid the soul of the idea of vindictive gods, of death as an evil, and of the prospect of postmortem suffering.[37] Although no surviving evidence makes the point explicit, it is hard to doubt that Epicurus must have conceived of poetic stories and narratives in terms of mimesis. Later sources sometimes ascribe to Epicurus, or to his school, the conviction that *all* poetry contains falsehood and is therefore to be shunned and removed from its traditional place at the center of musicoliterary education (*paideia*). "Hoist the sails of a little Epicurean boat and navigate in flight away from poetry," as a hostile formulation in Plutarch puts it, playing on Epicurus's own injunction to "hoist the sails of your little boat and flee from all *paideia*"; while the evidence of another source that Epicurus called poetry a "fatal ensnarement by stories" (*olethrion muthōn delear*) suggests that he saw it as involving the perverse pleasure (how else could it "ensnare"?) of dangerously misleading fictions.[38] In keeping with this subjection of poetry to the criteria of truth

[37] Derogatory references to (poetic) *muthoi* occur in Epicurus's writings at *Ep. Herod.* 81; *Ep. Pyth.* 87, 104, 115–61; *Ep. Men.* 134; *KD* 12. Particular Epicurean contempt for myths about the afterlife surfaces in the criticisms targeted against Plato's alleged hypocrisy in the *Republic* by Epicurus's direct associate Colotes of Lampsacus: see chapter 1, note 46. Asmis 1992c is the best synthesis of Epicurean attitudes to poetry and education.

[38] See Plut. *Aud. Poet.* 15d, playing on Diogenes Laertius 10.6 (= Epicurus fr. 163 Usener, fr. 89 Arrighetti; cf. Quintilian *Inst. Or.* 12.2.24); the "ensnarement" of stories is cited by Heraclitus *Alleg. Hom.* 4.2 (= Epicurus fr. 229 Usener), but should not be paraphrased as a "web of lies" (Asmis 1990a, 2405; contrast Asmis 1992c, 64: "a destructive lure of fictitious stories."). Cf. the vituperative Epicurean abuse of poets in general, and Homer in particular, quoted at Plutarch *Non Posse Suav.* 1087a. Epicurus's rejection of traditional *paideia* is also attested at Plutarch *Non Posse Suav.* 1094d (= Epicurus fr. 164 Usener), Athenaeus 13.588a–b (= Epicurus fr. 117 Usener, fr. 43 Arrighetti); cf. his own supposed conversion from "liter-

entailed by his own system, Epicurus is reported to have said that "only the wise person [i.e., the Epicurean philosopher] can discuss music and poetry correctly, though he will not actually compose poems."[39] But this last sentiment already seems to imply that at least some poetry might receive a degree of Epicurean approval; a stance of unqualified hostility would surely make "correct discourse" rather superfluous.[40] It has often been noticed in this connection that another remark ascribed to Epicurus, that the wise person "will take more pleasure than others do at the festivals," might well be understood to cover performances of epic and drama, as well as listening to music and viewing visual works of art, and therefore appears to give at least partial ratification to some of the essential traditions and institutions of Greek poetic culture.[41]

The mention of pleasure, Epicureanism's central value, opens up several alternative lines of thought. First, even if many poetic myths are false, why should Epicureans not seek out and derive pleasure from poetry whose subject matter is compatible with, or even expressive of, their own beliefs? Second, why should Epicureans not take pleasure in aspects of poetry other than, and unaffected by, the beliefs about reality thought to be contained in it? Third—an extension of the last consideration—why should poetic myths, and the contents of poetry at large, be necessarily regarded as aspiring to veridical status, rather than perhaps that of self-consciously pleasurable inventions? In Epicurus's own case, it is possible to say something about how he would have responded to the third of these questions. As regards the status of *muthoi* such as those depicting the gods and the afterlife, it is clear that, like Plato and, before him, Xenophanes, Epicurus regarded them as being fully embedded in the general belief systems of Greek culture, and therefore as too widely accepted and respected to be accorded a purely fictional or imaginative status in poetry. At the same time, we get one hint that Epicurus could at any rate contemplate the

---

ary" to philosophical education, put into anecdotal form, at Diogenes Laertius 10.2, Sextus Empiricus *Adv. Math.* 10.18–19, with Obbink 1995b, 189–93. Epicurean attitudes to poetry are extensively reflected in the arguments of Sextus Empiricus *Adv. Math.* 1.270–98 against the usefulness of poetry: see Blank 1998 for detailed commentary.

[39] Diogenes Laertius 10.120 (= Epicurus fr. 593 Usener, fr. 1.120a5 Arrighetti). Compare and contrast the Stoic formulation in note 21.

[40] It has to be said, however, that if Plutarch *Non Posse Suav.* 1095c–96c is reliable, Epicurus elsewhere rejected most discussion of poetry and music, so that "correct discourse" on these matters might well be of limited scope.

[41] Diogenes Laertius 10.120 (= Epicurus fr. 593 Usener, fr. 1.120a5 Arrighetti); the similar passage at Plutarch *Non Posse Suav.* 1095c–e (= Epicurus fr. 20 Usener, fr. 12.2 Arrighetti) actually specifies Dionysiac festivals and the theater; cf. the reference to the Anthesteria at Philod. *De piet.* col. 30.865–68 Obbink 1996 (= Epicurus fr. 157 Usener, fr. 86 Arrighetti). There is an allusion to looking at paintings, *qua* "likenesses" (a comparison for visual sense data in general), at Epicurus *Ep. Herod.* 51.

notion of treating some poetic statements as other than putatively or intentionally truth-bearing. In his *Epistle to Menoeceus* (126–27), in the course of expounding his distinctive attitude to death ("death means nothing to us"), Epicurus attacks the expression of a traditionally pessimistic sentiment found at Theognis 425–27, that it is best "never to have been born, but once born to pass through the gates of Hades as quickly as possible." Epicurus first rebuts this in a vigorously dialectical style, as though the speaker were a personal opponent ("if he says this because he believes it, why doesn't he make his exit from life?"), before adding: "but if he says it with irony [*mōkōmenos*], he must be treated as fatuous among those who do not accept [what he says]." It seems that Epicurus can at least entertain the idea that the poet's voice may here be a sort of pretense or fiction, perhaps part of the creation of a hypothetical character, mood, or view of life, rather than the unqualified assertion of the propositions enunciated in the passage. Even though he is dismissive of the value of such an interpretation for those who adhere to his own philosophy, Epicurus fleetingly recognizes the possibility of an approach to poetry that could escape from the strict confines of truth as construed by his own "natural philosophy."

We know of at least one later Epicurean who took such an approach further and directly linked it to mimesis. In (probably) the second century A.D., a certain Diogenianus wrote an Epicurean attack on the Stoic Chrysippus's treatise *On Fate*. Diogenianus criticized Chrysippus's use of Homer as a "witness" for his Stoic views, and he seems to have taken the opportunity to make his critique cover the wider Stoic practice of enlisting poets on the side of their own philosophy.[42] After showing that Homer's poetry contains conflicting statements and ideas about fate and therefore cannot be harmonized with a single philosophical doctrine, Diogenianus proceeds to undermine the whole principle of looking for doctrinal truth in poetry. The poet, he says, "does not promise us the truth about the nature of reality [*tēn alētheian . . . tēs tōn ontōn phuseōs*], but represents [*mimeisthai*] every sort of human emotion, character, and belief," so that it is entirely appropriate that his work should accommodate contradictory sentiments, whereas "a philosopher must not contradict himself and, for this very reason, must not use a poet as a witness." Diogenianus is here drawing together several earlier strands in ancient criticism. The problem of poetic (so-called) "self-contradiction" had been raised as early as the classical period. Plato, while sometimes exploiting the issue to the disadvantage of poetry, had made the same point as Diogenianus in a passage of

---

[42] Diogenianus's critique is reported by Eusebius *Praep. Ev.* 6.8.1–7 (= *SVF* 2.998); Eusebius's description of Diogenianus as a Peripatetic is erroneous. Stemplinger 1913, 25 n. 2, mistakenly takes Diogenianus's remarks on mimesis as evidence for Chrysippus's own position. On the old idea of treating poets as "witnesses," see Halliwell 2000a, esp. 94–95, 98.

the *Laws* that connects the question of self-contradiction to mimesis; and Aristotle, in *Poetics* 25, had attempted to elaborate critical principles that would largely diffuse the issue.[43] Similarly, the notion of using poets as "witnesses," in confirmatory support of a belief or doctrine, was well established by the time of Plato and Aristotle; its roots lie in the archaic Greek tradition of treating poets as sages and authorities on all the major matters of life. In his critique of Chrysippus, then, Diogenianus is in effect repudiating a very old Greek conception of poetry, and asserting against it a freer model of poetry as the imaginative and dramatic representation of possible human experiences and points of view. His conception of mimesis consequently detaches the ideas and beliefs expressed in poetry from the personal feelings or commitments of the poet and espouses a notion of fictionally hypothetical utterances whose status is directly contrasted with "the truth about the nature of reality."

This fragment of Diogenianus's thinking provides a fascinating glimpse of one radical Epicurean resolution of the issue of truth and falsehood in poetry that had for so long been a crux of mimeticism. But Diogenianus's position is so assured as to lose sight, it seems, of the problem that had originally exercised the school's own founder. For if poetic statements are always and only fictional, if they inhabit a world that is purely of the poet's dramatic invention, then why had Epicurus himself been moved to attack the myths of the poets and the system of cultural education (*paideia*) that institutionalized their transmission and their treatment in representational art? Epicurus, like Plato, clearly supposed that over and above (or even, in some sense, *through*) the poet's ascription of particular thoughts and feelings to individual characters, the shape and development of his stories could serve as the expressive foundation of a real perspective on the world, a perspective that might at some level, whether conscious or subconscious, be taken seriously by audience or reader, especially if it made contact with the prevailing values of the surrounding culture. So far as we can tell, Diogenianus has swept such concerns aside, at any rate for the purposes of criticizing the Stoic Chrysippus's dependence on poetic "witnesses" for his doctrine of fate. But if that is so, he has adopted a conception of mimesis, as self-contained fiction, that ostensibly lacks the capacity to explain why poetry had been the subject of so much contention in the earlier philosophical and critical tradition.

The only Epicurean thinker in whose work we can now trace the treatment of mimesis in any detail is Philodemus. Yet we face formidable problems in reconstructing his ideas on the basis of the fragments of those

---

[43] Plato *Laws* 4.719c–d; Aristotle *Poet.* 25.1461b15–18. On poetic "self-contradiction" see Halliwell 2000a, 102. Zeno the Stoic's distinction between truth and opinion in poetry, at Dio Chrysostom 53.5 (cf. my note 24), was designed in part to deal with the problem of Homer's supposed self-contradictions.

treatises which partially survive (and are still under meticulous scholarly reconstruction) in papyri from Herculaneum.[44] One of those treatises, *On Music*, received some detailed attention in the preceding chapter, where we saw that all mimetic models of music, together with associated ideas of music's emotional and ethical power, were rejected by Philodemus with unhesitating insistence. I want here to offer a synthesis of the wider evidence for Philodemus's standpoint on the concept of artistic mimesis, and to start by pointing out that his denial of mimetic status to music in *On Music* provides in itself an oblique pointer to his acceptance of the mimetic status of poetry. When Philodemus repudiates the Stoic Diogenes of Babylon's view of music as parallel to poetry "in terms of mimesis,"[45] he actually implies that poetry itself is uncontentiously mimetic. Elsewhere in *On Music* he claims to have established that it is false to suppose either that music can "represent [*mimeisthai*] the things spoken about," or that it can have ethically beneficial effects on the mind even when combined with "infinitely more mimetic media" (*tōn muriōi mimētikōterōn*): in both cases the reference must be to poetry, whose mimetic status is once more admitted without demur.[46]

But the force of this conclusion cannot be investigated any further in what survives of *On Music* itself. For possible illumination we need to turn to book 5 of Philodemus's treatise on poetry itself, *On Poems*; but here interpretative difficulties loom up at every turn. In discussing the criteria of poetic excellence, Philodemus asserts that poetry should render mimesis (*memimēsthai*) of the style or diction (*lexis*) "which contains useful instruction as an additional element [*ōphelima prosdidaskousan*]," and should contain a level of "thought" (*dianoia*) that is midway between that of the wise and the masses.[47] Working with a standard Hellenistic distinction between *lexis*, poetic diction or stylistic form, and *dianoia*, poetic thought or content, Philodemus uses the verb *mimeisthai*, as just cited, to describe the necessary qualities of *lexis*, but then goes on almost immediately to use the noun *mimēsis* itself of the resulting combination of diction and thought, stating with some emphasis that a poem (*poiēma*) is "that which is as mimetic as possible."[48] It seems, then, that Philodemus takes

---

[44] An informative account of the modern work of reconstruction, with special reference to Philodemus's writings on poetry and music, is provided by Janko 1992.

[45] *Mus.* col. 136.27–32 Delattre 2001 (= 4.22.27–32 Kemke); for Diogenes' view of musical mimesis, cf. chapter 8, note 52.

[46] *Mus.* col. 91.3–10 Delattre 2001 (= 3.55.3–10 Kemke).

[47] Philodemus *Poems* 5.xxv.34–xxvi.7 Mangoni. *Rhetoric* 4 (*PHerc.* 1423) col. v.12–16 (1:150 Sudhaus) is not a denial that language can be mimetic, but only that language *sounds* (*phōnai*) can be mimetic, except in a narrow sense: see my note 57. Erler 1994, 342, supplies no evidence for his assertion that Philodemus rejected mimesis as a criterion of poetry.

[48] *Poems* 5.xxvi.11–15 Mangoni; Greenberg 1990, 83, translates *hōs endechetai* as "it is accepted that . . .," but this can hardly be right: see Mangoni 1993, 286–87 (cf. Jensen 1923,

poetry to be mimetic, in some sense, at the level of both *lexis* and *dianoia*; mimesis is a dimension of the entire poetic enterprise.[49] It has been suggested that in using the phrase *memimēsthai tēn* (sc. *lexin*), "represent the style/diction," Philodemus may be deliberately echoing Plato's use of mimesis terminology for dramatic impersonation—that is, the direct mimesis of speech, in *Republic* 3.[50] But given the continuation of the passage of *On Poems*, as just indicated, it is hard to believe that Philodemus is using mimetic terminology in different senses, especially since he is here prescribing, or, rather, endorsing, principles of judgment that he claims to be established and widely shared.[51] It is safer to suppose that his concept of mimesis describes the status of a poem as a whole, and this would fit well with his general stress elsewhere on the conjoint, indeed interrelated, importance of style and content in poetry.

For Philodemus, then, as for both Plato and Aristotle, mimesis is the genus of human activity to which the art of poetry belongs. But the tenor of the passage just cited suggests that Philodemus is closer to Aristotle than to Plato in treating mimesis as a form of depiction that is not reducible either to the poet's own views or to putatively veridical statements about reality. By speaking of the need for poetry to represent a style or diction "which contains useful instruction as an additional element," Philodemus intimates his rejection of any position that judges poetry by exclusively ethical criteria, but simultaneously accepts that an ethical dimension to the depiction of speech (and therefore, presumably, of character) does or can contribute to the success of poetry. A later formulation, where Philodemus endorses the idea that poetic composition should "be like that which teaches something more/exceptional" ([*lexin*] *hōmoiōmenēn tēi perittoteron ti didaskousēi*), apparently corroborates this interpretation.[52] It looks

---

53: "die möglichst getreue Nachahmung"). It is also unlikely, though perhaps just conceivable (given the apparent clumsiness of Philodemus's Greek), that *hōs endechetai* here denotes the realm of "possibility," in quasi-Aristotelian fashion, as the object of poetic mimesis: see Koster 1970, 98–99. On the *lexis-dianoia* distinction, see, e.g., Asmis 1990b, 152–58.

[49] A further passage that reinforces this inference is the phrase "all the things which they [the poets] want to represent (*mimeisthai*)" at *Poems* 5.xxxv.28–32 (in the context of Philodemus's polemics on the subject of "appropriateness").

[50] See esp. *Rep.* 3.398b1–2, cited by Asmis 1992a, 149 (who translates the Philodemus passage; for a different translation, see Armstrong 1995, 264); Philodemus refers again to mimesis of *lexis* at *Poems* 5.xxxv.14–16 Mangoni, but apparently within the formulation of an opponent's views. Cf. also Asmis 1991, 7–11, but she strains to preserve Philodemus's consistency by maintaining that at *On Poems* 5.xxv–xxvi he is talking about morally good and bad poems, not good and bad poetry *simpliciter*.

[51] *Poems* 5.xxv.23–xxvi.1 Mangoni.

[52] *Poems* 5.xxxiii.15–20 Mangoni, though Philodemus is there taking over, and modifying the force of, a phrase from an opponent whose views he has just been criticizing (ibid., 1–4). I assume (cf. Mangoni 1993, 312) that the verb *homoiousthai* (be made like or made to resemble) is here (xxx.4, 15) virtually synonymous with mimesis: see, e.g., Plato *Rep.*

as though Philodemus is constructing a compromise with traditional Greek convictions of the didactic or edifying value of poetry: he maintains that "poems do not, *qua* poems, provide benefit,"[53] but also that poetry ought to incorporate elements of both style and thought that in some degree conform to ethical criteria. If this is right, it also and equally importantly amounts to a compromise with the doctrines of Epicurus himself. Philodemus does not reproduce Epicurus's own hostility toward poetic stories, and his principles do not require as stringent a judgment of the contents of poetry as Epicurus had pronounced. In one passage Philodemus allows that poetry can present the "most mythical" (i.e., utterly fictional) things with complete vividness. Far from seeing a problem in this, he accepts it as part of poetry's remit: it is indifferent to him whether poetry depicts known reality or a purely imaginary world.[54] Yet the shadow of Epicurus himself may lie over part of Philodemus's thinking about poetry, leading him to preserve a place for at least an ostensibly ethical component in poetry's representations of the world.

There is one other partially surviving stretch of *On Poems*, from the end of book 4, where Philodemus has occasion to use mimeticist terminology.[55] In criticizing the views of a Peripatetic work, possibly Aristotle's dialogue *On Poets*,[56] Philodemus several times refers to mimesis, most clearly in column viii, where he states his thesis, cognate with that expounded more extensively in *On Music*, that mimesis is possible only in the language or words (*logos*) of poetry, not in its sounds or its accompanying music, "because of the impossibility of using voices [*phōnai*] and

---

3.393c2–6, 396a3, b9. When Philodemus uses *homoiousthai* in a similar way at *Rhet.* 4 col. iv (1:149.8–9 Sudhaus), he appears to be speaking about sophistic-rhetorical stylistic "imitation" of philosophical language. It is entirely possible, however, that Philodemus did not distinguish clearly between mimesis as stylistic imitation and as verbal representation of a style of speaking.

[53] *Poems* 5.xxxii.18–19 Mangoni.

[54] Poetic narrative of the "most mythical" or "fictional" (*muthōdestata*) things, see *Poems* 5.vii.6–13 Mangoni; cf. the noun *muthos* at 5.x.25. The depiction of reality (*pragmata*): *Poems* 5.iv.31–v.11, where such depiction is implicitly acknowledged in Philodemus's criticisms of Heraclides Ponticus. As regards the verb *apaggellein* and noun *apaggelia* at 5.v.2–9, vii.8–13, Philodemus's use of these terms in *Poems* 4 cols. v-vi (Janko 1991, 13–14) preserves their application (by others) to the narrative as opposed to dramatic mode (see, e.g., Aristotle *Poet.* 3.1448a21, 5.1449b11); cf. my note 56. But this can hardly be so with our passage from book 5.

[55] I leave aside *Poems* 5.xxxiii.24–xxxiv.33 Mangoni, where mimetic vocabulary refers to a doctrine of literary imitation or emulation of earlier poets: see Asmis 1992b, 408–10, and cf. chapter 10, note 21.

[56] A forceful case for this hypothesis has been remade by Janko 1991, but his treatment of mimesis in this passage is tendentious (see notes 57, 59), and he plays down some problems with the hypothesis, e.g. the apparent fact that the opponent, col. v.11–13, stated that narrative was the only mode of epic (Janko 40–41 fudges the issue).

sounds [*psophoi*] to render mimesis of things [sc. in general], as opposed to mimesis merely *of* voices and the sounds of things."[57] As I explain in chapter 8, Philodemus's position here depends on the idea that musical sounds are entirely "irrational" (*alogos*) or nonsemantic, not on the premise that mimesis requires a direct match between the medium and the object of mimesis,[58] even though such a match obviously obtains in the case of the mimesis of sounds by sounds, which he concedes to music in this passage. In this latter case it may be appropriate to say that Philodemus allows, reductively, that (nonsemantic) sounds can "imitate" nothing other than sounds themselves, as when a musical instrument produces a simulation of birdsong. But it does not follow that Philodemus's concept of mimesis in general is a concept of imitation. It is, in fact, impossible to pin down Philodemus's view of mimesis any more precisely in the fragments of *On Poems* 4 than anywhere else.[59] Thus, when he contests a claim about the mimesis of action in Archilochus and Aristophanes by saying that "Archilochus would have maintained that he was not using mimesis," he may be alluding to the tradition that Archilochus wrote poems about real characters and events, rather than making a distinction between dramatic and

---

[57] *Poems* 4 col. viii.9–13 (Janko 1991, 15); on the use of *phōnai* for vocal pitches construed purely as sounds, see chapter 8, note 43. It is misleading of Janko 1991, 29, to ascribe to Philodemus a denial "that music is mimetic (imitative)," when this sentence shows precisely that he accepts that music *can* be, in a narrow respect, "imitative" (i.e., of other sounds) but *not* mimetic in the sense of a fuller representational and expressive capacity. Janko's translations, 15 and 31, are inconsistent, reflecting a larger confusion about the meaning of mimesis (see note 59). This sentence of *On Poems* is closely paralleled in *Rhetoric* 4 (*PHerc.* 1423) col. v.12–16 (1:150 Sudhaus), where Philodemus seems to be talking about sophistic or rhetorical exploitation of nonsemantic properties of language (the translation of *phōnai* as "words" by Hubbell 1920, 295, is wholly wrong). Janko 1991, 31, cannot be right to suppose that Philodemus thought language *tout court* could not render "mimesis of things"; this would make nonsense of his general references to poetic mimesis, esp. at *Poems* 5.xxvi.11–15 Mangoni (cf. note 48), which Janko 1991, 18 and 31 n. 138, tries to sidestep, and at *Mus.*, e.g., col. 136.27–32 Delattre 2001 (= 4.22.27–32 Kemke). *Poems* 5.xxxv.16–21 Mangoni apparently shows Philodemus rejecting the possibility of any kind of expressive correspondence ("likeness") between poetic sounds and subject matter; his target here is a certain concept of stylistic appropriateness and can hardly be linked to Stoic views of "mimetic etymology" (cf. my note 5), *contra* Grube 1965, 197 (read "xxxii" not "xxiii" in his n. 3), Mangoni 1993, 316–17.

[58] For the larger importance of this point, see chapter 8, section III.

[59] Janko 1991, 17–18, is overconfident in deciding when Philodemus means "imitation" and when he means "representation," and he confuses matters by some inconsistency of his own (compare 17, his commentary on col. i.1, with his translation of the same passage, 12); cf. my note 57. Moreover, as part I of this book has shown in detail, it is quite wrong to suppose, as Janko does, that mimesis *qua* "imitation" can be straightforwardly treated as the "Platonic" sense of the word.

nondramatic poetic modes.[60] But given his oblique formulation, couched in terms of what the poet himself might have said, it is hard to draw a solid inference about Philodemus's own estimation of mimesis. Here as often elsewhere, his relentlessly, even crudely, polemical reaction to the views of others leaves a very hazy impression of Philodemus's own version of the concepts he uses.

If we try, despite the formidable barrier of textual and interpretative problems, to discern what the overall importance of mimesis may have been in Philodemus's theory of poetry, we need to situate the question in relation to his principle that style or composition and thought or content are intertwined in poetry. On this view, mimesis will be the poetically successful presentation of a hypothetical world, regardless of the ontological status of the characters, actions, or thoughts that constitute that world. When Philodemus says that poetry is "that which is as mimetic as possible," he is effectively ascribing to poetry the aim of depiction for its own sake. But if that is right, there is, I suggest, a disquieting uncertainty at the heart of Philodemus's position. Many scholars have expressed admiration for Philodemus's supposedly sophisticated sense of the interrelationship between thought and content, but they have failed to see that Philodemus has no ultimate explanation for the pleasure he undoubtedly believes that the poetic combination of thought and content gives its audiences. Unlike Aristotle, Philodemus cannot appeal to a link between mimesis and the human desire to know and understand the world. Unlike his Stoic opponents, he cannot treat poetic representations as a kind of popular philosophy.

What, then, is the source of the pleasure of poetry? We do not have a clear version of Philodemus's answer to this question, if indeed he ever supplied one. No one, for sure, has yet managed to construct a cogent answer on his behalf. It is not enough to say that the mind enjoys the verbally fine expression or presentation of "thought," because that will not solve the conundrum: for Philodemus, this cannot be pleasure in the verbal as such, independently of the thought, yet he seems unprepared to place any limits on the "thought" that is suitable or acceptable for poetry— unprepared, at any rate, apart from the one passage, to which I have drawn attention, where he apparently endorses the requirement of a quasi-ethical

---

[60] *On Poems* 4 col. iv.8–10 (Janko 1991, 13). But Janko 1991, 38 is wrong to ascribe to Aristotle the view that Archilochean iambus is not poetry because it deals with particulars or individuals. Aristotle nowhere *limits* mimesis to the representation of universals; see chapter 6, section II, and cf. Halliwell 1986, 276 n. 36, which is not in tension with 270–71, misunderstood by Janko 1991, 38 n. 173: my point there was that iambus is different from *comic* mimesis, not that it is not mimesis at all.

element in both style and thought.[61] In the final analysis, therefore, we come back round to the problem of squaring this passage with Philodemus's general aversion to edification or ethical instruction as a criterion of poetic merit, and we are left with a conception of mimesis as the representation of a (thought) world that is suspended without any real bearings— a pretense without a purpose. It may be that the burden of Epicurus's own critique of poetry made it impossible for Philodemus to resolve the problem of how to "redeem" poetry in a philosophically respectable manner while continuing to exclude it from the sphere of philosophy itself. Philodemus certainly continued the Epicurean tradition of criticizing (some) poetry on theological grounds,[62] but he also went so far as to write a treatise, *On the Good King according to Homer*, in which he argued that some sound political and moral principles could be discerned, by the Epicurean interpreter at any rate, in the Homeric epics. Yet his treatise on poetry, in its extant fragments, leaves it quite uncertain why such criticism, whether negative or positive in its results, should be applicable to an art form whose raison d'être, on his own premises, is essentially amoral and disengaged from the realm of truth.

---

[61] *Poems* 5.xxv.34–xxvi.7 Mangoni, with my earlier comments. Porter 1996, 619, rightly speaks of Philodemus's "ambivalence towards (not outright denial of) the moral utility of poems"; cf. Porter's (to my mind, excessively generous) remarks, 625–28, on the elusiveness of Philodemus's concept of poetry (somewhat similarly, Asmis 1992b, 415). Gigante 1995, 36, is far too sweeping in saying that for Philodemus "poetry, like music, had nothing to do with ethics and education and should not be connected with reality or philosophy."

[62] For theological criticism of poetry, see, e.g., Philod. *De piet.* col. 85.2479–86B Obbink 1996, with Obbink 1996, 315–19, and Obbink 1995b; Asmis 1991 (cf. 1992c, 87–88) discusses Philodemus's *On the Good King according to Homer*.

Chapter Ten

❁

Images of Life: Mimesis and
Literary Criticism after Aristotle

Just as octopus is delicious to eat but gives one nightmares full
of disturbing, weird imaginings (so they say), likewise with
poetry too. (Plutarch)[1]

ARISTOPHANES OF BYZANTIUM, one of the leading literary scholars of Hellenistic Alexandria and the head of its library in the first part of the second century B.C., famously posed a rhetorical question about the comedies of Menander: "O Menander and Life, which of you took the other as your model?"[2] The standard rendering of the words *poteros . . . poteron apemimēsato* as "which of you imitated the other?", though hallowed by convention, is likely to blunt our appreciation of several facets of this quizzical bon mot. Aristophanes takes for granted an established and broadly Aristotelian concept of (dramatic) poetry as mimetic, more specifically as concerned with the representation of "life."[3] But his question also plays on a very general behavioral sense of mimesis, a sense appropriate to all the ways in which people can attempt to emulate or follow the example of others.[4] This combination of kinds of mimesis—artistic representation and

---

[1] Plutarch *Aud. Poet.* 15b–c, glossing the proverb "the octopus's head contains evil, but also good." This passage is taken by some scholars as a reference to cuttlefish or more generally to fish; but as at Plutarch *Mor.* 734f, where eating the head as such is in question (at 15b–c Plutarch's Greek probably implies that eating the whole creature is meant), there is no good reason not to take *po(u)lupous* in its standard sense of "octopus."

[2] The quotation, probably an iambic epigram in form (cf. Cantarella 1969, 190–91), is preserved by the fifth-century A.D. Neoplatonist rhetorician Syrianus *Comm. in Hermog.* 2: 23.6–11 (Rabe 1892–93) = Slater 1986, test. 7 = Menander test. 83 *PCG*; see the latter for other comparable judgments of Menander's art. Syrianus is himself commenting approvingly on Menander's use of character types as the basis of his plots.

[3] The earliest occurrence of the idea of the mimesis of life is at Plato *Rep.* 3.400a7, with reference to music (in a passage where mimesis is in part a concept of expression; cf. chapter 1, note 38); it then appears at Plato *Laws* 7.817b4 (where the reference to philosophy trades on existing views of poetry; cf. chapter 3, section I), in Aristotle *Poet.* 6.1450a16–17, and in a variety of later sources, e.g., Strabo *Geog.* 1.2.5 (see chapter 9, section I), Horace *AP* 317–18 (with Brink 1971, 342–44), and Homeric scholia that reflect traditions of Hellenistic criticism (see note 44). Mimesis of life may have been applied specifically to comedy by Theophrastus, although the threads of evidence are slight; see the sources in Janko 1984, 48–50, with his n. 111; cf. Dosi 1960, 601–23, 668–69, and my note 7 on Cicero *De rep.* 4.11, with Cantarella 1969, 189 n. 3, for some other related texts.

[4] Cf. note 20, with my introduction, note 33.

the adoption of behavioral models—allows him to construct his witty, proto-Wildean suggestion that Life itself might be a devotee of Menander's oeuvre.[5] Aristophanes can hardly have been intimating, of course, that individuals consciously modeled themselves on the plays of Menander. Nor, however, need he imply that the playwright used particular models "from life," or that his plays are realistic in any direct or immediate respect. He is much more likely to be evoking (as Syrianus, who reports him, certainly is) the types or classes of character and behavior that give Menandrean comedy its familiar qualities of stylized verisimilitude.[6] In other words, if Aristophanes' question teasingly manipulates an already existing notion of poetic "truth to life," the kind of mimesis this presupposes should not be understood as the transcription of the actual or ordinary, but more like the artistic capturing of what are taken to be stable, recurrent patterns of human experience.[7] We shall certainly discover that such interest in the relationship of mimetic art to something other than the "raw" phenomena of life is one important strand in the Hellenistic and imperial traditions of criticism that this chapter explores.

The investigation of Stoic and Epicurean attitudes to mimesis undertaken in the preceding chapter required some close inspection of rather partial and often difficult evidence. But Hellenistic philosophers lived in a culture where the language and ideas of mimeticism enjoyed much wider currency, and their own views were often shaped in part by response to this broader background. We saw one instance of this in the case of Strabo's reactions to the views of the scholar-scientist Eratosthenes, and the point is more extensively exemplified by Philodemus's polemical engagement with various critics and schools of criticism in book 5 of *On Poems*.[8] The most rudimentary generalization that can be made about the

[5] For Wilde's own inversion of art's "imitation" of life, see chapter 12, section II; Cantarella 1969, 193 n. 20, is right to speculate that Wilde knew Aristophanes' question, though wrong to suppose that Aristophanes was seriously repudiating the notion of artistic mimesis and adumbrating a doctrine of aesthetic autonomy.

[6] One of the best recent analyses of this aspect of the genre is Zagagi 1994, esp. ch. 5, though her statement (94) that for Aristophanes of Byzantium "Menander's realism was indistinguishable from the actual life it portrayed" is naive.

[7] Cicero's much-cited definition of comedy as "a representation of life, a mirror of social custom, an image of truth" (imitationem vitae, speculum consuetudinis, imaginem veritatis [*De rep.* 4.11], though the attribution to this work is speculative), which is a compound of older Greek ideas (cf. chapter 4, with its note 42, on the mirror metaphor), couples mimesis of life with "truth"; cf. Cicero *Rosc. Am.* 47 for New Comedy as an "imago vitae"; but the similar combination of "imitatio" and "veritas" at *Brutus* 70, with reference to visual art, is not a simple statement of realism but entails an interplay of lifelikeness with beauty: see Douglas 1973, 108–15, for a shrewd statement of this point, and cf. Cicero *De orat.* 2.94, 3.204 for "imitatio vitae/veritatis" in rhetorical contexts. Vitruvius *Arch.* 7.5.1–4 accommodates within the range of pictorial "truth" both what is (or has been) and what could be.

[8] For this component of Philodemus *Poems* 5, see esp. Asmis 1992b; on Strabo and Eratosthenes, see my chapter 9, section I.

whole course of Hellenistic and imperial mimeticism, and one that we have already glimpsed in my discussion of the philosophers, is that, building on the work of both Plato and Aristotle, it provided the basis of an almost universally shared concept of the mimetic arts as a coherent group of activities. This group centered principally on poetry and the figurative arts (above all, painting and sculpture), but also included dance and, for most though not all thinkers, music, as well as artistic role playing (in acting, mime performance, etc.). These activities were linked, on the prevailing view, first, by their representational-cum-expressive status and their consequently comparable appeals to human imagination, thought, and emotion and, second, by their culturally close affinities, especially the frequent conjunction of poetry with music and often with dance, together with the connected and overlapping uses of mythological material by poets and visual artists. The mimetic arts, on this account, were an extended "family" of cultural forms and practices, musicopoetic on the one side, pictorial and sculptural on the other—the same family whose basic relationships had been delineated by the original development of mimeticist terminology in the late archaic and early classical periods.[9]

Around the core of this "aesthetic" conception of mimesis as a set of art forms, other uses of mimetic terminology either continued or developed. Among new developments was the idea, never found in a text from the classical age, and apparently running counter to Aristotle's distinction between poetry and history in *Poetics* 9, that mimesis is both possible and desirable in historiography.[10] It may be no accident that this idea is first attested in a fragment of the early Hellenistic Samian historian, Duris, who is said to have been a pupil of Aristotle's pupil Theophrastus, and is known to have written separately on epic, tragedy, and the visual arts.[11] Duris complained that two major fourth-century historians, Ephorus and Theopompus, fell far short of doing justice to their material, because "they lacked both mimesis and pleasure in their recounting of events [*en tōi phrasai*], and took care only over their style of writing [*autou tou graph-*

[9] See my introduction, section III. Given the nature of the evidence for Hellenistic aesthetics, there is no basis for the claim of Tatarkiewicz 1970–74, 1:334, that the concept of mimesis "was employed less and less" in the Hellenistic period. Meijering 1987, 70–71, simplifies in limiting Hellenistic conceptions of mimesis to realism.

[10] Gray 1987 gives an overall view of this subject, to which Plutarch *Glor. Ath.* 346f-7c should be added, an important comparison of historiography to both poetry and painting (cf. Wardman 1974, 25–26). But Gray's definition of historical mimesis as "the recreation of reality . . . based on observation of what men do in real life" (469–70) is too broad, and her association of mimesis with stylistic propriety is partly misleading (propriety is a much wider rhetorical principle than historiographical mimesis), as is her repeated description of mimesis as a "technical term." A more appropriate emphasis is placed on quasi-poetic/theatrical vividness and emotional intensity by Strasburger 1966, 78–96.

[11] See Jex-Blake & Sellers 1896, xlvi–lxvii, for Duris's art-historical interests (cf. chapter 4, note 47).

ein]."[12] It is reasonable to assume that Duris's complaint pertains to a perceived lack of dramatic qualities and therefore implies a positive esteem for bringing historical scenes alive with the kinds of narrative technique and artistry that traditionally belonged to poetry. We know that Duris used the concept of mimesis elsewhere in connection with poetry. A fragment of his *Homeric Problems* criticizes Homer's simile at *Iliad* 21.257–62— where the river-god Scamander's pursuit of Achilles is compared to the gathering momentum of a stream in a garden—for failing to convey to readers a sufficiently imposing idea of the river's noise and danger.[13] Paradoxically, it might seem, Duris connects the putative failure of this passage with the precision or detail of the poet's mimesis, as indicated by the verb *ekmimeisthai*, whose intensifying prefix suggests here something like to represent "fully" or "meticulously." Duris's point is that the very specificity of the simile, its careful description of the gardener's creation of his miniature irrigation system, works against the drama of the epic situation, in which the immense river is threatening to engulf Achilles. Small-scale mimesis, so to speak, (supposedly) obscures the larger representational aims of the scene.

This second fragment ought not to confuse us about Duris's point in his remark on Ephorus and Theopompus, and we do not need to engage with his arguably shallow interpretation of Homer's simile in order to infer something about his guiding critical concepts and standards. Several things are clear enough, over and above the fact that here, as in most of the texts relevant to this book, to translate mimesis as "imitation" is simply an impediment to interpretation.[14] The first is that Duris uses the concept of mimesis to mean not representation *tout court* (otherwise it would be

[12] Duris *FGrH* 76 F1.

[13] Duris *FGrH* 76 F89. Gray 1987, 475, misinterprets Duris's point: it is not that mimesis allows the simile's inappropriateness to escape the reader's attention, but that mimesis in the simile distracts and detracts from an appropriate conception of the surrounding episode. Richardson 1993, 74 rightly criticizes Duris's own presuppositions.

[14] Yet "imitation" predictably turns up in, e.g., Walbank 1972, 35 (despite his own rejection of this at Walbank 1960, 218); Fornara 1983, 124 (using "imitation" and "representation" apparently interchangeably); Gray 1987, repeatedly (despite the caveat of her first sentence, 467); cf. "Nachahmung" in Strasburger 1966, 78. There are surveys of the interpretation of Duris F1, in particular the issue of so-called tragic history (i.e., history with the quasi-Aristotelian qualities of drama), in von Fritz 1956, 106–14; Walbank 1960, 217–20; Walbank 1972, 34–9; Kebric 1977, 15–18; Gray 1987, 476–83; Pédech 1989, 368–72; and, most recently, Leigh 1997, 33–38. The speculations of Walbank 1972, 36, regarding Aristotle's own attitude to history, are invalidated by the erroneous claim that the art forms of painting and sculpture are omitted in the first chapters of the *Poetics* (they are mentioned in both chs. 1 and 2). Aristotle could in principle have allowed that elements of mimesis might occur within a work of historiography (just as he could consider philosophical dialogues as mimetic, *Poet.* 1.1447b9–13, *On Poets* fr. 15 Gigon 1987); but he would presumably have maintained that such elements would strictly count as poetry, not history.

impossible for Ephorus's and Theopompus's history to be found wanting in it) but a certain kind or quality of representation, one that exhibits the objects of representation with imaginative directness or immediacy. At the same time, Duris's criticism of an Iliadic simile reveals that he judges the effectiveness of mimesis to be partly a matter of contextual coherence, and this leads him to see the image of the garden stream as mimetically clear in its own right but dramatically ineffective in its larger setting as a means of conveying (and thereby inducing a reader to react emotionally to) the awesome potency of the surging Scamander. This amounts to saying that Duris regards mimesis as a means to an end, not an end in itself—an important means for drawing the reader, whether of history or poetry, into a heightened visualization and grasp of the force of the situations depicted. Finally, in his comment on his fourth-century predecessors in historiography Duris associates mimesis with narrative pleasure, and this has caused some scholars to make a case for supposing that Duris was expressly attempting to adapt an Aristotelian theory of poetry to the interpretation of history—a genuine possibility, for sure, but one that needs cautious handling in view of the slender surviving evidence.[15] Although Duris linked mimesis with pleasure, we are simply not in a position to decode his conception of the pleasure of history. But since his aspersion on Ephorus's and Theopompus's lack of mimesis was part of a complaint that they had failed to do justice to the events covered by their histories, we can tentatively conclude that Duris saw a function for mimesis in not just evoking those events vividly but opening up their features to fuller understanding or appreciation.[16]

Whatever the further implications of Duris's position, the idea of the historian's use of mimesis remained in the critical tradition after his time, but in doing so it seems to have acquired a broader sense. It occurs, for example, in a general comment on historical writing by Diodorus Siculus, in the first century B.C., where history's "representation [*mimeisthai*] of events" is said, by virtue of its necessarily sequential treatment of occurrences that were in reality contemporaneous, to fall short of "their true configuration" [*tēs alēthous diatheseōs*].[17] Mimesis is here apparently a cate-

---

[15] Fornara 1983, 124–30, reconstructs Duris's Aristotelian "aesthetic" forcefully but rather too speculatively, not least in talking of "the imitation of the emotions raised by history" (124).

[16] It is worth adding that Duris (*FGrH* 76 F32) is the source of the anecdote at Pliny *NH* 34.61 about the painter Eupompus's remark that "Nature herself, not another artist, should be imitated," a remark which plays on two senses of mimesis—emulation of others (cf. note 21) and artistic representation of life—and is the earliest known case of "the mimesis of nature" as a general principle of representational art. Cf. my later comments, with chapter 12, section I.

[17] Diodorus Siculus 20.43.7; contrast the different emphasis of Aristotle's comments on the relationship of poetic narrative to real time at *Poet.* 24.1459b22–28. This passage of Diodorus

gorization applicable not just to a particular style or technique of historical writing but to all historiography in virtue of its narrative organization of the past; yet it is construed by Diodorus as to some degree artificially removed from "nature" and "the truth" of history, where "truth" designates the fundamental temporality of events rather than the details of specific occurrences. Historical mimesis here approximates to a concept of narrative reconstruction of the past.

Similarly wide, but carrying a somewhat different significance, is the use of mimetic terminology in connection with historiography by Diodorus's partial contemporary, Dionysius of Halicarnassus. At one point in his treatise on Thucydides, Dionysius describes the historian as "a writer who wanted to represent [*mimeisthai*] the truth," and in his letter to Gnaeus Pompeius he refers to "the mimesis of character and emotion" by both Herodotus and Thucydides.[18] These passages suggest that for Dionysius historiography's entire relationship to reality ("the truth") can be thought of in terms of mimesis, or representational accuracy, but also that particular aspects of historical writing can be highlighted as especially mimetic. The second of these points, which recurs in, for example, the second-century A.D. rhetorician Hermogenes of Tarsus,[19] depends, perhaps not unlike Duris's position, on a rhetorical-cum-poetic model of history's need to appeal to its readers by vividly dramatic presentation of the human and emotional substance of the events it reconstructs. The former point seems, prima facie, to be in tension with this, by signaling an acceptance of history's fundamental subservience to "the truth," its obligation to record and not to invent. But Dionysius's stance is not so simple, for his description of Thucydides as "a writer who wanted to represent the truth" occurs with an ironic edge in a context where he is criticizing the historian for failing to meet essentially *rhetorical* criteria of good historiography, failing, more precisely, to give Pericles utterances appropriate to his character and to the situation in which he depicts him.

So Dionysius, in the same breath as he appeals to a notion of historical truth or reality, betrays his own commitment to methods of historical writing that depend on much more than adherence to factual evidence. By advocating and applying rhetorical criteria of appropriateness, Dionysius shows that his concept of "the truth" is not restricted to literal particularity but embraces broader considerations of human nature and the psychology

---

is often taken to show the influence of Duris (e.g., Strasburger 1966, 85; Kebric 1977, 77), but their concepts of historical mimesis seem to me to have a very different thrust; cf. Gray 1987, 481–82.

[18] Dionysius of Halicarnassus *Thuc.* 45, *Gn. Pomp.* 3.18.

[19] Hermogenes *Peri id.* 2.12.124–25 cites the "highly poetic" mimesis of character (*ēthos*) and emotion (*pathos*) in Herodotus; cf. 2.12.62–64 on Xenophon. At 2.12.184 Hermogenes uses mimesis more specifically for the speeches and dialogues in Thucydides.

of human groups. But that in turn affects the connotations of the verb *mimeisthai* in Dionysius's phrase, "a writer who wanted to represent the truth"; indeed, it invites us to connect *mimeisthai* with Thucydides' own programmatic statement, at 1.22.1, that he had given his speakers appropriate words and thoughts, wherever he was unable to record exactly what they had said.[20] If we bear these qualifications in mind, it now starts to look as though mimesis is here not a simple canon of fidelity to fact but a more generously conceived conformity to the supposedly constant lineaments of (human) reality. And if that is so, then Dionysius's application of the idea of mimesis to history is not very far, after all, from some of the ways in which mimesis had been, and continued to be, understood with reference to poetry or visual art.

As it happens, we can see such a concept of mimesis at work in some other passages of Dionysius's writings. In addition to his very common use of mimetic vocabulary to refer to the creative emulation of their predecessors by writers and artists of various kinds,[21] which had by this date become a stock principle of Greco-Roman classicism, it is possible to observe Dionysius drawing in a number of places on a concept of mimesis more directly related to issues of artistic representation.[22] In the first place, Dionysius holds a conviction, probably compounded of various philosophical influences, that human beings are mimetic by nature; and he believes that a mimetic instinct is one of the roots of language itself. Although some of Dionysius's examples and comments in two passages of *De compositione* that explain these ideas illustrate specifically onomatopoeic phenomena,[23] it becomes clear that he is operating with a notion of

---

[20] Dionysius indicates his intention of judging Thucydides' speeches by this criterion at *Thuc.* 41.

[21] This sense of mimesis, in origin an extension from the idea of behavioral emulation or imitation (cf. my introduction, note 33), lies outside the scope of my argument, even though it may occasionally have come into conceptual contact or convergence with representational mimesis: for the relationship between the two ideas see Bompaire 1958, 21–32; Russell 1979, 4–5; Flashar 1979, 92–95; cf. my notes 26–27, 61 here, with chapter 9, note 55, and chapter 12, n. 18.

[22] Two nonliterary examples are *Antiq.* 7.72.10 (satyric dancing, where the very rare verb *katamimeisthai* denotes parodic representation), *De imit.* fr. VIa Usener & Radermacher (painting).

[23] *De comp.* chs. 16 and 20. The connection between mimesis and expressive language, including onomatopoeia, belongs to an ancient tradition of stylistic analysis found also, for example, in Demetrius *De elocutione*, a text of uncertain date but likely, on balance, to be earlier than Dionysius. See esp. *De eloc.* 72, 94, 176, for the classification of onomatopoeic effects as mimetic; the translators' use of "imitation" in these passages is too conventional and obscures the idea of expressiveness: cf., e.g., Dionysius Thrax *De nom. spec.* 18 (p. 42.3–4 Uhlig), with my note 47 for examples from the Homeric scholia, and Stanford 1967, 99–121, for a survey. As with Dionysius, Demetrius also has a broader concept of mimesis: see *De eloc.* 220, 226, 298, for "the mimetic" as the strong evocation of reality, practically

mimesis fluid enough to encompass other types of linguistic significance and expressiveness. In section 20 he observes that those recounting events of which they were eyewitnesses find themselves naturally shaping their discourse (such as their word order) in ways that reflect or express the qualities of the events themselves: literally, "they become mimetic of the things being narrated" (*mimētikoi ginontai tōn apangellomenōn*). From this observation he advances to the principle that poets and orators too need to use language mimetically: that is, to use words (in their lexical, syntactic, and rhythmical aspects) to represent and express the salient features of the things they wish to describe or evoke. But where these "literary" artists are concerned, the mimesis Dionysius enjoins is specifically said to be not a matter of nature but of art's so-called imitation of nature,[24] a principle whose significance became increasingly complicated in the Hellenistic period. Thus nature and artistry form an intricate partnership in Dionysius's argument: a general human instinct for mimesis becomes the basis of a highly artificial, self-conscious manipulation of language for the purpose of recreating, and rivaling, the vivid immediacy of "natural" events themselves.

Dionysius's model of art's mimetic relationship to nature recurs, and is clarified, in passages where he declares his admiration for Lysias's ability to convey an impression of ordinary speech or the common language. Here it is important to see why a notion of "imitation" is inadequate to Dionysius's arguments. Just as in *De compositione* 20 he emphasized that poetic and rhetorical effects are not those of nature but of the mimetic relationship in which art stands to nature, so in a passage of his treatise on Isaeus, when contrasting the *apparent* naturalness of Lysias's style with the too obviously contrived character of Isaeus's, he stresses that Lysias's achievement is precisely a matter of artifice, but artifice that has succeeded in effacing itself and creating an illusion of the wholly natural and "true."[25] The implication of this for Dionysius's concept of mimesis is that it is hardly reducible to one of "imitation" or copying.[26] It makes much better sense

---

synonymous with "vividness," *enargeia*; for this last equation cf., e.g., Josephus *Bell. Jud.* 7.142, Plutarch *Glor. Ath.* 347a, my note 60 here, chapter 5, note 45, and chapter 11, note 53 (with Manieri 1998, 97–192, for the fullest treatment of *enargeia*).

[24] More literally, "art attempting to give a mimesis of real events" (*technēs mimēsasthai peirōmenēs ta ginomena, Comp.* 20): even in isolation, there is no more reason why the verb *mimeisthai* should be translated "imitate" here than "represent," "express," or even "emulate." For the various senses of artistic mimesis of nature, see chapter 5, note 5, and chapter 12.

[25] *Isaeus* 16; see *Lysias* 4, 8, and 13, for Dionysius's other uses of mimetic language in connection with Lysias's style.

[26] The same is true of Dionysius's concept of mimesis as creative emulation; see Russell 1979.

to say that he takes Lysias to be a master at producing a verbal simulation or convincing representation of common speech, and at giving his representation a degree of credibility that deceives the hearer into taking it for reality itself, for the pure truth of the speaker's (i.e., in most cases, Lysias's client's) own voice. We can see, therefore, why Dionysius should want to bracket together poet and orator, as he does at *De compositione* 20, in terms of their mimetic mastery of language: he takes both to be artists in employing words to conjure up a supposed reality in which the hearer or reader will be persuaded to believe. But this means that Dionysius's concept of mimesis is deeply ambivalent, and one of the passages in which he commends the style of Lysias can help us trace a little further the consequences of this point even for his notion of historical mimesis.

Having just insisted that Lysias's style is only apparently artless, but in fact the work of accomplished artistry, Dionysius suggests that "anyone cultivating the truth, and wishing to be an expert in the mimesis of nature, would not go wrong by using Lysias's style of composition—for he could not find a truer style."[27] The paradoxical status of this advice is conspicuous: to achieve an effect of "the truth" or of "nature," adopt the "true" style of a writer who is a master of the artificial simulation of the natural! Moreover, Dionysius here employs phraseology, especially the words "wishing to be an expert in the mimesis of nature" (*phuseōs mimētēs ginesthai boulomenos*), reminiscent of his description of Thucydides, already quoted, as "a writer who wanted to represent the truth" (*tōi mimeisthai boulomenōi sungraphei tēn alētheian, Thuc.* 45). As I maintained earlier, in this last passage Dionysius faults Thucydides not for diverging from the evidence (for all that Dionysius says, Thucydides may actually have known that Pericles said the sort of things he attributes to him), but for a breach of (rhetorical) standards of appropriateness and plausibility. When we put that point together with Dionysius's explicit recognition that Lysias's "true" and "natural" style is itself a work of art, and can indeed be as good a model as reality itself, it becomes hard to resist the inference that Dionysius regards mimesis simultaneously as a kind of stylized fabrication or invention, yet also as a possible means of depicting and conveying truth or nature, where these are understood not as discrete facts but as embodiments of general, recurrent features of the (human) world. If I am right in diagnosing a tension within Dionysius's use of the language of mimesis, it would be fruitless to look in his writings for much self-awareness about this conceptual instability. But it is a nonetheless revealing symptom of the inheritance of mi-

---

[27] *Lysias* 8, which involves a kind of synthesis of two aspects of Dionysius's use of mimeticist terminology, equivalent to a recommendation that a writer seeking to represent (*mimeisthai*) reality could do worse than go about it by emulating (*mimeisthai*) Lysias!

meticism to which Dionysius is affiliated, that he finds himself, when discussing the status of both rhetoric and history, caught between mimesis as artifice and mimesis as the reflection of reality.

II

Issues akin to those that emerge obliquely in Dionysius's use of mimesis as a category within the framework of rhetorical stylistics reappear in the work of Plutarch, a century and a half later, in more explicit and fully formed connection with mimetic art. The writings of Plutarch exhibit a large range of usage of the mimesis word group, a range broadly typical of Greek of the Hellenistic and imperial periods.[28] But in his treatise *De audiendis poetis*, later to carry some influence with Renaissance neoclassicists, Plutarch approaches the subject of poetic mimesis from the distinctive vantage point of a moderate (and eclectic) Platonist bent on establishing the appropriate place of poetry in the education of the young men whose true intellectual destiny lies with philosophy itself. Poetry, he here affirms in a traditional credo, should be a preparation, a propaedeutic, for philosophy (15f–16a), and one moreover that combines pleasure with ethical value or utility—this latter formulation being an answer to the old challenge posed at Plato *Republic* 10.607d8 (the challenge to show that poetry is "not only pleasant but also beneficial to society and human life"), though not an answer original to Plutarch.[29] Rather than rejecting poetry outright, as Epicurus had done, Plutarch urges an educational theory that promises to eliminate harmful elements from the art while preserving what is potentially beneficial. Though he does not say so explicitly, Plutarch is attempting to design a philosophical attitude to poetry that can satisfy Platonist scruples while stopping short of the *Republic*'s expulsion of (many) poets from the well-governed city. Inevitably, then, Plutarch needs

---

[28] In addition to the passages discussed in my text, Plutarch refers to mimesis in connection with dance (*Theseus* 21.1, *Qu. Conv.* 748a–b, cf. ibid., 747c–e, for a special distinction), painting (e.g., *Cimon* 2.3, *Alex.* 4.2, *Qu. Conv.* 681e), sculpture (e.g., *Def. Orac.* 436b, *Qu. Conv.* 674b, *Alex. Fort.* 335b), acting (*Qu. Conv.* 673c–74c), music (*Lyc.* 20.5), and even architecture (*Per.* 13.5). Beyond the mimetic arts, Plutarch often applies the concept of mimesis to (quasi-)ritual reenactment (e.g., *Theseus* 23.3; *Romulus* 21.6, 29.4; *Qu. Graec.* 293c, 301e), and he uses it, sometimes with Platonic associations, of various metaphysical or symbolic correspondences (e.g., *De Iside* 372f, 377a; *Def. Orac.* 416e, 428d; *Virt. Mor.* 441f, *Tranq. Anim.* 477c).

[29] The combination of pleasure and ethical utility (*chrēsimon*): *Aud. Poet.* 14f, 15e–f, 16a. This combination had earlier been asserted by some Stoics: see Strabo 1.1.19. (It is uncertain, though, how much Stoic influence should be detected in Plutarch's treatise: see Babut 1969, 87–93, and Nussbaum 1993, 122–49, for contrasting arguments.) For another advocate of this "dualist" aesthetic, Neoptolemus of Parium, see Philodemus *Poems.* 5.xvi.9–13 Mangoni.

a strategy for dealing with what Plato's own writings had identified as the possible delusions of mimesis.

Plutarch prepares the ground for this strategy by accepting the proverbial saying that "bards tell many falsehoods," but construing its key term, *pseudos*, "falsehood" or "lie," which book 2 of Plato's *Republic* had given a partially pejorative twist, in such a way as to allow it, together with other items in Plutarch's critical vocabulary, something close to a benign notion of fiction.[30] The invention and fashioning of stories, of narrative fictions, is essential, Plutarch suggests, to the very existence of poetry (16c), and in a manner that might alarm a thoroughgoing Platonist he seems to treat it as sufficient protection against the potential harm of immoral statements made by immoral characters in poetry that the hearer or reader should keep in mind the "magic" of poetry's false or fictional nature. Plutarch here, in fact, takes over details from the *Republic*'s discussions of poetry,[31] but strives to address the anxieties underlying them by asserting the possibility of treating poetic *pseudos* as a sort of self-sufficient pretense, something the recipients of poetry need not connect with their beliefs about reality.

It is crucial, however, that Plutarch's argument (just like the arguments in Plato to which they respond) depends on the premise that the experience of mimesis can and will be controlled by a particular mentality, a set of guiding assumptions and expectations. He repeatedly stresses that the young must internalize this mentality, and he sums up its kernel by saying that they are not to regard what is successfully depicted in mimetic works as either "true" or "excellent," *kalon* (18b). This premise posits, in other words, a sort of self-censorship, replacing the political censorship proposed in Plato's *Republic*. But what if self-censorship fails or is lacking? What if the audience of poetry should confuse mimesis with "truth"?[32] The

---

[30] See esp. *Aud. Poet.* 16a–d. Plutarch associates *pseudos* with *to plattomenon* (literally "that which is molded/fabricated," e.g., 16b–f, 17a, 20c, f; for earlier poetic associations, see e.g., Xenophanes fr. 1.22 DK, Plato *Rep.* 2.377b6, Andocides 4.23) and with *muthos/muthologia* ("myth," "storytelling," e.g., 16b–c, f, 17a, 20c). I discuss Plato's use of *pseudos* and *muthos* in chapter 1. For "bards tell many falsehoods" (*polla pseudontai aoidoi*), see 16a, with, e.g., Solon fr. 29 (West 1989–92), Aristotle *Met.* 1.2, 983a3–4.

[31] In addition to the use of *pseudos* itself (see note 30), see, e.g., the idea of objectionable statements made by supposedly reputable characters (16d, where *ellogimos* echoes *Rep.* 3.387d2, 390d2), the notion of poetic "magic," *goēteia* (16d; cf. *Rep.* 10.598d3), and some of the particular Homeric examples cited (e.g., 16e, with *Rep.* 2.383b).

[32] Heirman 1972, 131–32, and Schenkeveld 1982, 67 n. 15, distinguish between use of the *alēth-* word group in this work for "reality" and "truth." But it is hard to anchor this distinction in Plutarch's own thinking, especially because his Platonism inclines him toward a normative conception of "truth" (cf. chapter 1, section II), as the argument in my text will proceed to show. Compare note 7 on the idealizing slant of Cicero's notion of "imitari veritatem" as including beauty.

consequences, Plutarch momentarily concedes, might be disastrous (16d).
And he goes on to make matters much harder for his own position by
admitting, albeit somewhat arbitrarily, that some things in poetry are not
deliberately invented but correspond to the real beliefs of the poets themselves, even if they are reinforced and embellished with fictional detail
(16f). Here, after all, Plutarch registers the central thrust of the critique of
poetry in both books 2–3 and book 10 of the *Republic*, namely that poetry
has the emotional power to infiltrate the minds of its audiences and "fill"
them with the convictions and feelings to which it gives expression, especially in regard to the idea of death as something pitiful and fearful. While
Plutarch does not in this immediate context reuse the term *pseudos* or its
cognates to denote a pejorative sense of poetic "falsehood," he will do so
later on.[33] Yet even after realigning himself with Plato's arguments on this
point, Plutarch falls back once more, apparently still satisfied with its co-
gency, on the consideration that "poetry is not much concerned with the
truth" (17d) and that anyone who remembers this will survive the experience of poetry without psychologically damaging effect.

By the point at which Plutarch introduces the concept of mimesis into
his argument (17f), therefore, two things above all have become salient.
The first is that at the core of his enterprise lies an attempt to seal off poetry
in a domain of fiction where it is incapable of infecting its audiences' systems of beliefs and values. The second is that this enterprise is fraught
with barely submerged difficulty in dealing with the Platonic premise that
poetry, as a culturally influential medium of expression and communication, does indeed have the psychological, especially the emotional, potency to impinge on, influence, and disturb the mind at a deep level. Can
Plutarch's concept of mimesis help him to resolve this strain within his
attitude to poetry? He begins this stage of his case from the traditional
doctrine that poetry is a mimetic art and, as such, comparable to painting,[34]
and, equally conventionally, he takes mimesis to be a matter of "likeness"
or resemblance (*homoiotēs*). But he exploits the idea of likeness in a move
intended to circumvent a hard-line Platonist critique: if likeness is a matter
of achieving a realistic approximation to, or simulation of, the sorts of
things that exist or occur in the world, then the mimetic artist fulfills his
defining task by rendering any object, whether beautiful or ugly, good or
bad, with adequate accuracy. In this way Plutarch ostensibly purports to

[33] See 18e, where the sentiments of certain characters in poetry are called "vicious and
false" (*mochthēroi . . . kai pseudeis*): "false," as sometimes in Plato, here means "based on
false values."

[34] *Aud. Poet.* 17f–18a is one of four passages in Plutarch where Simonides' apophthegm
that "poetry is speaking painting, painting silent poetry" is mentioned; the others are *Quomodo Adul.* 58b, *Glor. Ath.* 346f, *Qu. Conv.* 748a (only the last two cite Simonides by name).
For Lessing's response to this famous remark, see chapter 4, with note 5 there.

separate the technical accomplishment of representational art from ethical questions about its choice or treatment of subject matter: "mimesis is praised for achieving likeness, whether the object be bad or good" (18a); "we do not praise the action represented by mimesis, but the art itself, when it has represented the object fittingly" (18b). So the young must be taught to enjoy the artistry of painters and poets who can convincingly render even the grossest of characters and actions, at the same time as they learn to condemn and repudiate such figures and behavior in their own right. Plutarch's argument here works harder than ever to maintain a strict disjunction between "internal," technical considerations of artistic merit and external considerations of ethical value. The nature of what is at stake is betrayed by the strikingly un-Platonic formulation that Plutarch is induced to use: "it is not the same thing to represent [*mimeisthai*] something excellent [*kalon*] and to represent something excellently [*kalōs*]."[35]

But consider more closely Plutarch's statement of the need for the young (who remain, throughout the piece, a touchstone for larger cultural issues) to couple admiration of artistry with ethical disapproval for unwholesome characters in poetry. This statement implies a point of acute pressure in his position, because it exposes the fact that the exercise of ethical judgment *is an integral part* of the experience of mimetic art. As Plutarch's whole argument recognizes, mimetic works present images of a world saturated by human emotions, desires, and choices, both good and bad, and a world in which such things as madness, fear of death, infanticide, sexual passion, physical agony, malice, and avarice (the list is compiled from Plutarch's own text) play a part alongside courage and nobility. How could such a world be contemplated without the active engagement of ethical responses, without feelings of attraction or aversion, on the part of the audi-

---

[35] *Aud. Poet.* 18d, a flat contradiction of Plato *Laws* 2.654b11–c1 (Pausanias's point at *Symp.* 180e–81a is of a different kind); the attempt of Valgiglio 1973, 115, to find some affinity with *Laws* 2.668d–69b is misguided. (For a late Renaissance statement of a very similar aesthetic "amoralism," by Battista Guarini, see Weinberg 1961, 1:29–30.) This terse formulation of Plutarch's position, together with its context, is partly, but only partly, reminiscent of Aristotle *Poet.* 25.1460b13–15, "correctness in poetry is not the same as correctness in politics or in any other domain" (cf. *Magna Mor.* 1.19, 1190a30–32, but contrast the apparently Platonist view of the young Aristotle at *Protrep.* fr. 49 Düring). There are inadequate grounds for seeing a direct connection, but we should allow for a Peripatetic strand in the argument of *De audiendis poetis*: note, e.g., the partly Aristotelian cast of phrasing at 19e, the "silent" teaching (*didaskalia*) that emerges from "the events themselves" (*ek tōn pragmatōn autōn*), comparing Aristotle *Poet.* 16.1455a16–17, 19.1456b2–7. Flashar 1979, 106, notes the mixture of Platonic and Aristotelian elements in the work, but somewhat simplifies their relationship, as does the hostile account in Sicking 1998, 101–13; cf. also Tagliasacchi 1961, 83–88, who pushes Aristotelianism too hard. Plutarch's distinction between representational art and biography at *Per.* 2.1–3 appears to be based on the assumption that the practitioners of the former lack ethical purpose: see Wardman 1974, 22–26.

ences of art? Plutarch has ultimately to accept that it could not, despite all
that he has said about the fictional status of poetry. Thus, when at 18f he
suggests that in hearing wicked characters in poetry voice their wicked
thoughts the young will be protected by "suspicion against the character"
(*hē pros to prosōpon hupopsia*), which will color their reactions to both
words and deeds, he perceives an ineliminably evaluative dimension to
their response to mimetic representation; and this gives him a cue to em-
bark on discussion of the various ways in which the ethical views and
attitudes of the poets themselves can be incorporated, whether explicitly
or implicitly, in their works. Indeed, practically the whole of Plutarch's
treatise from this point onward amounts to an elaborate analysis of how
ethical judgment can and should be exercised in the experience and criticism of poetry.

What this means, then, is that having apparently set out to construct an
"aestheticized" domain of fiction whose standards are essentially technical
and internal ("mimesis is praised for achieving likeness, whether the object
be bad or good," "we do not praise the action represented by mimesis, but
the art itself, when it has represented the object fittingly," 18a–b), Plutarch
has gradually *remoralized* his conception of mimesis in such a way as to
allow ethical questions to move back toward the center of his perspective
on poetry. If mimesis represents "likenesses" of possible realities, and if,
as Plutarch the Platonist believes, good and bad are part of the fabric of
reality, then the judgment of mimetic works must go beyond matters of
internal consistency and appropriateness and must embrace evaluation of
the entire world of human experience depicted in those works.

The challenge Plutarch has set himself—to work out a modified version
of the approach to poetry put forward in the *Republic*—is one that brings
with it difficulties in terms both of his own "soft" Platonism and of the
concept of mimesis as such, with its ambivalent capacity to lend itself to
two contrasting models of artistic representation (as an inventor of independent worlds, or a reflector of the one real world) and to two correspondingly divergent interpretations of aesthetic experience. It is germane
to notice briefly how these difficulties resurface at a later juncture in *De
audiendis poetis*.[36] At 25b–c Plutarch attempts to express, and at the same
time to harmonize, the tug of opposing considerations that has marked
his argument so far: "we must remind the young, not once but again and
again, and point out to them that poetry's mimetic status means that while
it embellishes and enhances the actions and characters with which it deals,
it does not abandon likeness to the truth [*homoiotēs tou alēthous*], since

---

[36] The recurrence of these issues marks a larger feature of the structure of Plutarch's treatise, as discussed by Schenkeveld 1982; but I see more of an ongoing tension in Plutarch's
argument, and less of an orderly strategy, than Schenkeveld finds there.

the attractive power of mimesis depends on its credibility [*to pithanon*]." Mimesis, Plutarch now seems to be saying, is *both* the invention of worlds that differ from the reality we inhabit, *and* fundamentally dependent on resemblance to that reality.

This statement certainly places a qualification on his earlier stance, as we can observe by juxtaposing the principle that poetry "does not abandon likeness to the truth," a formulation redolent of traditional authority,[37] with his earlier remark that "poetry is not much concerned with the truth" (17d). The new emphasis not just on "likeness" but on "likeness to the truth" is intended in part, as Plutarch immediately indicates, to combat a Stoic model of absolute, and absolutely uncompromised, virtue and vice, right and wrong. The real world, he wants to insist, is one in which virtue and vice are complicatedly intertwined, and this is properly captured in the poetry of Homer, which "says a robust farewell to the Stoics" (25c). But there is a more far-reaching principle visible in this context, namely that the audience of poetry cannot afford to presuppose that characters (e.g., heroes) are ethically homogeneous, but must be prepared to respond in an appropriately inflected way to individual words and deeds, remembering always that "poetry is the mimesis of characters and lives, and of people who are neither perfect nor pure nor entirely beyond reproach but have a mixture of emotions, false beliefs, and ignorance" (26a). As this last sentence makes finally categorical, Plutarch takes mimesis to *entail* the poet's representation of, and the hearer's or reader's active judgment of, a world permeated, indeed partly constituted, by ethical qualities and values. Plutarch may not have abandoned his conviction that the stories of the poets are in some important sense "false" or fictional, but after grappling for some time with the framework of a Platonist analysis of poetry, he has given up any attempt to detach mimesis from the understanding of reality.

In conclusion, Plutarch's problem can be restated very simply, although the competing strands in his own psychological and philosophical temperament made it difficult for him to hold it in entirely clear focus for himself.[38] It stems above all from the essential legacy of ancient mimeticism. On the one hand, Plutarch wishes to connect mimesis to the idea of artistic invention, which he adumbrates, as I earlier explained, through the use of such terms as *pseudos* and *muthos*, and through a series of statements that contrast poetry with "the truth." At the same time, however, he inescapably defines mimesis in traditional terms of "likeness," terms that might be thought to commit poetry to some sort of fidelity to the way things

---

[37] See my introduction, note 48, for the traditional motif of "like the truth."

[38] Heirman 1972, 188, thinks that because Plutarch was a "moralist" he lacked a true concept of "art": this view both presupposes that a true concept of art can and should be amoral and simplifies the complexities I have tried to diagnose in Plutarch's thinking.

really are in the world (or, at the very least, as Aristotle had stressed, the way they are really thought to be). The version of mimesis that Plutarch partly puts together for himself, and partly inherits from the earlier critical-cum-philosophical tradition, is torn between conflicting models of self-contained fiction and world-reflecting realism. That might be a manageable tension if all that were at stake in issues of artistic representation were the "ontology" of the objects it presents us with. But there is much more than that at stake. For, as Plutarch knows but sometimes struggles to integrate into his philosophical aesthetics, poetic representation necessarily makes contact with its audience members' convictions about good and evil in their own world and their own (possible) lives. The problems of mimesis are problems rooted in imagining, and choosing between, different forms of life—problems, *au fond*, of ethics.

III

So far in this chapter I have focused on specific critical uses of the concept of mimesis made by three individual thinkers, Duris of Samos, Dionysius of Halicarnassus, and Plutarch. One way of filling out the broader picture of Hellenistic and imperial attitudes to mimesis is to work back from the vestiges of critical works of those periods traceable in the marginal annotations found in the medieval manuscripts of ancient literature. Modern scholarship has seen enormous progress in our understanding of the origins and nature of these scholia and has been able to develop methods of source analysis that permit us, within certain parameters of confidence, to discover in the scholia evidence for the ideas and approaches espoused by ancient critics. Nowhere has this proved more fruitful than with the Homeric scholia, which preserve elements, albeit at several removes, that derive from a whole succession of ancient critics, going all the way back to the major Alexandrian scholars Zenodotus, Aristophanes of Byzantium, and Aristarchus.[39] There is more than one side to the interest of this work of reconstruction, but my exclusive concern here is with the possibility of using the Homeric scholia, principally those on the *Iliad*, as a source of illumination on the general tendencies of mimeticist thinking in the Hellenistic and imperial periods. For this undertaking to be feasible, it is sufficient to accept that those scholia (the so-called old scholia, *scholia vetera*) whose production derives from the cumulative excerpting and summariz-

---

[39] An excellent sketch of the status and classification of different kinds of Homeric scholia can be found in Snipes 1988, 196–204. Meijering 1987 is a wide-ranging study of some of the literary and rhetorical categories found in the scholia and traceable back to ancient critics. Richardson 1980 gives a synthesis of such material in one particular class of Homeric scholia.

ing of ancient work on Homer can help to bolster our sense of the overall importance of mimeticist ideas and values within the critical trends of antiquity. I am not, however, trying here to pin down particular views to individual figures whose lost works may be reflected in the scholia, because the cases where this might be done are too tenuous to have much value for my main argument.[40]

Although we find more than one concept of mimesis in the Homeric scholia, the vast majority of uses of mimetic vocabulary converge on the broadly Aristotelian idea of poetry as the vivid and convincing representation of (possible) reality. In a number of places a notion of "the mimetic" (*to mimētikon*) stemming ultimately from Plato *Republic* 3 designates the dramatic or enactive mode of poetry as opposed to the narrative or "diegematic";[41] but this usage accounts for a minority of the occurrences of mimeticist terminology in the scholia. Elsewhere we find occasional references to mimesis of three other kinds: role playing in a wider (nonpoetic) sense, visual representation, and vocal mimicry.[42] But in most cases mimesis in the Homeric scholia indicates a flexible conception of poetry as verbal representation, a conception just as applicable to narrative and descriptive passages as to those in dramatic speech.[43] In many instances there is an explicit statement to the effect that Homeric mimesis is "lifelike" or taken "from life," or that it involves depiction of "the truth," and at least some of these passages belong to a quasi-Aristotelian tradition of defending the poems against charges of "irrationality." An example of this last point is the note in which the scholia say that it is not unreasonable or inconsistent, given the situation of consternation obtaining around him, that Odysseus should be shown striking and rebuking certain soldiers in the panic at *Iliad* 2.199, even though Athena had told him at 180

[40] It is particularly unfortunate that we cannot make any definite assertions about the role of mimesis in Aristarchus's views on poetry. Struck 1995, 215–24, detects a quasi-Aristotelian conception of mimesis at work in Aristarchus, but his position is shaky in various respects; Porter 1992, 74–75, and Richardson 1994, 23–25, make a more general case for Aristotelian influence. It seems likely, at any rate, that Aristarchus would have been broadly sympathetic to Aristotle's formulation of the range of possible objects of mimesis at *Poet.* 25.1460b8–11.

[41] See, e.g., Σ bT *Il.* 1.17; 4.127a, 303b; 6.45–46; 15.425–26; 19.282–302, with Matthaios 1999, 395–400. (All references to the scholia to the *Iliad* are taken from Erbse 1969–88; those to the *Odyssey* refer to Dindorf 1855.) Σ b *Il.* 2.494–877 gives a garbled version of the tripartite distinction of modes at Plato *Rep.* 3.392d: the third mode has been corrupted from *miktē* (mixed) to *mimētikē* (mimetic), which makes it identical with the first; for the correct version note Eustathius *Comm. Il.* 1.400–401. Cf. note 49 here, with chapter 5 note 44.

[42] Σ bT *Il.* 1.584b (Hephaestus's role playing), 16.104–5a (visual art, whose nontemporal character is noted negatively here), Σ PE *Od.* 4.279 (vocal mimicry).

[43] The most general statement of this kind is at Σ EQ *Od.* 8.100, "poetry is mimesis" (*mimēsis hē poiēsis*), where a point of characterization (cf. my note 45) is at issue.

to use "gentle words" (cf. 189): indeed, they add, it would be *unrealistic* (literally "unmimetic," *amimēton*) to show Odysseus as unperturbed by the situation.[44]

What matters to us here is not the scholia's attempted resolution of the "problem"—a resolution that seems to overlook a clearly marked distinction between Odysseus's behavior toward leaders and ordinary troops— but their appeal to a canon of psychological realism or "truth to life." In such passages, the scholia (and the tradition of criticism lying behind them) frequently admire Homer for depicting both events and characters (the mimesis of character is itself often picked out)[45] that conform to what are taken to be recurrent, general or even universal features of life: such things do and could happen, the scholiasts tell us.[46] However jejune some of these comments may strike us as being, they are manifestations, in a simplified form, of potentially far-reaching critical presuppositions; and it is significant that they do not just appeal to the idea of the general conditions of human behavior and experience but pick out passages that demonstrate Homer's ability to convey or capture these conditions with a credible particularity, a point amply borne out by the scholia's penchant for the verbally expressive mimesis embodied in onomatopoeia, striking rhythms, and related sound effects.[47] So the combination of, or interplay between, a standard of verisimilitude (ostensible conformity to the known condi-

---

[44] Σ bT *Il.* 2.199a; the adjective *amimētos*, which elsewhere normally means "inimitable" (though it does describe a formally "nonmimetic" mode in Σ b *Il.* 2.494–877; cf. my note 41), is reminiscent of the cognate adverb at Aristotle *Poet.* 25.1460b32: I am not aware of any other passage where one of the *amim-* word group is used evaluatively in this way before the Byzantine period (see, e.g., Σ Tricl. Aeschylus *Agam.* 1343b). References to mimesis of/ from life: see, e.g., Σ AbT *Il.* 1.547a, Σ bT *Il.* 6.467; the adjective *biōtikos* (lifelike), without explicit reference to mimesis, is sometimes used to make the same point (e.g., Σ bT *Il.* 5.370– 72, 8.407, 22.512–13; cf. *zōtikon* in the same sense at Σ T *Il.* 10.409–11, with chapter 4, note 17, and chapter 11, note 54). Mimesis and "the truth": e.g., Σ bT *Il.* 5.667b; 12.110a, 342–3; 14.342–51. For Aristotelian defenses against the supposedly "unreasonable" or "irrational" (*alogon*), see esp. *Poet.* 25.1461b14–21. Traces of other Aristotelian ideas (on poetic unity) in the Homeric scholia are discussed by Gallavotti 1969.

[45] See, e.g., Σ bT *Il.* 4.195, 6.450–54 (collective *ēthos* of barbarians), 15.201–2, 18.429–31, 23.543a.

[46] See esp. Σ bT *Il.* 5.799 ("such things still happen nowadays"), referring to the small detail of holding on to the chariot yoke. The same function is served by supporting generalizations in the scholia, e.g., Σ bT *Il.* 5.667b ("we often overlook things when rushing"), 6.467 (on the behavior of babies), 472b ("even a harsh person can be overcome by fondness for a baby"); the triteness of some of these observations should not be allowed to conceal the model of mimesis that underlies them. For a link to Aristotle's *Homeric Problems*, see Aristotle fr. 366 (Gigon 1987).

[47] See, e.g. Σ bT *Il.* 5.216a, 8.393b, 10.409–11, 13.409–10, 14.394b, 16.470a, 17.263–65. For the idea of "expression," as well as representation, encompassed by this notion of verbal mimesis, see, e.g., Σ T *Il.* 24.358–60, on the relation of the syntax to Priam's distraught state

tions of lived experience) and the power of vivid, credible immediacy (mimesis as the simulation of life) underpins many of the Homeric scholia's comments on mimesis.[48] This is tantamount to saying that behind the centuries of criticism that we find boiled down in these medieval marginalia lies something close to an Aristotelian conception of poetry, a conception in which the universals of which poetry is capable of "speaking" (*Poetics* 9.1451b6–7) are not the stuff of explicit statement but are communicated by means of the successfully specific representation of "actions and life" (*Poetics* 6.1450a16–17).

One particular scholion calls for closer individual attention. In book 3 of Plato's *Republic* (390b–c) Socrates had objected to the portrayal of Zeus in *Iliad* 14 as so overcome by sexual desire for his wife Hera (whose seduction of Zeus is a ploy to distract him from the intrigues of the gods) that he recalls memories of their earliest, surreptitious sexual passions, and insists on making love with her immediately on the ground, rather than going back to his bedchamber. The scholia on part of this passage record a response to the Platonic critique, suggesting that there are three modes of poetry (or three points of view from which poetry can be considered): first, that which represents the truth (*mimētikos tou alēthous*); second, that which involves imaginative elaboration of the truth (*kata phantasian tēs alētheias*) and should therefore not be scrutinized in precise detail, such as the (Homeric) description of disembodied souls in Hades as being capable of tasting and talking; third, that which involves "going beyond, as well as imaginative elaboration of, the truth" (*kat' huperthesin tēs alētheias kai phantasian*), as for example with Homeric characters like the Cyclopes and the Laestrygonians (in the *Odyssey*) and "these passages involving the gods."[49]

As I explained earlier, "the truth," *qua* object of mimesis, is to be understood as meaning the general conditions of reality, more particularly reality as experienced from a human perspective. Given this, we can see that the scheme of poetic modes propounded in this note marks an attempt to

---

of mind; to translate the verb *mimeisthai* here as "imitate," as does Richardson 1993, 311, totally obscures the point. See further in note 23.

[48] When Σ b *Il.* 19.4b says of Achilles' act of "embracing" the corpse of Patroclus that it is "so mimetically" rendered (*lian mimētikōs*), the comment on a single detail encapsulates the idea of an emotional power that contains some deep truth about the possibilities of human experience.

[49] Σ bT *Il.* 14.342–51; cf. Meijering 1987, 67–98, who considers aspects of the passage that I ignore for present purposes and is rightly cautious about its possible sources. Other references in the Homeric scholia to the critique of poetry in *Rep.* 2–3 occur in Σ bT *Il.* 14.176b (Plato "fails to realize that Homer introduces the gods as characters with human emotions"), 24.527–28b, Σ A *Il.* 18.22–35a (Porphyry). Cf. note 41.

argue that poetry can go beyond the sphere of possibilities that conform
to actual human experience, into realms of imagination (*phantasia*) that
either extend or in some cases quite transcend those possibilities. This
scheme purports to answer the ethical objections raised by Plato's Socrates
about Zeus's susceptibility to sexual passion by firmly including Homer's
depiction of the gods, at any rate in this passage, under the third mode,
and thus detaching divine behavior from the standards of "the truth." Now,
this strategy falls well short of constituting a cogent answer to the Platonic
criticism of Homer, for that critique depends on the prescriptive idea that
gods *should* be thought of as paradigmatically good and therefore not
portrayed as lacking the virtue of self-discipline (*sōphrosunē*)—a lack all
too patent, it might be supposed, in Zeus's insistence on the immediate
gratification of sex *al fresco* with his wife.[50] Plato's own argument does
appeal to a canon of "the truth," but it is truth construed as a normative
category that comes close to being synonymous with (ethical) goodness.[51]
Our passage from the Iliadic scholia fails, at least as it stands, to address
the nub of the Platonic critique, in which considerations of religious truth
and ethics are interwoven in a test of poetry's paradigmatic value. To say
that some poetry goes beyond "the truth" is, arguably, to sidestep but not
to meet Plato's question about the cultural and educational exemplarity
through which the psychologico-ethical influence of poetic representations operates.

Although we cannot now trace the source(s) of this particular Homeric
scholion, it is worth noting the possibility of at least an oblique connection
with an Aristotelian line of argument. In *Poetics* 25 Aristotle divides the
objects of poetic mimesis into three types, "the sorts of things that were
or are the case, the sorts of things that people say and think to be the case,
or the sorts of things that ought to be the case" (1460b10–11), and he
appeals to this scheme in suggesting how objections such as those of Xenophanes (and, though he does not say so, Plato) to poetic depictions of
the gods might be deflected: "if neither [sc. of the other defenses] is appli-

[50] The example of Zeus's passion in *Il.* 14 belongs to the argument concerning self-discipline that begins at *Rep.* 3.389d9; cf. 390a4. Observe that the scholia on *Il.* 14.342–51 actually
fail to recognize the ethical motivation of Plato's critique (though their ultimate source may
have done so); indeed, the note begins in a way that implies, wrongly, that Plato's text had
criticized Zeus's use of a golden cloud to hide himself and Hera from view. Recurrent concerns over this section of the *Iliad* made it a subject of ancient allegorism: see Buffière 1956,
106–15, 544–48, with Sheppard 1980, 62–74, for a full analysis of Proclus's allegorical interpretation of the scene. Plutarch *Aud. Poet.* 19f–20b rejects allegorical interpretations of the
episode and finds an ultimate ethical lesson (against female seductiveness) in the negative
upshot of Hera's deception.

[51] See my discussion of the normative, exemplary role of truth in *Rep.* 2–3 in chapter 1,
section II.

cable, there remains the principle that people say such things, as with matters concerning the gods; for perhaps it is neither ideal nor true to say such things [sc. about the gods], but maybe it is as Xenophanes thought. No matter, people do say them."[52] It is important that Aristotle's defense of poetic "theology" refers to both ethics and truth, thereby responding in principle to *Republic* books 2–3. It is equally important, however, not to take this passage as an Aristotelian endorsement of simply anything what-soever that poets might project onto the gods. As with other topics covered by the "solutions" to critical problems discussed in *Poetics* 25, Aristotle's position would require depictions of the gods to be tested by the criterion of relevance to a poem's overall structure and "goal" (see 1460b22–26, 1461b19–21 for the overarching priorities). Moreover, this chapter of the *Poetics* draws distinctions *within* the field of mimesis, here construed as a general category of artistic representation (embracing the visual arts as well as poetry, 1460b8–9), not between mimesis and something else, as in the Homeric scholia. Even so, it is possible that Aristotle's attempt to distinguish different objects of poetic representation gave stimulus to a Hellenistic scheme that modified his analysis by limiting the concept of mimesis, as elsewhere in the Homeric scholia, to representations of a world that conforms to the observable conditions of human life.

The scholion we have been considering purports to put Homer's pre-sentation of the gods beyond the reach of Platonic (ethical and theologi-cal) criticism, into a realm of the extravagantly and purely imaginary, though it does so, as already noted, by stressing the magical golden cloud (not mentioned by Plato) at the expense of the anthropomorphic psychol-ogy of the scene in *Iliad* 14. An Aristotelian would want to qualify this strategy by saying, first, that to depict the gods in any shape or form is still an exercise in mimesis or poetic "image making"; second, that while it is not appropriate to ask simply whether the depiction is true, or the behav-ior exhibited good in itself, it does not follow from this that the depiction can be severed from the question of what we are to make of such gods and how they fit into the picture of the world constructed by the poem. A Platonist would press this last point more robustly. However fictional or imaginary the gods of Homer may be, the ways in which hearers or readers of the poems react to the images of these gods are bound to be all too real and human; and this means that their reactions are connected to what they believe about the world—what, ultimately, they believe to be true, and what they believe to be good. The ethics of representation cannot simply be evaded by an appeal to the freedom of imagination.

[52] *Poet.* 25.1460b35–61a1.

The nub of that last claim is all the more worth pressing because of a standard but exaggerated view that the concept of *phantasia* came in antiquity to challenge the predominance of mimesis in critical and philosophical aesthetics.[53] The first thing to be said in this connection is that while the Homeric scholia use the concepts of both mimesis and *phantasia* in many places, the scholion on *Iliad* 14.342–51 is the *only* one where these concepts are explicitly contrasted. Insofar, therefore, as the scholia as a whole give us a sense of the priorities and prevailing patterns of Hellenistic and imperial Greek criticism, they supply little reason for positing an intrinsic tension between the categories of mimesis and *phantasia*. This is not surprising, because the term *phantasia*, though the subject of a complex philosophical and critical history, had a basic semantic connection with "appearance," "vision," and "visualization" that scarcely made it incompatible with the full range of ways in which the concept of mimesis was itself put to use.[54] Apart from the passage in question from the Homeric scholia, only one ancient text manifests a strong distinction between mimesis and *phantasia*, and this has become the endlessly repeated textbook example of a supposed reaction against mimeticism in the name of imaginative creativity. In his *Life of Apollonius* (6.19) written in the early third century A.D., Philostratus makes the Neopythagorean sage Apollonius of Tyana draw an explicit contrast between mimesis (as that which represents "what it has seen") and *phantasia* (capable of representing "that which it has not seen") when discussing the source of artistic inspiration behind Greek statues of the gods, as opposed to the theriomorphic Egyptian images that Apollonius belittles as unworthy of a serious conception of the divine. The twin premises behind this distinction are, first, that mimesis entails a connection (though not necessarily a direct correspondence) to the possibilities of human sensory experience and, second, that the power of visualization or imagination can transcend such a connection. But given that the specific topic of *divine* images, already an issue for mimeticist theories at an earlier date, is here under discussion, it is surely inadvisable to treat this passage of Philostratus, any more than the

---

[53] Schweitzer 1934, 297, speaks of *phantasia* coming to replace mimesis in later Greek conceptions of visual art; Verdenius 1983, 55, makes a related generalization in regard to literary criticism, Zagdoun 2000, 147–70, in regard to Stoic aesthetics.

[54] When Josephus *Antiq.* 12.75 contrasts *phantasia* (illusionistic appearance) of the natural world with artificial mimesis (*technēs mimēmata*), it is clear this is hyperbolic commendation of visual mimesis itself (cf. 12.77); *phantasia* and mimesis are intertwined at Proclus *In Remp.* 1.163.27–164.7 Kroll (and cf. chapter 11, section II on Proclus's other uses of *phantasia* terminology). Watson 1988a is the fullest survey of ancient ideas of *phantasia* (cf. Watson 1986 for an outline); see also Cocking 1991, chs. 1–4, and Meijering 1987, 67–72, 91–98. On the relationship of *phantasia/fantasia* to mimesis in the Renaissance, see Kemp 1977, esp. 361–81.

Homeric scholion discussed earlier, as evidence for a full *phantasia*-based alternative to a mimetic model of pictorial art.[55] The sentiment put in the mouth of Apollonius propounds a thesis about a special artistic application of imaginative or inventive visualization, not about the essential character of the figurative arts themselves.

Indeed, we find elsewhere in the same work that mimesis not only continues to provide the basis of a general account of representational art but is actually interpreted in such a way as to make it encompass an explicitly imaginative component.[56] In a memorably eloquent passage, at 2.22, Apollonius accepts his companion Damis's suggestion that all painting is mimesis ("of everything seen by the sun, and even of the sun itself"), before proposing that the images sometimes seen in cloud formations may be the work of god the artist, playfully making pictures like children drawing in sand. The two agree that pictorial and sculptural art involves a capacity to translate into visual images the mimetically conceived notions of the mind (*nous*). Apollonius describes mimesis as a natural facility of all humans, an originally Aristotelian idea that by this date had become a cliché of Greek thought. But he gives this idea a new impetus by arguing, on the basis of some remarks about the ability of even monochrome drawing to produce expressively rich depictions, that the viewers of visual art need to use their own mimetic capacity (*mimētikē*), their powers of forming mental images, to understand the works they contemplate. The experience of mimesis, he is maintaining, requires a kind of "projectional," interpretative response on the part of the beholder, a view that may much later have influenced the author of *Laokoon*.[57] The passage thus ties together the production and receptive appreciation of visual representation through a theory of mimesis that roots the latter in the image-forming powers of the human mind.

---

[55] For discussion of Philostratus *Vita Ap.* 6.19, see esp. Birmelin 1933, 392–414 (overstressing Aristotelian affinities), and Watson 1988a, 59–95 (emphasizing the conjunction of Platonic and Stoic elements); cf. my chapter 9, note 36. Elsner 1995, 27, prejudices the issue by speaking of "mere imitation" in his account of this passage (but see 48 for a qualification), while Panofsky 1968, 16, wrongly treats it as evidence for the idea of a "supreme art . . . completely emancipate[d]" from the empirical world: that is to extrapolate illegitimately from images of gods to the art form as a whole. Manieri 1998, 60–66, recognizes mimesis and *phantasia* as two parts of a Philostratean aesthetic. On the specific issue of divine images, see esp. Dio Chrysostom 12.54, 59, with chapter 9, note 30, and chapter 11, note 63. Pollitt 1974, 52–55, 201–5, offers a general account of *phantasia* in relation to visual art.

[56] This is also true of the collection of *Eikones* (*Imagines*) attributed to the elder Philostratus, whether or not this is the same author as that of the *Life of Apollonius*: see the proem 1–2, with 1.2.4–5, 1.21.3, 2.1.2–3; but note that 1.9.5 narrows the sense of mimesis to specifically realistic appearances.

[57] See the discussion of this passage in Birmelin 1933, 153–80 (overstressing the Aristotelian dimension: cf. Schweitzer 1934), and, more briefly, Cocking 1991, 45–47, with my chap-

Once we recognize that this theory itself has a strongly, actively "imaginative" dimension, it becomes easier to see that what we are offered in the contrast between mimesis and *phantasia* at 6.19 is not a pure distinction between imaginative and nonimaginative art but an insistence that the possibilities of representation extend beyond the boundaries of the observable world. Such a perspective was, in fact, entirely compatible with certain older conceptions of mimesis, such as that of Aristotle in *Poetics* 25.1460b8–11, which expressly allows for artistic idealism. But because some models of mimesis laid weight on realistic truth to *appearances*, Philostratus makes Apollonius distance idealistic religious art from canons of representation closely bound to the phenomena of visible reality. It remains uncertain, however, whether in doing so Philostratus was consciously aligning himself with a Middle Platonist, and subsequently Neoplatonist, strain of thought that ascribed to art, or at any rate to the artist's mind, the power to access a transcendent realm of truth.[58]

The term *phantasia* may have come to occupy an increasingly prominent part in the artistic and aesthetic theories of the imperial period, but we have insufficient grounds to believe that it posed a substantial threat to the older hegemony of mimeticist thinking, as a concluding glance at Longinus *On the Sublime* can help to confirm.[59] Longinus uses *phantasia*, especially in chapter 15, to refer to the capacity of writers, both poets and others, to visualize their ideas vividly and to convey them through appropriately expressive language. *Phantasia* is here akin to the traditional poetic-cum-rhetorical category of *enargeia*, though Longinus specifies that the latter is the specific concern only of rhetorical visualization, whereas poetic *phantasia* aims at powerful emotional "amazement," *ekplēxis*.[60] The point of this distinction is to allow for the scope of poetic

---

ter 4, for the very similar view in Lessing. Cf. the stimulation of the reader's *phantasia* by poetic mimesis at Proclus *In Remp.* 1.163.27–164.7 Kroll.

[58] Watson 1988a, 59–95, and 1988b argues for a Platonist background (together with a Stoicizing element) to Philostratus's use of *phantasia* in this passage; for the Middle Platonist developments in question here, see chapter 11, note 6. Schweitzer 1934 offers a more art-historically orientated perspective.

[59] Against the modern consensus that *On the Sublime* is an anonymous first-century A.D. work, Heath 1999 states a fresh case for accepting the ascription to the third-century rhetorician Cassius Longinus: I here continue to refer to the author as Longinus for convenience, without committing myself on this question. For an overview of imperial Greek criticism, see Russell 1989.

[60] The underlying continuity of critical ideas can be seen by comparison between the definition of *phantasia* (representation of absent things as though present; cf. my introduction, note 48) at Quintilian *Inst. Or.* 6.2.29 (referring to the Greek term) and Aristotle's idea of *enargeia* at *Poet.* 17.1455a22–6. Cf. note 23 on the association of *enargeia* with mimesis; for *ekplēxis*, see chapter 7, note 19.

imagination to outrun the realm of common experience, to take on what he calls a "rather mythical/fictional exorbitance" (*muthikōteran tēn huper-ekptōsin*) and to transcend credibility in every way (15.8). But it is not the case either that Longinus approves unequivocally of such flights of fancy, or that he thinks *phantasia*, even in poetry, intrinsically requires departure from the norms of credibility. Although chapter 15 ascribes "truthfulness" (*to enalēthes*) directly to rhetorical visualization, we find elsewhere that the best poetic imagination too keeps contact with the real: hence, in particular, the praise of the *Iliad* in chapter 9 for being "packed with visualizations drawn from the truth" (*tais ek tēs alētheias phantasiais*, 9.13), while the *Odyssey*, though admired, is placed firmly in second place for exhibiting precisely those features ("the mythical and the incredible," *tois muthōdesi kai apistois*) associated with exorbitant *phantasia* in chapter 15. Elsewhere Longinus famously extols the psychological potency of a love song by Sappho for expressing emotions that come supposedly "from the truth itself" (*ek tēs alētheias autēs*, 10.1), from an unmistakably authentic human reality.

We have seen throughout this book, including the earlier sections of this chapter, that "truth" was never a necessary, still less an unambiguous, touchstone of mimeticist aesthetics. But for the author of *On the Sublime* everything in the greatest writing converges on a truth that is identical with the greatness of "nature" itself, and there is no doubt that for him mimesis remains one way of speaking about creative contact between human thought and the dynamics of reality. In part Longinus continues to think of mimesis in a way comparable with the rhetorical traditions exemplified by passages of Dionysius of Halicarnassus discussed earlier: this is evident at 18.2, where, within his treatment of figures of speech, he comments on the capacity of rhetorical "self-questioning" to represent (*mimeisthai*) and give a strong sense of spontaneous emotion. But another passage later in the same stretch of the treatise, at 22.1, where Longinus states that the best writers' use of emotionally dislocated word order, hyperbaton, means that "mimesis is carried toward the effects of nature" (*hē mimēsis epi ta tēs phuseōs erga pheretai*), intimates that such ideas are not limited to the goal of merely manipulative artifice. What we have here is a special adaptation of the artistic "imitation of nature" (cf. 43.5): the whole concept of sublimity calls for an artistry that, at its highest, is indistinguishable from, and in some sense transmuted into, the inspiration of nature herself. *On the Sublime* embodies a remarkable sensibility that stretches the understanding of literary creativity well beyond anything found in most texts in the mimeticist tradition. Moreover, its interest in a whole spectrum of writings—rhetorical, historical, philosophical as well as poetic—makes it perhaps unsurprising that mimesis does not occupy a large or central position in

its critical outlook. But that does not mean, as some have supposed, that
the work simply replaces mimesis with *phantasia*, or that Longinus's concept of *phantasia* is an attempt to break free of one of the chief values
traditionally associated with mimesis, the goal of representational fidelity
to important ("spiritual" rather than "phenomenal") features of the living
world of "nature," whose contemplation is, according to *On the Sublime*
(35), the true destiny of the human mind.[61]

[61] Rostagni 1955, 501, claims that Longinus replaces mimesis with *phantasia*, which he
understands in terms of "intuition" and the "expression of an inner reality" (469); but he
ignores the implications of *Subl.* 9.13, quoted in my text, and of Longinus's references to
representational mimesis. More subtly, though his understanding of mimesis is too narrow,
Manieri 1998, 51–60, claims a transformation of mimesis by *phantasia*; Cocking 1991, 30–
32, sees the compatibility of *phantasia* and mimesis in Longinus. The clearest indication of
Longinus's interest in a more than merely "phenomenal" fidelity to nature is given by the
contrast with the "likeness" of sculpture at 36.3. On the "imitation of nature" at 43.5, cf.
chapter 12, note 19. For the relation between mimesis as representation and as emulation of
literary models (at, e.g., 13.2, 15.12, 34.2) in Longinus, see Flashar 1979, with my note 21.

Chapter Eleven

❀

Renewal and Transformation:
Neoplatonism and Mimesis

Dal mortale al divin non vanno gli occhi infermi.
(Michelangelo)
Nel crearsi dell'opera di poesia, si assiste come al mistero della
creazione del mondo. (Croce)[1]

THE CONCERNS explored in Plato's repeated dealings with mimesis set a large
part of the agenda for the history of ancient aesthetics. Together with the
countervailing views of Aristotle, which they themselves had helped to
prompt, they became, in ways my two preceding chapters have allowed
us to glimpse, a source of both stimulus and provocation that ran through
the core of the mimeticist tradition. But not until late antiquity did anybody
take up the topic of mimesis on the full scale of the Platonic precedent,
restoring it to a position with relevance for the entire gamut of philosophical issues from the sensory to the metaphysical domain. For this reason
the mimetic theories of Neoplatonism, above all those of Plotinus in the
third century and Proclus in the fifth, deserve to count as the most radical
and important developments in the ancient mimeticist tradition after the
foundational work of both Plato and Aristotle. In related yet substantially
distinct ways, Plotinus and Proclus elaborated new understandings of artistic mimesis by placing the subject within a grand, all-encompassing philosophical framework of thought. In doing so they were taking mimesis
back to one of its strongest but by this date deeply submerged roots, pursuing projects that were Platonic in the scope of their ambitiousness as
well as in much of their conceptual detail.

---

[1] Michelangelo ("eyes that are weak do not advance from the mortal to the divine"), poem
164.10–11 in Ryan 1996, 152; B. Croce, "Aesthetica in Nuce," in Croce 1990, 211 ("in the
creation of a work of poetry it is as if one is witnessing the mystery of the creation of the
world"). On Michelangelo's Neoplatonism, see, e.g., Blunt 1978, 58–81; Panofsky 1962, 171–
230 (with x–xiv), esp. 178–82; Panofsky 1968, 115–21; von Einem 1973, 260–64; Summers
1981, 11–17. Michelangelo's relationship to Plotinus *Enn.* 5.8.1, which states that the form of
a sculpture is not to be found *in* the stone (contrast Cicero *Div.* 2.21.48, Dio Chrysostom
12.44), fluctuates: compare poems 111 and 151 in Ryan 1996, 102, 138; cf. Clements 1963,
22. See also, but differently, Plotinus *Enn.* 1.6.9.8–11. On the idealist aesthetic of Croce, see
my note 6 here, my introduction, note 26, and, for the intellectual pedigree of the idea of
creativity exhibited in my Crocean epigraph, cf. Nahm 1947.

Yet it is not in any straightforward sense true of either Plotinus or Proclus that they were reconstructing a consistently or authentically Platonic perspective on mimesis. Both of them diverged from Platonic discussions of the theme in respects whose significance was to have lasting influence on the complex evolution of mimetic theorizing from the fifteenth-century Renaissance to the era of romanticism. In this as in other areas, Neoplatonism is so revisionist as to require a concept of Platonism as something more than a static affiliation—rather as a kind of philosophical spirit capable of perpetual revivification, though each time in a subtly different guise. It is tempting, indeed, to consider the two Neoplatonist aesthetics I examine in this chapter as themselves being edifices of *intellectual* mimesis, constructed from an intricate, highly self-conscious response to, and adaptation of, Platonic patterns of reasoning. Furthermore, Neoplatonism in its turn became a primary channel for the transmission of Plato's ideas beyond the boundaries of paganism, and in the penultimate section of this chapter I trace some of the delicate threads that connect Platonizing approaches to mimesis with the contested status of images in the debates of Byzantine Iconoclasm, particularly in the work of John Damascene.

Any investigation of the place of mimesis in the philosophy of Plotinus must start with the fundamental observation that the language of mimesis pervades his writings, forming a conceptual vein that leads to the heart of his thinking. Plotinus's use of mimetic terminology appears in several dozen passages of the *Enneads*, only a small proportion of which, however, refer directly to the mimetic arts. This recurrent strain of vocabulary can be readily accounted for, in broad terms at least, by reference to Plotinus's systematically and magisterially hierarchical worldview, which posits various levels of "higher" and "lower" realities in a sequence that descends from the ultimate, transcendent source of all being, the One, down through the mediating powers of *nous* (intellect) and *psuchē* (soul), to the lower reaches of material nature. Within this scheme, lower realities not only reflect the higher realities that constitute their origins and causes, but also constantly reach up to and strive to become like them. Plotinus frequently formulates this type of relationship, in which the lower both reflects and aspires to the higher, as one of mimesis. Metaphysical mimesis of this sort, which is a matter of asymmetrical "likeness" and assimilation to an "archetype,"[2] manifests itself in numerous dimensions of the Plotinean program. On the largest scale, Plotinus can speak of the relationship between *everything* and the One as a case of mimesis: all things aspire to the eternity and goodness embodied in the first principle of the cosmos (5.4.1.33). More commonly, Plotinus posits mimesis between comparable

---

[2] Plotinus uses the term *archetupon* in connection with mimesis at, e.g., 1.2.2.3, 5.3.7.32, 5.8.12.15. For the asymmetry of the relationship, see 1.2.2.1–10.

entities or components of reality at distinct levels of his system, or between these levels themselves. It exists, therefore, between human and divine logos, human and divine soul, human nature and the nature that is prior to humans; between soul and *nous*; between *nous* and the One; between time and eternity (an idea indelibly associated with the *Timaeus*); between the perceptible or sensory and the noetic world.[3] If, in Plotinus's scheme of things, being or reality "flows" down the cosmos from top to bottom, mimetic affinities are one way of talking about the process by which all being endeavors to revert, upward, to its source. To understand mimesis is, accordingly, to understand a key principle of the dynamics of reality.

In order to bridge the gap between this grand metaphysical apparatus and Plotinus's remarks on the mimetic arts in their own right, we need to remember that, like Plato, at any rate in his later dialogues, Plotinus regards human thought and language (both covered by the term *logos*) as themselves mimetic. "Just as the logos in the voice," he writes at 1.2.3.27–28, "is a *mimēma* [a model?] of the logos in the soul, so the latter is itself a *mimēma* of divine logos and *nous*." Language reflects thought, if imperfectly, and human thought in turn reflects, and is the "interpreter" (*hermēneus*) of, divine intellect and reason. Elsewhere Plotinus says that the soul, modeling itself (*mimoumenē*) on what it discerns of reality, uses the sounds of language to try to signify its own cognition of the nature of that reality, which itself contains mimetic traces of its origin in the ultimate One (5.5.5.23–27). This last passage well exemplifies the density of Plotinus's applications of mimetic terminology (here in triplicate, for the relationships between reality and the One, the soul and reality, language and the soul), while also reinforcing his tenet that the human soul depends on mimesis, *qua* a kind of self-likening attraction, in order to move toward a fuller grasp of reality. If the levels of reality are partial models, images or imprints of that which lies above them in the ontological hierarchy, in the case of the human soul this process is an especially active engagement in mimetic "assimilation." For the philosopher, this is to be understood above all as the goal, by this date shared by pagan and Christian thinkers, of fashioning oneself "in the likeness of god."[4] But the two passages cited earlier in this paragraph show that Plotinus considered all activity of the human soul to be a potential fulfillment of its mimetically aspiring movement toward the source of its own being. This implication has obvious pertinence to Plotinus's view of the mimetic arts themselves. But it might

---

[3] Human and divine logos: 1.2.3.28; human and divine soul: 2.1.5.8; human and "prior" nature: 2.1.8.26; soul and *nous*: 5.3.7.33; *nous* and the One: 2.9.2.3; time and eternity: 3.7.11.56, 3.7.13.37, 5.1.4.18 (with Plato *Tim.* 38a); sensory and noetic worlds: 2.4.4.8, 4.8.6.28, 6.2.22.38, 6.7.7.21.

[4] See esp. Plotinus *Enn.* 1.2.1–3, with chapter 9, note 29.

prompt us to wonder at the outset whether his position is one that can afford to esteem these arts for their participation in the soul's impulse towards higher reality, or alternatively one that, in keeping with certain Platonic texts, is destined to deem them inferior to other, more philosophical forms of mimetic yearning.

We find evidence, as it happens, for both these attitudes in the *Enneads*, and, what is more, sometimes in close proximity.[5] On the positive side is the fullest and most influential Plotinean discussion of mimetic art, which occurs at 5.8.1–2. But one must appreciate straightaway that art is mentioned here not for its own sake but by way of analogy, to help explicate what it means to contemplate the beauty of the noetic world, of intellect (*nous*), itself. Plotinus analyzes the beauty of an artwork (his example is a stone statue of a beautiful figure, divine or human) as deriving from the form (*eidos*) put into it by the maker, but which exists in the maker's mind prior to its realization in matter and is at the same time a reflection of the artist's art (*technē*) itself. The notion of the artist's mental "form" is very old, and it had already been used by earlier Platonists to give approval to some kinds of idealistic art.[6] But Plotinus takes an innovative step by claiming that the beauty "in the art" (*en tēi technēi*) is superior to, and purer than, the beauty produced in the stone. Art creates according to its own internal principle (*logos*) and is more beautiful, precisely in virtue of that principle, than the things it generates externally. This externalized beauty is weaker, because more diffuse, less concentrated, than its origin—a process of attenuation that exemplifies a larger aspect of Plotinean metaphysics: everything that creates is stronger and superior to that which it creates.

The brief but pregnant analysis of a statue's beauty in 5.8.1 adumbrates a metaphysics of representational art by accommodating the latter within the framework of Plotinus's whole system of thought. The beauty of the visible becomes, in short, an intimation of (and derivation from) higher beauties.[7] The claim is potentially momentous, but possibly also disquiet-

---

[5] Rich 1960 gives a survey of Plotinus's treatment of artistic mimesis.

[6] See Xenophon *Symp.* 4.21; Aristotle *Met.* 1.6, 988a4; 7.7, 1032a32–b1; cf. Plato *Gorg.* 503e, *Crat.* 389b, *Rep.* 10.596b. Middle Platonism, perhaps encouraged by Plato *Rep.* 5.472d, 6.500e–501c (cf. chapter 4, section II), appears to have adapted this concept to a more specifically Platonist notion of ideal forms. See Cicero *Orator* 8–10, where mimetic representation ("imitari") is still involved: some, including Theiler 1934, 17, Dillon 1996, 93–95, have posited Antiochus as Cicero's source; but Barnes 1989, 95–96, vigorously rebuts this hypothesis. Cf. Seneca *Epist.* 58.18–21, 65.7–10, with Theiler 1934, 15–19; Steckerl 1942; and Rich 1954 on the development of the notion of (Platonic) ideas in the mind of god. For a partial modern parallel to Plotinus's location of artistic form and beauty in the artist's mind, cf. the idealism of Croce, e.g., his reference to "works of art that exist nowhere other than in the souls that create or recreate them" (opere d'arte, le quali non altrove esistono che nelle anime che le creano o le ricreano; Croce 1990, 216).

[7] Gerson 1994, 212–18, offers one overview of Plotinus's conception of beauty.

ing. Does it, one might ask, cogently elevate art to a higher plane, or simply miss its point? Could there really be a greater beauty located in the sculptor's mind than in his finest statue? Does "the true statue," as Plotinus says elsewhere (in a significant modification of *Republic* 10), stay "within" the art, rather than the material image?[8] Plotinus himself is alert to the need to situate his position more carefully vis-à-vis existing aesthetics, and he continues by countering an expected objection that "the arts" (his own phrase)[9] are negligible because they operate through mimesis of nature (5.8.1.33). The fact that Plotinus can envisage such a point being made *negatively* indicates that he anticipates it as coming from within a Platonizing framework. Yet he immediately goes on to point out, first, that nature itself involves mimesis (on his own special metaphysical understanding, as sketched earlier); second, that the arts "do not simply produce mimetic representations of the visible realm (*to horōmenon*), but return (*anatrechousin*) to the principles from which nature comes";[10] and third, that the arts can "add" beauty, from their own resources, to the things they make, as in the case of Phidias's celebrated statue of Zeus at Olympia, which was based on no sensory model but on the artist's conception of what Zeus *would* look like, if he took on visible form.[11]

So Plotinus brings together three points in a compound defense of the mimetic arts against the implied slur that they are mere semblances or simulacra of the phenomena of nature: one, that mimesis itself is a pervasive principle of reality (so that to be mimetic is not per se to fall away from the real); two, that art can reach beyond the appearances to the underlying principles of nature (and in that respect emulate the mimetic activity of nature itself, 4.3.11.8–10); three, that art can enhance or improve on the beauty of nature. All three of these suggestions might, with suitable qualification, be described as forms of idealism; in conjunction, they delineate

[8] See 5.9.5.36–41, where Plotinus treats "statue" and "bed" as the same in relation to the shaping force of art, an explicit contradiction of Plato *Rep.* 10.596–97.

[9] Cf. my introduction, note 18.

[10] For Proclus's use of *anatrechein* (5.8.1.35–36), to "return/revert" to one's source, compare 4.5.7.1, 4.9.3.22.

[11] Plotinus here (5.8.1.39–40) uses a similar phrase, *hoios an genoito*, "what he could/would be like," to Aristotle's now famous formula at *Poet.* 9.1451b5 (the poet, unlike the historian, speaks of *hoia an genoito*, "things that could/would occur"), but its import is very different; cf. also Plato *Rep.* 5.472d5, with chapter 4, section II. Proclus, *In Tim.* 1.265.18–24 (Diehl 1903–6) was later to connect Phidias's inspiration to the influence of Homer's poetry—a passage that was often subsequently cited by idealists in aesthetics: see, e.g., Reynolds' third *Discourse* (Reynolds 1997, 42), Winckelmann's *Gedanken über die Nachahmung der griechischen Werke* (Winckelmann 1982, 3), and my chapter 12, section I, for the case of Bellori. Other pertinent passages on Phidias's Zeus include Strabo *Geog.* 8.3.30; Cicero *Orator* 8–9; Seneca maj. *Controv.* 10.5.8; Dio Chrysostom 12.26, 48–83; Philostratus *Vita Ap.* 4.7, 6.19 (with chapter 10, section III).

the possibility of a new philosophical aesthetic. Part of the significance of this aesthetic lies in the fact that Plotinus here stakes out a position that simultaneously involves an acceptance and a reinterpretation of mimesis.[12] Because his system as a whole correlates the idea of mimesis, *qua* reflection of higher realities, with the doctrine that reality is generated by emanation from higher to lower levels, it is not necessary for him to discard or depreciate the mimetic status of the arts. Instead, he can reconfigure artistic mimesis in terms of something more than a correspondence to appearances, converting it into a movement upward in the direction of the formative principles, *logoi*, which lie behind the world of mere phenomena.

Unfortunately it is difficult to make further headway with the elucidation of this intriguing passage, as Plotinus breaks off his analogy with mimetic art abruptly at the start of 5.8.2 ("let us put the arts aside") and returns to his main topic, the relationship between visible beauty in general and the higher realms of beauty to which it can direct us. He leaves us with a distinct indication that a mimetic artwork might be contemplated for more than its prima facie figuration; his argument about artistic form implies that the quality of a work will be commensurate with the quality of the artist's prior conception of the form to be imposed on it. But it remains deeply uncertain what this might mean in practice, or how it might shape the interpretation of particular artworks.[13] Moreover, Plotinus's position is complicated by ostensibly more disparaging views of artistic mimesis that appear elsewhere in his work. This is perhaps most notably so at 4.3.10.17–19, a comparison that stresses the inferiority of all "art" (*technē*) to the creative power of soul and nature and describes art as producing "murky and weak mimetic objects [*mimēmata*], playthings [*paignia*] of a sort, of little worth," and as "using many contrivances to produce a simulacrum [*eidōlon*] of nature."[14] Yet even this passage, despite its thick texture of Platonic reminiscences, does not dismiss art unequivocally. To call something a "plaything" *paignion*, is not, for Plotinus, to condemn it irredeemably. It is, certainly, to count it as insubstantial in the totality of things; but in that respect Plotinus regards all ordinary human life (the life of killing and being killed) as a matter of "playthings" and, likewise, the entire

---

[12] His position should therefore not be called a "non-mimetic defence of art" (Allen 1999, 440).

[13] Rich 1960, 239, thinks Plotinus may have been influenced by contemporary Roman portrait sculpture's attempt to express "inward meaning." There is little to anchor this suggestion in the *Enneads*; 2.9.16, which Rich cites, does intimate a possible sensitivity to portraiture, but it refers to painting, not sculpture.

[14] The term *paignion* is just one of a cluster of echoes suggesting that Plato *Polit.* 288c was particularly in Plotinus's mind in 4.3.10; cf. the similar passage at 3.8.5.6–9, also (probably) using *paignion* of the products of art.

domain of material phenomena.[15] At the same time, because all reality allows the possibility of turning upward and self-assimilation, via contemplation, to a higher level of being, even a "plaything" can have value. If Plotinus can explicitly say, in subtle modification of the *Symposium*, that those who have experienced noncorporeal beauty do not repudiate bodily beauty, because they recognize it as a "plaything," a kind of existential echo, of that higher beauty (3.5.1.62), then his description of mimetic artworks as "playthings" need not demote them below the level at which they might make some contribution to a truth-seeking life of contemplation.

But the presence of some ambivalence in Plotinus's attitudes to mimetic art is more salient at 5.9.11.1–6. Here he refers to a group of arts—painting, sculpture, dance,[16] mime—which he describes as using perceptible models (*paradeigmata*) and offering representations of visible forms and movements, but therefore as lacking access to the noetic realm, the realm of pure intellect. He does go on, however, to say that an art that rose from the properties of particular natural forms to natural forms in general *could* contribute to a process of noetic contemplation, and he explicitly ascribes some such capacity to the art of music, though this is owing to its quasi-mathematical character not to any mimetic component that he may or may not have recognized in it. Here, then, Plotinus seems more guarded than at 5.8.1 about the extent to which mimetic art can transcend a nonphilosophical, a merely spatiotemporal, view of the world. But these two passages, and even the "murky and weak *mimēmata*" of 4.3.10, can be harmonized if we take Plotinus to envisage a spectrum of mimetic art, running from the less to the more "idealistic." At 4.3.10 and 5.9.11 he appears to accept that much art is immersed in a humanly interesting subject matter that exhibits no aspiration to the contemplation of higher truths. At 5.8.1 (interestingly, the latest of these three treatises), on the other hand, he stresses the possibility of treating the beauty embodied in (some) mimetic works as a pointer to the formative principles, *logoi*, which run back, via the artist's conception and his art itself, toward a more-than-human source, though his only example of what this might amount to in artistic practice is a disappointingly trite one, Phidias's statue of Zeus at Olympia.

In all the passages so far cited Plotinus takes visual art, whether pictorial or plastic, as his main reference point for mimesis. In part this betokens

[15] *Paignion* is used repeatedly of human life, with its picture of constant killing, in 3.2.15; it is applied to all the phenomena that appear in material guise at 3.6.7.23.

[16] We learn more about Plotinus's view of, and apparent passion for, dance from the way he uses it memorably as metaphor in 3.2.16–17, 4.4.33–34, 6.1.27; cf. 6.7.7.17 (where a dancer is said to be given a "scenario," *drama*), and see Ferwerda 1965, 183–86. The idea of the dancer "making himself into everything" (6.1.27.20) is presumably synonymous with mimesis: passages such as Plato *Rep.* 3.397a–b, 398a1–2, 10.596c, and *Soph.* 233d–34b may have been at the back of Plotinus's mind here; cf. chapter 4, section III.

the larger fact that the general model of mimesis which pervades his meta-physics is heavily (though, of course, metaphorically) visual, at any rate in the sense that it is closely correlated, and often practically synonymous, with the language of the "image" (*eikōn*).[17] But this same point might also prompt a particular question and a further line of inquiry. The largest number of mimetic arts named by Plotinus is at 5.9.11 (mentioned earlier), where he specifies painting, sculpture, dance, and mime.[18] It is notable that neither here nor anywhere else does Plotinus explicitly mention poetry as a mimetic art—hence, a fortiori, he never avails himself directly of either of Plato's discussions of poetic mimesis in the *Republic*, even though he was undoubtedly familiar with those two stretches of the work.[19] But among his references to Homer, most of which take the form of brief quotation or allusion,[20] there is one, at 1.6.8.17–20 (the earliest of the treatises), where he cites Odysseus's decision to leave behind Circe and Calypso, despite the pleasures they offered, as instances of allegories of the soul's need to rise above the sphere of the corporeal. Now, it would be rash to infer that Plotinus simply did not consider poetry to be a mimetic art at all; the verb *mimeisthai* at 3.2.17.32, within an elaborate analogy between drama and life,[21] establishes that he recognized dramatic poetry, at least, as mimetic. But the idea of an allegorical interpretation of Odysseus's departure from Circe and Calypso broaches the possibility that Plotinus might have accommodated poetry to his idealized model of mimesis at 5.8.1 precisely by treating allegorical meaning as at any rate one poetic means of access to the underlying principles, the *logoi*, of nature. If 5.8.1 redefines the character of mimesis in terms of something more than a correspondence to appearances, then it is conceivable that Plotinus would have treated poetry as mimetic not so much for its vivid depiction of life as for its potential to gesture, and guide the mind, beyond the human to the higher zones of reality.

[17] Passages where mimesis and image are equivalent include 2.9.8.16–29, 3.7.11.28–29, 6.2.22.36–46. Armstrong 1988 gives one reading of Plotinus's metaphysics of images.

[18] Plotinus seems to presuppose a grouping of visual, verbal, and musical arts at the start of 1.6.1, but there is no reference to mimesis in that context. Even so, it would not be stretching things much to connect the discussion of beauty there with the discussion of beauty arising from (mimetic) form at 5.8.1, and thus to infer that Plotinus could readily have accepted the full gamut of mimetic arts.

[19] See Henry & Schwyzer 1982, 356, 358, for Plotinus's references to those parts of the dialogue. Cf. my note 8 for one tacit Plotinean modification of the argument of *Rep.* 10 on mimesis.

[20] Lamberton 1986, 90–107, provides an interesting discussion of the attitudes lying behind Plotinus's references to Homer.

[21] The analogy with drama appears first at 3.2.11.13–16, then becomes a leitmotif in 3.2.15–18; Plotinus here treats a conventional image with an intricacy that suggests firsthand experience of the theater; see Ferwerda 1965, 180–83, and Kokolakis 1960, 65–67, whose book

Given the paucity of Plotinus's references to poetry, it is not feasible to test the hypothesis just stated; but one other passage may have some bearing on it. After his grandiloquent description, at 6.9.11, of mystical union with the One (a condition lying "beyond beauty" and involving "a different mode of seeing" [*allos tropos tou idein*], yet equivalent, in another sense, to "nothing"), Plotinus says of his own metaphors, "these are all mimetic reflections [*mimēmata*]" (6.9.11.26–27), explaining that this is why the wise resort to allegory to try to convey "how that god is seen" in the highest state of contemplation. Plotinus invokes allegory (designated by *ainigma*, *ainittesthai*, never by *allēgor-* terms) in a number of other places in his essays,[22] including his reference to the *Odyssey* at 1.6.8; but what is not entirely clear at 6.9.11 is the relationship between mimesis and allegory. Although some sort of contrast seems to be involved, it is arguable that Plotinus is thinking of allegory not as simply distinct from mimesis, as Proclus was to do two centuries later,[23] but as working *through*, and adding deeper significance to, mimetic images of the world. After all, Plotinus's general metaphysics of mimesis, as outlined earlier, functions as a way of linking up different modes and elements of reality—a way, in other words, of passing between different levels of being and experience. If that is so, then it tallies with my suggestion that allegoresis was one way in which Plotinus would have adapted the idealist aesthetic of 5.8.1, where mimesis is not rejected but redefined, to literary texts.

If Plotinus's disinclination to pursue such an adaptation in any detail leaves us with inevitable inconclusiveness, we can perhaps glimpse beyond this point to a deeper uncertainty about his aesthetics, and one that reflects his relationship to the earlier philosophical tradition. That tradition, above all as embodied in the *Timaeus* but reaching back to the early Pythagoreans too, supplied Plotinus with the possibility of a thoroughly metaphysical concept of mimesis,[24] though the extent of his development of such a concept, as well as his partial application of it to mimetic art, went decisively further than any precedent. On the other hand, the philo-

---

gives a rudimentary survey of "all the world's a stage" imagery in antiquity; cf. chapter 3, note 13.

[22] He applies it to the interpretation of myth (4.3.14, 5.8.4.25–26, 6.9.9.31–32), the mysteries (1.6.6.3–5, 3.6.19.25–41, 5.1.7.33–36), and the work of Plato himself (3.4.5, 6.2.22.1–14); but it has often been noted that 4.3.14.17–19 suggests a somewhat cavalier attitude to allegorical interpretation.

[23] See, however, my subsequent argument that even Proclus does not suppose the mimetic function of poetry to be entirely suspended when allegory is in operation.

[24] Plotinus echoes, though hardly reproduces, an element of the Pythagorean heritage in his view that numbers involve mimesis of their origin in the One (5.5.4.21). He draws on the *Timaeus* (a work he echoes more than any other) for a mimetic model of the cosmos at, e.g., 2.9.8.16–29, 3.6.7.27–30; cf. my note 3, with chapter 4, notes 22, 53. On metaphysical mimesis, cf. my introduction, note 34, and chapter 9, notes 30–33.

sophicocritical tradition as a whole, not least in Plato's own writings, had
established the idea of artistic mimesis as tied to an anthropocentric perspective on the world, a perspective that views things at the level of physical perception, of embodied life, of human actions, desires, and emotions.
These two very different elements in the tradition have both left a mark
on Plotinus's thought, and the relation between them is inescapably a matter of tension. Plotinus recognizes that most mimetic art necessarily involves prima facie representations of imagined life in the material, phenomenal world. At the same time, he touches on the possibility, at any
rate at 5.8.1, of finding intimations of a higher, spiritualized reality within
the images of art. What this surely means, in the final reckoning, is that
the ambivalence discernible in Plotinus's references to art is a symptom of
an ambivalence in his system of thought as a whole, an ambivalence that
keeps Plotinean philosophy caught between ultimately irreconcilable ideals of "flight" from the merely physical and, on the other hand, a commitment to finding the echo of higher realities in what it continues to regard
as the rich and multiform "tapestry" of life itself.[25] Plotinus's body and soul,
like those of the Homeric Heracles to whom he refers on several occasions,
are not always in the same place.[26]

Despite the partly unanswered questions posed by the view of mimetic
art I have traced in the *Enneads*, Plotinus had done enough to create two
possible lines of influence on later thinkers in aesthetics. The first and
more obvious was his idealized model of mimesis at 5.8.1, whose claim
that the arts could make contact with the underlying principles of nature
was to prove attractive to Neoplatonizing theorists in the Renaissance and
to others who found congenial a sense of art's powers of spiritual revelation. The second, more radical possibility was of going beyond Plotinus's
own explicit remarks on mimetic representation and applying his larger
model of metaphysical contemplation, in ways he seems never to have
envisaged himself, to the experience of artistic beauty. This second possibility, absorbed into a complex convergence of currents in the history of
ideas, was ultimately to be realized within the specific trajectory of thought
that culminated in eighteenth-century models of aesthetic experience as
the disinterested contemplation of pure beauty.[27] Both these influences,

[25] Life produces its many beautiful forms as though by embroidery (*poikillein*): 3.2.15.32.
(Cf. Carlyle's expression, "tapestry of human life," in *Sartor Resartus* 1.10.) Clark 1996 bravely
attempts a positive account of Plotinus's dualism of body and soul.

[26] Plotinus refers to the Heracles of *Od.* 11.601–2 at 1.1.12.31–39, 4.3.27; cf. 6.4.16.40–43,
and see Lamberton 1986, 100–02.

[27] Plotinus's influence on aesthetics has recurrently been a ghostly presence, easier to
sense than to pin down. His affinities with, but lack of direct influence on, late ancient,
Byzantine, and medieval art are explored by Grabar 1945 and Mathew 1963, 17–22. On Neoplatonist aesthetic currents in the Renaissance, to which Plotinus was a real but partly indirect

which allowed Plotinus the Platonist to serve as a counterweight to Plato's own supposed hostility to art, may seem somewhat paradoxical if we reflect that Plotinus himself, unlike Plato, betrays little that could be called a passion for art, despite the occasional enthusiasm detectable in some of his references to dance, drama, and painting. But if this is a paradox, it reflects the circumstance that Plotinus's importance in the history of aesthetics stems less from his direct treatment of artistic representation than from the ways in which he made available a more comprehensive and metaphysically laden ideal of contemplation that others were subsequently able to appropriate for their own purposes.

II

Proclus, active in Athens from the 430s to 480s, and scholarch of the Academy for most of that period, has left us the most elaborate Neoplatonic attempt to reinterpret Plato's evaluation of poetry and thereby to bring about a rapprochement between philosophy and poetry. Among Proclus's prolific output is a "commentary" on the *Republic*, consisting of a series of essays or lectures on various aspects of the work. Proclus's analysis of the treatment of poetry in books 2–3 and book 10 of the *Republic* (but with extensive reference to other dialogues too) amounts to the longest stretch of the entire commentary. But it consists of two distinct lectures, the fifth and sixth in the series, which adopt rather different standpoints toward the major issues in Plato's critiques of poetry, not least the issue of mimesis.[28]

In the shorter lecture (i.e., the fifth) it is a general premise of Proclus, and one he evidently thinks is accepted by Plato himself, that all poetry is mimetic: he makes this point quite explicitly, more than once.[29] Proclus holds this position despite his awareness of Plato's use of the term mimesis in *Republic* 3 for one particular mode of poetry (the dramatic or enactive mode), but he is likely to have been influenced by his knowledge that this

---

contributor, see, e.g., Panofsky 1962, 129–230; Gombrich 1972, 31–81, 123–95; Allen 1999; for the case of Michelangelo, cf. my note 1. A later instance, Plotinus's influence on Goethe, is cited in my introduction, note 13. Abrams 1989, 20, 154, 167, notes Plotinus's significance for the course of ideas leading to the eighteenth century's concept of the distinterested contemplation of beauty.

[28] Sheppard 1980 gives excellent overall guidance to the character of the two essays; Lamberton 1986, 162–232 (cf. Lamberton 1992 for a briefer account) puts the sixth essay in the larger context of Proclus's work as an allegorist, though his almost total neglect of the fifth essay is regrettable (see, e.g., 188, where his remarks on Proclus's mimetic vocabulary are inconsistent with the fifth essay).

[29] The most straightforward statement of the premise is at 1.44.1–2 (all references to Proclus's commentary are to volume, pages, and lines of Kroll, 1899–1901), even though he is there discussing *Rep.* 2–3 (cf. my note 30). See also 1.67.12–13, 18 (the latter citing *Laws* 2.667c).

is the only passage in Plato where that specialized usage occurs.[30] But if in summarizing the critique of poetry in *Republic* 2–3 Proclus technically departs from Plato's own use of mimetic terminology as defined at 392d, he does so to allow mimesis to function as a comprehensive category of poetic representation in a way that is true to the larger thrust of Plato's work, including the treatment of mimesis in the *Laws*.[31] Thus, as we shall shortly see, Proclus translates the distinctions between true and false (or accurate and inaccurate), good and bad, in *Republic* 2–3 into distinctions within the whole field of representation; in doing so he shows a firm grasp of the overall concerns, both cognitive and ethical, that underlie this portion of Plato's text, even though he chooses to leave on one side book 3's investigation into the particular psychological implications of the dramatic or enactive mode of poetry, the "mimetic" mode in the restricted sense. Moreover, while he maintains the traditional link between mimesis and "likeness," Proclus does not here tie mimesis to a literalist or veridical standard: if a poem or painting[32] gives an unreliable or ethically objectionable picture of the world, it still counts, in his terms, as a mimetic work. The consequences of this point for Proclus's position cannot, however, be described as aesthetically generous. Apart from one moment of quasi-Aristotelian "anthropology," where he records the principle that "our minds naturally take pleasure in mimetic works, which is the reason why we are all fond of stories [*philomuthoi*],"[33] Proclus shows no inclination to liberate artistic mimesis from strict philosophical requirements of truth and morality. What matters to him is to bring the evaluation of poetry into line with a philosophical understanding of the world, and we can best see what this means for his concept of mimesis by observing how he reworks the particular line of argument in *Republic* 2–3 that focuses on the poetic depiction of heroes and gods.

[30] Proclus invokes the tripartite scheme (mimetic, narrative, mixed) of *Rep.* 3.392c–94c (cf. chapter 5, note 44) at *In Remp.* 1.14.15–15.19, when discussing the form of Plato's own dialogue; but he almost entirely ignores that passage elsewhere: the only other references to it are at 1.66.19–26, where Proclus almost immediately restores a general sense of mimesis at 1.67.7, 12–25, and 1.160.16–25; 1.163.21 may be an oblique allusion. Proclus could have noticed that elsewhere in *Rep.* 2–3 Plato uses the category of poetic mimesis more flexibly in several passages, esp. 3.388c3: cf. chapter 1, note 35, with note 34 here.

[31] Proclus refers to the *Laws* in direct connection with the broader conception of mimesis at 1.46.5–7, 67.17–21.

[32] Proclus introduces an analogy with painting at 1.46.3–7.

[33] *In Remp.* 1.46.14–15. The first part of this (and cf. the following reference to childhood mimesis, 46.15) need not show direct knowledge of Aristotle's *Poetics*; Proclus probably knew Aristotle's *On Poets*, to which 1.49.17–18 is likely to be an allusion (fr. 81 Rose, fr. 921 Gigon 1987, who treats it as of uncertain origin; see Janko 1987, 186; Laurenti 1984, 58–63; Laurenti 1987, 1:258–64; Sheppard 1980, 110–13). The word *philomuthoi* is an echo of Aristotle *Met.* 1.2, 982b18.

Employing, as already remarked, a more general concept of mimesis than the one developed at *Republic* 392c ff., Proclus states the nub of Plato's case as follows. All poetry is mimetic, and poetic mimesis can be defective in one of two ways: either by presenting its subjects without likeness or similarity (*anhomoiōs*) or, while achieving such likeness, presenting a shifting diversity (*poikilia*) of character and behavior that, by means of psychological assimilation (the effect of all mimesis), will produce comparable characteristics in the audience.[34] At first glance, it may look as though we have here a pair of distinct criteria, one of accuracy or likeness and the other of moral quality. But the situation is more complex, in a way that is related to Proclus's source text in the *Republic* itself.[35] The concept of mimesis that fails to achieve likeness or accuracy is taken directly from *Republic* 2.388c3, where the adverb *anhomoiōs* is correlated with *anaxiōs* "unworthily" (388d3). Although the Platonic Socrates accepts that poetry about gods and heroes lacks an exact model and must therefore be in a certain sense false or fictional (*pseudos, pseudēs*), he takes it as an indefeasible stipulation that the divine should be portrayed as wholly good, uncontaminated by quasi-human vices. So "likeness" or accuracy is here a matter of adherence or conformity to a theological tenet; and because that tenet is inescapably ethical, mimetic "likeness" must be construed here ethically too. But much the same is true of heroes as well, for as "children of the gods" they are to be thought of (supposedly) as paradigms of excellence.

It turns out, then, that if "likeness" encompasses factors of both truth and morality, truth itself is in effect conceived of in ethically normative terms. It is this intertwining of considerations that Proclus attempts to reproduce. He repeats the Platonic requirement that poetry must tell fine or good (*kalos*) "falsehoods" or "fictions" about the gods, and he stresses the accompanying need for depictions of heroes as virtuous. However, he partly confuses the matter by inconsistency. His initial statement of the two main species of poetic faults mentioned earlier is blurred, not to say contradicted, by his subsequent pronouncement that the depiction of psychological variation in human characters is itself one way in which poetry may fail to achieve "likeness."[36] Relatedly, he claims that Plato criticized

---

[34] *In Remp.* 1.43.26–47.19; *anhomoiōs* picks up Plato *Rep.* 3.388c3 (where it is pertinent that the verb *mimeisthai* has a broader sense than at 3.392d: see chapter 1, note 35); cf. Proclus's use of this notion at *In Tim.* 1.265.10–16 (Diehl 1903–6). On Plato's concept of *poikilia*, see chapter 2, note 47. In the longer essay, at 1.160.25–161.14, Proclus remarks that *poikilia* of mimetic characterization is a feature of Plato's own work.

[35] See chapter 1, esp. section II.

[36] *In Remp.* 1.46.7–10. In the summing-up at 1.47.14–19 Proclus reverts to his initial dichotomy (with *alēthōs*, "tru(thful)ly," corresponding to *homoiōs*, "in keeping with likeness/accuracy," at 1.44.4).

poetic representations of the gods for diverging from the truth in bad ways
(*ou kalōs pseudesthai*), but criticized representations of heroes for diverging from the truth (*pseudesthai*) *simpliciter*, whereas no such distinction
is to be found in Plato's own text.[37] What these details indicate, I believe,
is that Proclus has imperfectly grasped the complex relationship between
truth-related and ethical criteria in *Republic* 2–3's scrutiny of poetry. More
specifically, he has failed to see that Plato's argument both allows the notion of "falsehood" (*pseudos*) to operate partly as a concept of fiction, and
moves tacitly between distinct levels of what, in a previous chapter, I
called narrative and normative veracity.[38]

Despite this shortcoming, there is no doubt that in the fifth essay Proclus
takes over from Plato, and remains broadly faithful to the spirit of, an
attitude to poetry that relies on overriding standards of philosophical truth,
morality, and psychological benefit. But when we turn from the shorter to
the longer essay, we encounter a much more complex situation, one in
which an overt depreciation of poetic mimesis is accompanied by a positive revaluation of certain specimens of the art. Where the shorter essay is
mostly limited to an attempt to make sense of Plato's own arguments, the
longer is informed by a deep desire to vindicate poetry, above all Homeric
poetry, against the ethical, theological, and other imputations ostensibly
brought against it in Plato's writings. Proclus's strategy here is twofold: to
show that there is more to poetry than its literal meaning; and to show
that there is more to Plato's view of poetry than certain statements in the
dialogues might at first suggest. The first part of this strategy hinges on a
hermeneutics of allegory, while the second seeks to piece together a complex Platonic theory of poetry by blending elements from different parts
of his oeuvre. The ultimate aim is to merge Homer and Plato, poetry and
philosophy, into a synthesis of Neoplatonic insight and revelation. This
sophisticated if tendentious ambition is partly held together by Proclus's
acute sense of Plato's own indebtedness to Homer: Homer, he says in one
passage of fine eloquence, "is the teacher not only of tragedy" (a reference
to *Republic* 10.595c1–2) "but also of Plato's own entire use of mimesis and
his whole philosophical system."[39] Where Nietzsche was to see ultimate

---

[37] *In Remp.* 1.44.23–45.6: n.b. the negative *ou* has dropped out of Kroll's text before the
last word of 1.44.24 (see Kroll 1899–1901, 2:472, cf. Festugière 1970, 1:63); Rangos 1999, 252,
misses this and therefore garbles the context. *Rep.* 2.377d–e, referring to non-*kalos* falsehood
or fiction about *both* gods and heroes, shows Proclus to be simply wrong on this point; cf.,
likewise, Plato's use of the verb *katapseudesthai* (to denigrate falsely) in both cases (2.381d5,
3.391d3). It is important, indeed, that *Rep.* 2–3 never complains about *pseudesthai* pure and
simple, unlike some other Platonic texts, including *Laws* 2.668d, which Proclus interestingly
cites for something like a distinction between factual or perceptual and ethical likeness at
1.46.1–7 (where the analogy with painting is very unhelpful).

[38] See chapter 1, section II.

[39] *In Remp.* 1.196.9–13 (cf. chapter 2, note 29).

antagonism between the great poet and the great philosopher ("Plato gegen Homer: das ist der ganze, der ächte Antagonismus"),[40] Proclus perceives a pair of profoundly kindred spirits.

How, then, does this longer lecture engage with mimesis? It does so, in the section of which the sentence just quoted forms the conclusion, by placing it at the bottom of a tripartite hierarchy of poetic types: the inspired, the knowledge-based, and the mimetic (which is further subdivided, as shortly to be explained). This scheme marks a fundamental step outside the framework of the previous lecture, because it involves the abandonment of the earlier premise that *all* poetry is mimetic. Whether this difference is to be understood entirely as a development in Proclus's thinking is uncertain. Particularly pertinent here is a passage in the shorter lecture that stresses a distinction made in Plato's *Phaedrus* between inspired and uninspired poetry.[41] Proclus foregrounds this point when surveying different Platonic conceptions of *mousikē*, and he appears to reach the conclusion that only uninspired poetry is to be reckoned as mimetic, leaving the inspired kind on a higher level.[42] If this is right, it suggests that Proclus may already have had available to him, when writing the shorter lecture, a distinction between mimetic and "superior" types of poetry. In that case the best inference would be that the relatively expository level of the shorter lecture leads him to adhere to a broadly traditional version of poetic mimesis, with the exception of the one passage I have cited. Because the worldview and methodology of Neoplatonism is in all respects hierarchical, this would effectively mean that whether one talks about poetry in terms of mimesis depends on the level of intellectual insight that is being sought. For Proclus, it is only within the more ambitious and "theological" scope of the longer lecture that he needs, and can afford, to make explicit his tripartite scheme of poetic types, together with the demotion of mimesis entailed by this scheme.[43]

That scheme is set out at considerable length. It stems from a tripartite hierarchy of lives: the "divine" life, in which the soul is joined to the divine realm by assimilation; the "middle" life, in which human reason and knowledge contemplate the noetic essences of reality; and the inferior life, in which the soul fails to rise above the sphere of sense impressions.

---

[40] *Die Genealogie der Moral* 3.25 (Nietzsche 1988, 5:402–3); cf. chapter 2, note 1 for another part of this same passage.

[41] *In Remp.* 1.56.23–58.10, citing Plato *Phdr.* 245a and 248d.

[42] See 1.60.6–13.

[43] Compare the fact that there are allusions to allegorical interpretation, but no use of this method, in the shorter lecture: see 1.44.14, 19–20, with Sheppard 1980, 16–18, who stresses, however (18–20, 96), important differences between the inspired-uninspired distinction as it appears in the two essays, and makes a detailed case (15–38) for seeing a developmental relationship between the two pieces.

Corresponding to these lives are the three types of poetry, all of which, Proclus claims, are referred to as such in Platonic texts: first, divinely inspired poetry, which Proclus traces back especially to *Phaedrus* 245a and the *Ion*; second, knowledge-based poetry, which is full of virtue and therefore has didactic or educative value, and which Proclus finds acknowledged in the idea of Theognis's political sagacity at *Laws* 1.630a; and, third, mimetic poetry.[44] Proclus defines mimetic poetry in terms of the world of the senses, the world of "phenomena," which is effectively both the empirical-material domain and, more generally, the readily accessible domain of human impressions or imaginings (*phantasiai*), (insecure) beliefs (*doxai*), and emotions (*pathē*).[45] He proceeds, however, to subdivide the mimetic into the two species recognized in Plato's *Sophist*, the eicastic (or accurately proportional), which can be aligned with "correct belief," and the phantastic (or viewer-dependent), which is lowest of all and is taken by Proclus to be the target in the first part of *Republic* 10.[46] As a Homeric instance of phantastic-mimetic poetry Proclus mentions certain descriptions of sunrise and sunset, including *Odyssey* 3.1–2, which do not capture the truth about the world but only the way things appear to our senses. As an example of eicastic mimesis in Homer he cites the representation of the actions and (virtuous) characters of the heroes. But it is essential to Proclus's position to contend that Homer, the great inspired poet in whom the allegorical method can discover revelations of philosophicotheological truth, is only "mimetic" at all when this is unavoidable. To find poetry that is mimetic, indeed "phantastic," through and through, Proclus declares that we must turn to tragedy, a genre that aims only at the emotional thrills of its public and which is accordingly immersed in the realm of a purely human sensibility. Proclus, whose whole enterprise in this area thrives on explaining away difficulties, is not greatly disturbed at this stage by the fact that Plato had called Homer himself the "teacher" and "leader" of the tragedians.[47]

Proclus's demotion of mimesis in the longer essay on poetry is integral to his strategy of elevating parts of Homer's work onto the plane of philo-

[44] The three lives are classified at 1.177.7–178.5, followed by lengthy analysis of the three types of poetry, 1.178.6–196.13. For the influence of this tripartite hierarchy on Sir Philip Sidney's poetics, see chapter 12, note 4.

[45] Proclus connects "imagination" (*phantasia*) closely with emotion: see esp. 2.107.26–29, in a passage on the appeal exercised by the literal content of myths (cf. Sheppard 1980, 157–58). Consult Watson 1988a, 119–26, and Sheppard 1995 on the place of *phantasia* in Proclus's thinking as a whole.

[46] Eicastic/phantastic: 1.179.18–32, 188.28–192.3, etc., with Plato *Soph.* 235d–6c (see chapter 1, section III). For Proclus's view that *Rep.* 10 is an attack on phantastic mimesis, see esp. 1.196.18–199.28.

[47] *Rep.* 10.595c1–2, 598d8 (cf. 605c11, 607a3), with *In Remp.* 1.195.21–196.13, 203.1–205.14. On Plato's conception of Homer as a tragic poet see chapter 3, esp. section II.

sophical theology itself. The thesis that mimesis is trapped in a world of mere impressions ("all mimesis is tied to appearances [*phainomena*], not to the truth," 1.162.23–24) is the price that supposedly has to be paid for finding intimations of ultimate truth in the finest poetry. This strategy brings with it a contrast between symbols (*sumbola*), the instruments of inspired poetry, and mimesis.[48] The contrast is expressed most resoundingly at 1.198.13–19, where Proclus, after reiterating his view that *Republic* 10's critique of poetic mimesis is aimed at tragedy and comedy, not at Homer, proceeds: "How could poetry that conveys the divine through symbols be called 'mimetic'? Symbols are not mimetic representations of the things they symbolize. Opposites could never be the medium of mimesis. . . . But symbolic contemplation actually reveals the nature of things through complete opposites." The disjunction is apparently absolute. But there are two complicating factors that call for some attention at this juncture.

First, because the categories used in the tripartite hierarchy of types of poetry function evaluatively, and not simply descriptively, they do not exclude the possibility that the same passage or work could count as belonging theoretically in more than one of these categories. The most important implication of this point for my argument is that nothing in Proclus's longer essay requires the supposition that the higher forms of poetry—the inspired, and also the didactic or educative—are not also, when viewed from a certain angle, mimetic or representational.[49] This can be regarded as in part a proposition about interpretation: not simply the poetic work but also the mind of the interpreter will determine the level at which the poetry can and should be read.[50] This principle is also needed in order to keep a sufficient degree of compatibility between Proclus's fifth and sixth essays, because we have seen that it is an unquestioned premise of the former that all poetry is mimetic (though there mimesis is a descrip-

---

[48] For Proclus, "symbols" (*sumbola, sunthēmata*) are not arbitrary or merely conventional signs, but tokens whose significance reflects a system of cosmic connections or "sympathy": see Sheppard 1980, ch. 4, esp. 145–46, 151–53; cf. Coulter 1976, 43–45, 60–68.

[49] Sheppard 1980, 97, 182–83, 187, while accepting that inspired poetry remains, for Proclus, "representational," insists that "didactic" does not (though this leads her into a tangle regarding didactic and myth, 193–94). This can hardly be right: first, because the Homeric material encompassed by the "didactic" type at 1.192.12–15, 193.4–9, must include passages of narrative or dramatic presentation (such as the description of Heracles at *Od.* 11.601 ff.), and to that extent would count as representational, i.e., mimetic, at any rate in the terms of the fifth essay; second, because 1.199.23–28, 1.201.5–8 (see my note 55) specifically countenance mimesis in the educative-didactic type (a detail overlooked by Lamberton 1986, 191). Note that the idea of "teaching" (*didaskein*) cannot in itself mark off the didactic type: Proclus uses the verb of *both* inspired and "didactic" poetry (e.g., 1.193.5, 11).

[50] Proclus makes this point quite explicitly at 1.76.24–77.6, juxtaposing and coupling differentiation between types of poetry with differentiation between the minds of their potential audiences.

tive, not an evaluative category). Nor should it be overlooked that the
tenet that all poetry is mimetic reappears in the summary of *Republic* 10
given in the fifteenth essay of the commentary;[51] Proclus evidently finds it
easy to slip back into this assumption. Even in the sixth essay itself, the
existence of a mimetic dimension to all poetry (and/or its interpretation)
manifests itself from time to time. It emerges in a series of remarks on the
mimetic vividness and richness of Homeric poetry, often accompanied by
the observation that the same qualities are to be found in Plato's own
work. An example is the statement that the "multiform" (*polueidēs*) nature
of mimesis, reflecting a constantly changing, "imagistic" (*eidōlikē*) perspective, gives grounds for expelling *both* Homer's *and* Plato's work from
the "first" (i.e., ideal) state (*politeia*), though not for denying them any
value within less perfect states (163.1–9). In this acknowledgment, albeit
couched in low-key terms, of the representational richness (and, with it,
the diverse human interest) of what is, for Proclus, the "surface" of both
Homer's and Plato's text,[52] the wording of the passage leaves a pronounced impression that such surface constitutes a general feature, rather
than just one kind, of Homeric poetry. This impression is heightened by
the more positive and revealing formulation that follows soon, when Proclus describes Plato's use of dialogue as "woven on the model of Homeric
mimesis" and praises the comparable "vividness" (*enargeia*) of both writers: "their use of mimesis moves our imagination [*phantasia*] in every way,
changes our beliefs, and molds us to the events they present, so that many
readers weep with the wailing Apollodorus, and many share the grief of
Achilles as he laments his friend. . . . We seem to be present at the events
represented, thanks to the vivid impression [*phantasia*] arising from the
mimesis."[53]

Despite, then, the dominant emphasis of the longer essay on the higher
truths symbolically conveyed by the inspired mode of Homeric poetry,
Proclus seems to intimate in passages such as those just quoted[54] that mi-

[51] This essay, in summarizing four stages in book 10's critique of poetic mimesis, nowhere
suggests that the category of the mimetic is limited to certain kinds of poetry: quite the reverse, esp. at 2.87.8–10.

[52] As regards the contrast between textual surface and depth, note Proclus's metaphor of
"the interior" (*to entos*) of a myth or story at 1.85.22.

[53] *In Remp.* 1.163.19–164.7: "Apollodorus" is a reference to Plato *Phaedo* 59a, 117d (cf.
Halliwell 1984, 57–58); on the motif of seeming to be present at the events themselves, see
my introduction, note 48; on *enargeia*, chapter 10, note 23. Proclus calls Plato "most mimetic"
(*mimētikōtatos*), for his treatment of character in dialogue, at *In Crat.* 14 (p. 5.17 Pasquali).

[54] Cf. also 1.171.10 ff. For a parallel in the shorter essay, see the reference to *zōtikēn hom-
oiōsin*, "lifelike likeness," at 1.46.9, which is paradoxically part of Proclus's statement about
anhomoian mimēsin, "inaccurate mimesis" (i.e., a use of representation that is both vivid
and yet philosophically objectionable); *zōtikos* was standardly used in praise of mimetic
verisimilitude: for an early instance, see Xenophon *Mem.* 3.10.6 (with chapter 4, note 17);

mesis is nonetheless, as the fifth essay suggested, an integral, defining, mark of poetry, and that the three types of poetry, *qua* different levels or aspects of meaning, as well as different levels of interpretation, can in principle coexist in the same parts of the same text. This inference is corroborated by one or two passages that specifically countenance the simultaneous practice of mimesis and one of the other types of poetry.[55] In practice, however, Proclus does mostly use different passages to illustrate the separate presence of the three types of poetry in Homer, because it is no part of his brief to try actively to demonstrate the coexistence of which I have just spoken: his tripartite scheme remains resolutely hierarchical, and he is not committed to preaching the virtues of being simultaneously "inspired" and "mimetic." Indeed, a few passages of the commentary might be cited in support of the view that the three types are understood as confined to distinct parts of the text.[56] This is particularly true of 1.195.20–21, where we hear that "the mimetic and phantastic element" has been "removed" (*exhērēsthai*), except insofar as it is absolutely necessary, from Homer's poetry. If there are traces here of a certain ambivalence in Proclus's stance, the explanation, I suggest, must lie in the fact that within the totality of his treatment of poetry mimesis is *both* a descriptive *and* an evaluative concept. In the first respect, as seen principally in the shorter lecture, it serves to characterize the general representational status of poetry (as well as Platonic dialogue); in the second, it functions as the lowest rung on the ladder of poetic types.

A second complicating factor, a further layer of uncertainty, affects Proclus's conception of mimesis. Given his ostensibly absolute distinction between mimesis and symbolism (1.198.13–19, quoted earlier), it is puzzling that there are passages in the commentary that blur this distinction. The most conspicuous case is at 1.77.13–24, where Proclus has the following to say about "the fathers of myth-making [*muthopoiïa*]": Homer and Hesiod "observed that nature herself, in producing images of immaterial and noetic forms and embroidering this cosmos with mimetic representations of

---

later, e.g., Callistratus *Imag.* 2.3, 5.4, 7.2, 8.1, with chapter 10, note 44, and Plotinus *Enn.* 6.7.22.30 (though Plotinus's metaphysics of beauty goes beyond lifelikeness: cf. Mathew 1963, 17–19).

[55] See esp. 1.199.23–28, 1.201.5–8, where mimesis is said to be compatible with knowledge, which is part of the second, educative type of poetry; cf. too the explanation of how Homer can be *both* "divine" *and* "third from the truth" (1.204.8–11), or the same myth be "daimonic" on the surface, "divine" in its inner revelation (1.78.25–79.4). Note too, though somewhat differently, 1.152.9–11, 25–26, referring to the mimesis of actions that are in themselves "symbolic"; cf. Sheppard 1980, 76. My point here, however, is quite different from the notion of "symbolic mimesis" found in Coulter 1976, 48, 51, which seems merely a confusion (cf. Sheppard 1980, 197 n. 97).

[56] This seems to be the view of Sheppard 1980, 195, who refers to "the mimetic parts of Homer's text."

those things, uses divided matter to make images of the indivisible, temporal media to image the eternal, and perceptible media to image the noetic. . . . So, following nature and the emanation of the world of phenomena and sense impressions, they too shape images of the gods in words that are opposite to, and far removed from, their objects, and by doing so make mimetic representations [*apomimountai*] of the transcendent power of their models."

What is so remarkable about this passage is that Proclus insistently employs the language of mimesis, and the traditionally associated language of image making, both for the relationship between the visible, material world and the realm of immaterial, eternal "forms," and for that between the poetic myths of Homer and Hesiod and the transcendent reality of the divine. If we were confronted only with the first, metaphorical part of the passage (where nature is a mimetic artisan), with its unmistakable echoes of the *Timaeus*,[57] it would still raise an awkward question about Proclus's concept of mimesis, because even as a metaphor the idea of mimetic imaging of the immaterial in material media, the eternal in the temporal, is prima facie incompatible with the depreciation of mimesis elsewhere as tied to the domain of sense impressions and the purely phenomenal. But this question is made all the more pressing by the application of mimeticist vocabulary to Homeric and Hesiodic poetry's creation of myths that contain, on Proclus's terms, veiled truths about the divine—an application that seems in flat contradiction of the disjunction between mimesis and symbolism later in the essay.[58] Furthermore, in the passage under consideration Proclus's argument appears to hint at a qualification of the proposition, stated at 1.76.20–24,[59] that mimesis is limited to materials involving a natural likeness, though that is the very view to which Proclus will later commit himself at 1.198.13–19. How are these tensions in the essay to be explained?

[57] On the *Timaeus*, see note 24, and cf. Proclus *In Remp.* 1.68.3–69.1 on Apollo, the "cosmic poet," who makes the visible into mimetic representations of the invisible (68.15–16), something elsewhere predicated of symbolism (2.242.24–25).

[58] *In Remp.* 1.198.13–19; cf. Sheppard 1980, 199, who seems to me to understate the difficulty. Note that the contradiction is even more glaring between 1.198.13–19 (mimesis versus symbols) and 1.83.29–30, where mimesis "*through* symbols" is mentioned (the fact that Proclus is discarding the proposition in question does not affect the logic of my point). The attempt of Rangos 1999, 261–70, to harmonize symbolism and mimesis in Proclus founders in part on the mistaken claim (265; likewise Janko 1998, 105) that poetry can ever, for Proclus, "imitate" the Platonic forms themselves: of the two passages cited by Rangos 265 n. 47, one (1.199.1–2) is specifically *contrasted* to mimesis, the other (paraphrasing Plato *Rep.* 10.599a) has no reference to the forms.

[59] *Contra* Sheppard 1980, 199, Festugière 1970, 1:94, I tentatively take that proposition to supply the hypothetical grounds for the view (1.76.17ff.) Proclus is addressing, not an essential premise of his own argument; the particle *dēpou* (76.20) may indicate a subtle note of reservation.

The explanation I favor entails an unstable interplay between Proclus's overriding goal—to elevate the finest, mostly Homeric, poetry to the domain of theological philosophy—and the different conceptions of mimesis found in Plato. The *Timaeus*, which is so evidently in Proclus's mind in the reference to nature's production of temporal images of the timeless, is a crucial element in this intersection of Proclean with Platonic thought, because in that work, though not there alone, Plato himself is prepared to use the language of mimesis with reference to the relationship between the material, temporal world and the realm of transcendent, unchanging reality.[60] As I argued in part I of this book, Plato's writings make use of shifting conceptions of mimesis, and the *Timaeus* employs the concept on the largest scale of all, treating it as a sort of key to the system of correspondences that supposedly connect and hold together different zones of reality, especially the noetic and the sensory. Proclus's own commentary on the *Timaeus* abundantly acknowledges that work's use of mimetic terms and models of explanation in metaphysical contexts. Nowhere does Proclus explicitly face up to the problem of correlating different Platonic applications of the language of mimesis, but his familiarity with the full spectrum of Platonic usage is likely to be the ultimate cause of those fluctuations to which I have drawn attention in the *Republic* commentary. Here, as I have argued, Proclus has both a broader (essentially descriptive) and a narrower (essentially evaluative) concept of mimesis: whereas the former leaves open the relationship between any mimetic work and its objects, the latter attaches mimesis to the phenomenal world of ordinary human experience. In speaking of Homer and Hesiod in the passage just quoted (1.77.13–24), Proclus allows himself to develop his mimeticist language in a way that echoes the *Timaeus* yet simultaneously preserves something of the wider, less prejudicial sense of poetic mimesis. The result is a notion of certain poetic works as quasi-natural microcosms.

I have tried to show that the longer essay on poetry in Proclus's *Republic* commentary is far from marking an escape from the supposed trammels of a mimetic theory of poetry. All in all, the essay is unequivocal in its ambition to raise Homer above the region of poetry that is merely of "human" interest, up to the plane of theological philosophy itself. But if we read it closely, it can hardly strike us as unequivocal about the consequences of this ambition for the mimetic language that Proclus had relied on so heavily in his shorter essay and now seems somewhat reluctant to abandon altogether. In terms of overt theory, Proclus accords little impor-

---

[60] Note the double occurrence of the verb *apomimeisthai* at *Tim.* 44d4, 88d1, which may have prompted its use by Proclus at 1.77.23. On the place of the *Timaeus*'s treatment of mimesis in relation to other Platonic works, see Halliwell 1986, 115–21, with chapter 4. Proclus's own commentary on the *Timaeus* is pervaded by the language of mimesis but in metaphysical applications that reflect the dialogue's own usage and hardly ever refer to mimetic art (see *In Tim.* 1.58.4–11, 1.64.2–6 [Diehl 1903–6], for two rare exceptions).

tance to the representational "surfaces" of mimetic works in their own right, and he devotes slight effort to elucidating the kinds of experience that such surfaces can afford the mind. Yet I have highlighted several passages that betray his underlying recognition that, for most readers at any rate, these surfaces, with all their "multiform" appeal to human values, cannot simply be treated as symbolic of deeper, nonhuman truths, because they continue to define the primary world into which the reader of the poems must enter. Within that world, all the old Platonic anxieties—anxieties encapsulated by Proclus's reference to weeping with Achilles—remain resolutely alive, no matter how hard Proclus may try to reconfigure mimesis in such a way as to silence them. If the grand venture of these essays is an attempt to redeem Homer while staying faithful to Plato, and to turn both figures into equal devotees of the divine, it is scarcely surprising that the audacity of the undertaking should have left some moments of precarious coherence in Proclus's text.

III

Close to the boundaries of the pagan traditions of criticism and philosophical aesthetics in antiquity lies an episode of cultural history that invites some tangential attention here for the traces it bears of older arguments about mimetic conceptions of art. The Iconoclast controversies of eighth- and ninth-century Byzantium obviously extend, in their full political and theological ramifications, well beyond the scope of my project. But they deserve brief consideration on account of their points of contact with older issues relating to the nature of images and, more particularly, because they form a kind of Christian counterpart to the Neoplatonist developments that the preceding sections of this chapter have addressed.[61] At the level of theologicophilosophical dispute, which was certainly only one dimension of the issue, Iconoclasm can be seen as the confluence of two streams of thought: one an old and recurrent Judeo-Christian anxiety regarding religious images, the other a Greek tradition of philosophical thought, especially in a Platonist mold, about the problematic relationship between images and their putative models or "originals." Christianity had inherited the concerns, especially about idolatry, embodied in the Judaic prohibition

---

[61] The literature on Iconoclasm is vast; among recent items that give a good sense of the range of religious, political, social, and cultural factors involved, as well as citing earlier scholarship, are Herrin 1987, 307–89, 417–24, 466–75; Pelikan 1990; Belting 1990, esp. 164–84; and Cameron 1992; Alexander 1958, 23–53, 189–213, and Ladner 1983, 35–111, examine the concepts of images at stake in the dispute, as does Freedberg 1989, 378–428, within a larger art-historical study of responses to images: none of these works, however, explores the links between Iconoclast controversies and the concept of mimesis as such.

on images in Exodus and other Old Testament texts,[62] but it nonetheless gradually developed, particularly in the post-Constantinian era, an extensive art and iconography of its own, much of it involving depictions of Christ himself. If the impossibility of truly imaging or representing the divine, of giving material shape to the immaterial, was an idea that could be found in some pagan as well as Judaic texts, the subject took on a new and problematic urgency because of the special doctrines of Christology.[63] In addition to refurbishing the old Judaic attack on idolatry, Byzantine Iconoclasts relied, theologically at any rate, on the argument from the impossibility of divine images. In Christ's case, according to this line of attack, any claim that his earthly existence made it feasible to depict him would imply a separation of his human from his divine nature and thus amount to Nestorian heresy.

As I have shown in preceding parts of this book, ancient mimeticism had opened up a large range of positions on the possible representational relationship between (mimetic) images and the world, including various types of expression, symbolism, and noniconic significance. The resulting spectrum stretches all the way from notions of mirroring, or the close fidelity to appearances of eicastic mimesis in Plato's *Sophist*, to, at the other end, the Neoplatonist theories examined earlier in this chapter, where the language both of mimesis and of images is applied to many ontological relationships that could not be construed in terms, or on the analogy, of strictly visual correspondence. The direct influence of any variety of pagan mimeticism on the Christian defenders of images is hard to trace. But elements of affinity and indirect influence can reasonably be identified in the most intellectually interesting of the iconophiles, John Damascene (c. 675–750). John effectively challenged the narrow assumption that an image needed to be understood in terms of strict equivalence. He argued, instead, for recognition of a more flexible sense of the power of images to signify beyond the limits of the visible, though even he necessarily accepted that images could depict only the incarnate form, not the true divinity, of Jesus.

[62] Exodus 20.4–5 (= Deuteronomy 5.8) combines a prohibition on idols with a general repudiation of image making: for the former, cf. 20.23, 34.17, Isaiah 40.18–20, 44.9–20; for the broader reference to images, cf. Leviticus 26.1, Deuteronomy 4.15–18, 4.23, 27.15. On Judaic attitudes to (religious) images or art, see von Rad 1962, 212–19. Affinities and possible connections between Judaic-Christian and Islamic views of figural image making lie outside my scope; see Ettinghausen 1963 for a summary of Islamic positions and practices.

[63] Statements about the impossibility of imaging the divine, from a variety of religious standpoints, occur at, e.g., Philo Jud. *Leg.* 290; Josephus *Ap.* 2.191; Dio Chrysostom 12.54 (with chapter 9, note 30), 12.59 (with Geffcken 1916–19, 296–98); Lucian *Pro imag.* 23; Clement *Strom.* 6.18.163.1; on the importance of Stoic views on this subject, cf. Armstrong 1966. Different studies of early Christian attitudes to images or art can be found in, e.g., Baynes 1955, 116–43, and Murray 1977.

In his most sustained discussion of the subject, written around 730 in immediate response to the first outbreak of Iconoclasm under Leo III, he adopts a conventional definition of images in terms of "likeness," but stresses, in a manner reminiscent of Plato's *Cratylus*, that an image is inescapably different from its "prototype" (*prōtotupon*) or "archetype" (*archetupon*).[64] He also makes the important claim that "every image is revelatory and indicative of the hidden" (*pasa eikōn ekphantorikē tou kruphiou esti kai deiktikē*), and he glosses "the hidden" as everything either invisible or lying beyond the reach of sense perception.[65] Having thus laid the ground for a sophisticated conception of images as more than iconic equivalents, John proceeds to offer a scheme of six types or "modes" (*tropoi*) of image: first, the "natural" (*phusikē*), which he distinguishes from the artificial and mimetic (*kata thesin kai mimēsin*) and exemplifies, quoting Paul, by the son's (Christ's) relationship to the father, the invisible god, as well as that between the third and second persons of the Trinity;[66] second, god's knowledge and "predetermination" of the future, "engraved and imaged" in his will; third, man himself, brought into being by divine "mimesis," that is, in the words of Genesis 1.26–27, created "in the image and likeness" of god; fourth, scripture, which gives shape and form to the invisible (for the human mind cannot contemplate the immaterial world without mediation of "analogies"); fifth, symbols which preecho the future, such as the burning bush that prefigures the virgin mother of Christ; sixth and last, memorials of the past, whether in verbal or material form (John cites various biblical instances), that serve to glorify virtue and put vice to shame.[67]

This scheme rather strangely interweaves *species* of "image" (persons, mental ideas, visual representations, writing, physical objects) with the *functions* of images (as prefigurings, analogies, reminders, etc.). The results may strike us as awkward and lopsided, but the typology is clearly

---

[64] I concentrate here on *De imaginibus orationes* (= *Imag.*) 3.14–26 (all references are to the text of Kotter 1975), which discusses images through a series of five questions (what? what for? how many kinds? what can/cannot be imaged? who first made them?); the definition is at 3.16 (cf. 1.9), together with John's remarks on the differences between original and image (cf. Plato *Crat.* 432a–d, with chapter 1, section I).

[65] *Imag.* 3.17, picking up a very old pagan notion of the possibility of imaging the soul through the body (compare, e.g., Xenophon *Mem.* 3.10.3–8, with my chapter 4, section I); cf. the power of images to give a "murky conception" (*amudran katanoēsin*) of the invisible at 1.11 (with an intriguing theory of "imagination," *phantasia*, as using images to inform religious judgment), 3.21. For a superficial parallel to 3.17, cf. Lucian *De salt.* 36, where pantomime dancing is said to be "a kind of mimetic knowledge [*mimētikē tis epistēmē*] . . . and one which makes unseen things clear [*tōn aphanōn saphēnistikē*]," perhaps referring to expression of thought, mentioned in the same sentence.

[66] John's distinction between natural and artificial or mimetic images is not original to him: see Ladner 1959, 780–81; Ladner 1983, 98–102.

[67] The scheme of six types of image at *Imag.* 3.18–23 is partly but less systematically anticipated at 1.9–13.

meant to reinforce the two general tenets of John mentioned earlier—that images are not tied to relationships of strict equivalence, and that they have the power to reveal that which is, in some sense, "hidden"—and thereby to promote a series of options in the interpretation of religious images. Above all, it is designed to allow images, of various kinds, to be regarded as partial revelations of the nature of the divine and its purpose, on the Pauline principle that while the divine as such is undepictable, god's invisible realm can be "seen" in the whole of creation.[68] Although the status of John's scheme is in no sense a general "theory of art"—he does not even register the existence of nonreligious images in this context[69]—several points are worth making here in relation to my larger perspective on the history of mimeticism. The first is that there is an affinity between John's theology of images and a Neoplatonist philosophy like that of Plotinus which posits imagelike correspondences between different levels and domains of reality. This affinity is likely to have come via the work of pseudo-Dionysius the Areopagite (probably of the early sixth century), whom John cites more than once and to whom he owes the cardinal principle that "visible things are truly manifest images of the invisible."[70] What we have in John, as a result, is a Christianized version of Greek philosophical thinking, largely Platonic in origin, which had found a way to interpret the sensible world as bearing the traces of the suprasensible. The assimilation of such an interpretative procedure was all the easier in that the Judaic heritage of Christianity already contained an idea, parallel to that found in Plato's *Timaeus* and later texts, of god as maker or artificer of a world that could consequently be considered to be his "work of art."[71]

In developing the implications of such views for a conception of religious images, however, John Damascene makes limited use of mimetic terminology. But how significant is this? We are not entitled to suppose that it reflects a negative conception such as that found in Proclus, which treats mimesis as too limited, too tied to the representation of appearances, or (in John's case) too tainted by association with pagan art,[72] to

---

[68] *Imag.* 3.21 (cf. 1.11), quoting Paul, Romans 1.20. Cf. also pseudo-Dionysius Areopagita *Epist.* 10.1, "visible things are truly manifest images of the invisible" (see note 70).

[69] Pagan religious images are referred to elsewhere in the work, e.g., at 1.24, 2.17, and the passages cited in my note 72.

[70] *alēthōs emphaneis eikones eisi ta horata tōn ahoratōn*: pseudo-Dionysius Areopagita *Epist.* 10.1 (= John Damascene *Imag.* 3.43). Cf. the references to pseudo-Dionysius at *Imag.* 1.10–11, 3.19, 21. Neoplatonic influence, via pseudo-Dionysius, on the iconophile position is recognized by, e.g., Barnard 1974, 93–94, and some of its strands are unpicked in detail by Ladner 1983, 73–111.

[71] See Theiler 1957, Curtius 1953, 544–46.

[72] John accepted a mimetic conception of visual art in general: see, e.g., the references to painting and sculpture at *Imag.* I.50 = 2.46, the definition of an image in terms of mimesis at 3.64 (quoting Gregory Naz. *Orat.* 30.129B 7–8), and *De haer.* 3.12 (a reference to a specifically pagan tradition of various mimetic arts).

be serviceable for a theology of images. We saw in the passage summarized earlier that one of John's applications of the term *mimēsis* is to god's creation of human beings, which in itself rules out any pejorative color to his understanding of the concept.[73] Indeed, because John followed the by now orthodox interpretation of the act of creation "in the likeness and image" of god as pertaining to human soul and spirit, this passage encourages an elevated conception of the spiritual and more-than-literal scope of mimesis, even if the work of god the divine "artist" cannot be taken to have direct implications for the activities of human artists themselves.[74] That mimesis lacks any pejorative connotations for John is borne out by passages in which he practically equates image making with mimesis. The most instructive of these is in the second of the discourses on images. He writes here, in quasi-Platonic fashion, that all images should be judged by criteria of "truth" and "aim" (*skopos*): if true and good, they should be accepted and honored as "images and mimetic representations [*mimēmata*] and likenesses [*homoiōmata*]."[75] This interpretative principle, designed to justify the religious images of Christ in human form, as well as of Mary and the saints, depends on a heavily spiritualized notion of truth; John does not expect religious icons to be judged in terms of historical accuracy of visual depiction, but by reference to the ethicoreligious values expressed and conveyed by the images. That helps to show that this passage is compatible with the section of the third discourse inspected earlier, where an image is defined as a "likeness" but also as capable of embodying a meaning that cannot be accounted for in terms of direct equivalence. Taken together, these passages suggest that, like other iconophiles,[76] John was prepared to allow the concept of mimesis itself to encompass his view of spiritually significant visual images, though he stops short, as I mentioned at the outset, of claiming that an image or mimetic representation could ever be made of the invisible, immaterial, and infinite god himself.[77]

John's subjection of mimesis to the joint criteria of truth and ethical "aim" or "purport" (*skopos*) leads on to my final point. Throughout both

[73] Nor does the contrast between natural and mimetic images at *Imag.* 3.18 (see note 66) imply anything negative about mimesis as such: on this basis, god's creation of humans was itself not an act of "nature" but a kind of cosmic artistry.

[74] God's work is specifically compared to that of human painters in the quotation from Gregory Nys. *De opif. hom.* 137A3–10 (*PG*) at *Imag.* 1. 50 = 2.46. Such comparisons occur elsewhere too in patristic and Byzantine theology: see Ladner 1983, 84–92.

[75] *Imag.* 2.10. For the equation of image making and mimesis, see also *Imag.* 3.64 (quoting Gregory Naz. *Orat.* 30.129B 7–8), *Contra Man.* 3.15, 10.14.

[76] See esp. Theodorus Stud. *Epist.* 57.17–70, who explains all nonnatural images in terms of "likeness" (*homoiōsis*) and mimesis.

[77] No *mimēma* could be made of the invisible god: *De fide orth.* 89.24–25; cf. *Imag.*, e.g., 1.7–8, 15–16; 2.5, 11; 3.24.

his most substantial discussions of images, in *De imaginibus* and *De fide orthodoxa*, John displays a strong sense of the need to consider the significance of images partly from the angle of their effect on the beholder. His concern with the relationship between image and beholder has a central theological role to play, because a key issue raised by Iconoclasm, though of older origin within Christian debate, was whether the use and contemplation of religious images could be reconciled with the avoidance of idolatry. My own immediate interest, however, is not in this theological issue as such, on which John adopts a consistent view that the contemplation of the image is a medium for veneration or devotion not to the object itself but to its "archetype."[78] Rather, I want to stress that John's theology of images rests in part on a broad psychological basis whose roots lie in the Greek philosophical tradition. In short, John believes that images induce either positive or negative reactions: the desire either to assimilate oneself to, and emulate, that which is depicted, or to shun and deprecate it.[79] This model of the experience of images as intrinsically affective and at least implicitly evaluative, and thus as giving rise to processes of attraction or repulsion in those who behold them, is deeply embedded in the pagan Greek tradition, and comes to particular prominence in some of Plato's treatments of mimesis, as we saw in earlier chapters. So in this as in other respects, John offers us a Christianized version of one kind of mimeticism. This is shown with particular clarity by the way in which he connects the status of images with the Christian goal of emulating the lives of both Christ and the saints. In *De fide orthodoxa*, for example, he juxtaposes the idea of setting up images of the saints with an injunction that the faithful should themselves become "living images" of the saints by emulation (*mimēsis*) of their virtues.[80] Mimesis *qua* expressive image making and *qua* behavioral assimilation are connected by means of the spiritual psychology of "viewing."

The resemblance between various features of John's theology of images and the mimeticism of Plato, especially in the *Republic*, is hardly accidental. It is largely a matter, though, of indirect influence (John's own references to Plato are few and perfunctory). Here we might think especially of Basil of Caesarea, who was himself a direct influence on John's conception of images and whose own understanding of mimesis was partly

[78] See esp. *De fide orth*. 89.2–9, 89.46–84; *Imag.* 1.21, 3.15: all these passages refer to Basil *Spir*. 406.19–20 ("the honor given to the image passes over to the original/archetype [*prōtotupon*]," where the reference is to Christ as an image of god), a tenet frequently cited by other iconophiles too (see esp. Theodorus Stud. *Epist*. 57.29–30, 170.27, 380.152–53).

[79] *Imag.* 3.17.

[80] *De fide orth*. 88.61–62. On the principle of "imitatio Christi," see, e.g., Michaelis 1942, 668–78; Morrison 1982, 41–48 (on Paul); Eden 1986, 124–41 (on Augustine).

shaped by the reading of Plato's *Republic*.[81] But what matters most to me is not to speculate about the precise routes by which Platonic influence may have reached John Damascene, but to underline its consequences. John's defense of images couples arguments about the ontological status of images with considerations about their psychological (i.e., devotional) value, and we have seen that his position involves the application of twin criteria of "truth" and "aim," a combination itself reminiscent of Plato.[82] In doing so he is engaging in a discourse whose terminology and concepts are part of a larger fashioning of Christian theology out of the language of Greek philosophy. Mimesis is only one feature of this enormous process, but its absorption into the Iconoclast controversy made it part of an argument over the nature, limits, and effects of representation that allows us to hear one of antiquity's final echoes of an urgent set of Platonic questions, more than a millennium after they had first been posed.

IV

As a tailpiece to this chapter, as well as to the whole story of mimetic theories of art in antiquity, I offer some extremely brief remarks on the break in the mimeticist tradition that occurred during the medieval period in the West. Mimesis as an integrated category of artistic representation (though not as a canon of literary imitation or emulation) is very largely absent from medieval aesthetics, and with it disappears any unifying conception of the musicopoetic and visual arts.[83] Indeed, the erasure of such a conception by other ways of thinking is itself an important index of the distinction between ancient and medieval mentalities. In one sense, the overarching medieval category of *ars*, like its Roman antecedent, harks back to the original Greek category of *technē*: it accommodates many different kinds of intellectual, productive, and rule-based human activities, from carpentry to astronomy. But to make that observation is precisely to draw attention to the framework within which the idea of a group of

---

[81] Basil echoes the *Republic* on mimesis in his *Ad adolesc.*, esp. ch. 4, which adapts the arguments of Plato *Rep.* bks. 2–3 to the Christian reading of pagan texts; cf. also the echo of *Rep.* 6.472d at ibid. 6.8–11, with chapter 9, note 4. John's quotations from Basil on images are cited in note 78. Add too John's own allusion to the *Republic* in his statement that comic actors (*mimētai*, here especially mime players?) must be "expelled from our republic [*politeia*]," *Sacr. Par.* 96.77.34–37 PG.

[82] The resemblance is particulaly close to the discussion of poetry in *Rep.* 2–3: cf. chapter 1, section II.

[83] Townsend 1997, 67–68 is very misleading in connecting medieval theories of allegory with classical mimesis, and his claim, 88, that mimesis dominated the medieval period is therefore entirely groundless. Note, however, that my remarks on mimesis have no bearing on other areas in which continuity may have existed between medieval and Renaissance attitudes to poetry: Greenfield 1981, esp. 308–16, cogently synthesizes elements of such continuity, but she has nothing to say about the Renaissance rediscovery of mimesis.

distinctively mimetic arts, an idea so important for the previous millennium and more, rapidly becomes conspicuous by its absence in the Latin West. The category of the "liberal arts" did survive, in canonically defined form, into the Middle Ages. But the liberal arts—which considered poetry largely within the linguistic study of grammar, treated music mathematically, and omitted the visual arts altogether—were not the mimetic arts.[84]

Although it is hazardous to generalize about the large and complex field of medieval thought, it remains appropriate to say that medieval writings about poetry, figurative art, and music expose the forms and subject matter of these activities to criteria, whether of beauty or of meaning, whose tendency is ultimately theological. One effect of this tendency is a severely attenuated need for a conceptual model to address the relationship of works in these media to the human and natural worlds themselves. I have argued repeatedly that ancient mimeticism moved around, and was partly energized by the tension between, two major poles of thought, one a sense of mimesis as a reflection of and engagement with "external" reality, the other an inclination to think of mimesis as the creation or invention of self-contained, fictional worlds. In both these respects, the ancient traditions were ill-suited to meet the needs of medieval writers who came to poetry or painting within a context of Christian belief and, frequently, with a disposition toward didacticism. The nature of artistic representation as such could command little interest in this cultural environment; and even when we reach a period of intense Aristotelian influence on medieval philosophy, in thirteenth-century Scholasticism, it is noteworthy that "it eliminates the philosophical justification of poetry from Aristotelianism."[85] Of course, there were various ancient concepts of artistic mimesis that expanded their ambit to embrace questions of metaphysical and religious significance, and even incorporated elements of symbolism and allegory into the understanding of mimesis.[86] These concepts could in principle have been adapted to medieval Christian concerns, in which symbolism and allegory became so important. But the fact is that they were not—or, if they were, it was not *qua* vehicles of mimeticist thinking that they became influential.[87]

The lack of a medieval need for a unifying conception of artistic representation, or of the representational arts as a cultural ensemble, is brought out by what happened when a thinker in this tradition first attempted, even at second hand, to translate Aristotle's *Poetics*. In 1256 Hermannus Alemannus (Hermann the German), writing at Toledo, produced a Latin

[84] On the liberal arts see, e.g., Curtius 1953, 36–42, and the essays in Wagner 1983.

[85] Curtius 1953, 224.

[86] In addition to the varieties of Neoplatonism discussed earlier in this chapter, see chapter 9, section I.

[87] An example of this is Plotinus, whose importance for medieval aesthetics scarcely touches his ideas of mimesis: see note 27.

version of the so-called middle commentary on the *Poetics* compiled in
the previous century by the great Arab scholar Averroes (Ibn Rushd).[88] As
regards mimesis, the result is a serious blurring of Aristotle's ideas and
arguments. Hermann does preserve a vestigial concept of the "representational arts" (artes representativae), but this detail is confused by the
presence of a compound notion of "representation" that runs together a
thin trace of authentically Aristotelian mimesis with notions both of figurative language and of imagery in a more general sense.[89] This situation
echoes the position of Averroes himself, who followed an Arabic preoccupation with placing the status of poetic images (as emotionally stimulating mental processes) in contrastive relation to the strict rationality of
logic. The treatment of the *Poetics* within the framework of logic, something that the Arabic philosophers inherited from late-ancient Greek Aristotelianism, should not be as automatically deplored as has often been
the case in the past. It did allow potentially important questions to be
raised about the psychological, cognitive, and cultural status of poetry;
and in a tradition of thought that included such outstanding figures as
al-Farabi in the tenth-century, Avicenna (Ibn Sina) in the eleventh, and
Averroes in the twelfth, it led to the emergence of a model of poetry as a
kind of imaginative fiction with the power to move the mind to strong
feelings of approval or repulsion—feelings often associated with an Arabic division of poetry, derived from *Poetics* 5.1448b24–27 though perhaps
more Platonic in spirit, into panegyric-encomiastic and satirical-lam-
pooning types.[90]

[88] The text of Hermann's Latin is in Minio-Paluello 1968, 41–74; Minnis & Scott 1991, 277–
313, provide a convenient English translation and cite further secondary literature (note their
comments on mimesis, 282–83). Cf. Halliwell 1986, 290–91. For Averroes' own work, see
Butterworth 1986, with Butterworth 1977 for the "short commentary"; note too Averroes' treatment, in his commentary on the *Republic*, of Plato's concept of mimesis in book 3, where his
paraphrase of the relevant passage does not convince one that Averroes has firmly grasped
the essential conceptual and terminological points (see Rosenthal 1956, 130–33, for the relevant passage from the fourteenth-century Hebrew translation, the only surviving version).

[89] The situation is rather different with the much more reliable though deliberately literalist
version of the *Poetics* produced by William of Moerbeke in 1278, which uses "imitatio," "imitari" throughout: the text is printed in Minio-Paluello 1968, 30–37. My statement in Halliwell
1986, 291, that William's version was without influence, needs amending in the light of Kelly
1979, 187–93, and Kelly 1993, 117, 139–40, who traces familiarity with it in the Paduan humanist Albertino Mussato; but its influence seems to have been slender, and there is no basis
for the suggestion of Dod 1982, 64, that it became a standard text.

[90] Black 1990 offers a sophisticated reappraisal of the so-called context theory of the *Poetics*, which placed it, alongside the *Rhetoric*, within the study of logic; cf. Hardison 1962, 11–
18, for the medieval and Renaissance impact of the association of poetry with logic. Heinrichs
1969, 105–70, gives a detailed account of the impact of the *Poetics* on Arabic philosophy.
Overviews of philosophical Arabic poetics can be found in Dahiyat 1974, 3–58; Goodman
1992, 216–26 (though the latter's reference, 218, to a work of Alexander of Aphrodisias on
Aristotle's *Poetics* perpetuates an old mistake: see Heinrichs 1969, 107, Thillet 1987, 107–8).

It was, however, difficult for Arab philosophers to integrate this model effectively into the explication of the *Poetics*, above all because they almost entirely lacked a historical and cultural familiarity with Greek poetry itself, especially drama, a form unknown to Arabic tradition.[91] Moreover, both Avicenna and Averroes attempted to interpret the *Poetics* without any knowledge of Greek, and they labored under the difficulty of working at two removes from the original, using a tenth-century Arabic version of an earlier Syriac translation of the treatise. Where mimesis is concerned, the upshot is of predictably mixed character. On the one side, particularly in the writings of al-Farabi and Avicenna, there was a sophisticated construal of mimesis as "imaginative representation" that could, in more auspicious conditions, have generated a fruitful extension to Aristotle's own theory of poetry. On the other, there was a tendency, already noted in connection with Hermannus's rendering of Averroes, to focus on figurative language (especially metaphor and simile) to the preclusion of a fuller conception of poetry as verbal "image making" or imaginative representation, and the corresponding absence of an authentically Greek conception of poetry as one of a distinctive group of mimetic arts.[92] All in all, it is hardly surprising that the encounter of Latin with Arabic thought that Hermannus's translation occasioned was unable to direct much fresh attention either to the *Poetics* itself or to Greek ideas of mimesis. For many medieval philosophers and theorists, mimeticism had become an alien and unintelligible way of thinking.

The fullest attempt to make philosophical sense of Arabic poetics and aesthetics from a modern viewpoint is that of Kemal 1991.

[91] Averroes' treatment of tragedy, and the (limited) nature of its influence on the Middle Ages and early Renaissance, is fully discussed by Kelly 1979, Kelly 1993, 118–25.

[92] Heinrichs 1969, 121–23 (cf. 145ff.) analyzes the difficulties that the Arabic translator of the *Poetics* had with the term *mimēsis*. On the connection between "imaginative representation" and "imitation" in Avicenna, see Dahiyat 1974, 62 n. 4; Kemal 1991, 148–61; for the same Arabic terms in Averroes, but with their English translations reversed (!), see Butterworth 1986, 63 n. 18, who here and elsewhere (e.g., 12–13) overestimates Averroes' understanding of Aristotelian mimesis. The foregrounding of figurative language in Averroes' concept of representation occurs in both the "middle" (Butterworth 1986, 60–62) and the short commentary (Butterworth 1977, 83). Minnis & Scott 1991, 278 (with 240, 293), suggest that this last feature of Averroes' work, in Hermannus's version, influenced Aquinas *Summa Theologica* 1.1.9 ad. 1, where "repraesentatio," however, refers specifically to figurative language and thus loses the force of Aristotle's remark at *Poet.* 4.1448b5–6, which it echoes, about an instinct for mimesis. On "imitatio" in Hermann's rendering of Averroes, cf. Weinberg 1961, 1:356–58. The broadest sense of artistic representation in any of the major Arabic philosophers is perhaps that of Avicenna, in his commentary on the *Poetics*, ch. 2, para. 3 (Dahiyat 1974, 71), where he brings together poetry, visual art, and (possibly) dramatic acting; but even here the scope of the concept is murky, and figurative language is again foregrounded. Outside poetic theory as such, there is a particularly intriguing combination of mimesis, in various senses, with Aristotelian "imagination," *phantasia*, in the work of al-Farabi: see Walzer 1985, 211–27, with 416–17.

Chapter Twelve

❋

An Inheritance Contested:
Renaissance to Modernity

Drive your cart and your plow over the bones of the dead.
(Blake, "Proverbs of Hell")

DESPITE, or perhaps in part because of, its importance and influence within the history of aesthetics, the current status of mimesis as a concept (or family of concepts) in the theory of art is contentious and unstable. In an age when talk of representation has become increasingly subject to both ideological and epistemological suspicion, mimesis is, for many philosophers and critics, little more than a broken column surviving from a long-dilapidated classical edifice, a sadly obsolete relic of former certainties. According to such convictions, even the Renaissance and neoclassical revival of mimeticism was a phase of thought whose structure of presuppositions and values we have left irretrievably far behind. The rallying cry of the so-called imitation of nature may once, on this view, have served as an energizing element in attitudes to both the visual and the musicopoetic arts, but it came under mounting strain in the eighteenth century, when a new integrated category of "(fine) art" arose and, closely associated with it, the supposed invention of "aesthetics" itself; it was then decisively repudiated by romanticism; and in the past two hundred years it has become progressively alien to modern—not to say modernist and postmodernist—accounts of art. As regards both the practice and theory of art (a concept whose own validity has come under ever more wary scrutiny in recent times), we live, it is sometimes alleged, in a "postmimetic" era.

But such a perspective, however wide its contemporary appeal, is only patchily reliable. One of the chief aims of this concluding chapter will be to expose some of the simplifications, omissions, and even evasions on which it depends. I challenged in my introduction the proposition that the eighteenth-century emergence of new concepts of art and aesthetics marked a complete break with older, especially mimetic, ways of thinking. Here I put that challenge in a larger context, and expand its force, by exploring in more detail some of the complex, tangled ways in which versions of mimesis, especially in their Latinized form of "imitation" and its equivalents in other European languages, have continued to play a significant role in the philosophy and criticism of art from the Renaissance to the present.[1]

Even a cursory glance at twentieth-century criticism and philosophy suggests a more elaborate picture than the standard view already described would lead us to posit, and confirms that, contrary to much received opinion, the legacy of mimesis has proved both tenacious and protean. Thinkers as different as Adorno, Gadamer, Murdoch, Barthes, Ricoeur, Kendall Walton, and, not least, Derrida have regarded some or other notion of mimesis as possessing persisting relevance for modern reflections on art.[2] Despite the diversity of positions occupied by these theorists (from the Platonist-moralist Murdoch to the arch anti-Platonist Derrida), as well as the variable extent to which they connect their own understanding of mimesis to historical texts on the subject, they do share a sense that a cluster of issues associated with the name of mimesis continues to pose hard questions for the interpretation of such activities as literature, visual art, and even (especially in Adorno's case) music. While Gadamer, in pieces first written in the 1930s, suggested that mimesis might be revived as a distinctively "Greek" model of artistic meaning in an era when much art seemed to embody precisely the rejection of meaning, and while Ricoeur has used Aristotle to develop an interconnected set of senses of mimesis which he relates to the basic "narrativity" of human experience (the "refiguration of temporal experience" through narrative) and which he believes can help stabilize the idea of representation against peculiarly modern forms of skepticism, the profusely skeptical Derrida affirms that the dominance of mimesis in the whole history of the interpretation of literature and art is part of the larger imprint of "Platonism" on European metaphysics—an imprint from which Derrida seems to think that escape is possible only, if at all, by dissociating mimesis from any

---

[1] Assunto 1965 contains much useful documentation but is unreliable on interpretation, especially of ancient texts; Block 1966 is a helpful overview, though marred by a caricature of "Platonic" mimesis and thin on the twentieth century; Gebauer & Wulf 1992 is wide-ranging but runs together too many different concepts and issues. Complexity in the history of mimetic theorizing is shrewdly observed by Prendergast 1986, esp. 4–5. Eusterschulte 2001 appeared as my book was going to press.

[2] Adorno's frequent but obscure references to mimesis as a preconceptual instinct for assimilation, both inside and outside art, are discussed, with intermittent illumination, by Cahn 1984, 31–55; Nicholsen 1997, 137–80; Früchtl 1998, 23–25; and Gebauer & Wulf 1992, 389–405; cf. my note 64. Gadamer: "Kunst und Nachahmung," "Dichtung und Mimesis," in Gadamer 1977, 2:6–26, 4:228–33 (English translations in Gadamer 1986). Murdoch: see esp. "Art is the Imitation of Nature," in Murdoch 1997, 243–57; Conradi 1994 gives an overview of Murdoch's Platonism. On Barthes, see section III. Ricoeur's main discussions of mimesis are in Ricoeur 1981 and Ricoeur 1983, 55–129 (1984, 52–87); cf. chapter 5, with its note 60. Walton's theory of art as mimetic make-believe, explicated in terms of psychological "games," is in Walton 1990; cf. chapter 6, notes 5, 7. For Derrida, see section III.

sort of claim to make contact with truth or reality, and converting it into
something more like a self-referential field of play. I shall come back at
the end of this chapter to twentieth-century approaches to mimesis, and
particularly that of Derrida. But for the time being one can say with some
assurance that these approaches collectively reinforce my thesis that the
importance of mimesis to the history of aesthetics is far from being solely
a thing of the past.

My main aim in this final chapter is to try to make some overall sense
of the contribution of mimesis to certain major aspects of aesthetics between the Renaissance and the present. To write even a basic history of
mimeticism over this period would take, at the minimum, a large book in
its own right. What I offer here is not even a historical outline but a selective analysis of some of the key determinants of this history, an analysis
designed in part as a corrective to prevailing misapprehensions. At every
stage on the route I shall chart through the subject, we face problems in
which, as I stressed in my introduction, conceptualization and translation
easily become entwined. A pertinent illustration of this point, but one too
little considered by historians of aesthetics, is the fact that throughout the
neoclassicism (in the broadest sense of the term) of the fifteenth to eighteenth centuries the vocabulary of "imitation," in whatever language, is
characteristically used alongside and interchangeably with the vocabulary
of "representation" and related terms.[3] Already by the mid-sixteenth century it was possible for a literary theorist, Girolamo Fracastoro (better
known for his understanding of medical infection), to treat the Latin terms
imitari or *imitatio* and *repraesentare* or *repraesentatio* in this context as
entirely synonymous, as they would be in English too for Sir Philip Sidney,
a writer partly influenced by Fracastoro, at the end of the same century.[4]

---

[3] Cf. chapter 8, with its note 5, for some further instances, and Bollino 1995 for discussion
of the semantic overlap between imitation and expression in eighteenth-century aesthetics.
Note also that it was even possible for a neoclassical mind to produce a version of mimeticism that did not use "imitation" language at all: this is conspicuously true of Castelvetro's
commentary on the *Poetics*, where mimesis is rendered throughout by "rassomiglianza" (likeness or resemblance), "rappresentatione," and their cognates; Castelvetro 1978–79, 1:487, is
his one reference to the common contemporary use of "imitazione." Castelvetro's terminological treatment of mimesis, which was a deliberate divergence from existing Latin and
Italian versions of the *Poetics*, cannot be separated from his larger interpretative view of
poetry as a sort of simulated history (esp. Castelvetro 1978–79, 1:44, with Halliwell 2002).

[4] See Sidney's much-cited definition of mimesis: "Poesy therefore is an art of imitation, for
so Aristotle termeth it in the word *mimesis*—that is to say, a representing, counterfeiting, or
figuring forth" (in Duncan-Jones 1989, 217). Sidney's understanding of mimesis fluctuates
somewhat, partly owing to the influence on him of Proclus's tripartite scheme of poetic types
(cf. chapter 11, section II): see Trimpi 1999, 192–95. For examples of the equation of "imitate"
and "express" (deriving from Latin usage of the verb "exprimere"), which further diversifies
and complicates the historical terminology of mimeticism, see Weinberg 1961, 1:60 n. 32, 61
n. 33, 146 n. 54; English instances are found in Puttenham's *Arte of English Poesie* (1589),

In his dialogue on poetics, *Naugerius*, published posthumously in 1555, Fracastoro makes two humanist scholars, Navagero and Bardulone, agree on this synonymity in order to preserve a basically Platonic-Aristotelian categorization of poetry.[5] Bardulone distinguishes *imitari* from *docere* (teach) in a manner that suggests he wants to treat the products of the former as quasi-fictional. But Navagero complicates the discussion by suggesting that not everything a poet says should count as *imitatio* or *repraesentatio*, because all writers, including historians, "represent" their subject matter. He concedes that some critics consider imitation proper to be limited to the presentation of human characters, that is, to a narrative or dramatic conception of mimesis, but he himself prefers to expand its scope so as to embrace all forms of representation of the "natural realm" (naturalia).[6] His purpose in adopting this stance is to entitle poetry to be a vehicle not only of "ethical wisdom" (prudentia) but also of "general understanding" (cognitio or intellectio) of the world. This is part of Fracastoro's strategy for coming to terms with an ancient dichotomy between poetic pleasure and edification, as emblematized for the Renaissance by Horace's famous *delectare-prodesse* contrast at *Ars Poetica* 333, a contrast that frames the entirety of Fracastoro's dialogue. One notable consequence of this move is that Fracastoro abandons an Aristotelian version of mimesis by specifically overturning the exclusion of "science" from poetry in *Poetics* 1. Moreover, in the involved eclecticism of *Naugerius* an inclusive Latinized concept of mimesis *qua* representation is in due course overlaid both by a rhetorical preoccupation with style and by an idealism that blurs the universals of *Poetics* 9 into a Platonizing notion of perfect beauty. Even without being able to follow all these ramifications in detail, we can recognize that Fracastoro's work is a cautionary instance of the many intertwined conceptual and terminological twists in Renaissance mimeticism that inevitably become lost to view if we misguidedly look for doctrinal purity or orthodoxy in this area.

The importance of this point makes it profitable to consider briefly two further, prominent cases, one from the early and one from the later stages of neoclassical thought, in which mimesis functions as part of a whole network of vocabulary and ideas. In both the Italian and Latin versions of

---

bk. 1, ch. 1 (in Vickers 1999, 192), and Ben Jonson's *Timber* 2369–72 (Donaldson 1985, 582), published posthumously in 1640–41.

[5] See the facsimile in Fracastoro 1924, 25–48 (= facsimile pp. 153–64): on 32 (= fac. 156c) Bardulone refers to Plato's and Aristotle's view of poetry as an "imitatoriam artem," before adding "nihil autem refert, sive imitari sive repraesentare dicamus" (it makes no difference whether we speak of imitation or representation); Navagero agrees, and interchangeability prevails for the rest of the dialogue.

[6] See Fracastoro 1924, 32–34 (= fac. 156d–57c) for Navagero's discussion of *imitatio/repraesentatio*.

his treatise on painting, completed in 1435, Alberti fluctuates considerably in his terminology for pictorial representation, using both "imitari" and "repraesentare" in certain key passages, and *fingere, ripresentare, contraf-fare*, and *ritrarre* in Italian.[7] Alberti indubitably belongs in the mainstream of mimeticism. Indeed, he exemplifies the crucial sense in which, as I suggested at the end of my previous chapter, the recovery of a (Latinized) concept of mimesis, after its general absence in medieval theorizing about art, is a defining element in Renaissance aesthetics. But this does not make it either feasible or desirable to ascribe to him a simple concept of art as the "imitation of nature." On the contrary, I mentioned earlier in the book how the technically naturalistic foundations of Alberti's theory of painting are modified both by his adherence to a poeticizing notion of *(h)istoria*, which might be paraphrased as an image's narrative-cum-emotional interest (with all that entails for the viewer's psychological and ethical engagement with its content), and by his espousal of the need for the depiction of natural appearances to be adjusted to certain canons of beauty.[8] Against this background, Alberti's terminological fluctuations are neither superficial nor capricious; they are a pointer to a movement of thought that develops both a Latinate and vernacular version of mimesis without thereby locking itself into a reductive notion of artistic "imitation." The status of Albertian mimesis does not constitute a single, self-contained feature of his account of painting but is the result of an interplay between all the main components in that account: it is not a one-dimensional model of the relationship between art and nature, but a model in which a naturalistic framework of depiction is enriched and filled out by a strongly normative view of the obligation on artists to select, shape, and, to some degree, idealize the images they create.

A comparable proposition applies to the much later case of Samuel Johnson, whose famous preface to his edition of Shakespeare (1765) uses a critical vocabulary that is in large part paradigmatic of neoclassical literary mimeticism. One germane aspect of Johnson's usage is precisely its mixing of the language of imitation and representation. Tragedy and com-

---

[7] Some examples (references to Alberti 1973 in brackets): *De pictura* 1.2 (10–11) uses *imitari* in Latin, *fingere* in Italian; 2.30 (52–53) *repraesentare/ripresentare*; 2.31 (54–55) *imitari/contraffare*; 2.35 (62–63) and 2.46 (82–83) *imitari/imitare*; 2.49 (88–89) both *imitari* and *repraesentare* in Latin, *imitare* in Italian; 3.59 (100–101) *imitari/ritrarre*. Alberti is, in this respect, entirely typical of quattrocento and cinquecento art theory; cf. the notebooks of Leonardo, in which we find overlapping use of *imitare, rapresentare, figurare, ritrarre, significare*, and *fingere*: for some instances see, e.g., Richter 1970, 1:53–68, Farago 1992, 184–202, with Kemp 1977, 381–82. Summers 1981, 279–82 (cf. 337), referring to Vincenzo Danti and Michelangelo, illustrates how *imitare* could be given less narrow connotations than a verb like *ritrarre*.

[8] See chapter 4, section IV.

edy are, for Johnson, "two modes of imitation"; all drama "exhibits successive imitations of successive actions"; the actions depicted in plays are
"imitative actions."[9] Equally, however, Johnson refers to Shakespearean
and other poetry in terms of representation, as in his famous description
of the plays as containing "just representations of general nature"; and it
is clear that he feels no qualms about combining these two strands in his
vocabulary.[10] Something of the character of this section of Johnson's critical lexicon can be highlighted by passages in which he uses the verb
"copy" for poetry's treatment of the world. The first of these is the sentence
immediately following the reference to Shakespeare's "just representations
of general nature," where Johnson links the idea of poetic copying to the
presentation of "particular manners."[11] But if "copy" is here correlated with
particulars, and "representation" with the general or universal, other passages show that this is not consistently so, for in two later places Johnson
identifies the object of poetic copying as "nature" itself, that same "general
nature" or "sublunary nature" that he so admires Shakespeare for capturing.[12] Precisely because nature (or, equally, "real life") is not, for Johnson,
a collection of particulars but a pattern of general truths, tendencies, and
probabilities, to "copy nature" cannot be a particularist tenet, and this
holds even more certainly of his dual terminology of imitation and representation. Johnson's critical principles, therefore, cannot be grasped without a strong alertness to the shifts that have subsequently occurred in the
usage of his favored terms and that have brought about dislocations of
previous semantic alignments. This reinforces my wider contention that
the Latinized neoclassical terminology of mimesis needs always to be considered not as a discrete or static phenomenon, confidently expoundable
from a modern conviction of what "imitation" necessarily amounts to, but
as the flexible armature of a larger, evolving structure of artistic ideas and
standards.

What is at stake here, then, is in part an awareness of how our relationship to older mimetic interpretations of art is complicated by the history
of language and translation at the most basic level. No modern critic, I
think, would now independently use "imitate" in the manner of Johnson,
except in paraphrase of neoclassical criticism itself; yet "represent(ation)"

[9] Johnson 1977, 304, 312, 332.
[10] "Represent(ation)": see esp. Johnson 1977, 301 ("just representations . . ."), 303, 311,
312, 320; representation and imitation are combined at 312 ("may not the second imitation
represent an action . . ."). Boyd 1980, 269–97, gives one reading of Johnson's relationship to
the traditions of mimetic criticism.
[11] Johnson 1977, 301.
[12] See Johnson 1977, 314, 320, for the later uses of "copy" (in the second of which there
is also a reference to the emulation, also called "imitation," of poetic predecessors: cf. my
note 18); "general nature," together with "sublunary nature," occurs on 303 as well as 301.

remains immediately intelligible in these same contexts. Historical sensitivity accordingly requires us to realize that one feature of the cast of mind exemplified equally, for all their other differences, by Johnson and Alberti is their willingness, now no longer available to us, to invest the language of "imitation" with a weight and richness that derive, in their eyes, from its ancient ancestry—more particularly, from the Latin tradition of art criticism in Alberti's case, and the ideas of Aristotle's *Poetics*, occasionally cited and often palpably just beneath the surface, in that of Johnson's preface. This means that neoclassical theorists rarely allowed the idea of imitation to be burdened by the narrow connotations that now almost inescapably attach to the term. This is why the juxtaposition of mimetic terminology with the language of representation (as well as "fiction," "depiction," and much besides) needs to be interpreted as a sign not of naiveté but, above all, of participation in a process of devising vernacular vocabularies of criticism that could be responsive to contemporary cultural needs but nonetheless keep contact with essential classical roots.[13]

I want to carry over what has so far been said about terminological and conceptual associations into a more far-reaching observation. From the Renaissance rediscovery, or reinvention, of a central aesthetic concern (first in the visual arts, then in poetry and music) with the methods and aims of artistic figuration, narrative, and representation—in short, with the legacy of ancient mimeticism—right up to the mid-eighteenth-century "crisis" of mimetic thinking, we find, contrary to many modern assertions on the subject, no single, invariable understanding of mimesis but a whole range of competing and subtly differentiated options.[14] Most of these options lean on and adapt ancient texts and ideas (from Plato's dialogues, not least the *Republic, Sophist,* and *Laws;* Aristotle's *Poetics,* especially from the 1540s "revival" onward; excerpts from the Neoplatonism of Plotinus and Proclus; and the Latin tradition of art criticism represented by Vitruvius, Pliny the Elder, and Quintilian), but rework their sources through a mixture of Latinized and vernacular vocabularies of which we have already had revealing glimpses. The gamut of post-Renaissance mimeticism extends all the way from the pursuit of naturalistic effects (the "look" of the real) in the figurative arts—a standard that, as one interpretation of the "imitation of nature," starts to take a hold on aesthetic consciousness from

[13] Block 1966, 717–18, notes the gradual displacement of the term "imitation" by "representation" (and *Nachahmung* by *Darstellung*: cf. my note 46) from the late eighteenth century on; but he does not consider the older alignment of the two terms.

[14] Surveys of mimetic conceptions in Renaissance literary thinking can be found in Spingarn 1908, 27–47 (with a somewhat one-sided stress on idealism), Hathaway 1962, 3–125. On the visual arts, see my note 20.

the later fourteenth century[15]—to a more or less Platonically idealizing tendency that aims to preserve for representational art a capacity to transcend the empirical, sensory domain and achieve insight into the spiritual substructure of reality. The result is an almost pervasive eclecticism that eludes precise analysis in terms of the influence of individual ancient texts. It is important to register that this eclecticism was animated by the pressure of a need to maintain for art as distinctive and elevated a status as possible in relation to the potent cultural forces of religion and, increasingly, of science. Various elements in the ancient traditions of mimeticism offered scope not only for the construction of new critical models of individual arts—pictorial naturalism, genre-based theories of literature,[16] musical expressivity—but also for conceiving of artistic representation in general as an indispensable instrument of human attempts to comprehend and come to terms with the world. This endowed the idea of mimesis, in all its forms and construals, with the power to direct the development of neoclassical aesthetics toward the goal of enhancing the significance of art in the life both of individuals and of the culture as a whole.

A nodal point in the web of interests and problems that defined neoclassical mimeticism was the motto of the so-called imitation of nature. This catchphrase more than any other formulation has come to be associated, even identified, with mimesis, not least by opponents of mimetic conceptions of art. But this association is often embedded in a misleading narrative of the early modern history of aesthetics. The narrative in question takes a static doctrine of art's "imitation of nature" to have constituted the core of neoclassical thinking from the sixteenth to the eighteenth century, and then to have been the main target of new, explicitly antimimetic models of art that arose in the second half of the eighteenth century and during the period of romanticism. Having been repudiated by the romantics, it is thought, the artistic credo of "the imitation of nature" never recovered and has now become an aesthetic principle of intellectually antiquarian interest. But such a narrative is, at best, a collection of half truths that offers a seriously abridged account of the fate of mimesis from the Renaissance to the present. The alternative account that I advocate needs to be built around a recognition that there can be no straightforward equation between mimesis and "the imitation of nature," because the latter was never

[15] We have already seen, however, from the powerful cases of Alberti and Leonardo (in this chapter and chapter 4, section IV) that visual naturalism was often modified by other aesthetic values; cf. note 20.

[16] On the "liberating" importance of Aristotle's *Poetics* for sixteenth-century Italian genre theory, see the series of studies by Javitch 1994, 1998, and 1999; cf. Halliwell 1992b, 412–18. Babbitt 1910, 3–19, gives a supercilious view of neoclassical Aristotelianism, but he is himself unreliable on Aristotle's own views (9–10).

a unitary principle but a formula interpreted in various, and sometimes incompatible, ways. I shall contend in the central section of this chapter, moreover, that the relationship of romanticism to the "imitation of nature" was itself ambivalent; and this forms part of a larger thesis that romanticism did not bring about a complete rupture of the traditions of mimetic theory in aesthetics, let alone the "death" of mimesis.

In trying, within a short compass, to disentangle some of the confusions that have arisen from the long history of the sentiment now conventionally translated as "art imitates nature," we encounter once more a problematic interplay of concepts and translation. Variations and fluctuations in the significance of the phrase reflect shifts in the understanding of all three of its terms. As I stressed in chapter 5, Aristotle's use of the principle, contrary to still widespread opinion, is never applied to the mimetic arts as such, but belongs exclusively to the general philosophy of nature ("physics") and within settings that address the processes and supposed teleology of nature at large. The Aristotelian tenet tells us that all human *technē* (all productive craft, including such activities as medicine) follows principles comparable with or analogous to those of nature, above all in two respects, the orderly imposition of form on matter and the operation of final causes. Even where this tenet could apply to, say, poetry or painting, it does so in a quite different sense from the mimesis of the *Poetics*. While the latter denotes a conscious process of representation, the "mimesis of nature" appealed to in the *Physics* need not be conscious at all: house building, for example, is covered by the wider Aristotelian principle of the mimesis of nature, but this does not mean that the house builder knowingly models his work on natural processes. Moreover, mimesis in the mimetic arts is a matter of representational *content* (poetry's representation of "action(s) and life"), whereas nature is not the intentional object or content of human artistry in the formula of the *Physics*.[17]

But if for Aristotle himself artistic representation and the analogousness of human productivity to nature were separate *kinds* of mimesis, the later history of aesthetics was to allow them to merge. When art's "mimesis of nature" was taken up, probably in Aristotle's own lifetime, as a principle of pictorial art, it was already laden with fruitful ambiguity. Behind the remark attributed by Pliny the Elder to the fourth-century Greek painter Eupompus that "naturam ipsam, non artificem, imitandam" (the object of artistic *imitatio* should be nature herself, not another artist), we can discern two possible senses of the Greek verb *mimeisthai* lying behind the Latin translation: one denoting artistic depiction or representation, the other quasi-behavioral emulation. The painter, Eupompus seems to be saying, should try to render natural appearances convincingly but should

---

[17] See chapter 5, notes 5, 6; for some broader reflections, cf. Bien 1964.

also aim to emulate or *rival* nature rather than other artists.[18] Although these two senses might be made to converge on a single artistic principle of visual naturalism, they could also lead in divergent directions: a canon of "emulating" nature might, after all (and as the romantics were to realize), be fulfilled creatively by doing something *other* than recording natural appearances faithfully. Whatever Eupompus may have meant by such a remark, then, Pliny's anecdote contained the potential to underwrite more than one kind of aesthetic value.

Throughout antiquity, in fact, we find a plurality of glosses put on the idea of artistic "imitation of nature": in addition to the original Aristotelian principle explained earlier, these senses include the creation of an impression of natural spontaneity and expressiveness of human feeling, adherence to supposedly natural values of nobility or beauty, the artistic simulation of the visible world of nature, and the quasi-metaphysical embodiment of the underlying principles of nature.[19] Given such a spectrum of possibilities, it is hardly surprising that when the "imitation of nature" was reactivated as an artistic principle in the Renaissance,[20] ancient

---

[18] Pliny *NH* 34.61; Eupompus was probably active in the first half of the fourth century (see Robertson 1975, 1:484). The fact that Pliny's report comes via the Peripatetic historian Duris of Samos might mean that this application of the formula had been taken up in Aristotle's own school not long after his death; cf. chapter 10, note 16. Here, as throughout, I cannot pursue the use of mimetic vocabulary for the emulation of artistic predecessors: cf. my introduction, note 33, chapter 10, notes 21, 61; and for various aspects of this usage, including its interplay with representational mimesis, see McLaughlin 1996; Draper 1921, 373–83; Weinberg 1966; Lee 1967, 11–16; Block 1966, 705–6, 710–11.

[19] Quasi-natural spontaneity: Longinus *Subl.* 22.1 (with chapter 10, section III); cf. Dionysius of Halicarnassus *Isaeus* 16, *Lysias* 8 (with chapter 10, section I). Following natural principles of beauty etc.: Longinus *Subl.* 43.5. Simulation of natural appearances: e.g., Philo Jud. *Migr.* 167, Callistratus *Imag.* 14.3, Heliodorus *Aeth.* 1.28.2, Plotinus *Enn.* 4.3.10.17–18 (cf. chapter 11, section I). Contact with the underlying principles of nature: the Stoics consider their own wisdom a *mimēma* of nature (chapter 9, note 5); Plotinus *Enn.* 5.8.1.32–40 opposes a metaphysical to a "reproductive" conception of the imitation of nature (chapter 11, section I). Examples of the original Aristotelian principle occur at, e.g., Theophrastus *De lap.* 8.60, Seneca *Epist.* 65.3 (contrast 65.7–10, with my note 25). Note also the general invocations of the principle at Marcus Aurelius *Med.* 11.10, Athanasius *Contra gentes* 18.

[20] "Ars imitatur naturam" was a commonly cited principle in the Middle Ages, but it referred to human productive craft in general rather than to representational art, and its influence was mostly influenced by a combination of Aristotelian teleology and the cosmology of Plato's *Timaeus*: see Flasch 1965 for a detailed and instructive analysis, with Blumenberg 1957 for a larger purview on the implications of the principle for ideas of human creativity. The principle starts to become an axiom of Renaissance aesthetics in the visual arts from the late fourteenth century: see the instance from Filippo Villani cited by Baxandall 1971, 70–72 (Latin text, 146–48), with Boccaccio's famous remark on Giotto (*Decameron* 6.5); cf. Barasch 1985, 114–20. On the elusiveness of the principle in Renaissance contexts, see Baxandall 1988, 119–21, with Lee 1967, 9–16, and Clements 1963, 146–53, on the tension between "literal" and idealizing conceptions of imitation in Renaissance theories of visual art, a tension

variations in its interpretation reappeared and were extended. Alberti, for example, uses the idea in at least two distinct ways. In his treatise on architecture he conveys by it a principle for the combining of separate parts into coherent wholes, a principle he discerns, somewhat in the vein of chapter 7 of Aristotle's *Poetics*, organically exemplified in the animal world, and one he believes the architect must cultivate in order to produce beatiful buildings: "imitating" nature is here equivalent to learning from nature and striving consciously to embody quasi-natural principles, though hardly natural "appearances," in the products of human design.[21] In *De pictura*, on the other hand, the requirement that the painter should take his subjects "from nature" is certainly part of a theory of visual naturalism, though one that modifies the principle of truth-to-appearances by coupling it with the need to create works that are both beautiful and animated by human interest.[22] The difference between these two cases has something in common with that between the two kinds of Aristotelian mimesis mentioned earlier—mimesis as analogousness between human and natural productivity, and mimesis as artistic representation. But the two distinctions do not precisely match, because in the first Albertian example the architect is envisaged as deliberately seeking to emulate and sustain the principles of unity that he recognizes in the world of nature.

Diversity in the interpretation of the "imitation of nature," as of artistic "imitation" itself, in Renaissance and post-Renaissance aesthetics affected all the arts. Among the most striking illustrations of this fact from a modern point of view is the variety of respects in which, during the sixteenth century and beyond, mimeticist thinking was applied to music. For theorists of the period, "imitation" could cover such disparate ideas as musical "depiction" (especially in "imitare le parole," descriptively matching instrumental accompaniment to verbal text), the discovery or invention of musical correlates to the passions or emotions, conformity to the supposedly natural laws of harmony, and, last but not least, the musical development and exploitation of what were specifically taken to be the essential "tones" and qualities of the human voice or human speech.[23] All these ideas evince

---

that continues to run through much neoclassicism (cf., for instance, Morgan 1986 on different senses of *vraisemblance* in seventeenth-century France).

[21] *De architectura* 9.5 (Alberti 1966, 2:811–19); cf., e.g., 3.14 (Alberti 1966, 1:247), on the structure of vaults.

[22] *De pictura* bk. 2 (with my earlier comments here and in chapter 4, sction IV).

[23] See Carapetyan 1948 (who is wrong, however, to equate all talk of "imitation" with "imitation of nature"); Dahlhaus 1985, 16–29; Palisca 1985, 396–401; and, more briefly, Sachs 1996, 515–16; quite separate, of course, is the common technical sense of "imitation" as melodic and motivic repetition. Berger 2000, 120–33, charts the rise of a "mimetic" model of music in the mid-sixteenth century, but he does not discuss different senses of mimesis. For the history of concepts of musical mimesis in general, cf. now Guthknecht 2001.

a sense that music is not a purely formal or abstract art but has its place within a larger cultural network of relationships between human minds and reality as a whole. But beyond that basis they differ considerably both in the model of "imitation" employed or implied and in the interpretation of "nature," so that the upshot is a whole mélange of possibilities, spanning things that might now be most readily described as figurative representation, emotional expression (of more than one kind), formal order and beauty, and the creation of a musical style with affinities to the quasi-spontaneous vitality of human speech. There seem to have been no limits to the elasticity with which the language of imitation could be applied to music. In his *De vita* of 1489 Marsilio Ficino speaks of the capacity of music to "imitate" human passions, words, actions, characters, and even the celestial world (this last idea having a Pythagorean coloring). The astrological dimension of this passage is distinctively Neoplatonic, but Ficino's mimetic conception of music is otherwise broadly typical of Renaissance thinking.[24]

The complexity of the total picture of Renaissance principles of mimesis, including the "imitation of nature," can be clarified in some measure by noticing the influence of (Neo)platonizing patterns of sensibility. As Panofsky showed in his classic study, *Idea*, it became common from the second half of the sixteenth century for accounts of artistic creativity to take an idealistic turn that stressed both the artist's original mental conception of his subject and a more metaphysical understanding of "nature"—a cast of thought prefigured in a number of ancient texts (among them, passages of Cicero, Seneca, and Proclus) whose aesthetic goes back to developments that took place in the period of what we now know as Middle Platonism.[25] Such Platonizing factors helped to shape a debate in which what was principally at issue, behind the talk of "ideas," was the status of the "world" represented in art. This debate, which runs throughout the whole period of neoclassicism and into romanticism, generated a range of doctrines stretching all the way from a fully embedded naturalism of the phenomenal world (making art a faithful reflector of visible nature), through various intermediate positions that connect art to forms or "ideas" that inhere in and underlie nature in general, to, at the other end, a conception of art as transcending nature as ordinarily understood and reaching an elevated plane of idealism that could be equated with an ultimate and

---

[24] Ficino 1989, 358–59 (bk. 3, ch. 21); interestingly, Ficino speaks here also of an "imitative" psychological response in both the performer and the hearer of music, an idea with a Platonic pedigree (cf. chapter 2, section I).

[25] See Cicero *Orator* 8–10 (with chapter 11, note 6); Seneca *Epist.* 58.18–21, 65.7–10; Proclus *In Tim.* 1.265 Diehl (cf. chapter 11, note 11); with Panofsky 1968, 11–32, 71–99: Gombrich 1991 voices some reservations about Panofsky's approach.

permanent "nature." All these positions, with their attendant notions of "imitation" as fidelity to, discovery of, or insight into "nature," have important antecedents in the ancient traditions of mimeticism, though it is characteristic of Renaissance and post-Renaissance thinking to produce a highly syncretistic use of ancient sources, as well as exhibit a tendency to blur the distinctions between different conceptions of artistic representation. The imitation of nature can prove a mutable aspiration even in the hands of an individual thinker.[26]

This last observation is forcefully exemplified by one of the most influential documents in the (Neo)platonizing trend of late- and post-Renaissance aesthetics, Bellori's introduction (originally delivered as a lecture in 1664) to his *Lives* of the artists (1672), a piece of writing whose eclectic mixture of ancient citations includes both Platonic and Aristotelian elements, marshaled, with something less than historical meticulousness, in support of the central thesis that figurative art should embody "ideas" of beauty formed in the artist's mind and imagination.[27] The interest of the essay for my purposes lies partly in its attempt to argue for an idealized aesthetic that nonetheless remains, in an important but slippery sense, naturalistic: the artist's "idea" of beauty, Bellori proclaims, should rise "*above* the natural" (sopra le cose naturali), but yet be "derived from nature" (originata della natura) and indeed from "the continual contemplation of nature" (la continua contemplatione della natura). Bellori's somewhat involuted treatment of "imitation" is symptomatic of this aspect of the project. He can be seen, on close scrutiny, to employ perhaps half a dozen somewhat different versions of "imitation" within his rather overcrowded conceptual and metaphysical apparatus. Thus, Bellori's artist "imitates" God himself in virtue of his ability to create by reference to ideal forms; he also imitates the idea, sometimes *rather* than nature (as Bellori says of Phidias's statue of Zeus); but because figurative art is the represen-

---

[26] See the different uses of the principle cited from Ficino (applying both to representational art and to other human activities, and shifting between a concept of rational creativity and the simulation of natural appearances) by Allen 1989, 146–50, with 117–27 for connections with Ficino's (extremely free) interpretation of the eicastic-phantastic distinction in the *Sophist*; cf. Hankins 1991, 265–359 for a detailed contextualization of Ficino's project of Platonic translation and interpretation.

[27] The Italian text of the 1672 edition, together with a translation, is given in Panofsky 1968, 154–75; see 105–9 for Panofsky's discussion of Bellori's essay, which tries too hard, however, to identify a stable concept of representation in the work (cf. Lee 1967, 13–16). For one antecedent of Bellori's thinking, Giovanni Agucchi's *Trattato della pittura* of c. 1610 (of which only a fragment is preserved), see Mahon 1947, 125–31 (on the influence of Aristotle's *Poetics*, esp. the reference to idealized portraits at 15.1454b8–13, also quoted by Bellori), with 240–58 (esp. 242–43) for the Italian text. Bredvold 1934 discusses the kind of Neoplatonist aesthetics of which Bellori is a salient example. I note a possible Goethean echo of Bellori in my introduction, note 7.

tation of human action ("rappresentatione d'humana attione"), the objects of the artist's imitation must include the directly physical expression of emotion. On the other hand, Bellori also uses the language of "imitation" disparagingly for excessive visual naturalism (which he mistakenly equates with the notion of "(e)icastic mimesis" from Plato's *Sophist*), especially where ugly or unattractive subjects are concerned: this subjugation, as he sees it, to the senses rather than the mind, a subjugation with which he also associates the close imitation of defective artistic models (though the imitation of the best *ancient* sculptural models he aligns with pursuit of the "idea" itself), is sometimes also called "copying" (*copiare*), a term Bellori never applies to idealized depiction.

In this way, through a series of precariously balanced antitheses that depend on the possibility of distinguishing "perfect(ed)" nature from its purely empirico-sensual manifestations, and that permit approval of artworks derived from yet rising above nature, while requiring censure of those merely "depicted from nature" (le cose dipinte dal naturale), Bellori strives to achieve a stable conception of idealizing representation. His aesthetic, contained within a framework whose tripartite configuration of God (the ideas), nature, and human mimesis has an ancestry that goes all the way back to Plato *Republic* 10, amounts to a kind of spiritualized naturalism, in contrast to a purely visual, phenomenal naturalism. The same is accordingly true of his mimeticism, which depends on somehow retaining a basis of natural appearances in art while calling for the transformation of those appearances into intimations of a divinely ordained domain of beauty—a reversal of Plato's own apparent priorities carried out in the spirit of ancient Middle Platonism and Neoplatonism, as signaled by the essay's references to such figures as Philo, Maximus of Tyre, and Proclus. Bellori's ideal artist, we must conclude, both does and does not "imitate nature"; everything turns on precisely how each of the key terms is understood, and the resulting interpretation of mimesis spans a spectrum from servile copying to creative imagination. This point is nicely captured by an engraving in the *Lives* that shows an allegorical figure of "wise imitation" (Imitatio sapiens), who, classically draped and seated inside an architectural perspective, self-admiringly gazes into a mirror, symbol of her own idealized potential, but simultaneously treads resolutely on an unprepossessing "ape," traditional metaphor for the debasement of mimesis into the empty simulation of a world of vulgarly reflective surfaces.[28]

[28] See Panofsky 1968, 101, for a reproduction of the engraving (also in Bell 1999, 20; Suthor 2001, 1305–6), with 202–4 and Curtius 1953, 538–40, for the history of the "ape" metaphor.

II

Competing conceptions of mimesis and of the relationship between art and nature, rather than any monolithic orthodoxy, continue to lie at the heart of some central aesthetic debates for a century and more after Bellori.[29] Arthur Lovejoy rightly claimed that "nature" was the most protean term in the vocabulary of seventeenth- and eighteenth-century neoclassicism, and he documented a multiplicity of senses—on a scale, parallel to that already indicated for antiquity and the Renaissance, running from extreme realism, via generalized verisimilitude, to extreme idealism— which regulated its understanding within the increasingly trite yet elusive slogan of "the imitation of nature."[30] Lovejoy also observed that "the imitation of nature" became so flexible a maxim that it was available to and used by the opponents just as much as the upholders of neoclassicism.[31] In this respect Lovejoy was diverging from a standard and still prevalent view that it was an unqualified rejection of the "imitation of nature" that subsequently characterized romanticism, whose aesthetic impulses supposedly shifted from an outward-facing, so-called "pragmatic," to an inward-facing, "expressive," model of art.[32] Quite apart from other possible reservations about the sharpness of this account—which misses, for example, the extent to which mimesis itself had always been in part a concept of expression—I hope that even the sketch I have already offered of some aspects of the traditions of mimeticism lends plausibility to the alternative interpretation I want to defend here. On this alternative, romanticism (or, at any rate, some important lines of romantic thinking—the hazards of generalization in this area hardly need underlining) involves the "renegotiation" and redefinition, not the outright rejection, of certain strands in the intricate makeup of mimeticism.

[29] Block 1966, 706–17, supplies a convenient selection of examples; Draper 1921 documents eighteenth-century English attitudes, but his own understanding of Aristotelian mimesis is badly distorted by an idealistic interpretation derived from Butcher (cf. chapter 5, note 64). Dieckmann 1969 explores tensions and changes in the "imitation of nature" in eighteenth-century French thinking; Jauss 1969 and Preisendanz 1969 study the impact of ideas of the novel on the same principle.

[30] Lovejoy 1948, 69–77; cf. Lewis 1960, 54–58. Wilkinson & Willoughby 1982, 322–26, document multiplicity of usage in one particular thinker, Schiller.

[31] Lovejoy 1948, 76.

[32] In addition to Abrams 1953, see Iknayan 1983, esp. 3–64, on some of the complexities involved in the shift from "imitation" to "expression"; Burwick 1995 argues, rightly though not always perspicuously, that some forms of romanticism elided the distinction between imitation and expression. Culler 1981, 161–68, voices some reservations about Abrams' mirror-lamp contrast as an account of romanticism's antimimetic turn. Todorov 1977a, 141–203 (1977b, 111–70), traces tensions in eighteenth-century mimeticism (which he treats somewhat impatiently) and romantic reactions (whose completeness he overstates) against mime-

Consider, for example, Karl Philip Moritz's *On the Formative Imitation of the Beautiful* (*Über die bildende Nachahmung des Schönen*, 1788), parts of which were included by his friend Goethe in the latter's *Italienische Reise*. Moritz's term *Nachahmung* needs to be read as a conscious but, I suggest, paradoxical repositioning in relation to the traditional category of artistic "imitation."[33] His essay is a short but effusive rhapsody on the idea of creative genius, which he understands in terms of an active power both analogous to and reflective of the larger powers of nature. The work of genius is a unified "image" and microcosmic equivalent of nature's large-scale beauty. But Moritz concedes that it nonetheless exists at the level of secondary "phenomenon" (Erscheinung); it only "mirrors" nature (Moritz is happy to keep the familiar motif, though applying it to something more like a metaphysical than a sensory relationship) and does not actually constitute "what [its subject] represents" (was er darstellt). That last verb, *darstellen*, is used several times in the essay: Moritz still assumes that representation is a necessary part, an instrument, of creative art. But this yields the paradox that he employs the notion of imitation, *Nachahmung*, not for the correspondence between an artwork's representational content and the visible world, least of all the particular phenomena of that world, but for the creative analogy between the "formative" imagination of genius and the productive capacity of nature itself. The paradox resides, quite simply, in the circumstance that while Moritz is certainly not endorsing the time-honored formula of art's "imitation of nature," a principle he expressly rejected in an earlier essay on the fine arts, he continues to use exactly the same vocabulary for his own views.[34]

Moritz was not alone in combining repudiation of "imitation" as the supposedly lifeless, mechanical representation of mere appearances with a doctrine of art's (or, perhaps preferably, the artist's) metaphysical emulation of nature's own essential and creative energy. Something comparable can be found in an essay of Schelling to which I shall shortly turn. Such doctrines, however, though given an intensively and elaborately romantic cast by writers like Moritz and Schelling, are not wholly romantic in origin.

---

sis; Givens 1991b, with less than total conviction, renews the case for romanticism as the death of mimesis.

[33] See Moritz 1962, 63–93, with discussion in Macciantelli 1994 (who overlooks the older Neoplatonic background); Boyle 1991, 495–500 (esp. on the influence of Spinoza and Leibniz); and Boulby 1978, 151–52, 171–78. Further discussion of Moritz's place in the history of aesthetics, especially his contribution to the idea of pure, disinterested contemplative pleasure, can be found in Abrams 1981, 91–94; Abrams 1989, 165–70; Woodmansee 1994, 18–33; cf. also Todorov 1977a, 179–97 (Todorov 1977b, 148–64).

[34] Moritz's *Versuch einer Vereinigung aller schönen Künste und Wissenschaften unter dem Begriff des in sich selbst Vollendeten* (Attempt at a unification of all fine arts and sciences under the concept of the complete-in-itself, 1785) starts from an explicit rejection of imitation of nature (Moritz 1962, 3).

Versions of them can be found earlier in the eighteenth century, for example in Shaftesbury, who sees the artist as a "second maker," an "imitator" both of the formative power of nature itself and of God the true creator; and the roots of such ideas reach back, via Renaissance thought, to ancient traditions of Neoplatonic, especially Plotinean, mimesis.[35] Such notions remind us of how a conception of mimesis could be turned from a matter of "phenomenal" naturalism, directed to the production of worldlike appearances or impressions, into one of spiritual, organicist, and quasi-religious naturalism, concerned with the underlying forces and creative principles of nature—nature as total "system" and creator of worlds.

The relationship of romanticism, and more generally of eighteenth-century reactions against neoclassicism, to the language and ideas of mimeticism is complex. To simplify it is to risk distorting part of our own intellectual inheritance. The undoubtedly widespread romantic renunciation of mimesis, or equally of "the imitation of nature," *qua* supposed concern with the mere surface plausibility and verisimilitude of artistic images, became caught up in crosscurrents of aesthetic and critical argument that cannot ultimately be resolved into a clear-cut *pro* and *contra* dichotomy. In this regard, ideas belonging to the mimeticist tradition were consequently subject to reinterpretation and transformation rather than sheer repudiation.[36] A demonstration of this point can usefully be taken from the writings of August Wilhelm Schlegel, one of the most influential of all the German romantics. In his 1801 Berlin lectures on fine art and literature Schlegel draws a quintessentially romantic contrast between what he calls the "dead, empirical" (tote und empirische) view of the world as an inert collection of objects or facts, and the "philosophical" conception of the world as perpetual "becoming" (Werden) and "creation" (Schöpfung). Equally characteristically, he supplements this with a contrast between what is accessible to our "external senses" and that inner, spiritual element in us which connects us organically to the hidden, creative processes of nature.[37]

---

[35] Shaftesbury's "second maker" etc.: Shaftesbury 1999, 93, a passage that acknowledges the influence of the Cambridge Platonist Ralph Cudworth. Lieberg 1982, 159–73 (see 168 for Shaftesbury), underestimates how intertwined ideas of "creativity" and mimesis have often been.

[36] Eighteenth-century developments of mimeticist thinking predate romanticism proper. Moritz's concept of *Nachahmung* as quasi-natural creativity is partly anticipated, for example, by the ideas of the Swiss critic Johann Jakob Bodmer: see Abrams 1989, 169, 179, though Abrams exaggerates the extent to which Bodmer's own thinking was entirely new (it has affinities with earlier conceptions of the poet as a quasi-divine creator of "worlds"). Equally, Lessing's *Laokoon* is an example of how a notion of mimesis could be synthesized with concepts of imagination and expression: cf. chapter 4, section I.

[37] Schlegel 1962–74, 2:90–91. Cf. Ewton 1972, 60–71, on Schlegel's view of the relationship between art and nature.

What we have here is an archetypal romantic refusal of a clear dividing-line between the human mind and the natural world, with a corresponding preference for a dynamic interplay between them. Nature itself, far from being an externally inspectable order of phenomena, is a perpetually changing generative force. One of the things it generates is the mind's own active, imaginative, and speculative powers. Yet it is only in the exercise of those powers, only in some sense by thinking creatively ourselves, that we can have any chance of insight into the workings of nature. Whatever view one may now take of this romantic outlook, it ostensibly subverts the frame of reference on which many mimetic doctrines of art had depended. Yet even so Schlegel himself chooses to preserve a kind of place and sense for mimesis in his aesthetic. He does so, in this very same passage, by distinguishing between "imitation" (Nachahmung) as external "aping" (nachäffen) and, on the other hand, imitation as, in a less than transparent formulation, the adoption or appropriation of the principles of human action: "sich die Maximen seines Handelns zu eigen machen." In this latter sense, and on the understanding of nature as the generative force pervading everything, Schlegel emphatically affirms that "art *should* imitate nature" (die Kunst soll die Natur nachahmen). The function of authentically "imitative" art is to create "living works" (lebendige Werke) that contain their own principle of existence within themselves. This looks, after all, very much like a fresh reworking of older ideas, in particular the familiar trope of the "life" embodied in mimetic works, and the motif of the mimetic artist as a godlike creator of organic structures.[38]

There is, it turns out then, a partially submerged indebtedness to the past within Schlegel's thinking at this point. What is new, though, is that he has set these ideas within a romantic manifesto whose intensity of commitment to the notion of mind as itself part of nature's larger creativity has carried him far from the ethos of neoclassical aesthetics. But this makes it more, not less, worthwhile to see how Schlegel was unwilling to sacrifice every aspect of mimeticist thinking about art. In this respect Schlegel is a paradigm of a certain sort of romantic ambivalence. On the one hand, he defines his own romanticism partly in terms of an antineoclassical modernity, and this draws him into a rejection of what he regards as Aristotelian mimeticism. This slant becomes pronounced in his Vienna lectures of 1808, in the seventeenth of which his critique of French classicism induces him to hold Aristotle responsible not for the Unities as such but nonetheless for a purely "*external* definition of beauty" (eine . . . äußerliche Be-

---

[38] On the origins of the idea of "living" artworks, see my introduction, note 48; for the history of comparisons between human and divine artistry, see Theiler 1957. Benziger 1951 remains the best discussion of romantic accounts of "organic" unity, though he deliberately leaves ancient antecedents aside.

stimmung des Schönen) and an "*anatomical*" conception of poetic form
(solche bloß zergliedernde Begriffe—so much for Aristotle's conviction
that plot is the "soul" of tragedy!) that allegedly leads to the neglect of
imagination, feeling, and the free creation of the beautiful.[39] On the other
hand, as we have seen, Schlegel is attached to the notion of art as a creative
power comparable with that of nature itself. Hence, among much else, the
organicism of the material from the Berlin lectures mentioned earlier,
where Schlegel somewhat paradoxically combines an emphasis on the
fluid processes of nature's world of "becoming" with an insistence on the
importance of (organic) structure: his use of the verb *organisieren*, in the
description of creative nature as "organized and organizing" (organisiert
und organisierend), perhaps captures both sides of this stance, encompassing the "organic" and the "organized," we might say. The concept of
organic form, which was important for many of the romantics, takes us a
long way back in the tradition of mimeticism itself, not least to Aristotle's
Poetics, though Schlegel, preoccupied by what he sees as the Aristotelian-
French axis, never acknowledges its place in Aristotle's thinking.

   But a further dimension to Schlegel's ambivalence vis-à-vis mimesis deserves comment, namely its quasi-Platonic affiliations. Most romantics
were attached to the distinction between matter and spirit, (external) form
and (inner) idea, and were happy to claim Platonic precedents for this
element in their thinking.[40] Schlegel himself, in that same seventeenth Vienna lecture in which he makes several references to the higher sphere of
spirit and ideas, explicitly invokes Plato at one point, crediting him with an
"intuitive/contemplative inspiration" (anschauende Begeisterung) of true
beauty and, consequently, the germ of a true aesthetic.[41] This fits with
Schlegel's programmatic statement, in the first lecture, that in all poetry
(which he romantically widens to include all creation of beauty) "internal
[or inward] excellence alone is decisive" (innere Vortrefflichkeit ent-
scheidet allein), and external appearances are per se unimportant—so
much so that when Schlegel succumbs to the temptation to brandish the
old mimeticist metaphor of the artistic "mirror," it has to be "ideas," not
mere "actuality," that are to be reflected in it.[42] It is not, of course, that
Schlegel had much justification in Plato's own work for this ascription of

---

   [39] Schlegel 1962–74, 6:13–16.

   [40] Newsome 1974, 8–24, offers some reflections on Platonic tendencies in German and
English romanticism; cf. Baldwin & Hutton 1994.

   [41] Schlegel 1962–74, 6:15.

   [42] Schlegel 1962–74, 5:18. Schlegel's mirror (compare Moritz, noted earlier, and Schopenhauer and Nietzsche, notes 50, 54) is in the second Vienna lecture (Schlegel 1962–74, 5:34–
35): poetry must be a mirror of necessary and eternal ideas—"zum poetischen Gehalte ist
erforderlich, daß es Ideen, d.h. notwendige und ewig wahre Gedanken und Gefühle . . . in
sich abspiegle"—rather than reflecting the observation of mere "actuality" (das Wirkliche).

self-sufficient beauty to art itself. Rather, we have now reached the romantic culmination of a long process of adaptation, begun by ancient Neoplatonists, whereby, to put the point concisely, the distinction between appearances and reality that Plato himself had sometimes deployed *against* mimesis could now be used to the positive advantage of art by making it underwrite a romantic rhetoric of art as the creative workings of spirit and idea in the world of phenomenal form.

The consequences of this aesthetic "Platonism" for the cultural fortunes of mimetic thinking are ambiguous not only in Schlegel. In Friedrich Schelling's "On the Relation of the Formative Arts to Nature" (Über das Verhältnis der bildenden Künste zur Natur, 1807), we find a curt dismissal of the external "imitation of nature," and even of the imitation of *beautiful* nature (the doctrine of Winckelmann, and before him of Batteux and others), which Schelling takes to be an aesthetic idealism of mere appearances. Schelling regards nature in existing formulations to be a necessarily lifeless concept (he repeatedly depreciates various views of nature as "dead"), and he argues that only art created by "the spiritual eye" (das geistige Auge) can go beyond "empty external form" (die leere, abgezogene Form), move into the realm of pure ideas, and creatively emulate nature by embodying the eternal in a sensual form appropriate to it.[43] So we have here, as in Schlegel, both the rejection of the "imitation of nature" *qua* principle of the artistic reflection of the empiricophenomenal world, yet also its retention and reinterpretation as a principle of creativity itself: art must be "alive in its imitation" (lebendig nachahmend). However, having insisted that art must in one sense "withdraw from nature" (sich . . . von der Natur entfernen), Schelling proceeds to argue that in order to capture the unity of truth and beauty in which he quasi-Platonically believes, a unity equivalent to what he counts as "the indwelling spirit of nature" (des inwohnenden Naturgeistes), art must nonetheless "represent what actually exists in nature" (das in der Natur in der Tat Seiende darzustellen).[44]

Although I cannot claim to do justice to the many facets of Schelling's difficult position, it is very much germane to my purposes to notice that at any rate the paradoxical status of this last conclusion is the result of the Platonizing line of thought to which he is affiliated. Where some types of Platonism require a principle of transcendence that leaves an unbridgeable gap between appearances and reality, a romantic Platonist like Schelling attempts to *integrate* and harmonize the domains of form and idea, body and soul, nature and art. Schelling wishes to discard the view of nature as an external, mechanical reality whose surfaces are statically reproduced

---

[43] Schelling 1911, 387–425, at 388–95; on the motif of the "spiritual eye," cf. chapter 4, note 9.
[44] Schelling 1911, 395–98.

by art; instead, he proclaims that art is a kind of extension of the creativity of nature itself. He wants to abandon the aim of artistic realism as conventionally understood, because he thinks it cannot even be successful on its own terms. Yet at the same time he recycles some of the language of mimeticism by explaining that a genuine work of art can and should "resemble nature," albeit in virtue of an "unfathomable reality" (jene unergründliche Realität . . ., durch die es einem Naturwerk ähnlich erscheint); and, alert to the danger of characterless generality, he reaffirms the desirability of strong individuality in artistic representation, especially of the human form.[45] As one type of mimesis is repudiated, another seems subtly but irresistibly to occupy its place.

German romanticism created a mixture of attitudes toward the language and values of mimeticism whose repercussions can be traced in succeeding thinkers too.[46] This is so, for example, with Schopenhauer, who adopts an individual version of the doctrine of aesthetic "disinterestedness" that had emerged from Enlightenment, and especially from Kantian, aesthetics.[47] Within the terms of his own system he translates such disinterestedness into freedom from "willing," from the ceaseless, painful operation of the will that otherwise characterizes all life. Part of what makes Schopenhauer's philosophy of art pertinent to my own argument is that he manages to combine this notion with a larger model of art that does not disconnect it from the interest, meaning, and value of life as a whole. Works of art, for Schopenhauer, continue to depict and evoke possible features of experience, as well as to require in those who contemplate them—and here he diverges sharply from Kant—cognitive and emotional responses that draw on the general understanding of reality. At a very basic level, in fact, Schopenhauer remains a kind of mimeticist thinker, for he holds that all the arts, with the special exception of music (though even this, he believes, stands in a peculiar kind of "imitative" relationship to the ultimate ground of reality, the will itself), are species of "representation" (Darstellung) and produce objects that stand in the relation of "copy to original" (wie Nachbild zum Vorbilde).[48] But he turns his

[45] Schelling 1911, 396–97, 399–401.

[46] One of these repercussions was a tendency to separate "representation" (*Darstellung*) from "imitation" (*Nachahmung*) contrary to previous usage: we find this, for example, in Hegel, who offers a trenchant critique (with Platonic overtones) of one, reductive view of imitation (Hegel 1975, 1:41–6) but repeatedly discusses art in terms of representation.

[47] Cf. my introduction, section II.

[48] *Die Welt als Wille und Vorstellung*, vol. 1 §52 (Schophenhauer 1988, 1:338–53): note that, contrary to what is sometimes claimed, Schopenhauer here explicitly refers to music's "imitative relation to the world" (ihre nachbildliche Beziehung zur Welt, 339), though he regards it as different from that of the other arts and as something deeply obscure; on his concept of music, cf. Budd 1985, 76–103. In §45 (1:296–8) he rejects "Nachahmung der Natur," i.e., *qua* entirely empirical experience, as the source of artistic beauty (in visual art),

mimeticism into a strikingly Platonic, or rather Neoplatonic, form by maintaining that the particulars depicted in all artworks (*except* those of music)
become expressions, and promote knowledge, of quasi-Platonic ideas,
the universal forms that underlie all the phenomena of the world.[49] On
Schopenhauer's model, therefore, while aesthetic experience, as a will-
less, disinterested act of contemplation, is one of very few routes of escape
from the trammels of the individual's suffering existence, it is an experience that does not avert its gaze from reality but engages with it at a deeper
level of truth, the level of universal, eternal essences. This helps to explain
how Schopenhauer can preserve and adapt an old motif of mimetic thinking in referring to the will-less knowledge mediated through and experienced in art as the "pure, clear mirror of the world" (blosser, klarer Spiegel
der Welt), and can speak of the beautiful images of life that are possible
not in life itself but only in the "transfiguring mirror of art or of poetry" (im
verklärenden Spiegel der Kunst oder der Poesie).[50]

The force of my heterodox claim that at least some forms of romanticism
and its aftermath mark a renegotiated or redefined mimeticism, rather than
a clean break with the traditions of mimetic thought, is not applicable
only to German intellectuals. In England, Coleridge's repeated concern,
exhibited especially in his notebooks and his lectures on Shakespeare, to
elevate the notion of "imitation," in which likeness and difference, art and
nature, are joined together, over that of a "copy," exemplifies my thesis
equally well. In Coleridge's case, one line of continuity with older ways
of thinking consists of his equation of "imitation" with "representation,"
an equation whose earlier development I have already illustrated. Moreover, as Coleridge, like some other English romantics, was content to go
on using (interchangeably with that of "the fine arts") a category of "the
imitative arts" that was essentially coextensive with Plato and Aristotle's
class of the mimetic arts, his own stance toward earlier mimetic models of
aesthetics is anything but straightforwardly hostile.[51] Even more forcefully

---

which he traces instead to the artist's a priori grasp of ideas; at the same time he is in no
doubt that the best artists work from powerful, firsthand experience of life (cf. "vom Leben
und der Welt selbst unmittelbar," vol. 1 §49, Schopenhauer 1988, 1:314).

[49] Vol. 1 §§36, 41, 45, 49, 52. Note, however, that Schopenhauer's position here, formulating as it does the possibility of accessing ideas *in* or through particulars (§52, Schopenhauer
1988, 1:340–41: knowledge of ideas "durch Darstellung einzelner Dinge" [through the representation of individual objects]), might be regarded as (unintentionally) more Aristotelian
than Platonic.

[50] *Die Welt als Wille und Vorstellung*, vol. 1 §27 (Schopenhauer 1988, 1:215), vol. 2, ch. 30
(Schopenhauer 1988, 2:436). Cf. my note 54, on Nietzsche's use of the mirror motif.

[51] Coleridge's retention of "the imitative arts," paralleled in, e.g., Shelley's *Defence of Poetry* of 1821 (which refers to "mimetic representation" as well as "imitative arts": Jones 1916,
122–23), occurs in, e.g., *Biographia Literaria*, ch. 18 (Jackson 1985, 355), where both the
distinction between imitation and copy and the association of imitation with representation

than with the German romantics, we encounter here an appropriation and adaptation, not a jettisoning, of some of the vocabulary and the standards of mimeticism. Above all, by the insistence with which Coleridge asserts his separation between the "imitation" (in which the natural is transformed by the power of artistic remaking) and the "copy" ("cold," formal, mechanical reproduction)—a separation now obliterated, we need to notice, by the modern semantics of these terms—he contrives to salvage "imitation" for a place in his aesthetics of creativity, turning it into a fusion of sameness and difference that points toward his lifelong obsession with the reconciliation of opposites. Whatever may be made of that strategy within the larger reaches of Coleridge's mentality, it stands as a distinctively romantic response to the tension between world-reflecting and world-creating impulses that had characterized the whole of the preceding history of mimetic theorizing. Alongside the central value of imagination, Coleridge shared with Wordsworth a continuing belief in poetry's need for "a faithful adherence to the truth of nature."[52]

Another symptom of this same Coleridgean process of reorientation toward mimesis is the reworking of the motif of art as the mirror of nature— a motif that, as we have already observed, does not become obsolete in the late eighteenth and nineteenth centuries but is reinterpreted by various romantics in ways that convert the mirror of art from a reflective into a transformative instrument.[53] I earlier drew attention to Moritz's adaptation of artistic mirroring to his metaphysics of creative "imitation," where, however, mirroring is still linked to phenomenal "appearance" (Erscheinung). In Schopenhauer, as I have also mentioned, the mirror of art is expressly a "transfiguring" agent, insofar as it conveys universal, quasi-Platonic ideas rather than merely worldlike actuality; but the connection to artistic images is still not broken.

It was left to Nietzsche, in his own Schopenhauerian phase, to take the further, deeply paradoxical step of dissociating the idea of mirroring from the phenomena of life and attaching it to the artistic expression, especially by music, of the world's "inner truth"; and the paradox is reinforced by the fact that this "mirroring" (Wiederspiegelung) is directly opposed, in *Birth of Tragedy* 17, to "imitation" (Nachahmung, imitieren) of the surfaces

---

also occur. Related ideas appear in, e.g., *Biographia Literaria*, ch. 17 (Jackson 1985, 335), in the essay "On Poesy or Art" (Coleridge 1907, 2: 255–59, stressing imitation of "natura naturans" as against "natura naturata"), and in various passages of the lectures on Shakespeare: see Hawkes 1969, 48 ("imitation" synonymous with "representation"), 55 ("imitation," not copying, as "the universal principle of the fine arts"), 96–97 ("imitation" contrasted with "copy"). Marks 1981, 42–95, cites further material and argues for an "Aristotelian" rather than Neoplatonist cast to Coleridgean "imitation"; see also Metzger 1966.

[52] *Biographia Literaria*, ch. 14 (Jackson 1985, 314).

[53] See notes 42, 50, 54; cf. Abrams 1953, 31–35, 50, 127, for further examples.

of life.[54] Nietzsche's position here, for all its idiosyncrasy, can serve as a pungent instance of the tangled postromantic consequences of the reinterpretation of a mimeticist aesthetic. If, in chapter 17 of the *Birth of Tragedy*, Nietzsche feels impelled to reuse, with a new metaphysical significance, the classically mimeticist symbol of the artistic mirror, in chapter 2 he equally modifies the age-old formula of the "imitation of nature," doing so in a manner that consolidates the romantic turn toward a construal of this idea in terms of natural creativity rather than the production of naturalistic appearances. Nietzsche is able to do this because he takes his twin forces of the Dionysiac and the Apollonian to be, in the first instance, quasi-artistic drives (Kunsttriebe) in *nature itself*—a novel variant on the ancient notion of nature as "artist" or craftsman—so that, in relation to nature, every human artist is, he says, necessarily an "imitator" (Nachahmer), following the example revealed by nature through the experience of either dreaming or intoxication. In putting "Nachahmer" in inverted commas, as Nietzsche does here, he is self-consciously aiming, just as in the case of his renewal of the metaphor of mirroring in chapter 17, to retain yet reconfigure and recharge the vocabulary of much older traditions in aesthetics.[55] The same is true of his reference to Aristotle's idea of the "imitation of nature," which follows shortly afterward in this same context of the *Birth of Tragedy*. In the effort to transcend a tradition of Aristotelian poetics that had become fossilized by neoclassical canonization, Nietzsche finds himself, like the romantics before him, going back to a principle of Aristotelian *physics*, a principle, at base, of natural "productivity" and creativity.

The arguments I have been presenting in this section are not intended to deny that romanticism dealt a major blow to, and thus contributed to the long-term decline of, the (neoclassical) idiom of the artistic "imitation of nature." But the effects of the blow were more gradual than is often suggested, in part because the nineteenth century produced a reinvigorated interest in representationally "truthful" models of both visual and verbal, and even to some extent musical, art.[56] This interest is displayed most conspicuously, from the 1830s onward, in the history of new concepts, as well as new practices, of both "realism" and "naturalism" in literature and painting. The extensive critical debates that took place over these

---

[54] Nietzsche 1988, 1:109–15, associating "Erscheinung" with "Nachahmung" and "das imitatorische Konterfei der Erscheinung" (imitative counterfeiting of appearance), whereas music and the deepest poetic art operate as a "mirror" of the underlying truth, the (Schopenhauerian) "will," of nature. Cf. also *Birth of Tragedy* 22 (Nietzsche 1988, 1:141) for a contrast between godlike creation and "imitation of nature."

[55] Nietzsche 1988, 1:30–31; the editors' misleading reference (Nietzsche 1988, 14: 46), apropos "imitation of nature," to Aristotle *Poet.* 1.1447a16, perpetuates a common mistake (cf. chapter 5, notes 2, 5, 6).

[56] See Dahlhaus 1985 for nineteenth-century ideas of musical "realism."

aesthetic principles, especially in France, centered on interpretations of
the supposedly faithful and truthful representation of reality. It is well documented that the idea of artistic "imitation (of nature)," particularly in connection with visual art, remained a basic element in the critical vocabulary
of the period, though the issue of whether representation could justify
itself in wholly "realist" terms—that is, by exclusive reference to the depiction of the material conditions of life in the present—was at the very heart
of the debates.[57]

But if the nineteenth century saw the reinvigoration of older disagreements between aesthetic realists and idealists, a very different reaction to
the mimeticist legacy took the form of the efflorescence, directly in the
wake of romanticism, of self-conscious aestheticism, the doctrine of art
for art's sake. Aestheticism defined itself precisely by reaction against the
traditions of mimesis, including the contemporary embodiment of those
traditions in realist and naturalist theories of both pictorial and literary art.
No work epitomizes this aspect of aestheticism better than Oscar Wilde's
"Decay of Lying" (1889), many of whose most pointed aphorisms compose
themselves by picking up clichés of mimeticism and ostentatiously contradicting or inverting them. The result is a virtually parodic antimimeticism:
"novels which are so like life that no one can possibly believe in their
probability"; "it is the spectator, and not life, that art really mirrors"; art "is
a veil, rather than a mirror"; "life holds the mirror up to art"; and, above
all of course, "life imitates art far more than art imitates life." Given all that,
it should not be overlooked that in one central respect—the celebration
of art as "lying"—Wilde's speaker, Vivian, specifically if ironically invokes
a supposed precedent in the Platonic association of mimesis and "lies."[58]
Even Wilde's antimimeticism has some visible roots in the mimetic tradition, a perhaps not unintentionally piquant piece of witty derivativeness
(one of Wilde's special talents).

What is more, the epigrammatic bravura of Wilde's "new aesthetics"
only partially conceals the tensions in his position. Pushed through to its
obvious conclusion, the aversion to artistic realism, truth, and lifelikeness

[57] The best collection of evidence is in Weinberg 1937: see esp. 98–102 for common critical
formulations that relied on a notion of "imitation," with 106–14, 117–44, for the larger debates
in which questions of representation and imitation were involved. By contrast to new realist
tendencies, Quatremère de Quincy 1823 (first Eng. trans., 1837), making some reference to
both Plato (ch. 12) and Aristotle (ch. 11), had reasserted at length an idealizing concept of
"imitation" that resists the goal of full sensory fidelity and insists (a point as old as Plato *Crat.*
432a–d) on the incompleteness, artifice, and difference that distinguish mimetic works from
nature. Later in the century, ideas akin to the "imitation of nature" are prominent among
many impressionist critics and artists: see, for convenience, the views cited in Holt 1966, 17
(Laforgue), 46, 49, 51 (Renoir), 60 (Pissarro), 69–71 (Rodin), 92 (Cézanne).

[58] "The Decay of Lying" (1889), in Weintraub 1968, 165–96; the reference to Plato is at
168–69.

ought to point to the complete abandonment of human and natural subject matter in art (a step subsequently to be taken by others). Although a passage on Orientalism drifts toward such sheer formalism at one point in the dialogue, the inference is never fully drawn; Vivian's values continue to imply and require art forms with representational content. This is demonstrated by the ideal of "lying" itself, the related endorsement of "probability" (one of the oldest of mimetic criteria) as opposed to "truth," and, above all, the very idea of "life imitating art"—which, far from constituting the *ne plus ultra* of antimimeticism, actually echoes an ancient notion and, in Wilde's usage, does not so much negate mimesis as displace its purpose onto the artlike fashioning of life itself.[59] Despite yet also because of these inconsistencies ("who wants to be consistent?" exclaims Vivian at one point), "The Decay of Lying" brings out what is, from my standpoint, a crucial feature of nineteenth-century, postromantic aesthetics: the extreme polarization of attitudes and evaluations *pro* and *contra* the legacy of mimeticism. The degree of divergence between realism and aestheticism, between a kind of hypermimeticism and a would-be radical antimimeticism, stretches the spectrum of mimesis close to the limits. But not till the twentieth century, it seems, could anyone actually purport to move beyond the spectrum altogether.

III

When, in his book *After the End of Art*, Arthur Danto claims that mimesis, which he acknowledges as the dominant paradigm of art from Aristotle to the nineteenth and even into the twentieth century, "did not become ideologized until the age of modernism," he implies a startlingly abridged vision of the history of aesthetics.[60] It would be more accurate, as preceding parts of this book have tried to explain, to say that the definition and interpretation of mimesis have always been a locus of argument and contestation. It is hard, after all, to think of anyone for whom the issues of mimesis were *more* a matter of "ideology" than Plato himself, the great initiator of the mimeticist debate. Now, Danto makes the claim just quoted because he is understandably keen to emphasize the extent of the challenge that modernist art and art theory issued to aesthetics in the early twentieth century, and this causes him to overstate the homogeneity of mimetic thought for the purposes of his contrast. Modernism, with its abrupt turn away from existing styles of representation in all the arts, certainly delivered an unprecedentedly sharp jolt to the terms of the disputes which had been conducted around mimesis since the Renaissance: "all

[59] On the ancient idea of "life imitating art," see chapter 10, notes 2, 5.
[60] Danto 1997, 46.

forms of imitation are to be despised," as one of the futurist manifestos
stridently proclaimed (aiming, it goes without saying, both at the idea of
representation and at the emulation of older art).[61] But Danto is induced
by his awareness of the modernist revolution into characterizing the story
of mimeticism far too narrowly, especially when he asserts that "art criticism in the traditional or mimetic period was based on visual truth."[62] If
by "visual truth" Danto means a naturalistic fidelity to the appearance of
things, the "look of the real," then he is referring to an admittedly important
species or version of mimesis, but not, as we have seen at various junctures
of this book, its only version. In antiquity, thinkers as different as Aristotle
and Plotinus expressly allow for mimetic departure from "visual truth";
and from the Renaissance onward, as earlier sections of this final chapter
have documented, an unmodified naturalism is often criticized by leading
theorists of the figurative arts, especially on the idealist wing of the argument. Rather than producing an aesthetic consensus about visual, or any
other sort, of "truth," the traditions of mimetic theorizing had always set the
scene for divergent conceptions of the status, aims, and values of artistic
representation. I shall shortly return to this fundamental point when considering the perspectives on mimesis adopted by Derrida and Barthes.

It would be possible, of course, to draw up an elaborate "balance-sheet"
of twentieth-century thinkers, as well as of artistic movements themselves,
in terms of their *pro* or *contra* stance toward various (though often reductive) interpretations of artistic mimesis. It is not only in the visual arts that
the last hundred years have witnessed everything from the most radical
rejection of figurative or narrative representation per se to reassertions of
neorealist or similar aesthetic creeds. In virtually all artistic spheres, and
in the domains of both theory and practice, one of the main distinguishing
marks of modernism and its aftermath has been an unresolved, polarized
dialectic of values, between whose extremes an entire spectrum of positions, from outright formalism to outright moralism, from pure abstraction
to the most engaged styles of *verismo*, has stretched itself out. The impact
of this state of affairs on views of mimesis has been compounded by the
fact that at the level of more general philosophical aesthetics, as I indicated
at the start of this chapter, one can find revisionist advocacy of mimetic
theory and strong skepticism about the viability of such theory occupying
adjacent territories on the bewilderingly pluralist landscape of modern intellectual culture.[63] To attempt even an outline of how different parts of

[61] "Futurist Painting: Technical Manifesto," 11 April 1910, quoted from Chipp 1968, 292.

[62] Danto 1997, 47.

[63] Different treatments of mimesis in the modern scene can be found in Spariosu 1984a
(theoretically somewhat clotted), Lindenberger 1984 (an unsympathetic, rather superficial
analysis of what he calls the mimetic "bias" of modern Anglo-American criticism), Prendergast 1986 (a rich but balanced exploration of modern French treatments of mimesis). Nuttall

this teeming scene relate to the major themes I have pursued in this book would, in the space available to me, be wantonly overambitious. All I can offer, by way of conclusion, is a selection of extremely compressed reflections on what strike me as some of the most salient implications of the range of modern reactions to the legacy of mimeticism.

Mimesis has always been the object of divergent attitudes, but the romantic challenge to neoclassicism sharpened this divergence into conflicts that in the twentieth century hardened into apparently unmanageable polarization. Yet through and beyond this polarization mimesis has tenaciously remained a focus for a number of key issues in aesthetics and criticism, as well as in broader perspectives on culture.[64] The main reason for this situation, I believe, is that to think about mimesis, as the concept has been developed in the texts discussed in this book, is to come up against hard, foundational, and permanently worthwhile questions about artistic meaning, and, ultimately perhaps, about the status of meaning *tout court*. That, if my arguments in part I of this book were on the right lines, is something that Plato grasped, and even the most anti-Platonic of modern intellectuals cannot altogether escape from the challenge of mimesis that Plato was the first to adumbrate.

Among twentieth-century forms of aesthetics that maintain a manifest link with directly mimeticist traditions are Marxist or Marxizing theories of "socialist realism." That link is intricate, since such theories involve the double components of what can be called their professed attachment to

---

1983 offers an attempted rehabilitation of mimesis by a literary critic; Graff 1979, 63–101, considers antimimetic aesthetics within the broader context of modern cultural radicalism; Diamond 1997 explores a highly performative, nonrealist notion of mimesis within a feminist framework. Cf. Miner 1990, 58–60, on the tenacity of mimeticist categories (though he is wrong, here and elsewhere, to treat philosophical realism as a presupposition of mimetic theories). In the visual domain, one extreme symptom of complexity is the fact that even theorists of abstract or nonfigurative art can appropriate and adapt some of the language of mimeticism: see, e.g., Piet Mondrian's remarks on painting as the representation or expression of universal reality in Chipp 1968, 321–23, 349–64. The critique of ideas of visual mimesis in Bryson 1983, 37–66, relies on a reductive, question-begging construal of the key concept (38); contrast, e.g., Marin 1988 on the doubleness of mimesis (as what he calls "duplication" and "substitution"). For an overview of the history of visual models of mimesis, see now Suthor 2001.

[64] Among broader conceptions of mimesis, see, e.g., Walter Benjamin's quasi-anthropological view, which in turn influenced that of Adorno (cf. note 2), of "the mimetic faculty" in humans (Benjamin 1972–89, 2.1:204–13). The idea of a mimetic instinct was partly influenced by Frazer's theories of sympathetic magic, of which the homeopathic-imitative-mimetic is one branch (see *The Golden Bough* ch. 3 §§1–2, and cf. Gell 1998, 99–101; Gebauer & Wulf 1992, 374–88), but it goes back as far as Aristotle *Poet.* 4.1448b5–8 (cf. chapter 6, section I), and appears regularly in other writers (see chapter 6, note 5, with, e.g., Goethe *Wilhelm Meisters Wanderjahre* 2.12, Goethe 1985–98, 17:498; *Wilhelm Meisters Lehrjahre* 2.2, Goethe 1985–98, 5:80).

truth-to-life (the descriptively "realist" element in their makeup) and their idealization of political "heroes" (the normatively "socialist" element).[65] Something of this intricacy, with the paradoxes and instabilities resulting from it, can be traced in the special version or development of socialist realism contained in the ideas of Bertolt Brecht, not least in Brecht's formal statement of his theory of "non-Aristotelian" (nichtaristotelisch) drama- turgy in the *Kleines Organon für das Theater*, written in 1948 and first published the following year. Brecht's aesthetic of scientific-Marxist social commitment specifically repudiates nineteenth- and early twentieth-cen- tury artistic naturalism and realism as forms of "bourgeois" entertainment that are taken to be complicit in the maintenance of outmoded attitudes and, with them, outmoded social relations. Prima facie, and especially given his inclusion of such traditions under the umbrella-rubric of the "non-Aristotelian," it might be supposed that Brecht's rejection of theatrical "realism" and "naturalism" is a rejection of everything associated with mi- mesis. But this turns out to be far from the case.

Admittedly Brecht himself does on occasion, though not in the *Kleines Organon*, assert a need to discard the idea of mimesis as such.[66] But he does so only by treating this idea as synonymous with *false* or misleading representation, the kind of misrepresentation that allows for comfortable, indeed luxuriant, emotional empathy on the part of bourgeois audiences, but which is, for that very reason, the staging of a counterfeit, bogus "real- ity," untrue to the underlying processes of historical contingency and change revealed by dialectical materialism. That Brecht's own aesthetic is itself an aesthetic of (truthful) representation emerges right at the start of the *Kleines Organon*, where theater is defined as consisting of "living representations of recorded or invented events between human beings" (lebende Abbildungen von überlieferten oder erdachten Geschehnissen zwischen Menschen). The principle of representation, for which Brecht's favored term is *Abbildung*, is thereafter invoked repeatedly, and Brecht's critique of existing forms of theater is precisely that they involve, from one point of view, "such *poor*, inadequate reflections of reality" (mit einem so dürftigen Abklatsch der Welt, §27), though reflections which, as Brecht's theory compels him to admit, nonetheless succeed in producing the "nar- cotic" illusionism that bourgeois audiences are used to relishing. Further-

[65] That generalization needs refining, of course, for individual versions of socialist realism, whose relationship to mimesis fluctuates accordingly. This is so, for example, with the most complex proponent of the theory, Georg Lukács, whose late and monumental conception of mimesis as "reflection" (Widerspiegelung) involves a kind of representation of universals: see esp. Lukács 1963, 1: chs. 5–10, 2: ch. 14, with Lichtheim 1970, 116–29, for a concise analysis. Lukács's thinking lends itself much less well than Brecht's to brief treatment here.

[66] See esp. "Der Dreigroschenprozess" (1931), III.6 (Brecht 1988–2000, 21:477), which couples "empathy" (Einfühlung) and mimesis.

more, the *Kleines Organon* does not jettison the notion that theatrical performance is essentially a form of "imitation" (Nachahmung), albeit one modified by the special requirements of Brechtian dramaturgy.[67]

Modified mimeticism is a description that fits more generally Brecht's theory of epic dramaturgy, together with the larger aesthetic it expresses. It is tempting, in fact, to see this theory as defining itself by total commitment to one, and complete distancing from the other, of the two major poles of mimetic thinking I have emphasized throughout this book. That is to say, Brecht sets his face against the aesthetics of an *illusionistic* art that creates a world-in-itself, a self-contained "heterocosm," a mere counterfeit simulation of reality: in this respect, he is even to some degree a kind of Platonist in his strong aversion to illusionism (with its accompanying psychology of "empathy") and his alternative advocacy of an art of social understanding and judgment.[68] At the same time, however, Brecht remains wedded to the basic idea of artistic representation, to the goal of truth through representation, and therefore to what in his own terms counts as "realism." Outside the *Kleines Organon* Brecht is even prepared to continue speaking of the need for art to "imitate nature," despite his own association of "imitation" with "Aristotelian" categories of theater; and in the *Organon* itself he indicates a qualified adherence to what he knew to be a central, though always a problematic, symbol of mimeticism, the mirror: "if art reflects life," he remarks, "it does so with special mirrors" (wenn die Kunst das Leben abspiegelt, tut sie es mit besonderen Spiegeln).[69] Brecht is uncompromisingly opposed to styles and forms of art that allow the act of representation to become an end in itself; his interwoven dramaturgy and politics demand a principle of representation that gives access to, that lays bare, social reality without succumbing to the temptation to produce the "narcotic" of a fictionally convincing simulation. That formulation indicates that Brecht is firmly on the side of world-reflecting, not world-creating, mimesis, as well as being the proponent of a kind of mimesis that is an expressive and potent means of ideological communication. But it also brings out a central paradox in his position, namely that his

---

[67] *Kleines Organon* §54 (Brecht 1988–2000, 23:86): acting should be imitation modified by social observation and thought. Brecht is even prepared to claim, paradoxically, a kind of "naturalness" (Natürlichkeit) for the "V(erfremdungs)-Effekt" style of acting: see "Kurze Beschreibung einer neuen Technik der Schauspielkunst" (Short description of a new technique of acting, 1940), in Brecht 1988–2000, 22.2:647.

[68] On this point, cf. chapter 2, section II. It is tangentially interesting here to notice the overtones of Plato's Cave in the caricature of theatrical experience in *Kleines Organon* §26 (Brecht 1988–2000, 23:75–76); I cannot, however, trace a single reference to Plato's critique of (dramatic) poetry anywhere in Brecht's voluminous writings.

[69] *Kleines Organon* §73 (Brecht 1988–2000, 23:96). For Brecht's partial endorsement of art as "imitation of life" (Leben nachahmen), see "Couragemodell 1949" (Brecht 1988–2000, 25:172).

notion of "realism" actually requires an avoidance of the illusion of the "real."[70] The consequent tensions in a theory that at different times both does and does not seem to want to keep art close to "life" are the result of Brecht's attempt to define his own position through manipulations of a language and, in particular, through pairs of oppositions, substantially forged by the traditions of mimeticism.

Those traditions, as I have argued throughout this book, have always been complex, but ever since the eighteenth century's, and especially romanticism's, reaction against the "academic" orthodoxies into which some forms of neoclassicism had declined, those traditions have been especially vulnerable to simplification on the part of their critics. A primary source of mimeticism's complexity, as reflected in the structure of this book, is the dialectic built into its history by the interplay between Platonic and Aristotelian approaches to the subject, and the full thrust of that proposition can only be grasped if we allow "Platonic" and "Aristotelian" here to embrace everything that has been said and thought, however loosely, in the name of the two philosophers, not just in their own writings. Failure to do justice to this dialectic is the main weakness in Jacques Derrida's approach to the history of mimesis, an approach that construes that history as governed by a necessary commitment to the value of truth and which is almost entirely silent about the significance of Aristotle's non-Platonic understanding of mimesis for the tradition as a whole. But theories of mimesis are not, and need not be, tied to a uniform, let alone a uniformly Platonist, metaphysics.[71] Yet Derrida's perspective on the history of mimesis—and this is arguably a larger flaw in his perspective on the history of Western thought as a whole—is so fixated on Plato and "Platonism" (with obligatory inverted commas) that it seriously disregards other, especially Aristotelian, parts of the picture. In his essay "La double séance," which is initially written around the question of the nature of literature but very quickly expands to take in issues of metaphysics, Derrida claims that literature has always been construed in terms of a relationship to "truth," a

[70] The text that perhaps best illustrates this is again "Couragemodell 1949," where "realistic images" (realistische Abbildungen) are expressly opposed to the illusion of seeming to be present at a "real event" (einem . . . "echten" Vorgang bei, Brecht 1988–2000, 25:172, 176; for the Greek ancestry of the latter motif, see my introduction, note 48), though even here Brecht indicates the need for a *partial* theatrical "illusion."

[71] It is not only the intellectually radical Derrida who sees the traditions of mimetic thinking in excessively Platonist terms. Isaiah Berlin has claimed that "the aesthetic doctrine of mimesis . . . presupposes that there exist universal principles and eternal patterns to be incorporated or 'imitated,'" and he clearly connects this claim to the prevalence of "Platonic" as well as Christian metaphysics (Berlin 1990, 214). I do not understand the claim of Elam 1993, 579, that mimesis ("imitation") always "rests on a metaphysics within which fulfilment is possible."

relationship to whose history he sees mimesis as being central. For all his subtlety, especially in his shrewd remark that mimesis is a concept "qu'il ne faut pas se hâter de traduire (surtout par imitation),"[72] it is surprising that at an early stage of his reflections Derrida speaks of a mimetic "system." This system is taken to be essentially a manifestation of "Platonism," defined by an aspiration to make contact with truth, with real being, with "the *ontological*" (l'ontologique). According to Derrida, the concept of mimesis commits its holders to a metaphysics of truth because it supposedly always posits a reality that is prior and superior to that which represents it. The history of mimesis is "entirely ruled and regulated," on this view, "by the value of truth" (tout entière réglée par la valeur de vérité).[73]

Earlier chapters of this book have contended that the role and treatment of mimesis in Plato are far more intricate and inconclusive than many interpreters have appreciated. But even if Derrida were right, as I would dispute, to see Plato's own treatment of mimesis as utterly dependent on a metaphysics of truth and reality, it is mistaken to suppose, as Derrida seems to, that this dependence underlies virtually all subsequent versions of mimeticism (though Derrida's essay goes on to intimate its own idea of a kind of textual self-reference that can dispense with external referents). A vital fact about Aristotle's approach to mimesis, and therefore about its status for him as a concept of representation, is that he does not ascribe to mimesis either a single or a necessary relationship to reality but allows it to encompass a range of possible "objects," from fact to fiction, the realistic to the idealistic. If it is a usual premise of Plato's references to mimesis that questions of truth and falsehood (though not automatically at the level of metaphysics) are always in some way at stake, the same cannot so easily be said of Aristotle, for whom mimesis is embodied in a set of activities whose cognitive status is hypothetical and exploratory, though still anchored in beliefs about, and attitudes to, the real world. That difference between Platonic and Aristotelian models has proved a productive source of richness and diversity in the history of later mimeticism too, and the

[72] A "concept one should not hurry to translate, especially by imitation": Derrida 1972, 208. But Derrida himself had followed his own advice less well in "La pharmacie de Platon" (originally published in 1968), where he uses "l'imitation" freely (see Derrida 1972, 156–61, with just a brief reservation at 159 n. 58).

[73] Derrida 1972, 201–22, at 209; cf. 219 ("la *mimesis*, dans l'histoire de son interprétation, s'ordonne toujours au procès de la vérité": "mimesis, throughout the history of its interpretation, is always subject to the trial of truth"). Despite occasional allusions to the possibility of different notions of mimesis, Derrida's essay effectively makes mimeticism a monolithic model of art (and, in its metaphorical "Platonic" extensions, of all thought). The only (and extremely loose) reference to Aristotle is at 216 n. 12. Cf. Bennington 2000, 47–53, for a recent treatment of the essay, with Spariosu 1984b, 66–79, and Gebauer & Wulf 1992, 406–22, for other angles on Derrida's general critique of mimesis.

Derridean critique misses that diversity on account of its own paradoxically restrictive construal of mimesis.[74]

Moreover, Derrida's critique of mimeticism is vulnerable to an objection
that has been brought against his thinking more generally by Hilary Putnam, namely that it identifies a "Platonist" model of representation, which
seems to require unsustainable conditions of philosophical truth, with representation *tout court*, and counts the difficulties of the former as grounds
for challenging the validity of *any* concept of the latter.[75] But once mimesis
is seen as a locus of possibilities within a fully human perspective, a perspective that interprets "reality" through culturally structured but disputable (and amendable) frameworks of beliefs, standards, and conventions,
rather than by a set of metaphysically absolute reference points, it is far
from obvious that the Derridean critique gives us a purchase on anything
other than one extreme definition of (or aspiration to) mimesis. Derrida is
right to suppose that mimesis always implicitly posits an imagined reality
that could in principle be external to the work (representation must by
definition be representation *of* something); but he is wrong to suppose
that this need entail a "metaphysics of presence" or reference to a plane
of reality taken to be wholly independent of its artistic presentation. To
put the point more generally, if human thought and imagination are feasible and intelligible at all (and Derrida himself continues to engage in
them), then artistic mimesis has the only basis it requires. Representation,
whether inside or outside art, rests on the possibility of *some* publicly
shared understandings, but it lays no intrinsic claim to transcendent truth.

The issues summarily sketched in the preceding paragraphs are fundamental to much modern contention over the status of mimesis. At their
heart is an intellectual crisis of confidence brought about by a series of
twentieth-century assaults on the idea of representation, assaults stemming especially from parts of modernism (with its repudiation of humanist
traditions of art), from suspicion of cultural and political representation as
tools of ideology, and from the whole movement of poststructural skepticism about the possibility of stable meaning and interpretation. But none
of these assaults, or even their cumulative impetus, has succeeded in altogether discarding the idea or the currency of representational significance,
whether in art or in the practices of culture more generally. Even within
the radical epistemological skepticism of a Derrida there is acknowledged
room for, at any rate, partial and provisional determinacy of meaning.
Indeed, if there were not, it is hard to see how such skepticism could
articulate itself at all; even hard-core deconstruction actually depends on

---

[74] One recent version of mimeticism that specifically eschews a linkage with "truth" is that
of Lamarque & Olsen 1994, esp. 12–13, 398–439.

[75] Putnam 1992, 124.

the existence of widely shared semantic stability as the very framework against which to pit its own destabilizing operations.[76] The crucial point here is that no challenge to "foundationalist" systems of thought can proclaim unconditional victory for itself without appearing to arrogate the very certainty that it sets out to undermine; antirealism, in this sense, must avoid the danger of becoming a new kind of absolutism. But if skepticism, in theorizing itself, cannot aspire to, let alone achieve, the complete destabilization of meaning or interpretation, the upshot is that all discussion of representation must continue to work with acceptance of at least its culturally testable (and contestable) reality, its embodiment in various forms of socially recognized and interpretable artifacts, discourse, and behavior. The most pertinent implication of this heavily abbreviated case, whose ramifications obviously run beyond my own immediate scope, is quite simply that the intelligibility of mimetic conceptions of art—art as the imaging and "modeling" of life—has not been broken by modern skepticism. That this should be so is reinforced by my own central thesis that mimesis has never been an entirely homogeneous concept of art, but has always been marked by a contrast between world-reflecting and world-creating principles of representation. In that sense, indeed, the history of mimesis still has much to contribute to a better grasp of what is at stake in competing views of the relationship between art and reality.

One final illustration of the complex status of mimetic models of art in a modern context can be taken from the work of Roland Barthes. Barthes' convictions evolved through several distinct stages and have become a key instance of the transition from structuralist to poststructuralist ways of thinking. All I can afford to do here is draw attention to certain details of this intellectual and cultural trajectory that are revealing for the possibility of modern forms (or transformations) of mimetic thinking. In 1963 Barthes published an essay, "L'activité structuraliste," which actually uses a notion of mimesis to explain his own version of structuralist method. Structuralism itself depends, Barthes suggested, on mimesis, on the (re)constructive modeling of the objects of its inquiries, in order, by recomposing them, to set up and clarify the functioning of those objects. Structuralist activity, on this account, is the production of "simulacra," a kind of remaking of the world, but aimed not at replication but at rendering things intelligible: it is the "fabrication véritable," in Barthes' almost paradoxical terms, "d'un monde qui ressemble au premier, non pour le copier mais pour le rendre intelligible."[77] Part of the interest of this somewhat surprising reuse of a

[76] Abrams 1989, 299–312, gives a shrewd and fair analysis of the "doubleness" that marks Derrida's overall philosophy of meaning.

[77] "L'activité structuraliste," in Barthes 1993–95, 1:1328–33, at 1329 ("the fabrication of a world which resembles the primary world, not for the sake of copying it but in order to make it intelligible").

mimetic vocabulary and mode of thinking is that built into it is a subtle equivocation over the difference between the discovery and the invention of meaning, an equivocation that echoes the tension between mimetic truth and mimetic fiction that I have tried to show, throughout this book, was a hallmark of the mimeticist tradition at large. For Barthes, structuralist interpretation does not render the world simply as it finds it; it makes or remakes the world anew in the act of interpretation, and thereby exemplifies a conception of the human species as *Homo significans*, "man" the maker of signs or meanings. But Barthes does not here altogether or definitively detach human, cultural meanings from the larger, more-than-human context of nature. Human beings overlay nature with culture, but they nonetheless continue, as he puts it (in a phrase adapted from Hegel), to listen for the natural within the cultural (structuralist man "prête l'oreille au naturel de la culture"). Mimesis itself, it seems, is a prime act of cultural "fabrication," but it somehow remains, like culture in general, necessarily engaged in the attempt to establish a framework of significance through which humans place and orientate themselves in relation to a larger reality that is not purely of their own devising.

Not many years after this essay, Barthes can be found, in his well-known "Introduction à l'analyse structurale des récits" (1966), taking an apparently clear-cut antimimeticist turn, insofar as he now denies that the function of narrative, among the most primordial of forms of meaning, can be equated with mimesis *qua* "imitation." The function of narrative, he now insists, is not to represent, "la fonction du récit n'est pas de 'représenter'" (but why the self-conscious quotation marks at just this moment?), nor is it "of a mimetic order" (d'ordre mimétique); "narrative does not make us see, and does not imitate" (le récit ne fait pas voir, il n'imite pas).[78] We need to notice, for future reference, that Barthes here appears simply to equate imitation and representation, while his antirealist stance makes him protest too much: nothing *actually* happens, he tells us, and there is nothing *real*, in a (fictional) narrative—as though anyone could think otherwise. (One recalls Samuel Johnson's "imitations produce pain or pleasure not because they are mistaken for realities, but because they bring realities to mind.") Most troublingly of all, Barthes' denial of "representation" or "imitation" is accompanied by a statement that the function of narrative is "meaning" (sens). But why should representation and meaning be thus opposed? Barthes himself will have second thoughts.

Many other Barthesian texts, especially his *S/Z* (1970), could be produced to document his movement away from a structuralist standpoint toward a much more fluid, "playful" view of cultural activity, and with it the crystallization of an ostensibly decisive antimimeticist, antirealist aes-

[78] Barthes 1993–95, 2:74–103, at 103.

thetic.[79] But the story has a subplot. What I want to highlight here, with unavoidable brevity, is that a tension similar to that in the essay of 1963 resurfaces in some of Barthes' further dealings with mimesis and representation. In its later manifestation this tension can be encapsulated by saying that while Barthes comes to be ever more skeptical, even dismissive, of ideas such as the representation of reality, he nevertheless retains a sense of the ineradicable *appearance* of just that in literature and art (as well as other forms of cultural activity), and it is this phenomenon that he tries partly to contain in his concept of the "reality effect" (l'effet de réel) and the related idea of the "referential illusion" (l'illusion référentielle).[80] It is not farfetched to suggest that Barthes' reality effect is, at one level, a sort of redescription and a theoretical readmission of nothing other than the purportedly banished figure of mimesis. In addition, even when he continues to indicate some distance from the notion of mimesis as "imitation," Barthes comes to see very clearly the tenacity, indeed the *ineliminability*, of a "representational" posture toward the world. In his essay "Diderot, Brecht, Eisenstein" of 1973 he now deliberately introduces some space between imitation and representation—"la représentation ne se définit pas directement par l'imitation"—and proceeds to stress the crucial consequences with resigned eloquence: "se débarrasserait-on des notions de 'réel,' de 'vraisemblable,' de 'copie,' il restera toujours de la 'représentation,' tant qu'un sujet (auteur, lecteur, spectateur ou voyeur) portera son *regard* vers un horizon."[81] Theatrical, pictorial, and other representations frame particular tableaux of meaning (Barthes has abandoned his strange disjunction of representation and meaning), always offering a view from somewhere: "les choses sont toujours vues *de quelque part*."[82] Here, I claim, is what seems to be an unconscious acceptance of the basic conditions of mimesis, which might productively be thought of as the artistic construction of, and therefore the opportunity of gazing toward, hypothetical or imaginary horizons. It is precisely because the world is always humanly seen from a particular vantage point (as Plato himself had hinted in *Republic* 10.598a–b, albeit deprecatingly) that certain kinds of mimesis can make sense to their audiences.

---

[79] See the passages cited in Prendergast 1986, 12–18, 64–72, with his analysis of Barthes' struggle with the ambiguities of mimetic representation or reading; cf. Moriarty 1991, 117–42, though he works with a jejune concept of mimesis, esp. 128.

[80] The essay, "L'effet de réel" (1968), is reprinted in Barthes 1993–95, 2: 479–84. Cf. Prendergast 1986, 64–67 for some commentary.

[81] Barthes 1993–5, 2:1591–96, at 1591 ("representation is not defined directly by imitation," and "even if one rids oneself of ideas of 'the real,' 'the lifelike,' 'the copy,' there will always remain 'representation' so long as a subject [author, reader, spectator or voyeur] casts his or her *gaze* toward a horizon . . . ").

[82] Barthes 1993–95, 2:1591–96, at 1595 ("things are always seen *from somewhere*").

Barthes may still long for an escape from the frames of artistic narrative into the supposedly free world of what he sometimes (in a gesture harking back to French symbolism) calls "music," but he knows this is a utopian wish. When, accordingly, he develops his characteristic view of literature precisely as festive, "utopian" play, he can never quite snap the ostensible link between text and world. (Some) literature, he knows, has always been engaged in the supposed representation of "the real," and while Barthes asserts this to be impossible (largely, like Derrida, by projecting absolutist status onto "the real" and equating representation with *unmediated* access to the world) and affirms the perpetual function of literary texts to be a liberation from the delusions of fixity, he accepts an abiding tension between creative textual play and the impression of reality.[83] Through all his late reflections on the production of meaning by readers rather than authors, Barthes continues to recognize something like a mimetic surface, an image-making dimension, to writing (and other art forms). In a sense, I contend, he continues to be caught in the force field between the polarities of truth and fiction, between world-reflecting and world-creating paradigms of art, to which my analysis has appealed throughout this book and which had always helped to define the traditions of mimeticism.

In contrast to both Barthes and Derrida, I maintain that there is no central or consistent commitment in the history of mimeticism to the truth-bearing, as opposed to the sense-making, status of mimetic works. As preceding chapters of this book have explained, the relationship between mimesis and "truth," and, what is more, to different *kinds* of truth, has been construed in a multitude of ways by individual thinkers. What most versions of mimetic thinking, however, as well as arguably most forms of mimetic practice, do presuppose, is both the feasibility and the necessity of human attempts to explore and come to terms with the world through various means of depictive and expressive representation. The indispensable point of mimesis is the quest for meaning, whether that meaning is a matter of discovery or invention, or, most plausibly, both. To argue that this quest is doomed to fall short of finality is not, unless skepticism is compounded by nihilism, to negate its purpose or its value. Representational art forms, whatever their current cultural fortunes (and judgment on this depends greatly on where one stands on the spectrum between "popular" and "avant garde"), have a long past and a number of possible futures. For anyone to whom the past, present, and future of these arts remain vitally important, there is no alternative to continuing to wrestle

---

[83] See here, e.g., "Leçon" (1978, originally Barthes' inaugural lecture of 1977), in Barthes 1993–95, 3:801–14. As regards the tendency of Barthes and others to overstate the necessary pretensions of realist views, the remarks of Marshall 1981, 86 (cf. 94), on the reduction of the "rich and heterogenous tradition" of realism to "a brainless straw man," are apropos.

with the problems raised by the making, the experience, and the evaluation of their products. I have tried in this book to give reasons for supposing that coming to terms with the legacy of mimeticism is an important part of this ongoing enterprise. While the language and idiom of mimeticism may no longer be indispensable, their history remains an essential route to the understanding of issues that themselves remain inescapable. In aesthetics, the effort of finding possible paths of thought between antiquity and modernity involves traversing huge cultural distances across frequently perilous terrain. If this requires a journey over the bones of the dead, it also rewards us with precious glimpses of how the work of the past can nourish the prospects of the future.

Bibliography

Abrams, M. H. 1953. *The Mirror and the Lamp*. New York: Oxford University Press.
———. 1981. "Kant and the Theology of Art." *Notre Dame English Journal* 13:75–106.
———. 1989. *Doing Things with Texts*. New York: W. W. Norton.
Adam, J. 1963. *The Republic of Plato*. 2 vols. 2d ed. Cambridge: Cambridge University Press. Originally published 1902.
Aissen-Crewett, M. 1989. "Paideia und bildende Kunst." *Rheinisches Museum* 132:266–79.
Alberti, L. B. 1966. *L'Architettura*. Ed. G. Orlandi. 2 vols. Milan: Edizioni il Polifilo.
———. 1973. *Opere Volgari*. Ed. L. Grayson. Vol. 3. Bari: G. Laterza.
Alexander, P. J. 1958. *The Patriarch Nicephorus of Constantinople*. Oxford: Clarendon Press.
Allen, M.J.B. 1989. *Icastes: Marsilio Ficino's Interpretation of Plato's Sophist*. Berkeley: University of California Press.
———. 1999. "Renaissance Neoplatonism." In Norton 1999, 435–41.
Alpers, S. 1989. *The Art of Describing: Dutch Art in the Seventeenth Century*. Harmondsworth: Penguin Books.
Anderson, W. D. 1966. *Ethos and Education in Greek Music*. Cambridge, Mass.: Harvard University Press.
Annas, J. 1981. *An Introduction to Plato's Republic*. Oxford: Clarendon Press.
———. 1982. "Plato on the Triviality of Literature." In *Plato on Beauty Wisdom and the Arts*, ed. J. Moravcsik & P. Temko, 1–28. Totowa N.J.: Rowman & Allanheld.
———. 1992. *Hellenistic Philosophy of Mind*. Berkeley: University of California Press.
Ansell-Pearson, K. 1991. *Nietzsche contra Rousseau*. Cambridge: Cambridge University Press.
Armstrong, A. H. 1966. "Some Comments on the Development of the Theology of Images." *Studia Patristica* 9:117–26.
———. 1988. "Platonic Mirrors." *Eranos Jahrbuch* 55:147–81. Reprinted in *Hellenic and Christian Studies* (Aldershot: Variorum, 1990), ch. 6.
Armstrong, D. 1995. "Appendix 1: Philodemus, *On Poems* Book 5." In *Philodemus and Poetry*, ed. D. Obbink, 255–69. New York: Oxford University Press.
Armstrong, J. M. 1998. "Aristotle on the Philosophical Nature of Poetry." *Classical Quarterly* 48:447–55.
Arnould, D. 1990. *Le rire et les larmes dans la littérature grecque d'Homère à Platon*. Paris: Les Belles Lettres.
Arrighetti, G. 1973. *Epicuro Opere*. 2d ed. Turin: Einaudi.
Asmis, E. 1990a. "Philodemus's Epicureanism." *Aufstieg und Niedergang der Römischen Welt* 36.4:2369–2406.
———. 1990b. "The Poetic Theory of the Stoic 'Aristo.'" *Apeiron* 23:147–201.
———. 1991. "Philodemus's Poetic Theory and *On the Good King According to Homer*." *Classical Antiquity* 10:1–45.
———. 1992a. "Crates on Poetic Criticism." *Phoenix* 46:138–69.

Asmis, E. 1992b. "An Epicurean Survey of Poetic Theories (Philodemus *On Poems* 5, cols. 26–36)." *Classical Quarterly* 42:395–415.

———. 1992c. "Epicurean Poetics." In *Proceedings of the Boston Area Colloquium in Ancient Philosophy VII [1991]*, ed. J. J. Cleary, 63–93. Lanham, Md.: University Press of America.

———. 1992d. "Neoptolemus and the Classification of Poetry." *Classical Philology* 87:206–31.

———. 1992e. "Plato on Poetic Creativity." In *The Cambridge Companion to Plato*, ed. R. Kraut, 338–64. Cambridge: Cambridge University Press.

———. 1999. "Epicurean Epistemology." In *The Cambridge History of Hellenistic Philosophy*, ed. K. Algra, J. Barnes, J. Mansfeld, & M. Schofield, 260–94. Cambridge: Cambridge University Press.

Assunto, R. 1965. "Mimesis." In *Encyclopedia of World Art*, 10: 92–121. New York: McGraw-Hill.

Auerbach, E. 1953. *Mimesis: The Representation of Reality in Western Literature*. Trans. W. R. Trask. Princeton: Princeton University Press.

Babbitt, I. 1910. *The New Laokoon: An Essay on the Confusion of the Arts*. Boston: Houghton Mifflin.

Babut, D. 1969. *Plutarque et le Stoïcisme*. Paris: Presses Universitaires de France.

———. 1983. "L'unité du livre X de la *République* et sa fonction dans le dialogue." *Bulletin de l'Association Guillaume Budé* 42:31–54.

———. 1985a. "Sur la notion d' 'imitation' dans les doctrines esthétiques de la Grèce classique." *Revue des Études Grecques* 98:72–92.

———. 1985b. "Paradoxes et énigmes dans l'argumentation de Platon au livre X de la *République*." In *Histoire et structure: À la mémoire de Victor Goldschmidt*, ed. J. Brunschwig, C. Imbert, & A. Roger, 123–45. Paris: Librairie Philosophique J. Vrin.

Baldwin, A., & S. Hutton, eds. 1994. *Platonism and the English Imagination*. Cambridge: Cambridge University Press.

Banerjee, A. 1977. "Rousseau's Conception of Theatre." *British Journal of Aesthetics* 17:171–77.

Barasch, M. 1985. *Theories of Art from Plato to Winckelmann*. New York: New York University Press.

Barish, J. 1981. *The Antitheatrical Prejudice*. Berkeley: University of California Press.

Barker, A. 1984. *Greek Musical Writings I: The Musician and His Art*. Cambridge: Cambridge University Press.

Barnard, L. W. 1974. *The Graeco-Roman and Oriental Background of the Iconoclastic Controversy*. Leiden: E. J. Brill.

Barnes, J. 1982. *The Presocratic Philosophers*. 2d ed. London: Routledge.

———. 1987. *Early Greek Philosophy*. Harmondsworth: Penguin Books.

———. 1989. "Antiochus of Ascalon." In *Philosophia Togata I: Essays on Philosophy and Roman Society*, ed. M. Griffin & J. Barnes, 51–96. Oxford: Clarendon Press.

———. 1995. "Rhetoric and Poetics." In *The Cambridge Companion to Aristotle*, ed. J. Barnes, 259–85. Cambridge: Cambridge University Press.

Barnes, J. & D. M. Schenkeveld. 1999. "Linguistics." In *The Cambridge History of Hellenistic Philosophy*, ed. K. Algra, J. Barnes, J. Mansfeld, & M. Schofield 177–216. Cambridge: Cambridge University Press.

Barry, K. 1987. *Language, Music and the Sign*. Cambridge: Cambridge University Press.

Barthes, R. 1993–95. *Oeuvres complètes*, ed. É. Marty. 3 vols. Paris: Éditions du Seuil.

Bate, W. J. 1961. *From Classic to Romantic*. New York: Harper & Row.

Batteux, C. 1989. *Les Beaux-Arts réduits à un même principe*. Ed. J.-R. Mantion. Paris: Aux Amateurs de Livres. Originally published 1746.

Baumgarten, A. G. 1735. *Meditationes Philosophicae de Nonnullis ad Poema Pertinentibus*. Halle: J. H. Grunert.

———. 1954. *Reflections on Poetry: Meditationes Philosophicae de Nonnullis ad Poema Pertinentibus*. Trans. K. Aschenbrenner & W. B. Holther. Berkeley: University of California Press. Contains facsimile of 1735 original.

Baynes, N. H. 1955. *Byzantine Studies and Other Essays*. London: Athlone Press.

Baxandall, M. 1971. *Giotto and the Orators*. Oxford: Clarendon Press.

———. 1988. *Painting and Experience in Fifteenth Century Italy*. 2d ed. Oxford: Oxford University Press.

Baxter, T.M.S. 1992. *The Cratylus: Plato's Critique of Naming*. Leiden: E. J. Brill.

Belfiore, E. S. 1983. "Plato's Greatest Accusation against Poetry." *Canadian Journal of Philosophy*, supp. 9:39–62.

———. 1984. "A Theory of Imitation in Plato's *Republic*." *Transactions of the American Philological Association* 114:121–46.

———. 1985a. "Pleasure, Tragedy and Aristotelian Psychology." *Classical Quarterly* 35:349–61.

———. 1985b. " 'Lies Unlike the Truth': Plato on Hesiod, *Theogony* 27." *Transactions of the American Philological Association* 115:47–57.

———. 1992. *Tragic Pleasures: Aristotle on Plot and Emotion*. Princeton: Princeton University Press.

———. 2000a. *Murder among Friends: Violation of Philia in Greek Tragedy*. New York: Oxford University Press.

———. 2000b. "Narratological Plots and Aristotle's Mythos." *Arethusa* 33:37–70.

Bell, J. 1999. *What Is Painting? Representation and Modern Art*. London: Thames & Hudson.

Belting, H. 1990. *Bild und Kult: Eine Geschichte des Bildes vor dem Zeitalter der Kunst*. Munich: C. H. Beck. Translated as *Likeness and Presence: a History of the Image before the Era of Art*, by E. Jephcott (Chicago: University of Chicago Press, 1994.)

Benjamin, W. 1972–89. *Gesammelte Schriften*. Ed. R. Tiedemann & H. Schweppenhäuser. 7 vols. Frankfurt am Main: Suhrkamp.

Bennington, G. 2000. *Interrupting Derrida*. London: Routledge.

Benziger, J. 1951. "Organic Unity: Leibniz to Coleridge." *Proceedings of the Modern Language Association of America* 66.2:24–48.

Berger, K. 2000. *A Theory of Art*. New York: Oxford University Press.

386

BIBLIOGRAPHY

Berghahn, K. L. 1997. "German Literary Theory from Gottsched to Goethe." In *The Cambridge History of Literary Criticism 4: The Eighteenth Century*, ed. H. B. Nisbet & C. Rawson, 522–45. Cambridge: Cambridge University Press.

Berlin, I. 1990. *The Crooked Timber of Humanity*. London: John Murray.

Bien, G. 1964. "Bemerkungen zu Genesis und ursprünglicher Funktion des Theorems von der Kunst als Nachahmung der Natur." *Bogawus. Zeitschrift für Literatur, Kunst und Philosophie* 2:26–43.

Birmelin, E. 1933. "Die kunsttheoretischen Gedanken in Philostrats Apollonios." *Philologus* 88:149–80, 392–414.

Black, D. L. 1990. *Logic and Aristotle's Rhetoric and Poetics in Medieval Arabic Philosophy*. Leiden: E. J. Brill.

Blank, D. 1998. *Sextus Empiricus: Against the Grammarians*. Oxford: Clarendon Press.

Block, H. M. 1966. "The Concept of Imitation in Modern Criticism." In *Actes du IVe Congrès de l'Association Internationale de Littérature Comparée*, ed. F. Jost, 2:704–20. The Hague: Mouton.

Bluck, R. S. 1964. *Plato's Meno*. Cambridge: Cambridge University Press.

Blumenberg, H. 1957. "Nachahmung der Natur: Zur Vorgeschichte der Idee des schöpferischen Menschen." *Studium Generale* 10:266–83.

Blunt, A. 1978. *Artistic Theory in Italy, 1450–1600*. 4th rev. impression. Oxford: Clarendon Press.

Boal, A. 1979. *Theater of the Oppressed*. Trans. C. A. Leal McBride & M.-O. Leal McBride. London: Pluto Press.

Bollino, F. 1995. "Derive della mimesis. Il nesso imitazione-espressione fra Batteux e Kant." *Studi di Estetica* 11/12:85–136.

Bompaire, J. 1958. *Lucien écrivain*. Paris: de Boccard.

Booth, W. C. 1988. *The Company We Keep: An Ethics of Fiction*. Berkeley: University of California Press.

Bosanquet, B. 1892. *A History of Aesthetic*. London: Sonnenschein.

———. 1925. *A Companion to Plato's Republic*. London: Rivingtons.

Boulby, M. 1978. *Karl Philipp Moritz: At the Fringe of Genius*. Toronto: University of Toronto Press.

Bowman, W. D. 1998. *Philosophical Perspectives on Music*. New York: Oxford University Press.

Boyd, J. D. 1980. *The Function of Mimesis and Its Decline*. 2d ed. New York: Fordham University Press.

Boyle, N. 1991. *Goethe: The Poet and the Age*. Vol. 1, *The Poetry of Desire (1749–1790)*. Oxford: Oxford University Press.

———. 2000. *Goethe: The Poet and the Age*. Vol. 2, *Revolution and Renunciation (1790–1803)*. Oxford: Oxford University Press.

Braider, C. 1999. "The Paradoxical Sisterhood: 'ut pictura poesis'." In *The Cambridge History of Literary Criticism*; vol. 3, *the Renaissance*, ed. G. P. Norton, 168–75. Cambridge: Cambridge University Press.

Brandwood, L. 1990. *The Chronology of Plato's Dialogues*. Cambridge: Cambridge University Press.

Brecht, B. 1988–2000. *Werke*. Ed. W. Hecht et al. 31 vols. Berlin: Aufbau-Verlag.

Bredvold, L. I. 1934. "The Tendency toward Platonism in Neo-Classical Esthetics." *Journal of English Literary History* 1:91–119.

Brink, C. O. 1963. *Horace on Poetry: Prolegomena to the Literary Epistles*. Cambridge: Cambridge University Press.

———. 1971. *Horace on Poetry: The "Ars Poetica."* Cambridge: Cambridge University Press.

Brisson, L. 1998. *Plato the Myth Maker*. Trans. G. Naddaf. Chicago: University of Chicago Press.

———. 2000. *Lectures de Platon*. Paris: Librairie Philosophique J. Vrin.

Broadie, S. 1991. *Ethics with Aristotle*. New York: Oxford University Press.

Brock, R. 1990. "Plato and Comedy." In *"Owls to Athens": Essays on Classical Subjects Presented to Sir Kenneth Dover*, ed. E. M. Craik, 39–49. Oxford: Clarendon Press.

Brogan, T.V.F. 1993. "Representation and Mimesis." In *The New Princeton Encyclopedia of Poetry and Poetics*, ed. A. Preminger & T.V.F. Brogan, 1037–44. Princeton: Princeton University Press.

Bryson, N. 1983. *Vision and Painting*. London: Macmillan.

Buchheim, T. 1985. "Maler, Sprachbildner. Zur Verwandtschaft des Gorgias mit Empedokles." *Hermes* 113:417–29.

———. 1989. *Gorgias von Leontinoi: Reden, Fragmente und Testimonien*. Hamburg: Felix Meiner Verlag.

Budd, M. 1985. *Music and the Emotions*. London: Routledge.

———. 1995. *Values of Art: Pictures, Poetry and Music*. London: Allen Lane.

Buffière, F. 1956. *Les mythes d'Homère et la pensée Grecque*. Paris: Les Belles Lettres.

Bullough, E. 1957. *Aesthetics: Lectures and Essays*. London: Bowes & Bowes.

Burke, E. 1958. *A Philosophical Enquiry into the Origins of Our Ideas of the Sublime and the Beautiful*. Ed. J. T. Boulton. London: Routledge & Kegan Paul.

Burkert, W. 1987. *Ancient Mystery Cults*. Cambridge, Mass.: Harvard University Press.

Burnyeat, M. 1980. "Aristotle on Learning to be Good." In *Essays on Aristotle's Ethics*, ed. A. O. Rorty, 69–92. Berkeley: University of California Press.

———. 1999. "Culture and Society in Plato's *Republic*." *Tanner Lectures on Human Values* 20:217–324.

Burwick, F. 1995. "The Romantic Concept of Mimesis: *Idem et Alter*." In *Questioning Romanticism*, ed. J. Beer, 179–208. Baltimore: Johns Hopkins University Press.

Butcher, S. H. 1911. *Aristotle's Theory of Poetry and Fine Art*. 4th ed. Corrected reprint. London: Macmillan.

Butterworth, C. E. 1977. *Averroes' Three Short Commentaries on Aristotle's "Topics," "Rhetoric," and "Poetics."* Albany: State University of New York Press.

———. 1986. *Averroes' Middle Commentary on Aristotle's "Poetics."* Princeton: Princeton University Press.

Büttner, S. 2000. *Die Literaturtheorie bei Platon und ihre anthropologische Begründung*. Tübingen: Francke Verlag.

Cahn, M. 1984. "Subversive Mimesis: Theodor W. Adorno and the Modern Impasse of Critique." In *Mimesis in Contemporary Theory: An Interdisciplinary Approach*, ed. M. Spariosu, 27–64. Philadelphia: John Benjamins.

Cameron, Averil. 1992. "The Language of Images: The Rise of Icons and Christian Representation." In *The Church and the Arts*, ed. D. Wood, 1–42. Oxford: Blackwell.

Cantarella, R. 1969. "Aristofane di Bisanzio, Menandro e la mimesi." *Rendiconti dell' Accademia Nazionale dei Lincei (Classe di Scienze Morali, Storiche e Filologiche)* 24:189–94.

Cantor, P. A. 1991. "Aristotle and the History of Tragedy." In *Theoretical Issues in Literary History*, ed. D. Perkins, 60–84. Cambridge, Mass.: Harvard University Press.

Carapetyan, A. 1948. "The Concept of *Imitazione della Natura* in the Sixteenth Century." *Musica Disciplina* 1:47–67.

Carlisle, M. 1999. "Homeric Fictions: *Pseudo*-Words in Homer." In *Nine Essays on Homer*, ed. M. Carlisle & O. Levaniouk, 55–91. Lanham: Rowman & Littlefield.

Carpenter, R. 1959. *The Esthetic Basis of Greek Art*. Bloomington: Indiana University Press.

Carritt, E. F. 1949. *The Theory of Beauty*. 5th ed. London: Methuen.

Carroll, N. 1990. *The Philosophy of Horror*. New York: Routledge.

———. 1998. *A Philosophy of Mass Art*. Oxford: Oxford University Press.

Cartwright, D. E. 1984. "Kant, Schopenhauer, and Nietzsche on the Morality of Pity." *Journal of the History of Ideas* 45:83–98.

Cassirer, E. 1922–23. "Eidos und Eidolon: Das Problem des Schönen und der Kunst in Platons Dialogen." *Vorträge der Bibliothek Warburg* 2:1–27.

Castelvetro, L. 1978–79. *Poetica d'Aristotele vulgarizzata e sposta*. Ed. W. Romani. 2 vols. Rome: Laterza.

Cauer, P. 1920. "Terminologisches zu Platon und Aristoteles." *Rheinisches Museum* 73:161–73.

Cave, T. 1988. *Recognitions: A Study in Poetics*. Oxford: Clarendon Press.

Chantraine, P. 1984–90. *Dictionnaire étymologique de la lange grecque*. 2 vols. Paris: Klincksieck.

Chipp, H. B. 1968. *Theories of Modern Art*. Berkeley: University of California Press.

Clark, S. H. 1990. *Paul Ricoeur*. London: Routledge.

Clark, S.R.L. 1996. "Plotinus: Body and Soul." In *The Cambridge Companion to Plotinus*, ed. L. P. Gerson, 275–91. Cambridge: Cambridge University Press.

Clarke, K. 1999. *Between Geography and History: Hellenistic Constructions of the Roman World*. Oxford: Clarendon Press.

Clements, R. J. 1963. *Michelangelo's Theory of Art*. London: Routledge & Kegan Paul.

Cocking, J. M. 1991. *Imagination: A Study in the History of Ideas*. London: Routledge.

Cole, T. 1990. *Democritus and the Origins of Greek Anthropology*. Atlanta, Ga.: Scholars Press.

Coleridge, S. T. 1907. *Biographia Literaria*. Ed. J. Shawcross. 2 vols. Oxford: Clarendon Press.

Colvin, S. 1999. *Dialect in Aristophanes*. Oxford: Clarendon Press.

Conradi, P. 1994. "Platonism in Iris Murdoch." In *Platonism and the English Imagination*, ed. A. Baldwin and S. Hutton, 330–42. Cambridge: Cambridge University Press.

Cooper, J.M. 1975. *Reason and Human Good in Aristotle*. Cambridge, Mass.: Harvard University Press.

Cope, E. M. 1877. *The Rhetoric of Aristotle*. Cambridge: Cambridge University Press.

Corbelli, A. 1994. "Musica e imitazione in Jean-Jacques Rousseau." *Studi di Estetica* 10:41–54.

Coulter, J. A. 1976. *The Literary Microcosm: Theories of Interpretation of the Later Neoplatonists*. Leiden: E. J. Brill.

Cousin, V., ed. 1864. *Procli Philosophi Platonici Opera Inedita*. Paris: Durand.

Cowan, M., trans. 1962. *Friedrich Nietzsche: Philosophy in the Tragic Age of the Greeks*. Chicago: Regnery Gateway.

Croce, B. 1950. *Estetica come Scienza dell'espressione e linguistica generale*. 9th ed. Bari: Laterza.

———. 1990. *Breviario di estetica. Aesthetica in nuce*. Ed. G. Galasso. Milan: Adelphi Edizioni.

Croisille, J.-M., ed. 1985. *Pline l'Ancien: Histoire naturelle livre XXXV*. Paris: Les Belles Lettres.

Csapo, E., and W. J. Slater. 1995. *The Context of Ancient Drama*. Ann Arbor: University of Michigan Press.

Culler, J. 1981. *The Pursuit of Signs: Semiotics, Literature, Deconstruction*. London: Routledge & Kegan Paul.

Cunningham, I. C., ed. 1987. *Herodas Mimiambi*. Leipzig: Teubner.

Currie, G. 1995. *Image and Mind: Film, Philosophy and Cognitive Science*. Cambridge: Cambridge University Press.

Curtius, E. R. 1953. *European Literature and the Latin Middle Ages*. Trans. W. R. Trask. London: Routledge.

Dahiyat, I. M. 1974. *Avicenna's Commentary on the "Poetics" of Aristotle*. Leiden: E. J. Brill.

Dahlhaus, C. 1985. *Realism in Nineteenth-Century Music*. Trans. M. Whittall. Cambridge: Cambridge University Press.

Danto, A. C. 1986. *The Philosophical Disenfranchisement of Art*. New York: Columbia University Press.

———. 1997. *After the End of Art*. Princeton: Princeton University Press.

Davies, S. 1994. *Musical Meaning and Expression*. Ithaca: Cornell University Press.

Davis, W. M. 1979. "Plato on Egyptian Art." *Journal of Egyptian Archaeology* 65:121–27.

Dawson, D. 1992. *Allegorical Readers and Cultural Revision in Ancient Alexandria*. Berkeley: University of California Press.

De Angeli, S. 1988. "Mimesis e Techne." *Quaderni Urbinati di Cultura Classica* 28:27–45.

De Lacy, P. 1948. "Stoic Views of Poetry." *American Journal of Philology* 69:241–71.

———, ed. 1978–84. *Galen on the Doctrines of Hippocrates and Plato*. 3 vols. Berlin: Akademie-Verlag.

Delattre, D. 1989. "Philodème *De la musique*: Livre IV, colonnes 40* à 109*." *Cronache Ercolanesi* 19:49–144.

Delattre, D. 1997. "La parole et la musique chez Philodème de Gadara." In *Dire l'évidence*, ed. C. Lévy & L. Pernot, 177–94. Paris: L'Harmattan.

———. 2001. *Philodème de Gadara: Commentaires sur la musique, livre IV*. Paris: Les Belles Lettres.

Demand, N. 1975. "Plato and the Painters." *Phoenix* 29:1–20.

Denniston, J. D. 1960. *Greek Prose Style*. Corrected reprint. Oxford: Clarendon Press.

Dent, N.J.H. 1992. *A Rousseau Dictionary*. Oxford: Blackwell.

Depew, D. J. 1991. "Politics, Music, and Contemplation in Aristotle's Ideal State." In *A Companion to Aristotle's Politics*, ed. D. Keyt & F. D. Miller, 346–80. Oxford: Basil Blackwell.

Derrida, J. 1972. *La dissémination*. Paris: Éditions du Seuil.

Diamond, E. 1997. *Unmaking Mimesis: Essays on Feminism and Theater*. London: Routledge.

Diderot, D. 1957–79. *Salons*. Ed. J. Seznec & J. Adhémar. 4 vols. Oxford: Clarendon Press.

———. 1983. *Le neveu de Rameau*. Ed. J.-C. Bonnet. Paris: Flammarion.

Dieckmann, H. 1969. "Die Wandlung des Nachahmungsbegriffes in der französischen Ästhetik des 18. Jahrhunderts." In *Nachahmung und Illusion*, ed. H. Jauss, 28–59. Munich: Wilhelm Fink Verlag.

Diehl, E. ed. 1903–6. *Proclus Diadochus: In Platonis Timaeum Commentaria*. 3 vols. Leipzig: Teubner.

Diggle, J. 1998. *Tragicorum Graecorum Fragmenta Selecta*. Oxford: Clarendon Press.

Dilcher, R. 1996. "Furcht und Mitleid! Zu Lessing's Ehrenrettung." *Antike und Abendland* 42:85–102.

Dillon, J. 1996. *The Middle Platonists*. Rev. ed. London: Duckworth.

Dindorf, G. D. 1855. *Scholia Graeca in Homeri Odysseam*. 2 vols. Oxford: Oxford University Press.

Dobrov, G. 2001. *Figures of Play: Greek Drama and Metafictional Poetics*. New York: Oxford University Press.

Dod, B. G. 1982. "Aristoteles Latinus." In *The Cambridge History of Later Medieval Philosophy*, ed. N. Kretzmann, A. Kenny, & J. Pinborg, 45–79. Cambridge: Cambridge University Press.

Donaldson, I., ed. 1985. *Ben Jonson*. Oxford: Oxford University Press.

Donini, P. 1997. *Aristotele Opere 10**: Poetica*. Rome: Editori Laterza.

———. 1998. "La tragedia, senza la catarsi." *Phronesis* 43:26–41.

Dosi, A. 1960. "Sulle tracce della poetica di Teofrasto." *Rendiconti dell'Istituto Lombardo (Classe di Lettere)* 94:599–672.

Dostoevsky, F. 1994. *The Karamazov Brothers*. Trans. I. Avsey. Oxford: Oxford University Press.

Douglas, A. E. 1973. "The Intellectual Background of Cicero's Rhetorica." *Aufstieg und Niedergang der Römischen Welt* 1.3:95–138.

Dover, K. J. 1993. *Aristophanes: Frogs*. Oxford: Clarendon Press.

Draper, J. W. 1921. "Aristotelian 'Mimesis' in Eighteenth Century England." *Publications of the Modern Language Association of America* 36:372–400.

Dubos, J.-B. 1748. *Critical Reflections on Poetry, Painting and Music.* Trans. T. Nugent. Enlarged ed. 3 vols. London: John Nourse.

Duncan-Jones, K., ed. 1989. *Sir Philip Sidney.* Oxford: Oxford University Press.

Dupont-Roc, R., & J. Lallot. 1980. *Aristote: La Poétique.* Paris: Éditions du Seuil.

Düring, I. 1961. *Aristotle's Protrepticus.* Göteborg: University of Göteborg.

Dyson, M. 1988. "Poetic Imitation in Plato *Republic* 3." *Antichthon* 22:42–53.

Eaton, M. M. 2001. *Merit, Aesthetic and Ethical.* New York: Oxford University Press.

Edelstein, L. & I. G. Kidd. 1989. *Posidonius I: The Fragments.* 2d ed. Cambridge: Cambridge University Press.

Eden, K. 1986. *Poetic and Legal Fiction in the Aristotelian Tradition.* Princeton: Princeton University Press.

Elam, H. R. 1993. "Imitation, II: From the Modern Perspective." In *The New Princeton Encyclopedia of Poetry and Poetics,* ed. A. Preminger & T. V. F. Brogan, 577–79. Princeton: Princeton University Press.

Else, G. F. 1957. *Aristotle's Poetics: The Argument.* Cambridge, Mass.: Harvard University Press.

———. 1958. "'Imitation' in the Fifth Century." *Classical Philology* 53:73–90.

———. 1986. *Plato and Aristotle on Poetry.* Chapel Hill: University of North Carolina Press.

Elsner, J. 1995. *Art and the Roman Viewer.* Cambridge: Cambridge University Press.

England, E. B. 1921. *The Laws of Plato.* 2 vols. Manchester: Manchester University Press.

Entralgo, P. L. 1970. *The Therapy of the Word in Classical Antiquity.* Trans. L. J. Rather & J. M. Sharp. New Haven: Yale University Press.

Erbse, H. 1960. *Beiträge zur Überlieferung der Iliasscholien.* Munich: C. H. Beck.

———. 1969–88. *Scholia Graeca in Homeri Iliadem.* 7 vols. Berlin: de Gruyter.

Erler, M. 1994. "Philodem aus Gadara." In *Die Philosophie der Antike 4: Die Hellenistische Philosophie,* ed. H. Flashar, 289–362. Basel: Schwabe.

Ettinghausen, R. 1963. "Images and Iconoclasm: Islam." In *Encyclopedia of World Art,* 7:816–18. New York: McGraw-Hill.

Eusterschulte, A. 2001. "Mimesis." In *Historisches Wörterbuch der Rhetorik,* ed. G. Ueding, 5:1232–94. Tübingen: Max Niemeyer Verlag.

Everson, S. 1997. *Aristotle on Perception.* Oxford: Clarendon Press.

Ewton, R. W. 1972. *The Literary Theories of August Wilhelm Schlegel.* The Hague: Mouton.

Farago, C. J. 1992. *Leonardo da Vinci's Paragone.* Leiden: E. J. Brill.

Feagin, S. L. 1983. "The Pleasures of Tragedy." *American Philosophical Quarterly* 20:95–104.

———. 1996. *Reading with Feeling.* Ithaca: Cornell University Press.

Ferrari, G.R.F. 1989. "Plato and Poetry." In *The Cambridge History of Literary Criticism 1: Classical Criticism,* ed. G. A. Kennedy, 92–148. Cambridge: Cambridge University Press.

———. 1999. "Aristotle's Literary Aesthetics." *Phronesis* 44:181–98.

Ferwerda, R. 1965. *La signification des images et des métaphores dans la pensée de Plotin.* Groningen: J. B. Wolters.

Festugière, A. J. 1970. *Proclus: Commentaire sur la République.* 3 vols. Paris: Librairie Philosophique J. Vrin.

Ficino, M. 1989. *Three Books on Life.* Ed. C. V. Kaske and J. R. Clark. Tempe, Ariz.: Renaissance Society of America.

Fine, G. 1993. *On Ideas: Aristotle's Criticism of Plato's Theory of Forms.* Oxford: Clarendon Press.

Finkelberg, M. 1998. *The Birth of Literary Fiction in Ancient Greece.* Oxford: Clarendon Press.

Flasch, K. 1965. "Ars Imitatur Naturam: Platonischer Naturbegriff und mittelalterliche Philosophie der Kunst." In *Parusia: Studien zur Philosophie Platons und zur Problemgeschichte des Platonismus,* ed. K. Flasch, 265–306. Frankfurt am Main: Minerva.

Flashar, H. 1958. *Der Dialog Ion als Zeugnis Platonischer Philosophie.* Berlin: Akademie-Verlag.

———. 1972. "Furcht und Mitleid." In *Historisches Wörterbuch der Philosophie,* ed. J. Ritter, 2:1147–49. Basel: Schwabe.

———. 1979. "Die klassizistische Theorie der Mimesis." In *Le classicisme à Rome,* ed. H. Flashar, 79–111. Geneva: Fondation Hardt.

———. 1999. "Aristoteles." In *Die Musik in Geschichte und Gegenwart,* ed. L. Finscher, vol. 1 (Personenteil), 922–28. Kassel: Bärenreiter.

Foakes, R.A., ed. 1968. *Romantic Criticism, 1800–1850.* London: E. Arnold.

Ford, A. 1995. "*Katharsis*: The Ancient Problem." In *Performativity and Performance,* ed. A. Parker & E. Kosofsky Sedgwick, 109–32. London: Routledge.

———. 1999. "Performing Interpretation: Early Allegorical Exegesis of Homer." In *Epic Traditions in the Contemporary World,* ed. M. Beissinger, J. Tylus, & S. Wofford, 33–53. Berkeley: University of California Press.

Fornara, C. W. 1983. *The Nature of History in Ancient Greece and Rome.* Berkeley: University of California Press.

Fracastoro, G. 1924. *Naugerius, sive De Poetica Dialogus.* Trans. R. Kelso, intro. M. W. Bundy. University of Illinois Studies in Language & Literature, vol. 9.3. Illinois: University of Illinois Press.

Frazer, J.G. 1911–36. *The Golden Bough.* 3rd ed. 12 vols. London: Macmillan.

Frede, D. 1992. "Necessity, Chance, and 'What Happens for the Most Part' in Aristotle's *Poetics.*" In *Essays on Aristotle's Poetics,* ed. A. O. Rorty, 197–219. Princeton: Princeton University Press.

Freedberg, D. 1989. *The Power of Images.* Chicago: University of Chicago Press.

Freeland, C. A. 1992. "Plot Imitates Action: Aesthetic Evaluation and Moral Realism in Aristotle's *Poetics.*" In *Essays on Aristotle's Poetics,* ed. A. O. Rorty, 111–32. Princeton: Princeton University Press.

French, R. 1994. *Ancient Natural History.* London: Routledge.

Freud, S. 1953–66. *The Standard Edition of the Complete Psychological Works,* ed. J. Strachey. 24 vols. London: Hogarth Press.

———. 1989. *Studienausgabe.* Ed. A. Mitscherlich, A. Richards, & J. Strachey. 11 vols. Frankfurt am Main: S. Fischer Verlag.

Frontisi-Ducroux, F., & Vernant, J.-P. 1997. *Dans l'oeil du miroir.* Paris: Editions Odile Jacob.

Früchtl, J. 1998. "Adorno and Mimesis." In *The Encyclopedia of Aesthetics*, ed. M. Kelly, 1:23–25. New York: Oxford University Press.

Frye, N. 1957. *Anatomy of Criticism*. Princeton: Princeton University Press.

Fuhrmann, M. 1982. *Aristoteles Poetik*. 2d ed. Stuttgart: Philipp Reclam Jun.

Fusillo, M. 1986. "'Mythos' aristotelico e 'récit' narratologico." *Strumenti Critici* 52:381–92.

Gadamer, H.-G. 1977. *Kleine Schriften*. 4 vols. Tübingen: Mohr.

———. 1986. *The Relevance of the Beautiful and Other Essays*. Trans. N. Walker. Cambridge: Cambridge University Press.

Gage, J. 1993. *Colour and Culture*. London: Thames & Hudson.

Gallavotti, C. 1969. "Tracce della *Poetica* di Aristotele negli Scolii Omerici." *Maia* 21:203–14.

Galli, U. 1925. "La mimesi artistica secondo Aristotele." *Studi Italiani di Filologia Classica* 4:281–390.

Gallop. D. 1965. "Image and Reality in Plato's *Republic*." *Archiv für Geschichte der Philosophie* 47:113–31.

———. 1990. "Animals in the *Poetics*." *Oxford Studies in Ancient Philosophy* 8:145–71.

———. 1991. "Can Fiction Be Stranger Than Truth? An Aristotelian Answer." *Philosophy and Literature* 15:1–18.

———. 1999. "Aristotle: Aesthetics and Philosophy of Mind." In *From Aristotle to Augustine*, ed. D. Furley, 76–108. London: Routledge.

Gantz, T. 1993. *Early Greek Myth: A Guide to Literary and Artistic Sources*. Baltimore: Johns Hopkins University Press.

Gastaldi, S. 1998. "*Paideia/mythologia*." In *Platone: La Repubblica*, ed. M. Vegetti, 2:333–92. Naples: Bibliopolis.

Gauss, C. E. 1973. "Empathy." In *Dictionary of the History of Ideas*, ed. P. P. Wiener, 2:85–89. New York: Charles Scribner's.

Gebauer, G., & C. Wulf. 1992. *Mimesis: Kultur, Kunst, Gesellschaft*. Hamburg: Rowohlt Taschenbuch Verlag.

———. 1995. *Mimesis: Culture, Art, Society*. Trans. D. Reneau. Berkeley: University of California Press.

Geffcken, J. 1916–19. "Der Bilderstreit des heidnischen Altertums." *Archiv für Religionswissenschaft* 19:286–315.

Gell, A. 1998. *Art and Agency: An Anthropological Theory*. Oxford: Clarendon Press.

Gelzer, T. 1979. "Die Bedeutung der klassischen Vorbilder beim alten Goethe." In *Classical Influences on Western Thought, A.D. 1650–1870*, ed. R. R. Bolgar, 309–26. Cambridge: Cambridge University Press.

———. 1985. "Mimus und Kunsttheorie bei Herondas, Mimiambus 4." In *Catalepton: Festschrift für Bernhard Wyss zum 80. Geburtstag*, ed. C. Schäublin, 96–116. Basel: Seminar für Klassische Philologie der Universität Basel.

Genette, G. 1972. *Figures III*. Paris: Éditions du Seuil.

———. 1980. *Narrative Discourse*. Trans. J. E. Lewin. Oxford: Basil Blackwell.

———. 1988. *Narrative Discourse Revisited*. Trans. J. E. Lewin. Ithaca: Cornell University Press.

Gentili, B. 1988. *Poetry and Its Public in Ancient Greece.* Trans. A. T. Cole. Baltimore: Johns Hopkins University Press.

Gernez, B. 1997. *Aristote: La Poétique.* Paris: Les Belles Lettres.

Gerson, L. P. 1994. *Plotinus.* London: Routledge.

Gifford, M. 2001. "Dramatic Dialectic in *Republic* Book 1." *Oxford Studies in Ancient Philosophy* 20:35–106.

Gigante, M. 1961. "Σημαντικὸν ποίημα." *Parola del Passato* 16:40–53.

———. 1995. *Philodemus in Italy.* Trans. D. Obbink. Ann Arbor: University of Michigan Press.

Gigon, O. 1973. *Aristoteles Politik.* Munich: Deutscher Taschenbuch Verlag.

———. 1987. *Aristotelis Opera III, Librorum Deperditorum Fragmenta.* Berlin: de Gruyter.

Gilbert, K. 1936. "Aesthetic Imitation and Imitators in Aristotle." *Philosophical Review* 45:558–73.

Gilbert, K., & H. Kuhn. 1953. *A History of Aesthetics.* Rev. ed. Bloomington: Indiana University Press.

Gill, C. 1990. "The Character-Personality Distinction." In *Characterization and Individuality in Greek Literature,* ed. C. Pelling, 1–31. Oxford: Clarendon Press.

———. 1993. "Plato on Falsehood—Not Fiction." In *Lies and Fiction in the Ancient World,* ed. C. Gill and T. P. Wiseman, 38–87. Exeter: University of Exeter Press.

———. 1996. *Personality in Greek Epic, Tragedy, and Philosophy.* Oxford: Clarendon Press.

Givens, T. L. 1991a. "Aristotle's Critique of Mimesis: The Romantic Prelude." *Comparative Literature Studies* 28:121–36.

———. 1991b. "Blind Men and Hieroglyphs: The Collapse of Mimesis." *European Romantic Review* 2:61–80.

Goehr, L. 1992. *The Imaginary Museum of Musical Works.* Oxford: Clarendon Press.

Goethe, J. W. 1985–98. *Sämtliche Werke.* Münchner Ausgabe. 21 vols. Munich: Carl Hanser.

Golden, L., & O. B. Hardison. 1968. *Aristotle's Poetics.* Englewood Cliffs, N.J.: Prentice-Hall.

Goldhill, S. 1997. "The Audience of Athenian Tragedy." In *The Cambridge Companion to Greek Tragedy,* ed. P. E. Easterling, 54–68. Cambridge: Cambridge University Press.

Goldschmidt, V. 1982. *Temps physique et temps tragique chez Aristote.* Paris: Vrin.

Gombrich, E. H. 1972. *Symbolic Images.* London: Phaidon.

———. 1977. *Art and Illusion.* 5th ed. Oxford: Phaidon.

———. 1987. *Reflections on the History of Art.* Oxford: Phaidon.

———. 1991. "*Idea* in the Theory of Art: Philosophy or Rhetoric?" In *Idea: VI Colloquio Internazionale del Lessico Intellettuale Europeo,* ed. M. Fattori & M. L. Bianchi, 411–20. Rome: Edizioni dell'Ateneo.

Gomme, A. W. 1954. *The Greek Attitude to Poetry and History.* Berkeley: University of California Press.

Goodman, L. E. 1992. *Avicenna.* London: Routledge.

Gosse, E. 1970. *Father and Son.* Harmondsworth: Penguin Books.

Gould, J. 1992. "Plato and Performance." In *The Language of the Cave*, ed. A. Barker & M. Warner, 13–26. Edmonton, Alberta: Academic Printing & Publishing.

Gould, T. 1990. *The Ancient Quarrel between Poetry and Philosophy*. Princeton: Princeton University Press.

Grabar, A. 1945. "Plotin et les origines de l'esthétique médiévale." *Cahiers Archéologiques* 1:15–34.

Grabes, H. 1982. *The Mutable Glass: Mirror-Imagery in Titles and Texts of the Middle Ages and English Renaissance*. Trans. G. Collier. Cambridge: Cambridge University Press.

Graff, G. 1979. *Literature against Itself: Literary Ideas in Modern Society*. Chicago: Chicago University Press.

Graham, J. 1973. "Ut Pictura Poesis." In *Dictionary of the History of Ideas*, ed. P. P. Wiener, 3:465–76. New York: Charles Scribner's.

Grassi, E. 1962. *Die Theorie des Schönen in der Antike*. Cologne: Verlag M. DuMont.

Gray, V. 1987. "*Mimesis* in Greek Historical Theory." *American Journal of Philology* 108:467–86.

Greenberg, N. 1990. *The Poetic Theory of Philodemus*. New York: Garland.

Greenfield, C. C. 1981. *Humanist and Scholastic Poetics, 1250–1500*. Lewisburg: Bucknell University Press.

Gribble, D. 1997. "Rhetoric and History in [Andocides] 4, *Against Alcibiades*." *Classical Quarterly* 47:367–91.

Griffin, J. 1980. *Homer on Life and Death*. Oxford: Clarendon Press.

———. 1998. "The Social Function of Attic Tragedy." *Classical Quarterly* 48:39–61.

Grimm, J., & W. Grimm. 1854–1960. *Deutsches Wörterbuch*. 32 vols. Leipzig: S. Hirzel.

Grube, G.M.A. 1952. "Theophrastus as a Literary Critic." *Transactions of the American Philological Association* 83:172–83.

———. 1965. *The Greek and Roman Critics*. London: Methuen.

Grumach, E. 1949. *Goethe und die Antike*. 2 vols. Berlin: de Gruyter.

Gudeman, A. 1934. *Aristoteles Peri Poietikes*. Berlin: de Gruyter.

Gulley, N. 1979. "Aristotle on the Purposes of Literature." In *Articles on Aristotle 4: Psychology and Aesthetics*, ed. J. Barnes, M. Schofield, & R. Sorabji, 166–76. London: Duckworth.

Guthknecht, D. 2001. "Mimesis: *Musik*." In *Historisches Wörterbuch der Rhetorik*, ed. G. Ueding, 5:1316–27. Tübingen: Max Niemeyer Verlag.

Guthrie, W.K.C. 1962–81. *A History of Greek Philosophy*. 6 vols. Cambridge: Cambridge University Press.

Hall, E. 1996. "Is There a Polis in Aristotle's *Poetics?*" In *Tragedy and the Tragic*, ed. M. S. Silk, 295–309. Oxford: Clarendon Press.

———. 1997. "The Sociology of Athenian Tragedy." In *The Cambridge Companion to Greek Tragedy*, ed. P. E. Easterling, 93–126. Cambridge: Cambridge University Press.

Halliwell, S. 1984. "Plato and Aristotle on the Denial of Tragedy." *Proceedings of the Cambridge Philological Society* 30:49–71.

———. 1986. *Aristotle's Poetics*. London: Duckworth. Reprinted, with new intro. 1998.

———. 1987. *The Poetics of Aristotle: Translation and Commentary*. London: Duckworth.

———. 1988. *Plato Republic 10*. Warminster: Aris & Phillips.

———. 1990a. "Aristotelian Mimesis Reevaluated." *Journal of the History of Philosophy* 28:487–510.

———. 1990b. "Human Limits and the Religion of Greek Tragedy." *Journal of Literature and Theology* 4:169–80.

———. 1991a. "The Importance of Plato and Aristotle for Aesthetics." In *Proceedings of the Boston Area Colloquium in Ancient Philosophy V [1989]*, ed. J. J. Cleary, 321–48. Lanham, Md.: University Press of America.

———. 1991b. "Comic Satire and Freedom of Speech in Classical Athens." *Journal of Hellenic Studies* 111:48–70.

———. 1992a. "Pleasure, Understanding, and Emotion in Aristotle's *Poetics*." In *Essays on Aristotle's Poetics*, ed. A. O. Rorty, 241–60. Princeton: Princeton University Press.

———. 1992b. "Epilogue: The *Poetics* and Its Interpreters." In *Essays on Aristotle's Poetics*, ed. A. O. Rorty, 409–24. Princeton: Princeton University Press.

———. 1992c. "Plato and the Psychology of Drama." In *Antike Dramentheorien und ihre Rezeption* (= *Drama* 1), ed. B. Zimmermann, 55–73. Stuttgart: M & P Verlag.

———. 1992d. "Catharsis." In *A Companion to Aesthetics*, ed. D. E. Cooper, 61–63. Oxford: Blackwell.

———. 1993a. *Plato Republic 5*. Warminster: Aris & Phillips.

———. 1993b. "Philosophy and Literature: Settling a Quarrel?" *Philosophical Investigations* 16:1–17.

———. 1995a. "Plato, Imagination and Romanticism." In *The Passionate Intellect: Essays on the Transformation of the Classical Tradition*, ed. L. Ayres, 23–37. New Brunswick, N.J.: Transaction Publishers.

———. 1995b. "Tragedy, Reason and Pity: A Reply to Jonathan Lear." In *Aristotle and Moral Realism*, ed. R. Heinaman, 85–95. London: UCL Press.

———. 1996. "Plato's Repudiation of the Tragic." In *Tragedy and the Tragic*, ed. M. S. Silk, 332–49. Oxford: Clarendon Press.

———. 1997a. "The *Republic*'s Two Critiques of Poetry." In *Plato Politeia*, ed. O. Höffe, 313–32. Berlin: Akademie Verlag.

———. 1997b. Review of Nightingale 1995. *Ancient Philosophy* 17:452–57.

———. 1998. "Aristotle on Form and Unity." In *The Encyclopedia of Aesthetics*, ed. M. Kelly, 1:101–4. New York: Oxford University Press.

———. 1999. "Music and the Limits of Mimesis." *Colloquium Philosophicum* 4:9–30.

———. 2000a. "From Mythos to Logos: Plato's Citations of the Poets." *Classical Quarterly* 50:94–112.

———. 2000b. "Plato and Painting." In *Word and Image in Ancient Greece*, ed. K. Rutter and B. Sparkes, 99–116. Edinburgh: Edinburgh University Press.

———. 2001. "Aristotelian Mimesis and Human Understanding." In *Making Sense of Aristotle: Essays in Poetics*, ed. Ø. Andersen & J. Haarberg, 87–107. London: Duckworth.

———. 2002. "Aristotelianism and Anti-Aristotelianism in Attitudes to Theatre." In *Attitudes to Theatre from Plato to Milton*, ed. E. Theodorakopoulos. Bari: Levante Editori.

Hankins, J. 1991. *Plato in the Italian Renaissance*. 2d ed. Leiden: E. J. Brill.

Harding, D. W. 1968. "Psychological Processes in the Reading of Fiction." In *Aesthetics in the Modern World*, ed. H. Osborne, 300–317. London: Thames & Hudson.

Hardison, O. B. 1962. *The Enduring Monument*. Chapel Hill: University of North Carolina Press.

Harris, P. L. 1998. "Fictional Absorption: Emotional Responses to Make-Believe." In *Intersubjective Communication and Emotion in Early Ontogeny*, ed. S. Bråten, 336–53. Cambridge: Cambridge University Press.

Harriss, E. C. 1981. *Johann Mattheson's Der vollkommene Capellmeister: A Revised Translation with Critical Commentary*. Ann Arbor: UMI Research Press.

Harwood, J. T. 1986. *The Rhetorics of Thomas Hobbes and Bernard Lamy*. Carbondale: Southern Illinois University Press.

Haslam, M. W. 1972. "Plato, Sophron, and the Dramatic Dialogue." *Bulletin of the Institute of Classical Studies* 19:17–38.

Hathaway, B. 1962. *The Age of Criticism: The Late Renaissance in Italy*. Ithaca: Cornell University Press.

Havelock, E. A. 1963. *Preface to Plato*. Oxford: Blackwell.

Hawkes, T., ed. 1969. *Coleridge on Shakespeare*. Harmondsworth: Penguin Books.

Hawthorn, J. 1992. *A Glossary of Contemporary Literary Theory*. London: Edward Arnold.

Heath, M. 1987. *The Poetics of Greek Tragedy*. London: Duckworth.

———. 1989. *Unity in Greek Poetics*. Oxford: Clarendon Press.

———. 1991. "The Universality of Poetry in Aristotle's *Poetics*." *Classical Quarterly* 41:389–402.

———. 1996. *Aristotle Poetics*. Harmondsworth: Penguin Books.

———. 1999. "Longinus, *On Sublimity*." *Proceedings of the Cambridge Philological Society* 45:43–74.

Hegel, G.W.F. 1975. *Lectures on Aesthetics*. Trans. T. Knox. 2 vols. Oxford: Clarendon Press.

Heinrichs, W. 1969. *Arabische Dichtung und Griechische Poetik*. Beirut: Franz Steiner Verlag.

Heirman, L.J.R. 1972. *Plutarchus De Audiendis Poetis*. Leiden: Rijksuniversiteit te Leiden.

Held, G. F. 1984. "ΣΠΟΥΔΑΙΟΣ and Teleology in the Poetics." *Transactions of the American Philological Association* 114:159–76. Reprinted in Held 1995, 1–23.

———. 1995. *Aristotle's Teleological Theory of Tragedy and Epic*. Heidelberg: Universitätsverlag C. Winter.

Henry, P., & Schwyzer, H.-R. 1982. *Plotini Opera*. Vol. 3. Oxford: Clarendon Press.

Hense, O. 1905. *C. Musonii Rufi Reliquiae*. Leipzig: Teubner.

Hepburn, R. W. 1984. *"Wonder" and Other Essays: Eight Studies in Aesthetics and Neighbouring Fields*. Edinburgh: Edinburgh University Press.

Herington, J. 1985. *Poetry into Drama: Early Tragedy and the Greek Poetic Tradition*. Berkeley: University of California Press.

Herrin, J. 1987. *The Formation of Christendom*. Oxford: Blackwell.

Hobbes, T. 1991. *Leviathan*. Ed. R. Tuck. Cambridge: Cambridge University Press.

Holt, E. G. 1966. *From the Classicists to the Impressionists*. New York: Doubleday.

Hopkins, R. 1998. *Picture, Image and Experience*. Cambridge: Cambridge University Press.

Horn, H.-J. 1975. "Zur Begründung des Vorrangs der πρᾶξις vor dem ἦθος in der aristotelischen Tragödientheorie." *Hermes* 103:292–99.

House, H. 1956. *Aristotle's Poetics*. London: Rupert Hart-Davis.

Hubbell, H. M. 1920. "The Rhetorica of Philodemus." *Connecticut Academy of Arts and Sciences* 23:243–382.

Hume, D. 1993. *Selected Essays*. Ed. S. Copley & A. Edgar. Oxford: Oxford University Press.

Hwang, P. H. 1981. "Poetry in Plato's *Republic*." *Apeiron* 15:29–37.

Iknayan, M. 1983. *The Concave Mirror: From Imitation to Expression in French Esthetic Theory, 1800–1830*. Saratoga, Calif.: ANMA Libri.

Imbert, C. 1980. "Stoic Logic and Alexandrian Poetics." In *Doubt and Dogmatism*, ed. M. Schofield, M. Burnyeat, & J. Barnes, 182–216. Cambridge: Cambridge University Press.

Immisch, O. 1929. *Aristoteles: Politica*. 2d ed. Leipzig: Teubner.

Inwood, B. 1992. *The Poem of Empedocles*. Toronto: Toronto University Press.

Jackson, H. J., ed. 1985. *Samuel Taylor Coleridge*. Oxford: Oxford University Press.

Jaeger, W. 1948. *Aristotle*. 2d ed. Trans. R. Robinson. Oxford: Oxford University Press.

Jahanbegloo, R. 1993. *Conversations with Isaiah Berlin*. London: Orion Books.

Janaway, C. 1995. *Images of Excellence: Plato's Critique of the Arts*. Oxford: Clarendon Press.

Janko, R. 1984. *Aristotle on Comedy: Towards a Reconstruction of Poetics II*. London: Duckworth.

———. 1987. *Aristotle Poetics*. Indianapolis: Hackett.

———. 1991. "Philodemus' *On Poems* and Aristotle's *On Poets*." *Cronache Ercolanesi* 21:5–64.

———. 1992. "Philodemus Resartus: Progress in Reconstructing the Philosophical Papyri from Herculaneum." In *Proceedings of the Boston Area Colloquium in Ancient Philosophy 7 [1991]*, ed. J. J. Cleary, 271–308. Lanham, Md.: University Press of America.

———. 1998. "Reception of Aristotle in Antiquity." In *The Encyclopedia of Aesthetics*, ed. M. Kelly, 1:104–6. New York: Oxford University Press.

Jauss, H. R. 1969. "Nachahmungsprinzip und Wirklichkeitsbegriff in der Theorie des Romans von Diderot bis Stendhal." In *Nachahmung und Illusion*, ed. H. R. Jauss, 157–78. Munich: Wilhelm Fink Verlag.

———. 1974. "Levels of Identification of Hero and Audience." *New Literary History* 5:283–317.

Javitch, D. 1994. "Pioneer Genre Theory and the Opening of the Humanist Canon." *Common Knowledge* 3:54–66.

———. 1998. "The Emergence of Poetic Genre Theory in the Sixteenth Century." *Modern Language Quarterly* 59:139–69.

———. 1999. "The Assimilation of Aristotle's *Poetics* in Sixteenth-Century Italy." In Norton 1999, 53–65.

Jenny, L. 1984. "Poétique et Représentation." *Poétique* 15:171–95.

Jensen, C. 1923. *Philodemus über die Gedichte: Fünftes Buch.* Berlin: Weidmann.

Jex-Blake, J., & E. Sellers. 1896. *The Elder Pliny's Chapters on the History of Art.* London: Macmillan.

Johnson, S. 1977. *Selected Poetry and Prose.* Ed. F. Brady & W. K. Wimsatt. Berkeley: University of California Press.

Johnson, W. R. 1982. *The Idea of Lyric: Lyric Modes in Ancient and Modern Poetry.* Berkeley: University of California Press.

Jones, E. D., ed. 1916. *English Critical Essays (Nineteenth Century).* London: Oxford University Press.

Jones, J. 1971. *On Aristotle and Greek Tragedy.* London: Chatto & Windus.

Jost, F., ed. 1966. *Actes du IVe Congrès de l'Association Internationale de Littérature Comparée.* 2 vols. The Hague: Mouton.

Jouët-Pastré, E. 1998. "Le rire chez Platon: Un détour sur la voie de la vérité." In *Le rire des anciens,* ed. M. Trédé & P. Hoffmann, 273–79. Paris: Presses de L'École Normale Supérieure.

Kahn, C. H. 1979. *The Art and Thought of Heraclitus.* Cambridge: Cambridge University Press.

Kaimio, M. 1977. *Characterization of Sound in Early Greek Literature.* Helsinki: Societas Scientiarum Finnica.

Kannicht, R. 1980. "Der alte Streit zwischen Philosophie und Dichtung." *Der altsprachliche Unterricht* 23:6–36.

Kant, I. 1914. *Kritik der Urteilskraft.* Ed. O. Buek. Berlin: Bruno Cassirer.

Kardaun, M. 1993. *Der Mimesisbegriff in der griechischen Antike.* Amsterdam: Koninklijke Nederlandse Akademie van Wetenschappen.

Kassel, R. 1968. *Aristotelis: De Arte Poetica Liber.* Corrected ed. Oxford: Clarendon Press.

———. 1976. *Aristotelis Ars Rhetorica.* Berlin: de Gruyter.

Kaufmann, W. 1969. *Tragedy and Philosophy.* New York: Anchor Books.

Kebric, R. B. 1977. *In the Shadow of Macedonia: Duris of Samos.* Wiesbaden: Franz Steiner Verlag.

Keil, H. 1857–80. *Grammatici Latini.* 8 vols. Leipzig: Teubner.

Kelly, H. A. 1979. "Aristotle-Averroes-Alemannus on Tragedy: The Influence of the *Poetics* on the Latin Middle Ages." *Viator* 10:161–209.

———. 1993. *Ideas and Forms of Tragedy from Aristotle to the Middle Ages.* Cambridge: Cambridge University Press.

Kemal, S. 1991. *The Poetics of Alfarabi and Avicenna.* Leiden: E. J. Brill.

Kemke, J. 1884. *Philodemi de musica librorum quae exstant.* Leipzig: Teubner.

Kemp, M. 1977. "From 'Mimesis' to 'Fantasia': The Quattrocento Vocabulary of Creation, Inspiration and Genius in the Visual Arts." *Viator* 8:347–98.

Kennedy, G. A., ed. 1989. *The Cambridge History of Literary Criticism 1: Classical Criticism.* Cambridge: Cambridge University Press.

Kerkhecker, A. 1991. "'Furcht und Mitleid'." *Rheinisches Museum* 134:288–310.

Kerrane, K. J. 1968. "Aristotle's *Poetics* in Modern Literary Criticism." Ph.D. diss., University of North Carolina.

Keuls, E. C. 1978. *Plato and Greek Painting.* Leiden: E. J. Brill.

Kidd, I. G. 1988. *Posidonius II: The Commentary.* 2 vols. Cambridge: Cambridge University Press.

Kindstrand, J. F., ed. 1990. *[Plutarchi] de Homero.* Leipzig: Teubner.

Kirby, J. T. 1991. "Mimesis and Diegesis: Foundations of Aesthetic Theory in Plato and Aristotle." *Helios* 18:113–28.

Kirk, G. S. 1954. *Heraclitus: The Cosmic Fragments.* Cambridge: Cambrige University Press.

Kivy, P. 1980. *The Corded Shell.* Princeton: Princeton University Press.

———. 1984. *Sound and Semblance: Reflections on Musical Representation.* Princeton: Princeton University Press.

———. 1993. *The Fine Art of Repetition.* Cambridge: Cambridge University Press.

———. 1997. *Philosophies of Arts.* Cambridge: Cambridge University Press.

Kokolakis, M. M. 1960. *The Dramatic Simile of Life.* Athens.

Koller, H. 1954. *Die Mimesis in der Antike.* Bern: A. Francke.

———. 1980. "Mimesis." In *Historisches Wörterbuch der Philosophie*, ed. J. Ritter & K. Gründer, 5:1396–9. Basel: Schwabe.

Konstan, D. 1999a. "Philoctetes' Pity." *Proceedings of the Boston Area Colloquium in Ancient Philosophy XIII [1997]*, ed. J.J. Cleary & G. M. Gurtler, 276–82. Lanham, Md.: University Press of America.

———. 1999b. "The Tragic Emotions." *Comparative Drama* 33:1–21.

———. 2001. *Pity Transformed.* London: Duckworth.

Kosman, L. A. 1992. "Silence and Imitation in the Platonic Dialogues." In *Methods of Interpreting Plato and His Dialogues*, ed. J. C. Klagge & N. D. Smith, 73–92. *Oxford Studies in Ancient Philosophy*, supp. vol. Oxford: Clarendon Press.

Koster, S. 1970. *Antike Eposttheorien.* Wiesbaden: Franz Steiner.

Kotter, P. B. 1975. *Die Schriften des Johannes von Damaskos III: Contra Imaginum Calumniatores Orationes Tres.* Berlin: de Gruyter.

Krausz, M., ed. 1993. *The Interpretation of Music.* Oxford: Clarendon Press.

Kraut, R. 1997. *Aristotle Politics Books VII and VIII.* Oxford: Clarendon Press.

Kristeller, P. 1980. "The Modern System of the Fine Arts." In *Renaissance Thought and the Arts*, 163–227. Princeton: Princeton University Press. Originally published in *Journal of the History of Ideas* 12 (1951): 496–527; 13 (1952): 17–46.

Kroll, W. 1899–1901. *Procli Diadochi in Platonis Rem Publicam Commentarii.* 2 vols. Leipzig: Teubner.

Kugiumutzakis, G. 1998. "Neonatal Imitation in the Intersubjective Companion Space." In *Intersubjective Communication and Emotion in Early Ontogeny*, ed. S. Bråten, 63–88. Cambridge: Cambridge University Press.

Kuhn, H. 1941–42. "The True Tragedy: On the Relationship between Greek Tragedy and Plato." *Harvard Studies in Classical Philology* 52:1–40, 53:37–88.

Kyriakou, P. 1997. "Aristotle's *Poetics* and Stoic Literary Theory." *Rheinisches Museum* 140:257–80.

Laborderie, J. 1978. *Le dialogue platonicien de la maturité*. Paris: Les Belles Lettres.

Lada, I. 1993. "'Empathic Understanding': Emotion and Cognition in Classical Dramatic Audience-Response." *Proceedings of the Cambridge Philological Society* 39:94–140.

———. 1996. "'Weeping for Hecuba': Is It a 'Brechtian' Act?" *Arethusa* 29:87–124.

Ladner, G. B. 1959. "Eikon." In *Reallexikon für Antike und Christentum*, ed. T. Klauser, 4:771–86. Stuttgart: Anton Hiersemann.

———. 1983. *Images and Ideas in the Middle Ages*. Rome: Edizioni di Storia e Letteratura.

Lamarque, P. 1983. "Fiction and Reality." In *Philosophy and Fiction*, ed. P. Lamarque, 52–72. Aberdeen: Aberdeen University Press.

Lamarque, P., & S. H. Olsen. 1994. *Truth Fiction and Literature*. Oxford: Clarendon Press.

Lamberton, R. 1986. *Homer the Theologian: Neoplatonist Allegorical Reading and the Growth of the Epic Tradition*. Princeton: Princeton University Press.

———. 1992. "The Neoplatonists and the Spiritualization of Homer." In *Homer's Ancient Readers*, ed. R. Lamberton & J. J. Keaney, 115–33. Princeton: Princeton University Press.

Lampe, G. W. H. 1961. *A Patristic Greek Lexikon*. Oxford: Clarendon Press.

Laurenti, R. 1984. "Critica alla mimesi e recupero del pathos: Il *De Poetis* di Aristotele." *Aion* 6:51–63.

———. 1987. *Aristotele, i frammenti dei dialoghi*. 2 vols. Naples: Luigi Loffredo Editore.

Lausberg, H. 1990. *Handbuch der literarischen Rhetorik*. 3rd ed. Stuttgart: Fritz Steiner.

Lear, J. 1988. "Katharsis." *Phronesis* 33:297–326. Reprinted in Lear 1998, 191–218.

———. 1992. "Inside and Outside the *Republic*." *Phronesis* 37:184–215. Reprinted in Lear 1998, 219–46.

———. 1995. "Testing The Limits: the Place of Tragedy in Aristotle's Ethics." In *Aristotle and Moral Realism*, ed. R. Heinaman, 61–84. London: UCL Press. Reprinted in Lear 1998, 167–90.

———. 1998. *Open Minded: Working Out the Logic of the Soul*. Cambridge, Mass.: Harvard University Press.

Lee, R. W. 1967. *Ut Pictura Poesis: The Humanistic Theory of Painting*. New York: W. W. Norton.

Leigh, M. 1997. *Lucan: Spectacle and Engagement*. Oxford: Clarendon Press.

Lesky, A. 1966. *Gesammelte Schriften*. Bern: Francke Verlag.

Lessem, A. 1974. "Imitation and Expression: Opposing French and British Views in the 18th Century." *Journal of the American Musicological Society* 27:325–30.

Lessing, G. E. 1970–79. *Lessing: Werke*. Ed. H. G. Göpfert. 8 vols. Munich: Carl Hanser Verlag.

Levi, P. 1989. *Se questo è un uomo*. Turin: Einaudi.

Levin, S. B. 2001. *The Ancient Quarrel between Philosophy and Poetry Revisited*. New York: Oxford University Press.

Levinson, J. 1990. *Music, Art, and Metaphysics*. Ithaca: Cornell University Press.

———. 1996. *The Pleasures of Aesthetics*. Ithaca: Cornell University Press.

Lewis, C. S. 1960. *Studies in Words*. Cambridge: Cambridge University Press.

Lichtheim, G. 1970. *Lukács*. London: Fontana/Collins.

Lieberg, G. 1982. *Poeta Creator: Studien zu einer Figur der antiken Dichtung*. Amsterdam: Verlag J. C. Gieben.

Lindenberger, H. 1984. "The Mimetic Bias in Modern Anglo-American Criticism." In *Mimesis in Contemporary Theory: An Interdisciplinary Approach*, ed. M. Spariosu, 1–26. Philadelphia: John Benjamins.

Lippman, E. 1992. *A History of Western Musical Aesthetics*. Lincoln: University of Nebraska Press.

Liu, J.J.Y. 1975. *Chinese Theories of Literature*. Chicago: University of Chicago Press.

Lodge, R. C. 1953. *Plato's Theory of Art*. London: Routledge & Kegan Paul.

Long, A. A. 1971. "Language and Thought in Stoicism." In *Problems in Stoicism*, ed. A. A. Long, 75–113. London: Athlone Press.

———. 1992. "Stoic Readings of Homer." In *Homer's Ancient Readers*, ed. R. Lamberton & J. J. Keaney, 41–66. Princeton: Princeton University Press.

Lopes, D. 1996. *Understanding Pictures*. Oxford: Clarendon Press.

Lord, C. 1982. *Education and Culture in the Political Thought of Aristotle*. New York: Cornell University Press.

———. 1986. "On the Early History of the Aristotelian Corpus." *American Journal of Philology* 107:137–61.

Lovejoy, A. 1948. *Essays in the History of Ideas*. Baltimore: Johns Hopkins University Press.

Lowe, N. J. 2000. *The Classical Plot and the Invention of Western Literature*. Cambridge University Press.

Lucas, D. W. 1968. *Aristotle Poetics*. Oxford: Clarendon Press.

Lukács, G. 1963. *Die Eigenart des Ästhetischen*. 2 vols. Neuwied: Luchterhand.

McCall, M. H. 1969. *Ancient Rhetorical Theories of Simile and Comparison*. Cambridge, Mass.: Harvard University Press.

Macciantelli, M. 1994. "Karl Philipp Moritz e l'imitazione formatrice." *Studi di Estetica* 10:55–71.

McKeon, R. S. 1957. "Literary Criticism and the Concept of Imitation in Antiquity." In *Critics and Criticism*, abr. ed., ed. R. S. Crane, 117–45. Chicago: University of Chicago Press.

McLaughlin, M. L. 1996. *Literary Imitation in the Italian Renaissance*. Oxford: Clarendon Press.

Macleod, C. 1983. *Collected Essays*. Oxford: Clarendon Press.

McMahon, A. P. 1929. "Seven Questions on Aristotelian Definitions of Tragedy and Comedy." *Harvard Studies in Classical Philology* 40:97–198.

Mader, M. 1977. *Das Problem des Lachens und der Komödie bei Platon*. Stuttgart: Kohlhammer

Maehler, H. 1989. *Pindari Carmina cum Fragmentis: II, Fragmenta*. Leipzig: Teubner.

Magnien, M. 1990. *Aristote Poétique*. Paris: Le Livre de Poche.

Mahon, D. 1947. *Studies in Seicento Art and Theory*. London: Warburg Institute.

Mangoni, C. 1993. *Filodemo, Il quinto libro della Poetica*. Naples: Bibliopolis.

Manieri, A. 1998. *L'immagine poetica nella teoria degli antichi*. Pisa: Istituti Editoriali e Poligrafici Internazionali.

Marin, L. 1988. "Mimésis et description." *Word and Image* 4:25–35.

Markowitz, S. 1998. "Bullough, Edward." In *Encyclopedia of Aesthetics*, ed. M. Kelly, 1:316–18. New York: Oxford University Press.

Marks, E. R. 1981. *Coleridge on the Language of Verse*. Princeton: Princeton University Press.

Marshall, D. 1986. *The Figure of Theater*. New York: Columbia University Press.

————. 1988. *The Surprising Effects of Sympathy*. Chicago: University of Chicago Press.

————. 1997. "*Ut Pictura Poesis*." In *The Cambridge History of Literary Criticism 4: The Eighteenth Century*, ed. H. B. Nisbet & C. Rawson, 681–99. Cambridge: Cambridge University Press.

Marshall, D. G. 1981. "Aristotelian 'Imitation' as Non-Positivist Representation." *Annals of Scholarship* 2:85–95.

Mastrangelo, M., & J. Harris. 1998. "The Meaning of *REPUBLIC* 606a3-b5." *Classical Quarterly* 48:301–5.

Mathew, G. 1963. *Byzantine Aesthetics*. London: John Murray.

Matravers, D. 1998. *Art and Emotion*. Oxford: Clarendon Press.

Matthaios, S. 1999. *Untersuchungen zur Grammatik Aristarchs*. Göttingen: Vandenhoeck & Ruprecht.

Mattheson, J. 1739. *Der vollkommene Capellmeister*. Hamburg: Verlegts Christian Herold.

Meijering, R. 1987. *Literary and Rhetorical Theories in Greek Scholia*. Groningen: Egbert Forsten.

Melberg, A. 1995. *Theories of Mimesis*. Cambridge: Cambridge University Press.

Meltzoff, A. 1999. "Imitation." In *The MIT Encyclopedia of the Cognitive Sciences*, ed. R. A. Wilson & F. C. Keil, 389–91. Cambridge, Mass.: MIT Press.

Merki, P. H. 1952. *ὁμοίωσις θεῷ: Von der platonischen Angleichung an Gott zur Gottähnlichkeit bei Gregor von Nyssa*. Freiburg in der Schweiz: Paulusdruckerei.

Mette, H. J. 1936. *Sphairopoiia: Untersuchungen zur Kosmologie des Krates von Pergamon*. Munich: Beck.

————. 1988. *Kleine Schriften*. Frankfurt am Main: Athenäum.

Metzger, L. 1966. "Imitation and Illusion in Coleridge's Criticism." In *Actes du IVe Congrès de l'Association Internationale de Littérature Comparée*, ed. F. Jost, 2:781–88. The Hague: Mouton.

Michaelis, W. 1942. "μιμέομαι, μιμητής, συμμιμητής." In *Theologisches Wörterbuch zum Neuen Testament*, ed. G. Kittel, 4:661–78. Stuttgart: Kohlhammer.

Miller, W. I. 1997. *The Anatomy of Disgust*. Cambridge, Mass.: Harvard University Press.

Miner, E. 1990. *Comparative Poetics*. Princeton: Princeton University Press.

Minio-Paluello, L. 1968. *Aristoteles Latinus XXXIII: De Arte Poetica*. 2d ed. Leiden: E. J. Brill.

Minnis, A. J., & A. B. Scott. 1991. *Medieval Literary Theory and Criticism, c.1100–c. 1375*. Rev. ed. Oxford: Oxford University Press.

Moraux, P. 1955. "La 'mimesis' dans les théories anciennes de la danse, de la musique et de la poésie." *Les Études Classiques* 23:3–13.

Morgan, J. 1986. "The Meanings of *Vraisemblance* in French Classical Theory." *Modern Language Review* 81:293–304.

Morgan, M. 1990. "Plato and the Painters." *Apeiron* 23:121–45.

Moriarty, M. 1991. *Roland Barthes.* Cambridge: Polity Press.

Moritz, K. P. 1962. *Schriften zur Ästhetik und Poetik.* Ed. H. J. Schrimpf. Tübingen: Max Niemeyer.

Morris, S. P. 1992. *Daidalos and the Origins of Greek Art.* Princeton: Princeton University Press.

Morrison, K. F. 1982. *The Mimetic Tradition of Reform in the West.* Princeton: Princeton University Press.

Morrow, G. R. 1960. *Plato's Cretan City.* Princeton: Princeton University Press.

Morrow, M. S. 1997. *German Music Criticism in the Late Eighteenth Century.* Cambridge: Cambridge University Press.

Mortensen, P. 1994. "Shaftesbury and Art Appreciation." *Journal of the History of Ideas* 55:631–50.

Most, G. W. 1992. "Schöne (das)." In *Historisches Wörterbuch der Philosophie*, ed. J. Ritter & K. Gründer, 8:1343–51. Basel: Schwabe.

———. 1998. "Mimesis." In *Routledge Encyclopedia of Philosophy*, ed. E. Craig, 6:381–2. London: Routledge.

———. 2000. "Generating Genres: The Idea of the Tragic." In *Matrices of Genre*, ed. M. Depew & D. Obbink, 15–35. Cambridge, Mass.: Harvard University Press.

Moutsopoulos, E. 1959. *La musique dans l'oeuvre de Platon.* Paris: Presses Universitaires de France.

Müller, C. 1883. *Claudii Ptolemaei Geographia.* Paris: Didot.

Murdoch, I. 1997. *Existentialists and Mystics.* London: Chatto & Windus

Murnaghan, S. 1995. "Sucking the Juice without Biting the Rind: Aristotle and Tragic Mimesis." *New Literary History* 26:755–73.

Murray, C. 1977. "Art and the Early Church." *Journal of Theological Studies* 28:303–45.

Murray, P. 1981. "Poetic Inspiration in Early Greece." *Journal of Hellenic Studies* 101:87–100.

———. 1992. "Inspiration and Mimesis in Plato." In *The Language of the Cave*, ed. A. Barker and M. Warner, 27–46. Edmonton, Alberta: Academic Printing & Publishing.

———. 1996. *Plato on Poetry.* Cambridge: Cambridge University Press.

Nadel, J., and G. Butterworth, ed. 1999. *Imitation in Infancy.* Cambridge: Cambridge University Press.

Nagy, G. 1989. "Early Greek Views of Poets and Poetry." In *The Cambridge History of Literary Criticism 1: Classical Criticism*, ed. G. A. Kennedy, 1–77. Cambridge: Cambridge University Press.

———. 1990. *Pindar's Homer.* Baltimore: Johns Hopkins University Press.

Nahm, M. C. 1947. "The Theological Background of the Theory of the Artist as Creator." *Journal of the History of Ideas* 8:363–72.

Nauck, A. 1889. *Tragicorum Graecorum Fragmenta.* 2d ed. Leipzig: Teubner.

Neander, K. 1987. "Pictorial Representation: A Matter of Resemblance." *British Journal of Aesthetics* 27:213–26.

Nehamas, A. 1982. "Plato on Imitation and Poetry in *Republic* 10." In *Plato on Beauty Wisdom and the Arts*, ed. J. Moravcsik & P. Temko, 47–78. Totowa, N.J.: Rowman & Allanheld. Reprinted in Nehamas 1999, 251–78.

———. 1988. "Plato and the Mass Media." *Monist* 71:214–34. Reprinted in Nehamas 1999, 279–99.

———. 1992. "Pity and Fear in the *Rhetoric* and the *Poetics*." In *Essays on Aristotle's Poetics*, ed. A. O. Rorty, 291–314. Princeton: Princeton University Press.

———. 1999. *Virtues of Authenticity: Essays on Plato and Socrates*. Princeton: Princeton University Press.

Neill, A. 2001. "Tragedy." In *The Routledge Companion to Aesthetics*, ed. B. Gaut & D. M. Lopes, 363–73. London: Routledge.

Nesselrath, H.-G. 1990. *Die attische mittlere Komödie*. Berlin: de Gruyter.

Neubecker, A. J. 1986. *Philodemus Über die Musik IV. Buch*. Naples: Bibliopolis.

Newman, W. L. 1887–1902. *The Politics of Aristotle*. 4 vols. Oxford: Clarendon Press.

Newsome, D. 1974. *Two Classes of Men: Platonism and English Romantic Thought*. London: John Murray.

Nicholsen, S. W. 1997. *Exact Imagination, Late Work: On Adorno's Aesthetics*. Cambridge, Mass.: MIT Press.

Nietzsche, F. 1988. *Sämtliche Werke: Kritische Studienausgabe*. Ed. G. Colli & M. Montinari. 2d ed. 15 vols. Munich: Deutscher Taschenbuch Verlag.

Nightingale, A. W. 1995. *Genres in Dialogue: Plato and the Construct of Philosophy*. Cambridge: Cambridge University Press.

Nisbet, H. B. 1985. *German Aesthetic and Literary Criticism*. Cambridge: Cambridge University Press.

Nochlin, L. 1966. *Impressionism and Post-Impressionism, 1874–1904*. Englewood Cliffs, N.J.: Prentice-Hall.

Norton, G. P., ed. 1999. *The Cambridge History of Literary Criticism 3: The Renaissance*. Cambridge: Cambridge University Press.

Notomi, N. 1999. *The Unity of Plato's Sophist*. Cambridge: Cambridge University Press.

Nussbaum, M. C. 1978. *Aristotle's De Motu Animalium*. Princeton: Princeton University Press.

———. 1986. *The Fragility of Goodness: Luck and Ethics in Greek Tragedy and Philosophy*. Cambridge: Cambridge University Press.

———. 1990. *Love's Knowledge: Essays on Philosophy and Literature*. New York: Oxford University Press.

Nussbaum, M. C. 1991. "The Transfigurations of Intoxication: Nietzsche, Schopenhauer, and Dionysus." *Arion*, 3rd ser, 1.2:75–111. Revised version in *Cambridge Companion to Schopenhauer*, ed. C. Janaway (Cambridge: Cambridge University Press, 2000), 344–74.

———. 1992. "Tragedy and Self-Sufficiency: Plato and Aristotle on Fear and Pity." *Oxford Studies in Ancient Philosophy* 10:107–59. Shorter version in Rorty 1992, 261–90.

———. 1993. "Poetry and the Passions." In *Passions and Perceptions*, ed. J. Brunschwig & M. C. Nussbaum, 97–149. Cambridge: Cambridge University Press.

Nussbaum, M. C. 1994. "Pity and Mercy: Nietzsche's Stoicism." In *Nietzsche, Genealogy, Morality*, ed. R. Schacht, 139–67. Berkeley: University of California Press.

———. 1999. "Invisibility and Recognition: Sophocles' *Philoctetes* and Ellison's *Invisible Man*." *Philosophy and Literature* 23:257–83.

Nuttall, A. D. 1983. *A New Mimesis: Shakespeare and the Representation of Reality*. London: Methuen.

Obbink, D., ed. 1995a. *Philodemus and Poetry*. New York: Oxford University Press.

———. 1995b. "How to Read Poetry about Gods." In Obbink 1995a, 189–209.

———. 1996. *Philodemus On Piety: Critical Text with Commentary*. Oxford: Clarendon Press.

O'Connell, R. J. 1978. *Art and the Christian Intelligence in St. Augustine*. Oxford: Blackwell.

O'Gorman, D. 1971. *Diderot the Satirist*. Toronto: University of Toronto Press.

Ong, W. J. 1958. "A Dialectic of Aural and Objective Correlatives." *Essays in Criticism* 8:166–81.

Ortony, A., G. L. Clore, & A. Collins. 1988. *The Cognitive Structure of Emotions*. Cambridge: Cambridge University Press.

Osborne, C. 1987. "The Repudiation of Representation in Plato's *Republic*." *Proceedings of the Cambridge Philological Society* 33:53–73.

———. 1996. "Space, Time, Shape, and Direction: Creative Discourse in the *Timaeus*." In *Form and Argument in Late Plato*, ed. C. Gill & M. M. McCabe, 179–211. Oxford: Clarendon Press.

O'Sullivan, N. 1992. *Alcidamas, Aristophanes and the Beginnings of Greek Stylistic Theory*. Stuttgart: Franz Steiner Verlag.

Owen, W.J.B. & J. W. Smyser. eds. 1974. *The Prose Works of William Wordsworth*. 3 vols. Oxford: Clarendon Press.

Packer, M. 1984. "The Conditions of Aesthetic Feeling in Aristotle's *Poetics*." *British Journal of Aesthetics* 24:138–48.

Page, D. L. 1941. *Select Papyri III: Literary Papyri*. London: Heinemann.

Palisca, C. V. 1985. *Humanism in Italian Renaissance Musical Thought*. New Haven: Yale University Press.

Palmer, F. 1992. *Literature and Moral Understanding*. Oxford: Clarendon Press.

Palmer, J. A. 1999. *Plato's Reception of Parmenides*. Oxford: Clarendon Press.

Panofsky, E. 1962. *Studies in Iconology*. New York: Harper & Row.

———. 1968. *Idea: A Concept in Art Theory*. Trans. J.J.S. Peake. New York: Harper & Row.

———. 1970. *Meaning in the Visual Arts*. Harmondsworth: Penguin.

Pappas, N. 2001. "Aristotle." In *The Routledge Companion to Aesthetics*, ed. B. Gaut & D. M. Lopes, 15–26. London: Routledge.

Pasquali, G., ed. 1994. *Proclus Diadochus: In Platonis Cratylum Commentaria*. Stuttgart: Teubner.

Pater, W. 1901. *The Renaissance*. 6th ed. London: Macmillan.

Patterson, R. 1982. "The Platonic Art of Comedy and Tragedy." *Philosophy and Literature* 6:76–93.

———. 1985. *Image and Reality in Plato's Metaphysics*. Indianapolis: Hackett.

Pavel, T. G. 1975. "'Possible Worlds' in Literary Semantics." *Journal of Aesthetics and Art Criticism* 34:165–76.

Pédech, P. 1989. *Trois historiens méconnus*. Paris: Les Belles Lettres.

Peirce, C. S. 1931–58. *Collected Papers of Charles Sanders Peirce*. Ed. C. Hartshorne, P. Weiss, & A. W. Burks. 8 vols. Cambridge, Mass.: Harvard University Press.

Pelikan, J. 1990. *Imago Dei: The Byzantine Apologia for Icons*. Princeton: Princeton University Press.

Petersen, J. H. 1992. "'Mimesis' versus 'Nachahmung': Die *Poetik* des Aristoteles—nochmals neu gelesen." *Arcadia* 27:3–46.

Pfeiffer, R. 1968. *History of Classical Scholarship: From the Beginnings to the End of the Hellenistic Age*. Oxford: Clarendon Press.

Philip, J. A. 1961. "Mimesis in the *Sophistēs* of Plato." *Transactions of the American Philological Association* 92:453–68.

Philipp, H. 1968. *Tektonon Daidala: Der bildende Künstler und sein Werk im vorplatonischen Schrifttum*. Berlin: Verlag Bruno Hessling.

Pitcher, S. M. 1966. "The Concepts of Originality and Imitation in Plato and Aristotle." In *Actes du IVe Congrès de l'Association Internationale de Littérature Comparée*, ed. F. Jost, 2:721–29. The Hague: Mouton.

Plebe, A. 1957. *Filodemo e la Musica*. Turin: Edizioni di "Filosofia."

Podlecki, A. J. 1969. "The Peripatetics as Literary Critics." *Phoenix* 23:114–37.

Pole, D. 1983. *Aesthetics, Form and Emotion*. London: Duckworth.

Pollitt, J. J. 1974. *The Ancient View of Greek Art*. Student ed. New Haven: Yale University Press.

Pollmann, K. 1999. "Zwei Konzepte von Fiktionalität in der Philosophie des Hellenismus und in der Spätantike." In *Zur Rezeption der hellenistischen Philosophie in der Spätantike*, ed. T. Fuhrer & M. Erler, 261–78. Stuttgart: Franz Steiner Verlag.

Porter, J. I. 1992. "Hermeneutic Lines and Circles: Aristarchus and Crates on the Exegesis of Homer." In *Homer's Ancient Readers*, ed. R. Lamberton & J. J. Keaney, 67–114. Princeton: Princeton University Press.

———. 1995a. "Content and Form in Philodemus: The History of an Evasion." In *Philodemus and Poetry*, ed. D. Obbink, 97–147. New York: Oxford University Press.

———. 1995b. "οἱ κριτικοί: A Reassessment." In *Greek Literary Theory after Aristotle*, ed. J.G.J. Abbenes, S. R. Slings, & I. Sluiter, 83–109. Amsterdam: VU University Press.

———. 1996. "In Search of an Epicurean Aesthetics." In *L'epicureismo greco e romano*, ed. G. Giannantoni & M. Gigante, 611–28. Naples: Bibliopolis.

Pratt, L. H. 1993. *Lying and Poetry from Homer to Pindar: Falsehood and Deception in Archaic Greek Poetics*. Ann Arbor: University of Michigan Press.

Praz, M. 1970. *Mnemosyne: The Parallel between Literature and the Visual Arts*. London: Oxford University Press.

Preisendanz, W. 1969. "Die Auseinandersetzung mit dem Nachahmungsprinzip in Deutschland und die besondere Rolle der Romane Wielands (*Don Sylvio, Aga-*

thon)." In *Nachahmung und Illusion*, ed. H. Jauss, 72–95. Munich: Wilhelm Fink Verlag.

Preißhofen, F. 1974. "Sokrates im Gespräch mit Parrhasios und Kleiton." In *Studia Platonica: Festschrift für Hermann Gundert*, ed. K. Döring & W. Kullmann, 21–40. Amsterdam: Verlag B. R. Grüner.

Prendergast, C. 1986. *The Order of Mimesis: Balzac, Stendhal, Nerval, Flaubert.* Cambridge: Cambridge University Press.

Puelma, M. 1989. "Der Dichter und die Wahrheit in der griechischen Poetik." *Museum Helveticum* 46:65–100.

Putnam, H. 1992. *Renewing Philosophy.* Cambridge, Mass.: Harvard University Press.

Quatremère de Quincy, A.-C. 1823. *Essai sur la nature, le but et les moyens de l'imitation dans les beaux-arts.* Paris: J. Didot.

———. 1837. *An Essay on the Nature, the End, and the Means of Imitation in the Fine Arts.* Trans. J. C. Kent. London: Smith, Elder.

Rabe, H., ed. 1892–93. *Syriani in Hermogenem Commentaria.* 2 vols. Leipzig: Teubner.

Rabel, R. J. 1997. *Plot and Point of View in the Iliad.* Ann Arbor: University of Michigan Press.

Rad, G. von. 1962. *Old Testament Theology.* Trans. D.M.G. Stalker. Vol. 1. Edinburgh: Oliver & Boyd.

Radt, S. 1985. *Tragicorum Graecorum Fragmenta.* Vol. 3. Göttingen: Vandenhoeck & Ruprecht.

Raffman, D. 1993. *Language, Music, and Mind.* Cambridge, Mass.: MIT Press.

Rangos, S. 1999. "Proclus on Poetic Mimesis, Symbolism, and Truth." *Oxford Studies in Ancient Philosophy* 17:249–77.

Redfield, J. M. 1994. *Nature and Culture in the Iliad.* Expanded ed. Durham: Duke University Press.

Rée, J. 1999. *I See a Voice: A Philosophical History of Language, Deafness and the Senses.* London: Harper Collins.

Reeve, C.D.C. 1988. *Philosopher-Kings: The Argument of Plato's Republic.* Princeton: Princeton University Press.

———. 1998. *Aristotle Politics.* Indianapolis: Hackett.

Reiss, H. 1994. "The 'Naturalization' of the Term 'Ästhetik' in Eighteenth-Century German: Alexander Gottlieb Baumgarten and His Impact." *Modern Language Review* 89:645–58.

———. 1997. "The Rise of Aesthetics from Baumgarten to Humboldt." In *The Cambridge History of Literary Criticism 4: The Eighteenth Century*, ed. H. B. Nisbet & C. Rawson, 658–80. Cambridge: Cambridge University Press.

Rey, A. 1986. "Mimesis, poétique et iconisme." In *Iconicity: Essays on the Nature of Culture*, ed. P. Bouissac, M. Herzfeld, & R. Posner, 17–27. Tübingen: Stauffenburg.

Reynolds, J. 1997. *Discourses on Art.* Ed. R. R. Wark. New Haven: Yale University Press.

Rich, A.N.M. 1954. "The Platonic Ideas as the Thoughts of God." *Mnemosyne* 7:123–33.

———. 1960. "Plotinus and the Theory of Artistic Imitation." *Mnemosyne* 13:233–39.

Richards, I. A. 1928. 3d ed. *Principles of Literary Criticism*. London: Routledge.
———. 1929. *Practical Criticism*. London: Routledge.
Richardson, N. J. 1975. "Homeric Professors in the Age of the Sophists." *Proceedings of the Cambridge Philological Society* 21:65–81.
———. 1980. "Literary Criticism in the Exegetical Scholia to the *Iliad*." *Classical Quarterly* 30:265–87.
———. 1981. "The Contest of Homer and Hesiod and Alcidamas' *Mouseion*." *Classical Quarterly* 31:1–10.
———. 1993. *The Iliad: A Commentary, Books 21–24*. Cambridge: Cambridge University Press.
———. 1994. "Aristotle and Hellenistic Scholarship." In *La philologie grecque à l'époque hellénistique et romaine*, ed. F. Montanari, 7–28. Geneva: Fondation Hardt.
Richter, J. P. 1970. *The Literary Works of Leonardo da Vinci*. 3d ed. 2 vols. London: Phaidon.
Ricoeur, P. 1981. "Mimesis and Representation." *Annals of Scholarship* 2:15–32.
———. 1983. *Temps et récit*. Vol. 1. Paris: Éditions du Seuil.
———. 1984. *Time and Narrative*. Vol. 1. Trans. K. McLaughlin & D. Pellauer. Chicago: University of Chicago Press.
Riedel, W. 1993. "Mimesis." In *Literatur Lexikon*, ed. V. Meid, 14:91–4. Munich: Bertelsmann.
Riginos, A. S. 1976. *Platonica: The Anecdotes Concerning the Life and Writings of Plato*. Leiden: E. J. Brill.
Rispoli, G. M. 1983. "La 'Sensazione Scientifica.'" *Cronache Ercolanesi* 13:91–101.
———. 1991. "Elementi di fisica e di etica epicurea nella teoria musicale di Filodemo di Gadara." In *Harmonia mundi: Musica e filosofia nell'antichità*, ed. R. W. Wallace & B. MacLachlan, 69–103. Rome: Edizioni dell'Ateneo.
Ritoók, Z. 2001. "Damon: Sein Platz in der Geschichte des ästhetischen Denkens." *Wiener Studien* 114:59–68.
Ritter, J. 1971. "Ästhetik, ästhetisch." In *Historisches Wörterbuch der Philosophie*, ed. J. Ritter, 1:555–80. Basel: Schwabe.
Robb, K. 1994. *Literacy and Paideia in Ancient Greece*. New York: Oxford University Press.
Robertson, M. 1975. *A History of Greek Art*. 2 vols. Cambridge: Cambridge University Press.
Rorty, A. O., ed. 1992. *Essays on Aristotle's Poetics*. Princeton: Princeton University Press.
Rose, V. 1886. *Aristotelis qui ferebantur Librorum Fragmenta*. Leipzig: Teubner.
Rosenthal, E.I.J. 1956. *Averroes' Commentary on Plato's Republic*. Cambridge: Cambridge University Press.
Rösler, W. 1980. "Die Entdeckung der Fiktionalität in der Antike." *Poetica* 12:283–319.
Ross, D. 1949. *Aristotle*. 5th ed. London: Methuen.
Rostagni, A. 1945. *Aristotele Poetica*. Turin: Chiantore.
———. 1955. *Scritti minori I: Aesthetica*. Turin: Bottega d'Erasmo.
Rousseau, J.-J. 1959–95. *Oeuvres complètes*. Ed. B. Gagnebin & M. Raymond. 5 vols. Paris: Gallimard.

Rouveret, A. 1989. *Histoire et imaginaire de la peinture ancienne.* Rome: École Française de Rome.

Rowe, C. J. 1995. *Plato: Statesman.* Warminster: Aris & Phillips.

Rudowski, V. A. 1971. *Lessing's Aesthetica in Nuce.* Chapel Hill: University of North Carolina Press.

Russell, D. A. 1979. *"De imitatione."* In *Creative Imitation and Latin Literature,* ed. D. West and T. Woodman, 1–16. Cambridge: Cambridge University Press.

———. 1981. *Criticism in Antiquity.* London: Duckworth.

———. 1989. "Greek Criticism of the Empire." In *The Cambridge History of Literary Criticism I: Classical Criticism,* ed. G. A. Kennedy, 297–329. Cambridge: Cambridge University Press.

Rutherford, R. B. 1989. *The Meditations of Marcus Aurelius.* Oxford: Clarendon Press.

Ruthven, K. K. 1979. *Critical Assumptions.* Cambridge: Cambridge University Press.

Ryan, C., trans. 1996. *Michelangelo: The Poems.* London: J. M. Dent.

Sachs, K.-J. 1996. "Imitation." In *Die Musik in Geschichte und Gegenwart,* ed. L. Finscher, 4 (Sachteil):511–26. Kassel: Bärenreiter.

Sacks, O. 1991. *Seeing Voices.* London: Picador.

Sargeaunt, G. M. 1922–3. "Two Studies in Plato's *Laws.*" *Hibbert Journal* 21:493–502, 669–79.

Sartorius, M. 1896. "Plato und die Malerei." *Archiv für Philosophie* 9:123–48.

Sartwell, C. 1991. "Natural Generativity and Imitation." *British Journal of Aesthetics* 31:58–67.

Saunders, T. J. 1972. *Notes on the Laws of Plato.* BICS supp. 28. London: Institute of Classical Studies.

Savile, A. 1982. *The Test of Time: An Essay in Philosophical Aesthetics.* Oxford: Clarendon Press.

Schadewaldt, W. 1955. "Furcht und Mitleid? Zur Deutung des Aristotelischen Tragödiensatzes." *Hermes* 83:129–71.

Schaper, E. 1968. *Prelude to Aesthetics.* London: George Allen & Unwin.

———. 1979. *Studies in Kant's Aesthetics.* Edinburgh: Edinburgh University Press.

Schefold, K. 1992. *Gods and Heroes in Late Archaic Greek Art.* Trans. A. Griffiths. Cambridge: Cambridge University Press.

Schelling, F.W.J. von. 1911. *Schriften zur Philosophie der Kunst.* Ed. O. Weiss. Leipzig: Felix Meiner.

Schenkeveld, D. M. 1976. "Strabo on Homer." *Mnemosyne* 29:52–64.

———. 1982. "The Structure of Plutarch's *De audiendis poetis.*" *Mnemosyne* 35:60–71.

———. 1999. "Poetics." In *The Cambridge History of Hellenistic Philosophy,* ed. K. Algra, J. Barnes, J. Mansfeld, & M. Schofield, 221–5. Cambridge: Cambridge University Press.

Schier, F. 1983. "Tragedy and the Community of Sentiment." In *Philosophy and Fiction,* ed. P. Lamarque, 73–92. Aberdeen: Aberdeen University Press.

———. 1986. *Deeper into Pictures.* Cambridge: Cambridge University Press.

Schlegel, A. W. 1962–74. *Kritische Schriften und Briefe.* Ed. E. Lohner. 7 vols. Stuttgart: Kohlhammer.

Schlegel, F. 1964. *Kritische Schriften*. Ed. W. Rasch. Munich: Carl Hanser Verlag.

Schmitt, A. 1997. "Wesenzüge der griechischen Tragödie: Schicksal, Schuld, Tragik." In *Tragödie: Idee und Transformation*, ed. H. Flashar, 5–49. Stuttgart: Teubner.

Schofield, M. 1999. "Social and Political Thought." In *The Cambridge History of Hellenistic Philosophy*, ed. K. Algra, J. Barnes, J. Mansfeld, & M. Schofield, 739–70. Cambridge: Cambridge University Press.

Schopenhauer, A. 1988. *Werke*. Ed. L. Lütkehaus. 6 vols. Zurich: Haffmanns Verlag.

Schubert, A. 1995. *Platon: Der Staat*. Paderborn: Ferdinand Schöningh.

Schuhl, P.-M. 1952. *Platon et l'art de son temps*. 2d ed. Paris: Presses Universitaires de France.

Schütrumpf, E. 1970. *Die Bedeutung des Wortes ēthos in der Poetik des Aristoteles*. Munich: C. H. Beck.

———. 1989. "Traditional Elements in the Conception of *Hamartia* in Aristotle's *Poetics*." *Harvard Studies in Classical Philology* 92:137–56.

Schweitzer, B. 1934. "Mimesis und Phantasia." *Philologus* 89:286–300.

———. 1953. *Platon und die bildende Kunst der Griechen*. Tübingen: Max Niemeyer Verlag.

———. 1963. *Zur Kunst der Antike*. 2 vols. Tübingen: Verlag Ernst Wasmuth.

Schwinge, E.-R. 1997. "Griechische Tragödie und zeitgenössische Rezeption: Aristophanes und Gorgias." *Berichte aus den Sitzungen der Joachim Jungius-Gesellschaft der Wissenschaften* 15, no. 2:3–34.

Scodel, R. 1999. *Credible Impossibilities: Conventions and Strategies of Verisimilitude in Homer and Greek Tragedy*. Stuttgart: Teubner.

Scolnicov, S. 1988. *Plato's Metaphysics of Education*. London: Routledge.

Scott, D. 1999. "Platonic Pessimism and Moral Education." *Oxford Studies in Ancient Philosophy* 17:15–36.

Scott, G. 1999. "The *Poetics* of Performance: The Necessity of Spectacle, Music, and Dance in Aristotelian Tragedy." In *Performance and Authenticity in the Arts*, ed. I. Gaskell & S. Kemal, 15–48. Cambridge: Cambridge University Press.

Scruton, R. 1974. *Art and Imagination*. London: Methuen.

———. 1997. *The Aesthetics of Music*. Oxford: Clarendon Press.

Segal, C. P. 1962. "Gorgias and the Psychology of the Logos." *Harvard Studies in Classical Philology* 66:99–155.

Shaftesbury, Third Earl of (Anthony Ashley Cooper). 1999. *Characteristics of Men, Manners, Opinions, Times*. Ed. L. E. Klein. Cambridge: Cambridge University Press.

Shankman, S. 1983. "Led by the Light of the Maeonian Star: Aristotle on Tragedy and *Od.* 17.415–44." *Classical Antiquity* 2:108–16.

Sharpe, R. A. 2000. *Music and Humanism*. New York: Oxford University Press.

Sheppard, A.D.R. 1980. *Studies on the 5th and 6th Essays of Proclus' Commentary on the Republic*. Göttingen: Vandenhoeck & Ruprecht.

———. 1987. *Aesthetics*. Oxford: Oxford University Press.

———. 1994. "Plato and the Neoplatonists." In *Platonism and the English Imagination*, ed. A. Baldwin & S. Hutton, 3–18. Cambridge: Cambridge University Press.

Sheppard, A.D.R. 1995. "*Phantasia* and *Analogia* in Proclus." In *Ethics and Rhetoric: Classical Essays for Donald Russell*, ed. D. Innes, H. Hine, & C. Pelling, 343–51. Oxford: Clarendon Press.

Sherman, N. 1989. *The Fabric of Character: Aristotle's Theory of Virtue*. Oxford: Clarendon Press.

———. 1992. "*Hamartia* and Virtue." In Rorty 1992, 177–96.

Shorey, P., ed. 1930–35. *Plato Republic*. 2 vols. Cambridge, Mass.: Harvard University Press.

Sicking, C.M.J. 1998. *Distant Companions: Selected Papers*. Leiden: E. J. Brill.

Sier, K. 1990. "Zum Zeushymnus des Kleanthes." In *Beiträge zur hellenistischen Literatur und ihrer Rezeption in Rom*, ed. P. Steinmetz, 93–108. Stuttgart: Franz Steiner Verlag.

Sifakis, G. M. 1986. "Learning from Art and Pleasure in Learning: An Interpretation of Aristotle *Poetics* 4 1448b8–19." In *Studies in Honour of T.B.L. Webster*, ed. J. Betts et al., 1:211–22. Bristol: Bristol Classical Press.

Sikes, E. 1931. *The Greek View of Poetry*. London: Methuen.

Silk, M. S. 1994. "The 'Six Parts of Tragedy' in Aristotle's *Poetics*." *Proceedings of the Cambridge Philological Society* 40:108–15.

———, ed. 1996. *Tragedy and the Tragic*. Oxford: Clarendon Press.

Silk, M. S., & J. P. Stern. 1981. *Nietzsche on Tragedy*. Cambridge: Cambridge University Press.

Simpson, P.L.P. 1998. *A Philosophical Commentary on the Politics of Aristotle*. Chapel Hill: University of North Carolina Press.

Skillen, A. 1992. "Fiction Year Zero: Plato's *Republic*." *British Journal of Aesthetics* 32:201–8.

Slater, W. J. 1986. *Aristophanis Byzantii Fragmenta*. Berlin: de Gruyter.

Smith, A. 1976. *The Theory of Moral Sentiments*, 6th ed. Ed. D. D. Raphael & A. L. Macfie. Oxford: Clarendon Press. Originally published London, 1790.

———. 1980. *Essays on Philosophical Subjects*. Ed. W.P.D. Wightman & J. C. Bryce. Oxford: Clarendon Press.

———. 1983. *Lectures on Rhetoric and Belles Lettres*. Ed. J. C. Bryce. Oxford: Clarendon Press.

Smithson, I. 1983. "The Moral View of Aristotle's *Poetics*." *Journal of the History of Ideas* 44:3–17.

Snipes, K. 1988. "Literary Interpretation in the Homeric Scholia: The Similes of the *Iliad*." *American Journal of Philology* 109:196–222.

Solmsen, F. 1968. *Kleine Schriften*. 3 vols. Hildesheim: Georg Olms.

Sommerstein, A. H. 1997. "The Theatre Audience, the *Demos*, and the *Suppliants* of Aeschylus." In *Greek Tragedy and the Historian*, ed. C. Pelling, 63–79. Oxford: Clarendon Press.

Sorabji, R. 1972. *Aristotle on Memory*. London: Duckworth.

———. 2000. *Emotion and Peace of Mind: From Stoic Agitation to Christian Temptation*. Oxford: Oxford University Press.

Sörbom, G. 1966. *Mimesis and Art*. Stockholm: Svenska Bokförlaget.

Spariosu, M. 1984a. "Editor's Introduction." In *Mimesis in Contemporary Theory: An Interdisciplinary Approach*, ed. M. Spariosu, i–xxix. Philadelphia: John Benjamins.

———. 1984b. "Mimesis and Contemporary French Theory." In *Mimesis in Contemporary Theory: An Interdisciplinary Approach*, ed. M. Spariosu, 65–108. Philadelphia: John Benjamins.

Spingarn, J. E. 1908. *A History of Literary Criticism in the Renaissance*. 2d ed. New York: Columbia University Press.

Stanford, W. B. 1967. *The Sound of Greek*. Berkeley: University of California Press.

———. 1983. *Greek Tragedy and the Emotions*. London: Routledge.

Stansbury-O'Donnell, M. D. 1999. *Pictorial Narrative in Ancient Greek Art*. Cambridge: Cambridge University Press.

Staten, H. 1990. *Nietzsche's Voice*. Ithaca: Cornell University Press.

Steckerl, F. 1942. "On the Problem: Artefact and Idea." *Classical Philology* 37:288–98.

Steiner, G. 1989. *Real Presences*. London: Faber.

———. 1997. *Errata: An Examined Life*. London: Orion Books.

Steiner, W. 1982. *The Colors of Rhetoric: Problems in the Relation between Modern Literature and Painting*. Chicago: University of Chicago Press.

Stemplinger, E. 1913. "Mimesis im philosophischen und rhetorischen Sinne." *Neue Jahrbücher für klassisches Altertum*: 20–36.

Stern, J. P. 1973. *On Realism*. London: Routledge & Kegan Paul.

Steven, R. G. 1933. "Plato and the Art of His Time." *Classical Quarterly* 27:149–55.

Stevens, E. B. 1944. "Some Attic Commonplaces of Pity." *American Journal of Philology* 65:1–25.

Stewart, A. 1990. *Greek Sculpture*. 2 vols. New Haven: Yale University Press.

Stieber, M. 1994. "Aeschylus' *Theoroi* and Realism in Greek Art." *Transactions of the American Philological Association* 124:85–119.

Stinton, T.C.W. 1975. "*Hamartia* in Aristotle and Greek Tragedy." *Classical Quarterly* 25:221–54. Reprinted in *Collected Papers on Greek Tragedy* (Oxford: Clarendon Press, 1990), 143–85.

Stock, B. 1996. *Augustine the Reader*. Cambridge, Mass.: Harvard University Press.

Stohn, G. 1993. "Zur Agathonszene in den 'Thesmophoriazusen' des Aristophanes." *Hermes* 121:196–205.

Stolnitz, J. 1961. "On the Origins of 'Aesthetic Disinterestedness.'" *Journal of Aesthetics and Art Criticism* 20:131–43.

Storr, A. 1992. *Music and the Mind*. London: HarperCollins.

Strasburger, H. 1966. *Die Wesensbestimmung der Geschichte durch die antike Geschichtsschreibung*. Wiesbaden: Franz Steiner Verlag. Reprinted in *Studien zur alten Geschichte* (Hildesheim: Georg Olms, 1982), 2:963–1016.

Struck, P. T. 1995. "Allegory, Aenigma, and Anti-Mimesis: A Struggle against Aristotelian Rhetorical Literary Theory." In *Greek Literary Theory after Aristotle*, ed. J.G.J. Abbenes, S. R. Slings, & I. Sluiter, 215–34. Amsterdam: VU University Press.

Sudhaus, S. 1892–6. *Philodemi Volumina Rhetorica*. 2 vols. Leipzig: Teubner.

Summers, D. 1981. *Michelangelo and the Language of Art*. Princeton: Princeton University Press.

———. 1987. *The Judgment of Sense: Renaissance Naturalism and the Rise of Aesthetics*. Cambridge: Cambridge University Press.

Suthor, N. 2001. "Mimesis: *Bildende Kunst*." In *Historisches Wörterbuch der Rhetorik*, ed. G. Ueding, 5:1294–1316. Tübingen: Max Niemeyer Verlag.

Tagliasacchi, A. M. 1961. "Le teorie estetiche e la critica letteraria in Plutarco." *Acme* 14:71–117.

Tan, E. S. 1996. *Emotion and the Structure of Narrative Film.* Trans. B. Fasting. Mahwah, N.J.: Lawrence Erlbaum Associates.

Tanner, M. 1985. "Understanding Music." *Aristotelian Society, Supplementary Volumes* 59:215–32.

Taplin, O. 1977. *The Stagecraft of Aeschylus.* Oxford: Clarendon Press.

———. 1978. *Greek Tragedy in Action.* London: Methuen.

Tarot, R. 1970. "Mimesis und Imitatio: Grundlagen einer neuen Gattungspoetik." *Euphorion* 64:125–42.

Tarrant, D. 1955. "Plato as Dramatist." *Journal of Hellenic Studies* 75:82–89.

Tatarkiewicz, W. 1970–74. *History of Aesthetics.* 3 vols. The Hague: Mouton.

———. 1973. "Mimesis." In *Dictionary of the History of Ideas,* ed. P. P. Wiener, 3:225–30. New York: Charles Scribner's.

Tate, J. 1928. "'Imitation' in Plato's *Republic.*" *Classical Quarterly* 22:16–23.

———. 1929. "Plato and Allegorical Interpretation." *Classical Quarterly* 23:142–54.

———. 1930. "Plato and Allegorical Interpretation (Continued)." *Classical Quarterly* 24:1–10.

———. 1932. "Plato and 'Imitation.'" *Classical Quarterly* 26:161–69.

Taussig, M. 1993. *Mimesis and Alterity: A Particular History of the Senses.* New York: Routledge.

Taylor, A. E. 1928. *A Commentary on Plato's Timaeus.* Oxford: Clarendon Press.

Theiler, W. 1925. *Zur Geschichte der teleologischen Naturbetrachtung bis auf Aristoteles.* Zurich: Orell Füssli.

———. 1934. *Die Vorbereitung des Neuplatonismus.* Berlin: Weidmann.

———. 1957. "Demiurgos." In *Reallexikon für Antike und Christentum,* ed. T. Klauser, 3:694–711. Stuttgart: Anton Hiersemann.

Thillet, P. 1987. "Alexandre d'Aphrodise et la poésie." In *Aristoteles: Werk und Wirkung,* ed. J. Wiesner, 2:107–19. Berlin: de Gruyter.

Todorov, T. 1977a. *Théories du Symbole.* Paris: Éditions du Seuil.

———. 1977b. *Theories of the Symbol.* Trans. C. Porter. Oxford: Basil Blackwell.

Tolstoy, L. 1930. *What Is Art? And Essays on Art.* Trans. A. Maude. London: Oxford University Press.

Too, Y. L. 1998. *The Idea of Ancient Literary Criticism.* Oxford: Clarendon Press.

Townsend, D. 1997. *An Introduction to Aesthetics.* Oxford: Blackwell.

Tracy, H. L. 1946. "Aristotle on Aesthetic Pleasure." *Classical Philology* 41:43–46.

Trimpi, W. 1999. "Sir Philip Sidney's *An Apology for Poetry.*" In Norton 1999, 187–98.

Twining, T. 1812. *Aristotle's Treatise on Poetry.* 2d ed. 2 vols. London.

Uhlig, G. 1883. *Dionysii Thracis Ars Grammatica.* Leipzig: Teubner.

Unamuno, M. de. 1921. *The Tragic Sense of Life.* Trans. J.E.C. Flitch. London: Macmillan.

Usener, H. 1887. *Epicurea.* Leipzig: Teubner.

Usener, H., & L. Radermacher. 1904–29. *Dionysii Halicarnasei Opuscula.* Vol. 2. Leipzig: Teubner.

Valgiglio, E. 1973. *Plutarco: De Audiendis Poetis.* Turin: Loescher.

Velardi, R. 1989. *Enthousiasmos: Possessione Rituale e Teoria della Communicazione Poetica in Platone.* Rome: Edizioni dell'Ateneo.

Velotti, S. 1999. "Imitazione." In *Dizionario di Estetica*, ed. G. Carchia & P. D'Angelo, 146–51. Rome: Laterza.

Verdenius, W. J. 1949. *Mimesis: Plato's Doctrine of Artistic Imitation and its Meaning to Us.* Leiden: E. J. Brill.

————. 1981. "Gorgias's Doctrine of Deception." In *The Sophists and Their Legacy*, ed. G. Kerferd, 116–29. Wiesbaden: Franz Steiner Verlag.

————. 1983. "The Principles of Greek Literary Criticism." *Mnemosyne* 36:14–59.

Vernant, J.-P. 1991. "The Birth of Images." In Vernant *Mortals and Immortals*, ed. F. I. Zeitlin, 164–85. Princeton: Princeton University Press.

Vicaire, P. 1960. *Platon critique littéraire.* Paris: Klincksieck.

Vickers, B., ed. 1996. *Francis Bacon.* Oxford: Oxford University Press.

————, ed. 1999. *English Renaissance Literary Criticism.* Oxford: Clarendon Press.

Vico, G. 1968. *The New Science of Giambattista Vico.* Trans. T. G. Bergin & M. H. Fisch. Rev. ed. Ithaca: Cornell University Press.

von Einem, H. 1972. *Goethe-Studien.* Munich: Wilhelm Fink.

————. 1973. *Michelangelo.* Trans. R. Taylor. London: Methuen.

von Fritz. K. 1956. "Die Bedeutung des Aristoteles für die Geschichtsschreibung." In *Histoire et historiens dans l'antiquité*, ed. K. Latte, 85–128. Geneva: Fondation Hardt.

Wagner, D. L., ed. 1983.*The Seven Liberal Arts in the Middle Ages.* Bloomington: Indiana University Press.

Walbank, F. W. 1960. "History and Tragedy." *Historia* 9:216–34. Reprinted in *Selected Papers* (Cambridge: Cambridge University Press, 1985), 224–41.

————. 1972. *Polybius.* Berkeley: University of California Press.

Wallace, R. 1986. *Beethoven's Critics.* Cambridge: Cambridge University Press.

Wallace, R. W. 1995. "Music Theorists in Fourth-Century Athens." In *Mousike: Metrica ritmica e musica greca in memoria di Giovanni Comotti*, ed. B. Gentili & F. Perusino, 17–39. Pisa: Istituti Editoriali e Poligrafici Internazionali.

————. 1997. "Poet, Public, and 'Theatrocracy': Audience Performance in Classical Athens." In *Poet, Public, and Performance in Ancient Greece*, ed. L. Edmunds & R. W. Wallace, 97–111. Baltimore: Johns Hopkins University Press.

Walsh, G. B. 1984. *The Varieties of Enchantment: Early Greek Views of the Nature and Function of Poetry.* Chapel Hill: University of North Carolina Press.

Walter, J. 1893. *Die Geschichte der Ästhetik im Altertum.* Leipzig: Reisland Verlag. Reprint, Hildesheim: Georg Olms, 1967.

Walton, K. 1990. *Mimesis as Make-Believe.* Cambridge, Mass.: Harvard University Press.

Walzer, R. 1985. *Al-Farabi on the Perfect State.* Oxford: Clarendon Press.

Wardman, A. 1974. *Plutarch's Lives.* London: Paul Elek.

Warry, J. G. 1962. *Greek Aesthetic Theory.* London: Methuen.

Watson, G. 1986. "Imagination: The Greek Background." *Irish Theological Quarterly* 52:54–65.

————. 1988a. *Phantasia in Classical Thought.* Galway: Galway University Press.

Watson, G. 1988b. "Discovering the Imagination: Platonists and Stoics on *Phantasia*." In *The Question of "Eclecticism": Studies in Later Greek Philosophy*, ed. J. M. Dillon & A. A. Long, 208–33. Berkeley: University of California Press.

Watt, R., & R. Ash. 1998. "A Psychological Investigation of Meaning in Music." *Musicae Scientiae* 2.1:33–53.

Webster, T.B.L. 1939. "Greek Theories of Art and Literature down to 400 B.C." *Classical Quarterly* 33:166–79.

———. 1952. "Plato and Aristotle as Critics of Greek Art." *Symbolae Osloenses* 29:8–23.

Wehrli, F. 1957. "Die antike Kunsttheorie und das Schöpferische." *Museum Helveticum* 14:39–49.

———. 1967. *Die Schule des Aristoteles: Aristoxenos*. 2d ed. Basel: Schwabe.

———. 1969. *Die Schule des Aristoteles: Phainias, Chamaileon, Praxiphanes*. 2d ed. Basel: Schwabe.

Weinberg, B. 1937. *French Realism: The Critical Reaction, 1830–1870*. New York: Modern Language Association of America.

———. 1961. *A History of Literary Criticism in the Italian Renaissance*. 2 vols. Chicago: University of Chicago Press.

———. 1966. "L'imitation au XVIe et XVIIe siècles." In *Actes du IVe Congrès de l'Association Internationale de Littérature Comparée*, ed. F. Jost, 2:697–703. The Hague: Mouton.

Weinstock, S. 1927. "Die platonische Homerkritik und ihre Nachwirkung." *Philologus* 82:121–53.

Weintraub, S., ed. 1968. *Literary Criticism of Oscar Wilde*. Lincoln: University of Nebraska Press.

Weir Smyth, H., trans. 1957. *Aeschylus Agamemnon, Libation-Bearers, Eumenides, Fragments*. With app. and add. by H. Lloyd-Jones. Cambridge, Mass.: Harvard University Press.

Wellbery, D. 1984. *Lessing's Laocoon*. Cambridge: Cambridge University Press.

West, M. L. 1989–92. *Iambi et Elegi Graeci*. 2d ed. 2 vols. Oxford: Clarendon Press.

———. 1992a. *Ancient Greek Music*. Oxford: Clarendon Press.

———. 1992b. "Analecta Musica." *Zeitschrift für Papyrologie und Epigraphik* 92:1–54.

Westerink, L. G. 1962. *Anonymous Prolegomena to Platonic Philosophy*. Amsterdam: North-Holland.

White, N. P. 1979. *A Companion to Plato's Republic*. Indianapolis: Hackett.

Whitlock Blundell, M. 1989. *Helping Friends and Harming Enemies*. Cambridge: Cambridge University Press.

Wiles, D. 1997. *Tragedy in Athens*. Cambridge: Cambridge University Press.

Wilkinson, E. M., & L. A. Willoughby. 1982. *Friedrich Schiller: On the Aesthetic Education of Man*. Rev. ed. Oxford: Clarendon Press.

Wilson, P. J. 1996. "The Use of Tragedy in the Fourth Century." In *Tragedy and the Tragic*, ed. M. S. Silk, 310–31. Oxford: Clarendon Press.

———. 2000. *The Athenian Institution of the Khoregia*. Cambridge: Cambridge University Press.

Winckelmann, J. J. 1982. *Werke*. Ed. H. Holtzhauer. Berlin: Aufbau-Verlag.

Wind, E. 1983. *The Eloquence of Symbols*. Oxford: Clarendon Press.

Winnington-Ingram, R. P. 1980. *Sophocles: An Interpretation*. Cambridge: Cambridge University Press.

Wollheim, R. 1973. *On Art and the Mind*. London: Allen Lane.

———. 1980. *Art and Its Objects*. 2d ed. Cambridge: Cambridge University Press.

———. 1987. *Painting as an Art*. London: Thames and Hudson.

Wolterstorff, N. P. 1980. *Works and Worlds of Art*. Oxford: Clarendon Press.

Woodmansee, M. 1994. *The Author, Art, and the Market: Rereading the History of Aesthetics*. New York: Columbia University Press.

Woodruff, P. 1982. "What Could Go Wrong with Inspiration? Why Plato's Poets Fail." In *Plato on Beauty, Wisdom, and the Arts*, ed. J. Moravcsik & P. Temko, 137–50. Totowa, N.J.: Rowman & Allanheld.

———. 1992. "Aristotle on *Mimēsis*." In Rorty 1992, 73–95.

———. 1998. "Plato on Mimesis." In *Encyclopedia of Aesthetics*, ed. M. Kelly, 3:521–3. New York: Oxford University Press.

Wyrwa, D. 1983. *Die christliche Platonaneignung in den Stromateis des Clemens von des Alexandrien*. Berlin: de Gruyter.

Yanal, R. J. 1982. "Aristotle's Definition of Poetry." *Nous* 16:499–525.

———. 1999. *Paradoxes of Emotion and Fiction*. State College: Pennsylvania State University Press.

Zaffagnini, I. 1995. "Imitazione ed espressione nella *Critica del Giudizio*." *Studi di Estetica* 11/12:137–50.

Zagagi, N. 1994. *The Comedy of Menander*. London: Duckworth.

Zagdoun, M.-A. 2000. *La philosophie stoïcienne de l'art*. Paris: CNRS Editions.

Zierl, A. 1994. *Affekte in der Tragödie*. Berlin: Akademie Verlag.

Zimbrich, U. 1984. *Mimesis bei Platon*. Frankfurt am Main: Peter Lang.

Index

Gadamer, H.-G., 345
Galileo, V., 236
god(s), mimetic representation of, 42–43,
    108–9, 274n, 305–9, 325–26, 335n. *See
    also* Iconoclasm, Byzantine
Goethe, J. W. von, 1–6, 40, 212, 323n, 356n,
    359, 371n
Gombrich, E., 46n, 133, 143, 147
Goodman, N., 244
Gorgias, 20–21, 53n, 60n, 77, 100n, 111n,
    121, 134n, 212, 215n, 218, 221n, 231n,
    233n, 268n, 270n
Gosse, E., 74
Gregory of Nazianzus, 337n, 338n
Gregory of Nyssa, 338n

Hanslick, E., 257
Hegel, G.W.F., 98, 144n, 231n, 364n, 378
Heliodorus, 353n
Heraclides Ponticus, 250n, 283n
Heraclitus, 4, 15n, 42, 61, 153n, 210
Hermannus Alemannus, 341–43
Hermogenes of Tarsus, 292
Herodotus, 17n, 100, 218n, 292n
Hesiod, 20, 49n, 167n, 331–32
heterocosm, mimetic, 4–5, 9, 23, 373
Hippias of Elis, 121
Hippocrates, pseudo-, *De victu*, 15n, 121,
    154n, 275n
history, contrasted with mimesis/poetry,
    164–67, 170–71, 174, 193–99; mimetic ele-
    ments in, 289–96
Hobbes, T., 228
Homer, 20–21, 26, 30–32, 40, 55, 60–61,
    77n, 84n, 93, 98, 108–11, 164–65, 167–68,
    200, 207n, 212–13, 218–19, 229, 233n,
    269–72, 274–75, 290–91, 302–9, 311, 320–
    21, 326–34
Homeric Hymn to Apollo, 18–21
Horace, 118, 236n, 287n, 347
Hume, D., 83, 180

Iconoclasm, Byzantine, 32, 314, 334–40
idealism, aesthetic/artistic, 3–4, 25, 32, 67n,
    96, 129–31, 133n, 154n, 155n, 158n, 176,
    196–97, 306–12, 316–23, 351, 355–69
identification, aesthetic, 26, 52–54, 75–81,
    85–97. *See also* empathy (Einfühlung);
    sympathy, aesthetic
illusionism, mimetic, 2–3, 110–11, 120, 123,
    138–39, 373–74, 379. *See also* trompe
    l'oeil

imagination, vis-à-vis mimesis, 25–6, 52–55,
    73–74, 92–97, 119–20, 246, 308–12, 361–
    62. See also *phantasia* (imagination)
imitation, as problematic translation/inter-
    pretation of mimesis, 6, 13–14, 38n, 138,
    152, 274n, 284, 290, 293–95, 309n, 344–
    50, 354–69, 375n, 378
"imitation of nature," 2–5, 10, 28, 32–33,
    151, 153–54, 247, 291n, 294, 311–12,
    316–18, 348, 350–69, 373
impressionism, 368n
inspiration, vis-à-vis mimesis, in Longinus,
    311–12; in Philostratus 308–9; in Plato,
    40–42; in Proclus, 327–34
Isaeus, 294
Isidore, 50n
Isocrates, 42n, 98n, 100, 114n, 209n, 213–
    14, 218n, 269n

James, Henry, 168n, 177
Jauss, H. R., 87
John Damascene, 32, 314, 335–40
Johnson, Samuel, 27, 143–44, 180, 189,
    348–50, 378
Jonson, Ben, 347n
Josephus, 20n, 275n, 294n, 308n, 335n
Judaic attitudes to images, 334–35

Kant, I., 9–11, 180, 186, 203n, 230n, 235,
    364
Kivy, P., 245n, 247
Kristeller, P., 7–9

Laforgue, J., 95n
Leibniz, G. W., 154n
Leonardo da Vinci, 27, 144–46, 351n
Lessing, G. E., 4n, 83, 118–20, 123, 143,
    169–70, 178n, 180n, 212, 309, 360n
Levi, Primo, 81n
life "imitating" art, 287–88, 368–69
likeness, as criterion of mimesis, 20, 25, 44–
    48, 64, 126–28, 130n, 155–64, 180n, 184–
    85, 188–93, 240–47, 256, 278n, 298–302,
    324–25, 336–38, 365–66
Longinus, ?pseudo-, *On the Sublime*, 84n,
    168n, 180n, 243, 248n, 267n, 310–12,
    353n
Lovejoy, A., 358
Lucas, D. W., 187
Lucian, 272n, 335n, 336n
Lucretius, 251n
Lukács, G., 372n
Lysias, 294

Printed in Great Britain
by Amazon